Liz

WRITING

GREGORY COWAN
ELIZABETH COWAN

TEXAS A&M UNIVERSITY

Acknowledgments for all copyrighted material used are given on pages x-xvi after index.

Illustrations by Edward Malsberg and edward a. butler.

But I want first of all—in fact, as an end to these other desires—to be at peace with myself. I want a singleness of eye, a purity of intention, a central core to my life that will enable me to carry out these obligations and activities as well as I can. I want, in fact—to borrow from the language of the saints—to live "in grace" as much of the time as possible. I am not using this term in a strictly theological sense. By grace I mean an inner harmony, essentially spiritual, which can be translated into outward harmony. I am seeking perhaps what Socrates asked for in the prayer from the *Phaedrus* when he said, "May the outward and inward man be at one." I would like to achieve a state of inner spiritual grace from which I could function and give as I was meant to in the eye of God.

Anne Morrow Lindbergh, Gift from the Sea

Library of Congress Cataloging in Publication Data:
Author's name entry.

Cowan, Gregory.
  Writing.

  Includes index.
  1. English language—Rhetoric. I. Cowan, Elizabeth,
1940-   joint author. II. Title.

PE1408.C663	808'.042	79-24989
ISBN 0-471-01559-8		

Printed in the United States of America

10 9 8 7 6 5 4 3 2

PREFACE

Is there anything in this text that will make the teaching of writing and learning how to write easier and more successful? I believe so. Four years of workshops with hundreds of college, university, and secondary-school teachers across the country; a total of some thirty-five years, between the two of us, teaching writing; classtesting the concepts of the text with more than 300 students in community college, four-year college, and university classrooms; and working with graduate students in rhetoric and composition courses—all have combined to give us a feeling of confidence in the approach that this book takes.

The book has five main sections: Creating, Shaping, Completing, Applications to Practical Writing, and a Rhetoric Handbook. The first three of these follow the writing process from the first random word put down on paper, through the thesis formation/development stage, to the polished, revised, and edited final copy. The fourth section applies the concepts learned in the Creating, Shaping, and Completing stages to practical writing: research papers, essay examination questions, speech writing, business writing, writing about literature, and journal writing. The final section supplies the necessary information about conventions of grammar, punctuation, usage, and mechanics in a concise and complete handbook.

Throughout the text you will find:
- lively conversation
- visual reinforcement of concepts
- an attractive and functional design format
- a "divide-and-conquer" plan that makes writing more manageable
- traditional and basic principles of writing placed in contemporary contexts
- every aspect of writing illustrated copiously by both student and professional writing
- self-contained writing assignments, complete with readings, how-to instructions for students, and writing contexts for the essays
- application of writing principles to real-life writing situations
- a solid handbook that, in one reviewer's words, "could stand as a book in itself."

Stage One, Creating, concentrates on how to get ideas for writing. Covering invention from Aristotle to modern brain research, from the well-known Reporter's Formula to modern tagmemics, Stage One provides step-by-step instructions in how to find something authentic and interesting to say in a piece of writing. Specifically, this first section of the book teaches three heuristics in depth (called *Creating Techniques* in our text): Looping, Cubing, and Classical Invention. Studying these approaches will not only provide writers with a repertory of ways to think about a subject but also reinforce the fundamental concept: *find something to say before attempting to write the essay itself.* After studying Stage One, Creating, beginning writers will always have something beneficial to do when they sit down to write something for the first time. It is the aim of this first section of text to teach invention heuristics that are *directly* related to the writing of essays, research papers, speeches, and kindred applications. That is why we have not referred to creating as *prewriting:* we don't think that it is. Neither do we call it *free writing,* for it isn't that either. While there are warm-up exercises that are valuable to students in getting them to put pen to paper, we have not concentrated on such exercises in our text. Instead, in this first stage we have included heuristics that can lead directly to an essay or other piece of writing. There is a direct relationship between the writing the students learn to do in this Creating Stage and the final copy of their assignment. You will find that there is no time wasted in the process; the activities from Creating through Completing are of a piece: they are time- and work-efficient.

Stage Two, Shaping, begins with a down-to-earth discussion of current communication theory, emphasizing the crucial role that *audience* plays in any piece of writing. The differences between writing and talking, between private and public writing, are all discussed so that students can see why and how producing an essay, letter, research paper, speech, or résumé is different from writing for themselves. Shaping covers such crucial subjects as identifying and evaluating an audience, finding a good thesis, developing a thesis, forming the essay, recognizing and practicing various basic essay arrangements, writing first drafts, outlining, and rewriting. In Shaping you will find the essential concepts of structured, developed writing placed in a context that explains to students *why* such things are important. The writing assignments and application exercises reinforce these shaping concepts.

Stage Three, Completing, covers all of the basics for revision and editing. Revising for flow concentrates on the paragraph: topic sentence and function paragraphs, transition, and reminder signs. Revising for energy concentrates on the sentence: sentence combining, sentence variety, parallelism, subordination, coordination, and repetition and balance. Revising for punch concentrates on the word: vague v. specific, jargon v. concrete, colorless v. descriptive. Editing skills—correct spelling, punctuation, accepted usage, mechanics—are covered in detail for students as they finish a piece of work.

With the *Practical Applications* section of the text, students are taught how to apply the three stages of the writing process—Creating, Shaping, and Completing—to particular kinds of writing. There is a thorough chapter on the research paper, where students can actually follow a student's progress as she writes her first term paper. This chapter also contains an extremely valuable *ABC Guide of Useful Information in Writing a Research Paper*, a feature that has aided freshmen in English and experienced writers as well. The chapter on *Essay Examination Writing* in the Practical Applications section teaches students how to write good test answers in short time and contains many student examples for study and practice. The chapter on *Speech Writing* includes in-depth analysis of a speech and provides a checklist that many professional speakers have adopted for their own use after being exposed to it in our workshops.

The chapter on *Business Writing* is complete with business letters, job applications, résumés—everything a person might need to refer to as she or he enters and performs in the job market. Models and examples abound. And the *Writing about Literature* chapter not only provides models of fiction, poetry, and drama but also opens with a review of the elements of the three genres; it is, therefore, a self-contained "all about literature" chapter that has proved very helpful to students as they write about stories, poems, and plays that they have read. The chapter on *Journal Writing* is a compilation of journal excerpts and reasons for keeping a journal. It contains some of the most imaginative journal exercises that you will find anywhere.

Finally, the *Rhetoric Handbook* section is a compilation of information about parts of speech, diction and style, in-depth editing, spelling, punctuation, grammar, mechanics, and usage. One of the most usable features of this handbook section is the *ABC Guide to Correcting Your Writing*. With this quick reference guide, a student can find in alphabetical order almost *any* error marked on her or his paper and can see why it is wrong and how to correct it. There is thus no need to search for the error in a separate chapter of the handbook. This double presentation—first in a chapter itself and then, again, in alphabetical order in a special guide to correction—lets students study the rules in their contexts (in the chapters themselves) *or* quickly refer to a particular rule (in the *ABC Guide*) to understand some error marked on their papers.

In addition to the five major divisions of the text, there are ten mini-chapters scattered throughout the book: *Writing Assignments for Essays*. These assignments cover the following purposes for writing: personal experience, how-to, problem/solution, explanation, exploratory, personal viewpoint, assertion-with-proof, persuasion, information, and evaluation. Each type of essay is first discussed; next comes a group of readings, done both by students and by professional writers, illustrating the particular form of writing practiced. Students are then shown how to write their own essay of this type. Included in each writing-assignment minichapter are contexts that students can use to determine their audience and purpose for writing, as well as rules and information about the kind of rhetorical pattern(s) appropriate to that particular kind of essay. For example, when students learn to write an evaluation essay, they are taught in that same section rules about the comparison/contrast rhetorical pattern of thought, since comparison/contrast is critical to doing evaluative writing. Similarly, in the Personal Experience Essay section, students are taught about narration and description, again because these are necessary ingredients of good personal-experience writing. Explanation essays cover cause and effect, classification, and definition; how-to essays cover analysis by division and details; and so on. All the rhetorical patterns of thought are embedded in type-of-writing essay assignments based on real-life writing contexts. Instructors report that these assignment packages have been very successful in the classroom because students see a reason for the essays they are writing and find it easy to practice a particular rhetorical mode or pattern of thought since it is "organic" to the type of essay that they are writing at the time.

The book is filled with exercises for practice and discussion, writing assignments, and examples. There are approximately seventy-five to eighty pieces of student writing, both bad and good (see Special Index: Student Writing) and more than one hundred excerpts from professional writers, men and women from all over the world (see Special Index: Writers Cited). Because the book has sprung from our years of classroom teaching, it is practical as well as theoretical. Instructors using this text will have in their hands a coherent and sequential syllabus for teaching writing. Students using this book will have a step-by-step guide to writing that will stand them in good stead now — while they are writing in college — and later — when they write outside of school.

A quick glance at the dictionary entry for *preface* reveals that it is not only a statement of purpose and scope (covered in the paragraphs above), but also, in its liturgical definition, a statement of thanksgiving. It is appropriate that the word should be defined both ways, for as the coauthor of this text, I am humble when I recall the scores of people whose support of Greg and me as we wrote the book made the text possible.

First acknowledgment must go to Tom Gay, who saw the potential for the book and signed it, who served as our editor during the first three years of the book's development, and who continued to oversee the text through its final publication. Cliff Mills, who became our editor about a year ago, gave the most thorough and professional guidance during that critical time when the final form of the text was emerging and being refined. To both these friends, we owe the book.

There are others whom we want to acknowledge at Wiley. Butch Cooper, Jack Burton, Carol Luitjens, Rick Leyh, Wayne Anderson, Al Lesure, Don Wallin, and Larry Little advised, encouraged, and taught us. Angie Lee and Ed Burke provided the elegant design. Stella Kupferberg researched and provided the beautiful pictures. Suzanne Ingrao and Janet Sessa oversaw the book's production. Geraldine Ivins, Connie Rende, Justine Ollearis, and Elizabeth Doble were a support staff that handled dozens of details critical to the success of the book. Ronald Nelson oversaw the editorial care given our text, at times pitching in to set things right; he also supplied us with the suggestion for the book's title, as did Stephen Perine, and thanks are due to both. And Arthur Vergara, our depth editor and friend, expertly handled all the back-and-forths of our thought processes, the excesses and inexactnesses of our written language; he is responsible for the clarity, coherence, and structure of the text. To all these members of our Wiley family, we owe enormous thanks. Nor would we overlook the careful work of Marian Reiner, our permissions consultant, who pored over our many excerpts and selections.

To our professional colleagues who critiqued, advised, evaluated, and recommended as the book was being written we give grateful acknowledgment. Edward P.J. Corbett, Donald Stewart, Paul Bryant, and Marilyn Cooper reviewed the book. Harry Dean and Marilyn Fillers classtested it. Charles Anderson suggested some material; and Vicky Reinke researched and reviewed certain sections of the text.

The work of our two research assistants is almost beyond praise. Beatrice Egle researched the handbook section of the text; she is also responsible for the writing of significant parts of that section as well as of many of the application exercises throughout the text. Karen Davis prepared the ABC Guide to Correcting Your Writing, contributed significantly to the chapter on the research paper, proofread the galleys, wrote several examples in the text, researched and prepared materials for the writing-assignment minichapters scattered throughout the text, and gave such moral support and enthusiastic encouragement as enabled us to meet impossible deadlines and complete the book.

All of our students are acknowledged by the very existence of the book. To the last class taught by Greg and me, however, I would like to give special thanks: Mary Wolff, Patricia DeFloria, Teresa Harbich, Holly Jacobs, Jeannette Goodwin, Nancy Rutledge, Mary Russell, Charles McDaniel, Lillian Wesley, Karen Davis, and Nancy Hutson. Their response and success let us *know* that the book works. I also wish to express gratitude to all our students—this last class included—who allowed us to use their work as examples in the text.

The support of our families is at the core of our ability to conceive and write the text. Tommie and Rachel Harper, Pearl Cowan, Barbara and Wilson Walker, Frank and Peggy Harper: they admired, encouraged, reacted, and even helped revise. The book belongs as much to them as it does to us.

Finally, I acknowledge my coauthor, husband, partner, sweetheart, and friend, Greg Cowan. His knowledge, voice, enthusiasm, creativity, compassion, and love permeate every page of this text. He saw the book through to completion before that afternoon of his final jog—July 2, 1979. I have no words for the quality and totality of his contribution to his students, his friends, his family, and to me.

Elizabeth Cowan

TABLE OF CONTENTS

THE HANDBOOK 590

ELIZABETH COWAN received her B.S. and M. Ed. from the University of Chattanooga, and her Ph.D. from the University of Tennessee. She has taught English at Cleveland State Community College, where she was also the Head of the Division of Humanities, and is currently teaching at Texas A&M University. In addition to editing the A.D.E. Bulletin, and co-editing the STUDIES IN LANGUAGE AND LITERATURE series, Elizabeth has served as the Director of the English Program for the Modern Language Association and as coordinator of the Association of Departments of English.

GREGORY COWAN received his B.A. from Whitman College, his M.A. from the University of Washington, and did additional graduate work in English, Linguistics and Communication at Washington State University, Portland State University and the New School of Social Research. He taught English at Clark College, Forest Park Community College, City College of New York, and most recently at Texas A&M University. In addition to co-authoring six textbooks, including PLAIN ENGLISH PLEASE, and the PLAIN ENGLISH RHETORIC AND READER, Greg at various times served as the Chairman of the National Junior College Committee, panelist and discussion leader at many NCTE and CCCC national conventions, and consulting editor for college textbooks. He died in July of 1979.

BUILDING A CABIN, WRITING AN ESSAY

Does it seem strange to begin a textbook on writing with a photo essay on building a cabin?

Actually, there's a definite connection. Writing essays—what you will be doing in this class—is similar in several ways to building a cabin. The steps you go through, from first having the idea to finally completing the project, are very much the same. Let's consider these stages, one at a time.

STAGE 1

Naturally, a cabin doesn't simply materialize out of thin air. A lot of planning and preparation happen before you can sit in a cheerful room and enjoy the view through the brand-new windows. That planning and preparation may actually have begun so far back that it would be hard now to know just when the idea of building a cabin first occurred. It may have been at age four, when you got some Lincoln Logs for a birthday present and started building pioneer cabins. It could have begun with staying in cabins at camp. The planning or dreaming or thinking-about-it could have continued with seeing cabins in television shows and in movies. And perhaps along the way there were occasional stories about people who lived in cabins.

No matter when and how the thought about building a cabin first appeared, having the idea is at the center of the first stage. First there is an idea of building. During this stage you merely think about it, collect ideas, gather impressions.

When we look at this initial stage closely, we find that it has several specific characteristics.

Stage 1 Is Exploratory
You might buy cabin books, send off for floor plans, draw blueprints, build model cabins out of matchsticks, balsa wood, or cardboard, visit cabins, consider different locations to build on, save money for a cabin, collect pictures of cabins. You are just thinking of *all* the possibilities at this stage, and you want to range as far as you can.

Stage 1 Is Tentative
In this stage you're merely collecting ideas; you've made no commitment. You have not decided where the cabin is going to be built. You are not committed to a particular kind of cabin. You haven't invested in land or materials, only thought about them; you're just considering a lot of possibilities. It's all tentative, and you are totally free to change your mind as often as you want.

Stage 1 Is Enjoyable   You can dream your biggest dreams in this stage; it doesn't cost you a dime. You can say "I like this . . . I like that . . . I like the other" without having to choose among the contradictory ideas. You can experiment, change, adapt and be extravagant, wild, and impractical. The point is to collect as many ideas as possible — *and have fun while you are doing it.*

OK; now what about writing?

There's a comparable *Stage 1* in writing, when you collect ideas on a subject much as you would collect ideas for building a cabin. Perhaps you begin with an assignment or a simple urge to write. You merely think about it from time to time, maybe while you're vacuuming the rug or washing the car, or maybe while you're walking to algebra class or standing in line in the cafeteria. Thoughts about the subject simply come up, and you explore what you think about it, what you know about it, and how you feel about it. **Certainly, *Stage 1* in writing is *exploratory.***

You also get to experiment with the subject. You can try various approaches, arguing now for it, now against. You can pretend to be an amateur or an expert, an insider or a visitor, someone who is involved or someone who is merely an observer. And you can switch around as much as you like, seeing what works for you and what doesn't. The ideas are tentative.

But can it be *enjoyable* too? Why not? Humans naturally like to explore, to range widely. And we enjoy operating without limits sometimes, free from commitments and accountabilities. So this stage is enjoyable almost automatically, simply because it is exploratory and tentative. But more than that, it is enjoyable because it gives us something to do to get writing started. Doing those creating activities, we are active. Rather than sitting there worrying, we're engaged in generating ideas, pursuing thoughts and insights. Eventually, there's the delightful surprise of bumping into a new way of thinking about a thing, a new way of looking at it, a fresh seeing, a forgotten memory, a strong sense of clarity. But that reward comes at the end. At the beginning it is the sense of moving, of being on your way. If you approach this stage in order to stay open and see what you can discover, you'll enjoy it. In fact, if it's not enjoyable, you are probably doing Stage 1 all wrong.

STAGE 2

There comes a time in building a cabin when the dreaming stops and actual work begins. Here things get more serious. You don't have quite as much freedom as before because you must begin to make some firm decisions. You determine what kind of cabin you are going to build: log, A-frame, prefab, lean-to, or whatever. You start looking seriously for a site, and then you purchase one. You settle on a definite blueprint.

Stage 2 Requires Commitments   You make a series of decisions, plans, agreements, contracts. The project moves out of dreams and ideas into reality — *out of your mind and onto the ground.* Mistakes at this stage can cost something.

Stage 2 Requires Physical Work   After the plans, the land, the contracts, and the contractors have all been dealt with, *the physical work begins.* You clear the land, purchase materials, and start building. Down goes the foundation, up go the framing, roof, and walls.

Stage 2 Requires Clear Plans   At this point in the work *you need to be as clear and certain as possible* about the plan of the cabin. Although it is still possible to change a window here and add a partition there, any major changes — say to the foundation or roofline — would be very costly.

What is the comparable Stage 2 in writing?

Though the parallels are not exactly the same, there is a *Stage 2* in writing. That's where **you begin making definite choices and commit yourself to a specific topic, a particular purpose, an orderly plan.** Those *commitments* help you get the ideas out of your head and onto the paper. *Stage 2* moves from private to public writing. And while there was complete freedom in just collecting ideas for yourself, now some discipline needs to be imposed on that jumble of ideas if you want to make logical order of them for someone else.

To be sure, there is *physical work* involved. You can't "think" a piece of writing onto paper, or "talk" it there. You need to sit in one place with a pencil, pen, or typewriter, and **keep putting down one word after another,** one sentence after another, until the task is done. And serious changes at this point can lead to frustration. On the other hand, you have more leeway to change in *Stage 2* of writing than you would in cabin building. For example, if you don't like what you've written, all it costs you is your time and some paper. But it *does* cost something, and *clear plans can keep the cost to a minimum.*

STAGE 3

Finally, in cabin building there comes the finishing-up stage. Some people think this is the hardest part of building. (Prefab companies will sell their houses *much* more cheaply if the buyer agrees to do the finishing.) The frame, walls, cabinets, and countertops are all there. The rough work has been done; all the big pieces and major chunks are in the right places. Now it's time for the finishing touches.

Stage 3 Handles the Fine Details It's time to sand, rub, paint, stain, varnish, install fixtures, clean glass, haul away building scraps, make a path to the door, put up curtains — in general, turn the shell into a livable cabin. All the major decisions have been implemented at this point. The size, shape, and type of cabin, as well as the location, have all been taken care of. But *there are a thousand and one tiny details that have to be handled* before the cabin is really finished. It's rather picky work, often tedious, certainly time-consuming.

And, yes, there is a Stage 3 in writing.

In fact, many people mistakenly think that *Stage 3* is the whole writing process. Although *Stage 3* activities *can* occur any time during the writing process, it makes the most sense to do them at the end. Otherwise, it's like trying to vacuum your cabin while the roofers are sawing rafters overhead — that is to say, it's likely to get in the way unless it's left to the appropriate time.

Stage 3 completes the writing. It's the cleaning-up stage, the time to consider *fine details.* Are the words spelled right? Any grammatical errors? Is there enough information? Are the left margins even? Is anything left out? These picky, often tedious, time-consuming details do the same for the essay that they do for a cabin: they put on the finishing touches that make the cabin (or essay) presentable to other people. This stage completes the project, and nothing remains to be done. It's finished, ready for an appreciative world.

DIFFERENCES

You don't need to be told that there are differences between building a cabin and writing an essay — but it's a good idea to pay them some notice. For the *cabin*, people:

>**expect to plan,**
>**take the project in stages, and**
>**tend to enjoy each stage.**

For the *essay*, people often:

>**find writing more a chore than a pleasure,**
>**tend to give all the attention to the finished product,**
>**tend to ignore intermediate stages, and**
>**feel no accomplishment until the essay is completely finished.**

Furthermore, people for the most part have to write absolutely alone. (Of course it's possible and useful to discuss ideas and drafts with a friend or teacher; but most *productive* writers spend many more hours alone with paper and pencil than they do in conferences and discussions.) Finally, essays get graded and cabins don't.

SIMILARITIES

Despite these important differences, the similarities are even more important. In fact, the similarities show how you can learn to write more efficiently—and more enjoyably.

Let's look at those similarities right now.

As soon as writing is broken down into stages the way building a cabin is, it becomes *manageable*. Obviously, if you were trying to vacuum your cabin (a *Stage 3* activity) while the roofers were sawing rafters overhead (a *Stage 2* activity), you surely wouldn't get much done; you'd just be frustrated. In the same way, it's ridiculous to worry about spelling while you are collecting ideas in *Stage 1*. Yet we are all prone to do exactly that —to *unfocus* our attention and surrender our energy *by trying to handle all three stages at once*.

Paying attention to the similarities between building a cabin and writing an essay can brighten matters more than you think.

When you learn to deal with each stage in the writing process at the appropriate time and deal with that stage only, you will find that you not only accomplish the job but you also enjoy the feeling of satisfaction and success as you finish each separate part—rather than waiting until you get the entire essay completed.

Divide and conquer!
Stage 1: collect ideas on the topic. Enjoy doing this, and feel completion when you have finished.
Stage 2: make choices and commitments about subject and order. Shape up your ideas. When that stage is done, feel some additional satisfaction.
Stage 3: check for completeness and polish the essay. Enjoy getting the wording exactly right, the spelling absolutely accurate. Then enjoy the whole completed project.

Doing an essay this way, you experience rewards with each stage of the writing process. Those rest stops at the end of each stage are comforting and refreshing. You aren't a nervous wreck trying to do everything at once. In fact, you are calm and in control because you move only *one step at a time*. There's satisfaction *three* times instead of once, since you appreciate finishing each stage. Then there's the final sense of accomplishment when you hand the paper in.

Wouldn't it be great if, when you finished this book, you found that you could actually enjoy writing essays almost as much as you'd enjoy having a cabin?

STAGE 1

CABIN

Dreaming about a cabin
Wishing for a cabin
Playing with Lincoln Logs
Seeing different kinds of cabins
Buying cabin books
Making sketches and models of
  cabins
Talking with people about
  cabins
Saving money for a cabin
Sending off for cabin plans
Collecting pictures of cabins
Visiting cabins

ESSAY

Having an assignment and/or
  urge to write
Writing down everything you
  can think of about the subject
Talking to people about the
  subject
Reading about the subject
Doing discovery exercises to
  find out what you know on
  the subject
Collecting ideas/notes on the
  subject
Asking yourself questions about
  the subject
Thinking and daydreaming
  about the subject
Making lists of things to say
  about it

STAGE 2

CABIN

Moving from thoughts about it
  to doing something
Making specific commitments
Deciding exactly where cabin
  will be
Deciding on a specific plan for
  cabin
Clearing land
Putting material on site
Hiring help
Laying foundation
Raising walls, roof

ESSAY

Moving from thoughts about it
  to doing something
Narrowing what you are going
  to say to something specific
Deciding exactly what your aim
  or purpose will be
Making choices about what
  examples, illustrations, facts
  to use
Writing first and second rough
  draft copies
Deciding on order

CABIN
Completing inside: painting, sanding, varnishing
Cleaning up yard: planting, raking, burning trash
Scraping stickers off windows
Laying tile, linoleum, carpet
Hooking up electricity, plumbing
Putting up windows, screens
Waterproofing
Furnishing it

ESSAY
Reading essay aloud to yourself or someone else
Seeing where weak spots are and strengthening them
Checking spelling, punctuation, mechanics
Polishing essay for effectiveness
Typing or copying in final form

FINALLY

CABIN
Call friends and have a party to celebrate!

ESSAY
Hand in paper, call friends, and celebrate!

STAGE 1/CREATING

HOW TO FIND SOMETHING TO SAY

PURPOSE

During the creating stage you:

Set yourself up to have ideas on the subject

Follow specific activities to get started on a writing assignment or task

Tap your total resources by putting all thoughts on paper with no immediate evaluation of their significance or importance

Discover what you know and think about a particular subject

Get clear, at the end, exactly what you want to communicate to another person about a particular subject

To <u>CREATE:</u> To bring into existence: to cause, make; to produce through imaginative skill

To <u>INVENT:</u>
To think up or imagine; to create or produce for the first time; to make.

To <u>DISCOVER:</u>
To obtain sight or knowledge of; unearth; (presupposes exploration, investigation, or chance encounter, and always implies the previous existence of what becomes known; implies finding rather than making).

CREATING AND WRITING

How often have you sat down to write, only to find that you couldn't think of a single thing to say? You wrote a line or two, scratched it out, crumpled up the paper, threw it away, and started the whole cycle all over again. The thoughts just wouldn't come.

This situation occurs for all writers at some time or other, but it occurs most frequently for people who are waiting for a "good idea." *Somehow they developed the belief that it is possible to know what they want to say before they begin to write*—but that's not usually the way ideas come. Since "good ideas" and fully developed subjects almost never pop into the writer's head—especially during those first minutes or hours—there tends to be a lot of sitting and staring, and even some despair that any thoughts will *ever* come!

Actually, not knowing what to write when you sit down is a perfectly natural reaction to the situation. The feeling is uncomfortable, but it is normal. And the uncertainty can actually be *beneficial*.

"Not knowing what to say can actually be beneficial?" you exclaim, as you watch the clock ticking on the wall.

Yes.

If you sit down and write the very first thing that pops into your mind, you will often get clichés, worn-out information, stuff everybody already knows. You won't really care about what you are saying, and readers won't be involved or interested.

Beginning to write *before* you know what to say, and finding out as you go along—that's one of the best ways for you to think of something personal, fresh, and interesting on the subject, something out of your own experience, something that nobody but you might think of. It also allows you to find out what you think about a subject, to discover something about it, because *often you know a thing quite differently after you write about it than you did before you wrote*. In fact, often it turns out that just getting your thoughts down on paper will produce clarity or insight that you wouldn't have had otherwise.

"But this is Catch 22," you say; "I've got to write an essay on the topic and give it to someone else, and you say it's OK to start writing before I know what I'm going to tell the person! That will really go over big!"

Well, the way out of Catch 22 is to realize that the writing you do in this stage is *not* the essay; it is a collection of thoughts that will *lead* to the essay. You don't have to worry at this point about whether your thoughts are good or bad; you are just *exploring* the subject to find something to say. What you put down now is very *tentative* and is really being written just for you yourself (and your own *enjoyment*). This stage, in fact, is very private—just you and your subject. You aren't trying to be clear for anyone else; you aren't thinking of committing yourself to any specific part of the subject. You are just writing whatever comes into your head on the subject—maybe a list, a dialogue, even a heap of disjointed thoughts, so that you can later, with an objective eye, read through your private writing and find something you really want to develop into an essay.

choice of business and industry
BRAINSTORMING

Business leaders often employ a *brainstorming* session to discover ways to solve problems, create new products or services, or get a fresh approach to an old situation. Brainstorming is a group activity—*ideas spoken by someone else stimulate you to have ideas of your own*. It is this play back and forth that causes new thoughts to come. Brainstorm-

BRAINSTORM:
A sudden and violent disturbance in the brain; a sudden clever, whimsical, or foolish idea; a group of people freely calling out ideas on a subject; a session to explore a topic in order to produce as many ideas as possible.

ing can work particularly well for you as a creating technique if you and several of your friends have the same topic to write on or have the same assignment.

HERE ARE THE RULES FOR BRAINSTORMING

1 **Do it as a group activity.**
2 **Call out every idea you have on the subject.**
3 **Be absolutely nonjudgmental.** No idea should be made fun of or discarded. You and the others in the group must feel completely free to say whatever comes to mind and know that the idea won't be evaluated.
4 **Jot down all the ideas as they are spoken so that you will have a list to use later.**
5 **Do your own evaluation of the ideas privately sometime after the brainstorming session.**

You will probably have a long list of ideas when the brainstorming session is over. Now go through the list and mark out all the ideas that absolutely won't work or that you are just not interested in. Then, of the remaining ideas, pick the one or two that you can really see yourself writing on. Finally, run these ideas through one of the written creating techniques, and you will be well on your way to knowing what you want to say about this subject when you write.

"But I've got a deadline," you lament. "I don't have time to waste on writing personal stuff that isn't an essay."

This is The Great Paradox:

Although such exploratory writing won't be an essay, it will perhaps be the most important piece of writing you do for the essay. A good *creating* period will make the next two stages—*shaping* and *completing*—much easier, faster, and more productive. You will discover that you actually *save* time by spending it this way. It may seem strange now, but when you've tried it once or twice, you will see: *The freer you are with your time at this stage, the more efficiently your time is spent on the other two stages.* This is so because you will have a lot of material to use when you get to the point of deciding exactly what you want to say to a reader, and you will not have to stare at the sheet of paper, waiting for inspiration to strike. It's like already having bought all the groceries, measuring cups, knives, spoons, utensils, and the like, and having them ready on the kitchen counter *before* you begin to cook dinner. There's something there for you to work with, and you really will save time.

Dr. James Austin's
FOUR KINDS OF LUCK

KIND OF LUCK	ELEMENTS INVOLVED IN GETTING THIS LUCK TO HAPPEN TO YOU	PERSONALITY NEEDED FOR THIS KIND OF LUCK
1	"Blind luck." It just happens; there is nothing you need to do. You are just the fortunate recipient of the luck.	No special qualities at all.
2	Favors those *in motion*. Events are brought together to form "happy accidents" because you have applied your energies just by doing *something*.	Curiosity about many things; persistence; willingness to explore.
3	Favors the *prepared mind*. Some special attitude developed in the past allows/enables you to see a new fact or perceive ideas in a new relationship.	A background of knowledge, based on abilities to observe, remember, and quickly form new associations.
4	Favors one special individual because of who that person is; couldn't happen to anyone else. Is as personal as a signature and comes from some unique combination of past and present experiences.	Some unexpected, unplanned combination that connects what you've done in the past in a totally unrelated area with the subject at hand. There is nothing you can do specifically to prepare for this kind of luck.

THE CREATING STAGE BRINGS YOU LUCK #2.
IT ALSO ASSISTS IN LUCK #s 1, 3, AND 4.

The creating stage, as chaotic and unsure as it may seem, is not only efficient; it actually leads to a strong, interesting idea for your paper. You will always be able to come up finally with something to say — *if* you are willing to be in motion: curious, persistent, willing to explore. So, allow yourself to realize that the creating stage is every bit as valuable as a careful revision or a final draft, and you will truly be in touch with a major source of writing power.

Elizabeth Cade is president of the local Chamber of Commerce. She must prepare a report to mail to the membership in which she outlines new directions for the organization for the coming year. She dreads this writing task because *she isn't sure what she wants to say.* She sits down, however, and does a creating stage—and finds that ideas emerge which give her confidence that she'll be able to get the report done. Here is what she wrote in the creating stage:

Ideas for my Report

What do I want the Chamber of Commerce to do next year?

1 Get new business and industry into our town.
2 Sponsor a series of symphony concerts for young people.
3 Have more meetings.
4 Get a government grant to set up a tutoring center for adults in the community.
5 Buy the old Mansard House and convert it into a library and reception hall for the organization.

That list seemed to be everything she could think of right off the bat, so she reread what she had written and had this dialogue with herself:

WHAT DOES THIS LIST TELL ME?

• That I have long-range and short-range goals for the Chamber of Commerce.
• That I need to decide which of my goals I want the most.
• That I have lots of ideas on things to do but not many on where to get the money to do them.

"So I'd better do some serious thinking on this before I start my report."
"Serious thinking about what?"
"About *arranging goals into short- and long-term groups.*
About *arranging goals in order of importance.*
About *places to get money.*"
"Great. So now you know exactly what you need to think about."
"Right. And now that I have these ideas, I know what to develop before I get back to writing the actual report."

In this sample you can see how Ms. Cade uses the creating stage to make lists of things she'd like to do and how she talks to herself, in writing, in order to organize her thoughts and direct her energies. And you can also quite clearly see that Elizabeth is actually *discovering what she thinks* as she goes along. She is spotting areas she needs to concentrate on and seeing problems that she hadn't thought of until she sat down to put words on paper. Her final report will be much better because she has given herself this time to do a creating stage *before* she actually begins writing the report.

---

a familiar way to get ideas **MAKING A LIST**	

We all make lists in order not to forget. What about making lists in order to discover?

List-making can be a valuable first step in many writing situations, especially those that require you to recall or realize something you already know. For example, you might list the steps in a process — how to make a bookshelf — or list arguments for or against something.

As you settle down to write, a list can:

a give you a definite purpose and activity to get you started;
b cause you to have associations and thereby to think of something you might not have thought of before;
c provide you with a framework for your thinking at that moment.

You hardly need any rules for list-making, but you might want to remember these suggestions:

1 Put a title at the top of your list so you will stay on purpose and always know why you are making the list. ("Why I deserve a raise" or "Things our town could do for young adults.")
2 Write as fast as possible and use short words or phrases.
3 Don't be critical of any item on the list at this point; just collect as many things on the list as you possibly can in a limited time.

When you have finished the list, you can do several things: select the items on the list that seem to have the most promise for your writing; put the items on the list in some order — say, most important to least important; cross out items that you don't like; expand one or two items; add new items. The important thing is for the list to serve as a source of ideas for you as you begin to write your paper.

LIST:
An item-by-item printed or written entry of persons or things, often arranged in a particular order, and usually of a specified nature or category: a guest list; a shopping list; to itemize; to catalog.

APPLICATION

Choose one of the writing situations below and do a creating stage similar to the one in the sample above.

1 You are a student whose teacher has just assigned the term's first essay: a description of your home town. What would you write in the creating stage for this assignment?

2 You are looking for a job; the employment counselor tells you to write a short paper in which you describe all the jobs you have had in the past and what skills you developed on those jobs. What would you write in the creating stage for this assignment?

3 You have just been elected president of your hobby club or interest group; your local newspaper would like you to write an article that points out to the general public what is so interesting about your group. What would you write in the creating stage for this assignment?

TECHNIQUES FOR CREATING

You have just seen an example in which something as simple as making a list can be a creating activity in the writing process. Unfortunately, however, creating devices such as lists, dialogues, or brainstorming sessions don't *always* produce the best idea or enough ideas for a piece of writing. Because this is so, writers find it useful to have a whole catalog of creating techniques that they can choose from. These techniques, to be efficient and profitable, must result in more than motion for motion's sake. After all, if it were just *motion* we wanted, we would be as satisfied with seasickness as with an essay. **The creating stage must lead somewhere; it must move the writer toward a structured, developed piece of writing.** Even though the writing in the creating stage is for the writer's benefit and need not be finished (or addressed to any specific audience), still it must be *purposeful*. The purpose of the creating techniques is to assist you in coming up with ideas for your writing.

The following three creating techniques are designed to help *any* writer come up with something to say for *any* writing task. The techniques are directed toward the writing of essays because that is probably the kind of writing you will be doing most frequently in this course. You will see in the Applications section, however, how the three creating techniques can be used for all kinds of writing, including term papers, technical reports, memos, letters, and literary analyses. For now, however, you want simply to *practice* the three techniques so that you can experience how they assist you in having ideas on any subject. Become familiar with them. Make them a permanent part of your own personal repertory of ways to get ideas. *With such a repertory you should never have to worry again about not having something to say.*

REPERTORY:
The stock of songs, plays, operas, readings, or other pieces that a player or company is prepared to perform; the range or number of skills, aptitudes, or special accomplishments of a particular person or group.

1. LOOPING

LOOPING is a writing activity in which you start with a subject and, without planning or consciously thinking, write anything that comes into your mind on the topic. You write nonstop for *x* amount of minutes just to see what ideas emerge. At the end of the writing time—the loop—you stop writing and read what you've written. Look for the line of thought that seems to be developing, or the best idea that emerged, or the thought that seems to invite you to follow it—whatever it is about the writing that seems to stand out in bold relief. Then you write a single sentence expressing that loop's hot spot or center of gravity. Do at least three loops for each topic.

This technique lets you explore a subject to see what you know or think about it—without making any decisions about whether the ideas are good or bad, or whether they are important enough to do a paper on. The looping activity, too, gets other things that are on your mind out on paper so they don't block your mind as you work to come up with something to say on the subject. (You might like to know that this technique is based on an approach Peter Elbow discusses in his book *Writing without Teachers;* in fact, you might enjoy reading his version.)

FOUR RULES TO FOLLOW IN LOOPING

1 Begin with a specific topic.
2 Write nonstop for *x* amount of minutes.
3 Make no changes or corrections.
4 Write a center of gravity sentence for each loop before going on to the next one.

Rule 1: Begin with a Specific Topic At the top of the page, put down the subject (topic) you are going to write on in the loop. This allows your mind to focus on one particular thing at the beginning. As you write, you may discover that your mind gets off the subject and you are writing about something else entirely. When this happens, *go ahead and finish what you are writing about* and then go back to the subject you listed at the top of the page and concentrate on *that* subject. Often what you write that is "*off* the subject" will be something that is *on* your mind, perhaps worrying you; or it may be something that looks as if it were off the subject but is actually connected somehow. Either way, the "off-the-subject" writing is valuable because either it gets whatever is on your mind (and in the way of your sticking to the subject) out onto paper or it gives you an idea that you didn't at first think was connected to the topic. The aim of LOOPING, however, is to **come up with some idea on a specific subject** for a paper. So staying on that subject as closely as possible is the best thing to do.

Rule 2: Write Nonstop for X Minutes

This rule is simple but crucial. (Give ten minutes to each loop when you are first learning the technique. As you progress, you may want to increase the amount of time you spend on each loop.) Part of the "magic" of this technique comes about because you *must* keep writing. Do not take your pencil or pen off the page. *Keep it moving the whole ten minutes.* You can write things like "I can't think of anything on this topic," or "This topic is dumb," or "I despise this looping activity." You may even draw circles or make chicken-scratch marks on the paper, but **you must keep the pen moving.** This is to keep your thoughts stirred up and your mind open to whatever ideas may occur on the topic.

Rule 3: Make No Corrections

Whether a writer follows this rule or breaks it will determine the success or failure of LOOPING. It is just that simple. You absolutely cannot stop to think about whether a word is spelled right or whether a comma is in the wrong place. You cannot stop to make a judgment of whether a statement you have just written is stupid or smart. You cannot stop to decide whether you want to say something or don't. *Any kind of correcting or deliberating will cause the looping activity not to work.* (There *is*, of course, a time to correct your work; it *isn't*, however, during the *Creating Stage*.) The purpose of LOOPING is to scare up ideas, and to do that you need to forge ahead, not pausing or polishing. **So don't mark anything out; don't change anything.** Just keep writing.

Rule 4: Write a Center of Gravity Sentence for Each Loop before Going on to the Next One

LOOPING is designed to help you produce an idea to write on. It differs from *free writing* in that there is a broad focus to the writing; that broad focus in the general subject area on which you are going to be writing. Although you will sweep off and back to the subject from time to time as you write your loops, you are always moving toward finding a specific topic or idea. One way to ensure that this happens is to ***stop*** *when you have finished each loop,* ***read*** *what you have written, and* ***decide*** *what main thing you seem to be talking about in that loop.* What comes up again and again? What is the drift of that particular piece of writing? When you've read your writing and thought about it, **express in a single sentence a statement that catches the "hot spot" or essence of what you said in that loop.** This activity lets you see what seems to have the most potential at this point. The center of gravity sentence for each loop will give you a starting place for the next loop, a focus for the next piece of writing. The ultimate result is a zeroing in of your thoughts on the subject as you write.

PRACTICING LOOPING

To be sure that you understand how LOOPING helps you have ideas on a subject, let's do a dry run. We will take a very unspecific subject, a very broad one, and see how the technique leads you to have something quite specific and focused to say about the topic. The beauty of all three techniques in this chapter is that they will work on the most general subjects imaginable. In fact, if they couldn't, they wouldn't be of very much use to writers, because most of the time writers don't get to choose exciting and fantastic subjects; they must find a way to make an *assigned* subject (or the topic nearest to hand) interesting. LOOPING and the other creating techniques will show you how.

LET BOTH LOBES WORK FOR YOU

There are two main lobes, or parts, in the brain. These lobes act in completely different ways and actually provide us with two completely different ways of knowing things.

LEFT
- logical, orderly
- linear, purposeful
- makes sense of things
- stores facts, information
- involved in language, math, chemistry

RIGHT
- impulsive, emotional
- subjective, unordered
- has hunches, intuition
- thinks in images, pictures
- involved in painting, dance, music

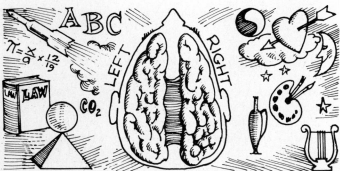

Our culture (but not all cultures) holds that the logic, order, analysis of the left lobe are more valuable than the hunches, intuition, non-verbal activities of the right. In some ways that makes sense: it's almost impossible to conceive of a cohesive, progressive society without language, order, and rational thinking. At the same time it is wasteful to ignore completely the activities of one half of our brain, as recent medical and psychological research has shown. In fact, many brilliant scientific discoveries had their lowly beginnings as "hunches" or "feelings."

In writing, particularly, it takes *both* lobes to be good. Writing with only the left lobe—rummaging among those facts and remembered bits of information—is like trying to lift a heavy cement block with one hand when you could be using both hands. Each lobe is a source of different kinds of strength.

Source of logical writing:
    organization
    coherence
    order.
Lets other people understand.

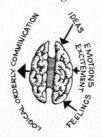

Source of exciting writing:
    original impressions
    personal knowledge
    emotion.
Your own unique way of seeing.

The creating stage sets up a situation where you can let both lobes work.

TOPIC: Money

To get ready to do a ten-minute loop writing on the subject of money, you will need some clean paper (be sure you have plenty) and a pen that won't run out of ink (you may want to have a spare handy). Write the word MONEY at the top of the first sheet. Have a clock, watch, or timer so that you can be sure when the ten minutes are up. Be clear about the rules: **no stopping, no changing, no correcting.**

OK. Ready?

Write the first ten-minute loop on MONEY.

Stop.

What happened during that ten minutes of writing? Did you write much on the subject itself? Did you find that your thoughts mostly rambled and didn't stay on the subject at all? Did you get bored? Did your hand hurt from writing?

Whatever you wrote about in this first loop is right! In the *Creating Stage* there is no wrong way; every word you write will contribute to your finding something to say. You will see later exactly why this is so.

Find the center of gravity in this first loop on MONEY.

Reread it. Your writing probably moved in several directions and raised a number of different points. But if you *had* to write a single sentence that expressed the hot spot, or the center of gravity of this loop, what would you write? This center of gravity sentence may not be the thing you *wrote the most* about; it may instead be the thing you *like most* in the writing or the thing you find *the most interesting*. Or it might be the idea or subject that you *returned to* several times in the loop. Just make a decision. If you can't figure out the main topic in that loop writing, just make up what you *think* the main topic is.

Write this center of gravity sentence at the end of your first loop.

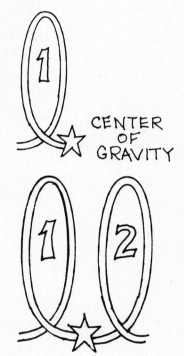

CENTER OF GRAVITY

Now you are ready for the second loop. Copy the center of gravity sentence on the top of a fresh sheet of paper. The rules are the same: your pen can't stop on the page; you can't correct. And, remember, there is *nothing* that can go wrong at this stage.

All set?

Write the second ten-minute loop on MONEY.

Stop.

Is your hand hurting? Shake it and rest. Shift around in your chair. Take two or three good deep breaths.

Now, read over what you wrote this time. Did anything pop up that didn't surface last time? Anything absolutely new? Or did you write about the same thing you wrote about last time? This loop may be closely related to the first one, may be something that *grew out of* the first loop, or may be *completely different from* the first loop. Any of these outcomes is completely all right!

Find the center of gravity in the second loop on MONEY.

Decide what the main thing was in this writing, and express that in a center of gravity sentence. Again, remember that the center of gravity sentence is whatever you think it is. It can be what you *wrote* about the most, what you *liked* the most, what seems *most interesting* to you. Anything you *think* is the main topic of the loop *is* the main topic.

Write one sentence expressing that.

CENTER OF GRAVITY

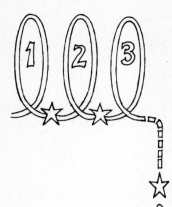

Get ready to repeat the process one more time. Write your second center of gravity sentence at the top of a fresh piece of paper, set your watch for ten minutes, and begin.

Write the third ten-minute loop on MONEY.

Stop.

When you finish this third loop, read it.

Then write the center of gravity sentence at the bottom of the page.

Congratulations!

You have finished the complete cycle. And you will probably be tired. Get up and stretch.

Usually by the end of the third loop you have come up with an idea that could be developed into an essay, something you could share with another person. Something will have stirred you or excited you or interested you; it may have just barely cropped up in the loop writings, but there are strong odds that you do see *something* to use as a slightly more focused subject than the broad word *money.* If so, you are ready at the end of the third loop to move on to the next step in the writing process, the *Shaping Stage,* in which you decide on a specific message to send to another person and put this message into organized, planned, orderly form. *If an idea has not surfaced by the end of the third loop, you might try writing an extra loop or two, or you might switch to another creating technique to see if it will work better.*

STUDENT SAMPLE: LOOPING
Money

LOOP 1   I need money bad. My parents gave me about $500 to start off with. I was foolish and bought 2 pairs of jeans, 2 shirts, a record and other junk. Now I have enough for rent and barely enough for electricity, phone bill and food. My parents will be furious when they find out I'm out of money. I've decided to sell Avon to get extra cash which would have worked but my schedule is so bad I don't have time to sell the avon because my first class starts at 8:00 or 9:00 every day and my last class doesn't end till 5:00. Now, I'm in a bind with selling Avon because I'm committed to it with no time. I also have been foolish spending my money on fussball, my new fling. Also all my drafting tools will probably amount to over $40 or $50. I won't have any money to do anything this week end.

Center of gravity sentence: *I have gotten myself into a bind with my money situation.*

Center of gravity sentence: *I have gotten myself into a bind with my* LOOP 2 *money situation.*

I feel a little better now. I got a call from my mom yesterday and she said she had gotten my letter asking for more money. She asked how much I needed and said she'd send me some and I'd get it in a couple of days—and, boy, do I need it. I've still got 3 books to buy and lots of tools. I feel like, now that I will have money, I should go out some, but that's really dumb. I'll probably get myself right back to the same situation—broke. But I love money. I love to spend it—that's why I never have . . . I went out yesterday to sell Avon to pick up some more money. I went to over 40 apartment houses and I only sold to four people. That's pretty depressing. I'll probably buy more Avon for myself than I sell. X X X X O O O O X O XXOO [loops and squiggles] One of these days I will open up a savings account and try to save some money, but I only *say* I'm going to do that. I probably never will. If I just had a rich relative that I could inherit money from. Gee, I'm getting pretty obsessed here with money but since I have to write about it for 10 minutes I guess that is all I can do. Now I have nothing else to say. I'm getting sick of thinking about money. I'd rather think about something more pleasant, like guys. But since I've picked the subject of money—money it is.

Center of gravity sentence: *I feel relieved after talking to my parents, but I think the same thing will happen again.*

———————

Center of gravity sentence: *I feel relieved after talking to my parents,* LOOP 3 *but I think the same things will happen again.*

Today I got in my bank balance and I figured it all out. Now I have $15 and something not too good. I hope I get a check from my parents soon. I have a lay-away payment due the day after tomorrow also—but no money to pay it with. I still haven't gotten the electric or the phone bill. I hope they come after I get a check from my mom. I also wanted to join a club—the Student Y—but that's another $4.00 just to join. I'm convinced this town is a big *ripoff* on money. Especially the book store—they'll take you for every penny. But I guess that's the way they make their money. I shouldn't talk about them. I'm the bad one for being so loose or foolish with all my money. I bought a lot I shouldn't have—but I wanted it all, of course there's a definite line between wanting and needing. I have to learn that difference if I expect to survive financially around here.

Center of gravity sentence: *My problem isn't money; it's not paying attention to the difference between wanting and needing.*

Vicki White

Do you see how Vicki actually makes an important discovery for herself as she writes? Her final center of gravity sentence will provide her with a focused aspect of the subject **money** *that she can turn into a thesis sentence for a paper that other people will read. She has hit upon something about money that she has energy on, something that means something to her. She will, therefore, be able to communicate* **to someone else** *something that matters* **to her.** *The next section of the text will show you exactly how this is done.*

STUDENT SAMPLE: LOOPING + ESSAY
Opportunity

LOOP 1   This may be the start of a bad habit. I bought this new pen today so I could write neater and now I'm doing a looping with it. Oh, well, I'll just be careful of my pen. First of all, to get some things off my mind before I write on opportunity (which is a very dumb topic for an English teacher to assign). Excuse me, but my pen's messing up. First of all, the coach of the football team resigned today and that's pretty sad because he's a human being and what will he do and where will he go from here. Also, I'm mad at my bestfriend because I was taking a nap and she turned the television on. Later I found out she wasn't even watching anything. Now, to zero in on opportunity. I have had opportunities to sing, to dance, to jog, to be me. I've had lots of opportunities throughout my life. I was brought up in a nice home with neat parents who never fought in front of me and who will be married for 25 years this August. I went to a great high school with a rotten football team, but that's o.k. because I guess I learned a lot about people while I was there. I learned a lot about boys anyway! Ha. In high school they were all nerds. Oh, well, what will be will be. I also went to a nice church and we had lots of kids and a fabulous choir director. We put on musicals and went all over the United States. I almost didn't take that opportunity, though, because I hated choir at first. I never did want to go to rehearsals. I really didn't want to spend my Saturdays all day practicing music and choreography. I'm glad I did, though. That was a neat opportunity my parents *made* me do.

Center of gravity sentence: *I've had lots of opportunities in my life, and some of them my parents made me take when I didn't want to.*

LOOP 2   **Center of gravity sentence:** *I've had lots of opportunities in my life, and some of them my parents made me take when I didn't want to.*

I really have . . . I guess I'm glad my parents made me do those things. In fact, I'm more than glad; I'm ecstatic. Really. I think my best opportunity is myself, though, how I am. I owe it to my parents for bringing me up the way they did, though. They instilled values and personality into me. But right now going to college, planning my biggest oppor-

tunity is about myself—IS myself. I guess that sounds conceited but . . .
I'm thinking about something a former teacher of mine told me, that
writing was an art and a writer didn't have to paint by number or follow drawn lines. Well, that's the way I feel about my opportunities to
get out there and make something of my life. See, I'm the artist; I hold
the brushes and the oils and my parents' training is the. . . . I have the
opportunity to be anybody I want this person to be. Conceit, conceit,
conceit. I better narrow this thing down further. I have grabbed opportunities and created opportunities by all the things I've done. One way
that I've realized this and changed my attitude about myself in the world
is by working in Colorado this summer cleaning cabins. I've always
thought of myself as a city girl, but I've always loved the mountains,
so when the opportunity came, I went to clean cabins. I look back on it
now and think, man, what all different opportunities there were. I
learned how to fly fish, how to flip gas refrigerators to make the frezon
circulate. I think, most of all, I had the opportunity to learn that it's
people who make a feeling, not a place. A place can bring back memories, but it can't make you feel things. I don't know, I thought I was
just going to clean cabins, and I ended up learning lots about business.

Center of gravity sentence: *My biggest opportunity is MYSELF, and I
proved this by working in Colorado this summer.*

Center of gravity sentence: *My biggest opportunity is MYSELF, and I*   *LOOP 3*
proved this by working in Colorado this summer.

When I was a little girl, we used to go to Taylor Park, Colorado, for
vacation, and we found this rickety place called Holt's Guest Ranch.
I'll never know what made me love that place so much except maybe it
was the childhood memories I feel there. Fishing with my dad. Dancing
at family night. Anyway, Mr. and Mrs. Holt always hired two college
girls to work with them. I used to tag along behind them, and Mrs.
Holt would always say, "Debbi, someday when you're in college, maybe
you can come work for us." I had all my plans made when I was nine. . . .
I realize as I write this that what looked like an opportunity last summer wasn't just a fluke or just good luck. I, myself, brought that opportunity about by keeping in touch with Mrs. Holt, even after they sold
the ranch to the Speers who almost ruined it, and then when they
bought it back. And, especially, I caused that opportunity to happen
when I told Mrs. Holt last year to call me if they kept the cabins. I
wonder how many things we call opportunities are really like this; we
do things that make the opportunities happen. I feel real encouraged
by thinking about this. If I—*MYSELF*—made that opportunity happen
last summer, can I do it again? And I am really proud of what I learned
by taking advantage of that opportunity. I remember that first night
there. I slept in Dad's flannel pajamas, long Fruit-of-the-Loom under-
wear and lined ski socks. We had two beds, but the thermal coupling in

the heater was broken, so my roommate and I slept in the same bed to keep warm. Also, I didn't want to sleep in my bed because there was a dead mouse in it. [Squiggles] I don't know what else to write. I'm tired of thinking about opportunities. I wish the timer would go off and I could stop this loop. Great, there it is.

Center of gravity sentence: *I made my own opportunity.*

When Debbi finished these three loops, she had a subject for an essay on personal experience, which her teacher had assigned. She decided to write on the idea that occurred in her second loop, "My biggest opportunity is MYSELF, and I proved this by working in Colorado this summer." Now read the essay she wrote on this subject for her class. You will easily see the connection between her creating activity and the content of the essay itself.

CONFIDENCE

Last April my telephone rang early in the morning, and it took me a full thirty seconds to recognize Mrs. Holt's voice. She wanted me to come to Colorado that summer and clean the guest cabins at her ranch. I thought about it a while and decided to go. I told myself, "This is a great opportunity to make money." What I learned during the summer, however, was that there is a bigger opportunity than making money. That opportunity is having confidence in yourself.

I flew from my hometown on May 19. When we arrived in Colorado, the temperature was 38 degrees. I got off the plane and realized that I had to carry both my suitcases and my clothes bag myself. This was just one of the things I was to discover during the summer that I had to do for myself. All the way up the drive in the canyon to the ranch, I keep thinking, "Don't forget how much money you are going to make. It will be worth it all." I was really scared.

It is true that the summer was a great opportunity to make money. I saved $500. My salary was $250. a month plus room and board. With all the baked potatoes and gravy and even some boiled cabbage that I finally learned to swallow, I felt I came out on the good end of the room and board part of the deal. I was able to save almost all my salary because there was nothing to spend it on except maybe an occasional tube of toothpaste at Sherm Cranor's Taylor Park Trading Post.

Sometime during the early summer, I quit thinking about the opportunity to make money. I began to experience the opportunity of proving myself and accomplishing hard and new things by myself. It was really rough running a guest ranch. There was always a pilot light that had gone out or a toilet that wouldn't flush. There was always a beaver to clog up the irrigation ditch or a customer who needed dry bath towels at the strangest moment. I learned all about leaky pipes and the parts of a toilet. I spent hours plunging with my plumber's friend. I even learned how to run a "snake" through sewer pipes. I made beds in three minutes flat, and I washed three million dirty bath and tea towels every day. I set thousands of mouse traps. I learned how to light the pilot on cooking and heating stoves. I helped flip refrigerators so their freon would circulate, and I exploded them when they wouldn't draw the air up. I painted signs and cleaned the fireplace and dusted furniture and even helped lay linoleum in the laundry room. (It got a big wrinkle down the middle. We nicknamed it the Continental Divide.)

So, what I had thought would be just an opportunity to make money turned out to be an opportunity to grow with myself. I found out so many things about me. I became very proud of myself and what I was able to learn and do. I found out I really liked people. It made me feel good to work hard and accomplish things. I even learned to like cabbage.

Someday, I'll go back. By then I am sure that I will have grabbed a lot more opportunities to make myself proud of me. And I will probably even make money on top of it.

Debbi Pigg

APPLICATION

1 Pick *one* of the topics and do three ten-minute loops on it:

FAMILIES   MUSIC   TRAVEL

Be sure to include a center of gravity sentence at the end of each loop.

2 Read over everything you have written during this looping activity. If you were required to write an essay on some idea that occurred to you during this loop writing, what would you write on?

Be prepared to discuss this topic (the one you picked) with the class. Were you surprised when you hit on it? Was it something you hadn't thought about for a long time? What did you like about it? What makes it seem like a good subject for an essay? What is there about the essay that you think would interest other people?

---

to discover ideas, have a conversation
DIALOGUE

The dictionary defines a dialogue as an exchange of ideas or opinions on a particular issue or subject. Writing a dialogue can be a novel way for you to see what you want to say about a particular topic. Imagine that you are discussing the subject you have to write on with another person, but you do the talking for both:

1:   I have to discuss some movie I have seen for my next English assignment.

2:   Well, which one do you want to do?

1:   I don't know. Maybe *Saturday Night Fever.*

DIALOGUE: A conversation between two or more people; a conversational passage in a play or narrative; an exchange of ideas or opinions; to express, talk, tell.

2: What would you say about that?

1: Oh, I don't know—that there's lots of action—that John Travolta is good —that the dancing is fun to watch.

2: Well, I don't hear an English paper in that one.

1: No, me either.

2: What else could you do?

1: I could discuss *Star Wars*.

2: OK! I think you've got something there. You could talk about the way *Star Wars* is like a western.

1: Yea, good versus bad.

2: And the way the opening is like the yellow brick road in *The Wizard of Oz*.

1: And I could discuss the words that the film opens with that sound like a fairy tale.

2: Or the take-off on old movies, like the bar scene that reminds you of *Casablanca*.

1: And that rod that made me think of King Arthur's sword.

2: What about Carrie Fisher—wasn't she like queens in medieval courts in that last scene when she was giving the medals away?

1: Yes. I see all kinds of possibilities now. I'll have to put these ideas down in some order and see what I can do with them in an organized way.

2: Good job!

The rules for writing a dialogue as a creating technique are simple

1 Write as though you were talking out loud to yourself.
2 When you get stuck or reach a dead end, use the second voice to ask a question in order to get the conversation going again.
3 Write short, quick answers so that you can keep the exchange moving. It is the fast action that stimulates the discovery of the ideas.

Consider *writing a dialogue* as a preliminary creating technique. Take the ideas that you get from this activity and use them in a second creating technique, if necessary, to get additional information for your writing.

2. CUBING

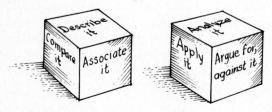

CUBING is a technique for swiftly considering a subject from 6 points of view. The emphasis is on *swiftly* and *6*.

Often writers can't get going on a subject because they are locked in on a single way of looking at the topic—and that's where CUBING works very well. CUBING **lets you have a single point of view for only 3 to 5 minutes, then moves you on to the next point of view.** When you've finished CUBING, you've spent 18 to 30 minutes, and you've really loosened up the soil of your mind. This technique moves very swiftly and is quite structured.

TWO RULES TO FOLLOW IN CUBING

1 Use all six sides of the cube.
2 Move fast. Don't allow yourself more than 3 to 5 minutes on each side of the cube.

Rule 1: Use All 6 Sides of the Cube
Imagine a cube—think of it as a solid block. Now imagine that each side has something different written on it.

One side of the cube says: **Describe it.**
Another side says: **Compare it.**
A third side says: **Associate it.**
The fourth says: **Analyze it.**
The fifth says: **Apply it.**
The sixth side says: **Argue for or against it.**

For the cubing technique, you need to use *all six sides.* This is *not* an exercise in describing, analyzing, or arguing. It *is* a technique to help you learn to look at a subject from a variety of perspectives. Consequently, *doing just one of the sides won't work.* Doing just one side is like a mechanical assignment—"describe this picture." You may decide after doing all six sides that you *do* want to describe it; but by then your decision will be meaningful and intelligent, based on your having something to say in the form of a description. So remember: **cubing takes all six sides.**

Rule 2: Move Fast. Don't Allow Yourself More Than 3 to 5 Minutes on Each Side of the Cube
The energy in this creating technique comes from shifting your perspective on the subject often. By moving around the cube, one side after another, in rapid-fire succession, you see that your subject can be looked at from a lot of different angles and that you can talk about it in a lot of different ways. *You are not hunting for something to say from each perspective;* you are taking a *quick* run into your mind for whatever presents itself on that angle, and the quickness of the run is important. **It is the quick switch that makes the CUBING work.**

PRACTICING CUBING

To practice this creating technique, let's use the picture of a luscious chocolate-covered cherry. Remember the rules: *use all 6 sides of the cube and move fast, allowing no more than 3 to 5 minutes per side.* Look at the chocolate-covered cherry. Get your paper and pen ready.

Begin. Do each of the 6 steps in order, spending no more than 3 to 5 minutes on each.

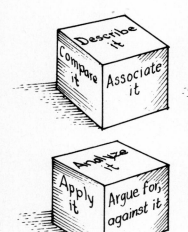

1 *Describe it.* Look at the subject closely and describe what you see. Colors, shapes, sizes, and so forth.
2 *Compare it.* What is it similar to? What is it different from?
3 *Associate it.* What does it make you think of? What comes into your mind? It can be similar things, or you can think of different things, different times, places, people. Just let your mind go and see what associations you have for this subject.
4 *Analyze it.* Tell how it's made. (You don't have to *know;* you can make it up.)
5 *Apply it.* Tell what you can do with it, how it can be used.
6 *Argue for or against it.* Go ahead and take a stand. Use any kind of reasons you want to—rational, silly, or anywhere in between.

When you have finished all six, read over what you have written. **If one angle or perspective strikes you as particularly promising, you probably have come up with a focus for an essay.** There very likely was one thing you really enjoyed writing during the cubing activity, something that made you smile, something that caused your pen to move faster, something you felt some interest in and even some excitement about. What is amazing and encouraging is that you can find *something* to say on this frivolous subject, a chocolate-covered cherry! Get used to the pleasure and security of having such a full repertory of creating techniques that you will *never* be given a subject without knowing *at once* how to find something you really want to say about it.

THE JOURNAL AS A SOURCE FOR IDEAS

"Have a lot of curiosity and be a good listener.

"Most writers want to talk all the time because they're alone so much. De Maupassant said, 'Put black on white.' That's the biggest step.

"Keep a journal. I keep a record of every day, and I don't spend much time on it. Every year I buy a new diary." He walks to the lower level and opens one of several drawers built in adjacent to the huge library. He held up an oversized appointment book.

"I write in this every night at bedtime. Not very much, but something. For instance, I saw you today. I'll make mention of that in my journal tonight.

"My kids saw me doing this, and they started doing it. It gave them a facility for writing; they got used to words coming out of them; they weren't afraid of a piece of paper. It's a breeze to switch and not be afraid of writing. My son's journal is more emotional, and my daughter does dreams.

"I'll give you an example of how I use my journal. I had a situation on the Orient Express, and I needed more details for a book. I located the journal when I'd taken a trip on the Orient Express and was able to recall the details."

—Irving Wallace

STUDENT SAMPLE: CUBING
Chocolate-Covered Cherry

TOPIC: Chocolate-covered cherry.

DESCRIBE IT

I see a chocolate-covered cherry. The brown outside covering is burst on one side; the inner cherry, red in color, is falling out. White cream is pouring out of it and around the cherry so pieces of chocolate are around the white cream. The cherry has some juice coming from it that has made a red streak in the white cream. The upper part of the chocolate shell is hollow and is dark, in a shadow. The whole object is making a shadow on the surface on which it sits. I can just taste it in my mouth, juicy and sweet and chocolate.

COMPARE IT

It looks like a typical chocolate candy except when it is burst it reveals its unique inside. It looks like a type of egg that has just been busted and is oozing out. It is quite different from a cracker, which is flat and thin. It could look like just an abstract picture if you just stared at it. It is like unveiling a surprise and finding what is beneath.

ASSOCIATE IT

It makes me think of Christmas. When we have Christmas parties at my grandmother's house, kids running everywhere, packages and paper crumpling and everybody laughing and having a good time. The chocolate cherries sit on the table with all the other goodies waiting to be devoured. One time I bought a box of chocolate-covered cherries and my brother and I sat out in the car, while waiting for my mother to shop, and ate the entire box. The taste of them and their sight always makes me think of Christmas.

ANALYZE IT First a tree has to be planted and then you have to wait until the tree produces cherries. Then they have to be picked and sent to a factory. Once there the cherry is dropped into the creamy sugar substance which is in a mold that has the form of the candy. The cream and cherry are then frozen while in the mold and then taken out of the mold and kept frozen. Chocolate is then poured. . . .

APPLY IT The cherry can be used for anything but usually is used for parties or things like that. It sets a festive mood when used at Christmas time because it seems to be a natural association with Christmas. It can be used to put in chairs for practical jokes. It makes a nice looking mess on somebody's clothes. It can also. . . .

ARGUE FOR OR AGAINST IT The cherry is definitely a needed thing in our society and without the chocolate cherry where would America be. It's like the old tradition — Christmas is not Christmas without a chocolate-covered cherry. After all, the father of our country, George Washington, brought our awareness to the cherry in his childhood, even before he was president and he was elected by the people so it is evident that Americans are totally aware of the cherry's heritage and as. . . .

— *Floyd Schexnayder*

You will notice that Floyd makes no attempt to keep his thoughts in any particular order as he moves around the cube. Whatever he thinks of as he describes or analyzes or argues goes down on the paper. When he got to analyze it *and* argue for it, *he started getting playful and putting things down even if he didn't know whether they were right or not. He probably has never been in a chocolate-covered-cherry factory, but he had fun pretending he knew about it. And who knows what those fantasies might bring into his mind and what thoughts they might lead to.*

Floyd definitely has the right attitude; he wasn't thinking he had to do anything serious or come up with anything profound as he cubed the picture. Instead, he was willing to take quick runs into his mind, just to see what might turn up. Later, he examined these cubes to see if there was *an idea significant enough to merit a public paper's being written about it. He decided to write a personal experience essay about the significance an inexpensive object can have when a lot of memories are connected to it, and he used the chocolate-covered-cherry story from his family Christmases as an illustration of his point. So, something a little serious and certainly true in a lot of people's lives came out of cubing what looked like just a light, playful topic. You will be surprised what fantastic ideas your mind will turn up for you on even the silliest of subjects.*

Whether the subjects are concrete or abstract, real or imaginary, pictures or words, cubing works. *Here is another student, David Hill, cubing the topic* My Home State, *which in David's case was Texas. Read his* cubings; *then see how he used that material in the theme he wrote later.*

MY HOME STATE (TEXAS)

Texas—big, bold, BIG, GIANT. Everything is big, so big that there's too many different things in it to mention. Texas has girls—girls on the beaches, in the cities, at the parks, in the country. The girls in Texas are something else! The main thing about Texas is that there isn't ONE MAIN THING. DIVERSITY. One can drive all night and never make it out of the state. There are so many different kinds of land—if you get tired of the desert, go to the mountains—if you get tired of the mountains—go to the beach. If you get tired of Texas get the H . . . OUT of here. Economically, it's great.

Texas is similar to and different from *itself*. Strange—instead of comparing the whole Texas to another whole anything you have to compare a little part of Texas to a whole something else. The beaches—let's compare the beaches—well, now which part? Aren't they all the same? No. Well, now, the South Padre beaches are white—not quite as beautiful as the Bahamas but you can't drink Lone Star on the Bahama beaches. The mountains are another thing. SOME ARE BIG—like the ones in the dramatic exploration movies. The rivers are like the ones in wilderness movies—movies—maybe that's why the movies are moving headquarters to Texas.

THE SUN—THE HOT, BIG, LONGTIME-RUNNING SUN. Cowboy hats—to keep the sun from burning. The sun of west Texas can make a person crazy if under it for a while—you can't make sandwiches out doors because the sun will toast the bread. Colors—bright colors— paisley colors—psychedelic SUN—old cowboys with leather necks and lines around their eyes from squinting while out in the sun—the weather —where else can it rain for one short 20 minutes and shine brightly soon after, then the next day it'll be cold and the day after hot again, with of course some rain and always THE SUN.

90,000,000 miles of sun, a million beautiful girls, natural flavor, natural psychedelic colors, no preservatives, nothing artificial added. Take above ingredients and mix in one large area—put a little jalepeño pepper in if Mexican flavor is your gig. The only thing left out are the cows—leave them out: they are messy. The Food and Drug administration said that Texas is good for indigestion. Texas is made of a little bit of everything.

You could use it as a wall decoration but you would have to have a BIG WALL!

You could use it for a place to meet a friend. "Meet me in Texas at 3:00." No—someone might want to use it for a place to go on vacation, but they might not leave. Look at me—I'm here on a life-long vacation. The only obvious thing to use Texas for is a place to live and stretch out.

ARGUE FOR OR AGAINST IT

Oh, yeah! Well, I happen to live in Texas, and I know that I not only don't have to pay state income tax (do you?) but sales tax is only 5%. There is no tax on groceries and the beef is local and fresh—best in the world. Where else can you drive on such good highways and don't forget the rest stops. Yes.

This cubing of the state of Texas has allowed David to explore what he thinks about the state and to see what ideas might surface in his mind about the topic. He actually got very excited about what he discovered when he did these cubes, and he chose one of the ideas as the thesis for his next writing assignment. Here is the essay he wrote:

THE LONE STAR?

Any veteran of fourth grade geography can tell you that Texas is the biggest state in the United States, next to Alaska. Many can also tell you that Texas is called the Lone Star State. But when one of these little scholars asked me *why* Texas is called the Lone Star State, I was stumped. I knew full well that the state flag has only one star on it, but I knew equally well that if I used that as the reason for Texas' nickname, the kid's next question would undoubtedly be,"Why does the flag have only one star?" I never did answer the question; I merely mumbled something about flags and retired to my library where I pondered the phrase "the Lone Star State."

The more I thought about it the more I convinced myself that Texas was anything except a lone star. As far as galactical comparisons go, Texas is more like the entire universe than a single star. Ask any cowboy if the ranches, pastures, and cattle-raising plains aren't the universe, and he will say if they aren't he isn't interested in knowing about it. Ask corporate leaders in oil and gas if there is a bigger place, and they are likely to answer no without even thinking. Stop in Houston and the citizens there will tell you how advanced science, technology, and medicine are in their city and that there is no other place like it. The people who live in Texas feel it is their universe. They can't imagine any need to live anywhere else.

This paradox is so typical of Texas. A symbol that is a lone star, which might suggest smallness, aloneness, tinyness; and a state that is so big, so varied, and so self-sufficient that its citizens think it is the universe. I turned off the light on my desk and headed for the door, mumbling aloud, "Nowhere except Texas—that's for sure." Just then I heard a small voice that sounded a lot like that fourth grader. Suddenly, I knew why a universe like Texas could be symbolized by a lone star. There absolutely is no other place like it!

THE REPORTER'S FORMULA

Rules: Take your subject and ask the following questions about it:

Who?   **Where?**   **Why?**
What?   **When?**   **How?**

Answering these questions could lead you to see a particular part of the subject that you know enough about—or are interested enough in—to use for the main idea in a piece of public writing. This is a particularly good creating technique to use when you have to write something in a hurry—such as an essay exam question or a newspaper article.

THE DRAMATISTIC APPROACH

Act 1, Scene I *(The Tragedy of Macbeth)*
Thunder and lightning. Enter three Witches.

1. Witch.   When shall we three meet again? In thunder, lightning, or in rain?

2. Witch.   When the hurly-burly's done, when the battle's lost and won.

3. Witch.   There will be ere the set of sun.

1. Witch.   Where the place?

2. Witch.   Upon the heath.

3. Witch.   There to meet with Macbeth.

1. Witch.   I come, Graymalkin.

(2. Witch.)   Paddock calls.

(3. Witch.)   Anon.

All.   Fair is foul, and foul is fair,
Hover through the fog and filthy air.   *(Exeunt)*

Notice how soon you find out the following things about this drama:
who is in the play? where is the play taking place? what is the action? how is the action going to take place? why?

If you were using the *Reporter's Formula*, you'd have answers to all your questions. However, in the *Dramatistic Approach*, you yourself set up the play and actually create the ideas and actions.

Kenneth Burke, a well-known writer, has developed this technique. He identifies five aspects of the subject:

AGENT   PURPOSE   ACT   MEANS   SCENE

According to Burke, the importance of these five aspects of a subject is really seen when you mix two of them together—*agent* and *means*, for example, or *purpose* and *act;* and there are many different combinations possible. (In fact, it is this mixing that makes the *Dramatistic Approach* different from other techniques, such as the *Reporter's Formula.*)

When two aspects of a subject are identified and then brought together, new sparks fly; and you think of still more ways of looking at the subject, still more insights. Using these five aspects of a subject, you can put on paper the actual "drama" that occurs when you think about a thing.

3. Classical Invention

INVENT:

To conceive of or devise first; originate.
To fabricate; to make up.
(From Middle English *enventen,* to come upon, to find.)

In ancient Athens there were people who gave speeches in public places as a way of life. These speeches were designed to persuade listeners on controversial subjects, and the arguments were often intense and always serious. One of the most distinguished of these ancient orators, Aristotle, decided to write a how-to manual for these speakers. In it, he covers subjects like how to make emotional yet ethical appeals to the listeners and how to deliver a speech most effectively; he also passes on valuable hints of the trade. Aristotle's advice summarized the best that was known in his time; it also added an extra dimension to the subject: his own particular clarity and insight. Not only has his work survived through the centuries, but it also continues to be very valuable today.

Although Aristotle's advice was aimed at speakers, not writers, and although his principles were mainly intended for debate and persuasion, many of his guidelines can be applied to written essays. For example, here is his original outline for preparing an argumentative speech:

<u>**Aristotle's Plan for Organizing Persuasion**</u>
Introduction
Statement of the topic under discussion
Outline of the points in the argument
Proof
Refutation of opposing arguments
Conclusion

This very same outline, or one with slight modification, appears in many textbooks today. Very likely you are familiar with the plan, even if you did not know that it originated with Aristotle.

In addition to giving sensible and useful advice on *organization* and *presentation,* Aristotle also gave advice on finding something to say, or finding the "best" thing to say. (Apparently the ancient Greeks had problems with that too. In a modified form, Aristotle's invention techniques can be as useful to you today as they have been for others down through the centuries.) Let's look first at Aristotle's original advice on finding ideas, then see how we can use this for our modern-day purposes.

Advice from Aristotle When you sit down to think of content for a speech, Aristotle suggested, picture your mind as a land with several kinds of places or regions or haunts in it. These places (called *topoi* in Greek; "topics" is a loose translation) stand for different *kinds* of ways to view or think of a subject. Just as each part of the country—desert or mountains—would have a climate of its own, so each area of the mind has its characteristic way of thinking.

Obviously, this is merely a figurative, picturesque way of describing different mental processes—and of course Aristotle lived many centuries before modern brain research. Nevertheless, **thinking of these different "areas" of the mind can serve as a kind of checklist, a way of seeing what ideas might occur to you as you examined the subject from each different perspective, or place.** For instance, a person intending to address the Athenian people on the subject of democratic government would prepare a speech systematically. The system would be to begin by self-questioning along such lines as the following:

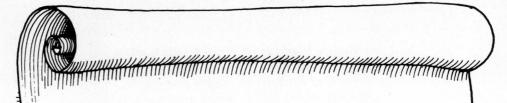

Definition:

    What is democratic government?

Comparison:

    How is democratic government similar to other forms of government?

    How is democratic government different from other forms of government?

    How is democratic government more like one form of government than another?

Relationships:

    What causes people to want democratic government?

    What is the effect of having democratic government?

    What consequences do people pay for having democratic government? for not having democratic government?

    What is contradictory about having democratic government?

Circumstances:

    What is possible in democratic government? impossible?

    What past democratic governments do we know about?

    What is likely to be the situation in the future for societies using democratic government?

Testimony:

    What have famous persons said about democratic government?

    Have people written in support of democratic government?

    What old sayings support an argument for democratic government?

    What laws support the concept of democratic government?

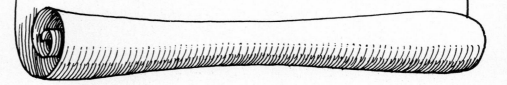

In other words, the Athenian speaker would be roaming around in "regions" of the mind, asking sets of questions appropriate to each region, in order to discover and collect ideas.

ARISTOTLE'S COMMON TOPICS

DEFINITION
  A. Genus
  B. Division

COMPARISON
  A. Similarity
  B. Difference
  C. Degree

RELATIONSHIP
  A. Cause and effect
  B. Antecedent and consequence
  C. Contraries
  D. Contradictions

CIRCUMSTANCE
  A. Possible and impossible
  B. Past fact and future fact

TESTIMONY
  A. Authority
  B. Testimonial
  C. Statistics
  D. Maxims
  E. Law
  F. Precedents

The *topoi*, or regions on the map of classical rhetoric, can do the same thing for any subject you want to get some ideas on. Using the place or region names that Aristotle suggested can remind you of things you had forgotten or make you think of something you had never thought of before. They, too, can work just like a checklist.

With your subject in mind you look at the topoi. The first one is *Definition*, so you ask yourself questions like "Does this subject *need* to be defined?" "If I defined it, what would I do with the definition?" "What if I broke my subject down into parts; what parts would I have?" "Is there any problem about my subject that defining it would show up?"—and so on until you felt you had asked enough questions about defining your subject. Then you would go to the next topic on the list, *Comparison*, and ask the questions that that topic made you think of. Somewhere along the line, this methodical, orderly, deliberate search for ideas will pay off; you will think of something you want to say on the subject.

After a little practice with this creating technique, you'll find that as soon as you know your subject, you instinctively go directly to the *topoi* that will work best with that subject, the *topoi* most likely to give you ideas. Until then, however, you will need to go through all five *topoi*, checking each one to see if, using that perspective, you can think of something to say.

CREATIVE JOGGING

Running Past Exams

By Hugh Burns

Like preparing for a marathon, preparing for doctoral exams is a harrowing, time-consuming, grueling experience. One's spirits crash and soar. Once-stable biorhythms fluctuate wildly in previously uncharted realms. And confidence—ah, confidence!—either asserts itself or wanes, depending on such incidental considerations as the color pen and type of paper to be used when writing the exam.

So, as one of those people who enjoys running when I need to think about things—call it therapeutic jogging or psychorunning—I logged a lot of miles preparing for my examinations. Since I passed all three exams without a problem, I believe I can show a cause-effect relationship between my running and effective studying.

I became rather systematic in my running routine by beginning my morning run with another warm-up exercise, namely stopping by my desk on the way to the door to read one of 60 possible questions for the first, four-hour examination. I would usually read the question aloud, repeating it to myself until I had a grasp on the issue and then I would trot out the door, through the sub-division and through the grazing pastures skirting Austin, Tex.

For the first part of the run, I would not think about the question very much except to repeat it to myself. After the first mile or two, as the kinks worked their way out of my body, the kinks would work their way out of my brain as well. Interesting notions about that morning's question began to occur. A cognitive psychologist or one interested in creativity might call this the end of the incubation phase and the beginning of the insight phase. Knowledge that had been internalized over the semester started to rise to the surface, to emerge from my long-term memory. Moreover, specific tactics for exploring these topics developed. For example, I would imagine that all the research designs I had ever read about had just exploded right in front of my eyes, and I would attempt to describe the debris which was flying past.

The point is that these study-runs enabled me to retrieve and sort out respectable ideas, to mentally arrange appropriate support material as well as suggest what support I still needed to uncover, and occasionally to prewrite a sentence or two. After the run, my shower, the footspray, the tumbler of ice water and the running log all had to wait until my typewriter cooled down as well.

Edward P. J. Corbett's formal method of search and discovery

QUESTIONS TO ASK ABOUT . . .

A—PHYSICAL OBJECTS
1 What are the physical characteristics of the object (shape, dimensions, materials, etc.)?
2 What sort of structure does it have?
3 What other object is it similar to?
4 How does it differ from things that resemble it?
5 Who or what produced it?
6 Who uses it? for what?

B—EVENTS
1 Exactly what happened? (who? what? when? where? why? how?)
2 What were its causes?
3 What were its consequences?
4 How was the event like or unlike similar events?
5 To what other events was it connected?
6 How might the event have been changed or avoided?

C—ABSTRACT CONCEPTS (*e.g., democracy, justice*)
1 How has the term been defined by others?
2 How do *you* define the term?
3 What other concepts have been associated with it?
4 In what ways has this concept affected the lives of people?
5 How might the concept be changed to work better?

D—PROPOSITIONS (statements to be proved or disproved)
1 What must be established before the reader will believe it?
2 What are the meanings of key words in the proposition?
3 By what kinds of evidence or argument can the proposition be proved or disproved?
4 What counterarguments must be confronted and refuted?
5 What are the practical consequences of the proposition?

FOUR RULES TO FOLLOW IN CLASSICAL INVENTION

1 Take the questions one at a time, thoughtfully.
2 Write brief notes about the answers.
3 If you get stuck or have nothing to say, move on.
4 When you finish the questions, reread your answers and check those that are most useful in generating material, information, or energy.

Rule 1: Take the Questions One at a Time, Thoughtfully   Following this rule is the key to using CLASSICAL INVENTION successfully. The power of CLASSICAL INVENTION comes from its relationship to common, ordinary patterns of human thought. There are probably a number of times each day when you are discovering the meaning of a new term (definition), comparing one thing to another, considering relationships, deciding whether to accept or reject some advertiser's claim, or weighing whether some action will or won't be possible (circumstance). *Taking the questions one at a time and allowing yourself to be thoughtful about answers (for example, giving more than a yes-or-no answer) will strengthen that particular way of thinking.* When you work on questions in the *Definition* section, you strengthen that mental skill in exactly the same way a weightlifter or violinist will practice specific movements to develop one specific physical skill. You may find some of the *topoi* less comfortable than some of the others. Remember that few of us can juggle, water ski, or type without a lot of practice; also, you may be exercising a kind of thinking that is entirely new to you. So be kind to yourself, and **allow this new mental skill to develop at its own rate, even if it means slowly, thoughtfully.**

Rule 2: Write Brief Notes About the Answers   You will want some kind of notes so that you can re-create your thinking later. Also, because your mind will probably range widely—especially on a question that seems particularly stimulating and appropriate to your subject—*you'll want to have some notes, outline, key words or phrases* that will let you retrace your thoughts. But you'll want to **keep the notes brief**—otherwise, you'll be writing long, sometimes exhaustive (and exhausting!) answers.

Rule 3: If You Get Stuck or Have Nothing to Say, Move On   Although you'll want to give yourself a reasonable amount of time to come up with an answer for every question—and sometimes several answers—*there are some questions that simply don't apply, or that you don't want to deal with.* For example, *Testimony* question 5 asks what sources you've looked into. That's a useful question if you need ideas on places to look for testimony, or if it jogs your memory about something you've recently read or heard. But unless you really intend to do research on a subject, it's best to use question 5 as a memory aid and let it go at that. If you find other questions that clearly just don't apply, pass them by. Remember, though, that surprises *can* happen; sometimes a seemingly useless question can provide a subject that you had never dreamed you would be interested in writing about.

Rule 4: When You Finish the Questions, Reread Your Answers and Star Those That Are Most Useful in Generating Material, Information, or Energy Your brief notes will have already established, for a while, thought patterns connected with each of the different *topoi* or questions. Later, when you reread your answers, you'll already know which areas look most promising. **You've used the process to *discover* which questions seem to work best for your subject.** You can follow up, perhaps by looping, to develop—in more detail and depth—those questions and answers that serve you best.

PRACTICING CLASSICAL INVENTION

Let's practice the creating technique of CLASSICAL INVENTION by using the subject *Romantic Love*. Don't groan! We're deliberately choosing an unpromising subject to demonstrate that the creating technique of CLASSICAL INVENTION really helps you come up with something to say on any topic. According to the Roman orator Cicero, a speaker relies on three things to find appropriate subject matter: native genius, diligence, and method (or art). As for genius, you're already operating on whatever level of native genius you've got; and as for diligence: you owe it to yourself, right? And method, fortunately, is something you *can* learn. That's comforting. Given your level of native genius and your willingness to look for ideas diligently, you can learn methods that will *always* work to find content for your writing.

And we believe any method you learn has to work on unpromising subjects just as well as on promising ones. Usually a person doesn't get sparkling subjects to write on in real-life, everyday situations, so we want you to know several methods for finding something to say that will enable you to feel confident about any subject you may be required to write about.

Here are the questions we will use in practicing CLASSICAL INVENTION. Go through these questions, seeing what ideas emerge about romantic love. Remember, too, that these same questions will work for any subject you might come across at a later time.

CLASSICAL INVENTION QUESTIONS

Definition
1 How does the dictionary define _____ ?
2 What earlier words did _____ come from?
3 What do *I* mean by _____ ?

4 What group of things does _____ seem to belong to? How is _____ different from other things in this group?
5 What parts can _____ be divided into?
6 Does _____ mean something now that it didn't years ago? If so, what?
7 What other words mean approximately the same as _____?
8 What are some concrete examples of _____?
9 When is the meaning of _____ misunderstood?

Comparison

1 What is _____ similar to? In what ways?
2 What is _____ different from? In what ways?
3 _____ is superior to what? In what ways?
4 _____ is inferior to what? In what ways?
5 _____ is most unlike what? (What is it opposite to?) In what ways?
6 _____ is most like what? In what ways?

Relationship

1 What causes _____?
2 What are the effects of _____?
3 What is the purpose of _____?
4 Why does _____ happen?
5 What is the consequence of _____?
6 What comes before _____?
7 What comes after _____?

Testimony

1 What have I heard people say about _____?
2 Do I know any facts or statistics about _____? If so, what?
3 Have I talked with anyone about _____?
4 Do I know any famous or well-known saying (e.g. "A bird in hand is worth two in the bush") about _____?
5 Can I quote any proverbs or any poems about _____?
6 Are there any laws about _____?
7 Do I remember any songs about _____? Do I remember anything I've read about _____ in books or magazines? Anything I've seen in a movie or on television?
8 Do I want to do any research on _____?

Circumstance

1 Is _____ possible or impossible?
2 What qualities, conditions, or circumstances make _____ possible or impossible?
3 Supposing that _____ is possible, is it also feasible? Why?
4 When did _____ happen previously?
5 Who has done or experienced _____?
6 Who can do _____?

7 If _____ starts, what makes it end?
8 What would it take for _____ to happen now?
9 What would prevent _____ from happening?

TOPIC: Romantic love

Begin. Go through each of the questions in each of the topoi *groups. Write your answers to the questions in brief notes. If other questions occur to you, make a note of them, too. If you get stuck or have nothing to say on any particular question, move on. When you've finished all the questions, reread your answers and star the ones that you think will be the most useful in giving you something to say on the subject.*

At the end of this process, you will have used several ways of thinking to consider your subject. Having a method like CLASSICAL INVENTION to know how to switch from one thought pattern to another deliberately lets you do a systematic, *thorough* investigation of your subject and arrive at ideas that have depth and a lot of potential for your writing.

Let's look at what one student—Joe Don Zant—discovered by using the CLASSICAL INVENTION creating technique:

STUDENT SAMPLE: CLASSICAL INVENTION
Romantic Love

1 How does the dictionary define _____ ?   *DEFINITION*
   Fanciful, extravagant, unreal, strangeness, suggests adventure, fantastic, fabulous, imaginary, not actual or real.

2 What earlier words did _____ come from?
   Latin; something written in common tongue.

* 3 What do *I* mean by _____ ?
   Passionate, free, uninhibited, caring and understanding, sensuous, exciting; involved, delicate situation, intense, free, sometimes strange.

* 4 What group of things does _____ seem to belong to?
   The great aesthetic things in life, free, pure, uninhibited communication.
   How is _____ different from other things in this group?
   It is totally different from anything in any group. Nothing.

5 What parts can _____ be divided into?
   Total understanding, pure loyalty, excitement, great times, moonlight.

6 Does _____ mean something now that it didn't years ago? If so, what?
Yes, it is more diluted, more superficial.

7 What other words mean approximately the same as _____ ?
Fantastic, idealistic, sentimental, tender feelings.

8 What are some concrete examples of _____ ?
Romeo and Juliet, looking into each other's eyes, serene happy feeling of being together. Exciting. Precarious.

* **9** When is the meaning of _____ misunderstood?
All the time. People today can't understand.

COMPARISON * **1** What is _____ similar to? in what ways?
Similar to the most exciting thing you have ever done, only ten times better. The most positive, delicate, good thing.

2 What is _____ different from? in what ways?
Different from the everyday, superficial life many people lead.

3 _____ is superior to what? in what ways?
It is superior to any . . .

4 _____ is inferior to what? In what ways?
Nothing; it is inferior to nothing except maybe God's love and grace. It's . . .

* **5** _____ is *most* unlike what? in what ways?
Most unlike the little games people play with each other's emotions. The superficial love. I hate it.

* **6** _____ is *most* like what? in what ways?
Most like finding something true and pure and exciting all in one ball.

RELATIONSHIP * **1** What causes _____ ?
Grace, timing and circumstance. It is a happening that is unexplainable.

* **2** What are the effects of _____ ?
It can change a person's life and the way a person views the world. It puts a person in a different perspective.

* **3** What is the purpose of _____ ?
To bring together two different thought processes and try to make them co-operate together.

* **4** Why does _____ happen?
I don't know—fate, maybe. Or because people want it to happen at the time?

* **5** What is the consequence of _____ ?
A person can get hurt feelings, but then again it may grow into a beautiful relationship. Romantic is relative.

* **6** What comes before _____ ?
Emptiness, hollow, void in person's life that the person may not be aware of.

* **7** What comes after _____ ?
Peace of mind, satisfaction, exciting great feelings.

TESTIMONY **1** What have I heard people say about _____ ?
That it's for the birds, that it is also the greatest feeling in the world. Like nothing they've ever experienced.

* 2 Do I know any facts or statistics about _____ ? If so, what?
  It is delicate, exciting, fun.

3 Have I talked with anyone about _____ ?
  Yes, my best friend. It's a delicate, personal subject.

4 Do I know any famous or well-known sayings (e.g. "A bird in hand is worth two in the bush") about _____ ?
  Love conquers all.

5 Can I quote any proverbs or poems about _____ ?

6 Are there any laws about _____ ?
  Can't do it in public; can't do it alone.

7 Do I remember any songs about _____ ?
  "Three Times a Lady," Reunited.
  Any books or magazines?
  No.
  Any movies or television shows?

8 Do I want to do any research on _____ ?
  No.

1 Is _____ possible or impossible?   *CIRCUMSTANCE*
  Possible.

2 What qualities, conditions, or circumstances make _____ possible or impossible?
  Two people in the same brain pattern, feeling the same things. Exciting understanding.

3 Supposing that _____ is possible, is it also feasible? Why?
  Yes, sometimes, if that's what they both need.

4 When did _____ happen previously?
  Last year.

5 Who has done or experienced _____ ?
  Myself, everyone probably.

6 Who can do _____ ?
  Anyone.

* 7 If _____ starts, what makes it end?
  A falling out, creating a void.

8 What would it take for _____ to happen now?
  A brick wall to hit and knock me off my feet.

9 What would prevent _____ from happening now?
  Most anything. This is a superficial world.

STUDENT SAMPLE: CLASSICAL INVENTION + ESSAY
My Retirement Place

* 1 How does the dictionary define _____ ?   *DEFINITION*
  A private or secluded place.

2 What earlier words did _____ come from?
  From French word which meant to withdraw.

3 What do *I* mean by _____?
A place that gives me pleasure and a sense of well-being.

4 What group of things does _____ seem to belong to?
Places to live.

How is _____ different from other things in this group?
It's different because a retirement place has to be really satisfying since you're in it all the time. Other places you might live can be not so satisfying because you're gone a lot.

* 5 What parts can _____ be divided into?
Different characteristics of the place, different ways to use it, reasons why it is nice.

6 Does _____ mean something now that it didn't years ago? If so, what?
It does to me because I've just retired. I used to not think much about the place I lived. Now it means a lot to me.

7 What other words mean approximately the same as _____?
resting place, vacationing place, easy place.

8 What are some concrete examples of _____?
Trailer villages, rest homes, senior-citizen communities.

9 When is the meaning of _____ misunderstood?
People think that a retirement place has to be where a lot of people have retired to.

COMPARISON * 1 What is _____ similar to? Why?
It's similar to a campground, a vacation spot, a state park.

2 What is _____ different from? In what ways?
Different from most senior-citizen communities, most apartment complexes. It's different from what people usually picture for a retirement place.

* 3 _____ is superior to what? In what ways?
Superior to any other retirement place I have ever visited because it doesn't feel or look like a retirement place. A lot of young people live here or they come for the weekend.

4 _____ is inferior to what? In what ways?
Inferior to . . .

5 _____ is most unlike what? In what ways?
Most unlike a jail, a hospital, room with no windows.

6 _____ is most like what? In what ways?
Most like a beautiful park

RELATIONSHIP 1 What causes _____?
The trees, lake, quietness.

* 2 What are the effects of _____?
Peace, easygoing life, satisfaction, quietness, being with nature.

3 What is the purpose of _____?
For people to get away from hustle and bustle of city life, be alone or with only a few people, be out of doors.

4 Why does _____ happen?
It happened for me because I was lucky and found it.

5 What is the consequence of _____ ?
I'm much happier and content.

6 What comes before _____ ?
A lot of frantic, hurried life.

7 What comes after _____ ?
Depends on how I live, I guess.

1 What have I heard people say about _____ ?
That my retirement place is ideal.

* 2 Do I know any facts or statistics about _____ ? If so, what?
Yes, I know that it was a fishing village first. I know it started around the turn of the century. There are about forty houses here and about twenty families live here year-round. I know that my retirement place is well cared for and protected because we have a full-time caretaker. I know a lot more.

3 Have I talked with anyone about _____ ?
Yes, a lot of people.

4 Do I know any famous or well-known sayings about _____ ?
"Too much work makes Jack a dull boy." "Here today, gone tomorrow."

5 Can I quote any proverbs or poems about _____ ?
A picture is worth a thousand words.
"Gather Ye Roses While Ye May."

6 Are there any laws about _____ ?
Yes, rules that keep the place nice.

* 7 Do I remember any songs about _____ ?
"A Little Bit of Heaven."
"By the Old Mill Stream."
"My Blue Heaven."
Any books or magazines I've read?
I've read enough to know how good mine is.
Anything I've seen in a movie or on television?
I've seen TV programs on the aged and where many of them live.

8 Do I want to do any research on _____ ?
No.

1 Is _____ possible or impossible?
Possible.

2 What qualities, conditions, or circumstances make _____ possible or impossible?
Having enough money to buy a place here; knowing about it in the first place.

3 Supposing that _____ is possible, is it also feasible? Why?
Yes. It's not too expensive.

4 When did _____ happen previously?
As early as 1900.

Four Rules to Follow in Classical Invention   41

5 Who has done or experienced _____?
A lot of people.
6 Who can do _____?
Anybody who likes this kind of environment.
7 If _____ starts, what makes it end?
Dying.
8 What would it take for _____ to happen now?
People to be ready to retire and to know about this place.
9 What would prevent _____ from happening now?
Not knowing about it; not liking the isolation or the quietness. Not having enough money.

MY RETIREMENT PLACE

There's an old saying that good luck comes when you least expect it. That was certainly true for me the day I discovered the clubgrounds which have now become my retirement place. I never dreamed that day about 15 years ago when some friends brought me to the Chickamauga Fly and Bait Casting Club for a picnic that I would come here to live when I quit work. I did, however, and I am extremely pleased. This club is a perfect place for a person who loves peace, quiet, and the out-of-doors.

The appearance of Chickamauga Fly and Bait Casting Club is one of its greatest assets. It certainly isn't grand, but it does look old in a comfortable sort of way. It started around the turn of the century as a fishing camp (in fact, that's how it got its name), and it looks settled and well developed. It's also very natural. Although the area is well taken care of, the trees and plants have been left to grow in their natural condition, so when you drive in you feel as if you are on a state campground. The club is also beautiful. The gravel road that you come in on ends at a large lake which has high mountains all around it. Many days I go down to the lake early just to see the mist rise off the water and into the trees of the mountains.

I think I would have chosen the club as my retirement place on its appearance alone, but it has even more good things about it. The management, for example. There is a full-time caretaker couple who keep the grounds in good shape and who protect the club. They lock the gate every night. If you are going away, they will check your mail or pick up your paper. There is also a pot-luck supper organized once a month by the club's officers. People who live at the club permanently and people who just belong get together for the meal and some kind of program. Every Wednesday the women who are on the grounds that day get together for some special activity. Once we painted the boatdock. Another time we went into town to a photography show. One day last winter we skated on the frozen lake. There's a governing board, also, that keeps very up-to-date on what the club needs and authorizes repairs and improvements. Right now they are getting a new water line so that people who have wells can hook up to county water, and they are inquiring about the cost of surfacing the road. I really couldn't ask for more from a management standpoint.

The appearance and management of my retirement place are great, but there's something even more important to me. That's how I *feel* living at the Chickamauga Fly and Bait Casting Club. I feel content, happy, and alive. I walk by myself a lot on Daddy Jack Trail. I take my pole some mornings about 5:00 and catch a big brim for breakfast. I watch the leaves turn, the dogwoods bloom. This is the most important thing to me—the happiness I feel daily in my retirement place. I think the luck that was with me 15 years ago is still holding. Every day I wake up feeling that I've come home.

— Rachel Harper

APPLICATION

1 Using the checklist for CLASSICAL INVENTION, explore one of these subjects to see what you have to say about it:

INDEPENDENCE   LONELINESS   HUNGER

Use the student sample on as a guide for your work.

2 Be prepared to discuss with the class what occurred as you used the classical invention technique. Where did you first become interested in the subject? What part caused you to think of something that really surprised you? What parts turned up ideas that you think would really appeal to a reader? Which parts were helpful in clarifying your own thinking?

Of all the the ideas you generated during the activity, which seems the most promising to you if you were to write an essay on the subject?

TAGMEMIC INVENTION AS A CREATING TECHNIQUE

Young, Becker, and Pike, in their book *Rhetoric: Discovery and Change*, present an invention approach based on language theory (tagmemics). Here is a simplified, adapted version of their technique. The writer asks questions such as these about certain qualities of the subject, and the questions generate ideas to be explored.

CONTRASTIVE

Look at your subject from a *contrastive* point of view.
How is the subject different from things similar to it?
How has this subject been different for me?
What would a snapshot of this subject be?
How is this subject made?

VARIATION

How much can this subject change and still be itself?

How is it changing?

How does the subject change from day to day?

What different varieties of the subject do I know or have I encountered?

What particular experiences do I have that illustrate the kinds of things I know or problems I have in relation to this subject?

How do I change in relation to this subject?

DISTRIBUTION

Where and when does this subject take place?

What is the larger thing of which this subject is a part?

What is the function of the subject in this larger thing?

How does this subject fit into my life?

What other things (experiences) preceded it? followed it? were similar for me?

SUMMARY

You have now practiced three distinctly different creating techniques, and you may already have your favorite among them, the one that works best when you are searching for ideas. You may also have practiced other techniques shown in the boxes scattered through this chapter. You will certainly have noticed the ways the techniques are different: Some work like a fishing expedition—you lower a net and catch whatever thoughts you have on the subject. Some work like a reminder or checklist to help you think up things you already knew but had forgotten. Some actually let you invent something new by rubbing together thoughts, ideas, information you already had to come up with new combinations, insights, relationships. Some work best when you don't have a single thing to say; others work best when you already have several ideas on a subject and need to decide which is the most promising. Some of the techniques are unstructured and loose; some are tightly controlled. No single one is inherently better than another. Each works for its own purpose.

*ALL MEN
(AND WOMEN!)*

Are created equal—but not all creating techniques are equal! Each, in fact, is different.

Learning what each technique will do for you may be trial and error at the beginning, but as you become more and more familiar with the ways to create, you will develop a feel for which one to use when. There will always be a unique mix of subject, what you already know and/or think about the subject, your mindset on a particular day, and many other variables that will affect which creating technique works best for you when.

The important thing to remember is that **there is a *creating stage* in the writing process—that you need to let yourself hunt for ideas *before* you begin writing a paper.** *Now* you know how to *get started*, no matter what the writing task or assignment is. You know something you *can* do. You know how to get *some* words on the page! You will never again have to say "But I can't think of anything to say. I don't know how to start." Because now you do know how to start. *You start by creating. You don't start by writing the piece of writing itself.* In fact, you don't worry at all in this stage about the essay or report or whatever you must write; you just set yourself to *have ideas* on the subject of that essay, report, or whatever by doing a creating technique.

And there is a bonus for you when you create: even if you never write the essay or the report, even if you never go a step further, **the creating activity gives *you* clarity by letting *you* see a thing and *know* it.** During the creating stage you find out what you actually think about this subject, what you believe, what you know. What is more, you not only come to *know* the subject by writing about it, but you also have *words on a page* to use as a starting point for sending your ideas to someone else. The creating stage serves both purposes. You find out what you know, and you get ideas that you can shape into a coherent message for another person.

> "Keep on going and the chances are you will stumble on something, perhaps when you are least expecting it. I have never heard of anyone stumbling on something sitting down."
> —Charles Kettering

APPLICATION: DOUBLE TECHNIQUE

Taking the same subject through *more than one* creating technique is an excellent way to see which techniques you find most beneficial for which kinds of subjects. To get practice in knowing the characteristics of various creating techniques, choose one of the topics below and **run it through two different creating techniques.** Be ready to discuss with the class what you discovered in this process, what one technique did that the other didn't, which you found most beneficial, what idea(s) you came up with that you could write on if you were required to do so, and the like.

1	CHOOSE ONE	CHOOSE TWO
	Getting along with (parents, children).	Cubing
	Finding work.	Looping
	Problems of growing up.	Classical Invention
2	CHOOSE ONE	CHOOSE TWO
	Things wrong with holidays.	Cubing
	A skill you have and are proud of.	Looping
	A problem you had and how you solved it.	Classical Invention
		Reporter's Formula
	Ways people act that you don't like.	Dramatistic Invention
	A movie you just saw.	Tagmemic Invention
	A book you just read.	Brainstorming
	Soap operas.	Writing a List
		Writing a Dialogue

		SUMMARY		
TECHNIQUE	CHARACTER-ISTIC	WORKS BEST FOR	STRENGTHS	WEAKNESSES
LOOP WRITING	unstructured; a fishing expedition	exploring in a free, wide-ranging way	uses right lobe, brings surprises and pleasures; lets the strongest thing emerge	usually takes several loops to work; may not always give depth
CUBING	fast-moving, structured; combination of fishing expedition and planned search	considering subject from six points of view to set up a variety of perspectives	"loosens the soil" of your mind; corresponds to way people usually think about subjects; shows writer perspective most likely to yield ideas for the essay	doesn't work on all classroom assignments; may not give enough depth
CLASSICAL INVENTION	structured; a planned search; goes into depth	exploring regions of the mind; handling subjects that benefit from logical, planned investigation	well-developed, traditionally useful, corresponds to human thought processes	can result in mechanical writing or writing that is more interesting in form than in content; takes considerable time
LISTING	simple, direct	gathering facts, details, points which already exist	quick, easy	limited application; requires the previous information to be there and within reach
DIALOGUE	conversational, a fishing expedition	exploring what you think or finding a strong angle you were not previously conscious of; letting two voices play off each other	lets writer ask and answer questions; questions and responses can generate new ideas	may seem awkward at first; difficult to get two points of view

TECHNIQUE	CHARACTER-ISTIC	WORKS BEST FOR	STRENGTHS	WEAKNESSES
BRAIN-STORMING	group activity	breaking mental blocks, getting fresh approaches	ranges widely; uncritical; works off other people's ideas	may seem merely silly, horseplay
REPORTER'S FORMULA	familiar, a set pattern	viewing subject as "thing" or separate entity; giving clear, objective information	produces factual information, detail; can suggest actual order/organization of finished writing	can be routine, unimaginative; can be applied only to *some* subjects (not all); separates writer from subject
DRAMATISTIC APPROACH	planned experimentation; structured	viewing subject as action, movement, a dynamic object	creates friction (energy) on subject by rubbing two agents together	may overwhelm beginning writer; ideas which emerge may not lead directly to thesis for writing
TAGMEMIC APPROACH	structured probe	taking a deep look into a subject; seeing familiar things in unfamiliar ways	corresponds to the physical qualities of a subject; gives depth	some overlap of areas considered; takes much time

Questions for Discussion

1 What is the difference between creating techniques and free writing?

2 What is the direct connection between the writing you do during the *Creating Stage* and the completely finished final essay?

3 What are some possible disadvantages of doing creating techniques?

4 What arguments would you give to a friend who said he or she didn't have to do a *Creating Stage* for a piece of writing?

5 What is the best state of mind to be in when you approach the *Creating Stage?*

6 Which technique works best for a subject you already know something about? Which works best for a subject you are absolutely blank on?

7 When would a quick technique, such as a list, work best?

WRITING ASSIGNMENT: THE PERSONAL EXPERIENCE ESSAY

You are now ready to put creating to the test by writing a complete essay. With each additional section of this book you will, of course, learn more and more about the writing process. However, you are at a good spot, right now, for a practical application of what you've been learning. Here is an opportunity for you to discover (and demonstrate) what a truly successful Creating Stage can contribute to a finished essay. If your experience is like ours, you know that every time you write, you learn something new, and you extend your command of writing skills. So consider this assignment as a chance to grow, specifically to increase your mastery of Creating and to increase your ability to incorporate the Creating Stage into a piece of finished writing.

The first assignment is a personal experience essay. People write about what happens to them for a number of reasons:

1 To tell something that happened to them which caused them to have an insight about life which they believe is universal enough or important enough for other people to take their time to read.

2 To relate an experience that the writer thinks will be interesting simply because the facts, description, and the like will be new, unfamiliar, or even unknown to the readers.

3 To use a personal experience to teach a lesson or warn the reader, sometimes explicitly or directly stated, sometimes not stated but understood.

4 To entertain the reader.

5 To write about something very emotional, disturbing, or upsetting that happened to the writer in order to get it off the writer's mind or to complete the experience.

6 To give the reader facts about the writer which the reader will be interested in knowing simply because the writer is so well known or famous.

On the following pages are examples of personal experience essays that illustrate these six reasons for writing. Some of the essays are written by professional writers, some by people who just like to write in their spare time, and some by students in freshman English classes. Reading them will probably give you some ideas for your own personal experience essay which you are about to write.

READINGS

1. PERSONAL EXPERIENCE TO MAKE A POINT

This first essay, written by the famous British novelist Virginia Woolf, illustrates the use of personal experience to share an insight or make a point the writer feels will be significant to a large number of readers. Notice that the writer doesn't just give details about her early life; she shows why *these details were important, what they caused her to realize. And then she relates this realization to all people. By going one step beyond merely stating the experience — by making a point about that experience — Virginia Woolf makes her personal life valuable to other people.*

A Sketch of the Past

Two days ago — Sunday 16th April 1939 to be precise — Nessa said that if I did not start writing my memoirs I should soon be too old. I should be eighty-five, and should have forgotten. . . . There are several difficulties. In the first place, the enormous number of things I can remember; in the second, the number of different ways in which memoirs can be written. As a great memoir reader, I know many different ways. But if I begin to go through them and to analyse them and their merits and faults, the mornings — I cannot take more than two or three at most — will be gone. So without stopping to choose my way, in the sure and certain knowledge that it will find itself — or if not it will not matter — I begin: the first memory.

This was of red and purple flowers on a black ground — my mother's dress; and she was sitting either in a train or in an omnibus, and I was on her lap. I therefore saw the flowers she was wearing very close; and can still see purple and red and blue, I think, against the black; they must have been anemones, I suppose. Perhaps we were going to St Ives; more probably, for from the light it must have been evening, we were coming back to London. But it is more convenient artistically to suppose that we were going to St Ives, for that will lead to my other memory, which also seems to be my first memory, and in fact it is the most important of all my memories. If life has a base that it stands upon, if it is a bowl that one fills and fills and fills — then my bowl without a doubt stands upon this memory. It is of lying half asleep, half awake, in bed in the nursery at St Ives. It is of hearing the waves breaking, one, two, one, two, and sending a splash of water over the beach; and then breaking, one, two, one, two, behind a yellow blind. It is of hearing the blind draw its little acorn across the floor as the wind blew the blind out. It is of lying and hearing this splash and seeing this light, and feeling, it is almost impossible that I should be here; of feeling the purest ecstasy I can conceive.

I could spend hours trying to write that as it should be written, in order to give the feeling which is even at this moment very strong in me.

But I should fail (unless I had some wonderful luck); I dare say I should only succeed in having the luck if I had begun by describing Virginia herself.

Here I come to one of the memoir writer's difficulties—one of the reasons why, though I read so many, so many are failures. They leave out the person to whom things happened. The reason is that it is so difficult to describe any human being. So they say: "This is what happened"; but they do not say what the person was like to whom it happened. And the events mean very little unless we know first to whom they happened. Who was I then? Adeline Virginia Stephen, the second daughter of Leslie and Julia Prinsep Stephen, born on 25th January 1882, descended from a great many people, some famous, others obscure; born into a large connection, born not of rich parents, but of well-to-do parents, born into a very communicative, literate, letter writing, visiting, articulate, late nineteenth century world; so that I could if I liked to take the trouble, write a great deal here not only about my mother and father but about uncles and aunts, cousins and friends. But I do not know how much of this, or what part of this, made me feel what I felt in the nursery at St Ives. I do not know how far I differ from other people. That is another memoir writer's difficulty. Yet to describe oneself truly one must have some standard of comparison; was I clever, stupid, good looking, ugly, passionate, cold—? Owing partly to the fact that I was never at school, never competed in any way with children of my own age, I have never been able to compare my gifts and defects with other people's. But of course there was one external reason for the intensity of this first impression: the impression of the waves and the acorn on the blind; the feeling, as I describe it sometimes to myself, of lying in a grape and seeing through a film of semi-transparent yellow—it was due partly to the many months we spent in London. The change of nursery was a great change. And there was the long train journey; and the excitement. I remember the dark; the lights; the stir of the going up to bed.

But to fix my mind upon the nursery—it had a balcony; there was a partition, but it joined the balcony of my father's and mother's bedroom. My mother would come out onto her balcony in a white dressing gown. There were passion flowers growing on the wall; they were great starry blossoms, with purple streaks, and large green buds, part empty, part full.

If I were a painter I should paint these first impressions in pale yellow, silver, and green. There was the pale yellow blind; the green sea; and the silver of the passion flowers. I should make a picture that was globular; semi-transparent. I should make a picture of curved petals; of shells; of things that were semi-transparent; I should make curved shapes, showing the light through, but not giving a clear outline. Everything would be large and dim; and what was seen would at the same time be heard; sounds would come through this petal or leaf—sounds indistinguishable from sights. Sound and sight seem to make equal parts of these first impressions. When I think of the early morning in bed I also hear the caw of rooks falling from a great height. The sound seems to fall through an elastic, gummy air; which holds it up; which prevents it from being sharp and distinct. The quality of the air above Talland House seemed to suspend sound, to let it sink down slowly, as if it were caught in a blue gummy veil. The rooks cawing is part of the waves breaking—one, two, one, two—and the splash as the wave drew back and then it gathered again, and I lay there half awake, half asleep, drawing in such ecstasy as I cannot describe.

The next memory—all these colour-and-sound memories hang together at St Ives—was much more robust; it was highly sensual. It was later. It still makes me feel warm; as if everything were ripe; humming; sunny; smelling so many smells at once; and all making a whole that even now makes me stop—as I stopped then going down to the beach; I stopped at the top to look down at the gardens. They were sunk beneath the road. The apples were on a level with one's head. The gardens gave off a murmur of bees; the apples were red and gold; there were also pink flowers; and grey and silver leaves. The buzz, the croon, the smell, all seemed to press voluptuously against some membrane; not to burst it; but to hum round one such a complete rapture of pleasure that I stopped, smelt; looked. But again I cannot describe that rapture. It was rapture rather than ecstasy.

The strength of these pictures—but sight was always then so much mixed with sound that picture is not the right word—the strength anyhow of these impressions makes me again digress. Those moments—in the nursery, on the road to the beach—can still be more real than the present moment. This I have just tested. For I got up and crossed the garden. Percy was digging the asparagus bed; Louie was shaking a mat in front of the bedroom door. But I was seeing them through the sight I saw here—the nursery and the road to the beach. At times I can go back to St Ives more completely than I can this morning. I can reach a state where I seem to be watching things happen as if I were there. That is, I suppose, that my memory supplies what I had forgotten, so that it seems as if it were happening independently, though I am really making it happen. In certain favourable moods, memories—what one has forgotten—come to the top. Now if this is so, is it not possible—I often wonder—that things we have felt with great intensity have an existence independent of our minds; are in fact still in existence? And if so, will it not be possible, in time, that some device will be invented by which we can tap them? I see it—the past—as an avenue lying behind; a long ribbon of scenes, emotions. There at the end of the avenue still, are the garden and the nursery. Instead of remembering here a scene and there a sound, I shall fit a plug into the wall; and listen in to the past. I shall turn up August 1890. I feel that strong emotion must leave its trace; and it is only a question of discovering how we can get ourselves again attached to it, so that we shall be able to live our lives through from the start.

But the peculiarity of these two strong memories is that each was very simple. I am hardly aware of myself, but only of the sensation. I am only the container of the feeling of ecstasy, of the feeling of rapture. Perhaps this is characteristic of all childhood memories; perhaps it accounts for their strength. Later we add to feelings much that makes them more complex; and therefore less strong; or if not less strong, less isolated, less complete. . . .

These then are some of my first memories. But of course as an account of my life they are misleading, because the things one does not remember are as important; perhaps they are more important. If I could remember one whole day I should be able to describe, superficially at least, what life was like as a child. Unfortunately, one only remembers what is exceptional. And there seems to be no reason why one thing is exceptional and another not. Why have I forgotten so many things that must have been, one would have thought, more memorable than what I do remember? Why remember the hum of bees in the garden going down to the beach, and forget completely being thrown naked by father into the sea? (Mrs Swanwick says she saw that happen.)

This leads to a digression, which perhaps may explain a little of my own psychology; even of other people's. Often when I have been writing one of my so-called novels I have been baffled by this same problem; that is, how to describe what I call in my private shorthand—"non-being". Every day includes much more non-being than being. Yesterday for example, Tuesday the 18th of April, was [as] it happened a good day; above the average in "being". It was fine; I enjoyed writing these first pages; my head was relieved of the pressure of writing about Roger; I walked over Mount Misery and along the river; and save that the tide was out, the country, which I notice very closely always, was coloured and shaded as I like—there were the willows, I remember, all plumy and soft green and purple against the blue. I also read Chaucer with pleasure; and began a book—the memoirs of Madame de la Fayette—which interested me. These separate moments of being were however embedded in many more moments of non-being. I have already forgotten what Leonard and I talked about at lunch; and at tea; although it was a good day the goodness was embedded in a kind of nondescript cotton wool. This is always so. A great part of every day is not lived consciously. One walks, eats, sees things, deals with what has to be done; the broken vacuum cleaner; ordering dinner; writing orders to Mabel; washing; cooking dinner; bookbinding. When it is a bad day the proportion of non-being is much larger. I had a slight temperature last week; almost the whole day was non-being. . . .

As a child then, my days, just as they do now, contained a large proportion of this cotton wool, this non-being. Week after week passed at St Ives and nothing made any dint upon me. Then, for no reason that I know about, there was a sudden violent shock; something happened so violently that I have remembered it all my life. I will give a few instances. The first: I was fighting with Thoby on the lawn. We were pommelling each other with our fists. Just as I raised my fist to hit him, I felt: why hurt another person? I dropped my hand instantly, and stood there, and let him beat me. I remember the feeling. It was a feeling of hopeless sadness. It was as if I became aware of something terrible; and of my own powerlessness. I slunk off alone, feeling horribly depressed. The second instance was also in the garden at St Ives. I was looking at the flower bed by the front door; "That is the whole", I said. I was looking at a plant with a spread of leaves; and it seemed suddenly plain that the flower itself was a part of the earth; that a ring enclosed what was the flower; and that was the real flower; part earth; part flower. It was a thought I put away as being likely to be very useful to me later. The third case was also at St Ives. Some people called Valpy had been staying at St Ives, and had left. We were waiting at dinner one night, when somehow I overheard my father or my mother say that Mr Valpy had killed himself. The next thing I remember is being in the garden at night and walking on the path by the apple tree. It seemed to me that the apple tree was connected with the horror of Mr Valpy's suicide. I could not pass it. I stood there looking at the grey-green creases of the bark—it was a moonlit night—in a trance of horror. I seemed to be dragged down, hopelessly, into some pit of absolute despair from which I could not escape. My body seemed paralysed.

These are three instances of exceptional moments. I often tell them over, or rather they come to the surface unexpectedly. But now that for the first time I have written them down, I realise something that I have never realised before. Two of these moments ended in a state of despair. The other ended, on the contrary, in a state of satisfaction. When I said about the flower "That is the whole," I felt that I had made a discovery. I felt that I had put away in my mind something that I should go back [to], to turn over and explore. It strikes me now that this was a profound difference. It was the difference in the first place between despair and satisfaction. This difference I think arose from the fact that I was quite unable to deal with the pain of discovering that people hurt each other; that a man I had seen had killed himself. The sense of horror held me powerless. But in the case of the flower I found a reason; and was thus able to deal with the sensation. I was not powerless. I was conscious—if only at a distance—that I should in time explain it. I do not know if I was older when I saw the flower than I was when I had the other two experiences. I only know that many of these exceptional moments brought with them a peculiar horror and a physical collapse; they seemed dominant; myself passive. This suggests that as one gets older one has a greater power through reason to provide an explanation; and that this explanation blunts the sledge-hammer force of the blow. I think this is true, because though I still have the peculiarity that I receive these sudden shocks, they are now always welcome; after the first surprise, I always feel instantly that they are particularly valuable. And so I go on to suppose that the shock-receiving capacity is what makes me a writer. I hazard the explanation that a shock is at once in my case followed by the desire to explain it. I feel that I have had a blow; but it is not, as I thought as a child, simply a blow from an enemy hidden behind the cotton wool of daily life; it is or will become a revelation of some order; it is a token of some real thing behind appearances; and I make it real by putting it into words. It is only by putting it into words that I make it whole; this wholeness means that it has lost its power to hurt me; it gives me, perhaps because by doing so I take away the pain, a great delight to put the severed parts together. Perhaps this is the strongest pleasure known to me. It is the rapture I get when in writing I seem to be discovering what belongs to what; making a scene come right; making a character come together. From this I reach what I might call a philosophy; at any rate it is a constant idea of mine; that behind the cotton wool is hidden a pattern; that we—I mean all human beings—are connected with this; that the whole world is a work of art; that we are parts of the work of art. . . .

2. PERSONAL EXPERIENCE TO GIVE UNFAMILIAR INFORMATION

This essay was written by Hans Rütimann, an executive in New York City who is an international authority on the application of computer technology to humanities research. Mr. Rütimann was invited by the Soviet Union to visit Russia and discuss the work he does. This essay, based on the personal experiences of that trip, is interesting because Mr. Rütimann discusses, in a lively and engaging form, customs and places unfamiliar to most readers.

A Stranger Goes to the Soviet Union

2 March. The briefing is short. The ride is smooth to Kennedy Airport. When the flight is announced, I go to the gate; there is a big crowd, a full flight. I don't like the airline—no class whatsoever, just the bare necessities. Meal lousy, wine so-so. The film is the pits; I sleep through it and wake up an hour before landing in London.

London: it is discovered that my bag was checked through only to London instead of through to Moscow. I have to clear customs, find my bag, check back through customs again, find the group—all in time to catch the flight to Moscow. The airline personnel are not helpful at all; I finally make it. The plane takes off on time; not many people on board. Smooth flight over Holland and Denmark. I go through my papers and practice some Russian expressions. (I do like this whole adventure.) I get excited about landing in Russia and spill coffee, a big mess. The approach into Moscow is announced, and I pick up my papers. What will happen?

3 March: This happened. After a 4-hour flight the plane goes low, over snow-covered fields, small clusters of houses, winding roads, nothing really unusual (come to think of it, what unusual things did I expect to see from the air—communism?). We have a good landing; the plane comes to a standstill quite a distance from the terminal. We get out;

several soldiers surround the plane. The passport check is very slow; the soldier checking mine looks at me, unsmilingly, several times, then down at the passport, then at my visa. Finally, he lets me go. A domestic flight has arrived at the same time, and some people wait for their bags. Otherwise, the terminal is deserted, unusual for the main airport of a capital of a country. I'm probably conditioned by my life in America, but there does seem to be a drabness, a dull monotony in the air; we passengers from the United States stick out like sore thumbs in our clothing and behavior. There is a ray of light: a small girl, about the age of my little daughter Sophie, bounces about and returns my smile. The Soviet officials whom I have come to meet greet me. Already, business cards are exchanged, something that will be repeated endless times over the next few days. (I actually run out of cards.) We pile into a limousine and dash over empty, spacious roads. Destination: Moscow. There is snow; everything is still frozen and a gray mist covers a faint outline of the sun, setting behind the city. The driver points out an intriguing monument of three stylized crosses. "Front," he says. I knew the Germans came close to Moscow, but this is hardly a stone's throw!

People go about their Saturday evening business, shopping, some standing in line. The city is quite beautiful on first impression; later I decide that Moscow is indeed a beautiful city with varied and interesting architecture. I catch sight of the Kremlin and the gold-covered roofs of the Assumption Church. When we arrive at the hotel, a modern structure, the lobby is spartan but filled with people. More officials are there to greet me, including Galina and Valentina who will be with me most of the time as guides, interpreters. Galina speaks English quite well; Valentina speaks only French and I wonder why she is assigned to me. To the end of the stay I could not figure out her role, but I suspect that her English is quite good. Anyway, formalities follow, passports are checked, this form gets you your key, that one is for the floor supervisor, etc. I am patient. There is a slow elevator to the sixth floor; the supervisor shows me my room, closes the window, "cold," she says, and I am finally alone in a small but comfortable room. I rest a short while before joining my hosts for dinner in the hotel restaurant.

The restaurant is full; a live band plays disco music and several young couples dance. The music is too loud; the fashions date from mid- to late-sixties. I look around a lot; it doesn't seem to matter since there is much confusion at our table. Ordering food is funny; my lack of Russian is not helped by the blaring music. Things are really getting out of hand, and I can hardly keep a straight face. Ordering food is far from finished when the week's program for my visit is distributed. There are numerous questions; the music gets louder; all conversation gets louder. To top it off, one of the officials insists on making a toast. Further, he insists that the toast be translated. Reluctantly, people raise their glasses. After a few words of toast, the waiters continue taking orders. The official gets furious at the waiters for interrupting him. The toast goes on endlessly, interspersed with Russian fables (I discover that, next to my own countrymen, the Swiss, the Russians have the greatest treasury of sayings and fables. Every time you ask a question, the answer starts with "There is a Russian fable . . .").

When the food comes, I look for my caviar. No caviar. I look for my blinis. No blinis. It turns out that the hour-long discussion over the menu was pointless; only steaks are available. The food is OK, excellent egg salad with olives, fine sourdough black bread, white wine (Georgian, I'm told) to go with the steaks. We are having a fine time; a ruble allocation is distributed — 75 rubles or about $110 per person. I finally look at the week's program for my stay: I am thrilled; tomorrow, as a birthday present, I will be getting a performance of *Anna Karenina* at the Bolshoi Theater. Back to the room, I prepare for the first conference tomorrow, take a hot bath, listen to some balalaika music on the radio. Streetcars rattle by from time to time. I make a mental note to get some food and wine for my room. Sink into the comfortable bed wondering, "What will tomorrow — my milestone fortieth birthday — bring?" With that thought — and the anticipation of a ten-year-old child — I fall asleep.

3. PERSONAL EXPERIENCE TO TEACH A LESSON, GIVE A WARNING, OR EFFECT A CHANGE IN READER

Paul Merriman, a student in a freshman English class, wrote this personal experience essay on catching a fish. Paul hoped that the reader, after reading the essay, might realize the same thing Paul did and make a similar decision. You will notice, however, that he does not "preach" to the reader or even suggest directly that the reader should change. Rather, he lets the drama of his own personal experience speak for itself.

Learning a Lesson

The large hungry redfish nosed along in the warm, knee-deep bay, unaware of my watchful eye. Twenty feet away in a small boat, I sat, my heart racing at the thought of catching this monster and showing him off back on the dock.

I gently picked up my fishing rod and tied on a gold spoon. Then I readied myself for the battle, realizing that this might be the only time in my life that I would ever get to battle such a fish. I cast the spoon about fifteen feet in front of the fish and then slowly reeled it in until it was about six feet away from his eyes. At that instant the fish darted away. Had I spooked it? No, he was on! Line shot off my reel, burning my thumb; I paid little attention to the pain, though, because I was loving the battle. The fish made one long run and almost stripped all the line off my reel. Fortunately, I had enough line. Eventually, the fish was tired enough so that I could slowly bring it towards the boat.

Finally, the fish was beside the boat, and I nimbly slipped the net under its streamlined body. I let out a whoop as I hauled him into the boat. I couldn't wait to get back to the dock to show him off to my parents and other admiring onlookers. I wanted to hear the praises roll in.

When I got back to the dock, I saw that everything was quiet. No problem, I thought. Everyone is inside the house out of the heat. I tied up the boat quickly and hurried inside to get my parents. Instead, I found a note saying that they had gone with a host of other people to cross the Mexican border and would be gone all day. When I read this note, I stormed out of the house and down to the dock, really upset that I had no one to show my fish off to.

I got back to the boat and lifted that monster out of the cooler. I stared at it for about a minute and then hurled its heavy body into the water. It hit with a resounding splat, but it didn't sink. Instead, it floated, and its dark eye seemed to be looking up at me. It was then that I felt very hollow. Why had I killed this beautiful fish? It wasn't for the food it could have provided. It wasn't for hanging on the wall. No, I had killed it just to go on an ego trip. I had done nature a gross injustice, and I felt terrible for the rest of that day. That night, in fact, I vowed to myself to never keep a fish again unless it was to be used as food.

To this day, I have lived by this promise. I now get as much thrill out of seeing a fish swim away healthy as I do catching him. After all, what better way to reward a fish for a good fight than to set it free so that it can fight again another day.

4. PERSONAL EXPERIENCES TO ENTERTAIN THE READER

No one can tell a funnier story than the American humorist Mark Twain. Here he describes his uncle's farm and pranks he used to play on his aunt and mother. There's nothing for the reader to do but sit back and enjoy.

Uncle's Farm

My uncle, John A. Quarles, was a farmer and his place was in the country four miles from Florida. He had eight children . . . and was also fortunate in other ways, particularly in his character. I have not come across a better man than he was. I was his guest for two or three months every year, from the fourth year after we removed to Hannibal till I was eleven or twelve years old. . . .

It was a heavenly place for a boy, that farm of my uncle John's. The house was a double log one with a spacious floor (roofed in) connecting it with the kitchen. In the summer the table was set in the middle of that shady and breezy floor, and the sumptuous meals — well, it makes me cry to think of them. Fried chicken, roast pig, wild and tame turkeys, ducks and geese, venison just killed, squirrels, rabbits, pheasants, partridges, prairie-chickens, biscuits, hot batter-cakes, hot buckwheat cakes, hot "wheat bread," hot rolls, hot corn pone; fresh corn boiled on the ear, succotash, butterbeans, string-beans, tomatoes, peas, Irish potatoes, sweet potatoes; buttermilk, sweet milk; "clabber"; water-melons, muskmelons, cantaloupes—all fresh from the garden—apple pie, peach pie, pumpkin pie, apple dumplings, peach cobbler—I can't remember the rest. . . .

I can see the farm yet with perfect clearness. I can see all its belongings, all its details: the family room of the house with a "trundle" bed in one corner and a spinning-wheel in another, a wheel whose rising and falling wail, heard from a distance, was the mournfulest of all sounds to me and made me homesick and low-spirited and filled my atmosphere with the wandering spirits of the dead; the vast fireplace, piled high on winter nights with flaming hickory logs from whose ends a sugary sap bubbled out but did not go to waste, for we scraped it off and ate it; the lazy cat spread out on the rough hearth-stones; the drowsy dogs braced against the jambs and blinking; my aunt in one chimney corner, knitting; my uncle in the other, smoking his corn-cob pipe; the slick and carpetless oak floor faintly mirroring the dancing flame-tongues and freckled with black indentations where fire-coals had popped out and died a leisurely death; half a dozen children romping in the background twilight; split-bottomed chairs here and there, some with rockers; a cradle, out of service but waiting with confidence; in the early cold mornings a snuggle of children in shirts and chemises occupying the hearth-stone and procrastinating—they could not bear to leave that comfortable place and go out on the wind-swept floor-space between the house and kitchen where the general tin basin stood, and wash.

Along outside of the front fence ran the country road, dusty in the summertime and a good place for snakes—they liked to lie in it and sun themselves; when they were rattlesnakes or puff adders, we killed them; when they were black snakes or racers or belonged to the fabled "hoop" breed, we fled, without shame; when they were "house-snakes" or "garters" we carried them home and put them in Aunt Patsy's work-basket for a surprise; for she was prejudiced against snakes and always when she took the basket in her lap and they began to climb out of it, it disordered her mind. She never could seem to get used to them, her opportunities went for nothing. And she was always cold toward bats, too, and could not bear them; and yet I think a bat is as friendly a bird as there is. My mother was Aunt Patsy's sister and had the same wild superstitions. A bat is beautifully soft and silky; I do not know any creature that is pleasanter to the touch or is more grateful for caressings, if offered in the right spirit. I know all about these coleoptera because our great cave, three miles below Hannibal, was multitudinously stocked with them and often I brought them home to amuse my mother with. It was easy to manage if it was a school-day, because then I had ostensibly been to school and hadn't any bats. She was not a suspicious person but full of trust and confidence, and when I said, "There's something in my coat-pocket for you," she would put her hand in. But she always took it out again, herself; I didn't have to tell her. It was remarkable, the way she couldn't learn to like private bats. The more experience she had, the more she could not change her views. . . .

As I have said, I spent some part of every year at the farm until I was twelve or thirteen years old. The life which I led there with my cousins was full of charm and so is the memory of it yet. . . .

5. PERSONAL EXPERIENCE TO CLEAR WRITER'S MIND

Often things happen to people that are so emotional—happy, sad, shocking, moving—that the experience needs to be written down so that the writer can get it off his or her mind. This kind of writing can be very powerful to read, because often the writer is able to recapture the experience so vividly that the readers feel they were there. Here a college freshman, Scott Mozisek, writes about the sudden death of his friend. This is a very personal essay, written in Scott's own style and as much for his purpose as anyone else's.

Death

Wade died today; coming home from school.
We were walking by the highway.
That car was coming so fast; we could hear the engine racing behind us.

Those two kids ran past us on the sidewalk.
They didn't stop at the corner; just kept running, right into the street.
They didn't see the car; didn't even look.

Wade started running.

A foot locked the brakes, and the car began singing.

The kids, they finally saw it.
But one kid froze.

Wade was at the corner.

The other kid made the side of the street.

Wade was in the street.

I was running, too.

The car was getting near(er).

Wade's long, lean strides ruffled the back of his shirt.

The car was beside me, sliding.

Miles in front of us, Wade was reaching out toward the kid.

The car was close. So close. Too close.

Wade was at the kid, grasping him under the arms, lifting, pushing him through the air.

The car was there. Time stopped; Wade had run out.

Wade twisted as the hood pushed in his hip, his knees molded like a bumper. He was the front of the car until his feet jerked out and up from under it, flipping him onto his back on the hood.

With his legs high above his body, he hit the windshield with his face and cracked it, his shoulder breaking it out. His chest caught the roof at the end of the window with such force that it hurled him up and over the back of the car toward the roadside.

The back of Wade's neck touched ground first, his legs coming down behind his head. He rolled and scraped in the gravel as he slid off the road into the grass.

When Wade finally came to rest he was flat on his back. Just lying there, with no contorted expression or twisted muscles. Just lying there, simply and quietly in the grass by the road.

The car stopped.

I was standing in the road, staring.

I walked across to Wade thinking about how long we had been friends. Always.

The things we did: swimming, traveling, running, fighting. How we were going out with Jill and Susan tonight.

Always "Wade and I."

So much we were going to do: college, business. How much we had planned.

Always "Wade and I."

Always together.

Standing over him, watching his living pour itself out of his body, I knew our friendship had been—postponed.

Wade's Dead.

6. PERSONAL EXPERIENCE TO GIVE FACTS

There are some people who become so interesting to the public, so well known, and so famous that readers want to hear about their personal experiences just because they happened to whom they did. Here is such an essay. Liv Ullman, the famous movie and Broadway actress, wrote a book called **Changing** *in which she describes various scenes, events, and persons in her life. It is very unlikely that anyone would be interested in these things, had Liv Ullman not been a* *well-known, interesting person. Ms. Ullman gives her personal experiences just for what they are: things that happened to her. The reader is interested in them because they happened to Liv Ullman.*

Christmas at Home

Christmas is one of my best memories. Sitting in the cathedral with the organ notes reaching into every corner of the great building. On the way home we would freeze all the way along Munkegaten, which was still paved with cobbles. Other families to the right and left of us with the same happiness we felt.

Then home. And the smell of roast pork and pickled cabbage. The wait in a darkened room—where my sister and I sat on the floor, tingling inside, because we knew that in the sitting room a tree was being dressed for celebration. The rustle of paper and quick footsteps signaling secrets.

And when at last the door opened and we, who were children, saw the Christmas tree for the first time, standing in the middle of the floor, glittering with candles, we almost swooned with joy.

Mamma at the piano. She who was much younger than I realized. With longings I only now perceive when it is too late to share them.

Stories on the edge of the bed. Cocoa and bread and butter with bananas and apple jelly. A woman sitting bowed over a book, her head with short brown hair turned slightly away from me. Looking up now and then and smiling.

That was happiness.

STEPS IN WRITING YOUR OWN PERSONAL EXPERIENCE ESSAY

STEP ONE

Look over the following writing contexts and decide on one that you would like to use as the basis for your own personal experience essay.

A

A close friend of yours has just really disappointed you. Because of this person's actions, you have discovered something about life that you hadn't realized before. You decide to write about this personal experience in order to share your insight with other peo-

B

You have just had a run-in with the police, for what you thought was a minor offense. You (a) took a plastic cone from the street where a work crew was painting the center line (b) were going ____ in a ____ mile zone and got stopped for speeding (c) had a party which

ple. Since your college newspaper solicits writing from the students, you decide to prepare your essay to submit to the editor, thinking that what you have learned will strike a responsive chord for a lot of your classmates because they have probably had similar experiences.

ended up moving out of doors at 2 A.M., and the neighbors complained to the authorities. You discover, however, much to your sorrow, that the police think the offense is much more serious than you do, and they take you down to the station. You have to appear before the judge to post bail. The judge says that the fine will be $200, but that $100 of it will be reduced if you write an account of this incident and get it published in your college newspaper as a warning to other students. You gladly agree to write the essay and get it published for your classmates to read. Perhaps, then, they won't make the same mistake.

C

You are taking an introductory geography course your freshman year in college, and the first assignment of the year is this: "Write an essay about the most unusual and interesting place you have ever been. Be sure that this place is likely to be a location your classmates will not have been." The instructor is planning to compile all the essays into a booklet; each member of the class will get a copy. The instructor believes this collection of essays will make the study of geography much more interesting and personal for everyone in the class. Write the essay you want printed.

D

A magazine like *Reader's Digest* is having an essay contest. Each contestant is asked to complete this sentence and write an essay about the experience: "The day I learned something I will never forget was when. . . ." The magazine announcement contains some sample essays: one about a birth, another about a death, a car wreck, a storm, an illness, a celebration. You want to enter the contest and win the $1000 first prize. Write the essay you will submit.

STEP TWO

After you have selected the writing context, you are ready to do the Creating Stage for the essay. Choose LOOPING, CUBING, or CLASSICAL INVENTION and do a complete *Creating Stage*. Don't worry at this point about the essay itself. Just follow the rules for the particular creating technique you choose and get your thoughts down on paper.

STEP THREE

After you complete the creating activity, you are ready to write the essay. You will learn many pointers about writing good essays in the *shaping* and *completing* sections later in this book. For now, however, here are just a few general facts that you can use to make your essay more interesting and worthwhile to your readers.

Remember that writing for the creating stage and writing for the essay are different in these ways:

CREATING	ESSAY
Has to matter only to you; doesn't have to be important to anyone else	Has to matter to someone else; must seem important or significant to him or her.
Can be messy	Has to be readable
Wanders around as your mind explores	Has one main idea and sticks to it
Is done to give you ideas on a subject	Is done to share with someone else something you think is important

What these differences highlight is that the creating stage is for *you* and the essay writing stage for *another person,* your *reader*. This means, then, that as you write the essay, you will want to keep your readers always in mind, *thinking about getting your message over to them.*

Remember that your readers want to see *the point* or *significance* of your personal experience; they are almost always bored by just a recounting of facts. Read these two short essays by college freshmen, and you will see that one has a point and the other one doesn't. You can check for yourself which one you find more interesting:

My Room	*The Bunk Bed*
Thinking back to when I was in the second grade and how my room looked at the time, there are things that come into my mind. As you walk into my room the bed was to your left and was in the middle of the room. It was a twin bed with a foam rubber pillow and	It wasn't much to look at. Just a plain old bunk bed covered with dull plain bedspread and at the end a ladder which led to the top far above. My toy box rested at the foot, making it a little easier for me to climb. This bed was my place in the world, and nothing since has

white sheets. It had a brown bed-spread with a picture of a cowboy on it. The bed also had a fold-down bed that rolled underneath it. The bed was not painted. Next to the bed was the dresser drawer. The dresser drawer had four large drawers in it and was painted a dark brown. The only other piece of furniture in my room was my desk. It was a small unpainted desk with a desk lamp on it. The drawer and the top were always piled full with junk I had collected.

The room itself was painted a light blue. It had four windows on two adjacent walls. The windows were wood frame windows with white plastic shades on them. There was a single light fixture hanging from the middle of the ceiling. In one of the corners was my closet. In the corner opposite from my closet were my fishing poles and BB gun. Pictures of the first moon landing hung on the wall. There was a wall socket on each wall and the light switch was next to the door. The floor in my room was made of dark oak floor-ing and was varnished and waxed. I still live in the same room. Its looks haven't changed a bit.

—*Ivan Mevnnich*

ever made me feel so safe and in control.

From the top bunk I could look out across the room, keeping it un-der constant surveillance without being seen by any intruders that might wander into my territory. Access up to my loft was almost impossible for anyone else, mak-ing my fortress invincible. When the enemy tried to flush me out, I quickly picked them off with my rifle, thus ending any threat to me.

Two pictures across the room on the wall near the closet mainly contained sailing ships with desert islands in the background. My bunk bed became those ships with pillows acting as cannon. The is-lands of the South Seas held many adventures and excitement until one day a great gale hit, leaving the ship virtually helpless. For days I drifted, the sun baking my skin, parching my throat, draining my energy. My mind wandered and I became delirious as fever set in. Only a call from Mom for supper saved me on that fateful day.

I'm an adult now, and I don't have fantasies any more about in-vaders and high sea adventures. Sometimes I wish I did. I miss those boyhood days when I could control the world and take care of myself against all odds—without ever leaving my top bunk. I don't know if I will ever again feel that I am as safe and as powerful as I did when my bed was the world and I was the king in it.

—*Brent Murphy*

Reading the two, you can see at once that the essay on the right has a point and that the one on the left doesn't. What makes for the difference?

ESSAY 1	ESSAY 2
Has no perspective; just tells reader *everything* in the room, with no emphasis or point to it	Chooses to concentrate on just one aspect of the room, the bunk bed, and lets reader know *why* that bunk bed was important
Tells only the personal experience; makes no point about it; doesn't say anything about "This experience is important because . . . ," or "I learned from this experience . . ."	Makes a point about the experience—that childhood fantasies, being powerful and safe, are sad to lose. Shares a general point that when we all become adults, we lose some wonderful things from the innocence of our childhood
Doesn't stick to any particular thing	Decides exactly what author is going to concentrate on and sticks to that all the way through; does not tell anything that doesn't relate to the point he is making or the experience he is telling
Doesn't mean anything to reader	Rings a familiar bell with reader because we all can remember our fantasies/daydreams from childhood when we could control the world
We don't learn anything about the writer	We learn that the writer loved his bed because it was his fortress and place of safety

DESCRIPTION: HOW TO PRESENT SHARP, FOCUSED PICTURES

1 Appeal to *all* the reader's senses: sight, smell, touch, hearing, taste. Be very specific.
2 *Select* the details you want to include in the description so that they give one main impression of the object, person, or scene. Don't try to describe everything at once. This means that you will choose details according to what your purpose is at the time.

Remember to *tell a good story* and use a lot of *vivid description* so that the reader can *see* the event. The successful personal experience essays you read earlier were interesting because the writers put their stories in an order you could follow easily, made you feel you were living the story with them, and used detail after detail to bring the scene to life. You want to do the same in your writing.

NARRATION: HOW TO TELL A GOOD STORY

1 Be sure to give the reader a clear time order. Provide a clear sequence of events. Often this sequence will be *chronological*—first this happened, then this, then that. . . . You may, however, use a *flashback* technique in which you show an earlier scene and then relate that scene to the main story you are telling at the moment.

2 Let your readers feel the *action* of your story. Don't just tell them *about* what happened. Let them *live* through what happened. Make a movie of the sequence of actions. The more *immediate* the details and the more *descriptive* the scenes, the more your readers will feel a part of what is going on in the story.

3 Be very *selective* in the details you choose. Don't give the readers a lot of information they don't need to understand or see your story. Stick to details that are directly related to your purpose in telling the story.

4 Decide on a *point of view.* Point of view is how the story is told. Very likely the *first person point of view* (when the author is a character in the story) will be the easiest way to tell a story that has happened to you. Later, however, when you are using narration as part of other pieces of writing, you may want to adopt the *omniscient point of view,* in which the writer knows everything and gives an objective, outside account of the sequence of events.

STEP FOUR

When you have finished writing the essay, be sure to put it in the best form possible for your reader. Make it neat and easy to read. After all, the essay will be the piece of "you" that the reader will have when the *real you* isn't there in person. Make it as impressive as you can.

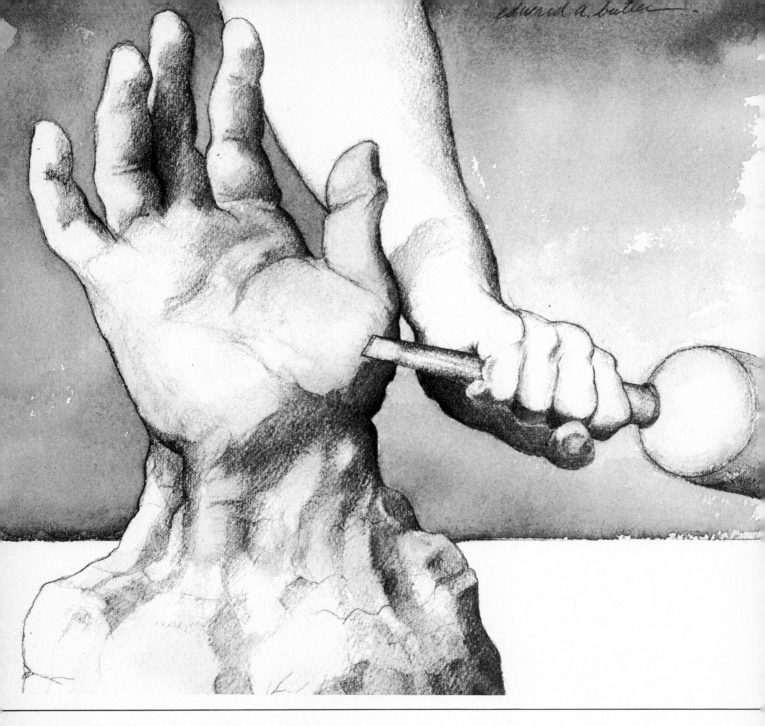

STAGE 2 /SHAPING

OUTLINE

HOW TO PUT WRITING IN ORDER

PURPOSE

During the shaping stage you:

Bridge the gap between private writing and public writing

Develop preliminary agreements about audience and thesis

Draft a rough version of the essay

Analyze and evaluate the overall organization

Create effective and well-developed beginnings, middles, and endings

GOING PUBLIC: WRITING FOR AN AUDIENCE

AUDIENCE:
THE READERS, HEARERS, OR VIEWERS REACHED BY A BOOK, BROAD-CAST, OR PERFORM-ANCE; AN OPPORTUNITY TO BE HEARD OR TO EXPRESS ONE'S VIEWS

PUBLIC:
Open to the knowledge or judgment of all; participated in by the people or community; connected with or acting on behalf of the people or community.

PRIVATE:
Of or confined to one person; not available for public use or participation.

In the *Creating Stage* of writing you are in your own private world, and you can be completely lost in it, totally unaware of everything else. It's like spending Saturday reading a mystery or building a bench or making a skirt, and then suddenly looking up and finding that it's night or snowing or 5:00, and you've been completely unaware of anything outside yourself and your project. During the *Creating Stage*, nothing outside yourself and your project matters much. It's a time for clearing your mind, learning what you think about a thing, having some ideas to write on, or just giving yourself pleasure. You explore *your* thoughts, images, associations, attitudes, ideas; you find what *you* want to say.

If you set out only to find out what *you* think on a subject, then you are finished when you have done the creating stage. If, however, you did the creating stage in order to have some ideas *to share with someone else*, you move into a second stage in the writing process — one determined by the demands of a *reader*, not one determined by you alone. **You move from your private world to the public world, from writing for yourself to writing for someone else.**

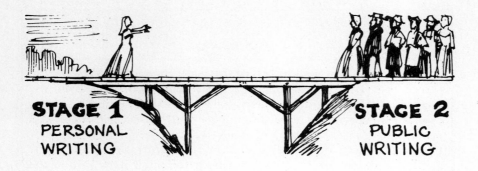

STAGE 1
PERSONAL
WRITING

STAGE 2
PUBLIC
WRITING

THE DIFFERENCE BETWEEN PUBLIC AND PRIVATE WRITING

Anyone who has ever peeked on the sly into another person's diary knows that private writing can be fun to read. People's journals—like Lewis and Clark's when they cut the Oregon Trail, or May Sarton's, when she moved to an isolated spot to live alone by the sea—illustrate that private writing can make good public reading. With private writing, however, the reader is always a visitor, a viewer on the outside looking in. The reader may get value or enjoyment or pleasure from reading the writer's private jottings, but that is just a by-product of the writing, which was written for the writer him- or herself. Later the writing may seem worthwhile to others. Perhaps they get a valuable insight into the writer's life. Perhaps they rediscover in the private writing some forgotten experiences or feelings that the writer has captured. Perhaps the private writing reveals some fascinating aspects of the period of history the writer lived in. Perhaps . . . but all that is really incidental and just a happy fringe benefit of the writing.

Even when private writing is considered interesting enough for the public to read, the reader has to make adjustments if any difficulty comes up in understanding what the writer meant. The writer does not explain who the people are in the diary or always date the writing or do anything specifically to aid the reader (unless, of course, the writer sees the writing becoming public one day—which isn't truly private writing). Also, when private writing goes public, almost always some editor goes through the writing, inserting footnotes and dates, putting the pieces in chronological or some other kind of order, and writing in as many explanations as possible. The reader may have to be willing to read both the private writing and the editor's additions to get the total picture.

In private writing, the writer doesn't have to do anything in the interests of any readers: *no explanations, no connections, no clarifications. It's totally up to the readers (and perhaps an editor who prepares the private writing) to make sense of the writing on their own.*

THE BEAR

In the evening, the men in two of the rear canoes discovered a large brown bear lying in the open grounds about 300 paces from the river, and six of them went out to attack him — all good hunters. They took the advantage of a small eminence which concealed them, and got within 40 paces of him, unperceived. Two of them reserved their fires as had been previously concerted; the four others fired nearly at the same time, and put each his bullet through him. Two of the balls passed through the bulk of both lobes of his lungs. In an instant, this monster ran at them with open mouth. The two who had reserved their fires discharged their pieces at him as he came toward them. Both of them struck him — one only slightly, and the other, fortunately, broke his shoulder. This, however, only retarded his motion for a moment.

The men, unable to reload their guns, took to flight. The bear pursued, and had very nearly overtaken them before they reached the river. Two of the party betook themselves to a canoe, and the others separated and concealed themselves, among the willows, [and] reloaded their pieces; each discharged his piece at him as they had an opportunity. They struck him several times again, but the guns served only to direct the bear to them. In this manner he pursued two of them, separately, so close that they were obliged to throw away their guns and pouches, and throw themselves into the river, although the bank was nearly twenty feet perpendicular. So enraged was this animal that he plunged into the river only a few feet behind the second man he had compelled to take refuge in the water.

When one of those who still remained on shore shot him through the head and finally killed him, they then took him on shore and butchered him, when they found eight balls had passed through him in different directions. . . . It was after the sun had set before these men came up with us, where we had been halted by an occurrence which I have now to recapitulate, and which, although happily passed without ruinous injury, I cannot recollect but with the utmost trepidation and horror.

The situation changes immediately, however, when a person intends from the outset to write something for somebody else. Instead of the reader having to make all the adjustment and take the role of the outsider being privileged to look into the writer's life, the writer has to take almost all the responsibility for getting the reader to understand and to be interested in what she or he has to say. In public writing, it's the *writer* who must see to it that there is something worthwhile enough to get and keep the reader's attention. In private writing, this is the *reader's* responsibility.

Wednesday, November 20th

GROWING OLD

A dismal day, rain, everything leaden. I forgot to say that yesterday when I was hurrying to get to an appointment on time I fell forward on the stairs and wrenched my shoulder. It shook me, because it brought vividly to mind the hazards of living alone. One feels fragile. And I realize that anxiety is never far away because what would happen to Tamas? The cat can get in and out through my bedroom window, but he would be trapped if anything happened to me and it might be days before I was found (Louise Bogan was found lying dead on the floor in her apartment in New York). Such anxiety should keep one alert and I believe that it does, alert and reminding oneself not to hurry. Most domestic accidents happen because someone is hurrying. . . . But on a deeper level than the mundane fact of a possible fall or heart attack I feel sure that after sixty everyone has death in the back of his or her consciousness much of the time.

Growing old . . . what is the opposite of "growing"? I ask myself. "Withering" perhaps? It is, I assume, quite easy to wither into old age, and hard to grow into it. . . . Growing old is certainly far easier for people like me who have no job from which to retire at a given age. I can't stop doing what I have always done, trying to sort out and shape experience. The journal is a good way to do this at a less intense level than by creating a work of art as highly organized as a poem, for instance, or the sustained effort a novel requires. I find it wonderful to have a receptacle into which to pour vivid momentary insights, and a way of ordering day-to-day experience. . . .

Also, in private writing, the *reader* wants something: a view into the writer's life. In public writing, however, it is the *writer* who wants something: the reader's attention and understanding. So, **in public writing, a writer must do everything possible to get the reader interested in what the writer has to say and to say it so clearly that the reader will experience no confusion.** That is why a writer *shapes* the ideas that have surfaced in the creating stage of the writing process. Readers want order, clarity, stimulation, and most of the time they are unwilling to provide these things themselves. Therefore, the writer must be aware of what readers demand and what conditions are usually present when communication actually occurs between a writer and a reader. With this knowledge—*about the nature of readers* and *the nature of communication*—a writer can plan and produce a piece of public writing that will do just exactly what he or she wants it to do: engage the reader in the act of understanding what the writer is saying.

PRIVATE WRITING	PUBLIC WRITING
The writer	The writer
has to think only of himself or herself	thinks always of another person, the reader
is under no obligation to explain or connect or make clear	must explain, connect, and make clear so that another person can understand what is being said
can be uninterested in whether anyone else would like the writing	is concerned at all points in whether the reader will start and complete the piece of writing
can ramble and roam wherever the mind travels	must decide what exactly is to be communicated to the reader and stick to that
can write things that would be totally insignificant or trivial to another person	cannot waste the reader's time or insult the reader by writing about things without thinking about their significance to other people
rules supreme.	is a partner with the reader in causing communication to happen.

HOW COMMUNICATION HAPPENS

Since the purpose of public writing is to communicate something, we should understand what happens when communication takes place. Let's take a look at what goes on when people talk (something you mastered so early and so thoroughly that you now take it pretty much for granted). Then we'll examine the differences between talking and writing (which you'll want to be aware of as you transform your own writing from private to public).

SPEAKING—"PERSON *A*"

When two people meet — say, Person *A* and Person *B* — they meet at some specific place (on a corner, at a laundromat, over a cup of coffee, at a dorm, in a hallway). Already Person *A* has some real advantages that she wouldn't have if she were writing:

> the audience is somebody specific;
> the place (location) is real;
> the person can be seen face to face.

If the meeting were arranged in advance, presumably that would help too. If it's a date, you say things appropriate about a date — maybe deciding about where to go for some food or a movie, or a walk or a ride, or to visit some other people or attend a game, go bowling — whatever. If it's a business appointment, you discuss the business at hand. If it's a chance meeting, then you know that, too. Some more advantages:

> the circumstances are known;
> the situation is known;
> subjects will fit the person and the
> situation (so will the words);
> all these elements enter the speaker's
> mind fairly automatically.

If Person *A* decides to communicate with Person *B* (more than "Hi" or "Hello"), that communication involves three more things: (1) Person *A* has a lifetime of stored knowledge, past experiences, feelings, attitudes, emotions, images. That's where it starts. (2) Person *A* makes a lightning-quick sorting and selecting from among all that's in the mind, choosing exactly the ideas, experiences, knowledge, emotions, attitudes — whatever — to be communicated to Person *B*. (3) After deciding what to communicate (and this happens so fast that we often don't even know we've done it) Person *A* "encodes" the message — puts the selected experience, knowledge, emotion, etc., into words and speaks those words to Person *B*.

An outline of communication in talking — at least for Person *A* — would look like this:

WHAT THE SPEAKER *KNOWS*

who the audience is   what the situation is
what the location is   what subjects are appropriate
how the audience is looking *right now*   what words are appropriate

WHAT THE SPEAKER *HAS*

a lifetime of stored knowledge, feelings, images, etc.
certain expectations about Person *B*, this situation, this communication

WHAT THE SPEAKER *DOES*

sort and select something to communicate
encode it into words that are spoken

LISTENING—"PERSON B"

So far, that's what Person *A* has done. Has any communication happened yet? Not until Person *B* gets involved. And Person *B*, to have communication take place, must hear what's said (not be hindered by mumbling, impaired hearing, or loud noises outside), understand the words (presumably *A* and *B* are using a common language), understand *A*'s intention, find it appropriate to the situation and circumstances, and be willing/able to re-create Person *A*'s idea—in effect, to build it again in *B*'s mind. That means that *B* has had experiences/knowledge/attitudes/images similar to *A*'s or that through some other way *B* is able to re-build *A*'s message.

Notice that the *memories* aren't the same as the original events—and that *words* about the memories aren't the same as either the original

THE WORD THE MAP THE SYMBOL **IS NOT** THE THING THE TERRITORY THE REFERENT

— S. I. HAYAKAWA

events or the memories. The original experiences are long gone; what remains is not the *originals* but *recollections* about the originals. If *A* wants to talk about breaking her arm this morning, the bone may still be broken, but the event—the breaking itself—is in the past. Further, when *A* tells *B* about it, *B* isn't getting the original experience: *B*'s arm won't break when he hears about *A*'s arm. Words about an experience aren't the experience: words about a delicious Thanksgiving dinner can't fill you up, and words about a mad dog can't bite you on the ankle.

What it all means is that for communication to happen, Person *B* must hear the words, understand them (recognize the language and the "meaning"), and reconstruct the message according to his own experience/knowledge/attitudes/images. **It is that re-creation that counts**—without *B*'s re-creation, not much happens. And if *B* re-creates something far, far different from what Person *A* sent, then there has been little if any communication.

WHAT THE LISTENER *KNOWS*
who the speaker is   what the situation is
what the location is   what subjects are appropriate
how the speaker is looking *right now*   what words are appropriate

WHAT THE LISTENER *HAS*
a lifetime of stored knowledge, feelings, images, etc.
certain expectations about Person *A*, this situation, this communication

WHAT THE LISTENER *DOES*
hears the words spoken, and the tone, volume, pitch, speed
recognizes the words (language) and meanings
matches the words to knowledge/feelings/images, etc.
re-creates *A*'s knowledge/feelings/images (or doesn't)

DR. RAYMOND S. ROSS' SPEECH COMMUNICATION MODEL

Momentary Set

Mutual Influence

Perception

Perception

Selecting and sorting

Encoding

Decoding

Selecting and sorting

Signs-symbols
Language
Arrangement
Voice Action

Situation Itself

Background Noise

Idea

Feedback

Idea reconstructed

Sending

Knowledge, Past experience, Feelings, Attitudes, Emotions, etc.

Knowledge, Past experience, Feelings, Attitudes, Emotions, etc.

Active Participation

The Ross Model shows how little overlap — *Mutual Influence* — there is when people communicate. Even so, mutual influence is vastly greater in speaking than in writing, simply because the two of you are together and because of the whole support system that goes with speaking.

GET IT?

Since both *A* and *B* have a lifetime accumulation of experiences and images in the mind plus a lifetime accumulation of associations for words that may be quite similar or quite different, the chance of *B* re-creating *A*'s message *exactly* is pretty small. Given good will, few distractions, and an appropriate setting, Person *A* has a lot going for her to help get through to Person *B:* spoken words, tone, facial expression, gesture, volume, pitch, delivery, visual contact to see how it's going and change whatever is necessary right on the spot.

You can ask questions. Looks on faces can be noticed. The speaker can say, "I don't think you see what I mean; let me start over." Or the listener can say, "I understand the first point but I don't see where you are going on the second." If the speaker sees a quizzical look on the listener's face, it's possible to give some more examples or explanations. If the listener looks bored, the speaker can stop or do something to get the listener's attention again. If there is a bulldozer that suddenly starts up outside the window while the conversation is going on, the speaker can say, "Let's go into another room." If the speaker wants to emphasize a point it's possible to talk louder or gesture with the hands and head. If the speaker can tell from the way the listener is acting that something touchy or upsetting has been mentioned, the speaker can do something about that immediately so that the communication doesn't get lost. In other words, the speaker's resources are plentiful. Indeed, when we list them, they look almost overwhelming.

Fortunately, we learned to use spoken words, tone, facial expression, gestures, volume, pitch, delivery, visual contact—and more—quite naturally as we were growing up. Somebody has remarked that if we had to go to school and take lessons on how to walk, we'd all still be crawling. Trial (lots of it) and error (some of it) gave us a mastery of walking and talking that leaves us so skilled that we never think, "Now I want to ease my weight slightly forward toward my left heel, pushing off slightly with my right toes, lifting my right leg at the same time I lower the left leg," and so on. In talking, we master all the nuances of voice, gesture and facial expression—the whole support system that lets us gauge our communication from moment to moment, to change wordings, to get new examples, to add emphasis, and to communicate over, under, on top of, and through the words themselves.

WRITING

So, what have you got going for yourself in writing? Nothing in sight except you, your pen, and some paper. *Blank* paper! And when you finally send your communication to someone else, what's in sight? Nothing but that same paper—this time with words on it.

SUPPORT SYSTEMS AVAILABLE

	FOR TALKING	FOR WRITING
words	yes	yes
paper	no	yes
pen	no	yes
audience present	yes	no
immediate feedback	yes	no
facial expression	yes	no
voice tone	yes	no
pitch	yes	no
loudness	yes	no
ability to switch as you go along	yes	yes
gestures	yes	no
location known	yes	no
situation known	yes	perhaps

WHAT'S MISSING IN WRITING?
- —an audience in person
- —feedback as you write
- —any indication whether it's working
- —any hint about whether your reader finds it appropriate
  some clue about whether the reader is still interested, or even if the reader is still reading
- —some way to fix it up as you go along, to make it fit whatever is happening

Because there is a big difference between the liveliness of talking to someone who is right there and the act of writing on blank paper all by yourself, it's no surprise to learn that many people don't really think of writing as *communicating* at all. But if writing isn't *communicating,* it is merely an empty and unsatisfactory activity to the writer, not to mention the reader.

However, writing *is* communication—when you intend it to be that. And since in writing you do not have the many advantages that you have when you speak, you'd better do what you can in advance to ensure that your reader will stick with you all the way.

What *can* you do?

This section on SHAPING shows you, exactly. Writing has its conventions that compensate for the absence of personal contact, voice, facial expressions, and the like. These conventions are almost like another language, and even people who do lots of reading and writing over a long period of time usually find explicit advice very helpful. In fact, that's why people study writing—**to learn how to compensate for not having the audience right there and not being able to change the message on the spot.**

Just realizing the differences between talking and writing can be a real step ahead. You soon begin to see that writing has got to change

IN WRITING,
If it doesn't happen
on paper,
It doesn't happen *at all!*

Public ↔ Communication ↔ Audience
Writing   Theory

from being a "guessing game" to becoming a "choosing game," where **you learn to control, as much as possible, the reader's reaction by making deliberate decisions about what will work.**

APPLICATION

1 Choose someone in your class to be your listener. Then tell him or her how to get from one specific place to another specific place. For instance, how to get from a building on one end of the campus to a fountain at the other end; or how to get from the campus to the bus station; or how to get from the dorm to the new pizza house.

Check how many things besides words that you use to communicate this information. Also check how many things the listener does to make the communication clear.

SPEAKER	LISTENER
_____ used hands to gesture or point	_____ used hands to indicate understanding or lack of understanding
_____ started over again when listener was not understanding	_____ showed by look on face that he/she was not understanding
_____ asked listener questions so would know what information to give	_____ asked speaker questions when did not understand
_____ others	_____ others

2 Now, write out the directions you gave orally just a little while ago, telling someone how to get from one specific place to another. (Use the same two places that you used in 1 above.) Give these written directions to someone else in class, not the person you just talked to.

First, make a list of all the ways writing the directions was harder for you than talking. Get as complete a list as you can. If it was easier in any ways, list those too.

Then, after your classmate has read the directions, talk with him or her about how well she or he understood them. Notice what wasn't clear that you thought would be. Notice what you assumed the reader would know that he/she didn't know.

3 Write a paragraph in which you summarize the differences you experienced between telling a message and writing it.

WRITING TO COMMUNICATE:
THE CONVENTIONS OF WRITING

It's because communicating in writing is such a different activity from communicating face to face that you even have to study writing at all. You especially have to study how to communicate in writing when that writing is *public* because no explanation can accompany the writing— **your writing must be its own explanation.** (There can be no counting on the public reader to know what you've left out the way a friend is able usually to fill in the gaps or to know enough of what you know to understand what you mean, even when you don't say it.) Public writing has its own peculiarities to a very great extent *because* you don't know the audience on an intimate level. And since you're writing for someone who isn't a close, personal friend with whom you share a lot of common experiences, you have to do a good many things *on the page* to make up for this absence of personal closeness.

The things you must do because the writing is public are what you may have heard called the *conventions* of writing. They are things you *must* do because the communication is written instead of spoken. It is not surprising that you actually have to study these; the writing conventions are not natural. They are not automatic. But they are necessary. You will perhaps be surprised to learn in this part of the book that many of the writing "rules" you have heard about in the past are important not because they are rules but because they have something to do with a public audience getting your message. For instance, you have probably heard since high school that an essay must have a *thesis*. You will see in the next few pages that this is true not because some English teacher thought it improved writing but because communicating in public writing is much more successful when the reader has a rope to hold onto all the way through the writing—and that's really what the thesis of a paper is!

We've gathered together the conventions that public writing depends upon and called these conventions **Shaping.** Shaping is exactly what works in public writing—shaping those thoughts that came to you in an unorganized, unstructured form during the *Creating Stage* and selecting some while discarding others, and arranging an orderly sequence that your readers can follow and understand. So, as you study the ways to shape, you are doing so because these ways are crucial to your being able to communicate in public writing. Everything in this *shaping section* is here because *it works,* not because it is "supposed" to be here.

NO RIGID BOUNDARIES

Even though *shaping* is much more structured and deliberate than *creating,* you will soon discover that in the *Shaping Stage* you also create (just as

Convention:

General agreement on or acceptance of certain practices; practice or procedure widely observed in a group, especially to facilitate social intercourse; widely used and accepted device or technique, as in drama, literature, or painting.

> All through *The Elements of Style* one finds evidences of the author's deep sympathy for the reader. Will felt that the reader was in serious trouble most of the time, a man floundering in a swamp, and that it was the duty of anyone attempting to write English to drain this swamp quickly and get his man up on dry ground, or at least throw him a rope.
>
> E. B. White

at times in the *Creating Stage* you actually begin to shape your public writing without even knowing it). It would be much simpler if writing actually happened in three totally separate stages that didn't overlap or contain each other at times. What actually happens, however, is that right in the middle of shaping your essay you may discover something new you want to say. Creating may happen without your even planning it. The three stages, however, can be separated as you learn them because each one—creating, shaping, and completing—does have its own characteristic activities that set it apart from the other two. Each has a specific purpose that the others do not have. *Inside each stage, of course, the other two stages are likely to pop up.*

You will see, for instance, that although shaping is for the most part much more organized and planned than creating, shaping itself begins with some steps that are exploratory (much like *creating*) and moves finally to some firm and concrete choices (much like *completing*). Actually writing is a recursive process: the stages happen once (*creating occurs* in the creating stage) and then later appear again, in a modified form, in other stages (*creating recurs*, in a lesser degree, in *shaping* and *completing*). So, just remember that **while you definitely do move through three distinct stages, each of these will also contain elements of the other two.** Because writing is recursive, you won't be able to finish the creating stage and say, "Well, that's that; I won't be creating any more in writing this essay!" What you *can* say is, "Well, I've finished the *Creating Stage* of the writing process, which allowed me to find something to say. I may actually do some more creating later in the other two stages, but not for the purpose of getting my initial ideas for the paper."

MORE DELIBERATE ACTIVITY

Shaping is a much more deliberate activity than creating. In shaping, you consider all the raw material you have generated or brought to the surface in the *Creating Stage.* From that, you choose what to focus on, what to develop for another person. Then you decide *how* that material is going to be put together—what comes first, second, third; what gets top billing and what comes in as supporting roles. All of these conscious decisions are necessary, because if you intend communication to happen, you need to do *in advance* everything possible to put the message into a form that will leave no room for misunderstanding or—worse yet—cause the reader to just stop reading in the middle of your paper.

EARLY SHAPING: PRELIMINARY AGREEMENTS

The *Shaping Stage* actually begins before you literally start organizing and arranging your material. **Shaping begins by your making some "preliminary agreements" about whom you are writing to and what you**

Recursive:
Each step depends on the step before; movement tends to return to point of origin, or to redo, with slight modification, something already done.

want them to know. Why these preliminary agreements? Simple: you *don't* have a live person right in front of you and you can't count on the support system you have in oral communication.

This idea of preliminary agreements is easy to grasp if you compare it with our second stage of cabin-building (see photo opening essay). To recall:

PRELIMINARY AGREEMENTS

FOR CABIN

LAND
BLUEPRINTS
CONTRACTOR

FOR ESSAY

PURPOSE
AUDIENCE
THESIS

You have made a firm decision to build a cabin. You are no longer dreaming, no longer collecting pictures or planning for the future. You are going to do it now. What will be some of the preliminary things that you will have to do before the actual building starts?

First, you will buy the land. You will select the contractors (or people to help, if *you* are going to be the contractor). You will decide exactly what size and shape the cabin will be. You'll hire someone to draw the blueprints. Only after you have done all these things—made these crucial preliminary decisions—will you start the actual laying of the foundation and putting up the boards.

That's how it is as you start the shaping stage in the writing process. You will already have gathered your ideas. You will already have collected information. Now you have to begin to make some firm decisions. **You decide to whom you are writing** (or review to whom you are writing, if the audience is assigned), **why you are writing, and what you want the writing to accomplish.** In other words, in early shaping you handle all "contracts" and preliminary agreements. Then, and only then, are you ready to start the rough work of indicating what shape the whole essay will take.

Let's take a look in detail at the preliminary agreements you have to make early in the shaping stage. A good place to start is with the concept of AUDIENCE. There are two principles involved here, and we'll take them one at a time.

1. INVENT AND KNOW YOUR AUDIENCE

This is one of the earliest conventions you have to think about when you begin to write because it is the most obvious difference between talking and writing. When you talk, you don't have to *invent an audience* because an audience is there. You may have to *analyze* your audience when you talk—for example, find out what age they are, what they already know about your subject, etc.—but you don't have to make up an audience. In writing, however, because the audience is not actually present in the room with you, you have both to make up your audience *and* to analyze that audience. That's what makes writing a totally different—and special—communication activity. *But what if I don't invent and know my audience before I start writing?*

Well, if you write a paper to no one, then the only audience you are likely to attract are people who like papers written with no particular audience in mind. How many people like that can there be? That's exactly what's wrong with the old schoolroom essay: it isn't aimed at anybody, and therefore it's boring and mechanical at best. Although teachers *will* read it (they have to!), they don't really enjoy it. Who can blame them? Nobody likes to be bored, and everybody likes to be stimulated. If you choose to write an essay with no audience in mind, or "forget" about the audience, or write for "a general audience," it all comes to the same thing: you are actually *deciding* that your audience will be those few souls in the universe who *like* dull prose. If you invent and/or know your audience in advance, however, you can actually plan the whole essay around this person or group of people. *You gain enormously by having your audience in mind from the very start.*

THE TRUTH ABOUT ALL AUDIENCES

No matter who your audience is, so long as it is made up of human beings, you can count on these things being true:

1 Readers do not like to be bored, and they **do** like to be stimulated.

According to people who study such things, all human beings have certain desires in common. Robert Ardrey, author of *Territorial Imperative,* writes that we all have a built-in system that causes us *to seek identity, security, and stimulus,* and *to avoid anonymity, boredom, and anxiety.*

Dear Nobody,
Nothing, nothing, nothing. Nothing at all. Nothing and nothing and blah blah blah......

2 Readers do not like to be bored, and they *do* like to be stimulated.
of the highest is a feeling of achievement or accomplishment.

Abraham Maslow, the famous psychologist, in *Psychology of Being*, puts these needs in a hierarchy, with the most basic at the bottom and the most sophisticated at the top:

Sophisticated	Self-Actualization, Achievement
↑	Esteem: Self-Esteem and Esteem of Others
	Love, Affiliation, Sense of Belonging
	Safety, Security
Basic	Psychological Survival

3 Readers want to get something out of what they read.
Sure. Don't you?

4 Readers resent being told what they already know, unless the writer brings a special expertise to the subject.
In fact, they tend to get "bored" and feel that they aren't "achieving" anything.

5 Readers are busy people; they will not tolerate having their time wasted.
Ask any ten people at random how much time they have for reading!

6 Readers are often reluctant to read; they would rather be watching television or playing tennis or even sleeping than reading.
People say, "Yea! I get to watch TV (or play tennis or sleep)."
Who says, "Hot dog! I get to read an essay!"?

7 Readers have to have ideas, opinions, and information explained; they demand expansion and development of points so that they can "see" what the writer means.
Seeing all that is involved in communicating (earlier in this section) explains why this is so.

8 Readers like order and hate chaos; they need to be able to sense where the writer is going.
They *presume* the writer has a plan and a purpose, and they like plenty of evidence that this is true.

What difference should these facts make to you?
For one thing, they ought to help you see that if you do not have the reader in mind from the very outset of the shaping stage, you are likely to do a lot of work for very little reward. The reader has specific needs, and when you know what they are, you can take them into account. For another thing, having the welfare of your reader at heart is almost the same as having your own welfare at heart, because if your reader does

not get your point, your interest, your sense of direction, your value, he or she will certainly not think much of your writing and may not even finish reading it. For you, the advantage in knowing about the nature of readers is that you'll be better able to get your message across to the reader (and all that work you put into your writing won't be wasted).

JOHN CHEEVER SAYS . . .

Writing is one of the few things in life that one cannot do alone. . . . When I write, I count very much on an intelligent reader agreeing with what I've put down on paper.

That has become more the case as I've grown older. I constantly keep the reader in mind. I ask myself repeatedly: "Is what I have to say urgent, and do I suppose it would be of any urgency to people who read my books?" And one always asks oneself: "Is it interesting?" But urgency is what I principally seek.

Readers are the only audience that cannot be isolated by computer surveys or polls. Nobody knows who the hell the reader is! As far as I'm concerned, the reader is an intelligent, well-informed man or woman anywhere in the world. I want to share with that reader the excitement of being alive or of comprehending the human condition.

PICTURE A **SPECIFIC** AUDIENCE

Knowing what's true of audiences *in general* is a great advantage to you as a writer. Even so, you want to have a *specific* audience in mind as you compose, for the problem with writing to "a general audience" is that you tend to shotgun your message rather than rifle it — to scatter your efforts broadly rather than train them on a real flesh-and-bones assemblage of live people awake and reading your paper. It's the difference between giving a tiny legacy to the whole population, or leaving a great fortune to a few heirs. It's the difference between sunlight falling on the broad earth and sunlight focused through a lens — one can light a fire, the other can't.

It is crucial to note who your specific audience is at the outset (or to invent an audience if the choice is yours) because your approach to the subject will be determined by who this audience is. Just suppose that you were writing an essay to inform your readers about the attractiveness of your home town as a vacation spot. Sure, why not? People always think they have to go *somewhere* to have a vacation. What might happen if they came to your home town? Of course, the question has more obvious answers if you live in a place like San Francisco or Las Vegas, but even the most unpromising places can be appealing — if you bother to work out the appeal. For example, whoever heard of

All: The will! Let's stay and hear the will.
Antony: Here is the will, and under Caesar's seal:
To every Roman citizen he gives,
To every several man, seventy-five cents.
Julius Caesar III, ii

Luckenbach, Texas, before the country-western song made it famous? Now it has tourists galore, and not a thing to offer beyond "the basics."

If you were to explain the attractions of your home town to potential tourists, what would you say? What would the differences be in how you approached the subject if your audience were

people your own age
people already living in your home town
people with small children
out-of-state visitors
foreign travelers
retired persons
culture lovers
all of these

You can see right away how many decisions would turn out one way for one group of people, another way for other people. Almost everything would depend on which audience you wanted to attract.

If you were writing for someone your own age, you would likely emphasize the things you like to do; you could probably count on your audience liking these things too. You could also be more informal; the words you used could sound like your normal conversation with friends, and you wouldn't have to worry much about the readers knowing the definitions or getting the drift of what you had to say. However, think of the difference in how you would write the essay if you were praising your home town as a vacation spot for foreign travelers, as contrasted to the way you would write for people who already live there. Foreign visitors would have to be given more background, would need directions, and would need to be persuaded to choose your hometown over a hundred other places they could visit while in America. If you were writing for people who already lived in your home town, however, you could skip much of the description, location, directions, and the like, and instead write about the places to go and things to do that even residents might have overlooked. For this audience, your purpose would be to write about the possibilities "right in their own backyard."

As you can see, not only the approach and purpose in writing are influenced by the audience, but also the very content of the writing itself—what points you make, what examples you use. **Getting to know your audience before you write the paper is crucial.** It's much more fundamental than making "stylistic" changes when you revise the paper (when you might change words or alter the tone slightly), touching up the prose here and there to make it fit more closely to the audience. Recognizing, inventing, and knowing your audience *before* you begin the trial draft will solve, in advance, the issue of how to approach the subject: approach it in a way that's appropriate to the audience you have decided to write to. And you'll find that it's then much easier to make the dozens of early decisions that have to be made, because you know with certainty the kind of person or persons you are writing for.

In fact, much of the work of preparing a piece of public writing is to
  (a) *decide what your audience is like and what it is likely to understand, find stimulating, need to know, and enjoy*
  and
  (b) *deliver that.*

One of the things you have to do in meeting this challenge is to anticipate just as much about your audience as you possibly can. What will they question, find unclear, not have any experience in, like or dislike? For instance, if you're describing a rock concert for people who generally attend them, you won't need to explain that the audience usually spends more time moving, dancing, clapping, standing, than they do sitting quietly in the seats. However, if your readers haven't been to that kind of concert, you'll need to tell them about it—and probably in a way that helps them to see that not only are the audience's antics pretty much expected and commonplace, but that it is a perfectly OK way to behave. (People who don't ordinarily bounce at concerts will need some help in seeing the point.) As a writer, many of the choices you make—about what details go into the paper, which ones are developed, which are made brief—will be made in light of what you think this specific reader will need.

INVENT AND KNOW YOUR AUDIENCE BEFORE YOU BEGIN TO WRITE TO THEM

CHECKLIST:
1 Know the truth about *all* audiences.
  They do not like to be bored; they do like to be stimulated.
  They want a feeling of achievement or accomplishment.
  They want to get something out of what they read.
  They are busy and don't want their time wasted.
  They often have things to do besides reading.
  They need explanations and details.
  They like order and hate chaos.
2 Picture a *specific* audience.
  Who is the audience?
  What do you know about this audience?
  How old? What educational background? What kind of work?
  What will be the audience's attitude toward the subject?
  How much does the audience already know about the subject?
  Will they already be interested in the subject? Why?
3 Decide what your audience is like and what it is likely to understand, find stimulating, need to know, enjoy . . . and
4 Deliver that.

APPLICATION

1   Think of writing an essay that would describe your home town as an attractive vacation spot. Make a list of things you would talk about for each of the following audiences:

> people already living in your home town
> people with small children
> retired people
> out-of-state visitors
> a group you make up yourself

When you finish your five lists, look at the ways each list differs from the others because of what is needed for the specific readers. Which audience seems to you easiest to write for? Which is hardest? Why? Which would you most enjoy writing for? Why? (Do you see, now, how having a *specific* set of readers in mind at the outset of your writing process takes care of a lot of those initial decisions?)

2   Imagine that it is your job to write the instruction sheet for assembling a bookshelf. You don't know who your specific audience will be because you don't know who is going to buy the bookshelf in the store. What will you still have to think about and do to be sure your writing matches your audience? Discuss this with your class.

3   Situation: You have just been assigned an essay to write for a college course you are taking in one of the following subjects: history, art, psychology, medical technology, computer science, sociology. You know that the reason you have to write the essay is that your instructor assigned it. Nobody else in the class is going to hear or see it. Question: even in this circumstance, what will be crucial for you to think about in terms of the audience for your paper? Discuss this with your class.

4   Adapting material for a specific audience. Choose one of these subjects and fill in the blank with something you know how to do:

> "How to cook a _____"

> "How to repair a _____"

Then consider: how would you explain that—in writing—to a child (ten or twelve years old) who had no experience with it whatsoever? If you explained it in writing to someone your own age, what would be different? Make three lists:

> *a.* What would you do specially for the child?
> *b.* What would you do specially for the person your age?
> *c.* What would you do for both?

2. TREAT THE READER LIKE A PERSON, NOT LIKE A WALL

If you want to write only for yourself, you can write merely to express, to unburden yourself of whatever opinions you have at the time, or to just ventilate your feelings. When you try to send *that* message to a reader, however, about all he or she will get is feelings, and probably not much of that. It's what happens when a writer says, "I want the reader to know how I feel." Here is an example of "Here's How I Feel" writing:

The color of a day makes life worth living. There are many interesting aspects to the colors of a day. To sit and observe them it is evident that you could be sitting and observing for an eternity. The mysterious blue sky with its billowing white clouds is like seeing imaginary objects returning a look. Also, in the sky is the beaming yellow sun. It is a gorgeous object that should bring happiness to everyone. It can brighten up even the saddest of days. There is a secret spy in the sky too, but he only comes out of hiding at night. He is like a wise old owl, only revealing himself at the appropriate time. Coming down to earth we find many new colors. There is green which includes many things. Trees can be many various colors of green. Variety is . . . .

There's nothing at all wrong with that kind of writing, as exploration or as private musing. But what's a *reader* likely to think? If we could get inside the reader's mind, it might be something like this:

ESSAY	READER'S REACTION
"The color of a day makes life worth living."	(Huh? What does "color of a day" mean? I haven't the foggiest idea! And how in the world can *it* make life worth living?)
"There are many interesting aspects to the colors of a day."	(I get sleepy reading glumpy stuff like "many interesting aspects." And I'm sure not interested in "aspects" of a thing I didn't understand in the first place.)
"To sit and observe them . . ."	(Observe *what?* Those silly aspects? Or colors? Or what?)
". . . it is evident . . ."	(*What* is evident? I don't even know what I am "observing.")
". . . that you could be sitting and observing for an eternity."	(Not me, baby! *You* sit there for an eternity if you want to, and observe away. As for me, forget it!)

Chances are, if you asked the writer what was intended by that paper, the answer might be something like, "I wanted to show how I felt about the colors of the day." And, in a kind of way, you'd probably agree that the paragraph does, hit or miss, show *something* about how the writer feels, though most of us would be hard put to say *what* exactly. But the point to notice here is: see how little there is for a *reader*. It's almost as though the writer were treating the reader like a wall and the message like a handball to be bounced off the reader. All the reader can do is stand there like a target while the writer bounces feelings. There's not any *participation* to speak of, and there certainly isn't any strategy on the part of the writer to get the reader to join in with the feelings.

If you want to persuade or convince your reader to *share* your position, judgment, attitude, strong feeling, or the like, then your purpose is different from just wanting to express your feelings. If you really want to get a message across, you have to treat the reader as a separate person, not merely as a wall to bounce your feelings off of. Treating the reader as a separate human being, like yourself but also different from yourself, you want to consider what, exactly, you might have to do to move that reader, to get him or her to join up with you, subscribe, agree, feel strongly, be convinced, know in the same way you, the writer, do. To do that, you may have to be sure *exactly* that he/she will have the same images for your words that you do. If you are using terms like "colors of the day," you had better make sure that you show or explain what you mean by them. And if you want your reader to share your wonder about a thing, you had better do more than *say* that it is wonderful — or that *you* think or feel that it is wonderful. You have to *show* the reader exactly *what* is so wonderful about it.

What you have to do is make your reader feel like a partner in the communication exchange. You have to act as though it were a privilege for you to be able to tell your reader whatever it is you are telling; you do not act as though it were the reader's obligation to read what you write just because you write it. Taking your reader into partnership with yourself by recognizing him/her as a person who is going to be listening to you is much different from simply expressing personal feeling and expecting the reader to be excited over that. You are not indiscriminately hollering; you are addressing yourself to someone quite distinct from you, a different human being, an *audience*. And you want this audience to be affected by your writing. You want the person to be moved, to agree, to understand, or at least to care about what you are saying. You want a response. When you say, "Hello; anybody out there?" you want a real live reader to answer, "Yes; I'm with you. I see what you mean. I get your message."

EARLY WARNING SYSTEM

Often, it is possible to tell from the first paragraph whether the reader is being treated as a wall or as a person. Compare these two opening paragraphs, for example. The first strains to catch the effect of the sunrise in the mountains, and concludes with an expression that is rather worn ("the first day of the rest of your life"). It's clear that the writer wants to describe the Great Outdoors. It is not clear that he cares at all whether the reader wants to read about the Great Outdoors. He doesn't seem to have taken into account any of the truths about general audiences—that they don't like to be bored, that they like to get something out of what they read, that they like to feel they will accomplish something by reading what is before them. He seems to be assuming that the reader is going to enjoy hearing about this scenery just because he enjoyed seeing it and writing about it.

There, on the horizon, are the majestic mountains, stretching their peaks so that they might be seen over the top of the towering bristlecone pines. You awaken in awe of this sight, and even more awed are you as you see the sky change from a shade of pink, to orange, to red, and finally, in a glorious burst of yellow light, the sun shoots up over the mountains, signaling the beginning of the first day of the rest of your life.

—*Howard Marshburn*

Now look at the opening of the next essay. It is written on the same subject, the out-of-doors, but from the very start the writer has been aware that he has to interest his audience, to write as though there were people out there, not walls, and that those people would put the writing down if it didn't provide them some sense of satisfaction. He begins by making the reader a partner, the person on the other end for whom he has done all this work.

An inaudible yawn was the best answer I could give to Bobby at six in the morning. Besides, what kind of a question is "Are you awake yet?" at this early hour? Slowly, my sleepy mind began to focus. Today was the day of our hike into the hill country. I was certain this day would be the low point of my visit with Bobby. However, Bobby was my older brother, as well as my host, and I felt that I should struggle through this journey for his sake. I could think of nothing more boring and worthless than wandering through some barren hills all day long. Nevertheless, I decided to crawl out of bed and get dressed, straining to open each eyelid. Before this day was over, I would realize that my eyes had never really been open before.

—*Tim Wold*

What has Tim done that Howard didn't do? He has "talked" to the reader by using vivid details, "drawing" the picture so that the reader can see exactly where the writer is. He has let the reader know what the reader can expect to read in this essay—about a day he hiked in the hill country. And even more important, he has been courteous enough to let the reader know more exactly what will be important about that day—that it was the day his eyes really opened to the out of doors. *The reader has been considered and included.* Tim took very little for granted; he wanted to tell the reader this particular thing, and he knew that to do so he would have to bring the reader into the transaction from the very start. *He did not take it for granted that someone would read his paper just because he wrote it.*

CHECKLIST: TREAT THE READER LIKE A PERSON, NOT LIKE A WALL
1 Have you considered and included the reader? 2 Does the writing let the reader participate, or does it merely fling feelings at him/her? 3 Have you used vivid details to "draw" a picture for the reader?

SUMMARY OF AUDIENCE

Knowing about audiences in general, inventing a specific one for each piece of writing that you do, and treating the reader as a person — all of these will assist you in making decisions about what details to put into your paper and how to arrange them so that *this* reader in *this* situation gets exactly the help he or she needs. Your chances for connecting with that reader are bound to improve dramatically, although you will never know for sure until you actually hand the message to someone else. But if you like playing with the odds in your favor, capitalizing on your own intuition and choices, then you will enjoy the game of audience.

Of course, as you practice you'll learn more exactly what works and what doesn't. But you are well started the minute you begin to think of your audience. You may even relish the strategy of answering *all* the questions before they are asked, out-guessing your readers, making things clear, giving examples. And the better you get at picturing your readers and anticipating their needs, the more effective you'll become as a writer, the more efficient your time spent in writing will be, the more reward you'll get for the work you put into it, and the more often you'll score by landing your message *exactly* where you aimed it.

APPLICATION

1   Divide the class into committees with four or five students in each. Have each committee read the essays (on biological clocks) that follow; then answer these questions:

    1 Who is the audience?
    2 How much does the audience know about the subject?
    3 Why would the audience read the piece?
    4 Where could the piece appear? (Give a *specific* title of an actual publication. Make titles up if you have to.)
    5 Why did you decide as you did in 1–4? That is, what clues in the *writing itself* tell you the answers?

(You will notice that the essays are incomplete; this is intentional because the point is to observe the stylistic adaptations to the various audiences rather than to read three complete essays.)

Recent studies have provided reasons to postulate that the primary timer for long-cycle biological rhythms that are closely similar in period to the natural geophysical ones and that persist in so-called constant conditions is, in fact, one of organismic response to subtle geophysical fluctuations which pervade ordinary constant conditions in the laboratory (Brown, 1959, 1960). In such constant laboratory conditions a wide variety of organisms has been demonstrated to display, nearly equally conspicuously, metabolic periodicities of both solar-day and lunar-day frequencies, with their interference derivative, the 29.5-day synodic month, and in some instances even the year. These metabolic cycles exhibit day-by-day irregularities and distortions which have been established to be highly significantly correlated with aperiodic meteorological and other geophysical changes. These correlations provide strong evidence for the exogenous origin of these biological periodisms themselves, since cycles exist in these meteorological and geophysical factors.

In addition to possessing these basic metabolic periodisms, many organisms exhibit also overt periodisms of numerous phenomena which in the laboratory in artificially controlled conditions of constancy of illumination and temperature may depart from a natural period. The literature contains many accounts, for a wide spectrum of kinds of plants and animals, of regular rhythmic periods ranging from about 20 to about 30 hours. The extent of departure from 24 hours is generally a function of the level of the illumination and temperature.

It has been commonly assumed, without any direct supporting evidence, that the phase- and frequency-labile periodisms persisting in constant conditions reflect inherited periods of fully autonomous internal oscillations. However, the relationships of period-length to the ambient illumination and temperature levels suggest that it is not the period-length itself which is inherited but rather the characteristics of some response mechanism which participates in the derivation of the periods in a reaction with the environment (Webb and Brown, 1959).

It has recently been alternatively postulated that the timing mechanism responsible for the periods of rhythms differing from a natural one involves, jointly, use of both the exogenous natural periodisms and a phenomenon of regular resetting, or "autophasing," of the phase-labile, 24-hour cycles in reaction of the rhythmic organisms to the ambient light and temperature (Brown, Shriner and Ralph, 1956; Webb and Brown, 1959; Brown, 1959). It is thus postulated that the exogenous metabolic periodisms function critically as temporal frames of reference for biological rhythms of approximately the same frequencies.

Most studies of mammalian diurnal rhythms have been concerned chiefly with the more conspicuous, phase- and . . . [Article incomplete]

One of the greatest riddles of the universe is the uncanny ability of living things to carry out their normal activities with clockwise precision at a particular time of the day, month and year. Why do oysters plucked from a Connecticut bay and shipped to a Midwest laboratory continue to time their lives to ocean tides 800 miles away? How do potatoes in hermetically sealed containers predict atmospheric pressure trends two days in advance? What effects do the lunar and solar rhythms have on the life habits of man? Living things clearly possess powerful adaptive capacities—but the explanation of whatever strange and permeative forces are concerned continues to challenge science. Let us consider the phenomena more closely.

Over the course of millions of years living organisms have evolved under complex environmental conditions, some obvious and some so subtle that we are only now beginning to understand their influence. One important factor of the environment is its rhythmicality. Contributing to this rhythmicality are movements of the earth relative to the sun and moon.

The earth's rotation relative to the sun gives us our 24-hour day; relative to the moon this rotation, together with the moon's revolution about the earth, gives us our lunar day of 24 hours and 50 minutes. The lunar day is the time from moonrise to moonrise.

The moon's arrival every 29.5 days at the same relative position between the earth and the sun marks what is called the synodical month. The earth with its tilted axis revolves about the sun every 365 days, 5 hours and 48 minutes, yielding the year and its seasons.

The daily and annual rhythms related to the sun are associated with the changes in light and temperature. The 24.8-hour lunar day and the 29.5-day synodical month are associated most obviously with the moon-dominated ocean tides and with changes in nighttime illumination. But all four types of rhythms include changes in forces such as gravity, barometric pressure, high energy radiation, and magnetic and electrical fields.

Considering the rhythmic daily changes in light and temperature, it is not surprising that living creatures display daily patterns in their activities. Cockroaches, earthworms and owls are nocturnal; songbirds and butterflies are diurnal; and still other creatures are crepuscular, like the crowing cock at daybreak and the serenading frogs on a springtime evening. Many plants show daily sleep movements of their leaves and flowers. Man himself exhibits daily rhythms in degrees of wakefulness, body temperature and blood-sugar level.

We take for granted the annual rhythms of growth and reproduction of animals and plants, and we now know that the migration periods of birds and the flowering periods of plants are determined by the seasonal changes in the lengths of day and night.

In a similar fashion creatures living on the seashore exhibit a rhythmic behavior corresponding to the lunar day. Oysters and clams open their shells for feeding only after the rising tide has covered them. Fiddler crabs and shore birds scour the beach for food exposed at ebb tide and retreat to rest at high tide. The reef heron, though living many miles inland, appears to know when low tide will occur and leaves . . . [Article incomplete]

3

Everyone knows that there are individuals who are able to awaken morning after morning at the same time to within a few minutes. Are they awakened by sensory cues received unconsciously, or is there some "biological clock" that keeps accurate account of the passage of time? Students of the behavior of animals in relation to their environment have long been interested in the biological clock question.

Most animals show a rhythmic behavior pattern of one sort or another. For instance, many animals that live along the ocean shores have behavior cycles which are repeated with the ebb and flow of the tides, each cycle averaging about 12½ hours in length. Intertidal animals, particularly those that live so far up on the beaches that they are usually submerged only by the very high semimonthly tides when the moon's pull upon the ocean waters is reinforced by the sun's, have cycles of behavior timed to those 15-day intervals. Great numbers of lower animals living in the seas have semilunar or lunar breeding cycles. As a result, all the members of a species within any given region carry on their breeding activities synchronously; this insures a high likelihood of fertilization of eggs and maintenance of the species. The Atlantic fireworm offers a very good example of how precise this timing can be. Each month during the summer for three or four evenings at a particular phase of the moon these luminescing animals swarm in the waters about Bermuda a few minutes after the official time of sunset. After an hour or two only occasional stragglers are in evidence. Perhaps even more spectacular is the case of the small surface fish, the grunion, of the U.S. Pacific coast. On the nights of the highest semilunar tides the male and female grunion swarm in from the sea just as the tide has reached its highest point. They are tossed by the waves onto the sandy beaches, quickly deposit their reproductive cells in the sand and then flip back into the water and are off to sea again. The fertilized eggs develop in the moist sand. At the time of the next high high tide, when the spot is again submerged by waves, the young leave the nest for the open sea.

Almost every species of animal is dependent upon an ability to carry out some activity at precisely the correct moment. One way to test whether these activities are set off by an internal biological clock, rather than by factors of signals in the environment, is to find out whether the organisms can anticipate the environmental events. The first well-controlled experimental evidence on the question was furnished by the Polish biologist J. S. Szymanski. In experiments conducted from 1914 to 1918 he found that animals exhibited a 24-hour activity cycle even when all external factors known to influence them, such as light and temperature, were kept constant. During the succeeding 20 years various investigators, especially Orland Park . . . [Article incomplete]

2   Here are the complete essays by Howard Marshburn and Tim Wold. Compare them, and you'll get a good deal of insight into the differences between treating the reader like a wall and treating the reader as a person. Because both essays have the same theme—an appreciation of nature—they have elements in common that invite comparison. Answer these questions:

> How does each author treat the encounter with a wild living thing —(the snake in Tim's essay, the trout in Howard's)?
>
> What is the event that causes each author to "realize" the significance of his experience?
>
> Which descriptions do you consider "seeable"? which bring no picture at all to your mind?
>
> Which conclusion relates back to the beginning of the essay, and how?
>
> Which author uses more exaggerated emotion? which uses more restraint? (give examples from each essay to support your opinion)
>
> What do you suppose led Howard to write the way he did?

When you finish this comparison, you will have a lot of concrete knowledge about how to know your audience and how to take your readers into partnership when you write. Be able to discuss the comparisons of the two essays with your class.

LIFE IN THE WILD

There, on the horizon, are the majestic mountains, stretching their peaks so that they might be seen over the top of the towering bristlecone pines. You awaken in awe of this sight, and even more awed are you as you see the sky change from a shade of pink, to orange, to red, and finally, in a glorious burst of yellow light, the sun shoots up over the mountains, signaling the beginning of the first day of the rest of your life.

1. Emma D. Terracini and Frank A. Brown, Jr., "Periodisms in Mouse Spontaneous Activities Synchronized with Major Geographical Cycles," *Physiological Zoology,* 35 (January 1962), 27–37.

2. Frank A. Brown, Jr., "Life's Mysterious Clocks," *Saturday Evening Post,* December 24, 1960, 18–19.

3. Frank A. Brown, Jr., "Biological Clocks and the Fiddler Crab," *Scientific American* 190 (April 1959), 34–37.

In this grandiose setting the human senses spark to life, as the air is filled with the pungent smells of cedar and pine, and tranquility is broken by the sounds of birds and animals frolicking in the sun of the newfound day. You realize then that you are either dreaming or you are truly experiencing some of the most beautiful sights in the world. You can imagine this scene, but I have and am experiencing it. After gazing at the beautiful scenario for a while, I reluctantly come back to reality.

I realize now that it is time to eat and all I have at my disposal is Mother Nature. I quickly set to work. My ears are way ahead of me as they have picked up the sound of running water over a nearby ridge. "Fish," I think out loud, "of course." I dart over the ridge and I come upon a babbling brook, and believe it or not, in the middle of this pool of Heaven's tears is the biggest rainbow trout ever beheld by human eyes. Can I catch it? The question becomes academic as I know I must if I wish to eat. So, I toss my baited hook into the stream and silently plead with the fish to take my morsel. Slowly he approaches the bait, and in an explosion of air and water that tears at the serenity of the surrounding area, the behemoth strikes and breakfast is mine.

After breakfast, one can do many things, including hiking through the wilderness and survey the splendor God hath wrought upon this land. As I top a ridge, overlooking the land our forefathers once fought for to make us free, I hear a sound that I think at first to be the whispering wind. I then recognize something that sounds like a storyteller, describing this land and how it got to be what it is today. Now I know what the sound is—it is the voice of the Spirit of the Pioneer. After hours of hearing the story of our land recreated, I grow proud to have the distinction of being able to say that by coexisting with nature I can contribute to our great land.

As I walk through this great land, I come upon an old tree and subconsciously wonder what stories it could tell me about this great land. Could it tell me how my forefathers treated this land as a frontier? I think of that and realize that, though my children will refer to this area as a landmark, I can call it home; for I know that I can appreciate the resources this land has to offer. Am I the last of a vanishing breed? I doubt it, for it is the instinct of Man to try to communicate with Nature and to be free. These feelings are the essence of life. This is the life, then, necessary for Man to truly live, and also the essence necessary for Man to break the bonds of humdrum routine of city life, for that can be called something less than living.

—*Howard Marshburn*

HILL COUNTRY HIKE

An inaudible yawn was the best answer I could give to Bobby at six in the morning. Besides, what kind of a question is 'Are you awake yet?' at this early hour? Slowly, my sleepy mind began to focus. Today was the day of our hike into the hill country. I was certain this day would be the low point of my visit with Bobby. However, Bobby was my older brother, as well as my host, and I felt that I should struggle through this journey for his sake. I could think of nothing more boring and worthless than wandering through some barren hills all day long. Nevertheless, I decided to crawl out of bed and get dressed, straining to open each eyelid. Before this day was over, I would realize that my eyes had never really been open before.

I could see a pale blue haze above the peaks of the hills as Bobby drove the Volkswagen farther away from the city. Soon the sun had risen completely, giving definition to the rocky hills on either side of the road. I was uncomfortable in hiking boots, and the drone of the car's engine made me sleepier. I felt miserable. Finally, Bobby led the VW off the road, parking on a flat, grassy plain at the crest of a steep incline. I got out of the car and followed Bobby, who waded through knee high grass, rather than walking down the worn trail many others had traveled before us. As Bobby and I labored up a rugged slope, I found myself wishing for the smooth trail we had passed by.

In any direction, as far as I could see, there was little else but rocks, grass, and an occasional mesquite. Yet there was a certain beauty about this place, a beauty I simply acknowledged rather than appreciated. Bobby spoke very little. He seemed to be interested in the smallest of details. After about thirty minutes of walking, I fell behind; Bobby and I were separated by a small ridge. I stopped in mid-stride, spotting a coral snake coiled beneath a rock in my intended path. I froze: not out of fear or even surprise. I simply stood still and watched. It seemed so odd to find life in such bare surroundings. I had never before encountered a snake and not felt the impulse to kill. Yet, all I wanted to do was watch. The snake jutted its tongue, sensing my presence, yet not the least bit anxious about it. It was so different from the snakes behind the window in a zoo. The colors were brilliant, and the symmetry was absolute perfection. Simply by taking the time to look, I noticed details no photograph could show or word could describe. The sun shifted, throwing light upon the snake and sending it racing for the shadows deep between two rocks. I walked on with a new impression of the land which surrounded me.

I ran over the ridge, catching up to Bobby, who had zig-zagged his way to the bottom of the ravine. We followed its sandy bottom for several hundred yards. I didn't mention the snake to Bobby, preferring to barrage him with questions about the kinds of plants and animals he had seen in the Hill Country. He answered my questions, half-smiling at the new interest I had taken in the surroundings. Before now, I had never understood why he was so observant of nature. Even now, I couldn't describe the feeling in words.

We followed the ravine between two hills where it led to a small pool of water, completely shaded from the afternoon sun. In the moist sand surrounding the water were the imprints of dozens of different animals.

Perhaps this was the only source of water for miles. My thoughts flashed back to the snake—there was a drama of survival here. Some animals lived by killing others; some lived because others were killed. There were those who were victims, those who were predators, and those who were scavengers. This land has literally thousands of different cacti; its rocks contain fossils of animals that no longer even exist! How could I ever have looked on this environment so superficially?

The day was such an awakening. Before it ended we were to spot several deer and actually watch a baby bird peck its way out of the shell. Exhausted, I settled into the seat of the VW with a strange feeling of contentment. Bobby returned my smile. I was proud of my older brother, for what he understood about life, and for teaching me the lesson I had only begun to learn.

—*Tim Wold*

Writing Assignment:
The How-To Essay

A how-to essay tells readers how to do a certain thing. A good how-to essay has these characteristics:

1 The content of the essay is directly related to the audience.

> Knowing who the readers will be, a writer makes decisions about just what kind of information to include and how much to include. Judging from how much the readers already know and how likely they are to be interested already, a writer can determine what kind of instructions or directions are needed and what details should be included.

2 The process being described in the essay is divided into clear, logical steps.

> The writer is careful to break the process down so that the readers can follow it easily, seeing exactly how one step leads to the next. The writer works to be certain there are no gaps in the directions, no faulty assumptions about what the readers will "automatically understand."

3 The essay is full of vivid, concrete details so that the reader can see exactly how to do the thing the writer is describing.

> The writer realizes that words have to do all the teaching in a how-to essay. These words must be as clear and sharp in detail as possible.

4 The information in the essay is presented in an interesting framework rather than just as cut and dried directions.

> The opening of a good how-to essay must get the reader's attention. It will have an interesting lead-in to or a frame around the information itself—something to move the reader into the subject. No writer expects anyone to be interested in just a set of dull instructions.

5 The essay sounds as though a human being, not a mechanical robot, wrote it.

> A good how-to essay is more than a list of directions; it is a *piece of communication* from one *person* to other *people*. The writer takes into account the fact that readers like to hear a "voice" behind the words, like to think someone alive and enthusiastic wrote the essay.

On the following pages are examples of how-to essays written by professional writers and by freshman students. Read these essays and ask yourself these questions:

> What has the writer done to adapt the *information* to this particular audience?

What does the writer do to get the reader interested? Place the information in a framework at the opening of the essay? Introduce the subject *before* the directions begin?

Is the process divided into clear, logical steps? How many? What are they?

What examples can you find of vivid details that let the reader see exactly how to do what the writer is describing?

What does the writer do to put a "voice" behind the words, to make it sound as though a *person* wrote the essay?

Be ready to discuss these questions and answers in class after you have read the sample essays. Studying these essays will help you know how to write your own how-to essay.

READINGS

How to Stop Procrastinating Today.

This essay, written by Richard Grossman, director of the Center for Health in Medicine at Montefiore Hospital and Medical Center in the Bronx, New York, and author of the book Choosing and Changing: A Guide to Self-Reliance, *gives a reader information on how to stop putting things off. The writer includes several specific actions a person can take who seems never to get things done when they should be done.*

The whole world is a stage, Shakespeare tells us in one of his most famous passages, and we are merely players. Unfortunately for most of us, there is no brilliant director to tell us when to move out of the wings and into the spotlight. We are not only the actors in our life drama, but script writers, producers and directors as well. It is we who prepare for the starring role, and we who must decide when the curtain rises to unveil the action. Yet, too many of us are still waiting backstage for some all-powerful voice to sound a loud cue signaling that it's time to move into our roles.

For an example of what I mean, consider three people who might seem familiar:

● Jerry Foley, an engineer for a large computer company, happens to be behind in his bills. Luckily, a local businessman has offered him a free-lance statistical assignment for which he will earn $750—just a few hundred dollars less than his backlog of debts. He must turn in his work, which he can do at home, within two weeks.

Jerry can be found at his desk, calculator and papers laid out in front of him, a freshly sharpened pencil in his hand. But wait—what is he doing? As we look over his shoulder he seems to be making several lists of figures. A closer look reveals that he is not doing his free-lance work; he is figuring out his bills again! There, in one column, are those he'd like to pay on the 15th; next to that is a column showing the bills he'll pay when he receives the check for the moonlighting work. Over and over them he goes, shifting his unpaid bills from one pile to another, re-figuring his plans for catching up. The statistical work that's to help pay the bills? Oh, he'll "get to that."

• Lily Corwin, a young social worker, is talking to her friend Francine. For the third time this week, Lily has invited a close friend to her home for coffee, to discuss whether she should apply for graduate school. Tonight, as with all the other times, the two women will spend three hours weighing the pros and cons of Lily's possible big move. By Friday at the latest, Lily must have the application mailed and postmarked. But she can't talk to her "really best" friend, Anne, until lunch on Friday. We hear her saying once more, "I just can't budge until I've sounded out my friends. I don't know what I'd do without them."

• A worried Polly Barnes is watching her husband switch the television set from channel to channel. Harry Barnes, a young lawyer unhappy in his present job, has become much less talkative lately. He has given up his regular weekend tennis game, and he has not wanted to take the children for the picnics the whole family so enjoyed last summer. Polly thinks of him as having "shrunk" over the past few months. He seems to her and the children to be listless and tired most of the time, as if he were going through the routines of his life in slow motion.

What is going on with these three people? Why is Jerry putting off the task that would help him? Why does Lily have to talk around and about her plans without acting on them? Why has Harry retreated from the intimacy of his family and the vigorous activities that formerly gave him so much pleasure?

In each instance, these people are avoiding decisions, dodging the choices that might move their lives on to a more meaningful and reward-ing course. Each displays a different variation on the theme of avoid-ance: Jerry is delaying the future by burying himself in the past; Lily is losing herself and her goals by refusing to step out of the present; Harry is blocking off *any* confrontation with his situation—present or future— simply by giving up.

We all do some of these things some of the time. We need not judge ourselves failures when we do, for one of the qualities of being human is that we are often afraid, nervous, unsure or ashamed to admit our terrors. But life is meant to be lived into the future, a future about which we have *some* choice. And we each must accept the responsibility of choosing.

Our lives are filled with acts of choosing: the little ones involving which tie or dress to wear; the ordinary and repeated ones of choosing what to eat, whether to smoke or drink or stay up late; the slightly more weighty ones of picking a nursery school for our children, or moving to a new house, or getting a car with better gas mileage. These are the logistical, housekeeping choices that affect our basic needs for food, shelter, clothing—survival—and our sense of belonging. Despite the number of them we make, and the thorny details they often entail, these choices are still relatively mechanical. Mechanical, that is, compared with the kinds of choices we must make to truly express our individuality and our uniqueness. These are the choices that make the difference between riding life as a passenger on a train driven by someone else, or taking charge of the trip ourselves. We may postpone them, talk them out without acting, or pretend that we do not have to make them—but we do so at the risk of disabling ourselves physically, mentally and spiritually.

The world, of course, limits our choices. We cannot shake our fists at a cloud-filled sky and "choose" sunshine. We cannot, at the age of 58, replace Reggie Jackson in right field. We cannot opt for blue eyes or the fingers of Arthur Rubinstein. Within our own physical reality, however, within the honestly assessed range of qualities we *do* possess, the opportunity and adventure of free choice are far more available to us than we usually think. The ability to choose freely—and well—is not automatic or instinctual; it is a unique capacity in each of us that must be nurtured and trained.

One good forward step in enhancing the power to choose for ourselves is to evaluate our choosing habits—and to make that evaluation with total candor. We have to be aware of whether we *are* aware of our choices. This can be done in a number of ways: by holding a family seminar or conference; by having a session with a friend who will give candid observations of your behavior; or by keeping a "Choice Diary" for a few weeks. Whichever way you select, take a long, hard look at your own style: Do you postpone hard choices, or ignore them—or distract yourself? Do you over-consult others, or withdraw into secrecy when you face a tough decision? Do you hurry through them, or pretend that big choices are a "piece of cake," denying that you're afraid? Do you think you have a variety of choices in life, or does the world look like a trap?

If you choose the diary form, set aside a regular period of time each day for two weeks, to examine your decision-making. Write down every instance you can recall of what choices presented themselves that day, and how you chose. Which choices were automatic (like brushing your teeth, having a second cup of coffee)? Which were unconscious (lifting the garage door, chewing a wad of gum too long)?

Now note the conscious decisions you made as a matter of principle: to tell your husband he had hurt your feelings; to ask for a change of assignment rather than put up with your discontent any longer; to write a letter telling your son you miss him.

In all this, the object is to find the patterns that have become your overall way of making—or not making—choices that will reflect who you think you really are, and what you think you might still become. We cannot "take charge" of our lives without these personal data. Most of us have grown to adulthood and beyond without ever examining the special ways we behave, and our choosing style is one of the traditionally unexamined issues we must face if we are to reclaim control of our lives.

But habit is a record of the past, and to the record of our prior performance we must add a plan for the future if we are to become healthier choosers. One way to do that is to make a "want list." Give yourself a quiet ten-minute period to make a list of *anything* you can (quickly) think of that you want at the moment. Your list may start with something as ordinary as a hamburger, but if you stick with it, you'll find yourself moving up a ladder of wants: traveling you'd like to do, special gifts for your children, a new skill like learning to knit or paint. And if you keep going you might well find yourself adding some cosmically ambitious things you'd like to see: a final cure for cancer, a solution to energy problems, or world peace. Your "want list," if you're honest, will probably be long and far-reaching.

Take another five minutes to review it. Giving serious, practical thought to the matter, select *five* things from your list that you, as an individual, might really be able to do something about. Do not allow yourself to use the standard choice-killers: "I'm too old to start racquetball"; "I'd become a nurse, but I should really have done that long ago. . ." Finally—and this is the big step—make one more short list. Write down one thing you might do in the next three weeks to go toward any one of the five wants you've specified.

Now throw away the first two lists. What is left is a plan designed by you and for you that might help you choose how to spend your time, your energy and your commitment. Life plans are made of this kind of basic self-assessment. No matter how small or vast, how modest or ambitious your special "want list" may be, it comes from your well-examined self, and it forms that challenge that makes your next three weeks worthwhile.

These exercises are only a beginning. They *start* the process of making conscious your past, present and future choices. None of us will ever, even with this new awareness, become perfect choosers through such devices. But we will have a better chance to make a difference in the world if we know what matters to us, and we will have a better chance to match our acts-in-the-world with the choices we make in private.

A Beach Cure That Works in Mysterious Ways and Lasts Forever

Joan K. Davidson has written a very enticing essay on how to go to the beach. She gives very explicit instructions on what to do to make a trip to the beach healing and rejuvenating.

Morning Instructions.
Early, while the rest of the world is still getting organized, hastily dispatch or ignore household chores; hop in car or on bicycle, and head for a saltwater bay. Leave before high noon, when the cars full of mothers, babies, nannies, umbrellas, blankets, floating rubber animals and suitcases of lunch begin rolling up.

For best results, choose a large bay with the following healthful properties: a long curving shoreline, white sand, cliffs, beach grass, seashells, sea gulls in conference, fishtraps on wood stakes and sailboats in the middle distance, and a pale island on the horizon.

What to bring.

Beach towel, shirt, hat, and a New York Public Library totebag with sunstuff and a few other necessities:

(a) The Ideal Book. Must have paper covers and be small, to provide easy hefting in odd positions. Should be interesting to read, but not that interesting, so as not to foreclose essential napping. Suggested titles: "Why Not the Best?" (Carter), "Tono Bungay" (Wells), "Mr. Sammler's Planet" (Bellow). Leave the New York Times, especially Sunday's, at home—trying to turn newspaper pages in the wind causes hives. No yellow legal pads either; they curl at the corners and bring sand into the house. A small notebook and pen are all right, for beginning a journal at last. Leave behind "The History of Serbia."

(b) Food. It is wise to recognize that hunger symptoms are automatically induced by beaches of any sort. Possible treatments: The *oeuf-en-gelée* dream picnic (too much bother); mass-produced peanut butter and jelly sandwiches (boring but good!); a peach or orange from the kitchen table, an honest tomato and/or a package of Pepperidge Farm Bordeaux cookies (recommended).

Who to Bring.

(a) Someone one has been looking for a chance for a conversation with. Spouse? Friend? Adolescent child? A still-deserted beach on a lazy morning is (with the possible exception of the long car ride) modern time's best setting for a Real Talk.

(b) Small or middle-range children, but only of the independent and cheerful sort. Whiners and naggers-for-attention impede the cure. Contributions of good children: ecstasy of the water squeal; the high seriousness of channel building and other sand construction; excitement (slightly nervous) in the presence of tiny sea animals; shining hair, smooth skin, the salt-white outline on tanned arms and legs.

(c) No one. A few hours at the beach alone is luxury, a gift. Do a long bay swim in clear water sweeter than the cold of a mountain lake and the chlorine of swimming pools; sweeter even than the warm blue of the Mediterranean and Caribbean. Think, walk, make a pass at collecting driftwood and pebbles, think some more, give up thinking, zzzz. . . .

Afternoon Instructions.

Arrive at an ocean beach toward the end of the day, the most beautiful moment, just as everybody else is packing up to leave. Breathe deeply, gaze at the sea in awe, contemplate the insignificance of human problems, the meaning of life, etc. Walk (jog if you must) along the water's edge, calling up the charging white horses of Virginia Woolf and feeling literary. Tick off the ancient beach markings: rock jetties, wind fences, a windmill, gray shingle roofs, Mr. Clean plastic bottles, logs, the distant mist, the curve of earth. Cry hosannah for one last beach still safe from hotels and condominiums and statement architects. Stumble across people it is pleasant to see, and note the curious fact that ocean beaches are improved by human noises — rumor and gossip, movies talk, politics talk — with or without something refreshing from a thermos. This is probably nature's answer to the cocktail party.

At sundown, assuming plenty of hands to divide up the work, take supper over coals that have been dug into the sand — clams, seaweed-flavored corn, bluefish . . . thus completing the perfect happiness prescription.

The beach cure works in mysterious ways and lasts forever. Neither peeling skin, nor suntan sicklied o'er and yellowing hideously, nor even car keys and contact lenses lost in the sand can take it away.

Virgie Richardson's 68-Year-Old Soap Recipe

This essay, which appeared in Progressive Farmer, *teaches the reader how to make soap. Notice, however, how the recipe itself is incorporated into the essay so that the reader is led into the subject.*

Many women swear by their recipes. However, Virgie Richardson's favorite recipe is a little bit different from most. She swears by her soap! Her ingredients are simpler than those in store-bought products — but her results are just as clean. And what more can you ask of a soap recipe?

The soap making process is more time consuming than buying it in the store. But Mrs. Richardson claims that her home made product is purer, cheaper, lasts longer, and has none of the fancy additives that sometimes irritate delicate complexions.

Besides these obvious advantages, she enjoys making it! Even though she began making soap out of necessity, she has continued the tradition for 68 years. And now, her soap making secrets have become the basis for an enjoyable craft demonstration at the Ozark Folk Center in Mountain View, Ark.

Her recipe yields 75 small bars and requires the following ingredients:
1 quart water
6 pounds of grease (purified)
1 can lye
Perhaps you'd like to try your hand at soap making! It should be done in a well ventilated area, preferably in a shed or outside.

If you use your own grease, skim off only the top for soap-making and add 1 cup borax. Mix the water and grease. Bring this mixture to a boil. Pour lye into boiled ingredients and bring to a second boil. Add 3 gallons of water. Cook it until it thickens, stirring constantly. Generally, if you boil the mixture for about three hours, the cast-iron pot will hold enough heat to finish cooking the soap.

Mrs. Richardson thinks a cast-iron pot is best because it holds the heat, but it isn't absolutely necessary.

After the soap is thick and creamy, pour it into molds. Standard molds are made of rectangular cardboard or wooden boxes, lined with freezer paper (wax side up). Decorative molds of cast-iron can also be used, but aluminum molds are not suitable because the lye will react with the metal.

Let the soap set about 24 hours until it hardens. Then cut the soap into squares and remove from mold. Next it must be cured because the lye is too strong for immediate use. Wrap the bars in cloths or waxed paper and store them in a cool, dry place for five weeks to six months.

Enjoy your own homemade soap. After mastering this technique, you may wish to try variations with perfumes and food coloring. And you may never notice the rising cost of soap again!

How to Borrow Money and Build Credit in Your Own Name

This essay, by Chris Barnett, is written to tell women how to achieve financial independence.

Today, there is absolutely no reason for you to cringe over credit. State and federal rules and regulations have been drastically rewritten to stamp out discrimination, bias and ingrained prejudices that have kept some women financial flunkies, hanging on the shirttails of their men, who doled out a weekly allowance or allowed them to sign on their charge accounts.

Now, thanks to the Equal Credit Opportunity Act (ECOA) passed in 1975, you have the same rights as men to borrow money in your own name—without having to grovel for a man's permission or cosignature. Even more important, you can now build your own separate credit history which, in most states, prevents a creditor from penalizing you if your past/present/future husband is a deadbeat who doesn't pay his bills.

Credit is not a right, it's a privilege. The ECOA doesn't guarantee credit. Banks, department stores and other credit grantors are not forced to give you a charge account. They just can't say no because you're a woman or divorced or single. But if you aren't creditworthy, in their subjective judgment, you won't get that credit card, charge account or bank loan.

So how do you become "creditworthy"? Start by setting up your own credit file in your name. If you're single, it's automatically set up once you're granted credit (although it doesn't make you automatically creditworthy). But if you are married, you have the right to set up a credit file in your own name.

Setting up your own credit file is probably the single most important thing a married woman can do. Especially since U.S. Census Bureau figures show that 85 percent of the women who are married today will someday find themselves single again—either divorced or widowed.

One reason so few married women have asked for their own credit file, apart from ignorance of this right, is fear—fear that their husbands will explode, feel threatened or think they're being set up for a divorce.

It's a real problem, but you shouldn't be deterred. Any man worth having should understand that if he died tomorrow, the family credit history would, in many cases, die with him. Today, you can set up your own credit file based on your own income or yours and your husband's joint income.

Your local credit bureau will set up a file for you free. But to have your information verified (place of employment, income) you might be charged a small fee of about five dollars. Pay it. It's a bargain at twice the price. Once you have a credit file, keep it spotlessly clean. When you apply for credit, the lender will check that file first to help determine your creditworthiness.

If you already have a credit history, it will spell out the details of most credit relationships you've had: Name of the credit grantor (Sears, Master Charge), date the account was opened, last transaction, high amount of credit extended, balance owing, any amount past due and the number of payments past due, if any.

But here's the killer for most people: That credit report also discloses how many times you've been thirty days late with your payment, sixty days late, ninety days late. Credit folks call these "derogs" (derogatory) and it's the one thing they hate. You can have a villa in Rome, a fleet of Rolls-Royces; but if you're consistently late in repaying loans, credit card agencies and department stores, you probably can't get a $100 line of credit at J. C. Penney.

Most lenders have a ten to fifteen-day grace period, but prompt payment habit is crucial because it shows you have enough pride in yourself to maintain your agreement with the lender.

Not every credit grantor reports to the credit bureau and this can be a two-edged sword. If you have an oil company credit card and pay it regularly, it will never show up on your credit file that you're a good risk. Even if you carry American Express, Diners Club or Carte Blanche — probably the three most difficult plastic money cards to get — the fact that you pay it off regularly won't help you get a Visa/BankAmericard or open a department store account. The reason: The oil companies and so-called "travel and entertainment" cards report only adverse information to the credit bureaus.

However, department stores, retail merchants, banks, finance companies, Visa and Master Charge give the credit reporting agencies a rundown of how you repay. They no longer report you as a slow pay, fair, good or excellent credit risk. You are reported as someone who "pays according to terms" (the best rating of all) or as having made three payments thirty days past due. (In reality, though, most department stores won't soil your credit record with a derogatory until you're sixty days past due. Then look out. Those stains are almost impossible to scrub off.)

And it's getting even tougher. Today fewer and fewer credit grantors are using judgment to determine your creditworthiness. Most retail stores and many banks use a computer to determine whether you're a good credit candidate, a poor risk or a deadbeat. They call it credit scoring and it's straight out of George Orwell. Remember, 1984 is only five years away.

Essentially, a credit grantor sets up a statistical formula based on its total lending experience and plugs in your application. You either score enough points and get credit or flunk and get turned down. It's that simple.

Everything counts for something. Having a home telephone is worth points. The amount of time on the job—current job and last job—are scored to show stability. If you have both a checking account and a savings account you get some points. Your education makes a difference. College graduates score higher than high school graduates. The type of occupation makes a big difference. A cocktail waitress would score low compared to a professional.

What's more, past transgressions—slow-pay track record—are held against you even if your account is now current and you haven't been tardy for the last three years. Those previous delinquencies have a bearing and never think they don't.

Red flags for credit grantors: A credit bureau report showing a flurry of applications at different stores and credit card organizations.

Other tips:

• It's "very, very, very" important for you to have your name on an individual credit account so you can build your credit history.

• If you are going through a divorce, you should make sure any joint credit which involves your name isn't neglected and is kept current. If your husband handles the bills and lets things go, it's going to hurt your credit, and you'll have no excuse since it's your responsibility, too.

• Never open a credit account in your husband's name where you are simply an authorized signer. Get a separate, individual account and don't get talked out of it.

The smart woman today should be as close to her banker as she is to her gynecologist. Your banker should be your financial confidante and you should start now to forge a solid relationship. After all, bankers are in the business to lend money, not hoard it. And since they are only human, they are more than a little leery of total strangers. If you're borrowing money for the first time, here are ten ways to impress your banker:

1 Dress conservatively and tastefully. Business suit or skirt and blouse but nothing sheer, flashy or gaudy, and no jeans. Theoretically, what you wear shouldn't affect your creditworthiness, but realistically, it does. Don't "dress down" to look as if you need the money; "dress up" so you look as if you can pay it back.

2 Phone the manager of your bank and make an appointment with his or her loan officer. Don't just walk in off the street and plop down in her chair. It shows that you realize the seriousness of your request and implies that you'll be just as diligent in repaying it. Be straightforward, self-confident. Don't, for instance, play the "little lost someone-who's-on-the-dole" role who needs help. Above all, don't try to trade on your sexuality.

3 As a first timer, make sure you have a good reason for borrowing the money. The best possible reason is to simply strengthen or help establish your credit history by borrowing the funds, putting them in a savings account at that bank (don't stick the money in a savings and loan association) and repaying the obligation on time every month. Just don't be frivolous. Your banker would rather see you buy a car with the money than jet off to Hong Kong. And be realistic. Don't go for a Porsche if you can only afford a Chevette.

4 Ask intelligent, relevant questions: What are the terms of the loan and the *total* finance charges. They vary widely but it's not always wise to shop other banks unless you can easily get a loan anywhere. Instead, stick with the bank that has your checking and savings accounts. Remember, you want to build that solid relationship.

5 Prepare a financial résumé. Similar to a career résumé, it also lists all your assets (savings, stocks, property, automobiles paid for) and liabilities (what you owe, to whom, outstanding balance) plus your credit cards and charge accounts complete with account numbers, addresses, average monthly payments, amounts owed. The more personal informational details it contains, the better. You'll always have to fill out a loan application and your credit will be checked, but it makes the loan officer's job easier and you never have to worry about overlooking an obscure asset that just might swing the loan for you.

6 If your credit history is blemished, tell your banker about it right up front, don't attempt to hide or ignore it. You can explain it verbally but back it up with a letter spelling out the precise circumstances of each transgression; i.e., your ex-husband went wild with your credit cards and you've subsequently paid them off, although the payments were late.

7 Be calm and sincere in discussing your loan. Don't get anxious, emotional or look the least bit desperate for the money. Your banker knows that too many "crisis loans" are forgotten once the crisis has passed.

8 You don't have to complete the loan application on the spot. Take it home with you, study it thoroughly (including all the fine print) and fill it out *completely*. (Bankers say partially completed applications are a good tip-off to a bad credit risk.)

9 Schedule a second appointment and make your "presentation"—the loan application, financial résumé, any explanatory letters. It's smart to preface it all with a covering memorandum spelling out some of your personal financial objectives.

10 Leave on friendly terms. If you are turned down for the loan, find out why and ask the loan officer what you should do before you reapply. Don't get angry. Even if you feel you've been discriminated against (he offhandedly asked when you were planning to marry and raise a family), don't threaten him. Go to the bank manager or the regional manager and file a complaint.

Under the Equal Credit Opportunity Act (ECOA), a lender can no longer:

• Refuse you credit because of your sex, age or marital status.

- Refuse to grant you credit because you are divorced or widowed.
- Deny a married woman a separate charge account or credit card if she'd qualify if she were single.
- Shoot down your request for individual credit if your husband has poor credit, unless you're applying for a joint account.
- Refuse to consider a divorcee's alimony or child support as income. (Before 1975, they were never included to help her qualify for credit.)
- Ignore *your* income when you and your husband apply for joint credit.
- Discount your income from regular part-time employment or retirement benefits.
- Ask if you practice birth control, which technique you use, or ask if and when you're planning to have children.
- Refuse to recognize a married person's legal name.
- Require your husband or anyone else to cosign for an unsecured loan if you are creditworthy.
- Deny your request to extend or continue credit because your age makes you ineligible.
- Terminate, or revise the terms of, or demand you reapply for a credit transaction because of retirement, or a change in borrower's name, or marital status.

What's more, you have some other extremely important rights under the Credit Consumer Protection Act that encompasses ECOA:

You can look at your credit bureau or reporting agency's file, usually for a small fee. If you're denied credit you can get a printout of your file free. You can ask the credit reporting agency to reinvestigate any inaccurate or outdated information in your file. After seven years, all derogatory information must, by law, be scrubbed off your record. If the credit bureau investigates and rules that the negative information is true, you can write a letter offering your version of the dispute and have it placed in your permanent file for all credit grantors to see.

Buying a Pickup Truck

In this essay Noel Perrin educates the reader on what to look for when shopping for a truck. He makes this process interesting to read about, even if the reader isn't looking for a pickup.

One of the ways a newcomer to the country knows he's getting acclimated is when he begins to notice trucks. (I say "he" strictly through obedience to grammar. The phenomenon happens to women almost as much as to men. Under age 25, I'd say just as much.)

Back in his other life, back when he was urban or suburban, it may have been sports cars that caught the newcomer's eye. Or maybe a showroom full of compacts, fresh and glittering from the factory. Now he finds himself eyeing some neighbor's sturdy green pickup with a big load of brush in the back and wondering how much one like it would cost. Welcome to the club.

Pickups aren't necessary in the country, but they are certainly handy. Any rural family that can afford two vehicles should probably make one of them a truck. And it is quite possible to have a truck as a family's sole transportation. It is also quite economical, since pickups begin almost as cheap as the cheapest cars, and go up in price, size, and quality at the same rate cars do—except that about halfway up the car price range, you have reached the most expensive pickups there are.

What's handiest about pickups is their versatility. First, obviously, in load. Because of that big open space in back, you can carry almost anything. Two beef cattle. Two full-length sofas that you're donating to the rummage. All the apples in a small orchard. With the tailgate down, a load of sixteen-foot boards. About 40 bales of hay. A full cord of firewood (provided it's dry). All your fence posts, your wire, and your tools, when you're building a fence. It's possible to get a little drunk with power, just thinking what a pickup can do.

Second, in range. Even without four-wheel drive, a pickup is a great deal freer than most cars to leave roads and drive over fields. Picking up hay bales, for example. Or to squeeze along homemade woods roads. This freedom comes partly because pickups are designed to have fairly high road clearance, even when loaded. Partly because they can take tires that will walk you right through a wet spot or over a (not-too-big) rock. Most pickup owners in rural New England keep a pair of over-size snow tires mounted on the rear wheels all year round. And partly because you can shift weight around in a truck to get maximum traction in a way that would cause the average car to collapse on its fat Detroit springs.

Third, a pickup is versatile in function. Besides its truck role, a pickup can do anything a car can do, with one exception—about which, more later. It can drive you to work, for example, using no more gas than a car, and when you arrive, it will not only park in the regular lot, it will do so in a smaller space than a Cadillac or an Oldsmobile.

Nor are you going to complain on the way that it drives like a truck, because it doesn't. It drives like a car. The ride is reasonably smooth, the surreptitious U-turn reasonably easy. Drivers of big highway trucks have ten gears to shift, and air brakes to worry about. Drivers of pickups have a standard shift and regular car brakes. And if they hate shifting, most pickups can be had with automatic transmission. For that matter, most can be equipped with a stereo tape deck, so that you barrel out to the woods playing Beethoven. I admit that a fully loaded pickup—say, a Chevrolet C-10 with a ton of rocks in the back, or a six-barrel gathering tank full of maple sap—doesn't corner quite so neatly as an MG, but it still drives essentially like a car.

The one exception is that a pickup is not much good for carrying a big load of people. At least, not in the winter or in wet weather. On a sunny summer day, its capacity is something else. Giving hayrides at our local fair, I once had fifteen children and two mothers back there in the hay, plus myself and a friend in the cab. I make that eighteen passengers.

Even if two couples are going out to dinner, a pickup is not handy. Four adults will fit not too uncomfortably in the cab of an American (though not a Japanese) pickup—but the law says three. The other husband may or may not want to crouch in back. Furthermore, it doesn't take many bags of groceries to produce a sense of claustrophobia in a pickup cab. A mother taking two children shopping on a rainy day in a pickup generally wishes she had a car.

There *is* a solution, to be sure. People who go out to dinner a lot, or mothers with four children, can get a crew-cab pickup. This is not what you'd call a glamour vehicle. It has two cabs, one behind the other, and looks something like a centipede dragging a large box. But it does seat six people. The only problem is that you now have a truck not only so ugly but so big that it is no longer versatile in the woods. I do not recommend it.

One last advantage of pickups should be mentioned. They never make hideous noises or refuse to start because you haven't fastened the seat belt. Like other trucks, they are exempt from that law. You can use the belts when you're roaring down the highway and skip them when you're going one mile an hour in the woods. Handy.

So much for pickups and their virtues. The time has now come to discuss the art of buying one. It *is* an art, incidentally, unlike car buying. A few wrong decisions on options can cut a farm pickup's usefulness by 50%.

The first decision, of course, is new or used. A really old pickup, small and square and no-nonsense, is about the most charming vehicle there is. Also one of the cheapest. You can get one for $200. Any children you know will adore the running boards and—if you have an old enough one—the windshield that pushes open for ventilation.

On the other hand, old pickups tend to have unreliable brakes and not notably reliable anything else. The 1947 Dodge I once owned—from its nineteenth to its twenty-first years—couldn't be counted on to start at any temperature much below freezing. That meant a long period of parking on hills and losing my temper, each October and November, until I finally gave up and put it in the barn until spring. One year I waited a week too late and had it frozen in the barnyard, in the way of practically everything, for three and a half months.

Even much newer pickups have generally led hard lives. (Little old ladies seldom own pickups.) Furthermore, it's difficult and expensive to have heavy-duty springs and other desirable country equipment installed in an existing truck. Probably only people with real mechanical ability should consider getting one.

But one last word. If you do get one, take a nice winter vacation and get it in some place like South Carolina. South Carolina pickups have never experienced road salt. At least the body won't rust out on you in a few years.

Now let's turn to new pickups. They come, basically, in three sizes and three styles. The sizes are called half-ton, three-quarter-ton, and one-ton. Not one of these names means what it says. Which is a good thing, because a bunch of trucks that could carry only 1,000 to 2,000 pounds wouldn't be worth much.

Let me define the three. A half-ton is the basic pickup: what you find at a car dealer, what people mean when they speak of a pickup. At the moment it comes in two avatars. It is a small Japanese-made truck that can carry almost a ton of cargo. Or it is a somewhat larger American-made truck that, with proper springs and tires, can manage a ton and a half.

A three-quarter-ton looks much the same, but has a much larger, truck-type rear axle. It costs more, gives a rougher ride, and carries loads of up to about three tons. People with campers put them on three-quarter-ton pickups—and then usually get about six miles to the gallon.

A one-ton has an even bigger rear axle. With dual rear wheels, it can carry up to near five tons. Neither it nor a three-quarter is what most people need for use on a country place. Not unless they plan to get into the lumber-delivery business, or maybe have always wanted, since they were kids, to have their own personal dump truck. (No fooling. There are truck shops in every New England state that will put a dump body on a three-quarter or a one-ton. The cost runs around $1,200. I have sometimes played with the notion.) But for general country use a half-ton is right; and for the rest of this article I shall talk about half-tons only.

Of the three styles, one can be dismissed right off. This is the tarted-up and chromed-up half-ton which attempts to pass itself off as a car. Chevrolet calls its El Camino; other makes have equally foolish names.

For families that are sincerely embarrassed at having to own a truck and that really think it would be preferable to drive something that looks like a scooped-out car, spending the extra money for an El Camino may make sense. Especially in those flat and treeless parts of the country where taking your truck out to the back forty must be something like driving across a very large football field. But to get one as a working truck on a rocky, hilly, wooded New England farm would be an act of insanity.

The other two styles are narrow-bed and wide-bed. Just as the half-ton is the classic American pickup, the narrow-bed is the classic half-ton. The design has been stable for 50 years now. Behind the cab you have —in most makes—a wooden-floored metal box four feet wide and six or eight feet long. (You get to pick.) This sits inside the rear wheels. Because it doesn't rust, and because it gives surer footing to any livestock you happen to be transporting, the wooden floor is a considerable advantage.

Until a few years ago, the narrow-bed was the cheapest of all pickups; now it costs exactly the same as a wide-bed. It retains two other advantages. Since the rear wheels don't stick up into the bed, you can slide slidable cargo in and out with great ease. And because this is the classic model, the tailgate in most makes is still the traditional kind that you hook with a chain on each side. That matters. You are able either to put such a tailgate down level, as an extension of the bed, if you are carrying a load of long boards, or to let it drop all the way down for ease in loading. Now that I no longer have one, I miss it.

All the Japanese-made pickups and most of the current American ones are wide-bed. These have a cargo space five and a half feet wide (American) or four and a half feet (Japanese). Obviously you can carry a lot more cargo. On the other hand, the rear wheel housings stick in on each side, which is sometimes inconvenient. (I will say they are handy for children to sit on.) And on many wide-beds you get a fancy one-handed tailgate, like a station wagon's, which won't drop down unless you disconnect the hinges. It's not difficult, it's just tedious. And when you want to close the tailgate, you have to reconnect them.

Which style is better? Myself, I used to have a narrow-bed and now have a wide-bed. I think the advantages and disadvantages of the two models just about balance. So on my current truck, I made the choice on esthetic grounds. The narrow-bed lost. Properly designed, it is the truest of trucks, the very platonic essence of a truck. But in the last five years Ford, Dodge, Chevrolet, Jeep, and International Harvester (a GMC pickup is just a relabeled Chevrolet)—all have moved to such enormously wide cabs that a new narrow-bed looks hydrocephalic. Wide-bed is now the handsomer truck.

As to whether Toyota, Datsun, LUV, or an American make, the decision really rests on how much highway driving you're going to do. The Japanese trucks, with their four-cylinder engines, get far better gas mileage. According to *Consumer Reports,* they average about twenty mpg, while American half-tons average fifteen. My own experience suggests that Japanese pickups do a little better than twenty, and American pickups a little worse than fifteen. For a vehicle that I was going to commute to work in, and just use as a truck on the occasional weekend, I would probably choose to save gas (plus about $300 in purchase price) and get a Japanese.

But for a truck that was to be mainly or even considerably a working farm vehicle, I still prefer the larger and more versatile American pickup. It's not just that you can carry more weight, it's that you can get a specially adapted country model. The Japanese trucks tend to be unadaptable, the same for an appliance dealer in New York City as for a family with 60 acres of woods in Colebrook, Connecticut.

The man delivering refrigerators in the Bronx doesn't need any special traction. He never leaves the pavement. But the family in Colebrook does. And one of the most humiliating things that can happen is to get stuck in your own truck on your own place. Especially since you're so unlikely to be able to jack, or rock, or bull your way out.

The trick is not to get stuck. Which means that you may want the four-wheel drive available as an option (a very expensive one) on all the American but none of the little Japanese trucks. Otherwise, you will certainly want limited-slip differential. This inexpensive ($75 to $100) option means a special rear axle designed so that when one rear wheel starts to spin, all the power goes to the other wheel. Normally when one wheel starts to spin, all the power goes to *it*, and that's why you get stuck. Limited-slip differential is said to have its dangers, especially in very fast highway driving, where you may fishtail in a skid, but it is highly desirable in a farm pickup. I would rate it, quite impressionistically, as making about a third of the difference between regular two-wheel drive and four-wheel drive. You can get it on American pickups, but not Japanese. It's only fair to add that I know farmers with Datsun pickups who say they have no trouble at all zipping up and down their rolling fields, even on dewy mornings, but I still commend limited-slip differential.

If you decide on a Japanese truck anyway, about all you have to do is go get it. Maybe settle whether or not you want a radio. But if you opt for an American truck, you still have to pick your engine, with at least six more country options to consider.

The engine is easy. Get a six-cylinder. Almost all pickups—including three-quarter and one-tons—can be had either six or eight cylinders. A six has all the power you will ever need, and wastes less gas. As to options, the first and most important is to specify heavy-duty springs in the rear, and heavy-duty shock absorbers front and rear. All this costs about $40; its value in increased usefulness must be about 50 times that much.

Second, for any pickup that's going to leave roads, either a four-speed shift or automatic transmission is a great asset. Why? Because going through a field with long grass (and hidden rocks), or up into the woods, you need to be able to creep along, almost literally feeling your way, and still not lose momentum. Low speed in a three-speed shift will not let you go slowly enough.

Here the Japanese trucks have an advantage, since all of them come with a four-speed shift. It costs an extra $125 on an American pickup. But even better than four-speed is an automatic transmission. You can creep with astonishing slowness, and still have power. I have never owned a car with automatic transmission and never plan to, but on my sturdy green pickup I find it marvelous. It does, of course, use too much gas, and my next truck will be four-speed manual.

Third, you ought to get a step-and-tow bumper. Unlike cars, trucks are sold with no rear bumper at all. (How much rear bumper have you ever seen on a tractor-trailer or on a gasoline truck?) But a step-and-tow—which is a broad bumper covered with sheet steel—really is handy for pulling, and as a rear step. The ones you get factory installed, for about $50, are not nearly as sturdy as they look, but are still worth having. The ideal is to have one made by a local welder. Rodney Palmer, the man who owns the garage in Thetford Center, is a superb welder; and for $101.50 I have a rear bumper that will fend off anything short of a Centurion tank, that is heavy enough to give me good traction with no load in the truck, and that will last for a hundred years. (Rodney designed it so that I can move it from pickup to pickup for the rest of my life. Then I'll will it to my daughters.) Incidentally, if you don't get a bumper like that, you should plan to keep a couple of large flat rocks or about four cement blocks in the back each winter. Way back. Otherwise you'll find yourself spinning to a halt halfway up icy hills. Better anchor them too, so that if you have to slam the brakes on hard they won't come hurtling through the back of the cab and kill you.

Fourth, for a family truck it is worth getting extra padding in the seat. A pickup has a reasonably smooth ride, but not so smooth that additional cushioning won't be pleasing to visiting grandparents, people with bad backs, and so on. If you're going to get stereo tapes, you might even want to pad the whole cab, so as to reduce road noise.

Fifth, if you can talk the dealer into it, get him to remove the four automobile tires the truck comes equipped with, and have him put on four truck tires. They should be not merely heavier ply, but if possible an inch larger in diameter. And as I said earlier, the rear ones should probably be snow tires, even if you get the truck in May. (Come winter, put snow tires on the front, too. They won't improve traction unless you have four-wheel drive, but they will help astonishingly in preventing sideslipping.)

If you can't talk the dealer into it, you're no horsetrader. In that case, resign yourself to your helpless condition, and pay extra for big tires. Or go to another dealer. Or hurry home and read Faulkner's *The Hamlet.* Then you will learn—from a master—how to trade.

Sixth, get the truck undercoated. Presumably any New Englander knows about undercoating anyway—but it's even more important on pickups than cars, since people usually keep pickups longer. The process called Ziebarting is probably the best and certainly the most expensive. If you can stand having your truck smell like fish oil for a month or so, I recommend it. If not, a grease undercoating is said to be adequate. But the full mysteries of Duracoat (acrylic resin), asphalt, and all the other undercoatings, I do not pretend to be a master of.

There are all sorts of other machismo things one can get with a pickup. You can have a snowplow mounted—in which case be sure to get four-wheel drive. Plan also to have the front end realigned frequently, because plowing will spoil the wheel alignment with surprising speed. You can have an electric winch put on the front, and thus be sure of freeing yourself 99% of the time when you get stuck. (Though a two-ton manual winch of the kind called a come-along will do nearly as well. You can get one for about $45, and keep it under the seat.) You can have a power take-off on most larger pickups, and run your own sawmill. You can merely buy a logging chain, keep that under the seat, too, and then when you find eight-foot poplars growing in the corners of your best field, you hook the chain on your step-and-tow bumper and pull them out by the roots. They don't grow back next year *that* way.

But just a basic pickup is machismo (or feminismo) enough. In fact, I can think of just one problem. Someday when you're going past the post office with a big load of brush, you'll glance up and see a whole row of summer people staring at you. With naked envy in their eyes.

How to Catch Speckled Trout

This essay was written by Paul Merriman, a student in a freshman English class. Notice that he includes the context and audience so the reader will know why and to whom he was writing.

CONTEXT
The student is using the persona of an owner of a bait stand. He is writing this essay to go in a pamphlet which he will give away to people who come to his stand to buy bait before they go fishing.

AUDIENCE
People who basically know how to fish but who have trouble catching speckled trout.

The young boy pulled in his tenth speckled trout within the hour. A few yards away from him, you sit in your boat with just one fish to show for your two hours' work. Convinced that the fishing gods are frowning on you, you rev up your motor and head for home. Actually, if you had just planned ahead and had used a few specific techniques, you could have had an ice chest full of specks just like that young boy did.

Planning ahead before you start fishing for speckled trout will set you up to achieve success. This planning involves four areas, the weather, the fishing location, the time, and the bait. The first thing you should do is check to see that the weather conditions are right before starting out. If it is a windy day, stay home. Wind will cause the water to churn up, and specks do not stay in cloudy water. They always head for clearer water if the wind is up.

The second thing you must do in this preparation stage is go where the fish are. This usually means taking a boat or a four-wheel drive vehicle. Speckled trout are found in large numbers almost always in back bays or other unpopulated areas. Sure, you could probably stand at a dock all day and catch, maybe, one, but to really get into the action, you must go where they live. That means taking the trouble to get there to those out-of-the-way fishing sites.

Planning ahead also means going fishing at the right time. The best time to catch specks is from just about an hour before dawn to around nine o'clock. This is when the trout is feeding on the small baitfish which swim on the surface. If you wait much later than nine o'clock, you will be wasting your time. Much earlier than a hour before dawn and you can't see what you are doing.

Finally, prepare by checking local reports to see how supplies of fresh shrimp are holding out. You must have live shrimp for bait. You could use lures, but nothing is as sure-fire as the frisky live bait. To put it in perspective, a live shrimp to a speck is like a filet mignon to a hungry football player. Live shrimp are not always available, so check before you head out.

This planning ahead must be followed up by some specific techniques at the fishing site. Once out on the bay, you are now ready to rig a bait so that it is most enticing to the fish. Here is what I have found to be the best method. Cut about a four foot section of line off your reel and set it aside for a moment. Now tie a small bobber on the end of the line on your reel. Then take the four-foot section and tie it under the bobber. Under this, tie a small treble hook. This hook is then baited with the live shrimp.

The next step is to cast the rig. When you cast, the bobber will float on top and the shrimp will swim for the bottom. This is when the fish will hit it. If the bobber just jumps and jiggles a little, then the fish is just lipping it. But when the bobber drops under water like a bullet shot out of a gun, that is when you should set your hook.

But be careful! Specks get off a hook very easily, so bring the fish in gingerly. When the fish is close enough, use a landing net. There is no sense in losing a fine fish because the line broke or the hook fell out just as you were lifting the trout on board.

It is true that speckled trout fishing is not something everybody excels in doing. It is something, however, that everybody can learn to do. By planning ahead—checking the wind, going to where the fish are and at the right time, and using the right bait—and using the right techniques when on the spot—rigging the bait and casting properly and using skill in bringing the fish into the boat—anyone can be successful at catching the specks. Once the skill is acquired, it can lead to many fun days and many fine fish.

WRITING YOUR OWN HOW-TO ESSAY

1. Context Choose one of the following contexts and write a how-to essay based upon the information. At the top of your essay state the context and the audience, following the model of the student essays you have just read.

CONTEXTS

A

The local Y is having a special summer sports program. Free lessons are available for all teenagers who have never played tennis, racketball, handball, basketball, or

B

Imagine that you are out of school and have a good job or perhaps even own your own business. As part of the publicity and advertising campaign for your company or

volleyball. When someone joins the program and signs up for lessons in one of the available sports, he or she receives a booklet which explains how to play that particular game. Write the how-to essay that will appear in the booklet.

C

You have been nominated by a local civic club as a candidate for Woman or Man of the Year. One of the things all candidates must do in the competition is write an essay in which they describe how to do something that most people don't know how to do. The information you have received from the club lists some possibilities:

If you collect stamps or records or books, tell how to make a really good collection.

If you can cook ethnic food, tell how to prepare an unusual, little known dish.

If you know how to build things, tell how to do some particular building project.

business, you plan to write a how-to essay telling your customers how to do something you think they will be interested in learning. (Paul Merriman did this in the essay he wrote to give away at his bait stand.) You plan to have this how-to essay printed up with a colorful cover and attractive format and give it to everyone who comes to your place of business. Write the essay which you are going to give away.

If you play a good game of chess or backgammon, tell how other people can perfect their game.

The information for the competition also tells you that you are to write the how-to essay for an audience who has had no experience in what you are describing. Your essay, as part of the competition, will be judged by the committee choosing Man or Woman of the Year on clearness, interest, and the ability of a person to follow your instructions and achieve success. Choose the thing you know how to do that most people might not and write the how-to essay that will win you the competition.

2. Creating Several of the creating techniques you have learned will help you find ideas for your how-to essay. You may, in fact, want to do a two part creating activity for this essay. First, if you have no idea what you want to use for your subject, write "What do I know how to do well that might interest other people?" at the top of the page and then do three 5-10 minute *loops*. (See Looping.) By the end of the third loop an idea will very likely have occurred to you. Second, after you know what you are going to talk about in the essay, a creating technique like LISTING (see Listing, earlier p. 62) will help you get the steps clearly in order. You could also use LOOPING again, this time writing the subject of your essay at the top of the page and then doing three 5-10 minute loops to get in your mind exactly what procedure you are going to use to tell your reader how to do whatever you're discussing.

3. Specific Audience After you have finished this creating stage, you are ready to write the essay. Now your audience becomes crucial. You have to think first about whether the subject you have settled on is one *(a)* you *really* do know enough about to teach to someone else and *(b)* your readers will get value from reading.

The aim of a how-to essay is to give value to the reader. This means that the subject must be something potentially interesting to the readers, not something ordinary like how to tie your shoes — unless you are writing for a preschooler's magazine. Nothing cute like how not to bowl — unless you are writing specifically for a light publication that solicits humorous, tongue-in-cheek pieces. Nobody would get value from a how-to essay on how to climb a tree — unless that somebody happened to be a hiker likely to come upon a bear.

Remember, you must be an insider. Don't try to tell someone how to change the points and plugs in a car if you don't really know how to do it yourself. Don't pick something that a reader is likely to know how to do in his or her sleep and will know as much about as you do. Pick something for your how-to essay that you know how to do extremely well and that you can safely assume your reader doesn't know how to do or might get value from learning to do the way you do it or who at least would be interested in just reading another way to do it. If you really want to tell how to bake a cake, why not set up an audience for the essay of ten-year-olds who have never cooked or a bachelor afraid of the oven and sure his cake will fall. Aim always to sound like an authority and to give value to the readers so that they do not feel they have wasted their time when they finish reading the essay.

You must also think about your audience in order to decide just what kind of, and how much, information to put into the essay. Your decision will be based on how much your readers are already likely to know. For instance, if you are writing an essay on how to water-ski, it would be very helpful to know if your readers have ever been in the water, have ever seen skis, or have any experience in other sports. Not only the amount of details and explanation but also the tone of the essay will be determined by who the audience is going to be.

In second-guessing your audience for a how-to essay, you have to think of even the simplest step in your process and include it in the discussion. You might know what a lug wrench is when you're telling about points and plugs, but your reader probably won't. If you are telling how to weatherproof a mobile home, you will just take it for granted that you pull the plastic tight over the windows before you staple it on, but your reader might never think of this and have plastic billowing out all winter sounding like clothes flapping on a line. Think through every step of your process and anticipate *anything* the reader might not understand or might overlook.

DETAILS: HOW TO BE SPECIFIC

1 Details are individual or minute parts of a whole. When included in a piece of writing, details give the reader a much clearer picture of what is being discussed.
2 Select details that are relevant to the point you are making. Don't try to include everything.
3 Among those relevant details, select only the most important ones to include.
4 Make the details as specific and concise as possible.

---

4. Final Check   When you have written your essay, read it to someone who does not know how to do what you have discussed. Find out if you have been thorough and clear enough for another person to understand the process. Ask the listener if the essay is *interesting* as well as informative. When you are satisfied that the essay can teach your reader how to do what you have discussed, put it in the best form you possibly can and turn it in.

RULES FOR A HOW-TO ESSAY

1 Be sure to choose a process that you know thoroughly.
2 Be certain that your essay will give value to the reader.
3 Know exactly what audience you are writing for and tailor your discussion of the process to that particular group of people.
4 Anticipate anything the reader might not know; make every step clear and in order.
5 Use vivid details.
6 Put the information into an interesting framework.

THESIS

1 Choose a single aspect of the subject to write on, and make a statement about it.
2 Be sure that you are an insider, that you can say something about the

subject that the reader doesn't already know or hasn't already thought of.

3 Be absolutely clear in stating exactly the message you want the reader to get.

4 Be reasonably sure this message is something that will *matter* to the reader.

HAVE A CLEAR THESIS

As you have just seen, many questions become resolved after you have made the preliminary agreements about the audience for your writing. You know a lot about level, approach, detail, tone, and vocabulary just by knowing clearly to whom you are writing. You almost never hear the advice, "Narrow your audience," but once you know the advantages that come from writing to a clearly defined and specific reader, "Narrow your audience" might strike you as sound advice.

On the other hand, nearly everyone at one time or another has heard the advice, "Narrow your subject." Most people think, "I feel that I don't have enough to say as it is; how in the world can I get anywhere by *narrowing* the topic?" As a matter of fact, though, you are not being asked to *begin* with a topic and then immediately start narrowing it down. What you've done is begin with a topic; then you've done CUBING and LOOPING and other invention techniques until you produced a pile of notes, sentences, points, approaches, angles. So it is not a matter of finding a subject or topic—it is rather a matter of selecting, sorting out, and narrowing down exactly what you are going to say about it. That's where the idea of THESIS is really helpful.

Many people make the mistake of thinking that having a "subject" is the same as having a "thesis" for a piece of writing. However, the thesis of your writing is something much more definite than the general subject. **The thesis expresses the *subject* of the writing, but also says what the *central point* of your writing about that subject will be. The thesis expresses the topic (thing you'll write about) and your assertion about the topic (what you'll say about it).**

The need for a thesis comes up when you have finished the *Invention Stage* on a subject. You have discovered a lot of ideas, written a lot of words, and had many thoughts about the subject. You can't just stop with the *Invention Stage*, though, and hand over all your notes to the reader and say, "Here is what I have to say on this subject." That would be like inviting some friends over for a meal and when they arrived handing them an uncooked steak, a box of Jell-o, and a raw potato and saying, "Here is dinner." To move from all your private writings on a subject, you have to prepare the thesis, the specific subject, and a statement *about* the subject—just as you have to prepare the ingredients before you can serve dinner. You have to choose, from all the ideas you had in the Creating Stage, *the thing* you want to discuss in your

THESIS:
A setting down; something set down; a proposition stated or put forward for consideration, especially to be discussed or proved or maintained.

IT'S NOT PRESENTABLE UNTIL IT'S PREPARED

HUNCHES
WORDS
IDEAS
THOUGHTS
WORDS
CONCEPTS
IDEAS
FEELINGS

writing. Somewhere during the *Creating Stage* you will have written something that you felt energetic about, something that really interested *you*—and that's where you begin, because it has to interest *you* before it can interest anybody else. Once you're clear about the subject (or topic, or thing) you want to write about, the next step is to decide exactly what you want to write *about* that subject. As you move through the process, you'll find that narrowing the topic will help you to find a thesis, and that finding a thesis will help you to narrow the topic still further.

1. To Find a Thesis, Narrow the Topic   Imagine that you had been asked to write a paper on "sports." You then spent an hour or so with two of the *creating* activities—CUBING and LOOPING—and at the end of that time you decided you could really write a fine paper on jogging. Now it's true that "jogging" is quite a bit narrower than "sports," but even though the topic is narrower, it isn't a *thesis* yet because there isn't any *assertion* about jogging. So you might ask yourself, "What *exactly* do I want to say about jogging?" A dialogue with yourself like this might follow:

You: I want to show the reader how to run three miles.

Little Voice: That's fine. Now *why* do you want to show the reader that?

You: Because it is interesting.

Little Voice: What's interesting about it?

You: It makes a person healthy.

Little Voice: Why will your reader care about that?

You: Everybody wants to live a long time and be healthy.

Little Voice: So, your purpose in writing would be to inform the reader about the value of jogging in order to live a long and healthy life?

You: Yes.

Little Voice: This means, then, that you'll tell the reader how to run three miles in order to live a long and happy life, and therefore you *won't* be talking about other aspects of jogging, like how to build distance or speed, or what kinds of shoes to wear.

You: Well, I could do that too . . .

Little Voice: No, *you can't.* Not if you are going to center on one purpose in the paper—to tell the readers why jogging will contribute to a long and healthy life.

You: Oh, I see.

Little Voice: I thought you would.

You: Yes, that's what *narrowing your topic* means. Not telling everything you know about a subject, but picking out the things you know that relate to the *one specific message* you are going to send to the reader.

Little Voice: You got it.

You: And when you express that *one specific message* in *one clear sentence*, that's a thesis?

Little Voice: Yep.

You: So that's what having a thesis is all about. Am I ever glad to learn it after all these years!

And that's exactly how it is. Of course you start out however you start—by CUBING or LOOPING, or just making lists, brainstorming, or woolgathering. But whether you *begin* with a thesis sentence, or produce one halfway through the *Creating Stage*, or develop one after the *Creating Stage* is completed, you'll need it eventually, simply because public writing must be structured and purposeful. However, it is our experience that the *Creating Stage* tends to be more fertile and productive if it is unrestricted—that is to say, if there is *no* thesis sentence around to inhibit the creative flow.

THE PROCESS OF ABSTRACTING

The "object" of our experience, then, is not the "thing in itself," but *an interaction between our nervous systems (with all their imperfections) and something outside them.* Bessie is unique—there is nothing else in the universe exactly like her in all respects. But we automatically *abstract* or select from the process-Bessie those features of hers in which she resembles other animals of like shape, functions, and habits, and we *classify* her as "cow."

When we say, then, that "Bessie is a cow," we are only noting the process-Bessie's resemblances to other "cows" and *ignoring differences.* What is more, we are leaping a huge chasm: from the dynamic process-Bessie, a whirl of electro-chemico-neural eventfulness, to a relatively static "idea," "concept," or *word,* "cow." In this connection, readers are referred to the diagram entitled "The Abstraction Ladder." . . .

As the diagram illustrates, the "object" we see is an abstraction of the lowest level; but it is still an abstraction, since it leaves out characteristics of the process that is the real Bessie. The *word* "Bessie" (cow$_1$) is the lowest *verbal* level of abstraction, leaving out further characteristics—the differences between Bessie yesterday and Bessie today, between Bessie today and Bessie tomorrow—and selecting only

"The Abstraction Ladder"

the similarities. The word "cow" selects only the similarities between Bessie (cow_1), Daisy (cow_2), Rosie (cow_3), and so on, and therefore leaves out still more about Bessie. The word "livestock" selects or abstracts only the features that Bessie has in common with pigs, chickens, goats, and sheep. The term "farm asset" abstracts only the features Bessie has in common with barns, fences, livestock, furniture, generating plants, and tractors, and is therefore on a very high level of abstraction.

For most people, those exploratory writings just develop as they happen, tending to wander around a good deal. That's natural. After all, you can't know what you want to say on a subject until you discover it. But that wandering, "unpurposeful" writing is definitely not for readers. In fact, it's boring. Here's a representative sample of writing from the *Creating Stage:*

The assignment is to write something about my state. How can I decide what to write about Iowa? Well, there's plenty of opportunity here. And it's kind of the heartland of America. I could talk about the politics here, and how they represent American values everywhere. And there are plenty of recreational opportunities too. Yeek! Did I just write "recreational opportunities?" Ugh, I'm getting to sound like a parks and recreation bulletin from the Department of the Interior. There's lots of farming here too. People are interested in farms, farming, livestock. There are lots of county fairs in the summers, and people love to swarm all over them.

That's fine for the *Creating Stage,* where the author is writing primarily for herself and primarily to discover what she wants to say. But, obviously, she's not going to take on the whole state in one small essay. And just as obviously, no reader is going to put up with an essay that rambles from point to point this way. Few would care to read further, once they saw that she jumps from one statement about the state to another.

After the author did some more creating activities, she found that one idea about Iowa really stuck out for her, and she felt really enthusiastic writing about it. The subject was *fairs,* and while "fairs" is certainly narrower than "something about Iowa," it still is only a topic, not yet a *thesis.* It is still a *topic without an assertion.* What *about* fairs? That's the question that has to be answered if someone is to read along with interest, if there is to be a message that will give value to the reader. Looking back over her *creating* material, the author discovered that several times she had talked about fairs taking some of the boredom out of long hot summers, and about the state fair being the biggest and best of them all.

Eureka! There was a thesis, something to *set forth,* to put out to the reader. She would write about the Iowa State Fair as a cure for summer

The question to ask is "What *exactly* do I want to say about it?"

$$\frac{\text{Narrowed Topic} \quad 1}{+ \text{Specific Message} \quad +1}$$
$$= \text{Thesis} \qquad = 2$$

(and it's not true if any piece is missing)

boredom. Her new introduction looked like this:

Summer months in Iowa seem long and boring. For most people, the highlight of the day is staying inside and listening to the drone of the air conditioner as it competes with the mindless gabble of daytime television. But just when you think you can't stand one more boring, long, dull day, the Iowa State Fair comes to town. Whoopee! Slip into your best western shirt and your most comfortable faded jeans. Fun times are just around the corner! For the next couple of days, the summer doldrums are cured.

This time the reader knows exactly what the thesis is—even if the thesis sentence doesn't appear in the paragraph. The subject "fairs" has been further narrowed to "the Iowa State Fair." And the assertion is clear too: *it's a cure for summer boredom.* Anyone could convert that to a sentence: **The Iowa State Fair is a cure for summer boredom.** And why will the reader be interested? That's obvious as well: anyone bored with a long, dull summer will benefit from finding out about the fair. *In this paragraph, unlike the first, there is a point to the whole thing, and the point is perfectly clear to the reader.*

2. Be an Insider   After coming up with a clear thesis to discuss in an essay, you must ask this crucial question: "Am I an insider in this matter?" The answer is "maybe" if you

> **know something about the subject or thesis that the reader doesn't know**

> or

> **have a special expertise in the matter.**

Figure out and establish your own special qualifications as an expert in this matter. Be certain that *you* are *the* appropriate person to write on this thesis. If that sounds too hard, you may need to look for another subject or another thesis, since you obviously don't want to waste your reader's time by latching onto a thesis and writing on it simply to have something to turn in. And, in fact, it wouldn't be a very good preparation for life after school, where "turning in assignments" means more than merely going through the motions.

YOUR INSIDE EDGE
But don't be too hasty in deciding that you're *not* an expert. Just be sure that you're thinking about it, and thinking about the ways that you *are* an insider. For example, the student who wrote about the Iowa State Fair didn't need to be a contestant in the baking contest, or a prize-hog exhibitor, or a calf-roper to be an expert about the fair. What she did need was to know a good deal about the fair, and she did need to tell the reader a lot of things the reader hasn't been thinking about lately. Concentrating on the fair as a cure for boredom, she can, if she has been to a few fairs, discuss the things going on there and tell or show what makes them interesting to her (and thus to the reader).

WRITE AS AN EXPERT, SPECIALIST, INSIDER

INNER CIRCLE

It's a point we can't emphasize too much: if you can't write about something you're an expert on, if you can't give the reader the insider's view, you'll probably be staying on the surface and you'll just wind up with a rehash of stuff you both already know. The way to get past that is to do some more work in the creating stage until something turns up that you *are* an insider on, *or* until you discover how to get the inside edge on the subject you want to write on. That's when *communication* begins — **when you're giving the reader your special, expert, inside view of the matter, your unique perception or special appreciation.**

3. State the Thesis Clearly After deciding on a thesis for the paper and determining if you are an insider on the matter and can give a personal approach to the topic, make sure the reader knows *exactly what your message is going to be.* **Somewhere early in the writing you should get that message out clearly.** Sometimes the message is expressed in the thesis sentence; other times it may come across to the reader through several sentences or even a whole paragraph, as it did in the example about the Iowa State Fair. But whether the thesis is expressed explicitly in one unmistakable sentence or whether it is imbedded in several sentences or a paragraph, it is almost always advisable to *let the reader know clearly what the rest of the essay is going to be about.*

Here's an opening paragraph that makes clear who the audience is, what the subject is, what the paper will say about the subject, and what the value to the reader will be:

This last summer thousands of people stamped up and down hundreds of miles of backpacking and hiking trails all across the United States and Canada, putting their feet through punishment and pain as they never had felt before. Blisters, corns, and painful swelling of joints plagued nearly everyone, including both the novice and the experienced trail guide. There is no sure way to prevent these discomforts, but the right type and fit of hiking boot can help make it a great deal easier, as I learned this last summer.

Who is the audience? Anyone who hikes or is planning to hike.
What is the subject? How to get the right type of fit in hiking boots.
What will the writer concentrate on? Giving the reader information on how to choose hiking boots.
What is the value to the reader? Information and, perhaps, more comfortable feet.

The thesis is expressed in the last sentence. The rest of the paper will expand on this thesis. A particular "thing to discuss" has been set up, and the rest of the paper will be devoted to discussing this thesis that the writer has selected.

Here is another example, the first two paragraphs of a student theme:

Soft, intriguing music plays in the background. Martha, a pretty brunette, walks into the living room. Her husband, Paul, is sitting anxiously on the couch. "Martha, where have you been?", then taking a closer look he adds, "You haven't been down at Ted's nightclub again, have you?" She remains silent for a moment and then speaks defensively: "What difference does it make to you? You spend every night working at the clinic! What do you expect me to do, stay home and watch TV by myself?" And so another dramatic episode begins.

Each weekday, many stories similar to this one are broadcast on TV. These soap operas are viewed by thousands of people across the country. Men are also enjoying what used to be considered shows for women only, and new soap operas are appearing during evening hours. "The soaps" have become an American pastime. Why do people watch soap operas? Why have they become so popular?

Here the writer has deferred any hint of a thesis until the end of the second paragraph — and by so doing she has generated a certain measure of suspense for the reader. However, it's clear at the end of the second paragraph that the topic is soap operas, that the paper will explore the reasons why people like them, and that the reader is probably someone who knows about soap operas and will be interested in an analysis of their appeal.

As you have seen, **it is almost vital to the success of the writing that the author have a clear grasp of the thesis.** On the other hand, sometimes a sentence can "look" like a thesis, yet because it is either too huge, or muddy, or both, it really doesn't serve either reader or writer very substantially. For example, you may remember Howard's essay, earlier in the text, about "Life in the Wild," which had "majestic mountains stretching their peaks" and the sun "shooting up over the mountains, signaling the beginning of the first day of the rest of your life." Howard's "thesis" was: "The beauty and splendor of the Great Outdoors is exhibited throughout the heritage of our country, and it is the exploration of this heritage that remains as one of the last frontiers." It looks a little like a thesis, and he calls it a thesis; but *is* it?

No. But it can be very useful to the writer, nonetheless, because if Howard (or you) examined it carefully, it would reveal exactly what needed to be done before the actual drafting could begin. For example, "the beauty and splendor of the Great Outdoors" *sounds* like a subject, but what picture do you have? Actually, there are so many kinds of beauty and so many varieties of splendor that just to list them all might take several days. So right away a writer can see that the subject is still too broad. OK — let's look further. What *about* the beauty and splendor? It is "exhibited throughout the heritage of our country." Well, that's a puzzler. What, in fact, does it mean? What *can* it mean? If beauty and splendor exist, how then can they be *exhibited*? And while it is possible to say that certain characteristics of the population are exhibited through certain *actions* and that the history of the country can therefore be partly accounted for by some of these traits, how does the character of the population relate to the Great Outdoors? Not only is the subject much, much too large; the assertion about the subject is completely unclear. The last part of the statement comes closer to making sense to the reader: "exploration of the beauty and splendor of the Great Outdoors

BEWARE OF A VAGUE THESIS.

remains as one of the last frontiers"—except that it's still too broad in the subject and a bit fuzzy, too, in the assertion (what makes the Great Outdoors like a "last frontier"?). So while this particular thesis fails to measure up to the criteria—and certainly there's no evidence of writing as an expert or insider—still it is extremely valuable in showing the writer that *he hasn't yet got enough mastery of either the subject or the approach.*

4. Check to See if the Thesis Will Matter to the Reader   It's always tempting to assume that anything interesting to *you* will also be interesting to the reader—but that's not always the case. You're interested in something simply because you're interested. And so you start out interested. The reader, though, starts wherever *he* or *she* starts from, and that may or may not be in alignment with what interests you. Clearly, that was a problem for the woman who wrote about the colors of the day —she started out interested, and she never considered that the reader might not share that interest. (Is it something that the reader will gain value from? What's in it for the reader?) Checking your thesis in advance can help you present a subject and approach that are exciting and satisfactory to you and also that really connect with the reader.

Knowing clearly who the reader is, having a detailed image of the audience, will let you realize whether or not you're likely to connect. Here is where Holly, the woman from Iowa, can take measures to guarantee her success. Her thesis clearly meets the first three requirements:

> **she does come up with one particular aspect of her subject and makes a statement about it,**
> **she is an insider on the subject (we assume),**
> **she clearly puts the thesis in the opening of her essay.**

Now the next question is, *who will care?* If she can think of readers who would be interested in the message, she can develop a strategy that will help her connect. If, for instance, she decided to write for a 4-H magazine in her home state, she could certainly make the thesis matter a lot to her readers. And if she were writing for her English classmates right before school was out for the summer, she would also know exactly what to do to connect with *that* audience. With some careful thought, she might make it work for people who live in other states, by making the fair seem so exciting and inviting that they would want to come even though they weren't particularly bored at home.

The point is, though, that Holly, or anybody, has to work on making the message matter. You can't just take for granted that readers are going to care deeply for what you are talking about. You have to **present the subject as significant;** you have to **find an audience that will get value from what you have to say** and you'll want to aim all the way through the writing to **make a difference to the reader.**

Nobody gains when the reader yawns and says, "So what?" Look at this opening of an essay, where clearly the writer has given no thought

to whether the thesis will matter to the reader:

Fall is seldom described as someone's favorite season, but I anticipate its arrival with great excitement. The heat of summer is nice for a while but it soon gets to be very bothersome. With fall come cool days and cold nights. The whole world begins to change. The sky starts getting more gray in it as the cold fronts begin to roll in. The leaves on the trees turn various colors with the yearly metamorphosis that converts the trees from plain green plants to enduring sculptures of intricate patterns and shapes.

Fall is similar to spring in one respect. Both seasons are preparing for the upcoming season. During fall, the world prepares to close shop for the winter. The world bursts out with great amounts of activity. Millions of birds fly south and soon leave behind deserted skies. Other animals, such as squirrels and bears, begin to gather food to get ready for hibernation.

Want to read any further? *Not on your life!* The writer evidently has as his thesis the fact that he likes the fall (although you can see a lot of wobbling around on this thesis, so he probably didn't really get clear what *single* message he wanted to get across to the reader). But giving him the benefit of the doubt and saying that he had settled on a thesis/message, "Fall is a good time of the year," all you can say is, *So what? What will this matter to the reader? Why should readers care about this?* The writer has to show why the message should matter or throw this essay away.

Here is another "So what?" thesis:

Learning is the process by which a person gains knowledge or understanding of a subject or skill. It is through this unique process that the human race has advanced as far as it has. There are many methods of learning, but the main three are instruction, observation, and practice.

Now, we won't even ask this writer the first three questions: **are you writing on *one specific aspect* of the subject? are you an *insider* on the matter? have you *clearly stated* the thesis *early* in the paper for the reader?** We will just put this last question to him: So what? Why does this matter to the reader? Why should the reader care about this at all? This writer has acted as though the reader didn't matter. He seems to be playing the game of putting *something* down in order to have *something* to turn in for his assignment. He isn't really intending to *communicate* something; if he were, he would **think constantly of ways to interest the reader, to give value to the reader.**

As we saw in the essay by Tim Wold ("Hill Country Hike"), even personal experience can give tremendous value to the reader—it's the approach that makes the difference. Here's a final example, this time from Cindy Rochford, about water-skiing. Her CUBING and LOOPING turned up loads of personal experience that she'd had as a water skier, but it remained personal—mostly an expression of what *she* liked or telling about good times *she* had had. She puzzled a good bit, trying to find a way to interest readers in her personal enthusiasm but had to give up again and again. The turning point came when Cindy realized that what was true for her would also be true for the reader—that if water-skiing was fun for her, it could also be fun for the reader. Thus, she shifted her focus and approach from "Wow, I really like it" to "You should try it; you'd like it too." Here's how it turned out:

> Do it if you can; do it if you dare. It's frustrating and vigorous. But the satisfaction of actually meeting the challenge of water-skiing is exhilarating.
>
> To the inexperienced water-skier each preparation step up to the point of take-off is strenuous. The mere act of just putting on the skis while in the water can become totally exhausting. The skis are difficult to manipulate in the hands of a novice. During my first time to ski, I must have struggled for a small eternity trying to get my tiny feet into the even tinier rubber foot holds on the skis. The skis were no help at all, either. They twisted and turned every which way except my way. I was worn out before I ever skied.

Checking out against the questions, Cindy gets a perfect score.

Is she writing on *one aspect* of the subject?
> Yes—she is writing on a single aspect of water-skiing—how it is frustrating to the novice but worth the effort.

Is she an *insider* in the matter?
> Yes—you can tell from the details that she is an expert on how it feels to be a novice skier.

Has she stated the thesis *clearly* and *early*?
> Yes—"the satisfaction of actually meeting the challenge of water-skiing is exhilarating" is perfectly clear and comes in the first paragraph.

Will the reader *care*?
> Yes—because Cindy has created an audience that have not skied before, and because Cindy clearly takes the approach that she has something of value to share with them and means to share it.

Even someone who already knew how to water-ski could read Cindy's paper with pleasure and satisfaction, as one insider can appreciate the *expertise* of another insider—or just to pick up some pointers that could be used to persuade nonskiing friends to give the sport a try.

YOU CAN'T BE SURE BUT . . .

Finally, the truth is that you can't always know whether the reader will be interested. A lot of very expensive shows open every year on Broadway, with all the people from author to cast to stage crew having done their best to interest the audience—and most of the shows don't last a full season. Still, there are new shows every season that open the curtains to long and successful runs. So it stands to reason that the more attention you give toward taking an approach that will interest the

reader, the more likely you are to be rewarded by the reader's interest, even though you never can be *absolutely* sure.

SUMMARY OF THESIS

Asking yourself exactly what the paper is going to accomplish for your readers is absolutely necessary. To be sure that readers will be willing to take their valuable time to read your writing, to be sure they'll get something out of your writing, to be sure that they will be interested and that you'll tell them something they don't already know, you can ask these questions:

> **Am I writing on a *single aspect* of the subject?**
> ***Am I writing as an *insider* in the matter?**
> ***Have I stated the thesis *early* and *clearly*?**
> ***Is the reader likely to *care*?**

When you can answer yes to these questions, you will know your specific purpose for writing and the specific message you want to send. Since there are hundreds of things you are an insider on, hundreds of subjects you can write about and thereby contribute to a reader's enjoyment, knowledge, and awareness, don't waste your time and theirs writing on some blah subject that doesn't matter to anybody. If you are keen on a subject, if you really have something to say about it, you can make it matter to anybody. It's being conscious about this and having the clear intention of making what you write matter to the reader that will take care of the problem for you.

A CHECKLIST FOR THESIS

1 The message I am communicating in this paper is _____ .
2 I am the appropriate person to write on this thesis because I am an insider on the subject. I know it from the point of view of _____ .
3 I have clearly let my reader know what I am writing about by telling him or her on page ____ in paragraph ____ .
4 This thesis will probably matter to my readers because _____ .

APPLICATIONS

1 Look at these opening paragraphs from student essays and see if the writers seem to be *insiders* on the subject. What passages, words, sentences, establish them as *insiders* (or *outsiders,* as the case may be)? Be able to discuss these paragraphs in class.

A

I came to college with high and mighty, yet customary, goals. The excitement of everything about college seemed enough to keep me propelled forward forever. But, after two months, I'm worried. The excitement flew out the window, and I'm left amidst the crowds of students sharing the same problem. Instead of something flashy and fairly easy, I found that college is dingy clothes and a D in Biology.

B

Dating is an important part of every young person's maturing process. One's social growth is very likely to be stunted by the limiting of himself or herself to a single steady date. Young adults are quick to believe they are in love and believe that marriage would be the only way to truly express it. True, some of these marriages work out fine but most result in divorces.

C

Racquetball is the youngest of the racquet sports. And, in many ways, it is the best. The game can be enjoyed at any level of competition. Almost anyone can hit a rubber ball against the wall, but few can do it with the power, velocity, and finesse of a racquetball champion.

D

"You know that class is awful. I never learn anything from it, but it seems to last for hours."

"I know what you mean. The lectures are so disorganized. He doesn't even know what he's talking about."

"Well, I won't be there next class. I have better ways to spend my time."

This conversation is often heard after many college classes. However, this attitude can be reversed through the efforts of the professor. By inspiring confidence in the student and through an organized and knowledgeable presentation of the material, a professor can make any class interesting as well as instructive.

Which of these paragraphs convince you the writer can give some unique value on the thesis? When you've finished making your decision, look closely at the convincing paragraphs and examine them for features that suggest the writer has the reader in mind. Explain what techniques a writer can use to convince the reader that there will be value in the writing.

A

Have you ever had the courage to work with little kids and not only try to teach them how to play soccer, but, at the same time, have them enjoy what you are teaching? Chances are your answer is no, but then again you probably never thought about it quite like that. This act of bravery is not a subject to be taken lightly. Mainly because teaching is one of the hardest ways to relate to kids. While you are teaching them, you need to do it in such a manner that they can enjoy what they are learning. Some people just do not understand that kids can enjoy what they are being taught.

B

The American way has always been toward progress but not always towards every aspect of the future ahead. Americans in their race for progressive happiness have damaged one integral part of their future, their own lands. Now the people are beginning to see their wrongs and are correcting these problems. The only natural wild lands they have left to save are those in the national parks and forests and their time for repenting their ways grows short.

C

I have some grim facts concerning the automobile's future. According to the Ryman's study (Standard Oil Co. of New Jersey) in 1967, there are 30–50×10^9 tons of oil on the North Slope. There are just 200×10^9 tons of oil in reserves in the U.S., with the average automobile using 2 tons of oil a year in the U.S. (1 ton $=$ 8 barrels). If the energy usage of the U.S. continues to go up at the present rate (1% and $3/10^9$ tons used per year), the U.S. will have to import as much oil from the Middle East in the 1980s as it produced in 1970. There is evidence that shows the automobile will have to use one-tenth less gasoline in the year 2000. According to most studies, the automobile is responsible for over half the energy consumption in the U.S. The excessive use (or waste) of gasoline will soon spell an end for the automobile.

3 Read the following paragraphs. Answer these questions about them:

Does each paragraph have a **clear thesis statement?** If so, what is this statement?

If a thesis statement is present, does the writer limit the subject to a **single aspect?**

Has the **writer been clear** about what she or he is going to say about the thesis?

Can the **reader** know what he or she is **going to get** from reading the paper?

Be able to discuss your answers for each paragraph in class.

A

"Gee, Mom, it smells good in here! What's cooking?" asks a boy as he walks through the kitchen. Slam! Mom watches her son come in and walk by without even noticing her presence. In tears she looks on as he hunts through the refrigerator for a mid-afternoon snack and thinks, "You call this a family."

B

It took me twelve years of school to finally realize that I did not know how to study. When I was in high school, I did about twenty minutes of studying a night (of course, excluding Fridays and Saturdays). Plus, for a test, I kicked in about thirty extra minutes. Despite the lack of study I still pulled out a 3.325. Then came the shock of my life, college.

C

I cannot believe that it is all over. When I was little, all I ever wanted to be was a teenager. I longed for the days when I would do nothing but chase boys, talk on the telephone and blast my stereo. I wonder now, if I had not talked quite so long on the phone and had not listened to my loud stereo quite so avidly, if my high school years would have gone by any slower. I never really took the time to stop and say, "Hey! I am now one normal, 100-percent, full-fledged teenager!" Instead, it seems as if I made a transition straight from babydoll little girl life into womanhood without even stopping to think twice.

D

The serene atmosphere surrounding the neighborhood was pierced by an echoing scream. A teenager turned and ran in the direction of the noise. Rounding a corner he was confronted by a mother and father standing over their son. The teenager took note of the situation and immediately began artificial respiration. Within a few minutes the child was conscious and active. Why was the teenager able to save the child while the mother and father stood helplessly by? Were they overcome by the shock of seeing their son in trouble, or did they not know how to administer first aid? In either case their son might have died if it had not been for a total stranger. The teenager was able to save the child's life because he had been taught first aid.

4   All of the following paragraphs fail to meet the conditions for **effective thesis development, effective adaptation to audience,** or both. Read them carefully; then be prepared to discuss exactly how each fails and what could be done to improve them. When you've finished, pick two and rewrite them.

A

Man is, at heart, a cruel animal injuring and attacking not for food or protection but for enjoyment. What is more, he does this fighting with each other. Those of the species who do not participate watch and cheer on their favorite, wishing all the time that they had the skill to be in his place. Of course I am speaking of man's sports, his vicious ways of recreating.

B

For many people, the idea of a restaurant brings to mind a place where one can relax and eat the food of his or her choice. Some people go to a restaurant to relax, have a few drinks and eat a good meal. After a hard day, nothing is better than to go to a quiet restaurant and let someone else, who is probably better than you anyway, cook the meal of your choice. You can also listen to the quiet music while you eat your delicious meal. With no interruptions like a telephone or a doorbell ringing, you can probably enjoy your meal more. You can take your time eating and enjoy every morsel of your delectable meal. Someone else will cook your meal to your specifications and will also serve it to you quietly and politely. The dishes will be taken away and you will not even have to clean them up.

C

There are many restaurants that specialize in certain types of food. My favorite varieties of food are seafood and Mexican food. One thing that annoys me is some people who go into a restaurant that specializes in one particular food and they order something completely off the menu. The customer should show some courtesy to the establishment. He could show this by leaving a tip for the waiter. A tip shows the customer's appreciation of a service which he considers the waiter deserved. In a few cases, I have encountered rude waiters who give none or very poor service. But these cases have been very few as I have been satisfied with most of the service I have received. A restaurant is still a good place to go to relax and enjoy the best food possible.

FORM: A THESIS WILL SUGGEST THE FORM THE ESSAY WILL TAKE

Nobody is sure exactly how writers decide the form that their writing will finally take. Usually a writer doesn't really *decide*. The essay, once the thesis is thought out, seems to take its form organically. This means that the *purpose* the writer has for doing the writing and the *thesis* (or point of the writing) somehow determine the form of the essay. Form is often a subconscious or automatic activity with experienced writers.

Look at these two examples to see how the *form* comes organically from the writer's *purpose* and *thesis:*

1   In this first example, the purpose is *to tell readers how to save money by changing their own oil in their cars.* The thesis might be something like this: "Car owners can save money learning to change their own oil." **The *purpose* and the *thesis* of this essay will determine to a very great extent the form this essay will take.** It would most likely start off by talking about the *value* of changing your own oil, particularly the *monetary* value. It would probably give some *comparison figures* of what it costs to have your oil changed at a service station and what it costs to do it yourself. Then the essay would probably take the reader step by step through the process of changing oil. The structure, in short, is a *brief introduction* giving some reason for reading, then the step by step directions. That is such a common pattern that the writer very likely won't make a lot of conscious choices about what to say first, second, third, and so on, because it makes sense to describe the steps of changing the oil in the order in which they occur; the order of the steps in the process determine the order of the paper.

This essay will "flow" naturally, in line with the subject, purpose, and thesis. There isn't a chance, for instance, that the paper would begin by telling the origin of oil or how cars are made or how people used to change oil in the early 1900s. These things just wouldn't fit the thesis: "Car owners can save money by learning to change their own oil."

2   The purpose in this second example is *to tell readers how it feels to have retired.* The thesis might be: "Retirement has required many adjustments." Do you see how, once again, the *purpose* and *thesis* to a very large extent set up the form of the essay? **The form is organic to the purpose and meaning.** This paper has no possibility for telling *how to* retire the way the first essay told how to change oil. That just isn't appropriate in light of the thesis. But a likely shape is there—right in the thesis itself: a form made up of *thesis plus examples.* The writer would probably give four or five specific adjustments that retired people must make and tell how each feels. It is just natural that, to deliver this thesis, the writer would *tell what those adjustments were.* The form, again, follows the thesis.

THE ACORN CONTAINS A MIGHTY OAK WITHIN.

There is a clear application for your own writing. When you wonder what form to arrange your writing into, don't look for some rules from outside to help you, to make it absolutely clear for all time. What researchers currently know about form is that the message itself—the main idea, the thesis that you are going to expand and develop—will determine to a very great extent the form the essay will take. And though there are no hard and fast textbook rules, there is one truth you can hold onto:

The message will have *the* form, or at least *a* form, inherent in it.

Yet, as we have seen before, beginning writers must often be more conscious and even maybe a little artificial when they are first learning to write, until they get the hang of it and can just "know" things automatically the way experienced writers often do.

What, then, can you learn specifically that will help you have form, arrangement, and organization in your essays as you develop that natural feel of writing? There are a few hints and suggestions that will probably help you in the beginning. Later, as you develop more sensitivity to form, the **shaping process** will become as organic and automatic for you as it often is for experienced writers.

SPECIFIC PATTERNS OF ORGANIZATION
TIME ORDER
    Narration
    Process
    Cause/Effect

SPATIAL ORDER
    Description

GENERAL–SPECIFIC ORDER
    Definition
    Induction

BREAK-DOWN ORDER
    Analysis
    Classification
    Examples

RELATIONSHIP ORDER
    Comparison/Contrast
    Analogy

Each of the specific patterns of organization you are about to examine come naturally and organically out of an essay thesis. They are "natural" patterns of thought that all human beings use every day. In fact, even if you wanted to, you couldn't stop yourself from thinking in these patterns. So it follows that you will also write in these patterns; in fact, you will find they come to you easily. The purpose of studying these patterns, then, is to become *(a)* aware of the types of thought patterns that are natural, and *(b)* alert to the combinations—that is, what kinds of thinking patterns usually occur with what kinds of thesis statements and writing purposes. **The more you write, the more proficient you will get in actually seeing the specific pattern of organization *in the thesis* before you start writing, or certainly by the end of your trial draft.**

Be aware of the Patterns;
Be alert to the Combinations

Your paper may fall into a *chronological* or *time order* if you have a thesis like this one:

THESIS: **The story of man's first landing on the moon excited the world.**

Here your purpose in writing the essay is to tell this story and to show why the story has excited the world. You naturally begin,

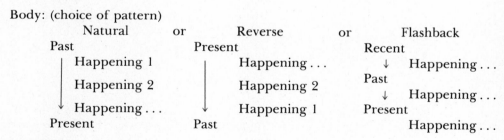

First, the rocket was launched . . .

Then, the team . . .

After that, the module . . .

Next this happened . . .

Finally, . . .

and on to the end of the story. You close off the essay with some discussion of the significance of this story for the reader, and there is your specific pattern of organization—*time order*, which you have not imposed arbitrarily. **The pattern of organization has emerged from the thesis of your essay.**

NARRATION

Introduction

Body: (choice of pattern)

Natural	or	Reverse	or	Flashback
Past		Present		Recent
↓ Happening 1		↓ Happening . . .		↓ Happening . . .
Happening 2		Happening 2		Past
				↓ Happening . . .
↓ Happening . . .		↓ Happening 1		Present
Present		Past		Happening . . .

Conclusion

Here is another thesis that leads naturally to *time order* as a pattern of organization in an essay:

THESIS: **Following these steps, a person can spend less for groceries, even in these days of high inflation.**

Do you see how the development that follows a process thesis will also just automatically take a chronological shape?

First, you do this . . .
Then, you do that . . .
After that, you do . . .
Another thing you can do is . . .
and so on to the end of the steps.

PROCESS

Introduction

Body: (choice of pattern)

Enumeration or	Steps	or	Sequence
1	Step one		First
2	Step two		Next
3	Step three		Then
4	Step . . .		After that
			Finally

Conclusion

Here is another thesis that would naturally produce a *time order* pattern of organization in an essay:

THESIS: **The 1954 Supreme Court decision on *Oliver Brown et al* v. *Board of Education of Topeka* caused American education to change.**

To develop this thesis you would follow a *time order* again because you would say first there is this cause—a court decision—and after that there are these effects—an historic shift in a nation's attitude. If *x* hadn't happened before, *y* wouldn't have happened afterwards. **It is an organic organization pattern for this thesis, then, when you discuss first the cause and then the effects.**

Sometimes the pattern might be reversed; you might want to discuss the effects first and then the cause, as in a paper written on a thesis like this:

THESIS: **Although integrated education is common in America today, it began in 1954 with the famous Supreme Court "Brown" decision.**

Then your paper would fall into a discussion of the effect first and then a longer discussion of the causes of this effect. You would still be moving in *time order*, however, because the cause occurred first and the effects second.

> "But after he has at least analyzed the subject in his mind and decided what his purpose requires . . . the writer will usually find that a satisfactory pattern suggests itself."
>
> —Randall E. Decker

CAUSE AND EFFECT

Introduction

Body: (choice of pattern)

Cause	Or	Effect
1		1
2		2
3		3
4		4
. . .		. . .
Effect		Cause
1		1
2		2
3		3
4		4
. . .		. . .

Conclusion

SPATIAL ORDER

Here is another specific pattern of organization that occurs again and again in writing because all of us see the world this way too, just as we all think in *time order*. The following thesis would result in a paper organized on *spatial order* principles:

THESIS: **The newest aid for tennis players is a specially designed ball thrower.**

It isn't hard to see how this thesis would have as its organic development a description of the new machine. The writer might describe the ball thrower from *left to right, inside to outside, top to bottom.* The important thing is that **the writer's pattern of organization should in some way be "built into" the thesis of the paper.**
Here's another example:

THESIS: **The most unusual costume I have ever seen was worn by the bass player in a family rock band.**

In the body of an essay written on this thesis you would naturally describe the costume, from top to bottom, or vice versa: *how it looked.* **Your organizational principle would come directly from the message you were sending in the paper.**

DESCRIPTION

Introduction

Body: (choice of pattern)

North	Top	Near	Inside	Left
↓	↓	↓	↓	↓
South	Bottom	Far	Outside	Right

Conclusion

GENERAL–SPECIFIC ORDER

A general statement is one that covers a lot, applies to many things, in-cluses a multitude of cases or instances or examples. A specific statement gives one *particular* example, incident, etc. Thought patterns that move from the general to the specific help us to understand new terms or concepts. A thesis like this would lead to a *general-to-specific order:*

THESIS: **Szechwan is a form of Chinese cooking closely tied to the region of the country where it first began.**

This thesis would lead to a definition of Szechwan cooking. It begins by a generalization: that Szechwan is a form of Chinese cooking. But, of course, there are many kinds of Chinese cooking, just as there are many kinds of American, French, German, and Italian cooking. So to move from the general to the specific, it will be necessary to show how Szechwan cooking stands out from all other kinds of Chinese cooking— Cantonese, Peking, Mandarin. The movement is broad-to-narrow (all cooking in China to Szechwan cooking), with the main part of the essay devoted to the definition of the more narrow, Szechwan, cooking. **Definition results in *general-to-specific order* because you are moving from a large group of things to show how one specific thing stands out from that larger group.**

DEFINITION
Introduction

Body: (choice of pattern)
        Define by synonym. Define by class. Define by origin. Define by details, description, etc.

Conclusion

Here is another thesis that would result in a general–specific order for an essay:

THESIS: **Lawyers are expected to have offices that look conservative, but nowadays some are showing a real individual flair in how they decorate the place in which they work.**

An essay written on this thesis would begin with a discussion of the generalization contained in the first part of the thesis: that lawyers are expected to have conservative-looking offices. After this discussion the writer would move to something more specific: evidence that some are now decorating with an individual flair. The shape and form of the essay is actually "predicted" and contained in the thesis sentence itself.

DEDUCTION
Introduction

Body:
        General
        Specific

Conclusion

The *general–specific order* can also be reversed. You might have a thesis like this:

THESIS: **Just because hunger and starvation have been on earth a long time is no reason to suppose that they will always be.**

You could develop that thesis nicely with a series of specific examples of things people used to believe but which are no longer true. You might use beliefs about the world being flat (which ended around 1492), that humans couldn't fly (which ended in 1903), that running a mile in under four minutes was physically impossible (which ended in 1954), that traveling to the moon was an unattainable dream (which ended in 1969). From those specifics you could move to a generalization: other "impossible" things have been achieved; we can also achieve the end of starvation. And the shape of the paper emerges effortlessly from the thesis.

INDUCTION

Introduction

Body:
      Specific 1
      Specific 2
      Specific 3
      Specific . . .
      Generalization

Conclusion

BREAK-DOWN ORDER

Another common thought pattern of organization is illustrated by this thesis:

THESIS: **All pieces of good writing have some characteristics in common.**

As you wrote the essay that developed this thesis, you would naturally discuss the *specific characteristics*—you would *analyze* good writing to see what its parts were.

   Here is another thesis that would just automatically result in a *break-down* pattern of organization:

THESIS: **This magazine advertisement is extremely effective in getting people to buy Vim chewing gum.**

The rest of your paper would consist of your analysis of the ad; you would talk first about one characteristic and then another. You would be breaking the subject down into *component parts* and that would provide the order for your paper.

ANALYSIS

Introduction

Body: (choice of pattern)

Part 1	Characteristic 1
Part 2	Characteristic 2
Part 3	Characteristic 3
Part . . .	Characteristic . . .

Conclusion

Another kind of thesis that results in a *break-down* pattern of organization is one like this:

THESIS: **Television shows can be divided into those that are produced to entertain and those that are produced to educate.**

As the writer who was going to develop this thesis, you would not even have to decide what organization pattern you were going to use. The parts of the essay would just naturally be (1) the shows that entertain, and discussion about these, and (2) the shows that educate, and discussion about these. *The thesis itself* produces the *break-down* organizational pattern with no effort to you the writer.

CLASSIFICATION

Introduction

Body:

Group 1

Group 2

Group 3

Group . . .

Conclusion

A third kind of *break-down* shape appears in this thesis sentence:

THESIS: **The Smoky Mountains in east Tennessee are a great vacation spot.**

To develop this thesis, you would give examples. Your aim in this essay would be to convince your reader by citing specifics that you think prove that the Smokies are good vacation country. You wouldn't have to worry about the overall shape of the essay because it's inherent in your thesis. (This is also known as the String-of-Beads Shape because examples follow the thesis like beads on a string.)

EXAMPLES

Introduction

Body:

      Example 1

      Example 2

      Example 3

      Example . . .

Conclusion

RELATIONSHIP ORDER

Imagine that the thesis of your essay was this:

THESIS: **City dwellers often dream of living in the country, but those dreams miss the reality by a country mile.**

You would be setting up your paper to discuss two things: dreams about life in the country, and the real life. This kind of *comparison/contrast* built into a thesis gives the writer his or her organizational pattern.

   Here is another example:

THESIS: **The question of whether to rent or to buy your own home is becoming more complex every day.**

The organization pattern for this essay will be to discuss renting and to discuss owning. The only decision you will have to make is whether to say everything you want to say about renting before going on to owning, or whether to talk about a *particular aspect* of the thesis—say, tax relief—and, in the discussion of tax relief, talk about *both* renting and owning, and then go on to *another aspect* of the thesis—say, initial investment—and talk about both renting and owning under that. At any rate, no matter which variation you choose, the basic pattern of organization —*comparison/contrast*—is an organic part of the thesis itself.

COMPARISON/CONTRAST

Introduction

Body (choice of pattern)

	I	Or	II
	Item A		Point 1
	Point 1		Item A
	2		B
	. . .		. . .

	Item B		Point 2
	Point 1		Item A
	2		B
	Item . . .		Point . . .
	Point 1		Item A
	2		B

Conclusion

Another relationship pattern is inherent in this thesis:

THESIS: **Partnership is a legal arrangement something like marriage.**

The organization pattern comes directly out of the thesis: a discussion of something probably unfamiliar to the reader (partnership) by comparing it to something familiar (marriage). This is a form of comparison that carries *one point extended all the way through the essay* with examples or details to show how the comparison is accurate.

ANALOGY

Introduction

Body:

Example 1: _____ is like _____ in this way
Example 2: _____ is like _____ in this way
Example . . .

Conclusion

MIXED FORMS

You have perhaps noticed that a group of essays might appear together in a collection and be introduced as, say, Essays of Definition. Then, when you started reading the essays, you saw that a lot of other ways of writing besides *defining* appeared in the essays—for instance, *describing, comparing, narrating*. Don't let this confuse you. Remember that terms like *comparing, defining, analyzing, classifying,* and the like are actually names of ways in which all of us human beings think. Any of these can be the *general form* of an essay and/or one of the *several specific ways* that the essay is developed within the *single general form.* Just remember that although the general overall *pattern* of your essay may be, say, comparison, you will use several other kinds of thinking to *develop* that essay.

Read the following student essay and notice (a) how the overall shape of the essay is determined by the writer's thesis and (b) how other forms of thinking also appear inside the overall shape or pattern.

OFTEN THE GENERAL FORM OF THE ESSAY IS DEVELOPED BY SEVERAL OTHER KINDS OF THINKING

COMPARISON	CONTRAST
CAUSE AND EFFECT	
DESCRIPTION	ANALYSIS
NARRATIVE	CHRONOLOGY

Freshman to Freshman: Surprises in English

Every time I go to get my hair cut, I ask the hairdresser if there isn't some way he could cut my hair so that I wouldn't have to wash it every-day, blow it dry, curl it, or roll it—and, of course, it would have to look perfect all the time. I would be willing to wash it occasionally and comb it once a day. Although I appear to be joking with the hairdresser, sub-consciously I think that, if he really knew his job, he ought to be able to perform this impossible task.

That's the same attitude I had about freshman composition. I didn't want to put out much effort, but I thought I should get good grades. My prof, after all, was being paid to teach me to write well. And I was paying that salary. Therefore, by the end of the semester I should be able to write well.

Very early in the semester I learned how wrong I was. I had to wash my hair everyday and keep it fixed if I wanted to look nice (oh, sure, some people can jump out of the swimming pool and look like a mil-lion dollars, but they're the exceptions); and I had to work on my writ-ing skills and put forth some effort on my own if I wanted my writing skills to improve.

I also discovered that writing was similar to hair styling in other ways. I never realized that, just as a beautician often looks at a picture of the finished hair style before he begins cutting my hair, I have to know what my finished theme should do before I ever begin writing. Hair has to be properly shaped to hold a certain style; themes, too, must be shaped to achieve their purposes. And, just like certain hair styles work on some people and don't on others, I had to decide how to write my theme to interest and convince the audience of readers.

Before I took freshman English, I had concentrated most of my efforts in writing on making sure that all words were spelled correctly and all commas were placed correctly. I soon discovered that that was like a hairdresser spending five minutes cutting, washing, drying, and styling hair and thirty minutes applying hairspray. When writing, all the correctly spelled words in the world won't help if the message is not carefully planned to be clear to the audience. I started spending much more time coming up with an interesting way to present my ideas and making sure that my audience understands my message.

That brings up another important part of writing. I've spent months sometimes going through magazines to find the exact hair style that would look right on me; I knew where to go to look for ideas. When preparing a theme, I had no idea that there were ways to create a topic and make my message more interesting and more effective. Finding a topic was always the worst part of writing; creating techniques—discovering ways to find a topic—were a welcomed surprise in freshman English.

I also quickly learned that my comp texts weren't much help. It seemed like the authors assumed that we already could write C+ essays and just needed help correcting mechanics so that we could all make A's or B's. Most of my help in freshman English came from the prof, from reading and discussing examples of good and bad essays, and from endless hours of writing and thinking.

I never expected my freshman comp course to have so much writing and thinking. Don't ask me why. Maybe it's because we really never wrote much in high school and I was hoping to make it through college English without writing.

But, now that I think about it, that would be like going to the hairdresser to have my car fixed.

—Karen Davis

This essay is written in the **Break-down** pattern with **Examples.** The writer's thesis is that **there were many surprises for her in freshman English.** The shape of the essay is organically present in this thesis: she gives examples of how she was surprised. These surprises turn out to be:

1 She had to work hard and put forth effort.
2 She learned that writing had to be shaped.
3 She learned there was more than editing to do when she wrote.
4 She learned about creating techniques.
5 She learned that her textbook wasn't much help.
6 She learned she had to do a lot of writing.

Notice, however, that even though this essay has the *Break-down* shaping pattern of examples as its overall form, **the writer does many other things inside the essay besides give examples.** She *narrates, describes, compares,* uses an *analogy,* and does other things, all in the overall *Break-down* pattern of shaping called *Examples.*

> "*Purpose* is the greatest influence on form."
> — Henry Boettinger

Here are the main points for you to remember about patterns of organization:

1 Be aware that a thesis does suggest its own pattern of organization.

2 Realize that although the overall pattern of organization may be defined as one word (classification, definition, etc.), *many* patterns of thinking will appear in the essay. The form of almost all essays is a *mixed form.*

3 Become familiar with and conscious of the basic patterns of organization, but don't make these patterns the reason you write.

Don't worry about memorizing such terms as *comparison, chronology, definition,* etc., because you will probably never have to stop and think that *analogy* produces *relationship order* while *definition* produces *general–specific* order, or the like. We are considering this matter simply to demonstrate how the thesis *does* result in its own appropriate form and to show that these forms can be discussed if need be. Knowing *this* form or *that* form, however, won't help you know how to write unless you really understand the central principle: *your thesis will lead automatically, especially the more you write, to a particular form for your writing.*

Writing in order to fit a pattern is writing backwards. Always begin with a *purpose,* an *audience,* and a *message.* Write because you have something to say to someone, and then be aware *after that* of the variety of methods of organization you might use for that message. Be confident, though, that *if you have a purpose for writing, a particular audience in mind, and a message you really want to send, then an organizing principle will naturally and organically follow.* Your essay will definitely have a shape.

APPLICATION

1 Read these thesis sentences and decide what organizational patterns are organically present in them:

 a The movie *The Godfather* is as popular today as it was when it first came out.
 b There are only three basic types of running shoes.
 c Nancy Lopez's rise in golf is a Cinderella story.
 d The new office building has a very unusual shape.
 e The book *Being Seventy* is extremely well written.
 f *Self-actualization* is a word everybody ought to learn.
 g The story of Jimmy Carter's gaining the presidency is fascinating.
 h People are eating better all over the country; this is causing some significant changes in health, illness, and death.

i The schools in this state are losing students every year.

j *Moving Mountains* tells the reader how to give an effective speech.

k Everything the commentator said on the news points to one fact.

l Stories abound about the danger of microwave ovens.

m Our new senator is a flamboyant person.

n *Poetry* is a hard word to pin down.

o Swimming doesn't use the same muscles that badminton does.

p Subways are picturesque.

2 Here are two lists of thesis sentences. Choose *one* from each list. When you've chosen, begin *at once* to write an essay on each subject.

The point is to notice how each thesis carries with it an organic shape. Therefore, deliberately avoid thinking about shape for the essay; bypass the creating stage too. Instead, move directly into the essay and watch the shape emerge.

You don't need to write two whole essays. Just write enough of each essay to experience how the shape is contained within the thesis.

GROUP 1

1 Red is not a good color to wear on a hot day.

2 Organizing recipes requires some kind of system.

3 Artificial respiration saved the life of a friend of mine.

4 The mountains were breathtaking.

5 You can recognize my neighborhood by its distinct boundaries.

6 My father's (mother's) face is a record of his (her) life.

7 Although my mother and father are both parents, each has a different role.

GROUP 2

1 Red is a better color than blue for decorating a playroom.

2 Recipes for making pie dough are easy to follow.

3 Artificial respiration causes a victim's lungs to continue functioning.

4 The mountains have interesting geological features.

5 My neighborhood has a feeling all its own.

6 There is more to fatherhood (or motherhood) than just producing offspring.

7 Although my mother and father each have very different roles, they both are described by the word *parent*.

WRITING ASSIGNMENT:
THE PROBLEM/SOLUTION ESSAY

All of us have probably experienced problems—perhaps plenty of them too. Certainly they have helped keep life challenging. Some of our time may be spent either being affected by problems or being relieved by solutions. Since dealing with problems and working on solutions can be an important part of our lives, it's no wonder that much of the writing required of us in life has to do with problems and/or solutions. The essay form you are about to practice will appear in your life probably in hundreds of guises—in reports you write, in speeches and talks you give, in letters you send, at meetings you attend. It is one of the most useful and common forms you can have. Fortunately, this form is also fairly simple and seems almost to write itself—provided you are discussing a problem you know something about.

A good problem/solution essay will have these characteristics:

1 The writer will thoroughly discuss *(a)* the problem, *(b)* the solution, or *(c)* both.

Problem/solution writing does not always cover both the problem and the solution with equal thoroughness. Sometimes a writer's purpose is to emphasize the problem so that people will think more about it. Perhaps the writer isn't even sure of the solution. Other times a writer's purpose will be to present the solution to a problem, and the problem itself will be mentioned only briefly. The writer will assume that the problem is evident to and agreed upon by the reader. At still other times the problem and the solution will be given equal space. The form that the problem/solution writing takes—emphasis on problem, emphasis on solution, or emphasis on both—depends on the purpose of the writer.

2 Examples and illustrations will be used in abundance.

The writer cannot expect the reader to understand the problem or to agree with the solution unless they are really *discussed* in the essay. The best way to help the reader see the situation as the writer sees it is to use many examples and illustrations. A problem/solution essay, then, will be filled with phrases like, "For instance . . . ," "An example of what I mean is . . . ," "To illustrate my point. . . . "

3 The writer will choose examples and illustrations that will have meaning for the particular audience to whom she or he is writing.

Just the presence of examples and illustrations won't get the problem and solution across. The examples must mean something to the people who will be reading the essay. They should, then, be about things, people, places familiar to the audience and preferably be examples that have a direct bearing on the readers' lives.

READINGS

The essays that follow have been written by both professional writers and by students. Reading them should be a useful preparation for writing your own problem/solution essay. As you go through the essays, ask yourself these questions:

> Does this essay emphasize the problem, the solution, or both?
> Does the writer make the problem/solution real *to me?* If so, how? If not, why?
> Does the writer use enough examples and illustrations? What kind does she or he use?
> Do I leave the essay convinced that the problem or solution is real or workable?
> What made me feel this way when I finished the essay?

Be ready to discuss the essays and your answers to these questions with your classmates.

How We Can Help Children Learn to Write

Margaret Mead, in this essay which appeared in Redbook *magazine, discusses solutions to the problem of illiteracy.*

Children *can* be taught to read and write, and to do both with some measure of ease and competence. In spite of all the evidence today to the contrary, that is one thing we must keep in mind. Now more than ever before, the ability to understand what others have written and to express oneself clearly are necessary adult skills. They are skills no one is born with and that everyone who is to become literate must learn.

Given a chance, children can learn to use words exactly and vividly to write about the world they are so busy discovering, as well as to express their thoughts and feelings. They can learn how to tell a story, how to describe accurately an event they have watched or taken part in, how to give directions to another person who wants to go somewhere or make something, how to organize an argument and how to share with others their moods of pleased excitement, anger, fright and happiness. This much is within the reach not of just a few especially talented or privileged children but of every child—or it should be. Given a proper chance to learn how to write, children can even learn to enjoy the process of discovering how to communicate more and more meaningfully.

An English philosopher, R. G. Collingwood, once said that you cannot fully know what the poem you are writing is about until you have finished writing it. It is equally true, I think, that you cannot fully know your own thought until you have succeeded in expressing it clearly, either orally or by writing it down. Learning to use words is not only a way of reaching out to others; it is also a way of finding yourself.

But the evidence cannot be dodged. Our children are not becoming competently literate. Great numbers of elementary-school children fail to grasp the basic elements of reading and writing and each year fall further behind. The majority of adolescents are incapable of expressing themselves in good, clear English. And the average adult has little confidence in her own ability to read rapidly and with understanding, to conceptualize what she wants to say and to say readily what she has in mind.

The facts are well known. The question is what we are to do.

First of all, I believe, we must scrap most of the current theories as to why our children are not learning. They are simply poor excuses for our own failures. It is said, for example, that television is so attractive to children that it is keeping them from reading. But watching television — for reasonable periods of time and with some attention paid by parents to the quality of the programs — is at least as useful in learning to read as the same number of hours spent roller skating or playing ball. It is certainly true that many children would benefit by more active play out of doors — but this would not turn them into readers. Just because children learned to read in the past does not mean that they spent all their free time reading or keeping diaries or writing stories. For one child who was a delighted bookworm or a precocious author, there were thousands who read no further than their school lessons required. But it is also true that children today who do learn to read and write do not treat television as their *only* resource.

We must also realize the pernicious effect on almost everyone of our continually rising anxiety about our children's education. Two generations ago the young adult who for some reason had not learned to read and write English could still get a job. Today this is not so; the illiterate person is a social cripple. And as we have raised our standards our ability to teach the necessary skills has diminished.

This is not the paradox it seems. For high standards can be used, not only to increase care and to provide timely warnings about things that may be going wrong, but also to frighten people with the specter of failure. And anxiety of this kind is paralyzing both to parents, who fear for their children's future, and to teachers in school systems where no one suggests workable remedies. In the end, of course, this adult anxiety paralyzes the children most of all, and they cannot learn.

Concern is legitimate in some cases. Parents and teachers must be alert to the needs of handicapped children and the special kinds of help they must have. But what I am speaking of here is the vague, unplaced worry that is extended to all children and that serves only to aggravate the difficulties along the way without providing remedies. In many schools, teachers, uncertain about the effectiveness of their methods, discourage any efforts made by parents — even though we know that the best way for a child to learn basic literacy is in the natural, everyday give-and-take with literate parents who are close to each child's interests and learning habits. Deprived of help, healthy children become handicapped, deprived of the ability to learn through no lack or failure of their own.

The children of illiterate parents need more help, and in the past we used to give it to many of them. And elsewhere in the world today, in new countries and postrevolutionary countries, whole adult populations have become literate almost overnight—because educational planners and teachers and students alike believed in the importance of reading and writing and had no doubt that these skills could be put within everyone's reach.

In our own country, in fact, during World War II, we had a splendid literacy program in the armed forces that was designed, not by educators who had given up on half the children it was their responsibility to teach, but by highly sophisticated people who respected their students as adults interested in adult things, who happened not to have learned to read and write but were perfectly capable of doing so. And they learned. Somehow we have forgotten what we have done and have not observed what others are doing.

Our most immediate task, then, is to change the level of our expectations. Instead of indulging in worry that carries with it the expectation of failure—and our contempt for those who fail—we must be convinced that what other children have done and are doing, all our children can do. We must establish a nationwide expectation that *all* children can and will be taught to be literate. And we must not be deterred by educators' quarrels over the methods of teaching or by shibboleths about such things as the McGuffey Readers or the dangers of permissiveness. Children have learned to read by being beaten—and also by learning their letters from cookies coated with honey. As long as the society—and so the teachers and parents—expect children to be able to learn, they will learn.

It is when that expectation falters, when a society believes that any group of children is incapable of learning—whether they are physically handicapped or the children of mountain people, whether they come from rural or urban slums or are Black or foreign-speaking, whether they are barefooted, or girls, or twitchy and unused to sitting still—then such children will become "social dyslectics," children who suffer from an impairment in the ability to learn to read that is social in origin.

Expectations have to change equally in the minds of educated, anxious parents who have accepted uncritically their children's failure to learn for complex psychiatric reasons. As I began by saying, we must keep firmly in mind that children *can* learn to read and write.

Our second task is to recognize the fact that education is costly as we now define it in a very complex world. And it is costly as it applies not only to beginners but also to all those in search of higher education—indeed, to everyone who wants to learn. There are those who say we should not raise our level of expectations until we are ready to pay for what we will need. Certainly the two go together. But on the whole, Americans are willing to commit themselves only to working hard for and spending money (especially tax money) on activities they accept as necessary and good and likely to succeed.

And in making plans for education and budgets to implement those plans, we must provide not only for children, adolescents and college students, but also for adults who want to advance and for the dropouts — the neglected, the deprived and the damaged — who want to enter the mainstream of living. As Americans we have never believed in penalizing people for their past, and any plan we make and advocate broadly must take into account those who have suffered. Today we have a vast number of parents who have been marred by the experience of their schooling. If we do not realistically give them a chance, we shall endanger the chances of their children, and so the well-being of still another generation.

But what about time? What about *my* children — now? Isn't there something we can begin to do now, immediately, for the children who are already in school and the still smaller ones who will come streaming into schools next spring and next fall? This is a legitimate demand. For every child, childhood happens only once and is always now.

There is, of course, a great deal we can do — parents and teachers and everyone involved in the teaching side of the educational process. We can begin by drawing on what we know worked in the past and adapt it intelligently to the kind of children we hope, at best, to bring up for tomorrow's world.

And we are not without help in the matter. Here and there in the country some children — a few — *are* learning to use their language very well. They are learning to write correctly and much more individually than the best-taught children did in the past. And there are teachers — not only very young teachers, and many more than we know about — who are struggling successfully with the problems of how to teach children the kind of literacy they will need and can take pride in as they are learning it. I have talked with some of these teachers and I have read some of the lively and interesting work that their pupils are producing.

One thing we have to realize is that the ability to read and to comprehend the meaning of written material does not give a child proficiency in writing. It is true that reading and writing are linked tightly together, so that unless a child understands that someone has written the words she is asked to read, and learns to write those words herself, reading remains a kind of mumbo jumbo. The child needs to see the teacher (or the parent as teacher) write the words that the child then reads. And then the child herself must write what she has read.

And she needs to practice writing all the time in order to begin to do it well — and better still as she goes along. We don't object to tennis players' or skaters' or jazz musicians' or ballet dancers' practicing incessantly, or to their knowing the technical names of the tools they use and how exactly to produce their formal, highly stylized actions. Why, then, should we let our old rebellions against admittedly outmoded disciplinary forms dominate us so that we call all practice and memorizing and technical study "dull drill"—and throw it out? Surely children have as much right to gain proficiency in a most basic skill as they do in learning a sport. And certainly they have as great a need to know how the language works and to have an accurate, specific way of talking about what they and others have tried to do in their writing.

In fact, children need to understand the whole wonderful literary process, from the first struggle with an idea, a fantasy or a muddled bunch of "facts" to printing and publication and reading and criticizing and weaving new patterns of ideas out of ones that have become familiar. And it can be done.

What is different now, I believe, and what differentiates the best of modern teaching and learning from the best of the past is that we recognize the fact that learning is a social process in which every participant plays a crucial role. The teacher respects the child, knows where the class is headed and how her students will proceed. But at the same time the teacher, like every child in the class, is a participant in the learning that is taking place for each child and for all the children together.

This is the true beginning, I believe, and it depends on a mutuality of trust and respect between teacher and pupil and among all the pupils. It depends on a belief shared within and outside the school that what the student learns is valuable to herself and her whole society. Learning to write takes time and much effort, but it can be done. And the joy of writing well is that this skill, learned early, stays with you and continues to grow through the whole of your life.

Can Sun Power Pay?

This essay, written by the staff of Newsweek *magazine, illustrates an effort to cover both the problem and the solution related to solar energy. The essay moves back and forth between the problems of using the sun for power and the solution to the energy crisis that the sun might offer.*

Its most vocal advocates are an uneasy alliance of "small-is-beautiful" zealots and profit-minded captains of industry. Much of its technology is uncertain and prohibitively expensive. But solar energy has popular appeal—and an important political supporter. "No cartel controls the sun," Jimmy Carter declared on Sun Day last May. "Its energy will not run out. It will not pollute the air, it will not poison our waters, it's free from stench and smog. The sun's power needs only to be collected, stored and used."

After a shaky start, solar energy and the industry growing up around it may soon be beyond the novelty stage. The new National Energy Act provides tax credits and financial assistance for users of solar energy, and a dozen states now offer their own incentives. Meanwhile, about 200 companies, ranging from tiny mom-and-pop outfits to such industry giants as Westinghouse and Exxon, are developing new technology and products. By some estimates, sales of solar-energy devices could grow from $150 million this year to $1 billion in 1982—and according to optimistic forecasts, to $100 billion by the turn of the century.

Much of solar power's future, however, depends on large-scale government support. Last week, the White House received a 53-page Domestic Policy Review of Solar Energy, compiled by more than 100 officials from 30 agencies, which states a strong case for a "maximum practical" effort by Federal, state and local governments on behalf of solar power. Among the suggestions: establishment of a solar bank to help homeowners finance solar equipment and substantial tax rebates for industries that convert to solar energy. Under the best circumstances, the report predicts that solar energy could supply as much as 20 per cent of America's energy needs by the year 2000.

Still, the solar industry is in for some serious growing pains. Zoning and tax laws work against those who want to invest in solar equipment. Legal pitfalls abound: can a would-be solar user, for example, force a neighbor to cut down a tree that blocks his sun? More important, solar technology is simply not ready to supply abundant cheap power. "Ultimately, economics are going to drive the system," warns William Brown, an energy expert at the Hudson Institute. "If solar is not competitive, you're not going to buy it unless you are Robert Redford—and even he has a backup system."

The need to back solar power with other sources of energy seems to be one of its major flaws. So far, science has found no simple way to store solar energy for use during long periods of sunless weather. As a result, both residential and industrial users of solar energy must have access to stand-by power that would prove expensive. A separate generator requires capital outlays, fuel supplies and maintenance. And utilities would almost certainly have to raise rates dramatically in order to maintain reserve capacity even as they lost regular customers.

To make solar power competitive with other energy sources, researchers are exploring a wide range of techniques and technologies. Some, designed for residential water and space heating, are quite simple—and already widely used. Others, aimed at providing energy for industry or turning sunlight into instant electricity, are in the experimental stage.

The rudimentary forms of solar energy are already fairly common. "Passive" solar design, which relies on architectural tricks to take maximum advantage of the sun's heat, is increasingly popular, especially in the Sun Belt. A well-designed solar building can save 50 per cent or more of the oil, electricity or natural gas that heats it. Solar water heaters are even more widespread. There are now about 80,000 units in use in the U.S. Most consist of a series of roof-mounted, flat-metal collectors, painted black for maximum heat absorption, which transfer heat from the sun's rays to a mixture of water and anti-freeze solution that circulates through them. The fluid is then pumped through a heat exchanger near a basement storage tank. But so far, solar water heaters are competitive only with electric hot-water heaters, which do the job for $10 per million BTU's; oil and gas units supply the same amount of hot water for just $2 to $4.

Several high-technology giants are trying to make solar heating better and cheaper. One of the most promising developments is General Electric's "evacuated-tube" collectors. Unlike the traditional flat-plate collectors, GE's tubes rely on the highly efficient insulation properties of a vacuum to collect the sun's heat. Each tube consists of three cylinders. The outside cylinder, made of clear glass, is fused to a second glass cylinder coated with highly light-absorptive material. Between the two lies the vacuum that allows very little of the collected heat to escape. The third cylinder, at the center of the unit, is made of copper or aluminum, and can be filled with either liquid or air, which is then pumped to a heat exchanger in the basement.

The big advantage of GE's invention is that it can produce higher temperatures than conventional flat-plate collectors. But so far, GE's "glass factory" can manufacture only about 400 evacuated tubes an hour; by contrast, it turns out fluorescent light bulbs, with similar technology, at the rate of 3,600 per minute.

In the longer run, residential use of solar energy may be dwarfed by the market in industry. Solar technology slightly more sophisticated than home systems is particularly useful in producing industrial process heat. An Anheuser-Busch plant in Jacksonville, Fla., for example, is using 4,600 square feet of solar collectors to supply the 150-degree water it needs to pasteurize beer. And ironically, one of the first industries to benefit substantially from solar energy may be the oil business. The Department of Energy is considering the use of big concentrating collectors to produce high-temperature steam for enhanced oil recovery.

But solar production of industrial process heat is still two or three times more expensive than other methods. And solar proponents say the tax codes work against would-be experimenters. The bulk of a solar system's costs are capital expenditures for equipment—which aren't treated as favorably by the tax man as the primary costs of conventional systems, that is, the price of the oil, gas or coal used as fuel.

Solar research is also focusing on how to make the sun produce electricity. One process, "solar thermal electric conversion," would collect sunlight, focus it on a boiler to make steam and thus provide the power that drives a conventional generator. With the help of Federal funds, Southern California Edison Co. plans to start operating the biggest such installation in 1982. Solar One in Barstow, Calif., will use about 2,000 mirrors called heliostats, each with about 400 square feet of reflecting surface. A computer will move the heliostats to track the sun and focus its rays on a boiler atop a 325-foot "power tower." At peak efficiency during the day, the 10-megawatt system will produce enough electrical power for a community of 6,000 to 8,000 people. The next step will be an attempt to build a 100-megawatt system. There's one big problem: with current technology, the plant would require more than 800 acres of mirrors.

To many experts, the most exciting solar prospect of all is "photovoltaics," a process almost magically simple. Sunlight strikes a semiconductor material such as silicon, and as light photons collide with atoms, electrons are jarred loose—instant electricity, without steam, boilers, condensers or moving parts. Photovoltaic cells are already used to power all U.S. space satellites, but they are formidably expensive; photovoltaic power costs ten to fifteen times as much as conventional energy.

The original photovoltaic technology fashioned ingots from molten silicon, then sliced them into wafers one-twenty-fifth of an inch thick. In the process, up to 70 per cent of the costly silicon was simply wasted. But researchers are experimenting with a variety of ways to bring down the costs—and most are convinced they can make photovoltaics competitive by the mid-1980s. Shell Oil Co. has poured $12 million into cells that substitute cheaper cadmium sulfide for silicon and hopes to have a $1 billion-a-year photovoltaic business in fifteen years. At the laboratories of Mobil Tyco in Waltham, Mass., scientists are trying to produce silicon ribbons of just the right thickness, eliminating waste caused by the shaving process. Solarex Corp. of Rockville, Md.—the photovoltaics "giant," with sales of $7 million projected for 1978—thinks it will soon succeed at a similar endeavor using polycrystalline, instead of single-crystal, silicon.

Meanwhile, a self-taught physicist named Stanford Ovshinsky announced last month that he has created a new material that might, after extensive development, produce cheap power. Ovshinsky's tiny firm, Energy Conversion Devices, Inc., has been experimenting with "amorphous" materials—semiconductor substances whose molecules are jumbled together without the regular patterns of materials like silicon. Amorphous materials are much cheaper than other semiconductors, and Ovshinsky says that if he can attract enough investment money, he can make photovoltaics competitive by 1986. But DOE officials caution that much more work remains to be done.

In the end, solar energy's fate depends in large part on what happens to prices of other energy sources. "If oil prices don't go up," says Richard Tabors, a solar expert from MIT, "all solar technologies will suffer." But if nuclear power and coal are rejected by the U.S. on environmental grounds, he adds, solar's prospects would improve dramatically.

The solar industry is well aware of the problems. For one thing, spokesmen for solar energy will have to work to erase the inequities of public policy; as Assistant Energy Secretary Omi Walden points out, "solar energy is competing against fuels that are heavily subsidized or, through regulation, have been held artificially cheap." For another, solar enthusiasts will have to convince corporations and consumers that their largely untried products are worth the investment. To many sun worshipers, the intrusion of giants like General Electric and Exxon seems distasteful. But the best hope for solar energy may well lie in the investment of big business—and in its staying power through the cloudy years ahead.

Solving the Problem at Dettmers' Greenery

CONTEXT
A student, Vicki White, wrote this essay to discuss solving the problems at the place she worked.

AUDIENCE
The owner and staff of Dettmers' Greenery

Last week while making out my annual report, I noticed something that has been happening so gradually that I hadn't noticed it before. Over the past year Dettmers' Greenery has been slowly losing business. Each quarter there has been a slight decline. I have taken out time to consider seriously this problem, and I have isolated two factors which I believe explain the loss. These two factors are our low plant sales and the improperly budgeted time of the staff. I have, therefore, several suggestions which could help the company if they are put into action.

The first and major concern involves raising the plant sales. These sales have dropped unnecessarily almost twenty percent over the past twelve months. I believe that by underselling certain produce, the greenery would profit in the long run. This would involve a series of special sales offered to our customers on a regular basis.

One such sale would be a "White Elephant Sale." In this sale we would separate all of the good plants from the damaged plants and offer the damaged ones at a discount. This would allow the customers to buy the plants they wanted (although slightly damaged) at a very low cost. Dettmers' Greenery, on the other hand, would save money by selling these plants instead of throwing them away, as has been done in the past.

A second sale would be the "Plant of the Month" sale. For this sale, a plant would be picked each month to be Plant of the Month. This plant would then be purchased through our wholesalers in mass quantity, resulting in a low price for us. We, in turn, could sell these plants at a reasonably low rate and still increase our income.

My last suggestion for raising sales would be to offer a ten percent discount to our regular customers. For example, last week while visiting the annex store of Dettmers', I ran into one such customer, Miss Schwarer. She comes in on a weekly basis and usually buys a good supply of merchandise. By offering customers such as Miss Schwarer a "club discount" of ten percent, we could continue to expect to have her business on a regular—and probably an increased—basis. And as these customers' buying increased, the extra business would overbalance any loss resulting from the discount.

Increased plant sales, however, will not solve our problem at Dettmers'. The staff's use of time must also be studied if we are to return to our healthy financial condition. One problem that arises frequently, and one that wastes an enormous amount of time, is the staff's failure to mark the prices of plants before they are put out to be sold. In the past, plants have been put out and then marked, often resulting in no prices being put on at all because the salesperson forgot to return to do the job. I recall many times when a customer has brought a plant to the cash register to buy it; nobody can find a price and nobody there at that time knows the price. The customer is irritated (sometimes to the point of leaving the plant and walking out of the store), and the staff is frustrated. This problem could be solved easily by a firm policy that *no* plant is to be put on the floor until its price has been marked.

Another way the staff time is wasted is in the decoration of pots. It takes more time than is recovered in the price of the flower to cover a pot neatly in colored foil and then tie a ribbon around it or add some other type of decoration. A lot of time could be saved if the company would invest in prefabricated baskets of various styles that the plants could be put directly into without further decoration. Although this would amount to more expense for the company initially, perhaps, the time savings of the staff would, in the long run, outweigh the expense. If hand-decorated pots were still used, they should be offered at an additional cost.

The last suggestion concerning the use of the staff's time most efficiently has to do with the assignment of duties to the employees. Just a short while back, when I was visiting our branch stores in the two new shopping centers in town, I noticed that the staff's schedules were in chaos. Both stores had been rotating daily the duties of spraying, watering, and feeding the plants. And at least once a week there was confusion on whose turn it was to feed the plants or give them their spraying, etc. This confusion results often in one of these jobs not getting done and perhaps another of the jobs being done twice in the same day by two different people, one of whom forgot what the exact assignment was for that day. This problem can be avoided by assigning each employee a specific duty, an allotted time to do it, and posting a chart stating each worker's duty. Then, if the plants are neglected, the problem can be pin-pointed very easily.

I have put much time and effort into both of the problems discussed here. If my proposals for solutions are put into action, the company will profit greatly. Not only will the earnings increase from the plant sales, but much time will also be saved. Since time is money, this improved budgeting of staff time will also improve the profits of Dettmers' Greenery. Very likely the company would realize the benefits of these changes as soon as the very next quarterly report.

The Elderly Are Being Swindled

This essay, done by Pam Evans in her freshman English class, was written to bring attention to a problem which Pam had recently experienced first hand.

CONTEXT
Student chooses persona of a person writing for the school newspaper. This essay, she hoped, would appear on the editorial page.

AUDIENCE
People her own age; readers of the school newspaper.

Do you have any idea what goes on in a house that has rooms rented to elderly men and women? Could you believe that the owners take the old folks' money and do not give them proper care? From experience I know what goes on behind the closed doors of a privately owned nursing home, and I now believe that the elderly in some of these establishments are bilked out of their money and treated shabbily in return.

When men and women pay $550, sometimes more, per month for a room in a private house, you would expect that the owner would provide them with the best of care. This, unfortunately, is not always the case. My own experience has taught me that an owner of a private nursing home pockets most of the $550 for her own use and keeps the residents on a diet suitable for a rabbit instead of a human being.

I visited my grandmother who works in such a home last week, and I was appalled at the conditions under which Goldie, the owner, operates the place. I discovered at meal time that Goldie feeds the women one teaspoon helping of vegetables and a piece of meat which she demands be no larger than three inches. I saw her purchase a large quantity of groceries with the money she received from the residents, but more than half those groceries went into her own personal freezer. Her family may eat well, but her boarders do not even receive a balanced meal. If my grandmother or I tried to give the ladies second helpings at one meal, we were in trouble. Goldie would lay down the rules for us. She would watch our every move at mealtimes. She reminded me of a hawk circling its prey.

Goldie was confronted, in the summer of 1979, by an official who keeps owners of private nursing homes in line. She was told that her nursing home violated several regulations set up by the state: having too many boarders, having too few workers, having no emergency exits, having no fire extinguishers. Usually there is a limit of five boarders to a four-bedroom house, but Goldie keeps seven. My grandmother is the only person to feed and dress the seven of them. It is a back-breaking job, especially when she has to lift a 230-pound elderly person. There are only two doors out of the house, and neither of these is close to the bedrooms. If there were a fire, the residents could not possibly rush to safety. No fire extinguisher is on the premises.

The state official threatened to close Goldie down, but she just changed her telephone number and will not open the door now for anyone she is not expecting. So far her methods have worked. I suppose the state thinks she has mended her ways.

How long does this have to go on? How can Goldie and other owners of this type be stopped? The only solution I can suggest is for the state to tighten its grip on the people who break the rules. We pay taxes so that the state government can make sure that people have proper care when they need it in their old age. When the elderly pay their life savings for a place to live, they expect, and should receive, the best of care.

WRITING YOUR OWN PROBLEM/SOLUTION ESSAY

1. Context   Choose one of the situations below as the basis of your problem/solution essay. At the top of the essay write the context and audience, following the model of the student essays you have just read.

A

You are running for a student government or city government position. All candidates have been asked to appear on a "Meet the Candidates" program sponsored by The Citizens for Voting. For this program you must prepare a position paper in which you discuss some problem you would solve if you won the election. Naturally, the audience will be making up their minds whom to vote for as they listen to the problems discussed and, more importantly, the solutions offered. You sit down to begin this position paper and realize that you aren't going to have any trouble thinking of the problem because so many come to mind. It will just be a matter of choosing the one you think the audience feels is most pressing in their lives. You think of things like parking space, library hours, quality of the food, lack of equal sports facilities for women and men if you're running for student government of-

B

Your boss has just held a special meeting of the employees. The company is going to adopt, you learn at the meeting, participatory management as its way of operating, and one of the first steps in this direction is to ask the employees to discuss the problems in the company and to present solutions to these problems. You now have the chance not only to get off your chest a complaint you've had about how things are done, but you also have an opportunity to make a contribution to the company. Write the paper that discusses these problems and solutions clearly and concisely, and watch changes that you have been longing for come to pass because of you.

fice. If you're running for a city seat, you think of things like taxes, school improvement, city spending, garbage pickup, corruption, etc. Choose the problem for which you have a really terrific solution, and write the essay that will win you the election.

C

You can't believe it! For years you have been plagued with (1) a problem around the house (2) a problem with a friend or relative (3) a personal problem (overweight, smoking). Suddenly you come up with the perfect solution. It's so simple or obvious or workable that you can't imagine why it took you so long to think about it. And it's something you think other people could profit from by hearing of your experience. Write about this problem/solution, inventing an appropriate context and audience for the essay.

D

You have just had an experience that *really* made you aware personally of a problem you'd heard a lot of people talk about but that you had never thought very much about until now. Perhaps it was having inflation really hit you in the face suddenly when you made a certain purchase. Or perhaps you realized how difficult life can be for someone trying to live on a fixed income like social security. You may have experienced the stereotyped attitudes toward people when they get old, the effect on a mother who does not work when all the children are gone, etc. You are motivated to write about this problem, perhaps for a sound-off column in your local newspaper, for your church bulletin, your club newsletter, etc. Prepare the essay you want published so that other people become aware of the problem.

2. Choosing a Problem   One of the pitfalls for students when they start to write a problem/solution essay is the inclination to pick a problem that is too big or too complex. Perhaps the subject will be something so complex that people working on it for the past fifty years haven't made a dent in the problem—like balancing the federal budget. Or maybe the solution the student decides to give is such a cliché that people get bored just hearing it—like "Don't be a litterbug." Here is the beginning of a student's problem/solution essay. Read it and see how long you stay interested:

Our society has forgotten the moral and social problems of the world, dedicating themselves to more technological problems. There has been a loss of faith by the individuals since many of their sociological problems have not been overcome throughout their lives. The self struggle to find a cause for which to live is, in many cases, hard to overcome. For instance, picture New York full of self-fulfilled individuals. It is not like that. The . . . life of the twentieth century is destroying most of the individuals that have the task to survive it.

Can you make any sense out of that at all? What in the world do you suppose this student is talking about? There is nothing here to indicate that the writer has any inside position on this problem or even cares about talking about it. The opening is just words. Empty words.

Here is another opening of a student's problem/solution essay. Notice how it begins with a discussion of conservation. Are you interested in reading on?

Once America was the land of plenty where nature's beauty seemed endless. The remaining greatness of these beauties is now packed into national parks. Every year the delicacy of these parks declines more. Yet, the American people can still save these elegant creations that have survived while they enjoy the beauty of our national parks.

Anything here that shows the writer has any special expertise? Anything that you haven't heard a hundred times? Somehow, when students think "problem," one of these all-time biggies like conservation is what comes to mind—together with war, energy crisis, environment, health care, and world peace. Resist such problems for all you are worth—unless you are truly an expert in the matter or have given a lot of thought to the problem and genuinely believe you have a solution to offer. If you don't know a good solution for the problem from your own first-hand experience, your own reading, or your own experience, don't write about it. Remember that, as always, you write to give your reader value.

"Well," you say, "there's nothing I can write about because I don't know about any problems that I have a solution for." Yes, you do. You tackle all manner of problems in your own life, and most of them you do actually solve. You may have had the problem in your home of a fireplace that costs you hundreds of dollars each year because of the heat you lost when the fire wasn't burning. You solved this by buying an inexpensive $50 fire door that not only keeps out the cold air when there is no fire but actually helps the fire draw better when it is burning. Or maybe you had the problem of how to tell someone goodbye, and you solved it by the unique solution of sending a singing telegram. Perhaps you know personally the problem of having a mentally retarded child in your home, and you can give some suggestions of solutions that alleviate the heartache and frustration that accompany this situation. There are hundreds of things you know about personally that will make very exciting problem/solution papers.

3. Creating Both CUBING and CLASSICAL INVENTION are excellent creating techniques for a problem/solution essay. If you cannot think of a problem to discuss, try *looping* the words "Problem/Solution Essay," and see if an idea doesn't emerge. Then take this idea through CUBING or CLASSICAL INVENTION because both of these will lead you to think about many aspects of the problem and solution. You will thus be able to go beyond a mere surface discussion—one that is not thought through but is merely an emotional or parroted reaction. Remember, too, that a problem/solution essay, to be effective for the most readers, must make its impact from its *evidence, examples, illustrations, facts, logic,* and *wisdom.* CUBING and CLASSICAL INVENTION will let you settle down and really look at what you know and *think* about the problem and its solution.

EXAMPLES AND ILLUSTRATIONS: HOW TO HELP THE READER SEE

1 An example or illustration is a specific instance that helps clarify a more general statement by allowing the reader to *see.* It is one single thing that shows the character of the whole.
2 Be as colorful, descriptive, detailed, and specific as you possibly can when you give examples and illustrations. Appeal to the readers' *senses.* Transport the readers to the spot and *show* what you mean.
3 Use *concrete* words. Abstract terms don't produce pictures in readers' minds. General words, too, can mean different things to different people. Concrete words appearing in examples and illustrations will let the readers know what *you* mean by the general terms. And if you've used any abstract terms, concrete words will help make them clear to the readers.
4 Choose examples and illustrations that will mean something to the particular audience for whom you are writing.
5 Be generous with examples and illustrations. A minimum ratio is one specific example or illustration to one general statement. Often, however, a higher ratio—say, two or three examples or illustrations to one general statement—will be necessary to let your reader *see* exactly what you mean. You will probably never err by having too many examples and illustrations.

---

4. Shaping The purpose of the problem/solution essay will produce its form or shape. If your purpose is to discuss the problem, then the essay can be arranged in an order that will answer these questions:

1 So, what's the problem?
2 Why should the reader care about this problem?
3 Here's a full description of the problem with several examples. Do you understand it?

4 So? What should the reader do or know as a result of reading this essay?

If your purpose in the essay is to discuss the solution to a problem, writing an essay which answers these questions in this order will provide the form of the essay.

1 So, what's the problem?
2 Why should you, the reader, care about this problem?
3 OK, here's the solution described fully with many examples. Do you understand it?
4 Why will this solution work?
5 So? What does the reader do or know as a result of this essay?

ANALYSIS: HOW TO HELP THE READER UNDERSTAND

1 The word *analyze* means to divide anything complex into its simple parts or pieces by separating a whole into its parts. It also means to show the relationship among the single parts of a larger, more complex subject.
2 A good analysis actually shows the reader how to *think* about the subject.
3 To use analysis in your writing, decide what parts you can break the larger subject down into. Then take these parts one at a time. Discuss or describe them, either on an individual basis or as a group, showing how they relate to each other. Finally, put the parts back together in a whole. The reader will then have been able to *understand* what may have otherwise been baffling or confusing.

If your purpose is to discuss both the problem and the solution, writing an essay that answers these questions in this order will give you an excellent shape for the essay.

1 So, what's the problem?
2 Why should you, the reader, care about this problem?
3 Here's a full description of the problem with many examples. Do you understand it?
4 OK, then what is the solution?
5 Here's a full description of the solution with many examples. Do you understand it?
6 So? And finally what?

If your essay answers these questions for the reader, you will have a clear and effective piece of writing.

And, as always, you must make decisions about your audience in this *Shaping Stage*. There is no way to answer the questions above unless you can picture who will be reading them. Decide in advance whom you want to read this essay and plan everything you do in light of those particular people.

5. Final Check   After you have written your essay, read it to someone to see if the listener
- —stays interested
- —understands the problem or finds the solution believable
- —feels that you, as writer, were genuinely concerned
- —feels that you, as writer, sounded like an insider on the subject.

When you are satisfied that the essay really communicates to another person, put it in the final form for turning in. Make it as correct and attractive as you possibly can. Don't let a hurriedly put together final draft steal all the effectiveness of the hard work you did in creating ideas and putting them into a shape that communicated to another person.

RULES FOR A PROBLEM/SOLUTION ESSAY

1 Select a problem and/or solution that you have experienced personally. Be positive that you have something to say on the subject.
2 Decide whether you want to discuss the problem, the solution, or both.
3 Know your audience and intend to give them value in the essay. Make certain that the subject is going to matter to them.
4 Use many examples and illustrations throughout the essay. Be sure these examples and illustrations will strike home to the audience.
5 Assist the readers in understanding any complex issues by breaking them down into their simpler parts.
6 End the essay by letting the readers know what to make of all you have said.

BASIC ESSAY ARRANGEMENTS

As you have seen, the thesis gives the general shape to your essay. Yet you suspect there's more to it than simply putting a thesis sentence at the top of the page and whizzing magically straight on through to the end of the perfectly-shaped essay. And you're right. Although you have a general method of development contained organically in the thesis sentence, you still need to arrange the writing.

The basic arrangement for all essays, regardless of what shape the thesis gives the body of the paper, is *beginning/middle/end.* This sounds so easy, but you would be surprised how many writers don't take advantage of the chance to capitalize on a good opening and a good closing for their writing. The middle of the essay will be handled, by and large, by the organically contained shape in the thesis (though you will learn later how to arrange even *that* organic shape to the very best advantage for you and the reader). It's the beginning and ending that you have to "concoct." They aren't present in the thesis—they have to be thought up, arranged before and after the thesis, fitting the thesis by leading up to it and gently closing off after it, but *they have to come entirely out of your head.* Here are some general principles that will help you learn how to concoct these necessary pieces of the essay.

THE BIG THREE:
BEGINNING
MIDDLE
END

ESSAY INTRODUCTIONS

The opening paragraphs of your paper have got to do three things:

1 **Get your readers' attention.**
2 **Reveal the message you intend to send in the essay.**
3 **Ease the readers into the very *aspect/perspective* of the subject that you want them to think about.**

Get Your Readers' Attention   This requirement of the introduction is easy enough to understand. Since you know that boredom is a writer's worst enemy and that there is enormous competition for your readers' attention, you have to begin with something that will make them listen to you instead of doing the thousand other things they could be doing. In real life, unfortunately, very few people will be paid to read your writing—as your English teacher is—so you must hook the reader immediately. **You probably have about two sentences, or 20 seconds, to do that.** David Pichaske, in *How to Do Well in Freshman English,* in the How-to Essay section, thinks you should look at your essay and ask, "If this were a novel at the drug store, would I pay $2.50 for it?" Of course it's an exaggeration to compare an essay with a novel, yet the point is clear: the reader should be strongly drawn into the writing at once, or else he or she is likely to wander off somewhere else, maybe to the record department or the magazine rack.

YOU'VE GOT 2 SENTENCES OR 20 SECONDS TO HOOK THE READER

2 OR 20

OVERALL ARRANGEMENTS AN ESSAY MIGHT TAKE	
I Shaughnessy's Questions and Answers	
Listener	Writer's Response
1 What's your point?	Thesis statement.
2 I don't quite get your meaning.	Restatement in different words.

3 Prove it to me.	Illustration, evidence, argument.
4 So what?	Conclusion.

II Borden's Formula

Step one: "Ho hum!" This step aims to "build a fire."

Step two: "Why bring that up?" This step builds a bridge between the reader's needs and the writer's thesis.

Step three: "For instance." Specific examples, etc., are cited in this step.

Step four: "So what?" Here appeals for the desired action are given.

III "Prospective Customer's Queries"

1 What are you selling?	Answer puts foot in door by establishing thesis.
2 What does it do?	Permits restatement and elaboration of thesis.
3 Why should I buy one?	Builds bridge to reader's needs and interests.
4 How does it suit my needs?	Illustrations and examples.
5 Can you prove it does what you say?	Conclusive argument.
6 How can I get one?	Indicates the action to be taken.

Reveal the Message You Intend to Send   You can almost always *get* anybody's attention for a second or two, but you won't *keep* it very long if there isn't something in what you say that seems clear and valuable. So after you have gotten your readers' attention, you must let them know what your purpose is, what you are going to write about; you must point them in the direction in which you want them to begin thinking. They can't simply be left in mid-air, entertained with some snazzy opening; they have also got to see your *point* in the essay.

Some students are inclined to write at the end of their introductions, "The purpose of this paper is . . ." or "In this paper I will. . . ." While discussed in the Practical Application section, readers usually enjoy less stiff, mechanical approaches. Don't leave a gap between the attention-getting part of the introduction and the point-telling part; but don't jar your reader with some klunky and obvious "I'm going to tell you about . . ." statement, either. Gaps and jars are hard on readers. Do remember, though, that **the introduction must contain, either explicitly or implicitly, the thesis of the writing.** Readers must know or be able to sense your point and purpose. Be sure that they can.

Ease the Readers Into the Very Aspect/Perspective of Your Subject That You Want Them to Think About   This is a more subtle use of your introduction, but it allows you to use the opening of the paper for double duty. You could spend the entire introduction talking about your subject in general, but it is more efficient to go directly to the angle of your subject that you are going to be discussing. The following two examples will show you the difference. Both deal with the same message—telling the reader that canning one's own pickles gives two advantages: the fun of canning and the pleasure of having good healthy food. Here is the first version, which begins—as you can see—far, far too wide.

Health foods. Do those words make you think of seaweed cookies and saw-dust-tasting soup? More and more people are beginning to learn that health foods can look and even taste just like ordinary food, yet they can really make a difference in length and quality of life. Health foods may be nothing more than ordinary foods grown or prepared in an organic and pure way, such as apples grown with no insecticide or peaches canned without additives. Realizing this, many people are more receptive to health foods and are willing to give them a try. A lot of people are beginning to do home canning. Pickles are a favorite thing to put up.

Well, this introduction finally *does* get to talking about canning pickles, but the reader has to wade through so much information about health food in general and the advantages of home canning in general. The writer is taking far too long to get to the subject and is not directing the reader's attention enough—or soon enough—to the very specific aspect that is the subject of the essay. She has to jump very awkwardly from people being willing to try health foods to home canning. The reader feels stretched and senses too big a gap there.

Let's look at the second version:

Home canning used to be a drag. Women would slave over a hot stove, heaving large pots of boiling water and taking all day to put up perhaps just one batch of beans. Home canning now is a hobby for men and women alike, and a lot of the pleasure comes from the ease of modern canning processes and the satisfaction of knowing that you are putting up clean, healthy food with no additives or preservatives. The new inexpensive equipment available for canners and the new awareness of the dangers of many commercially canned products makes even a job like making pickles a real pleasure. . . .

Here the writer gets immediately into the subject of home canning. While health foods in general is the broader subject in the first version, it takes too long to get from that big area to the smaller one. The second version does a much better job of moving right into the *aspect/perspective* of the essay. **It gives the reader a clear focus on the area to be concentrated on; it lets the reader know right away why the essay was**

written and what the reader ought to be thinking about immediately.
The more a writer can do this for a reader, the better the writing will
be received.

APPLICATION

1 Read the following introductions to essays, some by professional
writers, some by students. Notice how they *(a)* get the readers' attention, *(b)* tell the readers what the thesis of the writing is going to be,
either directly or indirectly, and *(c)* move quickly into the exact angle
of the subject the writer wants the reader to think about. Be able to
discuss the specifics of these introductions with your class.

A

We live in a country with the highest per capita income ever known
to mankind; yet of every 100 of our citizens who reach the age of 65,
95 are flat broke! Of every 100 who reach their "golden years," only 2
are financially independent, 23 must continue to work, and 75 are dependent on friends, relatives, or charity.

They lost the money game. The money game is not like any other
game. You cannot choose whether you'll play. You cannot choose to
sit out a hand or move to another game. For this game—the money
game—is the only game in town.

Since you have no choice but to play, then the only intelligent thing
to do is to learn the rules and play to win! Losing means spending 20
to 30 years of your life in angry frustration in a state of financial
insecurity.

Venita Van Caspel, *The New Money Dynamics* (Reston, Va.: Reston, 1978), p. xiii.

B

"What is my goal in life?" "What am I striving for?" "What is my
purpose?" These are questions which every individual asks himself at
one time or another, sometimes calmly and meditatively, sometimes in
agonizing uncertainty or despair. They are old, old questions which
have been asked and answered in every century of history. Yet they are
also questions which every individual must ask and answer for himself,
in his own way. They are questions which I, as a counselor, hear expressed in many differing ways as men and women in personal distress
try to learn, or understand, or choose, the directions which their lives
are taking.

In one sense there is nothing new which can be said about these
questions. Indeed the opening phrase in the title I have chosen for
this paper is taken from the writings of a man who wrestled with these
questions more than a century ago. Simply to express another personal
opinion about this whole issue of goals and purposes would seem pre-

sumptuous. But as I have worked for many years with troubled and maladjusted individuals I believe that I can discern a pattern, a trend, a commonality, an orderliness, in the tentative answers to these questions which they have found for themselves. And so I would like to share with you my perception of what human beings appear to be striving for, when they are free to choose.

C

Now that they've taught pigeons to play table tennis and chimpanzees to play word games and computers to play chess, it's becoming quite difficult to distinguish humans from the rest of the landscape. So, if you set out to ask what makes people people rather than animals or machines, bye and bye you have to look into the subject of music. It appears that the ability to make music is a characteristic of human nature only.

True, birds sing. But their repertoire is very limited, fixed in each species by its habits and family background. Take the starling. Its familiar song of "cheap, cheap, cheap" bespeaks its natural habitat: city halls and bank buildings. Or listen to the melody of the dove—"plop-plop, plop-plop." That is clearly a genetic message, as the original names of the dove reveal. In English, this bird is called the *pigeon,* a word clearly derived from *pig* (meaning "pig") + *eon* (meaning "eternal"). In Spanish, of course, the bird is called *plopaloma.*

Properly speaking, then, birds cannot really be said to make music even though they can do a number on you.

D

Teaching ten-year-olds how to play tennis is like teaching them how to play the piano. The only reason they are out on the court is because "Mommy" signed them up. And since learning tennis takes many hours of repetition and concentration, this causes a problem. The ten-year-old has an attention span only long enough to allow his or her little mind to come up with something mischievous. After the first ten minutes are up, well, Billy and Jim start to fight, Terry puts gum in Nancy's hair, Nancy starts to push him, and the tennis teacher is ready to call it a day.

The trick to solving this problem is keeping the kids from thinking they are being taught. They could be at home watching television or riding bicycles which would be fun. So, the teacher must make learning to play tennis look like fun. That is the key to effective teaching.

—Rick Jones

E

Last week while making out my annual report, I noticed something that I had not previously realized. Over the past year Dettmers' Greenery has been slowly declining in profits. So I took out time to consider seriously the problem, and I arrived at two factors which I feel are the reason for this decline. These two factors are low plant sales and improperly budgeted time. I do, however, have several suggestions which could help the company to correct these two problems if the suggestions were acted upon right away.

—Vicki White

F

An eight-year-old boy at summer camp lies on his bed crying. He feels empty, and he wants to go home. Ten years later, he stares out the window of his apartment with the same desolate feeling. Now, he realizes that he cannot run home, so he searches for some cure for his homesickness.

Most everyone has experienced this feeling at some point in his or her life. It is perfectly normal. It is the type of problem that must be confronted and then solved. As in all problems, there are ways to solve it.

—Mark Shelton

2 Read these opening paragraphs from student essays and notice how you respond as a reader. Are you interested? Can you tell what the writer is going to write to you about? Does the writer give you an angle on the subject? Be ready to discuss your answers in class.

A

What will happen to you the first few days of college life? Once you have settled into your class and study routine, what will you do with spare time for social pleasures? Where will you search for new friends?

There is no need to look far. Even though most friends made at home and in high school are left behind, there will still be a lot of people around who are looking for friends just like you.

The first place you will probably make a new friend will be. . . .

B

Chocolate-covered cherries have always been my favorite confectionery. They are always a special treat around our house especially around Christmas. This type of candy is, in my opinion, the best candy ever made. Plus it has a special kind of flavor made of ingredients that I do not particularly care for.

Christmas time around our house is something special. . . .

C

"Do you want to go to the show tonight?" "I don't know." "Aw, come on. I don't have anybody to go with." "Well, all right, I guess I will."

Oops, has another "yes" slipped out again when a "no" was intended? Don't worry. It's a common problem many people share. "No" seems to be a word that sticks to the tongue while "yes" blurts right on out and past it. How does a person learn to say "no"?

D

The small-block Chevrolet V8, without a doubt, has become the most popular engine in America. During the past 22 years, Chevrolet has produced more than 32,000,000 small-block V8's. Since its debut in 1955, enthusiasts quickly recognized the small-block's power-to-weight benefits. This started new development and almost total modification of the small-block. To improve performance, the factory increased the small-block's size from the original 265 inches to displacements as large as 400 cubic inches. They also tested and produced many off-road performance parts at unbelievably low prices.

But the development of the small-block by the factory was only the beginning. . . .

E

After waiting for what seemed like an eternity for my twenty-dollar steak, I noticed a wisp of smoke float over my shoulder. I glanced behind me to see if the kitchen was on fire and caught a blast of poisonous smoke in my face. The effects of this attack were immediate; my eyes became red and watery and my once-hungry stomach suddenly felt sick and queasy.

I am sure all of you nonsmokers can empathize with my feelings that night as I was attacked by a foe who was wielding that omnipotent weapon, the cigarette. The physical and mental strain that nonsmokers get from smokers is intolerable. My anticipated pleasant meal that evening was ruined by an inconsiderate smoker. How can we nonsmokers stop this assault on ourselves?

F

Wouldn't it be super if you could just swallow a pill about the size of a vitamin and in a few minutes know everything there is to know about a certain subject? Jump into a machine and have it pop you into the middle of an atom to watch the electrons whirl about you? How about slipping back into the 1800's and seeing Abraham Lincoln and the way he lived his life? Just imagine how much time we wouldn't have to spend in school and how much more interesting learning would be.

Well, getting back to reality, I think learning is a very difficult thing to get a hold of. It seems that a subject has to be interesting to enable it to sink into our head and stay there for a while. . . .

G

There are many things in this world that are known all over the globe. They are all vague ideas of universal concepts; they are vague because they are interpreted differently by each individual. One of these concepts is love. Love is a human emotion that is expressed in varying ways by different people.

3 Choose two of the introductions above (*A* through *G*) that need re-writing, and rewrite them.

ESSAY CONCLUSIONS
The ending of your paper ought to do three things:

1 **Remind the readers of what you have said.**
2 **Give the readers at least one new thing to think about.**
3 **Provide a gentle completing of the paper so that the reader is not left hanging in the air.**

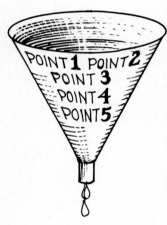

Remind the Readers of What You Have Said Since the whole purpose of your essay was to get a point across to your readers—some information that you wanted them to have, some opinions or experience of yours that you wanted to share—reminding them of what you have said and how this is significant (or what it means) is a very smart thing to do at the end of the writing. You don't want to insult the reader by simply saying over again what you have already said, using the same words, because the reader is likely to think, "How stupid does this writer think I am?" What you *do* want to do, however, is **assist the reader by summing up for him or her your main points, pulling together what you have said into one tight statement or group of statements, and in some way helping the reader know exactly what you said in the paper.** You want to bring back into the reader's attention the gist of what you have taken the whole paper to tell. Remember that readers have very short memory spans, (in fact, research shows that readers remember the linguistic form of a piece of writing about 20 seconds), and your ending must, in a very brief space, help the readers reconstruct what you said. Yet, you need only a few sentences because you have already explained it fully for the reader in the body of the essay. All you need at this point is to pull it together, say it one more time for the reader's benefit, and bring the writing to a close.

Give the Reader at Least One New Thing to Think About How can this be sound advice? Isn't the writer supposed to work hard to keep a reader's mind on the message being written? Why should the reader be told something *new* to think about at the end of the essay? Well, for this reason: **the something new will be some spin-off from the thesis of the essay, some sharp, *extra* point you can make about the thesis that you didn't make in the paper, some new way of saying something you have already said that will *cause the reader to continue to think* about your writing after the reading is over.** You want to make a difference to your reader, not have an essay that can be forgotten the minute the reading is finished. You want the reader to be affected by the writing, stimulated by it, intrigued by it, aggravated by it, entertained by it, etc., to the extent that the writing will have a ripple effect. Telling one new thing in the conclusion can be the pebble you drop into the well of his/her consciousness to produce those ripples.

Provide a Gentle Completing of the Paper So That the Reader Is Not Left Hanging in the Air   Be sure your reader knows when you are finished. Although we all like to be left hanging for a short period of time (during a murder mystery, a western, or a ferris wheel ride), we don't like to hang indefinitely. Your reader is willing to move with you through the essay while you prove your point or develop your message, but then she or he wants to be let down back to earth easily and told, "This is the end."

Concluding your paper merely carries out the principle of closure which is absolutely central to human beings: you have opened a discussion and brought the reader into this discussion with you; **not closing the discussion** *deliberately* **and** *clearly* **would leave your reader feeling unfinished, tricked, and waiting.** So, let your conclusion bring to a gentle and clear ending the exchange you began when you sat down to write.

In Closing* . . .   The important thing to remember for both the introduction and the conclusion is that they are not just there as window dressing. Having a clear opening and a clear closing will not make a bad essay good; in fact, they will only make a bad essay look even more mechanical and fake! Introductions and conclusions, however, can actually assist you in getting the message to your reader. They can be a valuable part of your strategy, not mere parts that are "supposed" to be there for custom or fashion.

* Q.: Does *this* paragraph satisfy any of the three criteria of a good conclusion?

HOW TO END A NUMBER

One trouble with a lot of books about how to play the piano is that they never tell you how to *stop* playing the piano. That is, you don't find out how to end a number until it is too late and you are removed bodily from the piano bench and wrapped in cool, wet sheets. So this book will make amends for the rest of the library.

When it comes to hymns, there is no difficulty about ending. It is *Amen*—two long chords or three.

But in the case of standard numbers, there is only an indication of how to treat a goodbye. And that hint is to be found in the *number of beats* in the final two bars.

In waltzes, usually, there are four beats to finish with. And they are played with separate, single-note attacks of the chord tones. While the final chord is sounded and dies away (your foot is on the sustaining pedal), you play the individual notes of the chord in a down-the-keyboard arpeggio—hitting the root, the 5th, the 3rd and the root again—to account for those final four beats. As a variation, you can use root, 3rd, 5th and root.

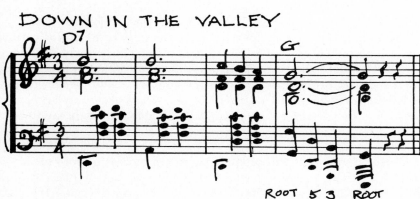

In the case of 4/4 time, the final two bars usually provide seven beats. So, the first four (the next-to-last bar) gets a skeleton bass-&-chord treatment. And the last bar, with its three beats, gets three attacks—the root, then the 5th and finally the root again—dropping down the keyboard.

182   *Stage Two/Shaping*

GOOD NIGHT READERS

APPLICATION

1 Read these conclusions from student essays. Decide if each conclusion meets the three requirements for a good ending:

does the ending remind the readers of what has been said?

does the ending give the readers one new thing to think about?

does the ending provide a gentle completing of the paper so that the readers are not left hanging in the air?

A

To sum up, here are the steps you should follow if you are interested in installing solar heating in your home. First, see your banker and see what kind of loan you can get. Next, talk to your local power company; some companies help citizens install the system. Some even put in the system free of charge so long as the owner lets them collect data from it. If your power company will not help you with your system, then see if you can find a nearby installer of solar equipment, or do it yourself. Design a system and its installation around your loan. Get your loan for as long a period as possible; the longer the loan the more likely it is that a solar system will pay for itself. And, finally, start installing the system knowing that you are one of a growing number of people who are tired of paying high utility bills and tired of worrying if they are going to be warm this winter and who have turned to the sun for their energy needs.

B

Campus life is not, then, an individual effort. It is learning, studying, and making conversation and friends. Look around, smile, and be friendly, because friends are one of the greatest assets a college student has.

C

Time management includes more than just studying and having fun. Good time management should tell you when to get up, when to go to class, what to do in between classes, and everything else almost. Good time management is the efficient use of the time you have. Therefore, good time management is very important to college students, especially freshmen.

D

With the use of these new parts and the parts perfected in the past, it is now possible to reach over 2 horsepower per cubic inch in the small-block. Each year the power-to-weight ratio has increased, but can this go on forever? Can the Chevy small-block engine continue to improve and stay the favorite of most Americans for the years to come? Even if it can't, the Chevy small-block has already achieved more success than any other American-made engine, and it will not soon be surpassed.

EARLY SHAPING: THE TRIAL DRAFT

HOW TO WRITE THE TRIAL DRAFT

1 Remind yourself why you are writing the essay.
2 Get started on the draft itself.
3 Write every idea you can think of to show your reader what you mean in your thesis statement.
4 Wrap up the essay.
5 Put the Trial Draft aside to cool.

You are now ready to do the first draft of your paper. You are clear who your audience is; you know why you are writing. You have decided on a *particular* thing you want to tell your readers. You can see, in general, the form your essay is likely to take, coming organically from your thesis. And you have an idea of the arrangement an essay has to take— beginning/middle/end. It is now time to see if the idea is going to fly. To check this out, you do a dry run of the paper, your **trial draft.**

It is really important that you accept that this *is* a trial draft. *Trial* means to test out to see what the results will be, and that is exactly what you will be doing in this first draft of the paper. **You are taking your idea and actually putting it into essay form to see if the idea is (***a***) what you *really* want to say and (***b***) something you can develop adequately.**

There is *no* way for you to know this until you do it. That is why it is crucial for you to be willing to let this first trial draft be whatever it turns

"How do I know what I think until I see what I say?"
— E. M. Forster

out to be. You may discover that you have to start over completely because you really don't know as much as you thought you did about your subject. You may find out that when you've stated your thesis you can't think of a single other thing to say. You may feel that you are sounding absolutely stupid. You may be certain by the second or third paragraph that no person in the universe would be interested in what you have to say. All of these feelings are legitimate. In fact, you will be lucky when you feel them—at least you won't be living in some blissful dream that's completely divorced from reality. Yet, you can handle the feelings, overcome them, merely by being willing to let your trial draft be just that—a *trial* effort. That way you'll at least be able to put some words on the paper. And, as an old French philosopher used to say, until you are willing to put black on white, you won't have anything to change, refine, improve, or fix. So just plow ahead and write the essay. Whatever you produce will bring you closer to that really fine essay you want eventually.

There is no question but that this trial draft can be rough, uneven, imperfect (unless you are writing that day under the luckiest stars in the heavens). In the first place, most of us have to do some writing to learn what we think; in the second place, most of us need to write some more to see how we want to say what we think. Writing is an act of discovery, whatever stage you are doing, and the trial draft is a perfect illustration of the back-and-forth motion that occurs between *creating*, *shaping*, and *completing*, the three stages of the writing process. Even though you may think you have in mind almost everything you are going to say before you begin the trial draft, you will often find that actually doing the draft itself will lead you to new and even better ideas on your subject.

There are some distinct differences, however, between writing this draft and *creating:*

1 **You are sticking to one subject** rather than exploring ideas on any and all subjects that might come into your consciousness;
2 **You have a definite audience in mind** rather than just yourself;
3 **You are now writing to** *communicate* **something you really want to say.**

You have a reason for writing and a goal you want to achieve. Everything you put in the trial draft is focused on that reason and that goal. Thus, though there is *creating* activity that occurs right in the middle of the *shaping* process, it is a *directed* activity rather than a strictly exploratory one.

When you think you have given the reader enough information so that he or she can understand exactly what you have been saying, it's time to bring the writing to a close. It would be easy if you could do what the writers suggest about bringing a hymn to a close—just write Amen, and let it go at that. Or THE END, and let the reader's feelings fall where they may. But you saw (in the section of the text on conclusions, that the reader needs an ending in order to feel finished about the writing. And you know that you as the writer can actually use the ending of the paper to tie up your message for the reader, to refresh his or her

Trial:
Act or process of testing, trying, or putting to the proof by actual or simulated use or experience.

Draft:
Preliminary version of a document.

Rough:
Having an uneven surface, full of bumps, ridges, or other irregularities; coarse, shaggy, uneven in texture; lacking polish or finesse; not perfected.

memory on the main things you have said, and to spark the reader to keep thinking about what you have said. Yet you may be so tired by the time you get to the conclusion part of the essay that you don't believe you could think an original thought if you had to.

The main thing to remember in this trial draft stage is to put *something* **down for a conclusion** — if for no other reason than to remind you to do a better one later. Maybe just summarize what you have said. Maybe come out and point-blank tell the reader what you want him or her to do with this message you have written (you can always rewrite later and make it more subtle then). Be sure that something *is there* as a conclusion.

When the rough conclusion is written, you have something you didn't have a few minutes ago — a completed trial draft. You will probably feel wonderful, and you're certainly entitled to. Whatever the faults of this draft, you have at least tested your idea and done a preliminary version of your writing. You are well on your way. Congratulations!

With the conclusion down on paper, you have finished the trial rough draft. Sure, it looks rough. And it definitely is a trial run. But you do have a complete paper, something you can work on later, and that is *exactly* what you set out to achieve. Put the paper aside with a sigh of contentment — or at least of relief. Leave it for several hours or more. Set it on the windowsill to cool. Recognize your accomplishment: you actually have got a complete draft of your paper. You can feel good about that!

If you are working on a very tight schedule and don't have time to let the paper cool for a few hours, at least do this: find a friend and read the paper out loud to him or her. Ask what message the person "hears" in the paper. Watch your listener's face and see if he or she looks confused as you read the paper. Listen to yourself and notice if you stumble anywhere as you read it *(research shows that wherever you stumble there is usually something that can stand to be changed in the writing)*. Ask your listener if the paper was boring. In general, get another person's response to what you have written.

If you do have time to let the paper sit for a while, go about your daily rounds. Study for other subjects, attend classes, take a walk, eat some food. Do what you normally do, and **let some psychic distance come between you and what you have written.** This psychic distance is exactly what you need to be able to look at the essay with new eyes and a clear head when you return to it. If you have been able to put this psychic distance between you and the essay, you will see — even before reading the paper to someone else — a number of places you want to rewrite or gaps you want to fill in. Then go over the trial draft, making notes to yourself as you read. Between your own sharp and rested eye and a listener's response, you will be in fantastic condition to move to the next stage in the writing process. You will be ready for LATE SHAPING: REWRITING.

HOW TO WRITE THE TRIAL DRAFT

1 Remind Yourself of "Why," "What," and "to Whom"   Begin your trial draft by putting three things at the top of the first page: **your purpose for writing, a short description of your audience,** and **your thesis.** These won't appear on the final paper itself, of course, but for now they will remind you of the *reason you are writing, the person or persons to whom you are writing,* and *the message you intend to deliver.* They will set your mind in the right channel as you begin.

2 Get Started on the Draft Itself   Actually start putting words on the page. Don't get caught in the cycle of writing and crossing out. And don't think of the hundred other things you could be doing—cleaning out your bureau drawers, washing the top of the refrigerator, calling your friend you haven't seen in four years. Handle this draft the way you handle swimming in cold water—just jump in! Start writing even if what you are putting down seems so obviously stupid that you are embarrassed to see it on the page. **Put it down.**

You already know that an essay always opens with some kind of introduction, so start there. Think of *anything* that can serve as an introduction. Tell a story; give a quote; ask some questions—anything that leads into what you want to discuss with the reader. Aim, if you can, for something interesting and catchy (since an introduction must finally be both). If you produce a workable introduction this time around, fine. If not, don't let that stop you. Keep moving; keep writing. **The point is to start the trial draft, not to get stuck in one part of it.** If all else fails, just write *Introduction* across the page and go on.

3 Develop Your Thesis   The body of your paper is the main part of your trial draft. Here you *develop* your thesis by making all the points you can think of to explain what you mean. *Develop* actually comes from Old French words that meant "to unwrap." And this is what you have to do in the body of your essay—unwrap for your reader the message you are sending. Your reader has very likely *not* been thinking about your thesis and certainly hasn't done the *creating* activities you have done. And the reader probably has a different background and set of experiences from yours, too. **So write plenty. Make all the points you can think of to *convince* or *inform* or *explain*.** And when you suppose you have given enough information for your message to be very clear, add about 10 percent. You really cannot underestimate how much development—unwrapping—your readers are going to need. This isn't because they aren't smart; it's just one of the limitations of written communication as opposed to spoken communication. Remember that *your reader can ask you nothing;* it's up to you to *explain, illustrate,* or *show* what your message is.

4 Don't Get Bogged Down!   Don't worry at this point whether *this* example should come before *that* one. Don't worry if you can't spell some of the words, or if you can't recall a specific thing you are trying to think of. *You have to keep moving on.* You can worry about all the rest later—you can take out, put in, fix up, skin down. Right now, however, you have to get the material onto the paper. Until you do, there simply isn't anything to revise.

LATE SHAPING: REWRITING

HOW TO REWRITE

1 Stick to the thesis. (Make your promise.)
2 Develop the thesis. (Deliver what you promise.)

What do you do after you have written your trial draft? By the very act of writing the essay in order to send a message to someone else, you have tacitly made an agreement with your readers. The agreement goes like this:

If you will read my essay, I promise to tell you this particular message so clearly and so thoroughly that you will know exactly what I mean.

The readers will then indicate whether they choose to join in the agreement with you or not—by continuing to read or by stopping. If they keep reading, or even if you just want them to, you are obliged to *deliver what you promised* and to *keep your agreement.* You may notice that most of the responsibility for this agreement falls on *your* side. That's because it is the *writer's* job to get the message across, and it is the *writer* who is asking others to trust that if they take their valuable time to read what's been written, they will get some kind of benefit from it. The responsibility is *yours,* then, because *you* started the whole arrangement, and because *you* get results when you keep your promise. Although it will never be so explicitly expressed, the agreement is something like this:

Promise:
A declaration that one will do or not do something; to afford a basis for expectation.

Deliver:
To take to the intended recipient; to perform as desired or promised; to transfer to another.

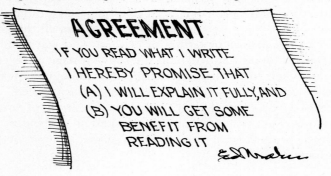

188 *Stage Two/Shaping*

Once you make that kind of serious agreement with your reader and intend to honor it, you can see the value in checking your trial draft to see whether you have actually delivered what you said you would.

1 STICK TO YOUR THESIS: MAKE CLEAR WHAT YOU ARE PROMISING

One of the first things to check is whether you veered off your subject when you wrote the trial draft. If you tell the readers in so many words, "You can count on me; I'm going to tell you this particular thing," and you get started on that but then think of something else and jump off in another direction, you are failing to keep your agreement; and the reader has every reason to just stop reading then and there. **You can't set up reader expectations and then ignore them.** Readers expect you to say exactly what you said you would say, period. They look for a discussion that stays on the subject throughout the essay; otherwise, they tend to feel frustrated, teased, or set up. They *don't* like changes, and they *do* like order. They don't want to be told to expect one thing and then have the writer surprise them with something else.

Campfire Dance   You can almost imagine the thesis working like a cheerful campfire, a bright and inviting spot where people can gather and feel cozy and quietly sociable. It's a natural place for tall tales, yarns, ghost stories. Everybody gets nicely settled, and one person begins a story. Then, a couple of sentences into a story about a shipwreck, he suddenly jumps into a story about graverobbers. Without finishing more than a sentence or two, suddenly he's telling about a magic beetle. In a

few more sentences he's begun describing a cold-blooded murder and then starts a new tale about a broken-hearted lover. It's as though he's jumping, hopping, and whirling all around the topic rather than really delivering on any *one* thing. And the folks who have settled down to hear a good story are certainly going to be put off by this disjointed drifting, shuffling, pouncing from one thing to another. We call this the *Campfire Dance*. The writer is bounding all around the campfire (the special subject for his essay) while the readers are forced to change position constantly in order to try to follow what's going on.

What causes a paper to be like this campfire dance? Sometimes the writer comes to the topic without any clear idea what to say—so he or she circles round and round the topic saying anything and everything that pops into mind. That can happen, and often does, when the writer has a *topic* but no clear *thesis*. A disjointed paper can also happen when the writer has *too many aspects* of the topic to cover in a single essay. Eager to cover them all, the writer shifts from position to position, and the reader is dragged along behind. When that happens, the problem usually is that *the writer has not narrowed the thesis enough*.

Here is an example of a student paper that does the Campfire Dance. We've made notes in the margin to help you see how the author jumps from aspect to aspect of the general topic.

FAMILY CLOSENESS

Title says that general subject is family closeness.

Can you find a main statement that the essay will discuss, consider, prove, etc.?

Special occasions, Christmas, relatives, small families, dinner, presents.

Special occasions seem to bring families together. There is usually a party consisting of the whole family during Christmas. Relatives from far away always come together to eat and enjoy each other's company. I have a relatively small family; my father has only one brother and my mother has none. Small families seem to be closer knit. During Christmas, nobody at the dinner table is shy to talk to one another because everybody is so closely related. It is a wonderful time of year; presents are passed about. Imagine yourself as a little kid and think about how excited you were when you opened the beautiful presents.

Parents' work, vacations, trips.

My father is a hard worker. He owns a restaurant, and my mother is a housewife. They are usually very busy, and it is a shame that they do not have time to enjoy themselves more. Another time that we are all together is the two weeks in June when my father takes off for a vacation. We usually go to a different part of the United States.

Trip to New York, grandfather, toy stores, streets, ice cream, June.

My first time to New York was when I was a child of 6. Things seemed so big. That was my first impression of New York. I can remember the time when my grandfather took me shopping at toy stores. We walked on endless streets and we went into all the shops. To close off the day, we would go to a drugstore and have ice cream. I always got chocolate and my grandpa got strawberry. In the month of June in New York, things are bright and warm.

I can still picture my grandparents' apartment. It consisted of four rooms, a kitchen, restroom, living room, and bedroom. It was an old beatup place. Walls were torn, and on one of the walls were two pictures, one of my grandmother and one of my grandfather. My grandfather is an outgoing person. He was the one who took my brother and me to see the streets of New York.

Grandparents' apartment, grandfather's character.

Last year was the last time I went to New York. This time the city gave me a drab feeling. It was cold and there was snow at least two feet high. New York did not feel the same as the time before.

Most recent trip to New York.

The first thing you can notice about this essay is that the writer had no clear message that he was sending. **Nowhere in the first paragraph or so of the essay can you find a statement/idea/subject that the writer is going to consider, discuss, prove, or maintain.** This, then, is the writer's first serious mistake. It leads directly, of course, to his doing the camp-fire dance. He takes the subject "family closeness" and then mentally hops from one thing to another.

Paragraph 1: He begins by talking about special occasions that bring families together. Then he gives some specific information about his family. Then he refers to Christmas and presents, with a strange reference to the reader that seems completely off the subject ("Imagine yourself as a little kid and think. . . .").

Paragraph 2: He talks about his father and mother, the work they do, and mentions that they go on vacations and take trips. But he doesn't relate this to family closeness.

Paragraph 3: Evidently when he mentioned vacations the writer next thought of a time when he went to New York—so, off we all go to New York. The Campfire Dance.

Paragraph 4: You can almost see the free association that is going on in the writer's mind. He thought of going to New York, then he thought

It is an ancient Mariner,
And he stoppeth one of
three.
"By thy long gray beard
and glittering eye,
Now wherefore stopp'st
thou me?

"The Bridegroom's doors
are opened wide,
And I am next of kin,
The guests are met, the
feast is set:
May'st hear the merry
din."

He holds him with his
skinny hand;
"There was a ship,"
quoth he.
"Hold off! unhand me,
gray-beard loon!"
Eftsoons his hand dropt
he.

He holds him with his
glittering eye—
The Wedding-Guest
stood still,
And listens like a three
years' child.
The Mariner hath his
will.

The Wedding-Guest sat
on a stone:
He cannot choose but
hear;
And thus spake on that
ancient man,
The bright-eyed Mariner.

—Samuel Taylor
Coleridge,
*The Rime of the
Ancient Mariner*

of his grandparents' apartment. Free association is a valuable creating device, and it's even fun just to play with when you are doing private writing for yourself only. But for *readers* it doesn't work very satisfactorily because readers expect *messages* to be delivered and are, therefore, mostly unsatisfied to follow anything that just pops into the writer's mind.

Paragraph 5: Finally, the writer tells us about one more time when he went to New York, and there is no connection with the subject of family closeness. We hear of the trip, and that's it.

Possibly this student was beginning to get in touch with the special closeness he felt toward his grandfather. Maybe the contrast in the moods of New York in June and in winter had something to do with his grandfather. There's just no way for the reader to tell. Most likely this student skipped EARLY SHAPING (A): AUDIENCE AND THESIS and thus stopped short of finding exactly what he wanted to discuss in this paper or how he meant to interest the reader. And that's enough to see how a paper looks and feels when it fails to stick to the subject and fails to develop one aspect of that subject.

Master Storyteller   The opposite of the Campfire Dance is the Master Storyteller, the one who settles down beside the fire with everyone else, and without stirring from that spot spins out a story so skillfully, so well developed, so tightly crafted that the listeners know exactly what it is about and are made to hang on every word and every detail.

Of course, everyone knows that the art of the master storyteller and the art of the essay writer are distinctly different. Yet in these two ways— *sticking to the subject* and *developing the subject*—they are similar enough to be profitably compared. Few people enjoy a story that hops and whirls from one point to another without any rhyme or reason, and fewer still enjoy a story that deals superficially with a dozen aspects of the same topic. **What audiences want, in a story or an essay, is to have the subject *clearly set down* and to have it *stuck to* and *developed* throughout.**

Here's a student paper that does clearly set down the subject and does indeed stick to it all the way through the paper and does indeed develop that point and that point only. You may remember having read the first two paragraphs earlier, in the section of our book that covers introductions. If you do, you'll probably be interested to see how the rest of the essay turned out.

AS THE SOAP TURNS

Soft, intriguing music plays in the background. Martha, a pretty brunette, walks into the living room. Her husband, Paul, is sitting anxiously on the couch. "Martha, where have you been?"; then, taking a closer look, he adds, "You haven't been down at Ted's Nightclub again, have you?" She remains silent for a moment and then speaks defensively, "What difference does it make to you? You spend every night at the clinic! What do you expect me to do, stay home and watch T.V. by myself?" And so another dramatic episode begins.

Dramatic beginning, to get readers' attention.

Transition to essay and main point.

Each weekday, many stories similar to this one are broadcast on T.V. Soap operas are viewed by thousands of people across the country. Now soap operas are also shown at night. Men are also enjoying what used to be considered shows for women. They have become an American pastime. Why do people watch soap operas? Why have they become so popular?

Generalization from the specific example.

Questions: an indirect way of putting the thesis.

Many people watch soap operas because they can identify with the characters. They can relate their own problems to those of the characters in the show. Lana, on *One Life to Live*, is contemplating whether to have an abortion or to have Brad's child. Her situation often occurs in the lives of real women. Their decision, as well as Lana's, will affect them for the rest of their lives. While watching the show, these women can see how Lana reacts to her problem and possibly make their decision according to hers.

First reason: people identify with the characters

Conclusion ties example back to main point: that watchers identify with characters

Divorce is another common situation in soap operas. Recently on *All My Children* Frank and Nancy got a divorce. Before they went to court, both of them wondered if divorce was what they really wanted. Men and women can see themselves in Frank and Nancy. The frustrations of indecision, the agonies encountered while carrying out a decision and the enjoyments of later realizing that the right decision was made are felt by the viewer in his or her own personal experiences. Seeing the same thing happening to someone else is comforting to the viewer.

Second example: divorce.

Tying this example to the point.

Tying example to point again.

Soap operas also provide a dream world in which an individual can fantasize. You can imagine what you might do if the same situation confronted you. If you were pregnant, or getting a divorce, or experiencing any one of the number of things that happen to the characters, would you make the same decision they did? Soap operas allow you to forget your own worries and momentarily focus on something else. Thinking about the character's problem creates a distraction from your own. This distraction sometimes makes your problems easier to take in stride.

Third point: dream world fantasy.

Tying example to point.

Tying example to point.

Soap operas are also beneficial in helping viewers see that their own life isn't as bad as it may seem. After watching a soap opera, you might find that the character's life is more complicated than your own. Almost any soap opera character's life could be considered complicated when compared to real life. For example, on *All My Children*, Mrs. Tyler, a wealthy doctor's wife, is an alcoholic. Her husband filed for divorce. She has blackmailed him by getting her chauffeur to take some pictures

Fourth point: related to paragraph above, but slightly different.

Specific example.

Tying example to point.

Return to examples used in introduction.

Again tying it to point.

Conclusion finishes essay, gives final reason why soap operas are popular.

and to record a telephone conversation. She has been sentenced to seven days in jail for driving without a license, her daughter is in a mental hospital, and her grandson has just disgraced the family by marrying a prostitute. Realizing that your life is not worse than theirs can encourage you. You have living evidence that things are much worse on the other side of the street.

Soap operas will remain part of American life. They are unending stories that are enjoyed by men and women alike. Martha and Paul may have reconciled their differences for today, but what will happen tomorrow? Will another argument arise? Why does Martha like to go to Ted's Nightclub? Does Paul really have to work nights at the clinic? The questions about the soap opera characters' lives never end. This is also true for people who watch the programs. Their lives are filled with questions needing to be answered.

Somehow it seems reassuring to think that all these questions and more might be answered in tomorrow's episode.

—Julie Meyer

Julie's purpose in writing the essay is stated at the end of the second paragraph: she is going to concentrate on telling the reader why people watch soap operas, why soap operas are so popular. She then gives three reasons that account for their popularity. Each reason is stated clearly and followed by enough explanation for the reader to be able to "see" what Julie means by the statement (paragraphs 3, 4, and 5). Then she closes the essay by giving the reader a final clue why soap operas are so popular. Nowhere does she get off on another topic. She clearly knew where she was going, and that's where she went. *Readers always appreciate this kind of clarity. In fact, they don't just appreciate it: they demand it.* If you are going to take up a reader's valuable time, you had better have something you want to say and then stick to getting it said. If you don't, you very likely have lost one more reader.

APPLICATION

Read the following student themes. In each, spot the thesis—the statement/position/subject to be discussed. Then decide whether the writer stays on this subject or does a Campfire Dance. If you spot a Campfire Dance, mark the places in the essay where the writer jumps from one aspect of the subject to another.

GOING TO COLLEGE

Going to college was something I dreaded in my younger years and that I looked forward to in my senior year in high school. I would ask my friends in college what it was like to be there. Elaine said, "Oh, you have a lot of free time, but you have to study a lot for tests. You can attend lectures if you want to and the professor won't get mad if you walk in late." I asked Mike, a graduate from my future college. "Don't worry, you don't have to study that hard. I know that you're just going to have so much fun!" I couldn't ask my dad since he graduated too long ago to be of any help. My high school counselor said that I would probably get a grade letter lower in college than in high school. Thanks a lot.

I had seen the campus life portrayed in movies and on television. The interpretation of the situation in college was this: you are always walking to and from class, you skip lectures, you are involved in civic activities, and you find yourself running amuck with your friends on the campus and in town. The campus always looks like a sunny afternoon in the second week of the first semester—with a football game going on.

Then, I found out things that I wasn't prepared for. My parents didn't come with me, so it was up to me to take care of necessary business the first day. I found myself studying really hard just to keep up with all of my subjects. I had to stay up late just like everybody else; which was something I wasn't used to. I had problems with Dr. Purdy, my math professor, and I didn't know where to run for help. I finally had the Dean of Engineering change my schedule for me. I was learning fast. You must make many of your own decisions in college.

There were a lot of things I took for granted that I had to take care of now that my parents weren't around. I wished that I had planned more for college. Maybe I should have asked more people and better questions about college. I learned that part of a college education is learning to make adult decisions. I just wished that I had taken care of my problems sooner before they became serious. College is fun, but it requires hard work to stay on top.

DISCO AND COUNTRY MUSIC

In this section of the country, two types of music are very popular: disco/rock and country/western. Disco is better for dancing; country is better for laid-back listening. Some students love disco, and some love country. Very rarely will you find someone who likes both.

Disco is fun and entertaining. It has a fast beat that makes you want to get on your feet and dance. There are many types of disco dances. One of the most popular is touch-disco. Touch-disco means that partners are actually in contact with each other throughout the entire dance. It consists of several loops, turns, and spins while holding hands. Some well-known types of these dances are the Hustle, Pretzel, and Latin-Hustle. Another type of disco dancing is freestyle. Freestyle is individual dancing with little or no partner contact. The Freak is a popular freestyle dance.

Country music can also be entertaining or at least funny. Most of the lyrics have to do with a man, his girlfriend, wife, lover, or mistress. (Sometimes his best dog or pick-up truck.) Almost all country music is very chauvinistic. Country is more to be listened to (if you like $99^{44}/_{100}$ percent pure love) than danced to. However, if you do want to dance to country, you will be dancing what is known as kikker. (I think this has something to do with the foreign matter found on most dancers' boots.) There are two popular kikker dances. One is known as the "Country Star" where everyone simply turns. The other is known as the "Cotton-eyed Joe." Now this is an interesting dance. People form lines and walk in a two-step circle. At the end of every 16 steps, a back step is taken, and everyone yells. It is quite amusing.

Dancing is a favorite pastime of many college students, and it's good exercise as well. No matter what type of dancing, it's fun. If you like fast dancing to good music, disco is the choice. If kikker is what you want, it's available. There are other types of music college students listen to, but disco and country seem to be the big rivals.

A FIVE-LETTER WORD

It is thin and crinkles when you handle it. It is just white paper with green printing on it. It is a small collection of silver and copper discs which jingle in your pocket when you walk. It is a commodity certain people say they cannot live without. How much of it one has determines a person's social status. "It" is a five-letter word—*money*.

According to certain theories, our present-day monetary system evolved from Primitive Man using seashells or coconuts or some other article in exchange for something that he wanted. Someone would trade a bunch of seashells for a piece of fruit someone else grew. This person would then give the seashells to someone else for a cutting utensil and so on. The amount of seashells one had determined one's wealth or social position. Over the years the seashells became gold and silver coins and finally evolved into the system we use today. As with the seashells, the amount of money one has determines one's social position.

There are three main social divisions in this country: the rich, who are few; the poor, who are many; and the middle class, who pay all the taxes and bear the brunt of every social crunch. The rich have more money than you can shake a stick at. They always have high-salaried lawyers who find every loophole they can to prevent their employer from paying "more than he or she truly owes" in taxes. The rich can also afford to hire people to lobby for those issues they feel will benefit themselves either immediately or in the long run. The rich also have benefits people do not usually think of, such as being well known if one is rich enough, and having the opportunity to rub elbows with other well-known individuals, like movie stars. But, then, what can you expect from someone whose main worry is how to spend $50,000 just to keep from paying that amount in taxes.

Then there are the poor. These are generally those people who live in what is referred to as the "inner city," "the ghetto," or the "poverty pocket." Whatever name you like, it all means the same. It means that these people have very little income and, subsequently, a lesser amount of money. These are the people who can really stretch a dollar, mainly because they usually have to. The poor also benefit in some ways from today's society, in a form of relief, i.e. welfare, medicare, and medicaid. Despite all the drawbacks, some of the happiest people in the world fall into this category of social status.

Last, but not least, there is the middle class. These people are the backbone and make up the fiber of today's society. These are the people that have to pay for the programs which give relief to the poor and the class that answers "How high" when the rich yell "Jump." The middle class is more mobile, in that one can still improve one's stature in society. This can be done many ways, but the main way is hard work. Some advantages for the middle class are that big business is set up to satisfy the average middle-class person; one can set up a small business with relatively little capital and move up in position; and the government is starting to swing toward the side of the average citizen. All things considered, middle class is pretty well off.

In going from seashells to dollar bills, the economic setup has changed and stayed the same. The rich have certain advantages over the other classes. The rich and poor can be more easily defined and distinguished now. There are three main classes with several divisions in each class. This is the main difference between now and seashells. People are still judged by how much they have.

2 DEVELOP YOUR THESIS: DELIVER WHAT YOU PROMISE

After you have looked at your trial draft to see if you stuck to the same point all the way through, you are ready to check to see if you gave your reader enough information. *You are ready to see how you need to expand what you wrote.*

There is no doubt about it: knowing how much to expand is a very thin line. How much development will the reader *really* need?

This is a big part of the "guessing game" we considered earlier. You, as the writer, have to anticipate what the reader is going to know and what the reader is *not* going to know. (All the more reason, of course, to know or invent your audience before you begin writing.) It's really a matter of second-guessing your readers. Will they be bored if you give them more examples on a particular point? Will they understand what you are saying if you don't give them a few more illustrations on another point?

Since you do have to guess about this, you may over- or underdevelop at times. Experience, however, teaches that **beginning writers *underdevelop* much more often than they *overdevelop*.** They assume readers

Develop:
To cause to grow or expand; to elaborate or expand in detail.

Expand:
To spread out or stretch out; to unfold; to express in fuller form or greater detail.

will see and understand—but the readers often don't! They have different backgrounds, different frames of reference, different experiences. What *they* picture when a writer says a particular thing may not be at all what the *writer* is picturing. So until you have had a lot of practice at second-guessing readers and really have a feel for how much or how little to develop and expand, **go for more instead of less.**

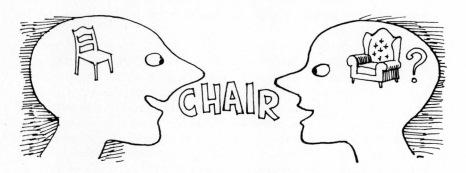

Another way of thinking about it is this: before the human mind can take in a new thought, it must first find something already there that is compatible with the new thought. According to this model, *the writer's job is is to put a thought, approach, idea or insight into such a form (or in such a way) that it is compatible with the reader's previous collection of information, facts, opinions, insights, and experiences.* You can appreciate how building that kind of compatibility takes a little time and a lot of awareness of the audience. You can also see how a point that is compatible with one reader might not match up in the mind of another reader—and so on. Of course the writer can never know for certain what is going to work for individual readers. The only thing to do is to give *enough* development or expansion of the idea so that there is a pretty

good chance that *most* readers in the audience will be able to find a match and a synthesis between what you are telling them and what they already know.

Now, how can you check to see how well you have developed matters in your trial draft so that you will know what you need to do when you rewrite? What follows is a sure-fire check that we call the BARE BONES OUTLINE. If you will put your essay up against the Bare Bones Outline, you can see *immediately* where you need more development. Here's how it works.

The Bare Bones Outline This Bare Bones Outline shows the structure of your essay in just the same way that an X-ray machine shows the skeleton of your body. By applying the Bare Bones Outline to your essay, you will be able to see exactly how many points you used to develop your thesis in your trial draft, how you developed each point, and whether there are gaps you need to fill in.

Here are the instructions for doing a Bare Bones Outline:

1 **Write your thesis at the top of the page.** (This may be actually stated in your essay or it may be implied. It is what you wrote the essay to say.)

I wrote this essay to tell the reader . . . .

2 **State how you began your paper.**

In my introduction, I. . . .

3 **Next, make a list of the points you made to develop and expand your thesis. Following each point, state *how* you developed that particular point.**

I made these points to develop the thesis, and I explained each point like this:

Point 1:

Developed by:

Point 2:

Developed by:

Point 3:

Developed by:

Outline:
To give the essential features or main aspects; to sketch the main points.

Point 4:

Developed by:

Point 5:

Developed by:

4 Finally, state how you closed your paper.

I closed the essay by saying. . . .

BARE BONES OUTLINE

Thesis: I wrote this essay to tell the reader. . . .
I began my essay by. . . .
I made these points to develop and expand my thesis; each point is developed this way:

1. (point)
    (developed by:)

2. (point)
    (developed by:)

3. (point)
    (developed by:)

4. (point)
    (developed by:)

5. (point)
    (developed by:)

I closed the essay by saying. . . .

What if you do the Bare Bones Outline and find out that you made only *one point* in the whole paper and maybe just said that single thing over and over again in different words? Well, there is no reason to despair. Finding out that you didn't make enough points is as valuable as finding out you made just the right number—it proves that your Bare Bones Outline is working for you, reporting what you have done. There is no reason to get mad at yourself if your Bare Bones Outline shows too little development. There is plenty of time (and a really enjoyable variety of ways) to put the development in. If you find out that you *have* enough development, fine and good; you can move on to the next stage. If you find out that you don't, no harm done. You will just get busy putting some in. A little more time but nothing more than that. You're still in good shape.

What Does Development Look Like?

First of all, let's see what *no* development looks like. Here is a student's paper that has no development of the message:

A controversy over taking vitamins is going on across the country. Some people say that vitamins will keep you from getting sick. Other people say that vitamins are a waste of money. Research shows that the people favoring vitamins are right.

There are articles that show that some vitamins can help clear the bloodstream of cholesterol. Vitamins also can make burns heal faster. Large dosages of vitamins can help people get over emotional problems. Vitamins can keep you from getting a cold. The people who believe in vitamins are definitely right.

That's it—the whole works. What will a Bare Bones Outline reveal? Let's take a look.

BARE BONES OUTLINE: Vitamin essay

Thesis: I wrote this essay to tell the reader that taking vitamins is a good thing.

I began this essay by stating that there is a controversy about vitamins.

I made these points to develop and expand my thesis. Each point is developed this way:

Point 1. Vitamins clear the bloodstream.
Developed . . . (nothing to put here—nothing in essay about point)
Point 2. Vitamins help heal burns.
Developed . . . (nothing to say here)
Point 3. Vitamins help people get over emotional problems.
Developed . . . (nothing here)
Point 4. Vitamins keep you from getting a cold.
Developed . . . (nothing here)

I closed this essay with one sentence: The people who believe in vitamins are definitely right.

And that tells the tale. *The student developed none of the points.*

There *is* a framework—a skeleton—to support the thesis of the paper, but this skeleton doesn't have any meat on it. If a reader didn't agree with the writer, there is nothing in the essay to convince, illustrate, or explain. The writer seems to be assuming that the reader is automatically going to accept the statements made (vitamins help heal burns, for example) *just because the writer says so.* Well, that isn't how it works. A reader will hardly accept anything—unless it is something he or she

Point:
A single, separate item in
a large whole; a detail.

already knows about and believes. This writer has got to back up what is being said with a *lot* of information, or else he has wasted his time in writing the essay.

If you look at your Bare Bones Outline and see that you need some development, what can you do? Well, here are some possibilities:

1 Give examples or illustrations.
Examples are specific objects, activities, conditions, data, etc., that make a general point clear. Illustrations are comparisons or examples (usually rather drawn out) intended to explain or support; something specific that gives clarity.

2 Tell a story.
The word *narrate* comes from Latin words that mean "to acquaint with"—so you could use a story, or narration, to make your reader know your point a little better.

3 Describe.
When you *describe* to develop a point, you draw images or impressions in words that *reveal* the thing described.

4 Give details.
Details are *specifics* that make something intelligible, or clear, and they help to dispel doubts. That is exactly what you want to do in the development of your message: *dispel all doubts the reader might have about what you are saying.*

5 Explain.
Explain means to give complete particulars that tell something fully and distinctly.

6 Compare.
When you *compare* to develop a point, what you are actually doing is finding something that "matches" it and will show in just another way what you mean. The word compare originally meant "to match together," and that is just exactly what you are doing when you find something to use that will help your reader see what you are saying in another way.

7 Give facts.
Facts can be defined as something known, by actual experience or observation, to be true. If it is appropriate to do so in the development of a point, *use plenty of facts* in order to convince your reader of what you are saying.

You can see from this list (and there are many other ways to develop; see development of the paragraph in the Completing Stage) that you really have a rich variety of ways to deliver what you promise your reader. *The important thing is that you do give the reader enough information for him or her to "see" what you are saying.* Did you notice how many of the words in the explanations above have to do with *seeing* or with getting the reader *closer* to the subject: *reveal, makes a point clear, something specific which gives clarity, to acquaint, to match, to convey an image.* **That's really all development is about: getting your reader up close to the subject in**

order to see clearly what you are trying to say. Let's look at these two brief essays—the first by James Fixx, the second by Shana Alexander—to see how the writers developed their messages:

Marathon Fever

Just as an aeronautical engineer using a wind tunnel can prove that a bumblebee can't fly, so any physiologist can demonstrate that human beings are incapable of running the 26.2 miles of a marathon. Somewhere around the eighteen-mile mark, even if you're well-trained and determined, the chemical that gives you energy is all too likely to fail you. When that happens, nothing can help. Not will power, not the roared encouragement of the crowd, not the most fervently heartfelt prayers. You simply stop. Period.

Begins with eye-catching comparison.
Gets reader's attention through narrative suspense.

Isn't it curious, then, that this month several thousand otherwise sober men and women will gather in a Massachusetts hamlet called Hopkinton to await the starter's gun and try to cover the long road that leads eventually to far-off Boston? What is it, exactly, that prompts them to attempt this exhausting and problematical feat?

Building down to thesis.

Mainly it is the lure of the incomparable Boston Marathon, an event that traces its history back to 1897, when a group of Bostonians, inspired by the 1896 Olympics, decided it would be interesting to have a long race in their own home town. For the first several years only a few runners, mostly local boys wearing homemade running shoes, turned out for it. With time, however, the race evolved into one of the world's great marathons. Part of its appeal lies in the participant's opportunity to run stride for stride with runners from every corner of the world, and at the finish line, to share a sweaty, joyous, and inarticulate embrace. And Boston's spectators! They are like the crowds at no other sports event. Because most have been watching the Patriots' Day runners since childhood, theirs is a reverence seldom accorded ordinary mortals like you and me. Children stand along the course, beseeching the contestants to accept ice cubes or slices of orange—at the very least, to touch palms in mystical communion. On that day, during those hours, you and I are heroes.

THESIS,
In the form of question. He'll discuss reasons people run marathons.

FIRST REASON:
Boston Marathon is special. Gives facts and some history.

Like any marathon, Boston summons us to transcend ourselves, to accomplish more than we have any right to hope we can do. Did I run a 3:12 last year? This year, in defiance of all logic I'll set out at an improbable 3:04 pace. Perhaps, it is true, I'll meet a cramped and breathless end on Heartbreak Hill. On the other hand—who, standing under the leafless trees in Hopkinton, can predict?—it may be that I will find myself miraculously invincible. It is worth the attempt and its attendant agonies. After all, it's not every day that we are granted such an opportunity to demonstrate that we are more than our workaday finitude suggests.

SECOND REASON:
In marathons people transcend themselves. Gives illustrations, word pictures.

Yes, marathons are special. Still, despite everything, it should be said that not everyone need run one, not this year or ever. Sometimes I find

CONCLUSION:
Repeats "marathons are

myself shaking my head in stunned disbelief when, having encountered a mile-a-day runner, I learn that his or her secret goal is to run 26.2 miles. I ask myself: Why? To run a marathon decently, most people find they need to train at least ten miles a day for several months—three times the distance anyone needs for health alone. Why, then, do it? Or if you can't bring yourself to resist the marathon, why not wait until you have two or three years of solid running under your belt? Then a marathon may turn out to be something more than a punishing and uncertain ordeal. With luck, it may even prove to be a triumph, something that beautifies rather than scourges the human spirit.

Motherliness

THESIS

"Motherly," to most of us, means gentle, open, warm, uncritical, and adoring. By these lights, some of the most motherly people I know are fathers.

EXAMPLE

Take a look at any beach in summertime. Here the motherly fathers are out in force. They help build the sand castles, they rub on the sun creme, go for the ice cream, and carry the toddlers into the surf. For this is the height of America's custody season and these are the weekend fathers. The bright summer sunshine reveals all the new patterns in part-time parenthood which our soaring divorce rate has forced us to devise.

FACTS

About a third of all American marriages now end in divorce. In some communities, like Southern California, the divorce rate has passed 120 per cent, which means that the mythical "average citizen" has been divorced one and one-fifth times. Divorce, here, is considered a normal part of marriage, much the same as death is accepted as a part of life.

DISCUSSION

But what of the children? What does a man do with a four-, or a six-, or an eight-year-old child, or perhaps all three of them, when "Daddy's Day" rolls around? Visits with the new wife or girl friend are difficult; Disneyland is expensive. Every spare cent Daddy has already goes for alimony and child-support. So it comes down to a choice of the beach—or visiting your children in your ex-wife's living room.

ILLUSTRATION

One stretch of California coastline has become so chockablock with weekend fathers and their offspring, it is known as Alimony Beach. The regulars here do not greet each other by name, but by number—"two-two-five," or "three-five-o," according to the amount the divorce is costing them per month, in cash. One day across the sand lurched a lone man festooned with beach towels, umbrella, hamper, and thermos jug, and followed by five small children. "That's seven-five-o!" someone whispered.

EXAMPLE WITH DESCRIPTION

I watched seven-five-o all the long day—finding lost sneakers, settling fights, and brushing sand out of the peanut butter—and I have never seen a more gentle, more patient, and—well—more motherly parent.

That qualities like "motherliness" or "fatherliness" are not inborn, nor God-given, but are really states of mind, is something men and women both must remember as drastic changes in patterns of marriage and family life tug at the fabric of our society.

CBS "Spectrum" — August 3, 1971

CONCLUSION: THE PROMISE AND DELIVERY SYSTEM — WHAT SHAPING IS ALL ABOUT

Do you see how an essay is just a chain of making an agreement with the readers to tell them a particular thing and then keeping that agreement by actually telling them? — and that the whole agreement set-up begins with the thesis that you promise to deliver? Then the agreements turn on smaller units — the individual points that you use to deliver your thesis. You have a secondary set of agreements with which to set up each point and then deliver it by developing the idea with examples, details, specifics of some sort or other. All along the way you are telling the readers that if they stick with you, they will find out *x, y,* or *z.* Keeping those agreements means the readers' expectations are fulfilled and your message gets delivered.

The system of agreements-plus-delivery also gives you a great way to check on the shaping of your paper. You have something to look for as you check to verify whether you have really communicated your message. Filling out a Bare Bones Outline after your trial draft and then again after the first revision will show you exactly where you have holes in your essay. You can plug them up *before* the reader ever sees the essay. Now that you know how to check your shaping carefully, you need never again miss the whole purpose by giving the reader so little information that he or she can't get your message.

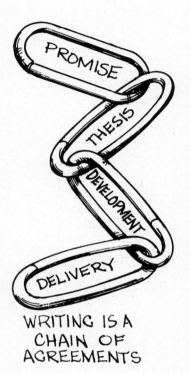

WRITING IS A CHAIN OF AGREEMENTS

APPLICATION

1 Read the following student essays. Answer these questions for each essay:

a Does the writer have a clear thesis?

b Is the writer an insider on this subject in a way that produces value for you, the reader?

c Does the entire paper stay on the thesis?

d Has the writer developed the thesis enough? Explain.

e What methods of development has the writer used? Be specific. Be able to point to sections in the essay to support your answer.

f Does the introduction attract you immediately? Does it start "close" enough to the exact subject of the paper?

g Does the conclusion remind the reader of what was said, provide one new thing to think about, and let you feel closure and completeness at the end of the essay?

Be ready to discuss these essays in class.

ONE PLUS ONE EQUALS FOUR

CONTEXT
Written as an assignment in a freshman sociology class

AUDIENCE
Classmates

I thought I was a hot shot in elementary school because I was one of the few kids who had two vacations every summer. I remember the first day of class every year. I would be asked to tell about my vacation that summer. I would show off by asking which vacation the teacher wanted to hear about, the one with my dad or the one with my mom? I usually got to tell about both.

I believe I am one of those lucky people who came from a split family. I say this with sincerity. Coming from a situation that gives me two sets of parents has been an advantage in many ways, some of which I am just now seeing, although I have felt lucky ever since I can remember.

My parents divorced when I was less than two years old. Each remarried when I was two and a half. By each remarrying, I had a total of three step-brothers, seven step-sisters, four parents, and more relatives than a family of monkeys.

Having two sets of parents gave me the opportunity to see two life-styles. With this came many more chances to see and meet many people, to go places, and to see and contrast four adults that were close to me. To see how my family lived on one side and then contrast that to the other gave me a choice of twice as many perspectives, ideas, and types of self-discipline.

I remember as a kid always being confused when I was spanked for something at one house and not at the other. This was a constant battle in my mind—I didn't know whom to believe, my mom or my dad. Discipline was always a big thing with both my mom and my dad, but they had different ideas about what deserved discipline and how that discipline was done. They were constantly telling me why it was wrong to do something, but it was usually a different thing. I can still recite 40 reasons why I should never have a dirty room, face, or clothes and why it is o.k. to do that but 40 reasons why I should study hard, go to church, and read science books. While this may sound as though having two families was a problem, actually this allowed me to learn early that everybody sets up life in a personal way. I learned early that all things are relative, actually, and based on how each person sees the world. This was a real contribution to my maturity.

I suppose the thing I have enjoyed most about all this is having two mothers. After all, what more can a guy want? I was never as close to my step-mother as to my mom, of course, but I love them both. My mom was always there to take care of me, no matter what. When I was away from home with my dad, my step-mother was always so glad to see me and cooked my favorite foods, making more things than I could possibly eat in one weekend.

I believe the real advantage is that I have been confronted with everything from four sides. I always had to hear about something when my mom and step-dad talked about it and when my dad and step-mother talked about it. Talk about getting mixed up—I was mixed up no matter what the topic was. I see now, though, that this has opened my mind, made me aware of alternatives, and made me richer in experience. I really am fortunate that one plus one equals four. There are, of course, disadvantages, but I believe the advantages outweigh them tenfold. I am very glad, in fact, that I have lived my life with four parents instead of two.

GARDENING FOR PROFIT

CONTEXT
Written for a community senior citizens' newsletter

AUDIENCE
Retired people, many of whom are on social security

Mrs. Sanford pointed to her garden and explained her admiration for it. As the chitchat continued, I got my turn and I explained how gardens were economical. Gardens on a small scale are similar to commercial farms that show a healthy, net profit every year. Hence, if large gardens are profitable, it follows that small gardens are profitable, also.

Gardens have only one major expense. That is a soil tiller which can run from $200 to $1,000 at any Montgomery Ward's. The size and type are dependent on the area of the garden. Gardens also have yearly costs. Water, for example, varies in cost from $10 to $100 per year. Fertilizer such as 10-15-10 will cost around $10 per year, while manure, mulch, seed, poison and plants will run from $5 to $100 per year, depending on size, geographic location, and thriftiness of the person running the operation.

You really can't measure the money made in a garden, because who can put a price on the taste of homegrown fresh vegetables? There is nothing like them. But, even putting the taste aside, if you go just on money spent and produce received, your final accounting will go something like this. If you have a garden 75 feet by 50 feet, filled with ¼ corn, ¼ beans, ⅛ okra, ⅛ sweet peppers, and the remainder in tomatoes, onions, cabbage and lettuce, you can produce enough vegetables to amount to about $1,000 if bought in the store. Your cost, after the purchase of the tiller, is about $150. per year for the above-mentioned things. This is a very good yearly profit margin.

THE EGGHEAD
IS NOT DEAD

CONTEXT
Written as an editorial for college newspaper

AUDIENCE
College students and faculty

Do you know those smart people in your classes, the ones who sit in the front of the room right in front of the teacher's desk? The ones who rarely speak and when they do it is to ask an impressive question or to remind the teacher to give the homework? Now you know who I am talking about, the so-called "brain" or "egghead." They usually wear glasses and clothes which are out of style. They do not participate in extracurricular activities. All they do is sit at home and study. Most likely, these people are not really this way. They want to participate in other activities, but they are shy and do not know how to make friends, plus they have been labeled "egghead." This word itself can ruin a person's entire social life.

Most of these "eggheads" have been pushed into their way of life by their parents. When they were young, their parents insisted on good grades, so all they have been striving for is academic awards. They finally reach high school and realize that they have been missing so much, such as doing things with their friends and just being a teenager. Since most of them do not know how to make friends, because up until now the only thing that was important was good grades, what can they do? How can they come out of their shell? Somehow their intelligence has outshined their other qualities.

If you have been labeled an "egghead," fear being labeled one, or even know someone who is a "brain," I have some good news! Here are a few tips on how to come out that "egghead" shell. Try to be more outgoing; get involved in clubs or organizations. Remember, academics are not everything. One *B* on your report card is not so much to pay for meeting new friends and having fun. Is it now? Help the people in your classes, but do not act like a "know-it-all." This will only confirm your peers' assumptions. Also, be more independent of your parents. I am not saying to disown them; just think more for yourself. Do things for yourself, too.

This advice may help someone you know. Help them out; give them a few tips, and, remember, the "egghead" is not dead—yet.

WRITING ASSIGNMENT: THE EXPLANATION ESSAY

One of the most frequent reasons that you will write after you get out of school is to explain something to somebody. An explanation always operates out of these conditions:

   —there must be someone who doesn't know or understand something

   —there must be someone else who does know and understand the thing

   —the person who knows must be able to discuss the matter so clearly that the one who doesn't know at the beginning will understand fully when the explanation is completed.

These conditions put a serious constraint on a writer who must be the one who understands and the one who can discuss the matter so clearly that someone else will also understand. The writer must attempt to explain, then, only those things she or he knows thoroughly. And the writer must find a way to explain so effectively that the person who doesn't know will be absolutely clear on the subject by the end of the explanation.

A good explanation essay, therefore, will have these characteristics:

1 Early in the essay the writer will identify what is going to be explained.

2 The essay will then center totally on this thesis.

3 The writer will take into account the particular audience who will be reading the explanation and will make decisions about how much and what kind of explanation is needed, based on the specific requirements of these readers.

4 The writer will give a *full* explanation so that the reader feels satisfied and complete at the end. This means that the writer must give enough information to resolve all tension in the reader's mind.

The following sample essays set out to explain something to a particular audience. Read them and decide how well they fit the four characteristics of a good explanation essay. Be able to discuss your evaluation of each essay when you come to class. This activity will help you recognize those characteristics and will also help when you write your own explanation essay.

To Explain:

To make plain or clear; render intelligible; to make known in detail; to assign a meaning to; to interpret; account for; to make clear the cause or reason for; to make understandable something not known or understood.

READINGS

Obtaining Power

In this essay, which came from a book called Power! How to Get It, How to Use It, *Michael Korda explains what people living in modern times have to do to obtain power. Although he is, in a sense, telling the reader how to do something, he has written more than a how-to essay. He has concentrated on* explaining *why each rule is necessary.*

My friend and I are sitting at the Central Park Zoo, on the terrace of the cafeteria, one of those hot summer afternoons when the park is so crowded with people that the animals seem more human than oneself. To our right are the towers of commercial New York, a high, brutal cliff of great buildings, rising through the layers of haze like the dreaded tower of Barad-Dûr in Tolkien's *The Lord of the Rings.* I can understand how one can become a powerful person in simpler societies and cultures; it may be a long, hard initiation, but the distractions are fewer. The sheer size of the city distorts the ego. We are either reduced to the impotence of a meaningless daily routine—sleep, eat, work—made even more painful by the knowledge that we have no power over our lives; or worse, we destroy ourselves by trying to become bigger, more famous, more powerful than the city itself. Can one have power here, I want to know, in a life full of compromises, decisions, worries, pressures, in a place where even the mayor seldom seems able to control anything at all? I can understand the meaning of power in the desert, the significance of the rites of power, the sudden illuminations of self-awareness that come when one is alone with Nature—all that makes sense. But in an office on the thirty-eighth floor of a huge building in which thousands of people work? How does one seek power there?

My friend smiles. There are rules, they are the same for everybody, this terrace is not so very different from a jungle clearing. The rules of power do not change because one is on the subway, or in Central Park, or in an office without windows, where everything is made of plastic. "The first rule," he says, "is simple. Act impeccably! Perform every act as if it were the only thing in the world that mattered."

I can understand that all right. It's an old Zen principle—you put your whole soul and being and life into the act you're performing. In Zen archery your entire being wills the arrow into the bull's-eye with an invisible force. It's not a question of winning, or even caring, it's making the everyday acts we all perform important to ourselves. No matter how small the task, we have to teach ourselves that it *matters.* If we are going to intervene in a meeting, we must do so at the right moment, prepare for what we want to say, speak up at the crucial point when our intervention will be heard and listened to, make sure that attention is paid. Otherwise, it's best to remain silent. It is better to do nothing than to do something badly.

"Second rule: never reveal all of yourself to other people, hold something back in reserve so that people are never quite sure if they really know you."

I can see that too. It's not that anybody seeking power should be secretive—secrecy isn't the trick at all. It's more a question of remaining slightly mysterious, as if one were always capable of doing something surprising and unexpected. Most people are so predictable and reveal so much of themselves that a person who isn't and who doesn't automatically acquires a kind of power. For this reason, it is important to give up the self-indulgent habit of talking about oneself. The power person listens instead, and when he *does* talk about himself, it is in order to change the subject of conversation. Good players can always tell when someone is about to ask them to do something they don't want to do, and they effortlessly but firmly move the conversation onto a personal level. One of the best players I know can talk about himself for hours at the slightest sign of opposition or a demand about to be made on him. Even so, he reveals nothing. Sometimes he gives the impression that he has two children, sometimes three, occasionally none, and he has at various times given people to understand that he was graduated from Yale, Harvard, Stanford, and Ol' Miss. Some confusion exists as to whether or not he is Jewish or Protestant, since he has claimed to be both, and also crosses himself when he passes St. Patrick's Cathedral. Nobody really knows the truth about him, and he is therefore respected. Once we know everything about a person, we have squeezed him dry like a juiced orange, he is no longer of any use or interest to us, we can throw him away.

"Third rule: learn to use time, think of it as a friend, not an enemy. Don't waste it in going after things you don't want."

Using time! Of course, but how seldom we do! Time uses us, we are merely its servants. We fight it as if it were the enemy, trying to force two hours' work into forty-five minutes if we're ambitious, or to stretch forty-five minutes' work into two hours if we're not. Powerful people devote exactly as much time to what they're doing as they need to or want to. They do not try to answer two telephones at once, or begin a meeting and then end it before a conclusion has been reached because "time has run out," or interrupt one conversation to begin another. They are willing to be late, to miss telephone calls, and to postpone today's work to tomorrow if they have to. Events do not control them— they control events.

"Fourth rule: learn to accept your mistakes. Don't be a perfectionist about everything."

True enough. Half the people we know are rendered powerless by their need to be perfect, as if making one mistake would destroy them. Powerful people accept the necessity of taking risks and of being wrong.

They don't waste time justifying their mistakes, either, or trying to transform them into correct decisions. Nothing makes one seem more foolish or impotent than the inability to admit a mistake.

"Last rule: don't make waves, move smoothly without disturbing things."

That makes sense too, even in our world. Half the art of power lies in arranging for things to happen the way we want them to, just as a good hunter stays in one place and draws the game toward him, instead of wearing himself out pursuing it. The skills of the hunter are not out of place in our world; they must merely be applied differently.

My friend smiles again. "What more can I say?" he asks, waving to the buildings south of the park. "It's your world. You picked it— telephones, Telex machines, credit cards and all. Myself, I wouldn't care to live in it all the time. I'm not interested in negotiating contracts, or buying a new car, or running a corporation—we don't have the same ambitions and desires. But I could live here as easily as I can anywhere else. You only need power. And since *you* live in it, you have to examine this world of yours coldly and clearly, as if your life depended on it. Because it *does*."

How Flowers Changed the World

In this essay Loren Eiseley, the famous scientist and naturalist, uses cause/effect analysis to explain how flowers affected the whole cycle of nature when they appeared. Does he make clear to you how the appearance of flowers affected the trees and animals already present in the world?

A little while ago—about one hundred million years, as the geologist estimates time in the history of our four-billion-year-old planet—flowers were not to be found anywhere on the five continents. Wherever one might have looked, from the poles to the equator, one would have seen only the cold dark monotonous green of a world whose plant life possessed no other color.

Somewhere, just a short time before the close of the Age of Reptiles, there occurred a soundless, violent explosion. It lasted millions of years, but it was an explosion, nevertheless. It marked the emergence of the angiosperms—the flowering plants. Even the great evolutionist, Charles Darwin, called them "an abominable mystery," because they appeared so suddenly and spread so fast.

Flowers changed the face of the planet. Without them, the world we know—even man himself—would never have existed. Francis Thompson, the English poet, once wrote that one could not pluck a flower without troubling a star. Intuitively he had sensed like a naturalist the enormous interlinked complexity of life. Today we know that the appearance of the flowers contained also the equally mystifying emergence of man. . . .

When the first simple flower bloomed on some raw upland late in the Dinosaur Age, it was wind pollinated, just like its early pine-cone relatives. It was a very inconspicuous flower because it had not yet evolved the idea of using the surer attraction of birds and insects to achieve the transportation of pollen. It sowed its own pollen and received the pollen of other flowers by the simple vagaries of the wind. Many plants in regions where insect life is scant still follow this principle today. Nevertheless, the true flower—and the seed that it produced—was a profound innovation in the world of life.

In a way, this event parallels, in the planet world, what happened among animals. Consider the relative chance for survival of the exteriorly deposited egg of a fish in contrast with the fertilized egg of a mammal, carefully retained for months in the mother's body until the young animal (or human being) is developed to a point where it may survive. The biological wastage is less—and so it is with the flowering plants. The primitive spore, a single cell fertilized in the beginning by a swimming sperm, did not promote rapid distribution, and the young plant, moreover, had to struggle up from nothing. No one had left it any food except what it could get by its own unaided efforts.

By contrast, the true flowering plants (angiosperm itself means "encased seed") grew a seed in the heart of a flower, a seed whose development was initiated by a fertilizing pollen grain independent of outside moisture. But the seed, unlike the developing spore, is already a fully equipped *embryonic plant* packed in a little enclosed box stuffed full of nutritious food. Moreover, by featherdown attachments, as in dandelion or milkweed seed, it can be wafted upward on gusts and ride the wind for miles; or with hooks it can cling to a bear's or a rabbit's hide; or like some of the berries, it can be covered with a juicy, attractive fruit to lure birds, pass undigested through their intestinal tracts and be voided miles away.

The ramifications of this biological invention were endless. Plants traveled as they had never traveled before. They got into strange environments heretofore never entered by the old spore plants or stiff pine-cone-seed plants. The well-fed, carefully cherished little embryos raised their heads everywhere. Many of the older plants with more primitive reproductive mechanisms began to fade away under this unequaled contest. They contracted their range into secluded environments. Some, like the giant redwoods, lingered on as relics; many vanished entirely.

The world of the giants was a dying world. These fantastic little seeds skipping and hopping and flying about the woods and valleys brought with them an amazing adaptability. If our whole lives had not been spent in the midst of it, it would astound us. The old, stiff, sky-reaching wooden world had changed into something that glowed here and there with strange colors, put out queer, unheard-of fruits and little intricately carved seed cases, and, most important of all, produced concentrated foods in a way that the land had never seen before, or dreamed of back in the fish-eating, leaf-crunching days of the dinosaurs.

That food came from three sources, all produced by the reproductive system of the flowering plants. There were the tantalizing nectars and pollens intended to draw insects for pollenizing purposes, and which are responsible also for that wonderful jeweled creation, the hummingbird. There were the juicy and enticing fruits to attract larger animals, and in which tough-coated seeds were concealed, as in the tomato, for example. Then, as if this were not enough, there was the food in the actual seed itself, the food intended to nourish the embryo. All over the world, like hot corn in a popper, these incredible elaborations of the flowering plants kept exploding. In a movement that was almost instantaneous, geologically speaking, the angiosperms had taken over the world. Grass was beginning to cover the bare earth until, today, there are over six thousand species. All kinds of vines and bushes squirmed and writhed under new trees with flying seeds.

The explosion was having its effect on animal life also. Specialized groups of insects were arising to feed on the new sources of food and, incidentally and unknowingly, to pollinate the plant. The flowers bloomed and bloomed in ever larger and more spectacular varieties. Some were pale unearthly night flowers intended to lure moths in the evening twilight, some among the orchids even took the shape of female spiders in order to attract wandering males, some flamed redly in the light of noon or twinkled modestly in the meadow grasses. Intricate mechanisms splashed pollen on the breasts of hummingbirds, or stamped it on the bellies of black, grumbling bees droning assiduously from blossom to blossom. Honey ran, insects multiplied, and even the descendants of that toothed and ancient lizard-bird had become strangely altered. Equipped with prodding beaks instead of biting teeth they pecked the seeds and gobbled the insects that were really converted nectar.

Across the planet grasslands were now spreading. A slow continental upthrust which had been a part of the early Age of Flowers had cooled the world's climates. The stalking reptiles and the leather-winged black imps of the seashore cliffs had vanished. Only birds roamed the air now, hot-blooded and high-speed metabolic machines.

The mammals, too, had survived and were venturing into new domains, staring about perhaps a bit bewildered at their sudden eminence now that the thunder lizards were gone. Many of them, beginning as small browsers upon leaves in the forest, began to venture out upon this new sunlit world of the grass. Grass has a high silica content and demands a new type of very tough and resistant tooth enamel, but the seeds taken incidentally in the cropping of the grass are highly nutritious. A new world had opened out for the warm-blooded mammals. Great herbivores like the mammoths, horses and bisons appeared. Skulking about them had arisen savage flesh-feeding carnivores like the now extinct dire wolves and the saber-toothed tiger. . . .

Apes were to become men, in the inscrutable wisdom of nature, because flowers had produced seeds and fruits in such tremendous quantities that a new and totally different store of energy had become available in concentrated form. Impressive as the slow-moving, dim-brained dinosaurs had been, it is doubtful if their age had supported anything like the diversity of life that now rioted across the planet or flashed in and out among the trees. Down on the grass by a streamside, one of those apes with inquisitive fingers turned over a stone and hefted it vaguely. The group clucked together in a throaty tongue and moved off through the tall grass foraging for seeds and insects. The one still held, sniffed, and hefted the stone he had found. He liked the feel of it in his fingers. The attack on the animal world was about to begin.

If one could run the story of that first human group like a speeded-up motion picture through a million years of time, one might see the stone in the hand change to the flint ax and the torch. All that swarming grassland world with its giant bison and trumpeting mammoths would go down in ruin to feed the insatiable and growing numbers of a carnivore who, like the great cats before him, was taking his energy indirectly from the grass. Later he found fire and it altered the tough meats and drained their energy even faster into a stomach ill adapted for the ferocious turn man's habits had taken.

His limbs grew longer, he strode more purposefully over the grass. The stolen energy that would take man across the continents would fail him at last. The great Ice Age herds were destined to vanish. When they did so, another hand like the hand that grasped the stone by the river long ago would pluck a handful of grass seed and hold it contemplatively.

In that moment, the golden towers of man, his swarming millions, his turning wheels, the vast learning of his packed libraries, would glimmer dimly there in the ancestor of wheat, a few seeds held in a muddy hand. Without the gift of flowers and the infinite diversity of their fruits, man and bird, if they had continued to exist at all, would be today unrecognizable. Archaeopteryx, the lizard-bird, might still be snapping at beetles on a sequoia limb; man might still be a nocturnal insectivore gnawing a roach in the dark. The weight of a petal has changed the face of the world and made it ours.

Winners and Losers

In this essay Muriel James and Dorothy Jongeward define the words winners and losers and explain the characteristics of each.

Each human being is born as something new, something that never existed before. Each is born with the capacity to win at life. Each person has a unique way of seeing, hearing, touching, tasting, and thinking. Each has his or her own unique potentials—capabilities and limitations. Each can be a significant, thinking, aware, and creative being—a productive person, a winner.

The words "winner" and "loser" have many meanings. When we refer to a person as a winner, we do not mean one who makes someone else lose. To us, a winner is one who responds authentically by being credible, trustworthy, responsive, and genuine, both as an individual and as a member of society. A loser is one who fails to respond authentically. Martin Buber makes this distinction as he retells the old story of the rabbi who, on his deathbed, is asked if he is ready for the world to come. The rabbi says yes. After all, he will not be asked, "Why were you not Moses?" He will only be asked, "Why were you not yourself. . . ."

Winners have different potentials. Achievement is not the most important thing. Authenticity is. The authentic person experiences self-reality by knowing, being, and becoming a credible, responsive person. Authentic people actualize their own unprecedented uniqueness and appreciate the uniqueness of others.

Authentic persons—winners—do not dedicate their lives to a concept of what they imagine they *should* be; rather, they are themselves and as such do not use their energy putting on a performance, maintaining pretence, and manipulating others. Winners can reveal themselves instead of projecting images that please, provoke, or entice others. They are aware that there is a difference between being loving and acting loving, between being stupid and acting stupid, between being knowledgeable and acting knowledgeable. Winners do not need to hide behind a mask. They throw off unrealistic self-images of inferiority or superiority. Autonomy does not frighten winners.

All people have moments of autonomy, if only fleeting. However, winners are able to sustain their autonomy over ever-increasing periods of time. Winners may lose ground occasionally and may even fail. Yet, in spite of setbacks winners maintain a basic self-confidence.

Winners are not afraid to do their own thinking and to use their own knowledge. They can separate facts from opinion and don't pretend to have all the answers. They listen to others, evaluate what they say, but come to their own conclusions. Although winners can admire and respect other people, they are not totally defined, demolished, bound, or awed by them.

Winners do not play "helpless," nor do they play the blaming game. Instead, they assume responsibility for their own lives. They do not give others a false authority over them. Winners are their own bosses and know it.

A winner's timing is right. Winners respond appropriately to the situation. Their responses are related to the message sent and preserve the significance, worth, well-being, and dignity of the people involved. Winners know that for everything there is a season and for every activity a time.

A time to be aggressive and a time to be passive,
A time to be together and a time to be alone,
A time to fight and a time to love,
A time to work and a time to play,
A time to cry and a time to laugh,
A time to confront and a time to withdraw,
A time to speak and a time to be silent,
A time to hurry and a time to wait.

To winners, time is precious. Winners don't kill it, but live it here and now. Living in the now does not mean that winners foolishly ignore their own past history or fail to prepare for the future. Rather, winners know their past, are aware and alive in the present, and look forward to the future.

Winners learn to know their feelings and limitations and to be unafraid of them. Winners are not stopped by their own contradictions and ambivalences. Being authentic, they know when they are angry and can listen when others are angry with them. Winners can give and receive affection. Winners are able to love and be loved.

Winners can be spontaneous. They do not have to respond in predetermined, rigid ways, but can change their plans when the situation calls for it. Winners have a zest for life, enjoying work, play, food, other people, sex, and the world of nature. Without guilt they enjoy their own accomplishments. Without envy they enjoy the accomplishments of others.

Although winners can freely enjoy themselves, they can also postpone enjoyment, can discipline themselves in the present to enhance their enjoyment in the future. Winners are not afraid to go after what they want, but they do so in appropriate ways. Winners do not get their security by controlling others. They do not set themselves up to lose.

A winner cares about the world and its peoples. A winner is not isolated from the general problems of society, but is concerned, compassionate, and committed to improving the quality of life. Even in the face of national and international adversity, a winner's self-image is not one of a powerless individual. A winner works to make the world a better place.

Although people are born to win, they are also born helpless and totally dependent on their environment. Winners successfully make the transition from total helplessness to independence, and then to interdependence. Losers do not. Somewhere along the line they begin to avoid becoming responsible for their own lives. . . .

A lack of response to dependency needs, poor nutrition, brutality, unhappy relationships, disease, continuing disappointments, inadequate physical care, and traumatic events are among the many experiences that contribute to making people losers. Such experiences interrupt, deter, or prevent the normal progress toward autonomy and self-actualization. To cope with negative experiences, children learn to manipulate themselves and others. These manipulative techniques are hard to give up later in life and often become set patterns. Winners work to shed them. Losers hang on to them.

Some losers speak of themselves as successful but anxious, successful but trapped, or successful but unhappy. Others speak of themselves as totally beaten, without purpose, unable to move, half dead, or bored to death. Losers may not recognize that, for the most part, they have been building their own cages, digging their own graves, and boring themselves.

A loser seldom lives in the present, but instead destroys the present by focusing on past memories or future expectations. The loser who lives in the past dwells on the good old days or on past personal misfortunes. Nostalgically, the loser either clings to the way things "used to be" or bemoans his or her bad luck. The loser is self-pitying and shifts the responsibility for an unsatisfactory life onto others. Blaming others and excusing oneself are often part of the loser's games. A loser who lives in the past may lament *if only:*

"If only I had married someone else . . ."
"If only I had a different job . . ."
"If only I had finished school . . ."
"If only I had been handsome (beautiful) . . ."
"If only my spouse had stopped drinking . . ."
"If only I had been born rich . . ."
"If only I had had better parents . . ."

People who live in the future may dream of some miracle after which they can "live happily ever after." Rather than pursuing their own lives, losers wait — wait for the magical rescue. How wonderful life will be *when:*

"When Prince Charming or the ideal woman finally comes . . ."
"When school is over . . ."
"When the kids grow up . . ."
"When that new job opens . . ."
"When the boss dies . . ."
"When my ship comes in . . ."

In contrast to those who live with the delusion of a magical rescue, some losers live constantly under the dread of future catastrophe. They conjure up expectations of *what if:*

"What if I lose my job . . ."
"What if I lose my mind . . ."
"What if something falls on me . . ."
"What if I break my leg . . ."
"What if they don't like me . . ."
"What if I make a mistake . . ."

By continually focusing on the future, these losers experience anxiety in the present. They are anxious over what they anticipate — either real or imagined — tests, bill paying, a love affair, crisis, illness, retirement, the weather, and so forth. Persons overly involved with imaginings let the actual possibilities of the moment pass them by. They occupy their minds with material that is irrelevant to the current situation. Anxiety tunes out current reality. Consequently, these people are unable to see for themselves, hear for themselves, feel for themselves, or taste, touch, or think for themselves.

Unable to bring the full potential of their senses into the immediate situation, losers' perceptions are incorrect or incomplete. They see themselves and others through a prismlike distortion. Their ability to deal effectively with the real world is hampered.

Losers spend much of their time play-acting, pretending, manipulating, and perpetuating old roles from childhood. Losers invest their energy in maintaining masks, often projecting a phony front. Karen Horney writes, "The fostering of the phony self is always at the expense of the real self, the latter being treated with disdain, at best like a poor relative." To the play-acting loser, performance is often more important than reality.

Losers repress their capacities to express spontaneously and appropriately the full range of possible behavior. They may be unaware of other options for a more productive, self-fulfilling life path. Losers are afraid to try new things and instead maintain their own status quo. Losers are repeaters, repeating not only their own mistakes, but often those of their families and culture as well.

A loser has difficulty giving and receiving affection and does not enter into intimate, honest, direct relationships with others. Instead, a loser tries to manipulate them into living up to his or her expectations. Losers' energies are often channeled into living up to the expectations of others.

People who are losers are not using their intellect appropriately, but instead are misusing it to rationalize and intellectualize. When rationalizing, losers give excuses to make their actions seem plausible. When intellectualizing, they try to snow others with verbiage. Consequently, much of their potential remains dormant, unrealized, and unrecognized. Like the frog-prince in the fairy tale, losers are spellbound and live their lives being something they aren't meant to be.

Few people are one hundred percent winners or one hundred percent losers. It's a matter of degree. Most people are winners in some areas of their lives and losers in others. Their winning or losing is influenced by what happens to them in childhood. However, once a person is on the road to being a winner, his or her chances are greater for becoming even more so.

The Three Stages of Man

Aristotle, in this essay, classifies men into three categories: young men, old men, and men in their prime. He then explains what it is like in each category.

Let us now consider the various types of human character, in relation to the emotions and moral qualities, showing how they correspond to our various ages and fortunes. By emotions I mean anger, desire, and the like; these we have discussed already. By moral qualities I mean virtues and vices; these also have been discussed already, as well as the various things that various types of men tend to will and to do. By ages I mean youth, the prime of life, and old age. By fortune I mean birth, wealth, power, and their opposites—in fact, good fortune and ill fortune.

Young men have strong passions, and tend to gratify them indiscriminately. Of the bodily desires, it is the sexual by which they are most swayed and in which they show absence of self-control. They are changeable and fickle in their desires, which are violent while they last, but quickly over: their impulses are keen but not deep-rooted, and are like sick people's attacks of hunger and thirst. They are hot-tempered and quick-tempered, and apt to give way to their anger; bad temper often gets the better of them, for owing to their love of honour they cannot bear being slighted, and are indignant if they imagine themselves unfairly treated. While they love honour, they love victory still more; for youth is eager for superiority over others, and victory is one form of this. They love both more than they love money, which indeed they love very little, not having yet learnt what it means to be without it—this is the point of Pittacus' remark about Amphiaraus. They look at the good side rather than the bad, not having yet witnessed many instances of wickedness. They trust others readily, because they have not yet often been cheated. They are sanguine; nature warms their blood as though with excess of wind; and besides that, they have as yet met with few disappointments. Their lives are mainly spent not in memory but in expectation; for expectation refers to the future, memory to the past, and youth has a long future before it and a short past behind it: on the first day of one's life one has nothing at all to remember, and can only look forward. They are easily cheated, owing to the sanguine disposition just mentioned. Their hot tempers and hopeful dispositions make them more courageous than older men are; the hot temper prevents fear, and the hopeful disposition creates confidence; we cannot feel fear so long as we are feeling angry, and any expectation of good makes us confident. They are shy, accepting the rules of society in which they have been trained, and not yet believing in any other standard of honour. They have exalted notions, because they have not yet been humbled by life or learnt its necessary limitations; moreover, their hopeful disposition makes them think themselves equal to great things—and that means having exalted notions. They would always rather do noble deeds than useful ones: their lives are regulated more by moral feeling than by reasoning; and whereas reasoning leads us to choose what is useful, moral goodness leads us to choose what is noble. They are fonder of their friends, intimates, and companions than older men are, because they like spending their days in the company of others, and have not yet come to value either their friends or anything else by their usefulness to themselves. All their mistakes are in the direction of doing things excessively and vehemently. They disobey Chilon's precept by overdoing everything; they love too much and hate too much, and the same with everything else. They think they know everything, and are always quite sure about it; this, in fact, is why they overdo everything. If they do wrong to others, it is because they mean to insult them, not to do them actual harm. They are ready to pity others, because they think everyone an honest man, or anyhow better than he is: they judge their neighbor by their own harmless natures, and so cannot think he deserves to be treated in that way. They are fond of fun and therefore witty, wit being well-bred insolence.

Such, then, is the character of the young. The character of Elderly Men—men who are past their prime—may be said to be formed for the most part of elements that are the contrary of all these. They have lived many years; they have often been taken in, and often made mistakes; and life on the whole is a bad business. The result is that they are sure about nothing and *under-do* everything. They 'think,' but they never 'know'; and because of their hesitation they always add a 'possibly' or a 'perhaps,' putting everything this way and nothing positively. They are cynical; that is, they tend to put the worse construction on everything. Further, their experience makes them distrustful and therefore suspicious of evil. Consequently they neither love warmly nor hate bitterly, but following the hint of Bias they love as though they will some day hate and hate as though they will some day love. They are small-minded, because they have been humbled by life; their desires are set upon nothing more exalted or unusual than what will help them to keep alive. They are not generous, because money is one of the things they must have, and at the same time their experience has taught them how hard it is to get and how easy to lose. They are cowardly, and are always anticipating danger; unlike that of the young, who are warm-blooded, their temperament is chilly; old age has paved the way for cowardice; fear is, in fact, a form of chill. They love life; and all the more when their last day has come, because the object of all desire is something we have not got, and also because we desire most strongly that which we need most urgently. They are too fond of themselves; this is one form that small-mindedness takes. Because of this, they guide their lives too much by considerations of what is useful and too little by what is noble—for the useful is what is good for oneself, and the noble what is good absolutely. They are not shy, but shameless rather; caring less for what is noble than for what is useful, they feel contempt for what people may think of them. They lack confidence in the future; partly through experience—for most things go wrong, or anyhow turn out worse than one expects; and partly because of their cowardice. They live by memory rather than by hope; for what is left to them of life is but little as compared with the long past; and hope is of the future, memory of the past. This, again, is the cause of their loquacity; they are continually talking of the past, because they enjoy remembering it. Their fits of anger are sudden but feeble. Their sensual passions have either altogether gone or have lost their vigour: consequently they do not feel their passions much, and their actions are inspired less by what they do feel than by the love of gain. Hence men at this time of life are often supposed to have a self-controlled character; the fact is that their passions have slackened, and they are slaves to the love of gain. They guide their lives by reasoning more than by moral feeling; reasoning being directed to utility and moral feeling to moral goodness. If they wrong others, they mean to injure them, not to insult them. Old men may feel pity, as well as young men, but not for the same reason. Young men feel it out of kindness; old men out of weakness, imagining that anything that befalls any one else might easily happen to them, which, as we saw it, is a thought that excites pity. Hence they are querulous, and not disposed to jesting or laughter—the love of laughter being the very opposite of querulousness.

Such are the characters of Young Men and Elderly Men. People always think well of speeches adapted to, and reflecting, their own character: and we can now see how to compose our speeches so as to adapt both them and ourselves to our audiences.

As for Men in their Prime, clearly we shall find that they have a character between that of the young and that of the old, free from the extremes of either. They have neither that excess of confidence which amounts to rashness, nor too much timidity, but the right amount of each. They neither trust everybody nor distrust everybody, but judge people correctly. Their lives will be guided not by the sole consideration either of what is noble or of what is useful, but by both; neither by parsimony nor by prodigality, but by what is fit and proper. So, too, in regard to anger and desire; they will be brave as well as temperate, and temperate as well as brave; these virtues are divided between the young and the old; the young are brave but intemperate, the old temperate but cowardly. To put it generally, all the valuable qualities that youth and age divide between them are united in the prime of life, while all their excesses or defects are replaced by moderation and fitness. The body is in its prime from thirty to five-and-thirty; the mind about forty-nine.

VACATION PICTURE FLOPS

In this essay Wade Dunn, a student in freshman English, explains what goes wrong so often in people's vacation pictures. Do you learn from his essay?

CONTEXT
This essay was written to be submitted to Family Circle *magazine as a possible piece for publication.*

AUDIENCE
Nonprofessional picture-takers who know very little about photography but who

want to shoot good pictures when they are on vacation. The general adult reader interested in photography will be the main audience.

The Miner family anxiously awaited the slides of the beautiful Mediterranean sunsets to light up their living room. As they waited, they joked over the mishaps that occurred on their vacation. Richie lost his suitcase somewhere between Venice and Marseilles. They missed their flight out of Frankfurt. The water in one town gave everybody in the family a nauseating case of the "jogs." All these mishaps, however, would be erased from memory, they were sure, when they saw the beautiful pictures they had made on the trip—little Tommy hanging over the edge of the Leaning Tower of Pisa and Mom biting into an eclair in Paris. But they were only to be disappointed. When the slides came on the screen, there were the none-too-magnificent sunsets and an out-of-focus Leaning Tower of Pisa. And Mom looked only like a blur. Mr. Miner looked at the pictures and shook his head.

There are several things that can explain why the Miners—and many people who take vacation snapshots with no instruction in photography—made mediocre pictures. The first and obvious explanation is that they did not know their camera. With today's technology, there are some cameras which will virtually say "cheese" for you. The amateur photographer can choose from hundreds of models that have all the gadgets you can imagine. Getting one of these "it-can-do-everything" cameras, however, won't help at all unless you learn how to use it. The Miners should have taken a short course at the store where they bought the camera, or they should have at least shot several rolls before they left for Europe. They, unfortunately, expected their new camera to do it all.

Another explanation of the Miners' bad luck with pictures was their unawareness that a camera does not see as the human eye does. Cameras cannot isolate, exhibit wide-angle capability, and zoom in all at the same time. Cameras cannot produce images in three dimensions. Although there are some cameras that can do some of these things, no camera records with the same perception as the human eye. Many people taking a picture mistakenly assume that the camera is seeing exactly what their eyes are seeing, and they are only disappointed when the photograph is returned.

Bad pictures almost always have been shot in the wrong light. While the human eye is capable of seeing with small amounts of light, film requires much more light. An example of the importance of light for film is seen in the picture Mr. Miner got of a mural in a chapel in Ravenna, Italy. The mural was painted on a forty-foot high ceiling. Mr. Miner placed his Blue Dot flash bulb on his camera, pointed towards the beautiful mural, and snapped his picture. This picture, of course, turned out black. Why? Mr. Miner was too far away from the subject. The light was too weak to reach the mural. Most flashes are not effective past eight feet in distance. Like a lot of people, Mr. Miner didn't think about the film needing extra light.

A final point that will explain why so many vacation pictures are mediocre is this: people do not get close enough to the subject. Pictures, to be good, must be easy to look at. They must be eye-catching, and they must be able to hold the attention of the observer. The photographer can accomplish this by "playing" with the arrangement of the subjects in the viewfinder. One absolute necessity is to get close to the subject. Do not overcrowd a picture with too many people or objects. Overcrowding will only draw attention away from the main subject. Getting close to the subject will automatically mean that the photographer is following a cardinal rule of picture taking which is, "Keep it simple."

Photos are a beautiful remembrance of the past. They say a thousand words. You can view an old photograph, then sit back and dream. As for the Miner family, I would be willing to bet that they buy a new camera "that does it all" for their next vacation. This really isn't necessary at all. All anyone has to do to make good vacation photographs is to understand why pictures go wrong. With this understanding everybody can make beautiful snapshots that will give pleasure for years. The Miners made mediocre pictures because they didn't know.

WRITING YOUR OWN EXPLANATION ESSAY

1. CONTEXT

Choose one of the following contexts as the basis for your essay. Be sure to indicate your context and audience on the top of the first page.

A

You have just missed the final exam in one of your most important courses. Although you have a legitimate, but complicated, excuse, the professor has not agreed to let you make up the test. She says that under school policy she is not allowed to do so. She has suggested, however, that you write a statement to the Dean of Student Affairs, explaining the situation and asking special permission to make up the exam. Write the essay that you are going to send to the Dean. Be sure that your explanation includes the facts about missing the test, the cause for your absence, the effect a decision not to let you take the test would have, and what you want the Dean to do.

B

One of your friends is unbelievable. Even though she is still in college, she is making over $5000 a year from part-time work which she does in her spare time. Most of these jobs she finds in magazine want ads and does at home: she has addressed envelopes, sold magazine subscriptions by phone, edited brochures, just to name a few. She has just discovered another job advertisement and is urging you to join her in the project. This is what you have to do.

A greeting card company that prints those little books on subjects like Happiness is . . . , A Friend is . . . , etc., is soliciting copy for additional books. If they buy the copy you send in, you will receive a $500 fee. The company will mail you $10, however, for every essay you send in, whether or not they buy it for use in their books. You are tempted. All the advertisement states is that persons interested should write an essay in which they define one of these terms:

Family togetherness is . . .
Bossiness is . . .
A vacation is . . .
Unhappiness is . . .
Success is . . .
An enemy is . . .
The good life is . . .

If the company feels your essay could be turned into copy for one of their books and would lend itself to great illustrations, they will buy it. Write them the essay. After all, you can't lose. At least you'll get the $10 for trying.

C

Someone once said that all persons in the world could be divided into two groups: those that eat oysters and those that don't. You thought about this the other night when you received a telephone call from a regional marketing company that wanted to hire you to give them some information about the people in your school. This marketing firm wants to know specifically how the people in your school dress. They represent several shoe and clothing companies that want to increase their sales in the area. The marketing firm offered you $250 to write an essay in which you describe the three basic ways people dress in your school. What they are actually asking you to do is to divide your classmates into three groups, based on how they dress. You realize that you will have to generalize to make this division, but you do think you could come up with three basic ways the people dress. The woman from the marketing firm said your report would have to be very descriptive, with a lot of specific details, because the firm would have to be able to make definite recommendations based upon what you have to say. You decide to write the report, using the general explanation essay format you have learned in school. It seems like something you might even enjoy doing.

D

Your manager or supervisor often has to hire people on a part-time basis during heavy workload periods to do the same job that you do on a regular basis. Every time someone new gets hired, your boss must take time out to explain to the temporary employee how the company operates, what to do on the job, etc. Realizing that much of this is a duplication of effort and a waste of time, the manager has asked you to write a pamphlet in which you explain everything the temporary help will need to know. The boss specifically asked you to include the rules of the company, the way to do the particular job (it's the same one you do), and how people get asked to stay on in a permanent position. You eagerly write the essay that the graphics department at the printing company will turn into a colorful pamphlet. After all, you're going to be saving yourself a lot of time, too, because you have to give out the same information time after time when the new employee has forgotten what the boss had to say.

E

The elementary schools in your area are starting a new program this spring: Super Saturdays. Various volunteers in the community will work with the children in subjects such as science, history, arts and crafts, writing, and music. The idea of these Super Saturdays (there will be two a month for three months) is to let the children learn new things in an informal, active environment. The science group, for instance, meets in the park. The ones signing up for arts and crafts will gather at a store that sells original paintings, drawings, and crafts. You love the whole idea and have agreed to be one of the teaching volunteers in the _____ group. For the first Saturday, you are going to explain one aspect of your subject that you think will really interest the children. (One of your friends in the history area is going to explain the effect of the discovery of the cotton gin one Saturday and the meaning of democracy another. Another

person in arts and crafts is going to explain to the children what weaving is, how and where it began, and the types of looms. The volunteer in science has several subjects in mind: why the sky is blue, types of clouds, what makes rain.)

You're preparing for your first meeting with the children (your group will be 10–12 years old) by writing out what you are going to discuss. This will take the form of an explanation essay which you studied in school. This essay will serve as your guide for the first Super Saturday meeting. Good luck.

F

You have just applied for Officer Candidate School in the Air Force. You receive this assignment:

The ability to communicate is an essential trait of a leader. In 500 words or less, express your reasons for desiring to be selected for participation in the Officer Candidate program. Since the Selection Board does not get to interview you in person, this statement is the only chance you get to express your motivation for a commission and to demonstrate your written communication skills. You may use a dictionary to assist you in writing your statement. Sign the statement when you have finished.

Write the essay which explains why you want to be accepted in Officer Candidate School.

CAUSE/EFFECT: HOW TO EXPLAIN THE REASONS AND CONSEQUENCES

1 Giving the cause and effect of a situation means that you (*a*) identify the thing/person/act that brings about a particular result and (*b*) show *how* it caused that result.

2 Be sure that the causes you give are sufficient to convince the reader. Even after you have isolated the cause of a situation in your mind, ask yourself, "Are there any other causes I should include?"

3 Be sure that there actually *is* a relationship between the cause and effect. If you can't prove this relationship exists in some logical, objective way, be sure that your reader understands that you are offering a personal view of the relationship between the cause and effect. Take the time in your essay to explain to the reader the connections you see.

4 Let the purpose of your writing determine the form your essay takes.

2. CREATING

The first thing you may want to do in the *Creating Stage* is to *loop* the contexts to see which one you want to choose as the basis for your essay. (You may also discover in the looping another context that you would rather write on. If so, discuss this new context with your instructor.) If you know immediately which context you want to use and don't need the looping activity to help you decide, you can move right into a creating technique that will produce ideas for the content of the essay itself. The best creating technique will depend upon the context you have chosen and upon your own preference. By this time you probably prefer one creating technique over the others and may also already be experiencing how different techniques work best for different purposes in writing and how they even lead to different ways of thinking. Whatever creating technique you choose, give yourself thirty to forty-five minutes or longer to come up with ideas for your essay.

CLASSIFICATION: HOW TO SHOW COMMON CHARACTERISTICS

1 *To classify* means *to organize into groups according to common characteristics, qualities, traits,* etc., *to put into basic categories,* or *to break down into component parts.*

2 When you set up a classification system, be certain that the categories don't overlap. Also make very clear to the reader what the groups are and how you decided what went into each group.

3 Don't oversimplify when you classify. Sometimes in an attempt to make everything orderly, a person will push a subject, person, item, etc., into a category where it doesn't really belong just to make the classification systematic. Don't undercut your credibility with your audience by forcing an item into a group where it doesn't clearly belong.

4 Use a classification system when it will help your reader follow your thoughts or explanation point by point.

3. SHAPING

1 Make your preliminary agreements. Know or invent the exact audience for whom you are writing. Even make a list of the characteristics describing these readers if it will help you stay clear on what they are likely to respond to. Write *to* (not *at*) your readers; remember they are people, not walls.

2 Check your thesis. Do you have one specific thing you are writing the essay to explain? Is this point very clearly stated early in the essay so that the reader knows from the beginning just where the writing is headed? Did you stay on this point all the way through the essay? Did you adequately explain it? Do you show that you are an insider on the matter and do actually have something to contribute to the reader? Does the essay sound like something you are *communicating* rather than something you are doing because you have a class assignment?

3 Do a Bare Bones Outline after you write the trial draft. This outline will show you any gaps or under-developed areas in the essay.

DEFINITION: HOW TO TELL WHAT SOMETHING MEANS

1 *To define* means *to explain the nature or essential qualities of a word, function*, etc. A definition determines or fixes the boundaries of the thing being discussed. The origin of the word *definition* was *to set boundaries*, and that is what a good definition does for the reader: it helps him or her stake out, limit, see the boundaries of a term.

2 A formal definition includes the term being defined, the class to which it belongs, and what differentiates it from other things in that class.

3 An informal definition takes several forms: defining by using a word that means approximately the same thing (*to gloat* means *to act superior and proud*); by using an opposite (*love* is *not using someone*); by showing the term's origin (*defining* originally meant *to set boundaries*); by using personal experience (*summer* means *time off, rest, and fun*); by giving examples (*eating well* is *having fresh vegetables and fruit, avoiding sugar, and staying off fried foods*).

4 Use definitions in your writing when there is any chance that your readers will not know the formal meaning of a word or the informal way you are using it. Being clear on the terms in a piece of writing is absolutely necessary for both the reader and the writer if communication is to occur.

---

4. FINAL CHECK

Write a second draft of the essay and read this to another person. Find out (*a*) if the person stayed interested all the way through (*b*) understood exactly what you were explaining (*c*) got value from the essay. After you have read the piece of writing to someone else and made any changes necessary after this reading, put the paper in its final form. Use a format that is as correct and attractive as you possibly can. Remember that the *appearance* itself of the essay can often make or break it as a piece of communication. How the essay looks is the first thing that strikes a reader. So don't undercut all the fine work you have done by letting the essay look incorrect and sloppy. Good luck!

edward a. cutler

STAGE THREE
COMPLETING

OUTLINE

HOW TO TURN GOOD WRITING
INTO EXCELLENT WRITING

PURPOSE

During the Completing Stage you:

Make life easier for yourself

Help the reader be more receptive to your message

Remove the last sources of confusion in the writing

Perfect what you say so that you can be proud of your writing

Release the paper and yourself

WHY COMPLETE?

You have now finished the first two stages of the writing process. In Stage 1 you CREATED something you wanted to say. In Stage 2 you SHAPED your writing by inventing your audience, turning your unruly thoughts into a single message that you could send to another person, and then doing everything you possibly could—organizing *beginning/ middle/end*, fully developing your points—to get that message delivered to the reader.

After all this, you may be asking *"What else is there to do?"*

Actually, all that *is* left to do is some check-up reviewing of the paper and some fine-tuning revisions. That's the third and final stage in the writing process—COMPLETING—and you're ready for it. **In the *Completing Stage* you turn a really critical eye on your writing to see what you have actually done.**

THE CONSTRUCTIVE CRITICAL EYE

When you turn a *critical eye* on your work, you are doing something you actually do in life many times a day. Have you ever hung posters or pictures on a wall and then stepped back to see how they looked? "That one is too high . . . no, a little too low, put it back up just an inch or so . . . that's just right; hold it while I get the hammer." That is turning a critical eye on your work.

Or you've looked at yourself in the mirror as you put the finishing touches on your hair, your outfit, your make-up. You think, "Should this shirt collar be on the outside of the sweater or on the inside?" Or you wonder, "Do I have that part in my hair straight; is it too far down on the left side?" Or you ask yourself whether your shoes can get by one more time without being polished. That's turning a *critical eye* on your appearance before you go out to meet the world.

Well, what you have done with pictures on a wall or your image in a mirror is exactly what you do to your writing when you move to the *Completing Stage* of the process. You examine it critically, but constructively. Your purpose isn't to find fault or to blame, but merely to see how it might look to someone else. Then see what you can do to make it better. *Have I made everything perfectly clear to my reader? Can the reader always see where I am going? Have I made any silly errors that will keep the reader from getting the message? What improvements and polish can I give this so that it is the very best writing I can possibly do?* Giving the paper the once-over—but not lightly—is exactly what you are now ready to do. And there is nothing negative about it. It is absolutely a golden opportunity for you to sit back—almost like a person who didn't write the paper—and see what can be done to make it the very best it can be. You aren't having to worry about what you want to say or how to put it into shape. Instead, you are free to be an editor now, pretending that someone else has handed you the paper for your suggestions on how to make the message 100 percent certain of getting across.

One big difference between putting the finishing touches on yourself before you go out and putting the finishing touches on your writing before you give it to someone else is that you *know* what to look for as you check yourself over in the mirror. It's not so easy with an essay. You're much more likely to read it over and think, "Well, that looks all right to me," because it takes a specially trained eye to know what to look for and to spot the ways the writing might be improved. This section will enable you to develop that "trained eye," and practice will perfect your use of it.

Although you might suppose that nobody would send out a paper without polishing, editing, and correcting it, experience shows that almost all beginning writers tend to skip this stage. Perhaps they lack the special skills required to do the job, or maybe they feel so burdened throughout the creating and shaping stages they figure that *any* kind of first draft is victory enough. Whatever the cause, many people omit this final stage. They shouldn't, however, and neither should you. To help you see the value of doing the *Completing Stage* on your own writing, and of doing it well, let's look at five substantial reasons.

WHY COMPLETING IS NECESSARY

1. **Completing makes life easier for you.**

There are certain things that we all do because they are proper or appropriate: we wipe our hands, if they are dirty, before we reach out for a handshake; we don't talk out loud at a wedding; we don't go out to dinner barefoot. These customs or established ways of doing things are violated only at the person's peril who breaks them. Don't observe the code = produce a hassle.

There are certain rules of correctness and propriety associated with writing. If you violate these established principles—say, have no margins or write in choppy, incomplete thoughts—then you are asking for the same kind of rebuff a barefoot person gets who tries to go into a roadside restaurant which clearly has a sign on the door: NO SHOES, NO SHIRT, NO SERVICE. There may be something to be proved by going against the rules, but in the case of writing, it's just plain smart to know the rules and to go by them. "*It's easier to ride the horse in the direction it's going.*"

2. **Completing makes the reader more receptive to your message.**

The *Completing Stage* is certainly a way of making life easier for your *message*. People do have certain expectations of a paper—they want it to be neat, to make sense, to be readable, to be correctly spelled and punctuated, and to have an order that they can follow. Because that's so, many people see only the error or weakness—the smudge, the misspelled word, the awkward sentence—and fail to see anything else in the paper, no matter how important that "anything else" might be. You may not think it is fair to equate mistakes in papers with sloppy thinking, but many people do just that. They pay so much attention to one or two faults that they miss the whole message. To give your message the best chance possible, you have to make it free of blemishes.

A story illustrates this human tendency to focus on a flaw and not see anything else. Uncle Elliot in late middle age noticed that his hair was getting quite thin—in fact, he was pretty bald on top. He decided to get a toupée, but was uneasy about the teasing he would get when he showed up at the next family gathering wearing the toupée for the first time. He hit on a brilliant scheme. He decided to put a large bandage on the tip of his chin the same day he started wearing his new wig. It worked like a charm, even for the family. Everybody asked how he had hurt himself, was it serious, would he have a scar, and so on. And nobody noticed his wig at all.

NO SHIRT NOT CORRECT
NO SHOES NOT POLISHED
NO SERVICE NOT READ

As surely as the tongue seeks the gap where the tooth is missing, so the reader will seek the gaps in your paper. And as surely as the family focused on Uncle Elliot's Band-Aid rather than seeing the rest of him, so the reader will focus on the errors in your paper and give that much less attention to your message. *Make life easier for your message.*

3. Completing removes the last sources of confusion.

Things written in haste sometimes confuse a reader because the message is actually blocked by gaps in the organization, too little development of the main points, or a lack of coherence. The *Completing Stage* gives you a final chance to make the message totally clear. Perhaps the reader will be tolerant, maybe he or she doesn't mind a smudge or is "understanding" about a misspelled word (although it's dangerous to count on that). But even if the errors or weaknesses don't upset the reader, they may still steal the punch or cloud the clarity of the message you are trying to get across. It is a shame to spend hours on a piece of writing, only to have it less effective than it could be simply because you didn't do a thorough *Completing Stage* and remove the last sources of confusion. The *Completing Stage* lets you find those things that could weaken the message; you have the leisure to sit back, relaxed and objective, and revise so that there is no confusion in your writing.

4. Completing lets you say what you mean in a way you can really be proud of.

There is nothing like the good feeling that is yours when you say something important in *just* the way you want it said. But it's impossible to check on the *way* it is said while the thoughts are still hot and rolling in. It's only after the words are "cold" that you can do the fine tuning that turns work from "OK" into "Good" or "Good" into "Best." Going back over your work gives you a chance to (*a*) say what you mean, (*b*) put on any finishing touches that you want to make, (*c*) rearrange for better effect, and (*d*) put your absolutely best foot forward. *It's your final chance to make the writing something you are very proud of—both for* what *you say and* how *you say it.*

5. Completing releases your paper and you.

Of the three stages of writing, the third one is very valuable to you symbolically because doing the third stage says, "*I'm finished!* It is the final act of this project in my life. I started it; I worked on it; I've finished it. I'm now ready to move on to something else." There is liberation and freedom in this act. You've in effect said, "This is the best I can do on this at the moment. I've finished it. I'm ready for a new thing." *Skipping the third stage will always leave you with an incomplete feeling and a knowledge that you did not give the writing your best.*

REVISING FOR FLOW: PARAGRAPHS

In the *Completing Stage*, the first thing you want to check with a critical eye is *how your writing flows. Flow* is a great concept: it means to proceed continuously and smoothly, and that is exactly what you want your writing to do. If your writing *flows*, not only will your thoughts proceed continuously and smoothly, but your reader, too, will be able to proceed continuously and smoothly along the course you have set.

However, there are several things that might keep the reader from proceeding continuously and smoothly. One is the overall *organization* and *development* of the essay. Of course, you have already done the Bare Bones Outline in the *Shaping Stage,* and you have become conscious of what your thesis is, how many points you used to "unwrap" or develop that thesis, and how you supported each of these points. So the basic organization and development are probably handled. **Now, in the *Completing Stage,* you can do a much more detailed internal analysis of your writing and develop more sophisticated and subtle means of having everything flow smoothly.**

To learn how to look critically at the flow of your writing, begin with the concept of PARAGRAPHING. Once you understand *what a paragraph does* and *how it* does it, you will be able to check your writing for smoothness. You will be able to revise it so that it really *flows*.

PARAGRAPHS

The root word for *paragraph* originated in Greece, where the term *paragraphos* meant a mark a writer put in the margin of a manuscript to set off part of a text. (*Para* = "beside"; *graph* = "mark.") Since these early writers didn't indent the way we do today, or actually write in paragraphs as we know them, they used these marks in the margins to draw the readers' eyes to certain main points. Our contemporary use of paragraphs is not too far removed from this.

Think of a paragraph as a container that holds words and sentences that you want to keep together for some reason or other, and you will have a good starting point for thinking about the concept of PARAGRAPHING. To see how this works, let's examine the two basic kinds of paragraphs.

Since *paragraph* is a term for the *container* that holds sentences and words, it stands to reason that the container can be used for different purposes. It's like having a jar that can contain berries or cherries or marbles or milk, or having a jar that you could use to prop up a window at your beach cabin, throw at a cat, or use as a magnifying glass. Paragraphs are similar. Sometimes they are containers for thought units, and sometimes they perform a function that serves the writer's needs at that moment in the writing. Let's look at these two uses of paragraphing:

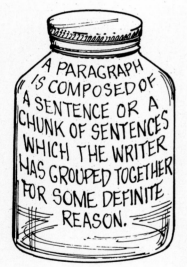

A PARAGRAPH IS COMPOSED OF A SENTENCE OR A CHUNK OF SENTENCES WHICH THE WRITER HAS GROUPED TOGETHER FOR SOME DEFINITE REASON.

Professional Writers
SURVEY ON PARAGRAPHING

We asked people who regularly write in connection with their work — people in management, sales, promotion, publishing — and also some professional creative writers, "When do you use paragraphs in your own writing?" Their answers covered quite a range and variety. Here are some of them:

When I'm writing a letter and move to a new point, I make a new paragraph.
> —*Sales supervisor who communicates mainly by letter to a sales force of about fifty people spread across the nation*

Often when I'm writing I'll make a point and then give an example. Then a second example occurs to me. I'll handle that by using three paragraphs— one for the point, and one each for the examples.
> —*Freelance magazine writer*

Usually I write in four to six paragraph clumps. That is, most ideas or points are good for about that much development. Almost like mini-essays. So I use paragraphs between those bunches to get the reader from one clump to the next.
> —*Textbook author*

Sometimes I need to keep writing on the same point but I'm afraid the reader may become confused, so I indent.
> —*Executive in sales and promotion*

It's strictly cosmetic. You look at the material and *see* where it needs indenting.
> —*Person responsible for corporate copywriting*

Paragraphs tend to be the same size, about 2½ to 3 inches, regardless of the number of words in the unit. Compare a book that has words all the way across the page to a magazine or journal, with words in several columns down each page. The book has lots more words to the line, but paragraphs tend to happen with the same frequency whether book or magazine—about every 2½ inches down the page.
> —*Person involved with layout and design of pages*

I switch them around, mix long ones with short ones, keep the reader interested and alert. Use them to vary the rhythm, nice leisurely long ones for easy and unhurried thinking, then "zip! biff!" I'll pop in a couple of short ones. If there was only one kind of paragraph, and only one length, the writing would be predictable and boring.
> —*Professional writer*

Finally, a corporate vice-president admitted to using the SWEG principle.

"What's that?" we asked.

"<u>S</u>cientific <u>W</u>ild-<u>E</u>yed <u>G</u>uess," she replied.

Although that survey left us a bit wild-eyed ourselves, we were determined not to stop there, so we simplified the answers and got this list. In short, people paragraph:

¶ to make a new point or change direction in their thinking.
¶ to develop a series of examples.
¶ to make transitions between sets of related thoughts.
¶ when the reader may become confused.
¶ for cosmetic purposes.

¶ for approximate size of units.
¶ to keep the reader alert and interested.
¶ by guess (wild-eyed or not).
¶ to show shift from one speaker to another (as in dialogue).

Two Kinds of Paragraphs The *Topic Sentence Paragraph* takes one main idea and develops it. The topic sentence (sometimes stated, sometimes implied) tells the readers what you are about to discuss, focuses the readers' minds on that particular thing, and then provides enough information to prove or explain or illustrate or otherwise develop that main idea. Thus it is possible to break a Topic Sentence Paragraph down into two parts: the TOPIC SENTENCE itself (the main idea, either stated or implied) and the ADDITIONAL SENTENCES (directly related to the topic sentence and developing it). It is this Topic Sentence Paragraph that carries the information or content of the writing and is essential in getting the message across to the reader.

1 TOPIC SENTENCE PARAGRAPH

Presents content *within the paragraph* in a way that defines or limits the reader's thoughts; contains a chunk of *complete thought;* provides the reader with a feeling of *completeness and satisfaction* by paragraph's end.

The *Function Paragraph* is a different matter entirely. In it, you won't find one main idea set forth and developed. In fact, at times a Function Paragraph may be only one sentence; it's a "paragraph" only because it is indented. Often a series of Function Paragraphs, taken all together, do indeed make up a single, related chunk of thought, but the writer chooses to break that chunk into smaller units. Some of the most common uses for Function Paragraphs are these:

1 To add drama to the writing, thereby keeping the reader's attention.
2 To make transitions.
3 To set off conversational dialogue.
4 To break up a paragraph that seems too long (or to keep all paragraphs in the piece of writing about the same length).
5 To accommodate the author's personal writing style.
6 To emphasize a point, to develop an example, or to add details.

2 FUNCTION PARAGRAPH

Directs the reader in *how to read* the essay; helps keep the reader interested; allows writer to emphasize or elaborate on certain points; lets the writer show her or his style in the writing.

Of course the descriptions of the two paragraph types are not exclusive. That is, it's possible to have a Topic Sentence Paragraph that is also dramatic, and it's possible to have a Function Paragraph that adds details. So there is some overlapping in the qualities that both paragraph types share. Yet in terms of *purpose* or *use* or *function*, the two types are quite distinguishable. The Topic Sentence Paragraph operates over and over, the same way. And although there are a variety of uses for the Function Paragraphs, they nearly always look and act like Function Paragraphs and not at all like Topic Sentence Paragraphs.

Let's look at an actual piece of writing to see how Topic Sentence Paragraphs and Function Paragraphs are used. This essay, written by a freshman, illustrates the individual (and lively) ways the concept of paragraphing can be applied.

Growing Up

I cannot believe that it is all over.

(1) Function Paragraph: to add drama and get reader's attention.

When I was little, all I ever wanted to be was a teenager. I longed for the days when I would do nothing but chase boys, talk on the telephone, and blast my stereo.

(2) Topic Sentence Paragraph: sets up main subject of being a teenager.

I wonder now, if I had not talked so long on the phone and had not listened to my loud stereo so avidly or run after so many boys, if my high school years would have gone by any slower. I really never took the time to stop and say, "Hey! I am now one normal, 100%, full-fledged teenager!" Instead, it seems as though I made a transition straight from babydoll little girl life into womanhood without even stopping to think twice.

(3) Function Paragraph: to emphasize a point. *(Actually, it is the continuation of the Topic Sentence Paragraph above; the two together make up one chunk unit of thought.)*

(Paragraph ends with the thesis the writer plans to develop in the rest of the paper.)

Looking back now, trying to recapture those years that were blurred with speed, seems virtually impossible. How does one write words that can convey the bliss of a first love, the heartache of a first good-by, and the first stark realization that the future is waiting breathlessly in one's hands? Decorating the quarterback's house and performing routines at the football games became more important than Thanksgiving, Christmas, and New Year's Day all put together. It was a time when Mrs. Bodkin's sophomore class became the most exciting class of the day because Kendall Carter always announced, "Here comes the farm news! The cows are up, the pigs are down, the corn is up, and the wheat is rising high!"

(4) Topic Sentence Paragraph: the main idea is the impossibility of recapturing those high school years. *(Everything else in the paragraph relates to that topic.)*

The nights were magical. When I close my eyes, I can still picture the lights whizzing by down Central Expressway as we laughed and sang to the radio and told jokes in the back seat. After the sun went down, my old 1960 blue Studebaker Lark would become a "Super Studie," and she would fly up and down the roads just about as fast as any 'Cuda, Trans-Am, or Corvette. Although the Studie broke down occasionally, we could always depend on that happening when we were where we were "supposed" to be: the library or the grocery store. The car never did break down on those great nights when we were racing on Forest

(5) Topic Sentence Paragraph: the main subject is nights the writer remembers from the past. *(All other sentences in the paragraph develop this subject.)*

Lane, cruising down Coit, dancing at "Chelsea Street's," or chasing Cessna 250's at Shiloh Airport.

(6) Topic Sentence Paragraph: the main idea is the summer as the grand finale. *(All the other sentences develop this idea.)*

Those magic nights, the senior prom, and graduation itself fade into background when I think about this past summer. It was a grand finale to everything. There was not much different from the previous years except that with this summer came the realization that it would soon all be over. It was right in the middle of laughing and joking that we would stop, turn to each other and realize that soon we wouldn't be together to laugh. It was a summer of smiling when we felt like crying, dancing when we felt like sitting still, and getting drunk when we felt like staying sober.

(7) Function Paragraph: to break a long paragraph, to change the focus slightly, even though still discussing the topic sentence from the paragraph above.

It was a summer of being nice to my little brother because I knew he wouldn't be around to pester me in the fall. He wouldn't be putting green plastic grasshoppers in my bed or howling over "George and his problem" jokes. I sat in my daddy's lap and did not feel silly and looked at my mother and really saw her for the first time. It was a mad rush to garage sales for kitchen utensils, a wild search for just the right pots and pans, and a scavenger hunt for the "perfect" shower curtain for me to use when I went away to school in September. Mother and daughter talks became a revered enjoyment, and the "one last shopping trip" became an almost holy ritual.

(8) Function Paragraph: to make transition and signal end of one part of the essay.

It was soon over. After one last spin by Jack-in-the-Box, one last night at the Roller Rink, and one last timid honk in front of Kendall's house, I knew the summer was gone.

(9) Topic Sentence Paragraph: the main idea is that writer is still the same person. *(Rest of paragraph develops this thought.)*

I am still the same person. I still wear the same clothes. My white phone may be sitting silently in my room at home, but my Studie is here with me and gets me around as well as it ever has. I live in an apartment now, but my stereo plays just as loud. I have an 8 x 10 glossy of Kendall Carter out, but every time I look at it, I have to realize that he isn't mine anymore and he really wasn't what I ever wanted in the first place. All of his dreams of playing university football and flying high in the sky got him nowhere except dropped out of high school.

(10) Topic Sentence Paragraph: the main idea is to show how writer is different.

Yes, I am the same person, yet I'm not the same. Every time I look at Kendall's mischievous cock-eyed grin, it makes me glad I am growing up. I *am* different now. I am 18. I cannot decide whether to vote for the Democrat or Republican in the next presidential election. I have had to realize that happiness and sadness cannot depend on whether things go my way or not. I have had to accept that I did let my high school years pass by almost unnoticed. I have jumped from child to adult, with only that blur in between.

(11) Function Paragraph: to provide drama and to emphasize a point.

And, yes, there's a loss.

(12) Function Paragraph: to emphasize a point and to follow the one-sentence function paragraph before it.

But I've come to accept that my true happiness will depend upon an agreement I have made with myself to do my best and to try to make the most of my new "adulthood." That's growing up.

—*Debbi Pigg*

You can see from this essay that without Topic Sentence Paragraphs there can be no developed message. Without Function Paragraphs, however, the reader would probably be bored by the sameness of the writing (a characteristic of a lot of classroom essays) and a lack of consideration for the reader's attention span. **Topic Sentence Paragraphs have a clear logic;** *there is a main idea, either stated or implied, and a group of sentences that develop that idea.* **Function Paragraphs usually have no logic except the author's own.** *They aren't caused by a new thought. They don't have main idea sentences. They don't develop a topic. They do, however, keep the reader moving, provide continuity in the essay, give a sense of drama, and reflect the individual personality of the writer.*

If an essay had to have one or the other, of course it would have to have Topic Sentence Paragraphs, else there would be little way to develop the thoughts. Fortunately, though, it is not an either/or case. Once there are good strong, fully developed Topic Sentence Paragraphs, a writer can add Function Paragraphs to make the writing lively, interesting and personal. Even though there isn't an either/or situation, *there is a priority situation:* **master the Topic Sentence Paragraph first.** Then revise and add Function Paragraphs. Perhaps you won't have to establish a priority; you may find yourself doing both kinds at once, almost automatically. If so, that is fine. If you aren't familiar with the concepts of each, however, start with the Topic Sentence Paragraph and build from there.

THE TOPIC SENTENCE PARAGRAPH

All essays must have several good Topic Sentence Paragraphs; it is these paragraphs that let you focus and limit the reader's attention to the particular thing you want the reader to think about. The Topic Sentence Paragraph also provides the reader with a sense of *satisfaction* or *completeness* because it *gives* the information or content of your message. A good Topic Sentence Paragraph will never leave your reader guessing. It will also never let the reader's mind wander from your subject.

By putting the main points of your message into Topic Sentence Paragraphs, you can be sure that your reader feels comfortable in knowing what you are trying to say and satisfied at the end that he/she got the message. Topic Sentence Paragraphs are a way of spiffing up all those untidy thoughts and presenting them in a controlled, predictable, orderly form. They state the message clearly and explicitly, leaving nothing for the reader to guess about.

That tends to sound a bit marvelous, a bit miraculous. Imagine having the reader think what *you* want her to think about, rather than what *she* wants to think about! Well, in a way it *is* kind of wonderful, but it is also quite *systematic* and a "miracle" that anyone can *repeat* again and again, once the principles are understood.

Watch how a Topic Sentence Paragraph operates:

The topic sentence paragraph presents and develops a point or thought within the paragraph, defines or limits the reader's thoughts, and provides the reader with a feeling of completeness.

"I knew a woman, lovely
   in her bones,
When small birds sighed,
   she would sigh back
   at them;
Ah, when she moved, she
   moved more ways than
   one:
The shapes a bright
   container can contain!"
   —Theodore Roethke

Here's a word:

$$Sea$$

I write it down, and you read it.

Then you "see" in your mind's eye whatever the word makes you think of. Perhaps a vacation you took at the beach, a program you saw on TV, the time you were in the Navy, jogging on sand, a storm, whales, or drowning. You think of whatever *you* think of; all I've done by writing down the word is to stimulate you to remember.

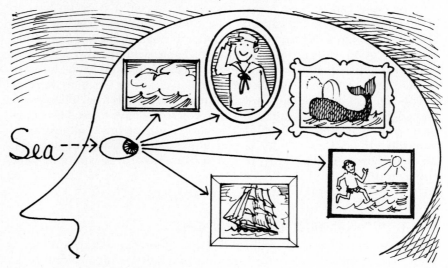

I add a few more words, giving you a phrase:

$$The\ Dead\ Sea$$

Now what has happened?

I've *limited* your thinking, directed it to what *I* am thinking about the word *sea*. Instead of entertaining any personal memory that you might remember connected with the word *sea*, now you are limiting your thinking (momentarily at least) to *The Dead Sea*. Maybe you think of Dead Sea Scrolls. Or you might think, "Isn't that where you float on top of the water?" or "I don't know anything about the Dead Sea." Whatever happens, you concentrate on *The Dead Sea* instead of just *sea*, simply because I have given you more information. I'm narrowing your attention.

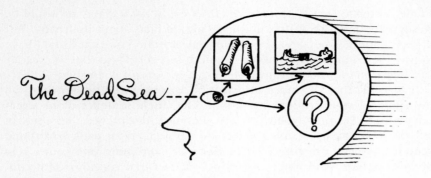

Now, watch this. I give you a whole sentence:

The Dead Sea is not a sea at all.

What will probably happen when I write this sentence is that you will stop looking into your own memory for something you know about the Dead Sea and will instead pay attention to me because I've caused you to be interested in what I have to say. If you aren't actually interested, at least **I've limited the things that at the moment you are thinking about *seas* in general and have directed you to the thing about seas that I want to say to you.** And, of course, this is the purpose of all communication from one person to another: getting the other person's attention so that you can tell him or her what you want to say in a way that will be really understandable.

So, the Topic Sentence Paragraph allows you to direct and control the reader's attention to what you want to communicate.

But is the sentence enough?

I've just written to you, *The Dead Sea is not a sea at all.* You're interested. I have your attention. What if I don't go on? How long would I keep your attention? If I added nothing to that sentence, you would be perfectly within your rights to say, "Well, what about it?" or "So what?"

Thus, if I want to keep your attention and get a message across to you that is complete, I have to add some more sentences to this one. So that's what I do:

Despite it's name, the Dead Sea is not a sea at all. It is actually a lake. The lake ranges in depth from 33 meters in the north basin to 2 meters in the south basin. The lake is 45 miles long by 9 miles wide. The two basins which make up the lake were joined in Biblical times by a neck of land which could be crossed on foot; today that neck of land is submerged and the lake looks like one continuous body of water.

— Harvey Arden

You can see now how a paragraph works. I can't deliver my complete message unless I give you enough additional information. Maybe the single sentence *Despite its name, the Dead Sea is not a sea at all* would be enough for me, the writer, if I know all the facts about it already. But if I want another person to believe or pay attention to what I say, I have to provide enough information—enough sentences—so that the reader will feel *complete* and *convinced* when the paragraph is finished.

It is ironic that the more information you give, the tighter you pull the circle of your reader's attention. The single sentence alone won't say enough. It's only when you put sentence to sentence that you can tell the reader any *meaning* about the subject. **With each additional sentence, you're drawing your reader more and more into your circle of information.** And you're directing—in fact to a certain extent controlling—what he or she thinks about your subject. A topic sentence paragraph can really put you in command and let you give the reader exactly the information you've chosen.

Topic Sentence Paragraph:
A group of sentences that are connected one to the other to cause the reader to know some particular point the writer is making; the smallest unit of writing that a writer can use to get a *developed message* over to the reader.

APPLICATION

1 Practice limiting your reader's thoughts by adding more information. You can do this by pretending to be both the writer and the reader. Start with a single word. Write down what you think of when you see the word:

Street: _____

Now, add some words to the single word *(street)* and make a phrase that limits the reader's thinking:

Phrase about *street:* _____

Now, turn the group of words into a sentence:

Sentence about *street:* _____

Do you see how with each step you are drawing a tighter circle around what your reader will think? You are directing the reader to what *you* want to say instead of letting the reader think whatever random thoughts might come up.

2 Do the same activity with the word *singing*. Begin by listing the random thoughts you have about the word.

Singing: _____

Add some words to *singing* that make a phrase to limit the reader's thinking:

Phrase about *singing:* _____

Now turn the group of words into a sentence:

Sentence about *singing:* _____

3 Take each of the following words through the same three steps. Notice every time how the writer can direct and control the reader's attention by giving additional information.

mountain   pizza   work   dancing   children

CHECKING YOUR WRITING FOR FLOW: LOOKING AT THE TOPIC SENTENCE PARAGRAPHS

Now, let's apply this information about Topic Sentence Paragraphs to one of your essays. First of all, go through the paper and label each paragraph that carried a message *TSP* for *Topic Sentence Paragraph.* Next, look at the paragraphs that you have labeled *TSP* and check them by answering the following questions:

1 Have you told the reader clearly the main idea that the paragraph is built around, or have you made that idea so clear by implication that the reader can't miss it?

2 Have you made sure that every sentence in the Topic Sentence Paragraph is related to the main idea?

3 Have you given the reader enough information so that the main idea gets across?

If there is anything that needs improvement in your Topic Sentence Paragraphs, it will probably be something in one of these three areas, so let's look at them carefully, one at a time.

Principle 1: Tell the Reader Clearly What the Paragraph Is About

The Topic Sentence Paragraph is named for its chief characteristic: the *topic sentence*. In a word, **the topic sentence tells the reader what the paragraph is about.** It expresses the organizing idea. All other sentences in the paragraph *relate to the topic sentence,* by explaining or developing or giving additional information. The topic sentence, then, is absolutely necessary for a paragraph that is to deliver a developed message. More accurately, it is the *order* and *structure* of the topic sentence that are absolutely necessary. How does it order and structure? In two ways:

1 **The topic sentence orders your readers' thoughts by directing them to think about that particular aspect of the subject that you want them to think about.** (Remember the Dead Sea examples earlier.)

2 **The topic sentence also orders your own thoughts.**

The topic sentence in a Topic Sentence Paragraph works like a classifying system. It lets you put those thoughts together that belong together. *What determines whether they belong together is the topic sentence.*

Here is how it works:

Imagine that you are packing to move, and you have one box marked "Take," one marked "Give away," and one marked "Burn." As you go through the closet, you put everything in the "Take" box that is going on the truck; anything you think someone else might use but that you don't want, you put in the "Give away" box; and what you don't feel anyone wants you throw into "Burn." The words on the box determine what goes into that box.

The topic sentence in a paragraph works like the words on those packing boxes. Whatever the topic sentence says determines what gets put into that particular paragraph. Look at this example about the Anasazi Indians, who built the famous cliff dwellings in Colorado:

The Anasazi were builders and settlers on a large and permanent scale, and it is for this that they are best remembered. At a time many centuries before the European discovery and settlement of the Americas, the Anasazi had developed a complex civilization of large and closely related communities. They erected massive and multistoried apartment buildings, walled cities, and cliff dwellings of shaped and mortared sandstone. They were dedicated farmers who planted, tilled, and even irrigated their crops, putting by the harvest to see them through the year. They were creative craftsmen of pottery and jewelry, and practiced a highly formalized religion in distinctive ceremonial chambers. The permanence and stability that they saw in their lives was reflected in the homes they built, but for reasons not yet completely understood their civilization lacked the durability of the building. The Anasazi abandoned their homeland, leaving the great stone cities and familiar farmlands for other areas in the Southwest, eventually to mix in the amalgam of modern Pueblo.

—Donald G. Pike

Because the topic sentence is what it is—*The Anasazi were builders and settlers on a large and permanent scale, and it is for this that they are best remembered*—the reader can see immediately why the six other sentences in the paragraph belong there. The topic sentence is the "leader" of the group, and gathered around it are the sentences that constitute the rest of the group. The topic sentence is the "boss" or "director" and determines everything else that goes into that particular paragraph.

You can now clearly see why it is absolutely necessary that you have a topic sentence for the paragraph. Without a topic sentence, there's nothing to direct the readers to the particular aspect of the subject you want them to think about, and there's nothing to hold the sentences together as a group. A paragraph without a topic sentence looks like this:

Jogging is a fast-growing sport. Sports really contribute to good health. There is a new sports magazine on the market this month. Playing ball was a sport done thousands of years ago in primitive societies. People get injured in sports every year. Tennis players do not have a wide variety of shoes available to them. Sports can be expensive.

Reading that jumble of sentences, you feel as though you were being pushed from this to that, never knowing what was coming up. There was not a single "leader" sentence in the bunch that directed your thoughts and served to hold all the other sentences together.

How *could* this paragraph become a good Topic Sentence Paragraph? In fact, it's impossible to use all these sentences in one coherent paragraph; the best you could do is choose *one* of them, make *it* the topic sentence, and add the necessary sentences to develop the point.

Playing ball was a sport done thousands of years ago in primitive societies. In fact, at Chichen Itza, an ancient Mayan Indian ruin on the Yucatán Peninsula in Mexico, you can still see the long ball court, the rings through which the ball was thrown, and the murals showing the two teams playing the game. The guides at Chichen Itza will tell you, too, how the winner of the ball game was rewarded. He was sacrificed to the rain god because that god deserved the very best. And by winning the game, he had proven he was the best.

To repeat: **the topic sentence lets the reader know, in general, what you are going to discuss and is the controlling idea for the rest of the sentences in the paragraph. All the other sentences are there because they discuss *in specific* the general subject set up in the topic sentence.**
It is absolutely in your own best interest to have topic sentences in your Topic Sentence Paragraphs. Since your whole purpose is to get a message across to another person, you need to do everything possible to make it *easy*. Remember that the reader gets impatient. The reader wants to *know* what you are going to talk about, and wants to know *quickly*. Remember, too, that the topic sentence helps *you* too because it sets up an expectation that the rest of the paragraph can fulfill. The topic sentence can order your thoughts as you write. It serves as a reminder to you of *what you are discussing at this time*.

APPLICATION

1   Here are some sentences that could be good topic sentences for a Topic Sentence Paragraph. Write the *additional* sentences that will develop, or relate to, the topic sentence.
    A Paying bills has its humorous side.
    B Apartment living is for the birds.
    C A woman who works has two exciting lives.
    D Going to college as an adult requires special skills.
    E Working and going to school at the same time is a drag.

2   Here are some "additional" sentences that might be added to a topic sentence. Write the *topic sentence* that will tie each unit together.

A

Red makes you feel aggressive and alive. Blue, on the other hand, can be calming or it can be depressing. If you wear yellow, you will probably feel cheerful, if for no other reason than because people say, "You look cheerful today dressed in yellow." Black can look smashing and chic, or it can look drab, depending on how you accent it. Probably the worst color to wear at all is gray. You just fade into the crowd.

Topic Sentence: _____

B

This is generally an excellent time, because you will be able to capture the attention of all those buyers who have been out looking at other open houses. Even though a Sunday afternoon open house does cut into the few remaining weekend hours, it is perhaps preferred by most because of the response gained. Buyers generally plan to set aside a certain portion of time during the week for their home inspections. Generally, they go out looking at a time when they will be able to inspect the most properties in the shortest amount of time. You might decide to stick with this trend.

—Ronald W. Jensen

Topic Sentence: _____

C

When the day is cloudy and gloomy, I get depressed. Even if I have a busy day planned, the gloominess of a day without sunshine makes it difficult for me to function effectively. But rainy days don't depress me at all. Sometimes, though, they make me angry—especially when I have to do a lot of walking that day. I hate to arrive at work soaking wet. Other times, rainy days cheer me up. There is nothing as refreshing as a rain shower after several days of hot, muggy weather. My best moods, however, occur on warm, sunny days. The brightness of the sun lifts my spirits; I feel energetic and ready to work. The only problem then is that I'd rather be outdoors than indoors.

Topic Sentence: _____

D

Some advertisers suggest that their cigarette will make you masculine or feminine. Marlboro and Virginia Slims ads are good examples of this. Others would like us to believe that their cigarettes will bring romance into our lives. Their ads feature happy couples usually strolling hand-in-hand; no doubt, we are to assume that the cigarette was instrumental in forming the romance. Still others claim that their cigarette is refreshing, that its taste will make you feel springtime fresh. Now that we know cigarette smoking may cause lung cancer, some advertisers try a logical appeal by comparing tar and nicotine levels: the smart smoker buys the cigarette with the least tar and nicotine and the best flavor. Actually, the smart person enjoys the ads and buys no cigarettes!

Topic Sentence: _____

PLACEMENT OF THE TOPIC SENTENCE IN A TOPIC SENTENCE PARAGRAPH

Where does the topic sentence go in the paragraph? Usually in one of three places:
1 At the beginning
2 At the end
3 Nowhere—it's just "understood"

1 Placing the Topic Sentence at the Beginning

By far the most common location for the topic sentence is at the beginning of a Topic Sentence Paragraph. It is easy to see the advantage of putting it there. **The reader knows *immediately* what you are going to talk about.** And *you* have a constant reminder too—from the very start—of what you are concentrating on in this paragraph. **The topic sentence will help *you* stay on the subject.** Knowing how fast thoughts can come—often faster than you can write them down—you're only too happy to have a system that weeds out the unnecessary ones immediately.

Here are two paragraphs written by college students. Both writers took pains to let the reader know *immediately* what they were going to talk about. See how their topic sentences signal the readers about what is going to be discussed.

Without a doubt, the small-block Chevrolet V8 engine has become the most popular automotive power plant in all aspects of motor sports. Its power-to-weight benefits were quickly recognized by enthusiasts, and its development continues even today. During the past 22 years its size has grown from the original 265 cubic inches to displacements up to 400 (not to mention what a few hot rodders have been able to come up with). Not only has the size increased, but virtually every part of the engine has been modified in one way or another to improve performance. Special light weight cylinder blocks and heads have been produced by manufacturers through the country. Even the Chevrolet factory has been caught up in the sharp demands for better performing parts. They actually developed several magnesium cylinder blocks that weighed only 35 pounds, but they proved unusable and never reached the market. The Chevrolet people and other companies continue to work on ideas of saving weight so that the Chevy V8 will retain its popularity.

What happens when ducks swallow lead? The pellets pass through the digestive tract to the gizzard where they are converted to a soluble form and absorbed by the bloodstream. Lead causes a reduction in oxygen supplies to all tissues. It interferes with the body's ability to break down glucose, leading to weight loss. Lead also disrupts the production of hemoglobin and anemia is the likely result. This imbalance in blood chemistry impairs the functioning of the liver and heart and causes severe damage to these organs. The external symptoms are an extreme loss of weight, wing droop, refusal to eat, a tendency to seek isolation and cover, and loss of the ability to walk or fly.

2 Placing the Topic Sentence at the End

One good reason for putting the topic sentence at the end of the paragraph is to keep the reader in suspense and, therefore, interested. **The reader reads on to see what you are going to say when you get through,** *but only if what comes first is really compelling.* Imagine a bicycle rider picking up a book that started, "You should study the interior and function of the muscle cell." Do you think she would be interested in reading on? But imagine the same cyclist with a different beginning for the paragraph:

Each of us is composed of a hundred trillion cells or more. With each movement the body requires the collaboration of thousands of nerve and muscle cells. The muscle cell in particular shows a remarkable ability for obtaining and using energy. *Exploring the interior and function of the muscle cell is an exciting beginning to the appreciation, knowledge, and understanding of the cycling body.*

—Irvin Faria and Peter Cavanagh

The reader is much more likely to be willing to read on because the writers built up to their point.

Another reason for putting the topic sentence at the end of a paragraph is **to build point by point toward the conclusion so that the reader will be prepared to agree** by the time he or she arrives. This type of paragraph is sometimes called *inductive,* since it induces the reader through a series of specific details toward a conclusion that draws those details all together. Here is an example:

Now that they've taught pigeons to play table tennis and chimpanzees to play word games and computers to play chess, it's becoming quite difficult to distinguish humans from the rest of the landscape. So, if you set out to ask what makes people people rather than animals or machines, bye and bye you have to look into the subject of music. *It appears that the ability to make music is a characteristic of human nature only.*

—Ward Cannel and Fred Marx

The first sample paragraph, about muscle cells, shows how a reader can be teased into reading further. This one, although rather light-hearted, shows how a reader can be taken, one step at a time, toward a particular conclusion. The first sets out to trap interest; the second sets out to trap agreement.

3 Placing the Topic Sentence Nowhere—Having It "Understood"
Sometimes you may feel that the reader will know the main idea in the paragraph without being told. In fact, **sometimes formally stating the main idea is somewhat artificial and stiff,** so you put in only the specific details. In the following example, Lawrence Durrell is describing the Greek island of Mykonos. There is no one sentence that says so; the main idea of the paragraph is, therefore, just understood.

Everywhere the white arcades and chapels repeat themselves in an obsessive rhythm of originality and congruence; and what is marvelous is that in Mykonos there are no foreign echoes from Venice, Genoa and the rest. Everything is as newly minted as a new-laid Easter egg, and just as beautiful. You can walk for hours in what is an imitation *souk* hung with carpets, brocades, island blankets, donkey bags, shawls in all their bewildering variety. Relentless perspectives of light and shade marry the voluptuous shapes of breasts translated into cupolas and apses, into squinches and dovecots. Take Picasso, Brancusi and Gaudi, knock their heads together, and you might get something like Mykonos by evening light, foundering into violet whiteness against a blue-black sea. At the end of every gyre or whorl (you are inside a seashell), you suddenly plunge out upon the harbor with its welcoming lines of cafés and chophouses, set out under brilliant awnings or in some places shaded by tall mulberries. Nightfall is the time, ouzo time, after an exhausting day of doing nothing purposefully (the opposite of killing time), when you feel the need of these cafés. The violets, pinks, rose and gray of the sinking sun on the walls — just before the wink of the green ray which says goodnight — are all the more haunting for being reproduced in the cloudy glass of ouzo before you on the table. It is like inhabiting a rainbow.

— Lawrence Durrell

And Please Note: It's very important to recognize the difference between a paragraph with an implied or understood topic sentence, such as the one above, and a paragraph that is just a collection of unconnected sentences. **If you are in the slightest doubt, put in the topic sentence.** That way you are *certain* not to go wrong.

APPLICATION

1 FINDING THE TOPIC SENTENCE:
Pick out the topic sentence in each paragraph below. If the topic sentence is implied, compose an appropriate sentence that describes the paragraph.

A

The alcohol-drunk driver usually finds it hard to hide his condition, if stopped by the police. But the pot-high driver often believes he can "come down" and carry on a seemingly normal conversation with a police officer. This apparent ability to "hide their high" gives many pot smokers confidence that they can drive stoned.

— Peggy Mann

B

The room in which I found myself was very large and lofty. The windows were long, narrow, and pointed, and at so vast a distance from the black oaken floor as to be altogether inaccessible from within. Feeble gleams of encrimsoned light made their way through the trellised panes, and served to render sufficiently distinct the more prominent objects around; the eye, however, struggled in vain to reach the remoter angles of the chamber, or the recesses of the vaulted and fretted ceiling. Dark draperies hung upon the walls. The general furniture was profuse, comfortless, antique, and tattered. Many books and musical instruments lay scattered about, but failed to give any vitality to the scene. I felt that I breathed an atmosphere of sorrow. An air of stern, deep, and irredeemable gloom hung over and pervaded all.

— Edgar Allen Poe

C

We get home from church around 12:30. After a late lunch, the afternoon seems to stretch before us unendingly. We leisurely read the Sunday paper — there's always more to it than there is to the weekly papers. Usually, there's homework to do, but no one feels like doing it, so we postpone it, choosing to nap or to go for a ride instead. Occasionally, there's an old movie worth watching on television. And, of course, it's always nice just to sit in the shade sipping a Coke or lemonade while the afternoon wears on.

D

In democracies, by definition, all human beings should have a say about technological developments that may profoundly change, even threaten, their lives: nuclear power, genetic engineering, the spread of microwave systems, the advance of satellite communications, and the ubiquitous use of computers, to name only a few. And yet, in order to participate fully in discussions of the implications of these technologies one must have training in at least physics, psychology, biology, philosophy, economics, and social and political theory. Any of these technologies has profound influence in all those areas. Because most of us are *not* so trained, all discussion takes place among our unelected surrogates, professionals and experts. They don't have this full range of training either, but they do have access to one or another area of it and can speak to each other in techno-jargon—"tradeoffs," "cost-benefits," "resource management"—and they therefore get to argue with each other over one side of the question or the other while the rest of us watch.

—Jerry Mander

E

When we first saw the barracks apartments, I told myself I would never live there. Five minutes later, we were turning the key to an apartment in one of those horrible buildings. (None of the nicer apartments were vacant, and we needed a place that day.) The first thing I didn't like was the stove that faced the door as you entered the apartment. Walking right into the kitchen as you came in reminded me of the crowded ghetto apartments I've seen on television. Then the couch looked like something you'd find in a cheaply furnished, rundown bus station. It was a gaudy orange vinyl and had no arms, and only two people could sit on it at a time because it was so small. There was no backboard on the bed, and the dresser drawer was made of brown, ugly metal. In the bathroom sink, there were separate hot and cold water faucets. I hated every thing about that apartment—but we lived there three years!

F

I think the stature of humor must vary some with the times. The court fool in Shakespeare's day had no social standing and was no better than a lackey, but he did have some artistic standing and was listened to with considerable attention, there being a well-founded belief that he had the truth hidden somewhere about his person. Artistically he stood probably higher than the humorist of today, who has gained social position but not the ear of the mighty. (Think of the trouble the world would save itself if it would pay some attention to nonsense!) A narrative poet at court, singing of great deeds, enjoyed a higher standing than the fool and was allowed to wear fine clothes; yet I suspect that the ballad singer was more often than not a second-rate stooge, flattering his monarch lyrically, while the fool must often have been a first-rate character, giving his monarch good advice in bad puns.

—E. B. White

2 TOPIC SENTENCE PARAGRAPHS IN YOUR OWN WORK

You have already marked the Topic Sentence Paragraphs in your trial draft. Now, for each paragraph that you marked *TSP* in your essay, find the topic sentence. *Underline it so that it really stands out.* If you don't have a topic sentence, either stated or implied, *now* is the time to find that out. It means that you reader will probably have no idea why you have grouped the sentences together that you did. As a result, you will lose the reader's attention while she or he tries to figure out the organizing idea of the paragraph. Mark any paragraph that does not have a topic sentence so that you can rewrite it when you get ready to make your next revision.

When you've checked and marked each topic sentence in your *TSP,* proceed to *Principle 2,* which follows.

Principle 2: Make Sure that Every Sentence in the Topic-Sentence Paragraph Is Related to the Topic Sentence

In the process of writing, ideas can pop up anywhere, sometimes even surprising to you, the writer. Often these surprising ideas are so original or intriguing that you veer off in happy pursuit of them. This is fine in the early stages of writing—in fact, it can even be desirable because you may discover some really good point that hadn't been thought of before. But when the writing process gets down to thinking about the reader and to making everything as easy as possible for the reader, **a topic sentence paragraph must be examined carefully to be sure that the reader doesn't get surprised.** Sudden veering off can be fun for the writer but confusing for the reader.

Because thoughts are at least as involuntary as they are deliberate, it's extremely useful to have a means of testing whether they are behaving—or dashing off in all directions. For example, this paragraph from a student paper shows how the writer's thoughts veered while the paragraph was in progress.

The sand dunes on the Oregon coast are as much fun as a carnival ride. You get into a modified pick-up truck, and the driver, who is probably 35, acts 14. He races up the dunes, stops suddenly, then takes off so fast that the truck—and you—leap several feet into the air. One man in our truck lost his glasses and his cigarette lighter on one of those leaps. His wife got very angry because the man could not find his belongings. The sand was so white and the truck had gone so far before the driver could hear us yelling "Stop!" that the glasses and lighter were nowhere to be seen. The wife wouldn't talk to the man all the way back to the ticket office. The spirit in the back of the truck just wasn't the same after that accident. The man was mad at the truck driver, and his wife was mad at him.

What has happened here? The writer began with a good topic sentence: *The sand dunes on the Oregon coast are as much fun as a carnival ride.* The next couple of sentences give additional information about *why* the dunes are fun and like a carnival ride. But *then* the writer veers off course: after telling about the man who lost his glasses and lighter, the writer gets onto a different topic—anger and resentful feelings associated with loss of the articles. Suddenly we've been shunted from *fun* to *anger*. And although there is some connection here—the articles got lost and the anger came up during the dune buggy ride—*the writer has not stayed on the topic as announced in the topic sentence.*

The paragraph could be easily fixed, and **attention to the topic sentence** makes the remedy obvious. Here's the revised version, with all the sentences related to the topic sentence.

The sand dunes on the Oregon coast are as much fun as a carnival ride. You get into a modified pick-up truck with a driver who is probably 35 but acts 14. He races up the dunes, stops suddenly, then takes off so fast that the truck—and you—leap several feet into the air. One man in our truck lost his glasses and his cigarette lighter on one of those leaps. The driver will also spot another truck in the distance. The two will run right toward each other, swerving only at the last minute to avoid a head-on collision. Once our truck ran to the top of a dune, and suddenly there was nowhere to go. The dune went straight down so suddenly that you couldn't see the bottom at all. We all thought we were sailing off into the far-blue yonder and said our last goodbyes. When the ride was over, we all jumped off the truck saying, "I'll never do that again," but in fact we could hardly wait to get back in line to take the ride again.

Here the writer sticks to telling *why the truck ride on the dunes is so much fun.* The writer doesn't get sidetracked onto the story about *the man's glasses* or *his wife's anger.* Everything in the paragraph connects to the topic sentence.

APPLICATION

1 PARAGRAPHS THAT DO OR DO NOT STAY ON TOPIC
Determine which of the paragraphs below stay on the topic and which stray off. Rewrite the ones that go off the topic.

A

Successful cooking can't be done quickly. The good cook reads recipes carefully *before* using them, and he rereads them as he goes along. He must assemble needed ingredients—or go out and buy them if they aren't available in his kitchen. He must gather utensils, and when the specified utensil isn't available, he must try to come up with a suitable substitute. As he begins the recipe, he measures patiently and exactly and adds things in the order specified. He follows instructions exactly, beating, cooking, and mixing for specified periods of time; he knows that failing to do this may result in a less than perfect product. Then, he cooks the whole thing for as long as the recipe says—not five or 10 minutes more or less. After everything is mixed and cooking, he takes time to clean up right away. Bowls, measuring spoons, beaters, and measuring cups must be washed. Unused ingredients must be returned to their proper places. Sometimes the kitchen floor must be mopped to clean up spilled flour or broken egg shells. But for the person who enjoys cooking, all this is time well spent.

B

These days, deciding how to spend your leisure time requires wisdom. If you watch television, you must determine which programs are worth watching and which should be turned off. Sometimes I think the people who produce TV programs aim to insult the public. There's nothing on but silly, unrealistic "sit-coms," violent, unrealistic adventure series, or ridiculous game shows. Do the producers think we have no taste when it comes to TV viewing? Do they think we don't use our minds when we watch television? The least they could do is offer something realistic. Sometimes I get so mad, I seriously consider getting rid of my set.

C

What I like most about going to college is the chance to meet new and exciting people. My roommate is one of the nicest persons I've ever met. He is good-natured, understanding, and generally easy to get along with. There's only one thing I don't like about him—he studies too much. He gets up early to study and stays up late. I can't sleep when his study lamp is on. And I don't appreciate being awakened at 6 A.M. by his alarm clock. I sure wish he'd ease up on his studying. He'll end up going through college without having any fun—and I'll go through college without enough sleep!

D

Many people today seem to be out of touch or out of reality. Psychiatrists and psychologists have many patients. The patients visit them regularly to return to reality and try to get problems out in the open and solved. The schizoid condition is a general condition of society. People take out loans at record high interests. Do these people really think that they will be able to pay these loans off? Some people think that a new car, boat or house are worth being in "hot water" for. Another problem that faces society today is the misuse of drugs. Many young people seem to want to be out of touch. For this purpose, they use mind-altering drugs. These people do not seem to know that natural highs are present throughout the universe. Professionals are not able to help all of the people in need. The entire world seems to be out of touch today. Wars are raging in the Far East today. Could not these people settle their differences and stop the loss of innocent lives?

2 FOR YOUR OWN WRITING

It is time now to do another check on the Topic Sentence Paragraphs in your essay. *Does each sentence in the paragraph clearly relate to the topic sentence?* A good way to check this is to **ask yourself about** *every sentence* **in the paragraph: how does this sentence relate to my main idea?** If you can't see that it does, mark the paragraph to be revised. If all the sentences do relate, you know you are in good shape in the "related" department.

Principle 3: Always Give the Reader Enough Information

The danger here is that the writer, who always knows more than the reader does at any given point in the paper (knows where the essay is going, knows what the purpose is), may overlook the reader's relative deluxe accommodations when it has only canvas cots. Of course, you —and after all that creating and all that shaping—the writer can easily underestimate the reader's *need to know*.

The old truth that *a confused or unsatisfied reader is a lost reader* holds here as much as anywhere else. If a writer raises the expectations of the reader and then doesn't fulfill them with enough information, the reader is likely to resent what feels like a set-up. It's like a hotel that advertises deluxe accommodations when it has only canvas cots. Of course you wouldn't deliberately mislead your reader; using the topic sentence check-up, you can always be certain of having provided plenty of information.

Here are two versions of a paragraph that illustrate this principle. The first version clearly does *not* give enough information:

Cooking southern food is something anybody can learn to do. The most important thing the cook has to learn is to be patient. The cook must also learn to think imaginatively. Finally, someone cooking southern food must think big instead of small.

This paragraph is almost provoking in its skimpiness of detail! Why is *patience* important? What makes *imagination* necessary? And what on earth does the writer mean by "think big instead of small"? This is a beautiful example of a paragraph in which the writer knows more than the reader *and* isn't telling enough. Perhaps if the reader already knew about southern cooking, the writer would not be in trouble. But if the reader didn't, the paragraph wouldn't tell very much.

Now see what happens when the writer rewrites the paragraph, this time *making sure* that the reader knows what the topic sentence means:

Cooking southern food is something anybody can learn to do. The most important thing the cook has to know how to do is to be patient. Almost all southern dishes cook for an enormously long time. Black-eyed peas simmer for half a day. Chicken and dumplings take hours. Green beans are cooked until they are pearl gray. The cook must also know how to use meat for seasoning, because almost all southern vegetable dishes are seasoned with meat. Green beans and black-eyed peas are cooked with fat-back or salted pork. Bacon grease is put into corn bread. Biscuits are made with lard. Finally, someone cooking southern food must think big instead of small. A southern meal is likely to have at least two meats, four or five vegetables, three pies, and several cakes. And the portions are large, too. So the cook has to make plenty and think in large menus. With these characteristics, however—patience, imagination, and willingness to think big—anybody can cook southern food.

These details added to the revision bring life to the paragraph and let the reader *know* what the message means.

What makes this principle—**give the reader enough information**—so important? There are two reasons:

1 **Readers do not remember *general statements* very long at all.** What they do remember are images, specifics, "pictures" that the writer gives them. This is why the topic sentence is not enough within itself. There must be concrete details, examples, that the reader can hold on to. It's the same principle at work when a set of instructions contains both written information *and* a picture or chart: you have a much better chance of understanding how to put an appliance or component together. And this is what you are doing in paragraphs when you give specifics to back up the topic sentence. You are giving the reader a double opportunity of getting the message: one way with the general topic sentence and another way with the specifics you give that paint pictures for the reader.

2 **Readers are more likely to get the message if you give it to them several times.** Not only are you sending it in two different ways—through a topic sentence and through back-up details—but you are also just plain sending it *x* amount of times. And you can hope that at least *one* of those times the reader will get it. This isn't because readers aren't smart. It's just because the communication process has to operate across space, time, and distance, and without the communicator even being present. That makes for certain difficulties. The reader's phone might ring; the reader might not have a particular interest in what you are communicating; a bird might fly by the reader's window —a lot of things might happen, including any or all of the things that distract *you* when *you* try to write. So you can see that if you are sending your message in just one sentence, just one time, just one way, the odds are stacked against you.

How Much is Enough?   How can you know what is *enough* information? There is no sure formula that answers this question. *Who your readers are* is part of the answer, because how much they already know or don't know will determine how much or how little you, the writer, have to explain. So, the first thing you can do as you look at your Topic Sentence Paragraphs to see if you have given enough information is to **make as good a guess as you can about *what your readers will need to be told*.** This will be an estimate on your part; and if you are undecided about whether they will or won't know something, go with the *won't* because it is better to give too much information than too little.

The second thing you can do when trying to decide how much information is enough is to **recognize some *givens* that are almost always true for all readers:**

1 **Readers do not remember** *general* **statements very long at all.**

2 *Readers are skeptical;* they often have a "show me" attitude, and you have to accept the responsibility for doing just that.

3 *Readers always want to be filled in.* "Fill me in, won't you?" says your friend who wants to get the whole picture, avoid confusion, and be in the know. So even readers who may know a lot about what you are writing on still want to be filled in on what *you* mean, on what *you* are attempting to say. You still have to give them enough information about *your thinking,* even if they know quite a bit about the subject.

METHODS FOR GIVING ENOUGH INFORMATION

Here are some ways you can use to add information to your Topic Sentence Paragraphs so that the readers will be satisfied that you have given them enough.

1 Illustrations, Examples, and Details   Here are some Topic Sentence Paragraphs that illustrate this method of providing enough information.

A

Isabella Bird, an adventuresome Englishwoman traveling alone in the West in the late 1800s, wrote a fascinating account of her travels in a book called *A Lady's Life in the Rockies.* In the Topic Sentence Paragraph she uses an example chock full of *details* to be sure that the reader "gets the picture."

<u>But oh! what a hard, narrow life it is with which I am now in contact!</u> Charlmers came from Illinois nine years ago, pronounced by the doctors to be far gone in consumption, and in two years he was strong. They are a queer family. . . . They have one hundred and sixty acres of land, a "Squatter's claim," and an invaluable water power. He is a lumberer, and has a saw-mill of a very primitive kind. I notice that every day something goes wrong with it, and this is the case throughout. If he wants to haul timber down, one or other of the oxen cannot be found; or if the timber is actually under way, a wheel or a part of the harness gives way, and the whole affair is at a standstill for days. The cabin is hardly a shelter, but is allowed to remain in ruins because the foundation of a frame house was once dug. A horse is always sure to be lame for want of a shoe nail, or a saddle to be useless from a broken buckle, and the wagon and harness are a marvel of temporary shifts, patchings, and insecure linkings with strands of rope. Nothing is ever ready or whole when it is wanted. . . .

B

In this next topic sentence paragraph, the writer uses details to give the reader a portrait of a shell she has just picked up on the beach. Notice how Anne Lindbergh, the writer, helps you, the reader, get a *picture* of the shell through the use of details.

But his shell—it is simple; it is bare, it is beautiful. Small, only the size of my thumb, its architecture is perfect, down to the finest detail. Its shape, swelling like a pear in the center, winds in a gentle spiral to the pointed apex. Its color, dull gold, is whitened by a wash of salt from the sea. Each whorl, each faint knob, each criss-cross vein in its egg-shell texture, is as clearly defined as on the day of creation. My eye follows with delight the outer circumference of that diminutive winding staircase up which this tenant used to travel.

C

In his fascinating account of how human consciousness evolved, Julian Jaynes uses *examples* to develop a point:

Examples of how little we are conscious of our everyday behavior can be multiplied almost anywhere we look. Playing the piano is a really extraordinary example. Here a complex array of various tasks is accomplished all at once with scarcely any consciousness of them whatever: two different lines of near hieroglyphics to be read at once, the right hand guided to one and the left to the other; ten fingers assigned to various tasks, the fingering solving motor problems without any awareness, and the mind interpreting sharps and flats and naturals into black and white keys, obeying the timing of whole or quarter or sixteenth notes and rests and trills, one hand perhaps in three beats to a measure while the other plays four, while the feet are softening or slurring or holding various other notes. And all this time the performer, the conscious performer, is in a seventh heaven of artistic rapture at the results of this tremendous business, or perchance lost in contemplation of the individual who turns the leaves of the music book. . . . Of course consciousness usually has a role in the learning of such complex activities, but not necessarily in their performance, and that is the only point I am trying to make here.

2. Description This method of adding information in Topic Sentence Paragraphs answers such questions for the reader as "What does it look like?" "What does it feel like?" When you *describe*, you actually picture the object, person, event for the reader. *You draw it with words.*

A

In this second excerpt from Anne Lindbergh, she is hoping to *show* the reader the snail shell she holds in her hand. *Describing* is drawing a picture in words for a reader who cannot "see" what you are seeing (or have seen) when you write.

This is a snail shell, round, full and glossy as a horse chestnut. Comfortable and compact, it sits curled up like a cat in the hollow of my hand. Milky and opaque, it has the pinkish bloom of the sky on a summer evening, ripening to rain. On its smooth symmetrical face is pencilled with precision a perfect spiral, winding inward to the pinpoint center of the shell, the tiny dark core of the apex, the pupil of the eye. It stares at me, this mysterious single eye—and I stare back.

B

John McPhee uses *description* to draw a picture for the reader of Frank L. Boyden, the headmaster of Deerfield Academy in Massachusetts.

McPhee wants readers who have never met Boyden to be able to see him anyway, through McPhee's words of *description*.

Boyden looked old when he was four, older when he was in college, and older still in the nineteen-twenties, but now he doesn't look particularly old at all. His hair is not white but slate-gray, and his demeanor, which hasn't changed in forty years, still suggests a small, grumpy Labrador. He sometimes dresses in gray trousers, a dark-blue jacket, and brown cordovan shoes—choices that are somewhat collegiate and could be taken as a mild sign of age, because for decades he wore dark-blue worsted suits and maroon ties almost exclusively, winter and summer, hanging on to each successive suit until it fell off him in threads. One of his jacket pockets today has a four-inch rip that has been bound with black thread. He doesn't care. He is an absolutely unself-conscious man. Let one scuff mark appear on a stair riser in his academy and he will quickly find a janitor and report it, but this kind of concern is entirely projected onto the school. He once got up on a cool July morning and put on an old leather coat covered with cracks and lined with sheepskin that was coming loose; he went off to New York in it and obliviously wore it all day in the sweltering city. After eighty-six years, his only impairment is bad hearing. "My ears are gone," he will say, and then he will walk into a roomful of people and pretend that there isn't a syllable he can't catch. He indulges himself in nothing. He will eat anything, and he usually doesn't notice the components of his meals, unless they happen to be root beer and animal crackers, which he occasionally eats for breakfast. He has been given honorary degrees by Harvard, Yale, Princeton, and seventeen other colleges and universities, but he apparently has not even a trace of a desire to be called Dr. Boyden, and no one calls him that except eraser salesmen and strangers whose sons are applying to the school.

3. Definition   At times you may want to *define* a term, process, etc., to add information in a Topic Sentence Paragraph. Look at the ways *defining* helps you understand the following excerpts:

A

In the first example Norma Skurka is discussing French styles of furniture. She is attempting to educate readers of *The New York Times Book of Interior Design and Decoration:*

To clarify some of the stylistic terms, let's see where they came from and what they meant. The word, *baroque*, is a corruption of the Spanish *barreuco*, which means a large, irregularly shaped pearl. The word was for a time confined to the jeweler's craft. It came to denote the extravagant fashions common in the first half of the seventeenth century, chiefly in Italy and France, in which everything was fantastic, florid, and lacking in restraint. The succeeding style, called *rococo* or Louis XV, is also a corruption of two French words drawn from nature: it is a contraction of *rocaille* and *coquille*, loosely translated as rock and shell work, a reference to two popular motifs used for decoration in the Louis XV style. Straight lines and symmetrically balanced arrangements rarely occur in wall paneling, furniture, or other decoration of the period.

B

Here is another Topic Sentence Paragraph that *defines* in order to give the reader enough information. Read what Eldridge Cleaver says:

Low rider [is]a Los Angeles nickname for ghetto youth. Originally the term was coined to describe the youth who had lowered the bodies of their cars so that they rode low, close to the ground; also implied was the style of driving that these youngsters perfected. Sitting behind the steering wheel and slumped low down in the seat, all that could be seen of them was from their eyes up, which used to be the cool way of driving. When these youthful hipsters alighted from their vehicles, the term *low rider* stuck with them, evolving to the point where all black ghetto youth—but *never the* soft offspring of the black bourgeoisie—are referred to as low riders.

4. Explanation and Analysis

A

Here are a couple of Topic Sentence Paragraphs that use *explanation* to give the reader enough information. They come from *Road & Track*'s 1971 article on the best cars in the world. *Road & Track* had two categories for this article, "Best Cars in the World" and "Best Car in Each of Ten Categories." These two paragraphs *explain* what those categories mean:

For the "Ten Best," we reasoned that some cars are "best" for one reason and some are "best" for another. So, if we established rigid criteria for the ten best, we would be restricting the final list in ways that would end up favoring one group or one type. And this, we didn't want. Each car that belonged on this list did have to be "best" for a specific reason, however, although it did not have to be a "best" for the same reason as another. We also decided that the cars on the Ten Best list need not be models that were sold in the U. S. Just because our benevolent and protective government has decreed that some of the world's best cars should be denied to Americans, we did not think this was a sufficient reason for a particular model's exclusion if we agreed that it qualified otherwise as one of the Ten Best.

For the "Best of Category," the criteria were more restrictive. Basically, the basic criterion was a judgment as to how well the car fulfilled the function for which it was intended in comparison with its direct competition. To make this decision it was of course necessary to include all the various facets that go into such an evaluation: engineering, assembly quality, handling, braking, reliability and so on. For the categories, we also restricted eligibility to those cars on which we had performed one of our normal road tests; that is, to those models that are available for sale in the U.S. at this time.

B

Here is another Topic Sentence Paragraph developed by explanation. The Indian writer Hyemeyohsts Storm is explaining a powerful symbol, the Medicine Wheel.

Among the People, a child's first Teaching is of the Four Great Powers of the Medicine Wheel. To the North on the Medicine Wheel is found wisdom. The Color of the Wisdom of the North is White, and its Medicine Animal is the Buffalo. The South is represented by the Sign of the Mouse, and its Medicine Color is Green. The South is the place of Innocence and Trust, and for perceiving closely our nature of heart. In the West is the Sign of the Bear. The

West is the Looks-Within Place, which speaks of the Introspective nature of man. The Color of this Place is Black. The East is marked by the Sign of the Eagle. It is the Place of Illumination, where we can see things clearly far and wide. Its Color is the Gold of the Morning Star.

5. Facts and Figures   Another way to develop a Topic Sentence Paragraph is to use *facts* and *figures* when appropriate. The only purpose of any form of development is to give the reader enough information so that she or he will believe what you say, agree with what you say, listen to what you say, notice what you say. *Statistics* and *factual information* will often add the weight to your assertions that will swing the reader your way. Here is a Topic Sentence Paragraph that uses *figures* and *facts* to give the reader enough information. Marie Winn writes:

Preschool children are the single largest television audience in America, spending a greater number of total hours and a greater proportion of their waking day watching television than any other age group. According to one survey made in 1970, children in the 2–5 age group spend an average of 30.4 hours each week watching television, while children in the 6–11 group spend 25.5 hours watching. The weekly average for adult viewers in 1971 was 23.3 hours. Another survey made in 1971 documented a weekly viewing time of 34.56 hours for preschool boys and 32.44 hours for preschool girls. Still other surveys suggest figures up to 54 hours a week for preschool viewers. Even the most conservative estimates indicate that preschool children in America are spending more than a third of their waking hours watching television.

6. Repetition   You may be surprised to learn that at times *repetition* is an excellent device for developing a Topic Sentence Paragraph. Often, repetition merely bores. And some writers may repeat simply because they don't have anything else to say—they said all they had to say in one sentence and hadn't anywhere else to go. By repeating, they at least fill up the page!

The kind of repetition we are considering here, however, is *valuable development* of the message you are sending. Since readers do not have a long memory span for the points you are making, you can develop the reader's mind in case they have been forgotten. The example below, from John Trimble, shows how valuable *repetition* can be when used in the right way:

Now for an essay writer, the chief desired effect is persuasion. Thus . . . writing really boils down to *the art of selling the reader.* Suppose you are that essay writer. You want the reader to buy two things: your ideas and you, their source. That is, you want him to view your ideas as sound and interesting, and you want him to view you as intelligent, informed, credible, and companionable. . . . If you don't persuade him to accept you, their advocate, it's doubtful that you'll persuade him to buy the ideas you're trying to sell him.

7. Comparison and Contrast   A very common way to help your reader "see" what you mean is to *compare* it to something else, showing how the two things are alike, or to *contrast* it with something else, showing how your idea is different from something else. Putting two things up together can throw light on the point that you, the writer, really want to get across.

A

Look at the way Annie Dillard uses a *comparison* of Nature with a children's puzzle to develop her thoughts:

It's all a matter of keeping my eyes open. Nature is like one of those line drawings of a tree that are puzzles for children: Can you find hidden in the leaves a duck, a house, a boy, a bucket, a zebra, and a boot? Specialists can find the most incredibly well-hidden things. . . .

B

Venita Van Caspel, a noted financial authority, is discussing how to be a wise investor. She has, in the paragraph preceding the one that follows, explained that an investor can't just buy blue-chip stocks and throw them in the drawer. Today's blue-chip stocks, she says, may become the "red chips," "white chips," or "buffalo chips" of tomorrow. Then she *compares* blue-chip stocks to other familiar items to make her point.

Just think back a few years. What car did the "man of distinction" drive? A Packard. I would have had difficulty convincing my father that only a few years later the manufacturers of the Packard automobile would be out of business. At the same time, what was the chief family home entertainment medium before television? It was radio, wasn't it? And who was the chief manufacturer of that half-egg-shaped wooden box in every home? Atwater-Kent. As you know, the Atwater-Kent Company no longer exists. You live in a world of constant change, and you must always be alert and ahead of this change if you want to become a millionaire through your investment know-how. You must sharpen your talents to predict trends before they happen, and move out before the trend has run its course.

8. Narrative "Once upon a time . . .": you can never fail to get a reader's attention if you *tell a story,* but in addition to that, a narrative can help you *explain* or *illustrate* the point you are making in a Topic Sentence Paragraph. In the paragraph below, Annie Dillard uses a *story* about her own personal experience to let the reader know what she means by the opening sentence of the paragraph.

Unfortunately, nature is very much a now-you-see-it, now-you-don't affair. A fish flashes, then dissolves in the water before my eyes like so much salt. Deer apparently ascend bodily into heaven; the brightest oriole fades into leaves. These disappearances stun me into stillness and concentration; they say of nature that it conceals with a grand nonchalance, and they say of vision that it is a deliberate gift, the revelation of a dancer who for my eyes only flings away her seven veils. For nature does reveal as well as conceal: now-you-don't see it, now-you-do. For a week last September migrating red-winged blackbirds were feeding heavily down by the creek at the back of the house. One day I went out to investigate the racket; I walked up to a tree, an Osage orange, and a hundred birds flew away. They simply materialized out of the tree. I saw a tree, then a whisk of color, then a tree again. I walked closer and another hundred blackbirds took flight. Not a branch, not a twig budged; the birds were apparently weightless as well as invisible. Or, it was as if the leaves of the Osage orange had been freed from a spell in the form of red-winged blackbirds; they flew from the tree, caught my eye in the sky, and vanished. When I looked again at the tree the leaves had reassembled as if nothing had happened. Finally I walked directly to the trunk of the tree and a final hundred, the real diehards, appeared, spread, and vanished. How could so many hide in the tree without my seeing them? The Osage orange, unruffled, looked just as it had looked from the house, when three hundred red-winged blackbirds cried from its crown. I looked downstream where they flew, and they were gone. . . . One show to a customer. These appearances catch at my throat; they are the free gifts, the bright coppers at the roots of trees.

APPLICATION

METHOD OF PARAGRAPH DEVELOPMENT

1 Read the paragraphs below and identify as closely as possible the method of development which has been used.

A

Shaking off from my spirit what *must* have been a dream, I scanned more narrowly the real aspect of the building. Its principal feature seemed to be that of an excessive antiquity. The discoloration of ages had been great. Minute fungi overspread the whole exterior, hanging in a fine tangled webwork from the eaves. Yet all this was apart from any extraordinary dilapidation. No portion of the masonry had fallen; and there appeared to be a wild inconsistency between its still perfect adaptation of parts and the crumbling condition of the individual stones. In this there was much that reminded me of the specious totality of old woodwork which had rotted for long years in some neglected vault, with no disturbance from the breath of the external air. Beyond this indication of excessive decay, however, the fabric gave little token of instability. Perhaps the eye of a scrutinizing observer might have discovered a barely perceptible fissure, which, extending from the roof of the building in front, made its way down the wall in a zigzag direction, until it became lost in the sullen waters of the tarn.

—Edgar Allen Poe

B

Have you ever noticed the kinds of shoppers you see in a grocery store? Some women dress up to go out and buy their groceries. Their hair and nails immaculately done and their outfits elegantly in style, they breeze from aisle to aisle leaving a whiff of expensive perfume lingering in the air. Other women don't seem to bother to change the sloppy clothes they were wearing at home. They dart from aisle to aisle in hair rollers, baggy, dirty shirts, and house shoes. Many times, they are trailed by a small army of equally sloppy, dirty children. Other shoppers are more noticeable for their approach to shopping rather than for their appearance. Some carry lists and carefully cross off each item as they put it in their baskets. Some spend minutes frugally comparing the "national" brand to the store brand. Others compare prices per pound for packages of different sizes. Others just take items off the shelves impulsively without regard for cost.

C

According to the story pieced together by astronomers, a star's life begins in swirling mists of hydrogen that surge and eddy through space. The Universe is filled with tenuous clouds of this abundant gas, which makes up 90 per cent of all the matter in the Cosmos. In the random motions of such clouds, atoms sometimes come together by accident to form small, condensed pockets of gas. Stars are born in these accidents.

—Robert Jastrow

D

I think this is the fourth spring the coon has occupied the big tree in front of the house, but I have lost count, so smoothly do the years run together. She is like a member of our family. She has her kittens in a hole in the tree about thirty-five feet above the ground, which places her bedchamber a few feet from my bedchamber but at a slightly greater elevation. It strikes me as odd (and quite satisfactory) that I should go to sleep every night so close to a litter of raccoons. The mother's comings and goings are as much a part of my life at this season of the year as my morning shave and my evening drink.

— E.B. White

E

Americans tend to think of Islam as just another religion, which explains in part why the Islamic revival has been so little understood in Washington. Actually, Islam is much more than a theology; it is also an idea of how society should be organized. The Koran and subsequent interpretations of Mohammad's thinking spell out rules for individual behavior from cradle to grave, and detailed precepts of how governments should conduct their affairs. The concept of separating church and state is meaningless to orthodox Muslims. Mohammad and his successors were not only the supreme religious leaders, but heads of government and commanders of its armies as well. Perhaps most important of all, Islam demands—and receives—an unquestioned faith from its believers. Western church-goers will listen politely while preachers thunder against immodest dress or sex in movies, but they hardly ever do anything about it. By contrast, the cry of a *mullah*, warning that Islam is in danger, is often enough in itself to send tens of thousands of Muslims surging through the streets.

—William E. Griffith

F

The past is completely eliminated in Orwell's *1984*. History is revised. Books are destroyed. Without print media, there is no evidence that anything has been different. Even keeping diaries is forbidden. People are expected to absorb and accept the new information delivered by the television sets even if it directly contradicts the news of a month ago. Since it is impossible to prove the contradiction, it is useless to try to resist. Without points of comparison, all information is equally real. The Underground, for example, or a distant war between Oceania and Eastasia, might have existed or they might not have; there is no way of knowing.

—Jerry Mander

G

The skin is the body's largest and one of its most complex organs. Spread flat, it would cover approximately 18 square feet, every square inch of which includes about a yard of blood vessels, four yards of nerves, a hundred sweat glands and more than three million cells. Without this natural spacesuit we would be prey to all sorts of deadly bacteria and, in any case, would quickly perish from loss of body heat.

—Reader's Digest

H

A basic understanding of euthanasia is needed before the controversy over it can be discussed. Euthanasia is the painless putting to death of a person terminally ill. In most cases these people are in pain and only kept alive by machines. In some cases, there is the question of whether the patient is human or vegetable. The term "vegetable" refers to the idea that because of no brain activity the "person" is dead. This mercy killing is usually accomplished by disconnecting the life-supporting machines. The controversy springs from the question of whether it is morally or legally right to take another person's life even though he would die without the life-supporting technology of this modern era.

UNDEVELOPED PARAGRAPHS

2 Each of the paragraphs in the two passages below is undeveloped. Using any of the methods discussed above rewrite each paragraph so that the topic is developed fully for the reader.

A

Although a college degree is a form of success in itself, only the individual can determine if that degree is the beginning or the end of the road. A person must want success in order to attain it.

In today's highly specialized and technical society, a university education is practically the only way to open doors of opportunity. Most good jobs require college degrees. But once on the job, a person must be willing to work hard and be the best that he can be.

Although a university education is not the only requirement for success, it is a necessary part of the make-up of a successful individual.

B

Euthanasia would prevent prolonged mourning by family and loved ones. It would ease the enormous financial burden that a family must bear in order to keep a person alive on life support systems.

This financial strain combined with the worry and sadness of having a person in the family in this condition brings strains on the rest of the family. These combined pressures often cause breakups in family life and sometimes lead to divorce.

No family should suffer these misfortunes and in most cases if a family is close, euthanasia will prevent this problem.

FOR YOUR WRITING

3 What we want to emphasize, now that you have seen *how* Topic Sentence Paragraphs can be developed, is the basic concept of **giving enough information.** The *method* you use is not the most important

thing; that you *give enough information to the reader* is. Now make a final check on the Topic Sentence Paragraphs in your essay. Read them with a critical eye to see if they are fully developed. Have you given the reader enough information? Have you given some *specific* statements for each *general* statement that you made? The principle of general > specific is at the heart of all good writing. The general statement guides the reader to know what you are going to communicate, and the specifics make sure that the communication happens.

In your final check to see whether you have developed each of your Topic Sentence Paragraphs, fill out a chart like this one:

CHART FOR CHECKING DEVELOPMENT IN TOPIC SENTENCE PARAGRAPHS

Here is my topic sentence: _____

_____

Here are the specifics I used to develop this topic sentence:

1 _____

2 _____

3 _____

4 _____

(for however many points you have)

For some of my specifics I gave *additional* information about something in that specific point, in order to further explain it:

To explain specific _____ , I gave this information: _____

_____

To explain specific _____ , I gave this information: _____

_____

(for howevermuch additional information you gave on specific points)

Actually, you can analyze any topic sentence paragraph in the world by using this chart. And if you apply the chart to your own topic sentence paragraphs, you'll see immediately whether you have developed your point fully. The chart works by making you look at *every sentence* to be sure you know *why* you put it there. And if you can see what the function of each sentence is, you can be pretty sure that each sentence is contributing to the *flow* of the paper.

APPLICATION

TOPIC SENTENCE PARAGRAPHS

1 The following paragraphs do *not* follow the three principles about writing good topic sentence paragraphs.

Three Principles for Topic Sentence Paragraphs:
1. Tell the reader clearly what the paragraph is about.
2. Make sure every sentence relates to the topic sentence.
3. Give the reader enough information.

(a) What principle is missing in each paragraph?
(b) Revise each paragraph so that the message has a better chance of getting across.

A

"No" is just a simple, one-syllable word used to express a negative answer. Agreed, the word "no" is easy to say, but to answer someone directly with it changes the entire situation.

B

Education concerning the harmful effects of smoking should be increased. This can be done through the schools, starting with health programs for children at an early age. Some schools have initiated such programs, but a more widespread and intensive approach must be employed.

C

Gardening of vegetables is one hobby that is money saving; not many hobbies can claim this. It is also fruitful, literally. Gardening of vegetables is relatively easy if you approach it in the right manner. First, you must have the proper location and tools. Pick a site that gets plenty of sunshine, is wind free, and preferably enclosed. You then must have some tool that breaks up the soil. I would recommend investing in a small tiller. You will also need an efficient watering system and common tools such as a hoe and garden rake.

D

Jogging requires determination. When a runner first begins, a thousand reasons come up for not going out. It will be too cold or too hot. Or the runner won't have any spare time. It is quite difficult to run in hot weather, and a runner has to train for it. The best thing to do is to run in the cool part of the day, stay in the shade, run slower, and drink something cold upon the return from the run. Running in cold weather just requires bundling up warm, but be careful not to wear too many clothes because the body gets hot fast when you are jogging.

PARAGRAPHS REPRESENTING ALL THREE TYPES OF ERRORS

2 Explain how the paragraphs below violate all three principles of paragraph writing. Then explain how each might be corrected through rewriting.

A

We are going to have to face the situation. We all have been brainwashed into the society we are by a variety of sources. Television is the main contributor of propaganda, followed by the government, other mass media, public education, the term "the American Dream," your neighbors, big business and labor, and, maybe even your own mother.

B

Although it was hard for the man working long hours and not getting paid a high salary, the woman's day was not easy. The average wife in the fifties stayed at home and cooked, cleaned and waited for her husband to come home. There is nothing wrong with this except for the fact that there was no diversion except for the radio. The television did not yet exist. The average couple had only one car which the husband would take to work. This meant the wife was stuck at home all day. To buy groceries, the wife would walk and either carry the bags home or pull them in a small cart. Although a couple starting out in the 1950s had a hard financial struggle, they appreciated all they had worked for.

C

To me the university is a place where I can go to fulfill my dream in life. Granted, the university is not for everyone—just those who want it. A carpenter, construction worker, a farmer have no reason to attend universities, but a doctor, scientist, businessman, or teacher all have to continue their education in universities, which sometimes can be expensive.

THE FUNCTION PARAGRAPH

Someone has said that if the only tool you have is a hammer, you tend to treat everything as if it were a nail. The same thing is true in writing an essay. If the only kind of paragraph you know about is the Topic Sentence Paragraph, you have to treat all your thoughts as if they were points to be developed.

Fortunately, this isn't the case.

As wonderful, useful, and necessary as the Topic Sentence Paragraph is, it isn't the only kind, even though it is the most commonly known. To get any *developed* message across, of course, Topic Sentence Paragraphs are necessary. But there are other uses of paragraphs—and you see lots of them in magazine articles and in books—that are *not* topic sentence + development. Rather, they are **Function Paragraphs,** paragraphs that do things other than give the reader information about a general statement, a topic sentence.

Function Paragraphs are amusing, quirky, and fascinating to learn about, but the main thing about them is that they are *useful.* Knowing about Function Paragraphs, you aren't confused when you look at writing in books and magazines and find paragraphs that don't always begin with a new thought and give a developed message. More importantly, however, when you know about Function Paragraphs you are aware of the many more choices available to you when you write. You can discover new ways of controlling your writing and your reader, and you will find new possibilities for putting energy, personality, and variety into your writing.

Function Paragraphs help you get attention, show what things you consider important to notice, and, in general, work like the time signatures and notations on a piece of music. They assist you in orchestrating the essay and in *telling the reader how to read it.*

The Function Paragraph guides the reader through the piece of writing, keeps the reader's interest whetted, and expresses the writer's personality, whims, style, and purposes.

List 20 things you can't do with a hammer:
1. Play the violin.
2. Comb your hair.
3.
4.

USES OF THE FUNCTION PARAGRAPH

1. Function Paragraphs Are Used to Add Drama and to Get the Reader's Attention Often when people are talking and really want to get someone's attention, they will shout or say emphatically, "Listen to me!" Or they will use their hands in a dramatic gesture to keep the listener's eye right on them. When you are writing, of course, you can do none of these things, so you have to depend on other means to get the reader's attention or to be dramatic. *Function Paragraphs will do this for you.* See how Isabella Bird uses a one-sentence Function Paragraph to set up the reader in anticipation for what is coming next.

I shall not soon forget my first night here.

Somewhat dazed by the rarefied air, entranced by the glorious beauty, slightly puzzled by the motley company, whose faces loomed not always quite distinctly through the cloud of smoke produced by eleven pipes, I went to my solitary cabin at nine, attended by Evans. It was very dark, and it seemed a long way off. Something howled — Evans said it was a wolf — and owls apparently innumerable hooted incessantly. The pole-star, exactly opposite my cabin door, burned like a lamp. The frost was sharp. Evans opened the door, lighted a candle, and left me, and I was soon in my hay bed. I was frightened — that is, afraid of being frightened, it was so eerie — but sleep soon got the better of my fears. I was awoke by a heavy breathing, a noise something like sawing under the floor, and a pushing and upheaving, all very loud. My candle was all burned, and, in truth, I dared not stir. The noise went on for an hour fully, when, just as I thought the floor had been made sufficiently thin for all purposes of ingress, the sounds abruptly ceased, and I fell asleep again. My hair was not, as it ought to have been, white in the morning!

FUNCTION PARAGRAPH

Paragraph to keep the reader alert and interested, to dramatize or quicken the pace.

That first sentence is so catchy that we tend not to even notice that *it is a paragraph all by itself.* You read "I shall not soon forget my first night here" and dash on to find out about that night and what was so unforgettable about it. Of course the author *could* have put that sentence with the next paragraph and thus have made *one* unit instead of *two.* And it would certainly have fit the rules for Topic Sentence Paragraphs, too. *But look at the drama that would have been lost!*

Here's another example of a Function Paragraph used for drama.

After the tour I stopped at the refreshment stand at the base of Masada and found myself sitting across from a rather elegant-looking white-haired woman. "Excuse me," she asked, "would you happen to know where I can find some mud?"

Mud?

The one-word response to the woman's request dramatizes Harvey Arden's incredulity and astonishment. And we get it with a punch, which would certainly have been lacking if the author had replaced that *single word* with a sentence or two that *explained* how he felt. Furthermore, the single word contributes to the pace, the lean, swift movement of the passage, as contrasted with **the loss of impact that would have resulted**

if there had been several lines of explanation. It's like the difference between someone who tells a joke and then lets it go, and someone who talks on for the next fifteen minutes to explain the punchline.

2. Function Paragraphs Are Used to Make a Transition from One Part of the Writing to Another

In a fascinating essay, "Toward a Theory of Creativity," Carl Rogers discusses what creativity is, what kind of people are most likely to be creative, what conditions must be present before creativity can emerge, and what some after-effects of creativity are. Then he prepares to discuss a new topic in the essay — how constructive creativity can be encouraged. To connect the parts of the essay, he had to write a paragraph that could work like a bridge that the reader could take to get from one part of the writing to the next. Here is that paragraph:

Thus far I have tried to describe the nature of creativity, to indicate that quality of individual experience which increases the likelihood that creativity will be constructive, to set forth the necessary conditions for the creative act and to state some of its concomitants. But if we are to make progress in meeting the social need which was presented initially, we must know whether constructive creativity can be fostered, and if so, how.

From the very nature of the inner conditions of creativity it is clear that they cannot be forced, but must be permitted to emerge. The farmer cannot make the germ develop and sprout from the seed; he can only supply the nurturing conditions which will permit the seed to develop its own potentialities. So it is with creativity. How can we establish the external conditions which will foster and nourish the internal conditions described above? My experience in psychotherapy leads me to believe that by setting up conditions of psychological safety and freedom, we maximize the likelihood of an emergence of constructive creativity. Let me spell out these conditions in some detail, labeling them as x and y.

Can you see in the first paragraph how Rogers wraps up the earlier section of the essay and introduces the next? A transition paragraph like this is a real courtesy to the reader. You can see, however, that the Function Paragraph that works like a transition does *not* have a topic sentence or main idea that is developed. **The Function Paragraph serving as a bridge is *only* a bridge. It simply gets the reader from here to there;** it does not present developed information. *It isn't supposed to.* It is merely to be like a road sign that says, "Turn here and now proceed in *this* direction."

3. Function Paragraphs Are Used to Set Off Conversational Dialogue

At times writers will use conversational dialogue in order to get the reader's attention and make a point by *showing* instead of *telling.* When such dialogue is used, each conversational response is put in a new paragraph. So you may see multiple paragraph indentations *simply because a conversation between two people is being recorded.*

Here is a student essay that uses conversational dialogue and that emerges with Function Paragraphs as a result.

"You know, this class is awful. I never learn anything from it, but it seems to go on for hours."

"I know what you mean. The lectures are so disorganized. The professor doesn't ever act as though any time has been spent in preparing for class."

"Well, I won't be here for the next class. I have better ways to spend my time."

This conversation is often heard after many college classes. These attitudes, however, could be reversed by a concerned professor. By inspiring confidence in the students and by organizing a knowledgeable presentation, a professor could make any class interesting as well as instructive.

All that you, as a writer, need to know about this use of the Function Paragraph is that **conversational dialogues are indented so that the reader will know when one person finishes talking and the other begins.** Again, you can see how the Function Paragraph helps a reader know *how to read the essay*. So many uses of the Function Paragraph are just courtesies for the reader. But what an important consideration! Because if the reader doesn't get your message for *any* reason, you've wasted your time in writing it.

4. Function Paragraphs Are Used to Break up Long Paragraphs or to Make Paragraphs of About Equal Length.

Sometimes authors make new paragraphs simply because they think **the reader's eyes will get tired if a paragraph is too long.** Readers do need a break periodically —*a psychological break if nothing else*—and a paragraph indention can be just the break they need when the writing is long. In this example below Martin Luther King is writing what has now become a very famous document, "Letter from Birmingham Jail." When you look at these two paragraphs, you can sense that Dr. King divided them to avoid having one really long paragraph. Of course, we can't know his motive for sure, but there doesn't seem to be any other recognizable reason for the division of the two paragraphs except to break the length.

You speak of our activity in Birmingham as extreme. At first I was rather disappointed that fellow clergymen would see my nonviolent efforts as those of an extremist. I began thinking about the fact that I stand in the middle of two opposing forces in the Negro community. One is a force of complacency, made up in part of Negroes who, as a result of long years of oppression, are so drained of self-respect and a sense of "somebodiness" that they have adjusted to segregation; and in part of a few middle-class Negroes who, because of a degree of academic and economic security and because in some ways they profit by segregation, have become insensitive to the problems of the masses. The other force is one of bitterness and hatred, and it comes perilously close to advocating violence. It is expressed in the various black nationalist groups that are springing up across the nation, the largest and best-known being Elijah Muhammad's

Muslim movement. Nourished by the Negro's frustration over the continued existence of racial discrimination, this movement is made up of people who have lost faith in America, who have absolutely repudiated Christianity, and who have concluded that the white man is an incorrigible "devil."

I have tried to stand between these two forces, saying that we need emulate neither the "do-nothingism" of the complacent nor the hatred and despair of the black nationalist. For there is the more excellent way of love and nonviolent protest. I am grateful to God that, through the influence of the Negro church, the way of nonviolence became an integral part of our struggle.

Here is another example of an otherwise single paragraph becoming two paragraphs probably for reason of length.

Despite its name, the Dead Sea is not a sea at all. It's actually a lake with a deep northern basin 331 meters (1,086 feet) deep, and a smaller southern basin averaging only about two meters deep. The two, totaling 75 kilometers (45 miles) long by 15 kilometers (9 miles) wide, are joined across a now submerged neck of land that could be crossed on foot in Biblical times, when the water was lower.

The deep northern section—almost as deep again as its surface lies below sea level—is cupped in the bottommost cranny of that colossal fracture in earth's crust called the Great Rift. Since it has no outlet, you'd think the Dead Sea would eventually fill up with the inflow from the Jordan and other streams. But, in fact, evaporation caused by dryness and heat—routinely topping 40°C (104°F) in summer—roughly balanced inflow.

Even the shrewdest observer would have a hard time rationally explaining the indentation between 1 and 2. But show the two paragraphs to an artist or someone who does layout for magazine or newspaper copy, and you'll get an answer that is simple and obvious.

"Sure, you need a new paragraph there. All the paragraphs are about the same length; it wouldn't look right to have one twice as long. Besides, that is the maximum length the magazine will allow."

And if you look all the way through the Dead Sea essay, from which these paragraphs came, you will find that the longest paragraphs run only up to about ten lines—exactly what we have here. It is likely that National Geographic's column width particularly lends itself to paragraphs of about this length. At any rate, the paragraph was broken not because a new subject was introduced or a new example inserted, but simply because the writer decided to have a new paragraph. The logic was all her own.

5. Function Paragraphs are Used to Accommodate the Author's Personal Writing Style

After you have read enough of a particular writer's work, you can often recognize his or her style without even seeing the author's name. **Many things make up a writer's personal style, but how he or she paragraphs is definitely part of it.** Here is an example from *Everything You've Always Wanted to Know about Energy but Were Too Weak to Ask.* You can probably tell from the title that the writing is going to be flippant, maybe a little breathless; and you are right. Naura

Hayden, the author, writes in an excited, personal style. *She paragraphs when she wants to,* and you see the same style all the way through her book.

> If you were to ask people what they would like if they could have anything in the whole world they wanted, most would say energy. Energy is everything. Energy is good health. Energy, rightly channeled, will get you anything you want—love, friendship, money, power, success, fun—*everything!*
>
> Loaded with energy, you'll feel like a million bucks—you'll feel as though there's nothing you can't do. And you know something? There *will* be nothing you can't do. Anxiety and depression will disappear. Your whole life will change drastically for the better when your body is surging with energy. Believe me, a whole new world of adventure and accomplishment will open up for you.
>
> Now what most people don't know is that energy is not that hard to get once you know the secret.
>
> Before I learned this secret, I smoked a lot and drank cups and cups of coffee to stimulate myself. These were the "uppers" I needed to get through the day. I've since found that most people need these things plus lots of sugar. Sugar is mistakenly thought of as an energy booster; all it does is give you a short spurt up, then you plummet down and get depressed until you eat more sugar—a vicious circle. It's *Bad* for you—and it's found not only in the sugar bowl, but in cakes, pies, cookies, soft drinks, and in donuts, bread, spaghetti, macaroni and other starchy things.
>
> Before I discovered my great energy secret, I was tired a lot and falling apart physically at a very young age. . . .

Hayden's writing style approximates her enthusiasm for what she has to say, and her approach to paragraphing seems to be all her own. If there weren't such things as Function Paragraphs, however, she would not be able to write as she talks.

6. Function Paragraphs are Used to Emphasize a Point, to Develop an Example, and to Add Detail

In this use of the Function Paragraph the writer will begin a new paragraph to emphasize a point, to develop an example, or to add detail. Of course, without the preceding paragraph, the reader wouldn't have a context for the Function Paragraph used for this purpose. So, the Function Paragraph with the details, examples, etc., is definitely connected to the Topic Sentence Paragraph preceding it and must rely on it for meaning. The writer has made the example details a separate paragraph perhaps for emphasis or perhaps because developing the example in the same paragraph would make the paragraph too long.

Here is an example from Henry Boettinger:

> The key to getting and holding attention lies in having something *new* happen continually. This calls for a sense of *movement* forward or backward, development, or the feeling of "something going on." Development suggests that what we are seeing *now* grew out of something before, and is going to turn into something else. Consider the difference between the attention a child gives to a basket of eggs on the kitchen table and his [her] concentration on an egg that is being cracked from the inside by a chick straining to emerge.

Another illustration, probably old when the pyramids were under construction, is the attention given to workers and their machinery on a large building project by sidewalk superintendents. The same project on a Sunday morning will hold no interest from passing crowds, because "there is nothing going on." Yet the structure's design is clear, and all the machinery stands ready, but silent. Clearly, the sense of development is dead, and with it dies attention. The fundamental aspect of development derives from its continuity with the past and the future. This unfolding of your presentation must parallel nature. Even the most spectacular and dramatic event in the story must be related to what has gone before. . . . Clear problem-statement is important because it allows a development related constantly to both aspects of any problem: that which exists and that which is desired.

Here is another example of a Function Paragraph that emphasizes a point. You will notice that the first paragraph is a Topic Sentence Paragraph with two examples of games for specific development of the topic sentence. Then there is a new paragraph, a Function Paragraph, for the next game. One can only guess at the writer's purpose. Evidently, he wanted the snow game to get special attention—perhaps he thought it was especially interesting—or perhaps he thought it would get lost if he left it in the same paragraph. Clearly, however, the snow snake game "belongs" in the Topic Sentence Paragraph as a specific example of the kinds of games the Iroquois played. Of the three games mentioned, however, the snow snake game is the only one to get its own paragraph.

Diversion in the form of games of chance and skill played an important part in Iroquois religious and social life. The contests were between individuals or teams organized within a community or beyond it, even including different tribes. The teams generally seem to have been divided along clan lines. These people were avid gamblers, and betting on the outcome of a game was intense. A man might even gamble all of his property on the outcome of a game. The favorite game was lacrosse, played on a field about 450 yards long. Each of the six to eight players on a team carried a crook that had netting strung from the curved end to about halfway up the stick; the ball could be moved only with this racket. The object was to drive a deerskin ball from midfield through the opposing team's goal, which consisted of two poles near each other at one end of the field. The rules allowed a variation from five to seven in the number of goals necessary to win a game. Another game was to throw a javelin through a rolling hoop or to throw it farther than an opponent could.

The snow snake game was played mainly by children. The snow snake was a thin, smoothed hickory shaft some six feet in length, with the forward end increased in diameter and slightly upturned. There were up to six players, with three to a side, and each hurled his snow snake across a snow surface. The game was scored according to the distance achieved until the specified number of points had been reached by one side. The snow boat game was based on the snow snake principle. A snow boat, constructed from a solid piece of beech wood, looked like a round-bottomed vessel with an upturned bow. The boat had small feathers at the top of the stern and an oblong central opening in which was placed an arched piece of wood hung with rattles. On a hillside each player trampled a runway in the snow, iced the depression, and propelled two or three boats down the chute and as far as possible across the snow below.

APPLICATION

FUNCTION PARAGRAPHS

Explain which of the paragraphs in the following passages are function paragraphs. Describe what their function is in each passage.

A

Try to remember a time when you *first* read a book or heard a radio show and then *later* saw a film or a television program on the same work.

If you read, say, *Gone With the Wind, Roots, Marjorie Morningstar* or *From Here to Eternity,* or heard any radio show such as "The Lone Ranger" first, you created your own internal image of the events described while you read or listened. You imagined the characters, the events and the ambience. You made pictures in your mind. These pictures were yours. Of course, they were influenced by the author—what he or she told you—but the creation of the actual image was up to you.

Marjorie Morningstar was an image in your mind *before* you saw the film. Then you saw the film with Natalie Wood playing Marjorie. Once you had seen Natalie Wood in the role, could you recover the image you had made up?

—Jerry Mander

B

Style is organic to the person doing the writing, as much a part of him as his hair, or, if he is bald, his lack of it. Trying to add style is like adding a toupée. At first glance the formerly bald man looks young and even handsome. But at second glance—and with a toupée there is always a second glance—he doesn't look quite right. The problem is not that he doesn't look well groomed; he does, and we can only admire the wigmaker's almost perfect skill. The point is that he doesn't look like himself.

This is the problem of the writer who sets out deliberately to garnish his prose. You lose whatever it is that makes you unique. The reader will usually notice if you are putting on airs. He wants the person who is talking to him to sound genuine. Therefore a fundamental rule is: be yourself.

—William Zinsser

C

I have never been as scared as I was that day.

We had driven to the top of the mountain to get a better view of the lake. We scrambled out of the car and ran to the edge of the mountain, being careful not to get too close lest we tumble down the steep, rocky side. As we returned to the car, Mike casually pointed to the darkening, swirling clouds above. Those weren't ordinary clouds. Herman shouted, "That's a tornado forming and about to touch down right on us!"

We didn't know what to do. If we stayed on the mountain, the tornado was sure to hit us. We tried driving down, but the swirling leaves and dust on the dirt road ahead told us the tornado was right in front. After frantically—and futilely—signaling for help on his CB radio, Herman decided to risk the drive down. We made it safely, but a few minutes later we heard on the radio that it had touched down on the other side of the mountain, killing several residents of a mobile home park.

Come on, admit it.

You've been living with someone for a while now and you sometimes think you've made a mistake, a big mistake. There are things you want to do that you can't because the person you are living with gets in the way.

You feel cheated. You're missing a lot. You can't stand thinking about it because it hurts so much. Sometimes you just want to be alone, free to be and do whatever you want.

—David Viscott

CHUNK UNITS OF THOUGHT: THE TOPIC SENTENCE PARAGRAPH AND FUNCTION PARAGRAPH BROUGHT TOGETHER

This last use of the Function Paragraph—to emphasize a point, develop an example, or give details—is an excellent illustration of the way *Topic Sentence Paragraphs and Function Paragraphs operate together to make up* CHUNK UNITS OF THOUGHT.

A CHUNK UNIT OF THOUGHT can be defined as a main TOPIC SENTENCE PARAGRAPH *plus* as many FUNCTION PARAGRAPHS and additional TOPIC SENTENCE PARAGRAPHS as are necessary to complete the thought.

In Chunk Units of Thought there will be a subject or point introduced; the reader has to start there to know the meaning of the rest of the paragraphs. The main Topic Sentence Paragraph sets up the context for understanding what follows—it is the mold that the rest of the paragraphs "fit" into. Look at this example of a Chunk Unit of Thought. This unit is part of an essay Henry Boettinger wrote on the subject of *where to get ideas*. He has been talking about a lot of sources for ideas; and when this particular Chunk Unit begins, he is moving to the subject of *reading and ideas*.

One of the evils of what has come to be tiresomely known as the information explosion is its relentless tendency to narrow our reading The pressures to confine ourselves more and more to reading in our primary field of interest must be resisted, if we are serious about generating new ideas. Those supple minds that make the great contributions have always been exercised by many interests. The narrowing specialist who tries to hone his skill by greater and greater concentration deteriorates in effectiveness. Shaw aptly described his terminal condition: He knows more and more about less and less until he knows everything about nothing. Such men are useful only as auxiliaries for better and broader minds, to be called on as one would grab an ice pick for a specific and well-defined task.

The best antidote for this is a wide range of reading. If an expert is really sharp, "outside reading" produces a flood of associations which drench his mind and allow promising and original approaches to sprout in his own field. One of the best comptrollers I know is good enough at

MAIN TOPIC SENTENCE PARAGRAPH:

Everything else in Chunk Unit will fit into this subject.

The first two sentences combine to be the topic sentence of the paragraph.

TOPIC SENTENCE PARAGRAPH:

Although this paragraph has a topic sentence, without the

preceding paragraph, the reader would not know what this meant in the opening sentence. So the paragraphs have to be read in a chunk in order to get the meaning.

geology to teach it in college. He has far more books on geology than on accounting in his home. The best experimental physicist I ever met was a recognized authority on beetles. The most humane and cultured financial officer I know is a national skeet champion and an ardent conservationist. Other acquaintances have similar "paired skills": An expert on financial operations has a profound grasp of Slavic history; an outstanding personnel specialist is learned in Post-Impressionist art; a first-class public relations practitioner is an authority on Mayan archeology; a management consultant's knowledge of geography would put world travelers to shame; a noted economist is a fine wood sculptor; and so on and on. I have little doubt that they are better in their chosen occupations *because of,* not in spite of, their interests and competence in other fields. In fact, it is difficult to find someone in the top drawer of contributions to his profession who does not do wide and lively reading outside it.

FUNCTION PARAGRAPH:

This paragraph makes a transition between the argument the writer has just used and the information that will follow. Again, notice how this paragraph wouldn't make sense if it weren't a piece of the whole Chunk Unit of Thought.

A senior editor once told me of the ways he used to keep oriented in our complex world. I have since used them myself and found them so productive of ideas and insights that I set them down here. They are based on one method used by surveyors to establish their positions. This method is called *triangulation,* i.e., three angles. Surveyors take sights to three known objects at some distance from their position, preferably in widely different directions. The place where the three lines of sight intersect determines the position sought. (This is also the basis of celestial navigation; the "known objects" sighted are stars, planets, sun, and moon.)

TOPIC SENTENCE PARAGRAPH:

Again, however, this topic sentence paragraph wouldn't make too much sense to the reader if it were isolated. For one thing, the reader wouldn't know what "take sights" meant. So this Topic Sentence Paragraph has to be read in the context of the opening main Topic Sentence Paragraph.

How does one "take sights" through his reading? Here are the editor's suggestions: 1. Skim an entire daily newspaper. 2. Read a weekly news magazine or review; select different ones from time to time. 3. Pick up a trade paper remote from your own field, every now and then. 4. Buy different monthly "opinion" periodicals, even if their editorial policy is repugnant to you. 5. Dip into so-called learned journals in other fields. If you grasp only the titles, you're ahead. 6. Scan a book review magazine of some kind. You may stimulate a latent interest. *Buy* some books; don't rely on friends. Use library copies if you can't afford them. 7. Read a foreign periodical frequently. If you know only English, use English, Scottish, Canadian, or Australian magazines. Some others are translated. 8. Reread a fine novel or classic untouched since your youth. You will be surprised at how different it is today. 9. Select a subject or a period in history for a few weeks of concentrated interest. Make it fun, not a chore. Stop when it becomes a bore or overtaxes your powers. Historical patterns help illuminate today's events. 10. Do not be afraid of being called a dilettante. You are after stimuli, not professional standing.

FUNCTION PARAGRAPH:

To emphasize a point and bring the Chunk Unit to a close.

After a while, these become almost habitual. Every excursion is like a sightseeing tour taken at your own pace. You will be a rare person indeed if you do not discover unexpected delights or get a new perspective on your own work.

It is the interrelatedness of Topic Sentence and Function Paragraphs

in whole Chunk Units of Thought that makes for "real writing," where each paragraph does *not* stick out as a separate isolated entity. Chunk Units of Thought *flow,* and the paragraphs are just the means for that flow to happen. *The reason why you, as a beginning writer, have to look so hard at your paragraphs is that you have not had much practice in having something important enough to say and in developing it well enough so that your paragraphs will just fall into place.* You still have to look hard at your own paragraphs to see what they are contributing to the message you are trying to get across.

APPLICATION TO YOUR WRITING

Now, in the *Completing Stage,* you have the time to look at your essay to see what you can do to make it move faster, interest the reader more, be better connected, or emphasize just what you want emphasized. You've checked all the Topic Sentence Paragraphs, and they are in good order. Now you can look to see if you want to add any Function Paragraphs. You may need some *transition paragraphs* to get the reader from one point to another. You may see some places you could use a little drama — maybe wake up the readers and keep them interested. Perhaps one of your thoughts could use another example, and you'll put in a Function Paragraph to highlight that extra information.

What you want to do is make your decisions according to what you believe is best for the reader and for your own presentation of the material. But remember: **almost no writing in the real world is ever one Topic Sentence Paragraph after another.** Real messages usually don't fall into these neat packages. **Function paragraphs add interest and assure flow.** You will want some if for no other reason than to sound like *yourself* when you write instead of like some dull "voice of the past."

This doesn't mean, however, that you can be oblivious to rules for paragraphing. You can't just paragraph anywhere and everywhere — with no rhyme or reason and no thought on your part — and have your writing really work. *If* you are conscious about *why* you are paragraphing — *what purpose each paragraph serves* — then you *do* get to make the paragraphs wherever you want to. But if you don't have some explanation and are unconscious in making your paragraphs, the result will inevitably be a disjointed, undeveloped, incommunicative piece of writing.

There is, then, truth to the old saying, "You learn the rules in order to know how to break them." You learn Topic Sentence paragraphing and Function paragraphing in order to know how to be individual and independent in your use of them. *But you have to know the basic concepts thoroughly.* You won't be able to fool anybody by claiming, "Oh, I just felt like putting a paragraph there." Good writers may put paragraphs in because they "feel" like it, but these paragraphs *contribute* to the flow of the work, not stop it. These writers can trust their feelings; **for your part, you must be *sure* that you arrange your paragraphs so that your readers don't have problems with them.** Because, again, even if you have the "right" to make a paragraph wherever you want to, you'll win the battle but lose the war if the paragraphs don't contribute to your writing's meaning something to your readers. Queer paragraphing only wastes your time, because the whole purpose of writing in the first place —to get a message across to someone else—will have been lost. So be fair—*to yourself!* Learn paragraphing and be honest in its use.

Now that you know about the two basic types of paragraphs and the varieties available within those two types, you'll be considerably freer to exercise your own style, both during the *Shaping Stage* and in the *Completing Stage*. You can make your writing more effective and orderly by mastering the Topic Sentence Paragraph, that backbone of the communication process; and as you master the various forms of the multipurpose Functional Paragraph, you'll be mastering techniques for getting across a sense of style, class, persuasion, and rhythm.

For some, a sense of paragraphs comes naturally—it's like having a sense of rhythm about dancing. In such cases, the paragraphs tend to almost shape themselves, with a natural and pleasing and effective variety—just the right blend of topic sentence and multipurpose functional types. For other people, paragraphs are more a matter of conscious design and are added after the content of the paper has been written and then rewritten at least once into the shaped form. The final version, though, inevitably reveals something of the personal preference and style of the writer. For example, we've noticed that people who depend on lots of one-sentence paragraphs often talk with their hands too! And writers who produce long, detailed paragraphs are often long-winded talkers—and often too have a reputation for being "heavy" and "serious." The balance between "too breezy" and "too heavy" isn't usually taught—in fact, it usually isn't even discussed in many texts. Yet sophisticated writers somehow learn about such things, and the discovery almost inevitably leads to an extension of the range of a writer's possibilities—how to be more precise, and how to more effectively be and express yourself.

As you do the *Completing Stage* of your essay, watch for the **flow** of the message. Sometimes a Topic Sentence Paragraph will be most appropriate, other times a functional paragraph will work just right. **Just keep your eye out for ways of moving the essay along smoothly and continuously;** that's the point of it all.

Application Here is a portion of the essay on the Dead Sea, which we have been quoting in this section. The beginning of the essay has been annotated so that you can see exactly how professional writers combine Topic Sentence Paragraphs and Functional Paragraphs in their writing. Beginning with paragraph (5), you should attempt to supply your own annotation or notes—your own analysis, in other words—similar to those provided for paragraphs (1) to (4).

You will observe how much (or how little) rhyme and reason there is to how professional writers use paragraphs. When you finish, you'll know and understand that there is no firm rule about paragraphing.

Yet at the same time, you'll have a broader concept of how paragraphs can be effectively used in your own writing. This understanding should allow you more control and more energy in the essays that you write.

The Living Dead Sea

By Harvey Arden
National Geographic Staff

(1) Getting to the bottom of it all is not so difficult. If you happen to be in Jerusalem, as I was one rainy November, you need only hail a taxi and ask to be taken to the Dead Sea—the lowest spot on the surface of the earth.

(1) FUNCTION PARAGRAPH: TO GET THE READER'S ATTENTION. The two-sentence introduction sets the scene and gets the essay moving swiftly. Writer gets reader's attention by being a little mysterious as he begins.

(2) It's only a half-hour drive from Jerusalem's 760-meter spiritual <u>height to the Dead Sea's netherworldish shore—399 meters (1,309 feet) *below* sea level.</u> Snaking through sere Judaean hills where Abraham and Jesus once walked, you pass a sign that says "SEA LEVEL" in Hebrew, Arabic, and English. It may vaguely occur to you that there aren't too many places in the world where you can dip below sea level in a taxicab and keep going, but such thoughts are now shunted out of mind by the fact that your ears have begun to pop, your head is ringing slightly, and the wool sweater you'd snuggled into back in Jerusalem's 10°C (50°F) chill has become uncomfortably warm.

(2) TOPIC SENTENCE PARAGRAPH: MAIN IDEA IS DEAD SEA; REST OF SENTENCES DEVELOP THIS MAIN IDEA.

(3) Your Israeli driver, Shlomo, informs you that this new-looking road was modernized by Jordan's King Hussein just before the six-day war of 1967 brought the West Bank under Israeli military control.

(3) FUNCTION PARAGRAPH: TO BREAK UP A LONG PARAGRAPH.

(4) "Nice of the king," Shlomo remarks wryly, and you slouch back in your seat just a bit uncomfortably at the thought that this is occupied territory. Before 1967 only the southwest quadrant of the Dead Sea belonged to Israel. An Israeli in West Jerusalem, unable to cross into Jordanian territory, had to take an hours-long roundabout drive through Beersheba to get to the Dead Sea. Nowadays, using "King Hussein's road" across the West Bank, it's just a short trip. . . .

(4) FUNCTION PARAGRAPH: TO MAKE TRANSITION. This paragraph hooks a new train of thought onto previous remark. The paragraph also allows writer to give additional detail about the road.

(5) Off to the left a splash of green brightens the ocher landscape. "That's Jericho," Shlomo says. "Oldest known town in the world. Been there 10,000 years. And that's the River Jordan just beyond, where Jesus was baptized by John. Over there"—he points to some caveriddled cliffs to the right—"is Qumran, where most of the Dead Sea Scrolls were found. And see those mountains? One of them is Mount Nebo, where Moses died. Joshua then led the Israelites into the Promised Land right down there, across the Jordan above the Dead Sea."

(6)   He smiles. "It's easy to believe in the Bible when you come to a place like this."

Ten minutes later you reach the Dead Sea shore at a former Jordanian spa called the Lido. Like most first-time visitors, you

(7)   cross the salt-encrusted beach to the water's edge, crouch down, poke one finger through the oily-looking surface, then gingerly put it to your tongue.

(8)   *Arghhh-h!* The taste is as strong and stinging as lye. "Worst-tasting stuff in the world!" Shlomo laughs, and you don't argue. . . .

(9)   Despite its name, the Dead Sea is not a sea at all. It's actually a lake with a deep northern basin 331 meters (1,086 feet) deep, and a smaller southern basin averaging only about two meters deep. The two, totaling 75 kilometers (45 miles) long by 15 kilometers (9 miles) wide, are joined across a now submerged neck of land that could be crossed on foot in Biblical times, when the water was lower. . . .

(10)   Nor is the Dead Sea "dead." While it's true that fish can't live in it, scientists have discovered in its waters a number of halophilic—salt-loving—microorganisms. One of them, *Halobacterium halobium*, has recently been found by U.S. scientist Dr. Walther Stoeckenius to yield a purple pigment that is the only known biological substance other than chlorophyll capable of photosynthesis—the conversion of sunlight directly into energy.

REVISING FOR FLOW: TRANSITIONS AND REMINDER SIGNS

TRANSITIONS AND REMINDER SIGNS

There is one final thing you need to check before you can be sure your writing is moving smoothly and continuously for the reader. You need to see if you have all along given the reader **signals** that indicate your direction *(transitions)* and **reminder signs** that help the reader remember what you are writing about. *Transitions* you have probably heard about since high school, at least. The *reminder signs* will probably be something you haven't thought much about but that you probably use occasionally. Turning a critical eye on these two areas will be the final part of revising for flow and will complete this part of the *Completing Stage* of the writing process.

TRANSITIONS

Once you know the *concept* of "transitioning," you'll master the *forms* almost without effort.

The word *transition* comes from the Latin word *transire* which means "to pass from one place to another." As you learned in studying Function Paragraphs, **transitions help the reader to pass from one place (or point) in your writing to the next.** And while, as you have seen, transitions may indeed be whole paragraphs in length, they may also be only a sentence or even a few words—*anything that indicates for the reader that you are changing from one point to another.* Although the *forms* vary, it is the *concept* of "transitioning" you want to learn, because once you understand the concept you will be able to insert transitions into your work in *any* form—paragraphs, sentences, or even single words—and you will be able to judge for yourself *which* form will do the best job for any given situation.

  Let's begin by examining the work of other writers to see how they indicate transitions, how they show the movement from thought to thought. Once you can spot the transitions in someone else's writing, and understand how they function (regardless of form), you'll be in good shape to look at your own writing to see whether there are enough (and adequate) transitions. In the essay by John Stewart and Gary d'Angelo that follows, the transition signals are marked.

Giving What You Say a Sense of Wholeness

(1)   If your experience is anything like ours, people have been telling you to <u>"get organized"</u> ever since you were in diapers. Your toy box was to help you learn to <u>organize your room.</u> School and work taught you to <u>organize your time.</u> And invariably, one goal of English, speech, philosophy, and science classes is to teach you to <u>organize your thinking</u> and the ways to express yourself. Sometimes, I wonder whether we tend to go a little overboard. Gary's got a carton on his office door that shows a high-school-age girl deep in thought, and the caption is: "Sometimes they teach things out of me. And I feel like saying, 'I wanted to keep that.'" We sometimes wonder whether spontaneous chaos is one of those things that schools "teach out of us" that we might enjoy—and profit from—keeping.   *[Key word repeated.]*

(2)   <u>On the other hand,</u> most psychologists believe that we *naturally* structure our world, i.e., that order is more characteristically human than is disorder. <u>But whether structure is natural or is an artifact of Western culture, it's here.</u> We *do* tend to see things and people in wholes made up of parts that are somehow related to one another. <u>Therefore, communication that has a sense of wholeness is usually easier for us to comprehend clearly than is communication that doesn't.</u>   *[Signals contrast. Signals contrast. Signals conclusion.]*

(3)   <u>When people perceive something that's "incomplete" or "disordered," they sometimes fill in or add details so that it makes more sense to them.</u> For example, as you watch a television program you may see an actor put a coffee cup to his lips and make drinking movements. Even though you don't actually see the coffee itself, you mentally "put" coffee in the cup—you fill in the detail. <u>This same kind of process</u> can occur when you're talking with another person. If you don't provide a "whole" message, the other person   *[Shift from conclusion to how people act. Signals example. Signals similarity.]*

may fill in missing details or examples and in so doing may make your message into something you didn't intend. To the extent that you don't come across as a "whole" person, the other person may fill in or infer things about you that don't adequately characterize you as an individual. In short, giving a sense of wholeness and some structure to your communication gives you some control over how *you* and your *ideas* are perceived by others.

Signals summary.

Shift to general principle about formal/informal contexts.

(4) The more formal the communication context, the more obvious that sense of wholeness can be. Persons listening to a public speech usually expect the talk to be clearly structured. A public speech doesn't have to sound as if it's coming from a robot; the speaker can still promote some person-to-person contact. But the speech should usually be pretty clearly organized. Your contribution to a group discussion should also have fairly clear structure, although it can be less formal than the organization of a speech.

Signals contrast.

Signals addition.
Signals contrast.
Signals difference.

(5) An informal conversation, however, is obviously different from both a speech and a group discussion. You don't sit down beforehand to organize a conversation—not usually, anyway. (Your first date might have been an exception to that rule. I remember frantically trying to plan topics of conversation for my first major boy-girl social engagements. You know how well that worked.)

Signals reassertion.
Signals example.

(6) Yet structure is important, even in conversational communication. For example, have you ever had a conversation like this?

Fred: How many Christmas presents do we have left to get?

Wilma: Just a couple. You have any ideas for your brother? I don't remember what we got him last year.

Fred: That reminds me, I forgot to call that woman.

Wilma: Hunh? Should we call Ann and ask her? I always feel like. . . .

Fred: *Damn*, that makes me mad! Oh, well, he still does a lot of hunting.

Wilma: She remembers *Halloween* even.

Fred: Who?

Wilma: Was it you who told me about that guy who killed one of the six remaining animals of that one species?

Fred: Yeah, but how does *that* relate to Sam's present?

Reminds reader of example.

(7) In a conversation like that, the problem is *not* that there's a total lack of structure. Fred's contributions make all kinds of sense to him, and so do Wilma's—to Wilma. *The problem is that the implicit structure is not made explicit.* Fred knows the connections among his own statements, but he doesn't bother to show Wilma those relationships, and Wilma doesn't bother to explain anything to Fred.

Signals example.

(8) For example, when Wilma mentions Fred's brother (Sam), Fred pictures Sam on the job—Sam counsels handicapped children—which reminds Fred that he forgot to call a psychologist he works with—"that woman." Wilma hears "that woman" and assumes that Fred is talking about Sam's wife, Ann. Wilma feels uncomfortable

around Ann and so begins to say to Fred, "I always feel like . . ." Fred doesn't even hear her. He's thinking that they might get Sam something he can use while hunting; when Wilma hears the word "hunting," she remembers a story Fred told her that she's been wanting to share with a friend, but forgot about until now, and so on.

(9)   The point we're trying to make is that there's structure even in an informal conversation, in the sense that each person's contributions "fit in" or "follow logically" or "make sense"—in short, connect—*for that person*. Problems arise when two (or more) persons' structures don't merge or fit together. Then you get the kind of confusing exchange Fred and Wilma had. You can avoid such confusion by thinking of the other person as unique, as someone who doesn't structure the world or the conversation as you do. Your thought patterns, the connections you see between ideas, are different from his or hers. So if you reveal your thought patterns, if you make them explicit by bringing them to the surface with verbal cues, then the structure of each person's contributions to the conversation becomes apparent to the other, and there will be less room for misinterpretation.

Signals point.

Signals summary.

Signals conclusion.
Signals condition.

(10)   In other words, there are ways to structure even informal conversation so that it makes sense. You don't necessarily have to give your conversation a beginning (introduction), middle (body), and end (conclusion). It would sound a little phony if you said to someone in an informal conversation: "Hi, I'm really glad to be talking with you today. As our conversation progresses I'd like to talk about three things: (1) the weather, (2) the movie I saw last night, and (3) our relationship." That kind of organization or structure fits many public speeches, but most people prefer spontaneity in informal conversation.

Signals rephrasing.

Signals contrast.

(11)   Even in an informal conversation, however, you can verbalize the implicit structure, that is, talk about the links you're seeing between ideas. When you don't, you leave open the possibility for all kinds of misinterpretation. When you do, you significantly improve your chances of adequately limiting the range of interpretations, i.e., you improve your chances of "being clear."

Signals qualification.
Signals rephrasing.
Contrasts conditions.

Signals rephrasing.

This selection is rich with connectors that act as a map to guide the reader from major point to major point, and also as a blueprint of structure even within the sentences themselves. The reader appreciates this wealth of clues, too, even though some of them may not register on the conscious level. In fact, sometimes clues work best when they are so smooth and subtle that the reader doesn't even notice them, but rather takes them for granted. However, by means of such clues the writer's ideas are made to flow smoothly and steadily for the reader. Without the clues, the reader's head bobs from point to point in a hopelessly wobbling fashion.

This essay, with its signals marked in the margins, makes clear exactly how these signals work. They *do* help the reader see where the writer is going at all times. And you will probably find that *you* usually put transitions into your own writing quite naturally and automatically, without thinking much about it. Yet sometimes as you're writing, your mind twists, turns, and shifts so fast that you forget to tell the reader where you have gone—or where you're headed. So it is always worthwhile to look over your paper to check if the transition signals are there. If they are, you are in good shape (and probably haven't lost much time in checking). If they are not, **you can provide a thoughtful service—a courtesy—for your reader by inserting enough transition signal words so that the reader will always know exactly where you are going.**

TRANSITION SIGNAL WORDS

A short list of words and phrases mainly used to indicate relationships between one piece of writing and another. (Although there are many such words and phrases, this is a fairly illustrative list.)

TRANSITION SIGNAL WORDS	MEANING
for example, for instance, e.g.	"Here's an example of that principle or generalization."
because, consequently, since, therefore	"This caused that, or is a reason for that."
in other words, that is, so, i.e.	"Here is a restatement or a clarification."
but, however, on the other hand, yet, nevertheless, on the contrary	"This is different from that."

EXAMPLE

CAUSE

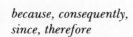

RESTATEMENT

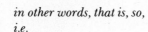

DIFFERENCE

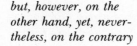

TRANSITION SIGNAL WORDS	MEANING	
similarly, likewise, in the same manner, in the same way	"This is similar to that."	SIMILARITY
also, too, in addition, and, furthermore, moreover	"Here comes another one, just like the other one."	ANOTHER ONE
first, next, then, last, before, prior, subsequently, earlier, later	"These exist in time relationship."	TIME SEQUENCE
aboard, above, beyond, on top of, under, alongside, upon, beneath, to the left	"These are related in space."	SPACE RELATIONSHIP
finally, at last, after all, in conclusion, to conclude, to sum up	"This wraps it up. The end is in sight."	THE END

REMINDER SIGNS

People generally have a short memory of what they read. In fact, some recent research indicates that within twenty seconds they forget the *form* of the message and remember only the *gist* of the message. (Of course that's a good reason to be sure that you do have a message in there in the first place!) Since we have considered this aspect of the message in the *Creating* and *Shaping* stages, what bearing has this for us in the *Completing Stage?* Just this: **since a reader will tend to forget the order of the words themselves so easily, you must use reminder signs all along the way in your writing to refresh the reader's memory and to keep your subject clearly visible.**

What are reminder signs in writing? They are simply *key words or phrases repeated throughout the writing.* Sometimes it is the *same* word repeated exactly (as the word *organize* was repeated in the last sample essay); other times it is a *variation* of that word, a *synonym* for the word, or a *pronoun* that stands for the word. The important thing about this repeating is that it keeps the reader pointed in a straight line without looking back to rediscover what you're talking about. It's the principle of "courteous repetition."

Here's a paragraph that illustrates the principle.

Specials for Your Hair

Leaves fall in an annual cycle, and there is a natural cyclical pattern of normal hair loss on the human head, too. The greatest amount of hair loss occurs in November; the least amount in May. A single hair grows on your head for a little less than three years. Then it rests. After about three months of rest, it falls out and a new hair grows in its place in the same hair follicle, and the cycle begins again. This is the end of that resting period for old hair, so you can expect heavier accumulations than usual in your brush and comb. Up to one hundred hairs a day may fall out in the normal course of things, but healthy new hairs are growing as you read this. If you suspect that your hair loss is greater than normal, count the hairs that come out in your comb. If the total is higher than one hundred, take measures. See the hairologist at a good salon for treatments.

—Vidal and Beverly Sassoon

Examining this paragraph, you can see that the key words are *cycle, normal hair loss, rest,* and *one hundred.* These key words are repeated all the way through the paragraph, and the reader is never allowed to forget what the subject is, never is obliged to double back to pick up the thought. In your own writing, you naturally have to beware of sounding monotonous, and so you will want to vary the wording, using pronouns or synonyms. However, you *will* need to do a certain amount of repeating of the main word or words in your message if you are going to keep the idea directly before your reader. This may finally—

with the transitions—be the most important thing in your writing that causes it to really *flow. A reader can't move in a straight line toward the goal—your total message—unless all along the way you give reminder signs to help overcome that twenty-second memory risk and to remember exactly what you are talking about at all times.*

"One should not aim at being possible to understand, but at being impossible to misunderstand."

—Quintilian

APPLICATION

TRANSITIONS AND REMINDER SIGNS

1   In the two samples below, find all the *transitions* and *reminder signs.* Underline them and be prepared to explain how they keep the reader moving smoothly through the paragraph and how they keep the subject at the front of the reader's attention.

A

Shopping around for a car loan is not as much fun as shopping for the car. But just as the savvy shopper checks out several car dealers before that final handshake, he should also check out competing lenders. To help him, the Federal Trade Commission has prepared a handy pocket *Credit Shopping Guide.* It includes tips on borrowing and a series of tables so you can compare the cost of car loans, home improvement loans and mortgages at various interest rates and over different time periods.

The total finance charge on a loan can depend on where you borrow. Let's say you need $3,000 for three years to buy a new car. If you finance it through the car dealer, where the average annual percentage rate—the true rate of interest—is 13½%, that $3,000 loan is likely to cost you $665. But if you go to a bank, where the average rate is 11%, the loan may cost $536; and if you can borrow against your life insurance, the rate will average 6%—for a cost of $286. . . .

To get a copy of the free credit guide, write the Public Reference Branch, Federal Trade Commission, Washington, D.C. 20580.

—Money Magazine

B

Samuel Johnson has fascinated more people than any other writer except Shakespeare. Statesmen, lawyers, and physicians quote him, as do writers and scientists, philosophers and farmers, manufacturers and leaders of labor unions. For generations people have been discovering new details about him and re-examining and correcting old ones. Interest in Johnson is by no means confined to the English-speaking world, though naturally it is strongest there. In Asia, Africa, and South America, groups of Johnsonians meet every year to talk about every aspect of him. The reason why Johnson has always fascinated so many people of different kinds is not simply that Johnson is so vividly picturesque and quotable, though these are the qualities that first catch our attention. The deeper secret of his hypnotic attraction, especially during our own generation, lies in the immense reassurance he gives to human nature, which needs—and quickly begins to value—every friend it can get.

—Walter Jackson Bate

2 Here are two examples that show just how effective your writing can be *when you constantly keep the subject before the reader by using reminder signs.* The first is by Chief Joseph of the Nez Perce Indians (published in 1879). What are the key terms? How often are they repeated? How does this contribute to the force of this paragraph?

The second example, by Don Fabun, is about the ways people use space to communicate. Examine this one for two things: the way Fabun *repeats* the key terms (which he is discussing) and the way he *signals* the reader at the beginning of each sentence. Underline both devices: *repeated key terms* and *signals,* and be prepared to discuss how Fabun uses each to lead the reader from sentence to sentence and to keep the main point always before the reader.

A

I have heard talk and talk, but nothing is done. Good words do not last long unless they amount to something. Words do not pay for my dead people. They do not pay for my country, now overrun by white men. . . . Good words will not give my people good health and stop them from dying. Good words will not get my people a home where they can live in peace and take care of themselves. I am tired of talk that comes to nothing. It makes my heart sick when I remember all the good words and broken promises. . . .

B

The way we use space is another way that we communicate with one another. The distance between you and someone else may determine the nature of the communication. If you are a few inches away from someone's ear, chances are that you will whisper and the nature of the communication will be "secret." At a distance of several feet, the communication may still be private, but its tone and nature will have changed. The change is even greater if you are speaking to a large audience. Here the nature of the message may be determined in part by the distance between you and the most distant members of the audience.

3 For your own writing: Look over your essay now to see if you have given the reader enough *transitions* and *reminder signs.* If not, reword some of the sentences to allow you to repeat the key words from a *previous* sentence early in the *next* sentences to be sure that you will take the reader along with you.

USE TRANSITIONS AND REMINDER SIGNS BECAUSE

1 Your readers forget easily, within twenty seconds.
2 You have a lot of competition for your readers' attention.
3 The best way to keep your readers with you is to keep them moving in a straight line, never causing them to double back to see what you are talking about.

WRITING ASSIGNMENT: THE EVALUATION ESSAY

"This car isn't running as fast as it did before the tune up."
"That was really a good concert."
"The price of real estate in this town is too high."
"That book isn't worth reading."
"She may be the best president we have ever had."

A hundred times a day we evaluate things around us, determining their value, quality, importance, or worth. The presence of some kind of standard against which the thing being measured is judged is what distinguishes evaluative writing. Sometimes these standards are *external:* this blender is better than those because *(a)* it has a stronger motor, *(b)* it is easier to wash, and *(c)* it has an unbreakable glass bowl. These features can be observed by everyone who wants to check on them and are external to the person writing the evaluation. The only thing the evaluator is taking for granted is that the reader agrees that stronger motors, easy washability, and unbreakable glass bowls are more desirable.

In other kinds of evaluative writing, the standards the writer uses for judging are *internal:* this book isn't worth reading because *(a)* there is too much description, *(b)* the main character is unattractive, and *(c)* the plot has too many angles. In a case like this, the writer cannot assume that the reader will necessarily agree that a lot of description is bad, that a particular kind of person is unattractive, or that a complicated plot is not desirable. The evaluation is based on the internal standards of the writer, standards which may or may not be the same as the readers'. (Usually, we like an evaluation more quickly if the writer has the same standards we do. One of the finest ways to broaden oneself, however, is to read evaluative writing done by people who think very differently.) The use of internal criteria for judging assumes that the writer has some special expertise, knowledge, experience, or the like to merit being listened to. One of the first things readers want to know when they read an evaluation is, "What are the writer's qualifications?" Any person using internal criteria, then, runs a greater risk of disagreement and can only counteract this by making very clear and convincing to the reader why her or his personal standards should prevail.

A good evaluation will always make very clear *(a)* what the criteria for the evaluation are and *(b)* whether these standards against which the thing is being judged are *external* (capable of being checked on or proved) or are *internal* (based on writer's personal experience, knowledge, view, or the like and not capable of being proved). Whether the

<u>To Evaluate:</u>
To determine or set the value of; to estimate the nature, quality, or importance of; to determine the worth of.

criteria are external and objective or internal and subjective, the value in an evaluation essay finally lies in the relationship between the person doing the evaluation and the thing being evaluated. It is this interface or friction between the one doing the judging and the thing being judged that the reader is finally left with, rather than some kind of absolute proof or truth. Even when a writer has used *external* criteria, for example, the human nature of the evaluator still intrudes on the evaluation—how many blenders were tested the day this one was proved best, does the evaluator work for the company whose blender won, do other blenders have outstanding features that are more important than motor strength, washability, or the kind of glass?

There is little use, of course, even to attempt to separate an evaluation from the person doing the evaluation, and it's not even desirable. To do so would be to lose the quality—the variable—that makes evaluations interesting, real, and valuable or not valuable. Instead, when we write (and read) evaluations, we should realize that we are having the opportunity to observe both the person doing the evaluating and the thing being evaluated. We can't avoid learning about both.

A good evaluation essay will have these characteristics:

1 The criteria used will be clear to the reader.
2 The writer will explain how these criteria are appropriate to be used in the evaluation unless she or he can assume that the reader will automatically know.
3 The nature of the criteria—whether it is internal or external—will be established early in the essay.
4 The writer's qualifications for doing the evaluation will be apparent to the reader.
5 The writer will give ample facts, specific details, or examples to support the final judgment made in the evaluation.

The following essays are evaluations done by both professional writers and students. Read them and then answer these questions. Be ready to discuss your answers in class.

— What are the criteria the writer uses for the evaluation? Are these criteria *external* or *internal*?
— Does the writer make any assumptions about what the readers will already agree with, believe, accept, or know?
— What are the writer's qualifications for making this evaluation?
— What kind of specific facts, details, and examples did the writer use to support the evaluation? Were you convinced?
— What did you learn about the writer when you read this evaluation?

READINGS:

American Space, Chinese Place

Evaluative writing often takes the form of comparing and contrasting two things in order to get at the nature of each. This essay, contrasting the American's sense of space with the Chinese's sense of place, is Professor Yi-Fu Tuan's attempt to identify the nature of two different cultures. The essay answers the question of evaluation: what is the nature, quality, or importance of . . . ?

Americans have a sense of space, not of place. Go to an American home in exurbia, and almost the first thing you do is drift toward the picture window. How curious that the first compliment you pay your host inside his house is to say how lovely it is outside his house! He is pleased that you should admire his vistas. The distant horizon is not merely a line separating earth from sky, it is a symbol of the future. The American is not rooted in his place, however lovely: his eyes are drawn by the expanding space to a point on the horizon, which is his future.

By contrast, consider the traditional Chinese home. Blank walls enclose it. Step behind the spirit wall and you are in a courtyard with perhaps a miniature garden around a corner. Once inside his private compound you are wrapped in an ambiance of calm beauty, an ordered world of buildings, pavement, rock, and decorative vegetation. But you have no distant view: nowhere does space open out before you. Raw nature in such a home is experienced only as weather, and the only open space is the sky above. The Chinese is rooted in his place. When he has to leave, it is not for the promised land on the terrestrial horizon, but for another world altogether along the vertical, religious axis of his imagination.

The Chinese tie to place is deeply felt. Wanderlust is an alien sentiment. The Taoist classic *Tao Te Ching* captures the ideal of rootedness in place with these words: "Though there may be another country in the neighborhood so close that they are within sight of each other and the crowing of cocks and barking of dogs in one place can be heard in the other, yet there is no traffic between them; and throughout their lives the two peoples have nothing to do with each other." In theory if not in practice, farmers have ranked high in Chinese society. The reason is not only that they are engaged in a "root" industry of producing food but that, unlike pecuniary merchants, they are tied to the land and do not abandon their country when it is in danger.

Nostalgia is a recurrent theme in Chinese poetry. An American reader of translated Chinese poems may well be taken aback — even put off — by the frequency, as well as the sentimentality, of the lament for home. To understand the strength of this sentiment, we need to know that the Chinese desire for stability and rootedness in place is prompted by the constant threat of war, exile, and the natural disasters of flood and drought. Forcible removal makes the Chinese keenly aware of their loss. By contrast, Americans move, for the most part, voluntarily. Their nostalgia for home town is really longing for a childhood to which they cannot return: in the meantime the future beckons and the future is "out there," in open space. When we criticize American rootlessness, we tend to forget that it is a result of ideals we admire, namely, social mobility and optimism about the future. When we admire Chinese rootedness, we forget that the word "place" means both a location in space and position in society: to be tied to place is also to be bound to one's station in life, with little hope of betterment. Space symbolizes hope; place, achievement and stability.

E. M. Forster's Tribute to Mahatma Gandhi

When Mahatma Gandhi died, E. M. Forster, a famous British novelist, attempted in this beautiful tribute to estimate the Indian leader's importance to the world. His words are an evaluation: they set out "to determine the worth" of Mahatma Gandhi and to get at the "quality and importance" of the famous man.

The organizers of this meeting have asked me . . . to pay a short tribute myself. In doing so I do not desire to emphasize the note of grief. Grief is for those who knew Mahatma Gandhi personally, or who are close to his teaching. I have neither of these claims. Nor would it be seemly to speak with compassion and pity of him, as though it were on him rather than on India and the world that the blow has fallen. If I have understood him rightly, he was always indifferent to death. His work and the welfare of others was what mattered to him, and if the work could have been furthered by dying rather than living, he would have been content. He was accustomed to regard an interruption as an instrument, and he remarks in his *Autobiography* that God seldom intended for him what he had planned. And he would have regarded death, the supreme interruption, as an instrument and perhaps the supreme one—preferable to the full 125 years of life for which in his innocence he had hoped. The murder seems so hideous and senseless to us—as an English friend of mine put it, one would have liked that old saint to fade away magically. But we must remember that we are looking at it all from outside; it was not a defeat to him.

But although neither grief nor pity are in place this evening, we may well entertain a feeling of awe and a sense of our own smallness. When the news came to me last week, I realized intensely how small I was, how small those around me, how impotent and circumscribed are the lives of most of us spiritually, and how in comparison with that mature goodness the so-called great men of our age are no more than blustering school boys. Read the newspapers tomorrow, see what they advertise and whom, observe the values they imply and the actions they emphasize. Then think anew of the career and character of Mahatma Gandhi, and the feeling of awe will return with a salutary shock. We, to-day—we are inventive and adaptable, we are stoical and learning to bear things, our young men have acquired what may be termed the "returned warrior" attitude, and that is all very well. But we are losing the sense of wonder. We are forgetting what human nature can do, and upon what a vast stage it is set. The death of this very great man may remind us, he has indicated by his existence the possibilities still to be explored.

His character was intricate, and this is not the place to analyze it. But all who met him, even the critical, have testified to the goodness in it, a goodness irradiated by no ordinary light. His practical teachings—the doctrine of non-violence and the doctrine of simplicity, symbolized by the spinning wheel—proceeded from that goodness, and it also inspired his willingness to suffer. He was not only good. He made good and ordinary men all over the world now look up to him in consequence. He has placed India on their spiritual map. It was always on that map for the student and scholar, but the ordinary man demands tangible evidence, spiritual proofs of moral firmness, and he has found them in the imprisonments, the fastings, the willingness to suffer, and in this death. The other day I passed a taxi-rank, and heard the drivers talking to one another about "Old Gandhi" and praising him in their own way. He would have valued it more than any tribute the scholar or the student can bring. For it sprang from simplicity.

"A very great man" I have called him. He is likely to be the greatest of our century. Lenin is sometimes bracketed with him, but Lenin's kingdom was of this world, and we do not know yet what the world will do with it. Gandhi's was not. Though he impinged upon events and influenced politics, he had his roots outside time, and drew strength thence. He is with the founders of religion, whether he founds a religion or not. He is with the great artists, though art was not his medium. He is with all the men and women who have sought something in life that is neither chaos nor mechanism, who have not confused happiness with possessiveness, or victory with success, and who have believed in love.

Didion Finds Nuggets in Most Unlikely Places

This short essay, written by Martha Liebrum, is a particular kind of evaluation that is very common: the book review. In such an evaluation, the writer is answering questions such as, "Is the book good or bad?" "What is the book's importance? its value?" In a book review evaluation, the reader must pay special attention to the writer's qualifications for judging the book and look carefully at the evaluator's qualifications and notice especially the internal criteria used for making the final judgment on the book.

THE WHITE ALBUM, by Joan Didion. 223 pp. New York: Simon and Schuster. $9.95.

Little more than a week ago, 600 workers walked out of the Department of Water Resources, temporarily shutting down the California Aqueduct, which supplies water to the San Joaquin Valley farmlands.

This is news which would not ordinarily provoke much interest this side of California . . . unless one had just completed Joan Didion's new book, a compilation of essays written during the last 10 years.

"Holy Water" is about the ebb and flow of water through the state of California and it is a sample of Didion's fine writing and inordinate attention to things most people take for granted, or simply ignore. Didion has been possessed most of her life by the thoughts of how water flows through California, she writes, and with disappointment she notes, "Not many people I know carry their end of the conversation when I want to talk about water deliveries, even when I stress that these deliveries affect their lives, indirectly, every day. 'Indirectly' is not quite enough for most people I know."

Things that affect us indirectly are plenty for Didion, enough to fuel pages and pages of intellectual essays. She is without doubt one of the finest journalist-essayists writing in America. Though she often tends to see life through a dark glass, she also has wit. In her essay on living in Malibu, she explains that community was not at all the way America perceived it, not the core of easy living (it was a community of neighbors, who knew and cared for each other, she says). Even so, she eventually moved out and knew this truth about Malibu: "I had not before 1971 and will probably not again live in a place with a Chevrolet named after it."

The publishers assert this book fully examines the "vibrations and fears that began in the late Sixties, that age of self-discovery and belief in the possibility of change whose spiritual center was California, Didion's homeland in fact and spirit," and that the book brings us full circle to today.

It does less than that, and more than that. Joan Didion's perceptions are often too personal to be considered reportage of how things were. But she almost never misses the bizarre within the ordinary.

Some fine moments: She describes a TV crew "setting up" a "natural" interview with Nancy Reagan in her garden. They want to run through her plucking a flower, but just a rehearsal. The cameraman explains, "Fake the nip, yeah, fake the nip."

She spent hours roaming the greenhouse of the greatest orchid grower in California, getting to know the man who raises the precious blooms.

She writes of her delight in Georgia O'Keeffe; her disenchantment with the women's movement and Doris Lessing. She covers migraines, Bogota, Bishop James Pike and Hawaii.

My chief complaint is that, having read so many of these pieces in print in various magazines over the years, I get a sense of reading very dated material. Did she have no second thoughts on the women's movement since 1972?

The title essay "The White Album," is an incredible piece. In it, she explains "THE times," (the Manson Family, a Doors recording session, Huey Newton) and HER own times, going through a mental breakdown, sensing that she'd lost the script she was supposed to be following in life, while she was at the same moment being named a Los Angeles Times "Woman of the Year."

Polish up on Your Insults

This amusing description of The Book of Insults, Ancient and Modern, *is an informal, light-hearted evaluation that attempts to go no further than saying what is good about the new book. Lynn Ashby, who wrote the essay, clearly likes the book and thinks his readers will, too. Notice how Ashby's style, tone, and approach correspond to the subject of the book he is evaluating.*

"Why don't you get a haircut," P. G. Wodehouse once chided. "You look like a chrysanthemum." A nice put-down. On par with Mark Twain's "In the first place, God made idiots; this was for practice; then he made school boards." Or Winston Churchill's comment as Clement Attlee passed by: "A sheep in sheep's clothing."

Yes, there are ways to insult which require every bit as much wit and venom as highflown praise requires fawning phrase-making. But we seem to have lost this talent of late. You bump some fellow motorist on the freeway and he will scream one or two ill-chosen profanities, with a total lack of style. And you will answer back with an equal lack of elegance. A possible answer to this problem may be found in this insulting little book called *The Book of Insults, Ancient and Modern,* by a Canadian, Nancy McPhee. (It costs $6.96 and is published by St. Martin's Press, Inc. So don't write me asking where to get it, you shallow-brained nerd.)

This book shows how a truly refined writer can stab his fellow man with a well-honed dagger. For instance, Oscar Wilde's observation after coming over for a visit: "Of course, America had often been discovered before Columbus, but it had always been hushed up." And Dorothy Parker, who reviewed a book with this remark, "This is not a novel to be tossed aside lightly. It should be thrown with great force." Thomas Carlyle, explaining why he did not want to meet the poet Swinburne, said he was "sitting in a sewer, and adding to it." Then again, Samuel Butler had this view of Carlyle: "It was very good of God to let Carlyle and Mrs. Carlyle marry one another and so make only two people miserable instead of four."

Writers and critics and others of the trendy set took great glee in dreaming up the best insults to fling at foes. Oscar Wilde on Shaw: "Bernard Shaw is an excellent man; he has not an enemy in the world, and none of his friends like him." Then there was the time that James McNeill Whistler, the American artist, made a snappy comment, to which Wilde said: "I wish I had said that." And Whistler replied: "You will, Oscar, you will."

The author of this little book, being a Canadian, has collected some great insults by, for and about her country. Such as Al Capone's observation: "I don't even know what street Canada is on." And fellow-Canadian Gordie Howe: "All pro athletes are bilingual. They speak English and profanity." After reading Nancy McPhee's collection, I think Canadian politicians are better shooting from the lip than are their U. S. counterparts. The late Prime Minister John Diefenbaker on a former premier of Quebec: "Jean Lesage is the only person I know who can strut sitting down." That's a great line. Like Oscar Wilde, I wish I'd said that, and plan to.

Prime Minister Pierre Trudeau in Parliament: "The Honorable Member disagrees. I can hear him shaking his head." The prime minister caught a few jabs, too. "In Pierre Elliott Trudeau, Canada has at last produced a political leader worthy of assassination." And, across the ocean, we have this from Aneurin Bevan in Parliament, preferring to address Prime Minister Churchill rather than Foreign Secretary Anthony Eden: "Why should I question the monkey when I can question the organ grinder?"

We just can't come up with angry goodies like that in the U.S., but we used to: "That dark designing sordid ambitious vain proud arrogant and vindictive knave," said Gen. Charles Lee. Thomas Paine wrote: ". . . and as to you, sir, treacherous in private friendship . . . and a hypocrite in public life, the world will be puzzled to decide whether you have abandoned good principles, or whether you ever had any." And who, pray tell, was their target? None other than George Washington. Nothing was sacred in those days.

So you can see by this how far we have come from really scurrilous insults. Someone pushes in front of you on the freeway and all you can come up with is "Go to hell!" Hardly an original direction. Now, if you were D. H. Lawrence, commenting on the critics and readers who failed to appreciate his genius, you would write: "Curse the blasted, jelly-boned swines, the slimy, the belly-wriggling invertebrates, the miserable sodding rotters, the flaming sods, the snivelling, dribbling, dithering, palsied, pulseless lot that make up England today. They've got white of egg in their veins. . . . They *can* nothing but frogspawn—the gibberers! God how I hate them!"

Still, after all is insulted, we must remember how much easier it is to condemn than to construct. With that in mind, we have this 1863 editorial in the *Chicago Times:* "We did not conceive it possible that even Mr. Lincoln would produce a paper so slipshod, so loosejoined, so peurile, not alone in literary construction, but in its ideas, its sentiments, its grasp. He has outdone himself. He has literally come out of the little end of his own horn. By the side of it, mediocrity is superb."

The *Times* was reviewing the Gettysburg Address.

Suzuki or Honda: Which One?

In this essay, Ivan Meunnich, a freshman English student, evaluates two motorcycles by comparing and contrasting their engines, maintenance requirements, performance, and price.

CONTEXT:
This essay was written to be submitted to a national motorcycle periodical.

AUDIENCE:
Persons interested in motorcycles and possibly thinking of buying one.

It is a hot, sunny day and despite the heat hundreds of fans anxiously watch the final turn on the track to see who the winner of the motocross is going to be. Finally, the long-awaited moment arrives, and the two cycles are running neck and neck with each other. As expected, the two cyclists are riding a Suzuki and a Honda. As they negotiate the turn, the rider on the Honda momentarily slips off the seat, and the rider on the Suzuki inches ahead. The riders then come barreling down the home stretch. The rider of the Suzuki opens up the throttle of his cycle all the way, and his machine responds instantly by lurching forward. The Suzuki then begins pulling further ahead of the Honda to win the race by three lengths of a motorcycle.

This scene is just one of many which happen every year on the motocross circuit as the two largest manufacturers of motorcycles compete: Suzuki and Honda. Much is learned about the capabilities and merits of each cycle in these races. This information is, in turn, very helpful in deciding which make of cycle to buy. Here is some of the most important information compiled from the performances in these races.

When looking at this information and comparing these two makes of cycles, the first thing one checks is the engine. The engines in Suzukis and Hondas are very different. Honda is powered by a four-stroke engine, the type of engines cars have in them. This engine fires once out of every four strokes the piston makes. It has valves which let either the air-gas mixture into the cylinder or let the exhaust out. This four-stroke engine is much heavier than the two-stroke engine which is found in the Suzuki. Suzuki, however, will soon be putting four-stroke engines in their motorcycles. This is because of the federal government's recent ban on the sale of motorcycles with two-stroke engines after 1979. The two-stroke engine fires once out of every two strokes the piston makes. It also has no valves and, consequently, must run at a higher rpm than the four-stroke engine in Hondas. This constant higher rpm sometimes leads to a burned piston if the cycle is run very hard. When taken care of, however, both of these engines are very dependable.

The maintenance of the Honda and the Suzuki is very similar in the ordinary areas such as tightening the chain and keeping nuts and bolts tight. The cycles have other types of maintenance, however, that are very different. One of these areas is in filling the oil reservoirs. The Suzuki has a reservoir for oil which mixes with the gas; this reservoir must be kept full. If it runs empty, the engine will get too hot and seize up. The Honda lacks this reservoir since it does not have any oil that will mix with the gas. It does, however, have a crankcase which must be kept properly filled. This crankcase is also the source of an additional maintenance in the Honda since it must be periodically drained and the oil changed. The Suzuki has no crankcase to fill with oil.

Another area of maintenance on the Honda is the keeping of the valve tappets adjusted. A valve tappet is a rocking arm with springs on it which controls the opening and closing of the valves. These tappets have to be adjusted periodically or else the engine will not run well. Since the Suzuki has no valves, this maintenance is eliminated. The Honda, also, has a points-condenser ignition system. Because of this type of ignition system, the Honda has another maintenance. The points and condenser must be periodically adjusted or replaced in order to keep the engine running efficiently. Suzukis have a CDI which is a form of electronic ignition system. Since this type is maintenance free, it never needs any adjustment.

Since Hondas have generators, their batteries must be constantly kept well charged. The electric current produced by the generator goes to the battery and from there goes to the ignition system. If the battery has a low charge, it makes the Honda nearly impossible to start either by the kick start or by pushing. The Suzuki, on the other hand, has a magneto to generate electricity. This sends the current it produces directly to the ignition system. This enables the Suzuki to be started even when the battery is dead. Thus, the Honda has an added maintenance in keeping the battery well charged and making sure the generator is charging properly.

The Suzuki greatly outclasses the Honda in performance. A cycle's performance includes how it runs and how the cycle handles. The Honda does not put out as much horsepower as the Suzuki. The Suzuki also has more torque or power than the Honda. This greater torque enables the Suzuki to have a faster time when running the quarter mile. The Suzuki's high torque is due to its two-stroke engine. Two-stroke engines respond very well to sudden increases in throttle. The Honda, however, responds sluggishly to sudden increases in throttle, causing it to sometimes flood out and die when the engine is still cold.

Another reason for Suzuki's great performance is its lighter weight. Less weight means the engine has less work to do. This lighter weight also makes the Suzuki easier to handle. By handling, I mean how easy it is to make turns or keep your balance when riding the cycle. The lighter weight makes riding easier and less tiring because you do not have to fight constantly the weight of the cycle to keep it under control. The suspension system also has much to do with the cycle's performance. A good suspension will reduce jars and keep the traction of its wheels at a maximum. The Suzuki has a better suspension system than the Honda, and this greatly improves its performance. This allows the Suzuki to negotiate corners at a faster speed than a Honda. The tires a Suzuki comes stocked with are also better than Hondas'. The Suzuki tires are very good at keeping the cycle from slipping or sliding out from under the rider. This is very important in that you are not as likely to lose control of the cycle and have an accident.

The initial price of the Honda is considerably higher than that of the Suzuki. The amount of money one has to shell out of pocket can be a very strong factor in determining which cycle to buy. Replacement parts for Hondas are higher, too. The time it takes to repair a Honda is longer than for a Suzuki. This makes repairs more costly because of the increased labor time. The Honda also has more costs because of its greater amount of maintenance.

When analyzing all the facts, the Suzuki is the better all-around cycle due to its performance, maintenance, engines and parts, and price. Proof of the Suzuki's greater performance is the fact that a Suzuki has won the United States Grand Prix of motocross the last four years straight. And those grueling tracks don't lie!

In this essay an editor from Road & Track *continues an evaluation of the Rabbit Diesel which has been going on since the car was new. The writer is answering the questions "What is good; what is bad?" about the car.*

Rabbit Diesel: 60,000-mile Update

We've decided to keep you more frequently informed of the progress of our long-term test cars, reporting approximately every 12,000 miles from now on instead of our previous 24,000-mile updates. In the case of the Volkswagen Rabbit Diesel, we last checked its progress in the pages of the March 1979 issue as the odometer ticked over 48,000 miles — here's what we've learned through 60,000 miles.

Fuel efficiency is still the Rabbit Diesel's long suit, as our car turned in

41.5 mpg for the most recent 12,000-mile stretch, maintaining and even slightly bettering its 41.0-mpg average for the entire 60,000 miles completed thus far. We noted in our last report that we were experimenting with a fuel additive, Surefire Diesel Power. Contributing Editor James T. Crow made two lengthy trips in the Rabbit during this latest stage of the test and carried on further experimentation with the additive. In the course of a 2230-mile trip the length of Baja California, Mexico and back, Crow reports the Rabbit with the additive averaged 48.6 mpg, while on the return leg without the Surefire, the mpg figure was 43.7. (Diesel fuel, incidentally, costs an average of 12¢ per gal. in Baja California, so Crow was able to make the journey for a total fuel cost of $5.80!) On his second outing, from California to Wyoming and back, Crow measured the mpg without the additive at 38.0, while with the special mix, it rose to 44.0 mpg. It would seem that Surefire Diesel Power additive will make a measurable difference in fuel consumption, but as we noted in our last report, with a car that already manages 40-plus mpg, how much incentive is there to measure out the tiny amount that goes into each tankful?

That's obviously a question that each owner will have to answer for himself and one that will increase in significance as fuel costs continue to rise.

In reviewing the repair and maintenance expenses for the past 12,000 miles, we're somewhat dismayed to discover that we've spent $824 keeping the Rabbit in tip-top condition. Regular readers may recall from our last report that at 31,738 miles, we had a serious engine problem that resulted in replacement of the crankshaft, rod bearings and main bearings. Unfortunately, the dealership that did that work failed to tell us that the head should be retorqued and the valves adjusted at 1000 miles and 15,000 miles after the work is done. So, we had both of those things done by our local dealer when we started having trouble with a leaking head gasket at just over 58,000 miles. Unfortunately, this was but a temporary fix and just before we hit 60,000, we had to have the head gasket replaced at a cost of $150.

Other relatively costly items that came up included having the ignition key break off in the ignition—putting that right cost $62; the Bilstein Corp of America provided us with new shock absorbers for the Rabbit and the installation of those plus going back to have the spring perches refitted when we discovered they were too large added up to $110; repair of a dented fender was another $113; we finally replaced the original equipment tires at 54,858 miles (impressive durability) with a set of Uniroyal 180 Series tires, the all-weather version we wanted to try in the ice and snow of Wyoming and closer-to-home ski resorts around California. The tires were supplied by Couderc Marketing Systems, Inc of Roslyn, New York. But the mounting and balancing along with the required front-end alignment cost $76. Then there were a lot of minor annoyances and maintenance items one expects with any car, such as replacing light bulbs, repairing a broken hood release cable, replacing windshield wiper blades, putting back pieces of body molding that fell off when the clips holding them wore out, etc.

Another item cropped up that deserves special attention. The oil line running from the block to the brake booster vacuum pump broke and was replaced at a cost of $17, parts and labor. That is the same oil line that broke and produced the serious engine problem alluded to earlier in this report—and the bill for that was $700.10. Diesel owners may want to make it a habit to periodically check that line because on our car it seems to be a weak point and it can obviously cause serious damage if undetected.

A few other items that came up were replacing the heater control in the dash at 59,438 miles because we couldn't get the heater to stop warming us up, repacking the CV joints ($55) when various drivers began to note a graunching noise coming from that area, and clutch adjustments. As we said, it all added up to more than $800 during the latest 12,000 miles and we were very surprised that we've been spending that amount of money keeping the Rabbit Diesel in shape. We'll be back with another report at 72,000 miles as we continue our longest extended-use report ever, and we're anxious to see what further adventures await us.

Writing Your Own Evaluation Essay

1. CONTEXT
Choose one of the following contexts for the basis of your essay, or make up a context for yourself.

A

You have been invited to be the guest (book, music, dance, food, or film) reviewer for the local newspaper while the regular reviewer goes on vacation. This delights you because you have been wanting to see a variety of types of _____ reviewed, and you welcome the chance to see your own standards and preferences reflected on the review page. The editor has just called to say the first review is due Tuesday. Write the essay that will put *you* in the public eye!

B

You have just heard from your brother, who lives in another state. He is shopping for a new car and wants your ad-
vice: what kind of car should he buy? You have a very decided opinion that a _____ is the best car on the market for his purposes and you sit right down to write him an evaluation of this car.

C

You are president of an organization and in this capacity must serve on a national committee which selects the next site of the annual convention of the club. You and the group have now visited over a half dozen possible sites for the convention, and each of you has been asked to narrow your choices down to two. You must write an evaluation of these two cities to give to the chair of the committee who will do a composite report for voting on by the whole membership. Write the evaluation of the two cities that you liked best as possible places for the organization to meet, emphasizing the advantages and disadvantages of each.

D

Your neighborhood is being considered as the site for a large city park and playground. Some of the people who live in the community are against the park because they think it will become an eyesore and encourage loitering. You are on the local Citizens Committee for Neighborhood Governance and have been asked to write an evaluation of what value the park will have for the neighborhood. Since the negative aspects of the park have already been aired, you will center your evaluation on the value of the park to the community.

E

A national rating organization has been hired by a television network to gather evaluations of their programs. You have been asked to watch all the programs on this particular network from 7:00–10:00 P.M. for 3 nights and then write your evaluation of what you have seen. The network is interested in knowing what you liked, what you didn't like (and why), what you felt had value and what didn't, etc. You will receive a hefty $300.00 for this research and evaluation—and all you have to do is watch TV and write the evaluation. You say yes—and fast.

F

A very good music group is coming to your college. Unfortunately, many of the students do not know much about them. You have been asked to write an evaluation of the group, highlighting their history, accomplishments, strong points, etc., for the school paper—so that people will be interested in coming to see them and informed once they get there.

G

The principal of your elementary (or high) school (or one of your favorite teachers) is retiring. You have been asked to come to the banquet in this person's honor and give an evaluation of the value this person has given to the school and the students. You know this will be a hard assignment, but you are looking forward to paying this tribute to a person who has meant a lot to you and your friends. You sit down to prepare the remarks you will deliver and the evaluation of this person's worth and value comes easier than you think. You find that the words just tumble onto the page.

H

You belong to a lively young adults group that even has its own monthly newsletter. One of the columns in the newsletter is called "Personal Finance," and the editor has asked you to write a piece for the next issue to be used in this "Personal Finance" column. You have been asked to evaluate the good and bad aspects of renting an apartment and buying a house. Since you have done both—in fact, had pleasant experiences both renting and owning —you are a good choice to give a balanced evaluation. You look forward to writing the essay.

2. CREATING

Once you have decided upon the context for your evaluation essay, the creating stage will follow very naturally. A creating technique many writers find especially useful when they evaluate is the simple *list*. For instance, one person writing on Context *C* made a list early in her creating stage that looked like this:

Possible convention sites

New Orleans	Santa Fe
great food	Old-World atmosphere
distinct Cajun culture	few hotels
many hotels	wonderful distinctive
high prices	New Mexico food
Mississippi River	great opera
Dixieland jazz	Chimayo weaving nearby
French Market	much fascinating history
great shopping	breathtaking scenery
Bourbon Street	unbelievable light
hard to get around in car because	not easily accessible by air
of traffic	pueblos nearby
easy to get to by air	very high quality arts and crafts
plantations nearby	available

The writer then decided to *loop* the two cities, too, just to be sure she had thought of every advantage and disadvantage that she wanted to include in the evaluation.

Another person, who chose Context *G,* did the *classical invention* activity and got more ideas for his essay than he could finally use. He remembered during the classical invention creating incidents that he had long forgotten and uncovered several unexpected memories, even of smells and tastes in the school.

As you certainly know by this time, there is no right or wrong way to get ideas on your subject. The important thing is that you set aside time to do the *Creating Stage,* a time when you feel absolutely free to go wherever your mind takes you as you write.

3. SHAPING:

A As you move in doing the evaluation essay from private writing in the *Creating Stage* to public writing in the *Shaping Stage,* you need to be very conscious of some specific requirements of evaluative writing:

1 Be sure to let the reader know immediately what criteria you are using in making the evaluation.

2 Be sure that your criteria are fair, logical, and consistent.

3 If you have many criteria that you could choose among, pick those most likely to convince the specific readers for whom you are writing.

4 Let the reader know your qualifications for making the evaluation.

5 Use *many* details, facts, and examples to support your evaluation.

B By now you are familiar with the various requirements of the *Shaping Stage:*

1 Write to a specific audience and treat them like people, not a wall.

2 Have a thesis that is (1) clear to the reader, (2) something you are an insider on, (3) the promise that the rest of the essay delivers, (4) something you can be reasonably sure the reader will find valuable.

3 Write a trial draft.

4 Do a Bare Bones Outline that checks for promise and delivery and for full development.

5 Rewrite the trial draft.

If you follow this progression in your writing and keep these courtesies to the reader always in mind, you will find that at the end of the *Shaping Stage* you will have an essay that actually does communicate exactly what you want to say to *another person* when you aren't present—the miracle of the pen! And you are the one doing it!

4. COMPLETING:

A In this evaluation essay you will have a chance to refine your work in the *Completing Stage* by checking to see if all your Topic Sentence Paragraphs are fully developed, if you have used function paragraphs for drama, emphasis, transition, and so forth and if you have clearly tied the paragraphs together with transition and signal words so that the writing flows for the reader smoothly and effortlessly.

B When you have revised the essay for flow, put it in the best possible form—check the spelling, punctuation, any typos, correctness—and present it to your readers with a feeling of pride.

COMPARISON AND CONTRAST: HOW TO SHOW SIMILARITIES AND DIFFERENCES

1 *Compare* comes from a Latin word which means *equal* and means to examine in order to observe or discover similarities or differences.

2 *Contrast* comes from an Italian word that meant *to stand opposed to* and implies a comparing for the purpose of emphasizing differences.

3 When comparing two things, you will probably use one of two common patterns: discussing *A* completely and then discussing *B* or discussing a particular characteristic of *A* and *B*, then another characteristic of *A* and *B*, then another . . . until you've completed the comparison.

4 You may discover that an item is similar to another thing in an exact way—that house has the same floor plan as the one I lived in as a child—or is similar in a nonliteral way—that house is like a tomb. Both kinds of comparison are valuable to a reader who is attempting to understand your subject just the way you do.

5 Differences you spot among things may be differences of characteristics—*their car has bench seats; ours has bucket seats*—or the differences may be differences of degree—*the back seat of the Volkswagen Rabbit is bigger than the back seat of the Volkswagen Beetle*. Both kinds of contrast help the reader see the subject the way you wish to communicate it.

REVISING FOR ENERGY

If you have ever heard the old saying "Where there's life, there's hope," it may just occur to you that the converse of that statement is usually true, too—and particularly when it comes to writing. If the writing has no life, there's little hope for it. A reader will react to dead writing the same way a bird will react to a bug that's playing dead—nose it around a bit, this way and that, then get bored, discouraged, and finally go off and leave it. But if there is some *life* in what you write, then there is real hope that the reader will stick with you long enough to get the message.

What makes writing have life? What can you do to be sure there is a lot of *energy* in what you put on the page?

When you are reading really *energetic* writing, you don't think, "Oh, look! There is energy here because the writer has done such-and-such!" You simply respond to the energy without even thinking. What is true, however, is that the writer did several things in the *Completing Stage* to make sure that you, the reader, felt the energy. Of course, sometimes the writing may have energy from the very beginning because the writer was *excited* about the subject; more often than not, though, **the writer revises to put *energy* into the paper.** It's like adding a few ounces of kerosene to a fire you have laid in the fireplace. You wad up the paper, then arrange the kindling, then the logs. When it's all tidy and ready to go, *then* you put on the kerosene, and light it. There's plenty of energy in the paper, kindling, and wood—but just that extra little bit of kerosene makes it all take off.

Now—how can you put energy into your writing?

Here are a few suggestions:

2 EFFECTIVE WAYS OF GETTING YOUR WRITING OFF THE SEAT AND OUT THE DOOR

1 Give the reader a *variety* of kinds of sentences.
2 Combine sentences to make your main points shout out loud and your supporting points hum in the background.
   In other words: develop a little style.

SENTENCE COMBINING

One principle that will handle both suggestions for giving your writing more life is SENTENCE COMBINING. When you have caught on to the trick of this technique, you will be able to handle (1) giving the reader a variety of kinds of sentences and (2) giving the reader a way to distinguish more important from less important information.

One of the reasons you need variety in the kinds of sentences you write is to keep from sounding simple and monotonous. Here is a passage from a third-grade reader that really shows how sentences that are too short and choppy give the reader an impression that most smart adults wouldn't want to create:

Most of the ways to turn salt water into fresh water cost a lot of money. The Symi factory on an island in Greece uses a way that costs very little.

Right in the middle of the town are some long ponds. They are only a few inches deep. The men of Symi dug out earth to make the ponds.

Over each pond is a low tent. It is made of plastic that you can see through.

At night, sea water is pumped into the ponds. The next day, the hot sun shines through the tents. The sun's heat turns the water into vapor that rises from the ponds. The salt is left behind.

Of course, the very short paragraphs and the very simple vocabulary also contribute to the too-simple effect. But it is the repetition of sentence after sentence, *each in the same pattern, each containing only a single unit of information,* which makes that passage sound so childlike, immature, and undeveloped. The deadness, for adult readers, comes from dragging on and on through sentence after sentence, picking up only one lifeless bit of message per sentence. *Combining those informational bits into longer, more varied sentences, would make them much more attractive and effective.*

Now look at this passage from a college-level government book:

John F. Kennedy's assassination on November 21, 1963, probably evoked—in the period that followed his death—greater feeling on the part of more people than the death of any other American. His assassination was as close to formal tragedy as is conceivable in a democracy. Kennedy had all the attributes of a hero: power, prestige, presence, the heroism of the warrior, affability, social standing, youth, physical attraction, religious belief, and wealth. He embodied all of these qualities with a special grace, and his death seemed associated with the death of youth in America.

—Theodore Gross

ENERGY:

Vigor or power in action; vitality and intensity of expression; the capacity for action or accomplishment; power exercised with vigor and determination.

By comparing this passage with the earlier one, you can see immediately the effect of short, simple sentences and the effect of longer, more varied sentences. The short little sentences are perfect for the third graders in elementary school, but unless that is your audience, you may insult your readers with sentences that sound as though they were written for eight-year-olds. **The more you combine short, simple sentences together, the more sophisticated your writing seems to the reader—and the more information units the reader gets per sentence, too**—which really facilitates communication by making it seem effortless. For example, take these two sentences:

Over each pond is a low tent.
It is made of plastic that you can see through.

Each one offers a niggling bit of information, yet the reader has to come to a complete stop at the end of each, and do all the work a reader does in beginning and ending sentences. However, *combining* them allows the information to come together in a neat and orderly way, and the reader is spared much unnecessary effort:

> Over each pond is a low plastic tent that you can see through.

What's happened? You've produced some variation on that same dreary repeated sentence pattern, *and* you've shown what really *is* important— *that there is a tent over each pond.* The information about what material the tent is made of is clearly less important, and the combined sentence helps the reader to keep clear what's important and what isn't.

In much the same way, you could perversely create dreariness out of the Kennedy passage by *un*coupling the sentences and separating the items out into single bits.

> Kennedy had all the attributes of a hero.
> He had power.
> He had prestige.
> He had presence.
> Etc. Yawn, yawn, and ho-hum!

Oh, oh, Dick!
Oh, oh, Jane!
Oh, oh, *Phooey!*

No, it is not the *separation*, but the *combination* of those bits that obviously makes the sense of the passage much easier to follow. And that's how sentence-combining works: it lets you send complex thoughts in an easy-to-follow form. (*For a detailed explanation of how to combine sentences, see the Handbook section.*)

APPLICATION

SENTENCE COMBINING FOR CHOPPY SENTENCES

1   Rewrite the following paragraphs combining short, simple sentences to make the writing sound more mature.

I was fortunate enough to be able to travel to Europe during my senior year in high school. We went during our spring break, March 17–26. The travelers consisted of eighteen students and two teachers. We traveled in a group known as the American Leadership Study Group.

There was question of whether or not I would be able to go. During the Christmas holidays we had a family reunion. My parents asked me if I wanted to go on the European trip. I said no immediately because I thought it was out of the question. The trip was too expensive. I began thinking about the trip more and more, and I finally decided I wanted to go. I had done quite a bit of baby-sitting and saved the money.

We proceeded to find out more information about the trip. My mother and I thought the only obstacle would be getting the passport in time. However, my teacher told me there was a waiting list for the trip. He told me he was an area representative for ALSG and that a friend of his owed him a favor. That information lifted our spirits. I would probably be first on the waiting list.

My mother and I went to the post office to apply for a passport. We learned that we could receive a passport very quickly if we paid an extra fee. We paid the fee and received the passport in a week.

2 For your own writing. The first application of the sentence-combining principle, then, is to examine your paper to see if you have so many short, simple sentences that it sounds as though you were writing for children. If that's what you find, put some of those little dinky ones into longer, more sophisticated forms. But remember: **variety** is the key word. An essay chock full of similarly long sentences isn't any more interesting than an eassy full of short, choppy ones. *Chu-whuffety, chu-whuffety, chu-whuffety* is about as monotonous as *thump, thump, thump.* **Variation, the feel for change of movement and pace, a sense of when to spin it out and when to make it short and punchy**—these are what make up *variety* and *style*.

MAKING VARIETY HAPPEN IN YOUR SENTENCES

You know that there are several possible patterns and that you can experiment with them as you revise for energy. That knowledge will not only enable you to cut out the choppiness but will let you—even with longer sentences—give variety so that the reader will stay interested and not get bored. Let's now take a closer look at these patterns; you will want to get the hang of them, the knack of knowing when and how to couple or uncouple them, to develop a feel for the impact and effect of this kind over that kind. In short, you want to learn the techniques for producing *energy* in your writing.

Linguists tell us that basic English sentence patterns are few and simple, like these:

Cows	eat.	
Cows	eat	grass.
Grass	is	green.

Even though these basic sentence patterns are English, we rarely use such simple patterns in regular conversation or writing. Our "real" sentences are longer—*they carry more information.* We vary the basic patterns and add information to them through a process called *expansion,* adding single words or groups of words here and there.

This is an example of such an expansion:

John has a job.
Finally, John has a job.
After three months of hunting, John has a job.
John has a job after three months of hunting.
Although he spent three months looking, John finally has a job.

When you are revising for energy in your writing, check to see if you use the simple patterns over and over again. If you do, you can probably count on your readers getting bored. *Give them some variety.* Begin sometimes with the end of the sentence first. At other times, start with a single phrase or a word and then put the main subject and verb of the sentence. You don't actually have to know a lot of terminology to do this (though knowing the names of the grammatical parts of the sentence will help you master sentence-combining for variety, and these are discussed in the handbook). For now, however, during this *Completing Stage* of the writing process, you can vary your sentences by modeling the variations after some of the ones that follow even if you don't know the formal names for the parts of the sentence you are moving about. Take a simple, basic sentence like:

Green pepper is good in spaghetti sauce.

Now look at the variations you can make of this basic pattern:

To make really good spaghetti sauce, you should add green pepper.
With green pepper added, spaghetti sauce is much better.
By adding green pepper, you can really make good spaghetti sauce.
Spaghetti is better with green pepper in the sauce.
That green pepper which has been added makes this spaghetti sauce better.
The spaghetti sauce, with green pepper added, is better.
The spaghetti sauce, which has had green pepper added to it, is better.

Just for practice, see how many variations you can make of this sentence:

A grocery list aids shopping.

You can even make a kind of game out of seeing how many ways you can write a sentence — sometimes just by moving one word.

ONLY I saw Howard Smith in the morning.
I ONLY saw Howard Smith in the morning.
I saw ONLY Howard Smith in the morning.
I saw Howard Smith ONLY in the morning.
I saw Howard Smith in the morning ONLY.

Each shift produces a slight variation. Making a game of it, and keeping alert for the various implications of each combination, you can enjoy revising your sentences for energy, and maybe even have fun with it.

The bonus for you, besides an increased mastery of sentence varieties, is that you'll have gained a technique for helping the reader to stay interested and stick with you all the way to the end of the paper.

APPLICATION

SENTENCE COMBINING FOR VARIETY

Rewrite the sentences in the following paragraph with the aim of improving variety in sentence patterns.

It was the last track meet of the season. The state championship. I was going to long jump and run the mile relay. Now the long jump is the first event at any track meet, so I got there early. The long jump started at 10:00 and went on until 12:30. Then the mile relay was at 5:00. I got to the field at about 8:30. I ran around the track four times to loosen up and stretch out. All this took about an hour. By 9:30 the stands were packed, and that's when this terrible nervousness hit me. I realized that over 2,000 people would be watching me as I would run down the runway and take my jump. I got a cold sweat; my entire body was shaking worse than jello in an earthquake. Then everyone started giving orders at once. My two other teammates were telling me what to do and what not to do. The official was telling me to get ready to jump. My coach was yelling at me to get a good jump the first time, and the crowd in the stands was going crazy because we were about to start. As I stepped out onto the runway, my entire mind and body went blank. I couldn't see anything or anybody except the long jump pit 104′ 6″ down the runway. My head was pounding, and all I could hear was the blood rushing through my body. I waited a second, said a little prayer and took off. It felt like I was moving in slow motion. My legs felt like lead weights. My arms didn't want to move the right way, and I thought I'd never get to the end of the runway to the take-off board. Finally, I saw it closing in on me.

SHOW THE READER WHAT'S IMPORTANT

After you have revised your sentences for variety to get more energy into your writing, you need to look at them to see if you have put, right up front, the information that you think is most important. One of the most valuable uses of sentence-combining is to let you show the reader what you want him or her to see, without seeming obvious about this at all. That is a better way than just saying, "What's important to me is . . ." As we saw, two sentences can be combined into one:

Over each pond is a low tent.
It is made of plastic that you can see through.

can become

Over each pond is a low, clear plastic tent.

And the result of the combining is not only sleeker and more adult-sounding, but **it also combines the elements in a way that shows what's important** (there's a tent over each pond) **and what's not so important** (the tent is made of clear plastic). This technique, *combining to show emphasis,* lets you control what the reader notices *and* lets you highlight the important thoughts efficiently and energetically.

Combining for emphasis

To see clearly how to combine sentences for the best emphasis, you'll need to consult two words:

COORDINATE and SUBORDINATE

These Latinate words may not immediately ring a bell, but getting clear on *co-ordinate* and *subordinate* will help you considerably in getting energy in your writing. Once you have the idea each term represents, you will have extended your mastery as a writer, and to a quite considerable degree.

Coordinate you can associate with co-partner or co-worker, someone you are on an equal basis with, someone in the same position as you. *Subordinate* you can associate with subfloor or a substitute player in a ballgame—not the main one; somewhat less important than the main players. It may also help to know that the roots are from the Latin *sub-,* "below," *co-,* "equal," and *ordinare,* "to arrange in order." Thus *subordinate* is in the "lower order" and *coordinate* is of an "equal order."

When two sentences in your writing are of equal importance, they are *coordinate.* **When the thought in one sentence is more important than the thought in the other, the less important one is** *subordinate* **to the more important one.**

Why do you need to know this?

Because when you are revising for energy and are combining sentences to emphasize what you really want the reader to notice, you will have to think about coordination and subordination, even if you don't use precisely those words.

COORDINATE: EQUAL
copartner
coworker
co-owner

SUBORDINATE: SECOND-ARY
subfloor
substitute
subcommittee

Coordination   Coordination—*linking together words, groups of words, or sentences of equal type and importance*—puts energy into your writing. Look at how this works:

Two subjects are supposed to be the hardest for freshmen.
One is math.
The other is English.

Linking the two words *math* and *English* makes perfect sense—they have equal value in the sentence: they are "of equal hardness for freshmen." That can be crisply expressed in this combination:

WORDS: *Math and English* are supposed to be the hardest subjects for freshmen.

And that handles it. Here is the way the sentence-combining works with phrases:

He spent the evening typing his essay.
He also spent the evening studying for his chemistry test.

Linking the two phrases, *typing his essay* and *studying for his chemistry test,* cuts out a lot of extra words and suggests that his evening was spent fairly evenly divided between the typing and the studying.

PHRASES: He spent the evening *typing his essay* and *studying for his chemistry test.*

The same principle works for clauses, too.

John went to the concert for two reasons.
One reason was that he had nothing else to do.
Another reason was that he had sort of promised his sister he would go.

Look at the streamlining sentence-combining gives to this example:

CLAUSES: *Since he had nothing else to do* and *since he had sort of promised his sister that he would go,* John went to the concert.

You can also combine whole sentences.

I had planned to spend the afternoon in the library.
I took a nap instead.

SENTENCES: *I had planned to spend the afternoon in the library,* but *I took a nap instead.*

Adding the word *but* allows the reader to move more quickly through the information and makes the two sentences one thought. Coordination in your writing does two things:

1 By combining words and groups of words, you avoid the monotonous repetition that steals energy from what you say;
2 By combining whole sentences you reveal the relationship between the thoughts.

When sentences are joined together by a conjunction that shows that the sentences are equal, the reader knows that one sentence is as important as the other. This example will make it perfectly clear.

Here are two sentences:

John doesn't plan to go to college.
He believes that experience in the working world is more valuable than an academic degree.

COORDINATING CONJUNCTIONS

and
or
nor
for
but
so
yet
either/or
neither/nor

Looking at them, we can *infer* that the second is somehow related to the first, but we have to produce the inference in our own imaginations — the writer gives no clues, merely sets forth two sentences, period. But look what happens when the sentences are linked in a way that shows, explicitly, exactly how the two items relate to each other:

John doesn't plan to go to college, *for* he believes that experience in the working world is more valuable than an academic degree.

In the combined form, you *know* that **the second sentence explains the first,** *and* that **the two ideas are of equal importance** to the understanding of the writer's message.

APPLICATION

COORDINATION

Rewrite the following groups of sentences using coordination to link clauses, phrases, and words.

1 Many times cooking for a crowd can be fun.
  It can be expensive.
  It can be time-consuming.
  It can be frustrating.

2 To save money Andrew's parents have decided not to travel to Yosemite this summer.
  They will spend a few weeks at a local lake instead.

3 Americans constantly criticize their leaders.
  They don't make an effort to vote in national elections.
  They forget to vote in local elections.

4 Many people consider a college education vital for success in the business world.
  Few professionals have reached their positions without at least one degree.

5 The energy crisis has made many people seriously consider their driving habits.
  Many people have bought smaller cars that use less gas.
  Many people are doing more walking and bicycling.

6 John had to make a decision about the summer.
  He could go to the local junior college and gain some extra hours toward his degree.
  He could work full-time for his uncle's construction firm.

7 Wearing clothes that are in style is very important to some people.
Others don't seem at all concerned about their appearance.
They wear jeans and T-shirts everywhere.

8 Everywhere you look you see people jogging.
You see people walking.
You see people climbing stairs instead of riding the elevator.
More and more people are growing conscious of the importance of good health.

9 Julie knew she could easily get tickets to tonight's rock concert.
She knew that if she went she wouldn't study for Friday's big chemistry exam.

10 Doing your own car repairs saves you money.
It can be as personally rewarding as a hobby.

Coordination:
All parts are created equal.

Subordination:
Some parts are more equal than others.

Subordination   Using *coordination* is like setting up a democracy, with everybody having an equal vote in the matter. *Subordination*, though, is more like a monarchy, and royalty matter more than commoners in that system. **Subordination puts energy in your writing by clearly emphasizing what is important and by displaying that importance in a way that the reader picks up clearly, promptly, without any doubt or wondering.**

Music provides an example of subordination, since it is the *variation* in music that makes it interesting, not just the sameness. Music moves from "important" chords, with lots of instruments, to relatively "unimportant" notes, with only one or two instruments. And the important notes or chords usually get played with more loudness—and get held longer—than the unimportant ones do. This fact is easy to see in the example from Beethoven's Fifth Symphony, the famous "V for Victory" symphony. Even if you can't read music, you can see the pattern of three short notes followed by an "important" note. The opening passage goes like this:

and then repeats

Ta - ta - ta - DA

Between these two full and massive statements there is a dramatic pause. Then the various parts of the orchestra restate the theme, quickly, in a series of three:

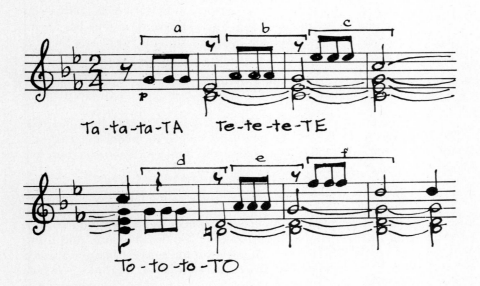

Ta - ta - ta - TA   Te - te - te - TE

To - to - to - TO

Can you imagine how boring that symphony would be if every note were the same and were given equal value:

Ta-ta-ta-ta-ta-ta-ta-ta-ta-ta-ta-ta-ta- . . . ?

Puts you to sleep just reading it, doesn't it? There would be no interest because the listener would have no way of hearing the theme the composer built all the rest of the symphony around. The notes, instead of sounding like music, would sound as flat and boring as a faucet dripping. It's the change in pace, the shift in emphasis, the subordinating of some sounds to others that give the music its form. You wouldn't be interested in it if there were no spots in the music "less important" so that the "more important" spots would really stand out for what they were.

You've seen this same kind of subordination and shift in emphasis in photography, in painting, in architecture. We all soon get very tired of looking at pictures if there is no focal point, no main thing to see in the picture. (Probably one reason home slide shows bore most people; is that the shots are usually the same — scenic views with no subordination of part of the background to a more important item/person as the focal point of the shot.) In fact, almost anything we examine has some parts that deserve emphasis, others that serve best by being in the background. With subordination, you can clearly determine the "foreground" and "background" of your message in writing, too. The variety gives emphasis *and* relief.

Using Subordination in Your Own Writing

How, exactly, can subordination work for you? It's not at all complicated, actually, and in fact you already use it quite naturally in a lot of what you say and write. The point here is just to become conscious and aware of it, so that you can use it intentionally during Stage 3 to improve what may have been a less conscious, less aware version of your writing in Stage 1 or Stage 2. Here's an example:

We were unable to go to the show last night.
The car wouldn't start.

Both are equal, and they don't seem related (although a kind-hearted, imaginative, generous reader might be willing to invent or create an inference that the second sentence caused the first). Subordination sets matters straight:

We were unable to go to the show *because* the car wouldn't start.

Superficially, it seems that little has happened; *because* was added — not a big deal. But you can see that coupling the two sentences and using *because* shows that the second sentence wouldn't be very important if it weren't for the first one. *The car wouldn't start.* Well, what of it? *Because the car wouldn't start, we were unable to go to the show.* So there was a

SAVE ENERGY: Subordinate

consequence! By linking the two sentences and showing how they relate to each other—how one part *causes* the other part—the writer saves the reader from having to process the relationship. And it provides energy in the writing because the *writer* has handled it already for the reader. The reader is spared the necessity for wondering and puzzling and imagining and creating the relationship—there's nothing at all to do but to *get the message*. And the message is *already* in motion.

Admittedly, this discussion is like watching a movie in slow motion. Actually, the reader skims from word to word and sentence to sentence quite swiftly, and the mind either makes connections or it doesn't, and that happens in fractions of a second. Yet sometimes slow-motion films let us study what passes in a flash, so that we can become very clear about exactly what did happen, and therefore do something differently or more efficiently, as football players do in studying game films to see why the left side of the line didn't give the quarterback any protection on screen pass plays. Incredibly enough, saving the reader those tiny bits of energy and those millisecond decisions can amount to the difference between a reader who is cheerful and enthusiastic about your writing and one who is worn out and half-hearted about it. Give the reader that sense of complete clarity and certainty, instant-to-instant-to-instant. A word as simple as *because* alone could do the trick.

SUBORDINATE CONJUNCTIONS

TIME: when, after, whenever, while, before
PLACE: where, wherever
CAUSE: because, since, in order that, so that
CONTRAST: although, though, while
CONDITION: if, unless, since, as long as

By subordinating one sentence to another when you combine them, you are carrying your reader's eye to the thing you think most important, and you are at the same time showing the relationship of one part of the sentence to the other, something that can only help the reader move easily and effortlessly through the essay.

APPLICATION

SUBORDINATION

Rewrite the following groups of sentences using subordination wherever possible.

1 Mary hates housecleaning.
   She claims she's basically a neat person.

2 You can chop the vegetables for the stew.
   I can brown the meat and prepare the gravy.

3 We want to visit the college campus next month.
   We want to make sure we have chosen the right courses.

4 John's uncle may offer him a job in his grocery store.
   John may have a job this summer.

5 The rain may stop soon.
   We may have to cancel the picnic scheduled for tomorrow.

6 Most people seem willing to cut down on their use of electricity, gas, and heating fuels.
   They don't want energy conservation to interfere with their established lifestyles.

7 We spent the afternoon in the library working on our history project.
   We all went out for pizza.

8 Old movies seem to get more popular every year.
   They offer plot and drama that modern movies often lack.

9 Writing involves grammar and punctuation rules that are hard to remember.
   Many students don't enjoy writing.

10 For many students, writing is fun.
   They are more interested in expressing their ideas than in following rules.

GETTING ENERGY THROUGH STYLE

Anybody who has ever heard Aretha Franklin or Janice Joplin sing knows that rhythm produces energy. The same thing is true of writing. Writing that has rhythm will often have energy, and people who know about rhythm also know about style. One kind of rhythm, in speech and writing, is PARALLELISM. You've heard it much of your life and probably already use it in your writing, but you may not be consciously aware of it. It is almost fascinating to see how it works, psychologically: setting up a reader's or a listener's expectations, then satisfying those expectations—a kind of suspense and conclusion, tension and release.

Parallelism:
a kind of rhythm

Becoming aware of this kind of rhythm and learning how to put it into your own writing, you will master a good bit of style and will control a source of energy and vigor of the sort that has even moved nations!

PARALLELISM

Using parallelism as a rhythm-making, energy-producing technique in your writing works because of ever-present factors: *the reader's sense of order* and *the reader's demand for fulfillment of expectations* (balance and delivery).

Let's examine some parallel sentences written by Mary McCarthy to see what we can discover about *order* and *expectation/fulfillment:*

Sheridan was then about six years old, and this [tin] butterfly immediately became his most cherished possession—indeed, one of the few he had. He carried it about the house with him all the next week clutched in his hand or pinned to his shirt, and my other two brothers followed him, begging him to be allowed to play with it, which slightly disgusted me, at the age of ten, for I knew that I was too sophisticated to care for tin butterflies and I felt in this whole affair the instigation of my uncle.

In the second sentence, the parallelism looks like this:

He carried it about the house with him all the next week
> *clutched in his hand*
> or
> *pinned to his shirt,*

and my other two brothers followed him, begging him to be allowed to play with it, which slightly disgusted me, at the age of ten,
> for
> *I knew* that I was too sophisticated to care for tin butterflies
> and
> *I felt* in this whole affair the instigation of my uncle.

The parallelism is in the arranging of the sentence to have neatly recurring patterns or parts:

clutched in his hand **or** pinned to his shirt
For I knew . . . and I felt . . .

The effect of parallelism can be *swift* and *punchy,* as in this sentence by Malcolm X:

In those days only three things in the world scared me: jail, a job, and the army.

The effect, likewise, can be formal and elegant, deliberate and thoughtful. Look at Adrienne Rich's sentence:

For the first time in history, a pervasive recognition is developing
> that the patriarchal system cannot answer for itself;
> that it is not inevitable;
> that it is transitory;
> and that the cross-cultural, global domination of women by men can no
> longer be
> denied
> or
> defended.

Parallelism was a device well known by Winston Churchill, and he became a master at using it:

We shall not flag or fail, we shall go on to the end, we shall fight in France, we shall fight on the seas and oceans, we shall fight with growing confidence and growing strength in the air, we shall defend our island, whatever the cost may be, we shall fight on the beaches, we shall fight on the landing grounds, we shall fight in the fields and in the streets, we shall fight in the hills; we shall never surrender.

Another of Churchill's resonant passages is the famous sentence:

Never before in the field of human conflict was so much owed by so many to so few.

With the parallel parts broken down, the sentence looks like this:

was so much owed
by so many
to so few.

John F. Kennedy used parallelism frequently, too, as in this speech delivered at the University of North Carolina in 1961:

Our policy must blend whatever degree of firmness and flexibility is necessary to protect our vital interests, by peaceful means if possible, by resolute action if necessary. . . . While we do not intend to see the free world give up, we shall make every effort to prevent the world from being blown up.

And Lincoln, in the Gettysburg Address, managed in few words to produce writing so resonant and enduring that readers are shocked again and again to discover that the entire address is only 266 words long. In fact, the main speaker of the occasion was Edward Everett, who later wrote to Lincoln, "I should be glad if I could flatter myself that I came as near to the central idea of the occasion in two hours as you did in two minutes." The whole piece contains only three paragraphs. It is the last that is so full of parallelisms and so richly enduring:

But, in a larger sense, we cannot dedicate — we cannot consecrate — we cannot hallow — this ground. The brave men, living and dead, who struggled here, have consecrated it far above our poor power to add or detract. The world will little note nor long remember what we say here, but it can never forget what they did here. It is for us, the living, rather, to be dedicated here to the unfinished work which they who fought here have thus far so nobly advanced. It is rather for us to be here dedicated to the great task remaining before us — that from these honored dead we take increased devotion to that cause for which they gave the last full measure of devotion; that we here highly resolve that these dead shall not have died in vain; that this nation, under God, shall have a new birth of freedom; and that government of the people, by the people, for the people, shall not perish from the earth.

Whether in the speech of presidents or prime ministers, or in the musings about a child's toy, parallelism moves with a kind of stately force. For one thing, **since the human mind responds to rhythm and order, the reader automatically responds to the rhythmic repetition of the parallel parts of sentences.** Readers get started with the particular structured order you set up in the first piece, then just move on with you quickly and satisfactorily through the second, and even third, parallel constructions. You have also set up an expectation for the reader, at least by the second parallel item, and **by continuing with that particular pattern you are fulfilling the reader's subconscious expectations and giving pleasure, even though the reader may not actually know why.**

PARALLEL: having comparable parts, readily recognized similarities; having the same tendency or direction; moving consistently by the same intervals; near similarity or exact agreement in particulars.

APPLICATION

PARALLELISM

1   Transform each group of sentences below into a sentence that contains parallel elements.

1 My grandmother bakes cookies and cakes for all of our birthdays.
   She rides horses.
   She gardens.
   She models.
   My grandmother is a remarkable woman.

2 Studying requires determination.
   It frequently means sacrificing fun times.
   To study effectively, you must have a serious attitude toward your
      education.

3 A good teacher is someone who thinks of each student as a person.
   He is willing to spend additional hours at school to counsel troubled
      students.
   He doesn't care if class discussions veer toward a relevant topic not
      scheduled for discussion.

4 Walking whenever possible shows that a person is concerned with
      good health.

Exercising regularly shows a concern with good health.
Watching the kinds of foods you eat is important if you want to be healthy.

5 I expected to feel independent when I moved away from home to go to college.
I knew I would enjoy making my own rules.
I expected to feel grown-up about paying my own bills.

2 Identify all the instances of parallelism you can find in the passage below by Norman Mailer.

But what will America look like? How will its architecture appear? Will it be the architecture of a Great Society, or continue to be the architecture of an empty promiscuous panorama where no one can distinguish between hospitals and housing projects, factories and colleges, concert halls, civic centers, and airport terminals? The mind recoils from the thought of an America rebuilt completely in the shape of those blank skyscrapers forty stories high, their walls dead as an empty television screen, their form as interesting as a box of cleansing tissue propped on end. They are buildings which reveal nothing so much as the deterioration in real value of the dollar bill. They are denuded of ornament (which costs money); their windows are not subtly recessed into the wall but are laid flush with the surface like a patch of collodion on the skin; there is no instant where a roof with a tower, a gable, a spire, a mansard, a ridge or even a mooring mast for a dirigible intrudes itself into the sky, reminding us that every previous culture of man attempted to engage the heavens.

No, our modern buildings go flat, flat at the top, flat as eternal monotony, flat as the last penny in a dollar. There is so much corruption in the building codes, overinflation in the value of land, featherbedding built into union rules, so much graft, so much waste, so much public relations, and so much emptiness inflated upon so much emptiness that no one tries to do more with the roof than leave it flat.

3 For your own writing. Parallelism can certainly supply your reader with a sense of order. If you start off a list of things, and move from one kind of construction to another, you'll surely interrupt the expected pattern, the flow, and the energy. So check to see whether your writing is structured with sequences, and if it is, **be sure they're developed in the same kinds of grammatical patterns.** Keeping a series of things in the same kind of construction will contribute immeasurably to the clarity and energy that the reader gets from you.

Next, check to see whether you may have used *too much* parallelism. Because parallelism tends to be elegant and formal, a little will contribute some class and style to your writing, but too much of it makes everything you say sound like a proclamation, whether you are commemorating the birth of a nation or simply calling the kids in to dinner. As you revise your writing for energy, insert parallelisms where they will really work for you, but *don't over-formalize everything.* Used appropriately, parallel constructions work beautifully to add style, rhythm, and clarity to your writing—and that results in energy for your reader.

AVOID MISMATCHED PARALLELISM

NO: Drivers need to know about starting a car, stopping a car, and periodic maintenance.

YES: Drivers need to know about starting, stopping, and maintaining a car.

BALANCE AND REPETITION

Another way to revise for energy through stylistic changes is to use *balance* and *repetition* in some of your sentences. Here is a good example of balance from Bennett Cerf:

He [Faulkner] saw all of the tragedy of the Old South, but he also saw the humor.

The symmetry isn't quite perfect, but the repetition of "he saw the ..." gives this short sentence a certain gravity, a touch of sobriety that is appropriate to the message—visions of tragedy and of humor.

Here is another balanced sentence, this time from Abraham Maslow:

A husband's conviction that his wife is beautiful, or a wife's firm belief that her husband is courageous, to some extent creates the beauty or the courage.

Chances are that if you were simply reading along, you'd go right past it; most people would. Yet closely examined, it's a wonderful sentence. Look how the parts match:

A husband's conviction	that his wife is beautiful,
or a wife's firm belief	that her husband is courageous,
to some extent creates	the beauty or the courage.

Not only do the parts match; the last part also manages to echo the main pieces of the first part: *beauty* and *courage*.

Now that your eyes are sharpened and you know what to look for, examine this longer sentence from Tillie Olsen's *Silences*. Notice particularly how she uses "fortunate are those" to introduce each particular assertion about the kind of environment that encourages rather than stifles talent.

Fortunate are those of us who are daughters born into knowledgeable, ambitious families where no sons were born; fortunate are those in economic circumstance beyond the basic imperatives, thus affording some choice; fortunate are those in whose lives is another human being "protecting and stimulating the health of highest productivity"; fortunate are those of us to whom encouragement, approval, grants, publication, come at the foundering time before it is too late; fortunate as has been indicated here are those born into the better climates, when a movement has created a special interest in one's sex, or in one's special subject; fortunate are those who live where relationships, opportunities, not everywhere available are.

APPLICATION

BALANCE

1 Rewrite each group of sentences below into a single sentence that uses balance.

1 I don't avoid jogging because I don't like running.
   I refuse to jog because everyone keeps telling me how great it is and that I should do it.

2 Television can be used wisely as a means of dispersing important information.
   Television can be abused grossly as a source of pointless, unimaginative "entertainment."

3 A good student knows that diligent studying yields the satisfaction of good grades.
   A poor student can only hope that her half-hearted efforts will get her a passing grade.

4 To work without praise can be disheartening.
   To strive without results can be discouraging.
   To set a goal and reach it is always revitalizing.

5 Friendship can be one of the greatest pleasures in life.
   Friendship can be the source of some of life's greatest pains.

2 Pick out the balanced structures in the passage below by Charles Dickens.

It was the best of times, it was the worst of times, it was the age of wisdom, it was the age of foolishness, it was the epoch of belief, it was the epoch of incredulity, it was the season of Light, it was the season of Darkness, it was the spring of hope, it was the winter of despair, we had everything before us, we had nothing before us, we were all going direct to Heaven, we were all going direct the other way—in short, the period was so far like the present period, that some of its noisiest authorities insisted on its being received, for good or for evil, in the superlative degree of comparison only.
There were a king with a large jaw and a queen with a plain face, on the throne of England; there were a king with a large jaw and a queen with a fair face, on the throne of France. In both countries it was clearer than crystal to the lords of

the State preserves of loaves and fishes, that things in general were settled for ever.

IMITATING PATTERNS

1 Rewrite each group of sentences below as a single sentence that follows Cerf's, Maslow's, or Olsen's patterns.

1 He acknowledged the importance of a college education.
He recognized his immediate need for a job.

2 A student's response to class discussion contributes to the tone of the class.
A teacher's encouragement of comments improves the quality of the comments.

3 I knew that planning the party would be a lot of work.
I knew that everyone was eager to get together.

4 Women born into open-minded families where no stereotypes exist can be considered liberated.
Those women who are not forced into roles they don't want, who feel free to change and choose their lifestyles, are also liberated.
Liberated women are encouraged by equally liberated husbands, children, parents, and friends.
Liberated women have been lucky enough to have been born in this generation, when the world is beginning to recognize the human, intellectual, and economic worth of women.
Liberated women live in a country which offers them the educational and business opportunities other countries would deny.

5 A student's determination to enjoy a required, basic course is often the only reason that the course is interesting.
A professor's effort to create interest usually results in an enjoyable class.

6 My father had endured the hardships of Illinois winters.
My father had enjoyed the pleasures of mild Illinois summers.

7 I enjoyed the weekly paycheck from my first job.
I enjoyed the responsibility my first job gave me.

8 A teacher's belief that her students have the ability to learn often improves the quality of the effort expended by the students.
The students' desire to prove that they have the motivation to learn controls their level of performance.

9 A person born into a family which values an active life can look forward to a healthy life.
The person who makes time for exercise and recreation will almost always be healthy.

A person will be healthy if she is encouraged to watch her diet, to exercise regularly, and to avoid a totally sedentary life.

The person who lives in this time when the importance of good health and the need for exercise are almost national obsessions should be healthy.

A person has every opportunity for being healthy if she lives in this country where jogging, tennis, swimming, bicycling, boating thrive through commercial enterprise and public interest.

10 Dr. Adams makes chemistry an enjoyable class.
He makes it intellectually demanding.

2   For your own writing. You may be saying to yourself "That's all well and good, but I never write sentences like those." Indeed, most people don't write sentences like those—but that doesn't mean that we can't imitate those patterns if we choose to do so. Why not try your hand at imitating Cerf, Maslow, and Olsen? Simply follow their *patterns* and put in your own content. For example, here's a spin-off from Cerf's sentence:

Grandmother knew all of the work of raising five children, but she also knew the satisfaction.

Simply replace the nouns and verbs with new ones, and keep the structure the same. To get the full benefit from this activity, you should probably do at least five each of the Cerf and Maslow patterns. The Olsen one is so long that you may want to do only two or three of them.

REPETITION AND PLEASURE

Repetition of words and phrases gives energy to your writing the way a drumbeat gives energy to music—by carrying the movement along. We have already learned the necessity for repeating words in order to keep the message in front of the reader because of the brief memory span. But **repetition is also pleasing esthetically, simply because readers respond favorably to the rhythm, to repetition.** Here are some examples, the first by Noel Perrin:

Most country dwellers in New England sooner or later think about doing a little maple sugaring. About nine-tenths of them never actually get around to it. They don't have enough trees, or they don't have enough time, or they don't have the $700 that even a small evaporator costs.

Here, Perrin leads off with two short sentences, then builds a longer one with a series of three clauses, each introduced by "they don't have." He could have condensed that sentence further and written

They don't have enough trees or time or the $700 that even a small evaporator costs.

Certainly that would be correct enough in terms of combining basic elements and compressing them into the most direct, least wordy message. Yet that would lose the easiness of motion, the casual tone, the effect of relaxed and rather casual conversation. The version Perrin offers sounds like one *neighbor* or friend *talking* to another; the second sounds like a much more distant, formal *expert* who is *explaining* something, perhaps in a textbook. The first is casual, approachable; the second is rather formidable. In both, it is the rhythm and the use of repetition (or absence of it) that produces the effect on the reader.

Here is another sample, this time by Theodore Sorensen. It describes young John Fitzgerald Kennedy, but you'll want to notice how much data is compressed into the first sentence ("At the age of twenty-three . . ."), how the second sentence carries out the same idea but in much briefer form ("At the age of thirty-five . . ."), and how the third sentence —short, unadorned, tart—expresses the point Sorensen means to emphasize ("But he had little interest . . .").

At the age of twenty-three he had expanded his highly regarded senior thesis —representing, he wrote his father, "more *work* than I've ever done in my life"— into a distinguished book on *Why England Slept*, a well-reasoned and well-regarded analysis of that nation's lack of preparedness for the Second World War. At the age of thirty-five he continued to be widely read in history, biography and politics. But he had little interest in abstract theories. He primarily sought truths upon which he could act and ideas he could use in his office.

This kind of repetition and variation will often provide your writing with a splash of style; your readers will probably also stay with you longer and much more happily.

Here is a longer passage written by E. B. White, one of the best essayists and stylists America has produced.

[1]It is a miracle that New York works at all. [2]The whole thing is implausible. [3]Every time the residents brush their teeth, millions of gallons of water must be drawn from the Catskills and the hills of Westchester. [4]When a young man in Manhattan writes a letter to his girl in Brooklyn, the love message gets blown to her through a pneumatic tube—*pfft*—just like that. [5]The subterranean system of telephone cables, power lines, steam pipes, gas mains, and sewer pipes is reason enough to abandon the island to the gods and the weevils. [6]Everytime an incision is made in the pavement, the noisy surgeons expose ganglia that are tangled beyond belief. [7]By rights New York should have destroyed itself long ago, from panic or fire or rioting or failure of some vital supply line in its circulatory system or from some deep labyrinthine short circuit. [8]Long ago the city should have experienced an insoluble traffic snarl at some impossible bottleneck. [9]It should have perished of hunger when food lines failed for a few days. [10]It

should have been wiped out by a plague starting in its slums or carried in by ships' rats. [11]It should have been overwhelmed by the sea that licks at it on every side. [12]The workers in its myriad cells should have succumbed to nerves, from the fearful pall of smoke-fog that drifts over every few days from Jersey, blotting out all light at noon and leaving the high offices suspended, men groping and depressed, and the sense of world's end. [13]It should have been touched in the head by the August heat and gone off its rocker.

This paragraph beautifully illustrates *effective repetition*. The whole paragraph is a response to the assertion that it is a miracle that New York City works at all. In substantiating that claim, White arranges the paragraph into two "groups," the first beginning with sentence 3 and the second group beginning with sentence 7. The first group is tied together by the repetition of *time* tags:

> *Every time* the residents brush their teeth, . . .
> *When* a young man in Manhattan . . .
> *Every time* an incision is made in the pavement . . .

Sentence 7 sets up the pattern that is repeated throughout the remaining sentences: what *should* have happened to New York. Thus White produces a kind of sleight-of-hand: he chronicles the chaos and nonsense that, for him, makes New York "implausible," and offers a welter of details that *shows* what he means—and yet he manages, through careful repetition of patterns, to present that picture of chaos in a way that gives the reader a sense of coherence and control about the writing. *He manages to create, with his paragraph, almost the same effect that he is describing* about New York—it's too chaotic and complicated to work, yet not only does it work, it does so dynamically and wonderfully.

People often ask how much consciousness is needed to produce such masterpieces, and how much is simply the result of natural art or genius. It's a good question but essentially unanswerable. Certainly E. B. White has demonstrated his abilities more often and more highly than most of us are likely to do. Yet that's no reason or excuse for not gaining as much mastery as we are able to. After all, it is *training* that extends whatever native art or genius we possess, whether for running, writing, or playing the violin. The point of this whole discussion, and this conscious-level examination of all these examples, is simply to show you *what is possible* and to suggest that you **imitate the models** in order to extend what is *possible for you*.

And, of course, it is possible for all of us to extend what is possible. That's just another form of "learning," after all. Here's a good example from a student paper of what can happen when an "ordinary" person decides to gain energy by using balance and repetition.

A hero is someone whom we all admire and respect. Either he has performed some spectacular task or he has set an example that is worthy enough for others to follow. Such a man needs not to have done something of earth-shattering importance, though he may be more easily recognized as a hero for doing so. He may be a man who has walked on the moon, or he may be a father who is gentle but firm. He may have climbed Mount Everest, or he may be a patient school teacher. He may have saved the lives of his fellow soldiers in combat, or he may have cared for a child's scraped knee. No one says a hero has to have done something of world-wide significance.

The point of this passage is to *contrast the two concepts of heroism.* Through the use of *balance* (he may be *this* **or** he may be *that*), and through *repetition* of this pattern through three sentences, the writer effectively uses structure to reinforce meaning.

APPLICATION

REPETITION

1 Rewrite these sentences in a paragraph illustrating repetition for emphasis.

1 My grandmother was a woman of remarkable energy.
   She canned the fruit and vegetables which grew in her garden in the summer.
   In the early spring, she always planted a garden in her backyard.
   When autumn came, she made fruit pies—some to eat right away, some to freeze and save for winter.
   During the winter, she knitted warm clothes to give to her grandchildren as Christmas presents.
   She even helped shovel snow when necessary.

2 It was an unprecedented time in the history of the country.
   The president had resigned.
   The office of the president had never before yielded so dramatically to public pressure.
   The voting public had at no other time exercised its democratic privileges with such results.
   Criminal accusations had never before tainted the president himself.
   The public had never felt so deceived by the leaders they had elected.

2 Explain how repetition is used for emphasis in the passage below.

   It won't do to say that the snoozing reader is too dumb or too lazy to keep pace with the train of thought. My sympathies are with him. If a reader is lost, it is generally because the writer has not been careful enough to keep him on the path.
   This carelessness can take any number of forms. Perhaps a sentence is so excessively cluttered that the reader, hacking his way through the verbiage, simply doesn't know what it means. Perhaps a sentence has been so shoddily constructed that the reader could read it in any of several ways. Perhaps the writer has switched pronouns in mid-sentence, or has switched tenses, so the reader loses

track of who is talking or when the action took place. Perhaps Sentence B is not a logical sequel to Sentence A—the writer, in whose head the connection is clear, has not bothered to provide the missing link. Perhaps the writer has used an important word incorrectly by not taking the trouble to look it up. He may think that "sanguine" and "sanguinary" mean the same thing, but the difference is a bloody big one. The reader can only infer (speaking of big differences) what the writer is trying to imply.

3 For your own writing:

Although ultimately every writer has his or her own style, most beginning writers may not be aware of such stylistic touches as *parallelism, balance,* and *repetition.* If that's so for you, you might **try some of these constructions deliberately as you revise to add energy to your work.** Don't do so much stylistic revision, however, that you sound fake and artificial. It may take a while for you to develop the "feel" for putting stylistic touches on your writing, which is perfectly all right. It also takes a while to grow an oak tree from an acorn, but nobody scolds the acorn on that account. The best advice is this: until you get full mastery of these elements, **do less rather than more.** But by all means practice a lot; that's the greatest way to develop as fast as you can. However in writing for other people—public writing—it is easy to *overdo,* to produce writing that is so flowery and fancy with parallelisms, balanced sentences, and repeating words that the reader gets no sense of personal voice from the writer, no experience that the writer "means it." Used sparingly, however, these stylistic touches can give little pockets of surprise and pleasure to the reader. And these never hurt.

WORDS: PICTURES OF HAPPINESS, JOY, AND LOVE
Woody Guthrie

We laughed in the wind and the wind swung around us lots harder. We done little goofy jig dances on the concrete slab of the Sixty-Six. Glad to hit the concrete and glad to kiss the Sixty-Six. Glad that we had made it this far. Glad to be here. Glad it was winter time. Glad it was cold. Glad it was dusty and glad it was blowing dirt in our faces while we talked. Glad to be parting. Glad to be leaving. Glad to say good-bye and gladder to get together a little bit later on down the road. Glad that Paw Jerry was doing such a good job of leading us through the dirt and through this wind so far. Glad to be coming through such a bad blizzard. Glad to be rolling. Glad to go walking apart from one another. Glad to climb back up inside the truck again. Glad to wave and to whoop our good-byes again. Glad to make our promises once more to find the mine fast and to get back together quick and warm. Glad we always had found some way to keep warm in the coldest northers that drifted and blew. Glad to see Helen and Irene go walking their ways off down the little dirt turn-off road to Ray and Stella's fence gate and to their warm door.

WRITING ASSIGNMENT: THE INFORMATION ESSAY

It's not hard to see that in most pieces of writing the readers learn about as much about the writer as they do the subject of the essay. For example, when a person evaluates a thing and then writes about it, the readers are clearly getting the "truth" filtered through the eyes, perceptions, and opinions of the person doing the evaluating. And when people write about personal experiences or give personal viewpoints, the emphasis is almost always totally on the writer. In the writing assignment you are about to do, however, the emphasis shifts radically. In fact, in the *information essay* the writer almost disappears. Now, naturally, the writer can never *really* disappear because facts don't just jump onto a page without having been gathered, sorted, and arranged by some human being. But the *emphasis* in an information essay is clearly on the *information*, the facts, rather than on the writer. When people read *for information*, they read to learn something that is quite objective, something that doesn't carry the stamp of the writer, her or his viewpoint, insight, or personal experience.

We write information essays in life for a variety of reasons:

1 To tell people something that they don't already know, something they might find interesting, important, educational.
2 To add to the readers' knowledge about something they are already familiar with by giving some "inside" information, little-known facts, etc.
3 To teach the readers some new information they need/want to know.
4 To record events that are happening at the present or that happened in the past.
5 To help readers understand ideas, concepts, principles, or situations that they might find difficult to understand without education or training in specific fields.
6 To present information/facts that will add to the readers' general knowledge or broaden their education.

A good information essay will have these characteristics:

1 The information itself will be the center of attention in the essay, not the writer's perceptions, experiences, insights, etc.
2 The writer will present this information as lively and interestingly as possible to avoid boring the reader with lifeless, monotonous facts.
3 The writer will do everything possible to help the reader relate the new information to something already familiar to the reader. The

TO INFORM:
To give knowledge of something; to tell; to teach; to acquaint with a fact

essay, therefore, will be filled with specific details, colorful word pictures, familiar examples or references so that the readers are engaged by the essay and are able to relate the new information to something they already know, thereby assimilating it into their store of knowledge.

Read the information essays that follow and ask yourself these questions:

— How would this essay be different if the emphasis were on the writer instead of on the information itself?
— What has the writer done to liven up this information so that it is not boring to the readers?
— How does the writer relate this new information to something the reader might already know?

Be able to discuss your answers in class.

READINGS

The Meanings of the Kiss

In this essay, Carol Tavris and Leonore Tiefer give interesting information about the kiss down through the ages.

Throughout history, people have found occasion to kiss almost every object that didn't fight back, and a few that did. We kiss icons, dice, the Bible and lottery tickets for luck; we kiss the Blarney Stone for the gift of gab; we kiss religious garments in reverence; we kiss to say hello, good-by, get well, get lost.

There have been so many kinds of kisses that from time to time scholars feel obliged to try to sort them into categories. The ancient rabbis divided kisses into three kinds: greeting, farewell and respect. The Romans identified *oscula* (friendly kisses), *basia* (love kisses) and *suavia* (passionate kisses)—it appears that they were somewhat bawdier than the ancient rabbis. The German language had no fewer than 30 types of kisses at the turn of the century, from *Abschiedkuss* (farewell kiss) to *Zuckerkuss* (sweet kiss). They have since lost, unfortunately, *nachküssen*, which in 1901 meant "making up for kisses that have been omitted."

However many types of kisses one makes up, though, they boil down into only a few basic messages:

"I am your subordinate and I respect you." The kiss as a symbol of deference and duty has a long tradition. In the Middle Ages the location of the kiss was a precise clue to the status of the participants: one kissed

the mouth or cheek of an equal, the hand of a political or religious leader, the hem of the robe of a truly great figure and—to express extreme respect—the foot or ground in front of a king, saint or revered hero. The further away one was in status from the kissee, the farther away from the face one kissed.

"I am your friend." To allow someone close enough to kiss you requires a measure of trust; in its earliest form the kiss of greeting undoubtedly meant, "It's safe. I will not bite your ear or stab your back." The kiss of reconciliation preceded the handshake in many societies, and even today children—and sometimes grownups—are encouraged to "kiss and make up."

"The bargain is sealed." Originally the kiss exchanged between bride and groom was a business kiss—a pagan practice that meant the couple were officially assuming their legal and economic obligations. When all the guests kissed the new wife, they were publicly recognizing the legality of the union.

"I will take care of you and ward off evil." Mothers kiss their children's scraped knees, feverish foreheads and bruised arms to "make the hurt go away," just as faith healers "kiss away" the ailments of grown-up penitents. Belief in the magical powers of kisses has filtered into everyday superstition: When you kiss dice or a cross (or your crossed fingers) or any object "for luck," you are enlisting the aid of fortune, God or the fates.

"We are in and you are out." The "ins" may be family, neighborhood, community or religious fellowship. When St. Paul instructed the faithful to "salute one another with an holy kiss," he established a ritual that came to reflect public adherence to the faith. St. Paul's kiss of peace, as it came to be known, was exchanged among Christians variously at services, baptism, confession, ordination and communion.

Because the kiss implies trust, solidarity and affection, deceptive kisses are everywhere despised. Judas's betrayal of Christ in the garden of Gethsemane was, of course, the most famous Western example. The Judas kiss is practiced ritually even today. Among some Mafiosi, a man who has betrayed the organization will be kissed on the mouth by his assassin—a sign of loving farewell.

On the Track of the Devil Wind

Sherwood B. Idso uses something familiar, a tornado, to assist readers of this essay in understanding something unfamiliar, the devil winds of the Southwest.

The year was 1934. In the eastern face of a 300-yard-long spur of the Castle Mountains, about 10 miles west of the Papago village of Santa Rosa, two workmen for an archaeological expedition camped in a large cave. It was winter; a relentless rain was falling outside, and they were cold. They had heard the legend of the cave, but their predicament apparently dulled their memory. So, without much thought, they built a fire with some ironwood branches. Food and the delicate warmth of the flames soon lulled them to sleep.

Suddenly, an explosion of firebrands filled the air, and menacing flames swirled about them, setting their blankets ablaze. Still drunk with sleep, the men tried desperately to react rationally to the cascading messages of their overloaded senses. But what could they do? Fumbling about in confusion and semi-panic, one of them grasped the large flat stone that lay nearby. Remembering its purported powers, he flung the talisman onto the flames . . . their fury abated; the spirits of the cave were appeased.

Ventana Cave. *Hewultki.* Indians call it "Whirlwind House" and "Home of the Dust Devil." For Wind *did* live there; and daily in summer small dust devils would issue forth from its mouth to grow into tall columns that marched for miles across the desert. Had not each son been told the story by his own father, while gathering the fruit of the giant saguaro?

It was true; it had always been so.

The day was bright and sunny some 40 years later when my young sons and I ventured forth onto the Gila River Indian Reservation just south of Phoenix. Like the Papagos of untold generations before us, we too had come to admire the beauty and majesty of the desert dust devil.

I pulled the car to the side of the road. Almost before it stopped, my fourth-grader, Grant, jumped from the back seat and dashed out on the powdery mulch of the recently leveled field. There, a tiny column of dust began to rise before him.

"Dad," he shouted, "I've created a dust devil!"

Tumbling out behind him, eager to see what all the excitement was about, came Keith and Craig, Grant's two younger brothers. Together, they all raced along in pursuit of the meandering whirlwind. Suddenly, however, it stopped its lateral movement and began to stretch vertically and expand in diameter. Then came the sound. Imperceptible at first, it gradually increased in intensity, as the wind whipped the loose surface soil into a frenzy.

I shouted to the boys to dash into the funnel and release the colored balloons they carried into its swirling updraft, so I could photographically determine their rate of ascent; but my encouragement was to no avail. As the ominous vortex churned violently before them, their own better judgment told them that here was a phenomenon to be observed from a respectable distance.

Musing upon the reactions of my young sons, my mind wandered back to Ventana Cave and the Papagos who christened it *Hewultki.* Did their sons and daughters ever chase the desert dust devil? Were they as awed by the spectacle as my young brood?

"It's dissifading!" Craig's booming voice jolted me back to reality.

"You mean dissipating," laughed Grant and Keith, as the sleek-looking funnel gracefully lifted from the ground and dissolved into the milky atmosphere. Even before its last tell-tale traces had vanished, however, the great vortex was replaced by a group of smaller funnels that seemed to revolve about a common center. These were more the boys' size; and they happily galloped after them to release their balloons.

Just how are dust devils formed? Grant's protestations of exuberant boyhood notwithstanding, conventional wisdom has it that they are born in thermal updrafts resulting from the intense heating of the earth's surface by the rays of the sun. So they are most common over dry surfaces that can be raised to very high temperatures, and, of course, most visible over ground having a good supply of fine loose particles that can be swept into the air.

As the sun climbs in the sky each day, heating anew the barren ground, a layer of very warm and unstable air begins to form near the surface of the soil. Being lighter than the cooler air above it, this layer has a tendency to rise. However, it cannot rise all at once in an intact sheet; so discreet "bubbles" of this warm air begin to waft upward as the thermals so familiar to sailplane pilots and birds of prey.

When the rate of ascent of these thermals surpasses some critical velocity, the inrush of air (to replace that which is transported upward) takes on a rotary motion, much like the swirling water that exits in a bathtub once the stopper is pulled. This influx of additional low-level warm air further fuels the developing spiral wind field; and, as it rushes upward in the small cross-sectional area of the young vortex, its rotational speed is increased in much the same way a figure skater increases her rotation rate when she pulls in her arms and legs to a contracted central position.

Although most people think of dust devils as rather innocuous, such is not always the case. Indeed, one of the world's foremost authorities on vortex wind phenomena, Professor T. Theodore Fujita of the University of Chicago, has written that a strong dust devil is generally more powerful than over one-fourth of all the tornadoes that occur in the world. So it is not unusual to turn on the radio and hear of a house trailer being overturned by a dust devil, or to pick up a newspaper and read of minor structural damage done to houses and farm buildings by these whirlwinds.

Most cases of severe damage, however, occurred in earlier days. The old handwritten weather records of Phoenix, for instance, record that on 29 May 1902 a dust devil "demolished a livery stable, throwing outward the walls on the northeast corner, and carrying the whole roof some distance from the stable, while various debris were found carried several hundred feet away." On the very next day it was also recorded that a dust devil of destructive violence "unroofed the store of H. A. Diehl, near the corner of Washington and Center streets at 2 P.M." Even as late as 1964 a large dust devil destroyed a church that was under construction in Tucson.

In addition to sometimes rivaling tornadoes in intensity, dust devils often mimic them in other ways. The most important of these similarities has to do with the common existence of small but very intense "mini-funnels" within the basic vortex of each type of whirlwind. Scientists believe that these small subsidiary swirls are the cause of most of the damage wrought by tornadoes, and that they are the explanation for the common observance that many times a tornado will completely demolish a house but leave almost unscathed the residence next door to it. It is thought that this peculiar type of behavior is due to the small size "suction vortices," as the mini-funnels are called, that may exist for only a matter of seconds yet do considerable localized damage. Tornadoes generally are believed to have only about three suction vortices in simultaneous existence. However, I have observed as many as 12 to 16 little funnels churning about the outer periphery of a large 200-yard-diameter dust devil.

Dust devils and tornadoes also exhibit similarities when they dissipate. Oftentimes their funnels become stretched into very long, narrow, and contorted structures, called, in the case of the tornado, a "rope cloud." I have observed dust devils at this stage of their life that extended a full thousand feet into the air and yet were no wider across than the shoulders of one of my sons. Indeed, my sons have often charged into such dust devils and greatly hastened their demise. In the case of larger dust devils, more drastic measures are required. It is reported that a dust devil once formed over a railroad embankment that was under construction and removed about a cubic yard of sand per hour from it for four hours. Its erosive action could not be stopped until a bulldozer was finally driven into it!

In addition to small boys and the hot desert sun, the Arizona Apaches can be counted on as being equally adept at creating dust devils—and rather unusual ones at that. They deliberately created them in times past by setting fire to the spines of large cacti. Even today huge whirlwinds are often set in motion by many of the local Indians when they burn stubble on their fields after a harvest. I have observed vortices of such an origin that have stretched a full mile into the sky and were as wide across as a football field.

But what about that most intriguing of situations—Ventana Cave? Why has it to this day continued to spew forth little dust devils from its mouth? And what about the legend of the ironwood fire? Was there really a "hexed" region, where a fire would set up a whirlwind that would "blow your head off," as the Indians claimed?

To find out, I contacted Julian D. Hayden who directed much of the actual digging at the cave during the mid-1930s. He essentially confirmed what was contained in the Papago legend, noting that when he and his men would begin work, "tiny whirls of dust would start up in the rear of the cave, increase in size as they approached the mouth of the cave, and by the time they reached the top of the talus, they were powerful enough to take our wheelbarrows and planking with them." He further said that they could watch them for miles in their progress across the desert to the east, "rising to several hundred feet in height."

In the published record of the excavations at Ventana Cave, the University of Arizona's E. W. Haury, leader of the expedition, gives additional support for the legend and some further insights into possible explanations. He too observed the air currents that moved through the cave, and mentioned that a fire in the wrong spot, especially a hot iron-wood fire, "might easily set up a draft to give the story a basis." In mapping the distribution of wood ash in the cave, Dr. Haury also noted that one area about two yards square was found to be practically ash free, whereas nearby, just outside the "hexed" region, ash was abundant.

And so the legend was de-mystified, and at the same time reestablished. But will I ever explain the nuts and bolts of it to my children? I think not; for as I was preparing this article, one of my younger sons came to me, begging for a bedtime story. Having long ago run out of fresh material, I began to relate the tale of *Hewultki* to him, much as I imagine Papago fathers did to their children long ago. His eyes sparkled and he quivered with delight, as I recounted each little detail. Afterward, he hugged me tightly and tucked his blanket up close under his chin. I know what he will dream tonight; and I know what we will surely seek this summer.

The dust devil—that denizen of the desert—holds an unfathomable fascination for the human mind. Though they may unravel many of its still-hidden secrets long after my time, I hope that my children will never fully comprehend all that there is to know about this marvelous whirlwind. It is too great an inspiration to be reduced to a set of cold equations and numbers.

Long live *Hewultki!*

Showing Off Prize Chickens

W. E. Harris is able, in this short article, to make a chicken show interesting even to someone who is not likely to ever be around a chicken. What does he do to put the readers into the room where the show is going on? How does he make the unfamiliar familiar?

In the chill gray dawn, shadowy figures scurry back and forth from pick-up trucks, vans and cars across parking areas to exhibition buildings carrying crates, boxes and coops.

As one enters the building, he is beset by a medley of sights, sounds, and odors. The bright lights reveal a mass of people and hundreds of chickens. Each rooster seems to be yelling his defiance to the world. There is a sweet aromatic odor of fresh wood shaving mingled with the smell of fresh brewing coffee and the unmistakable pungent aroma of almost two thousand chickens.

Among the rows and rows of coops, exhibitors preen and polish their prize chickens for that last time before the judges arrive. Every feather is subject to the sharp scrutiny of experienced judges.

Near the front entrance the crew of Dr. Bill Adams of the Georgia Poultry Laboratory has set up their equipment to blood test all of the chickens in order to protect the exhibitors and our poultry industry from disease. The poultry team is always ready with a bit of veterinary advice to a breeder.

This scene will be repeated all over Georgia almost every weekend in spring and fall as the numerous poultry clubs set up their meets. Exhibitors come from many states and travel many miles to show their proud offerings.

Raising poultry for exhibition is an art and science, demanding the best of both. An exhibition chicken is a living art form of color, conformation and size.

Poultry club shows are family affairs. They are open to the public and are free. Anyone is welcome as a visitor and guest.

Hope to see you at one of Georgia's finest and fastest growing hobby shows.

Don't Step on the Bugs

In this information essay, a student, Arthur Akard, discusses the demise of the Volkswagen Beetle. Arthur is a car buff who gathered these facts from his general reading and then sorted and arranged the facts into an essay.

CONTEXT:
Written for a regional car-buff newsletter and also sent to a weekly national magazine.

AUDIENCE:
Persons interested in cars in even a mild way.

The Volkwagen Beetle is as American as apple pie. Of course, that sounds a little ironic since the VW is made in Germany, but, nevertheless, it is still very true.

But after 40-plus years of faithful service, the bug will no longer be made. The reason is the same as for the Jaguar Roadster and the American-made convertibles: declining sales.

Back before the Second World War, Hitler promised the people of Germany that he would put a car in every faithful German's garage. So, he appointed a staff to come up with a "people's car," or a "volkswagen." What resulted from their study was the Volkswagen.

By the late 1930's things were looking up for this new Nazi car, but then a small delay came up in production — the war. With the outbreak of World War II, the VW plants in Wolfsburg, Germany, were converted into factories to make military vehicles for the Reich. Fortunately for the world, the Nazis lost. But with their defeat, it seemed that the bug, too, was dead. However, there was a group of Englishmen that had fallen in love with the beetle before the war. They pooled their money and put the bug back into production in 1946.

On a cool autumn day, in 1949, 6 beetle-looking cars were unloaded on the docks in New York City. As the months rolled by, more and more of these "bugs" were shipped to the U. S. By the mid-50's, the reign of the bug began. People from all walks of life started to buy the car: from farmers to college students, from juvenile delinquents to the policemen who arrested them. Everybody was starting to notice that bug.

The boom was really in full swing by the mid-60's. The VW was quickly becoming a universally recognized car. In fact, 1965 was a very special year for VW. The reason was because the 23rd millionth beetle rolled off the assembly line. This even topped the record set by that car so many Americans had driven — the Model-T Ford.

But with the ups also came the downs. The late 1960's became the down time for Volkswagens. Sales started to go down, and the cost of production started to go up. The sun was setting on the VW empire.

As the seventh decade neared, the bosses at VW became aware that sales were starting to drop now alarmingly. So in 1968, the plans for the Rabbit, Dasher, and the Scirocco were drawn up. In 1973, Volkswagen went into the red for all four financial quarters. In 1974 the new VW's hit the road.

But 1976 was the worst year for the bug. The heads at VW spoke those words dreaded by beetle lovers all over the world. "The year 1977 will be the last year for the hardtop beetle and 1978 will be the last year for the beetle convertibles."

From the brainchild of Nazi officers to the largest selling car in America, the Volkswagen bug has covered many a mile. Even though the beetle will no longer be produced, it will never die. Remember the Model-T? VW may have given up hope on the bug, but just remember this — like the Model-T, there will always be a bug on the road. Anything as American as apple pie isn't going to completely disappear.

Writing Your Own Information Essay:

1. CONTEXTS

A

The local Chamber of Commerce has organized a travel tour to a country (or state) with which you are very familiar. Over one hundred Chamber members — both male and female business leaders — have signed up for the tour. The Chamber president has asked you to write a short essay for the next edition of the *Chamber News,* which will go out to all who are going on the trip. He has requested that your essay focus on something about the country (or state) that will not likely appear in an average tourist guidebook. Write the essay that will appear in the *Chamber News.*

B

You are taking an introductory course in world religions. Your instructor is putting together a set of supplementary readings which will give students a different perspective on various religions. The instructor has assigned an essay to each student in the class on this topic: "Write an essay about the religious influences on daily life in your hometown." An alternative topic is "Write an essay in which you discuss the identifying aspects of the religious organization you know best." Every student will receive a set of the supplementary readings, which will be the basis for class discussion. Write your essay.

C

The teacher of a sixth grade class in a local school wants your help in preparing a learning package on hobbies to be used to get the students interested in taking up some hobby for themselves. He has asked you to write an essay for the package which will inform the students about your own hobby. He wants you to give the pupils enough information to let them know what the hobby requires, why it is fun, and what benefits can be gained from it. You know this is a tough assignment because you have to put your information on a level that sixth graders can understand, but give it a try. Write the essay for the learning package and enjoy making a contribution to the sixth graders. And they just might take up the hobby that you love best.

D

Be creative. Ask yourself what you know a lot about (or want to learn a lot about) that would interest or inform other people. Then make up a specific context and audience for presenting your information essay. All of us have some pockets of information tucked away in our heads that other people would be interested in finding out about. What is yours?

2. CREATING

Now you are ready to do the creating stage for your essay. Remember that the creating activity helps you explore ideas you already have and create new ones. The point is to get your ideas moving; when you start thinking on paper, you'll be surprised how easily more and even better ideas will trip along behind. So, do a complete creating stage now, following the rules for the particular creating technique you choose.

3. SHAPING

You may have the idea that informative writing needs to be dry and boring, always just a serious recitation of facts and figures. *But*, remember our discussion of the *Shaping Stage?* We noted, you recall, several very important characteristics of an audience. Above all, readers do *not* like to be bored, and this holds true for *anything* they are reading. Remember, too, that they want to get something out of what they read; they must have ideas and information explained. Moreover, readers are busy people, so don't waste their time with unnecessary detail. Here are some suggestions to help you succeed in informing your audience:

1 "A picture is worth a thousand words." Consider this throughout your essay and wherever possible use the techniques of description (discussed in previous unit) to help the reader develop mental images of the facts you are presenting.
2 Carefully weave facts into the essay in a manner which makes them interesting to the reader. Remember: if the readers wanted only the straight facts, they could read an encyclopedia. You must convince them you have more to offer than a "fact book."
3 Show the significance of the information you're offering to the reader. Do this by drawing comparisons or contrasts with something the reader is already familiar with.
4 Let the readers know you are taking them somewhere worth going, and then move along briskly. Stick to the point. Don't ramble and don't get bogged down in unnecessary details. Tell the readers only what is important and necessary; don't try to tell them everything.

Before you begin to shape your essay, review these rules for audience:

1 Make preliminary agreements about your audience and your purpose.
2 Invent and know your audience.
3 Picture a specific audience.
4 Treat your reader like a person, not a wall.

Take a few minutes now to be sure you have a clear view of your audience for the context you have chosen; see how many characteristics of

your readers-to-be you can think of: _____

_____

_____

_____ .

Also, remember to do a Bare Bones Outline after you finish your trial draft. If that outline shows any weakness in the promise and delivery system or any lack of development, be sure to correct these faults in the second draft.

4. COMPLETING

You can now revise your essay both for flow—by checking your topic-sentence paragraphs and your function paragraphs—and for energy—by seeing if the reader would be served if you varied the sentences, combined them, or used devices such as parallelism or balance to keep the writing interesting. After you have completed your revision, prepare the essay in the best way you possibly can. Polish it, correct it, and check the final copy for any mistake that might have crept in at the last minute. When you have finished, pass the essay along to your readers with pride and satisfaction.

REVISING FOR PUNCH: WORDS

REVISING FOR POWER AND PUNCH

You are very near the end of the *Completing Stage* of the writing process. We have gone through the various steps in revising your writing, from the large units in the essay—paragraphs and chunk units of thought in *Revising for Flow*, sentences in *Revising for Energy*. Now we are ready for the smallest units in your writing—the *words* themselves. Again, as in all other revising, the process *could* go on and on indefinitely and you could be exchanging this word for that until doomsday. This section will instead suggest just a few main things, which you will want to check to see whether they are true about the words you have used. If they are, you can be sure that your writing will have punch, will hit the reader squarely with its exactness and directness. And you'll be amazed how much you will get from so little effort!

Exactness, Specifics, Pictures, and Images   There is no doubt that you are writing for a television generation. This means that your readers are visually oriented; they are accustomed to *seeing* a thing instead of *reading* about it. To hold their attention—perhaps even to catch them enough to begin to get your message across—**you are going to have to draw pictures for them, pictures in words.**

Very likely, these *specific pictures* will be the thing your reader most remembers, so you should in the *Completing Stage* of the writing process make sure that you have many of these *specific pictures, exact references, images* that the reader can remember. Giving your writing power and punch through choice of words can mean the difference between being read and remembered and being read and dismissed.

As this part of the text was being written, image after image and exact word after exact word jumped into the authors' minds from books read as long as 8 or 10 years ago! It's really true that **it is the pictures that stay with a reader, that last beyond the reading itself.** One passage very well remembered is this letter written in 1854, from a father to a son away at college:

> Maybank Plantation, Liberty County, Georgia
> *Monday Morning,* May 22nd, 1854
>
> I do not think, my dear son, that anyone wrote you last week. I did not, it having been a busy week. Mother is always busy, you know, and has had company. She is remarkably well, and was never so <u>fleshy</u>. I must give you a sketch of her daily life.
>
> She rises about <u>six</u> in the morning, or now <u>half-past five</u>; takes her bath, reads, and is ready for family worship about seven; then breakfasts with a moderate appetite and enjoys a cup of <u>good tea</u>. Breakfast concluded and the cups, etc., washed up and dinner ordered, Little Jack gathers up his "<u>*weepons*</u>," as he calls them—the <u>flower trowel</u>, the

---

Confucius is reported to have stated that if he were made emperor of China, his first official act would be to establish a precise meaning for every word.

...fleshy...

..."weepons"...

trimming saw, the nippers and pruning shears and two garden hoes—and follows his mistress, with her sunbonnet on and her large India-rubber-cloth working gloves, into the flower and vegetable gardens. In these places she spends sometimes near two hours hoeing, planting, pruning, etc., Little Jack and frequently Beck and several other little fellows and Gilbert in the bargain all kept as busy as bees about her—one sweeping, another watering, another weeding, another planting and trimming, and another carrying off the limbs and trash. Then she dismisses the forces, and they go off in separate detachments to their respective duties about the house and premises, and she takes a walk of observation and superintendence about the kitchen yard and through the orchard and lawn, accompanied by any friends she may have with her and who may be disposed to take a walk of a quiet domestic nature.

. . . a walk of observation and superintendence . . .

About ten her outdoor exercise is over, and she comes in, sets aside her bonnet, draws off her gloves, and refreshes herself with a basin of cool water, after which she disposes of her seamstresses and looks that the house has been well put to rights and in point and in perfect order — flowerpots dressed, etc. She now devotes herself to cutting out, planning, fitting, or sewing, giving attention to the clothing department and to the condition of the furniture of chambers, curtains, towels, linens, etc. The wants of the servants' wardrobe are inquired into, and all the thousand and one cares of the family attended to.

. . . refreshes herself . . .

Meanwhile the yards have been swept, the walk sanded, and Patience has her culinary world all in neat order. The two milk-white cats have had their breakfast, and are lying in each other's paws in the shade on the green grass in the flower garden; and the young dog *Rex*, having enjoyed his repast, has stretched himself at full length in the sun, and ever and anon rolls over and wallows and kicks his feet into the air. The old turkey hen has spread her young ones like scouts around her, and is slowly picking along the green, and the gobbler is strutting with two or three idle dames in another direction. The fowls have scattered themselves everywhere in the lot, crowing and cackling and scratching; the sheep have finished their early browse, and are lying down beneath the great hickory tree; and overhead and all around is one general concert of birds.

. . . the young dog Rex . . .

. . . wallows . . .

The glorious sunlight, the soft south wind, and the green earth and the blue heavens—Mother sees and enjoys it all; but she is too busy now to come out and take a view. If she has visitors, she is sitting at work and in conversation with them, or for an hour or two before dinner takes her book or pen in hand. But sometimes she indulges in a quiet little doze, and gets up refreshed just before we are called to dinner. This meal she usually enjoys, but is never much of an eater; enjoys her food, but in much moderation.

. . . glorious sunlight . . .
. . . soft south wind . . .
. . . green earth . . .
. . . blue heaven . . .
. . . indulges . . .
. . . doze . . .

For an hour or two after dinner she retires, and about the middle of the afternoon makes her appearance dressed for the evening. Then she is full of her uniform cheerfulness, and attracts everybody to her—husband, children, servants, visitors, old and young. The sea breeze is blowing sweetly. Our friends have driven over; the horses have been

. . . uniform cheerfulness . . .

taken from the carriage, and the drivers have gone to pay their calls in the servants' quarters. The chairs are set out in the piazza, and here we spend a social hour and take tea. Our friends take leave, and then we have family worship. Sometimes they unite with us before they go. We all retire now to our study or rooms, and when the business of the day is over, then Mother enjoys the quiet, and loves to sit up reading and writing and conversing. She says this is the pleasantest part of *the day* to her.

You will recognize all this as very natural—what you have seen many times. Surely our hearts should be full of gratitude to God for all His unnumbered and undeserved favors to us as a family. May we all through riches of grace be saved in a brighter, better, and more enduring world than this! . . . All in the house—Mother, Brother, Sister, Aunt Susan, and Cousin Laura—send much love. <u>I hear Mary Sharpe and Laura singing at the piano, and your brother talking to Mother.</u> He is all the time quite busy. The Lord be with and bless you, my dear son!

I hear . . . singing at the piano . . .

> Your ever affectionate father,
> C. C. Jones.

From Robert Manson Myers, ed., *The Children of Pride: A True Story of Georgia and the Civil War* (New Haven: Yale University Press, 1972), pp. 35–6.

The underlined words highlight the *pictures* of Mrs Jones and her daily activities, and also the delicate appreciation Mr Jones has—almost a savoring—for exactly the right word. We're especially fond of Mrs Jones "refreshing herself with a basin of cool water" and "indulging in a quiet little doze." And of "the young dog Rex," who "wallows and kicks his feet into the air."

Another favorite for exact words, color, pictures, and images is Woody Guthrie's last book, *Seeds of Man*. You are challenged to read these two passages, the first about cornbread and the second about supper fixings, and then *try* to forget the pictures they'll put into your mind! Here's the first:

"I'll always remember Grandmaw Tanner's good cornbread. Wonder what th' secret was about it."

"Well, Mammy Ollie could dish it up just as good as your grandma Tanner could, any old time. Main secret was that she didn't put any sugar in her batter. Maybe an egg or so, which sometimes she did have and sometimes she didn't have, but anyway, she put in lots of salt and left out the sugar. Said that the sugar made cornbread taste too much like oatmeal cookies. She greased her pan with good hot lard, bacon grease, hog lard, whatever kind of grease she had, and she heated her pan in the oven, or up on the stove before she would pour her dough-batter into the pan. She used a good bit of buttermilk."

"<u>Likkum my slikkum.</u> Starvin' me t' death. Keep on."

"Mainest secret, I suppose, was lots of hot lard. And she shoved it into the oven when the oven was scorching hot. And she threw the wood to the fire till she nearly burnt the whole place up, summer, winter, all of the time. She always did say that she had to chase her whole family out from the house before she could bake up good cornbread. But they always came a-running back after a bit when they got the smells of it cooking up their nose holes."

"I 'mem'er. Yeahhhm."

"Always did bake it a long time. Most of us liked it good and curly brown all around the edges. Most of us would fight to get the corner piece, or at least an outside chunk."

"I remember. Me, too."

"I guess this was where I learned how to be such a good fighting hand in the first place. Fighting to get the best piece of Mammy Ollie's cornbread. Browny. Crispish. Real hot."

"Big glass o' buttermilk. Yeahhhmmmannn."

"Big slice of green onion—I mean, dry onion. No wonder that Pawpaw Jerry swung onto Mammy Ollie the way that he did. He always did say that it was her cracklin' bread that brought them together and it was this same bread that kept them together. This same cornbread that kept the whole family fighting and growing all of the time. I can just feel it sticking out of my belly button, here, right this minute. Mmmmm. Mmmm. Mmmm." Papa's face lit up with thoughts he was seeing walk acrost the places of his memory.

"Ymmm."

If you haven't put this book down yet to go fix yourself a snack, then you might as well read the second of Woody's passages; but you'll *surely* want to eat after this one:

Skinny Mammy beat the bottom of a skillet with her wooden stirring spoon. "Break it up, you harvest hands!" she yelled. "Chow is now on! Red bean a green bean a white bean a flitter, corn bread dry bread a wheat bread fritter! Come get it before I throw it to th' hogs in th' pen! Got ham hock. Got beef steak. Come on! Come on! Slop it up and slip it down. Gotta kiss th' cook or you can't ride to town! Eats! Eats. C'mon git 'em!"

"I'll sign up!" I yelled.

"If you would be kind enough, Skinny, or Hell Cat," Papa said as we staggered up off the floor, "to twist my arm and to force me to eat just a few mouthfuls . . ."

Reenie and Helen filled all of our eating plates high and dry and soupy and droopy and all down dripping and saggling and smoking and moving and running all down over the sides; both of them forked and ladled and spooned and poured the soupy thick cementy concretey stewbrowny hamhockery stuff steamyhot from our cooking pot, and next dropped a big oversized chunk of Skinny's rusty brownish red-

Mainest secret, . . .

. . . smells of it cooking up their nose holes . . .

. . . curly brown . . .

Browny. Crispish. Real hot.

. . . sticking out of my belly button . . .

. . . walk acrost the places of his memory.

"Ymmm."

. . . the soupy thick cementy concretey stewbrowny hamhockery stuff . . .

derish goldedged yellerneck yallerback cornponey rough salty greasy cornmeal bread off down around our plates in the general direction of Skinny's black-eye peas. Both girls filled their own plates as they stood by the table's edge dumping ours full; then, whenever all of ours were ready to be claimstaked and blasted and forked and shoveled and dynamited into, they both grabbed their own burnyhot plates to forkle and gobble them down like hungry hogs.

Isn't that fantastic? Can't you just *see* those plates "high and dry and soupy and droopy and . . ." And will you forget the description of that wonderful cornbread? Those onions? Those black-eyed peas? No, the question is not whether you will memorize the words in this passage and be able to recite them. Not at all. The question is, *did you get a powerful picture, or not?* The answer is most probably, *Yes.* And obviously the words contribute to that magic: "they both grabbed their own burnyhot plates to forkle and gobble them down like hungry hogs."

Bean Soup

In this passage from Families, *sociologist Jane Howard describes how she often wishes she had a child. Notice all the concrete words she uses, and see how they give energy and vividness to her writing:*

. . . breeding and chasing small children . . .

Many women in their forties and fifties only groan and roll their eyes at the very mention of breeding and chasing small children. But my own sympathies are with the elderly primigravidas.* May their ranks increase; may their offspring be whole and bright. Meanwhile I talk in daydreams to children I don't have. The ice is thin and dangerous, I tell one in such a daydream, and I hold you in my arms now as we skate, so you won't drop. There's a lot I've got to teach you. You have to learn to look up at the tops of buildings, not just at what is at eye level. You have to learn to notice the <u>fragrance</u> of clothes dried outdoors, the look of leaves against wet November pavements. You must learn to make angel wingprints in the new-fallen snow, and to bring people flowers, and to decorate walls with <u>topographic</u> maps, and to look up *evensong* and *crankshaft* and *aubergine* and *hogshead* in the dictionary. You must learn where to look—to your father, perhaps—for the things I cannot teach you, which are endless.

. . . fragrance . . .

. . . topographic . . .

We'll make bean soup together, and find people to feed it to. When we go to foreign cities (if there's fuel enough to go there when you're older), we will look for marketplaces, zoos, weddings, and funerals. We'll go when we can to houses near water, and while our <u>clothes</u> are <u>flapping dry</u> on the line in the wind we'll walk over rocks with our <u>sneakers laced together</u> and slung over our shoulders, in case we come to a place too sharp for bare feet. I'll show you how to cut a slice of bread, and when to pull back in your own lane after you have passed

. . . clothes flapping dry . . .

. . . sneakers laced together . . .

*pregnant for the first time

another car (if cars still exist when you're older). I shall try to make you understand that certain mysteries are meant to remain mysterious, that hellos imply farewells, that much of what you'll ever learn, from me or from anyone else, is subject to change, and that it is well to speak plainly, and on occasion to lift your voice in song.

...hellos imply farewells ...

Here is a short excerpt from George Orwell's "Shooting an Elephant." Even though the passage is brief, it clearly shows the kind of mastery Orwell had in fashioning comparisons that make the picture not only vivid but also unforgettable. The point of the essay is that, for fear of appearing foolish or being laughed at, we often go to extreme lengths and sometimes even allow ourselves to be forced into quite hideous acts. The vivid details in this description assist the reader in *feeling* the message as well as understanding it.

When I pulled the trigger I did not hear the bang or feel the kick— one never does when a shot goes home—but I heard the devilish roar of glee that went up from the crowd. In that instant, in too short a time, one would have thought, even for the bullet to get there, a mysterious, terrible change had come over the elephant. He neither stirred nor fell, but every line of his body had altered. He looked suddenly stricken, shrunken, immensely old, as though the frightful impact of the bullet had paralysed him without knocking him down. At last, after what seemed a long time—it might have been five seconds, I dare say—he sagged flabbily to his knees. His mouth slobbered. An enormous senility seemed to have settled upon him. One could have imagined him thousands of years old. I fired again into the same spot. At the second shot he did not collapse but climbed with desperate slowness to his feet and stood weakly upright, with legs sagging and head drooping. I fired a third time. That was the shot that did for him. You could see the agony of it jolt his whole body and knock the last remnant of strength from his legs. But in falling he seemed for a moment to rise, for as his hind legs collapsed beneath him he seemed to tower upwards like a huge rock toppling, his trunk reaching skywards like a tree. He trumpeted, for the first and only time. And then down he came, his belly towards me, with a crash that seemed to shake the ground even where I lay.
    I got up. The Burmans were already racing past me across the mud. It was obvious that the elephant would never rise again, but he was not dead. He was breathing very rhythmically with long rattling gasps, his great mound of a side painfully rising and falling. His mouth was wide open—I could see far down into caverns of pale pink throat. I waited a long time for him to die, but his breathing did not weaken. Finally I fired my two remaining shots into the spot where I thought his heart must be. The thick blood welled out of him like red velvet, but still he did not die. His body did not even jerk when the shots hit him, the tortured breathing continued without a pause. He was dying,

...bang ... kick ...
...devilish roar of glee ...

...mysterious, terrible change ...
...altered ...

...sagged flabbily ... slobbered ...
...thousands of years old ...

...agony ...jolt ...remnant ...

...not dead ... rattling gasps ...
...caverns of pale pink ...
...red velvet ...

very slowly and in great agony, but in some world <u>remote</u> from me where not even a bullet could damage him further. I felt that I had got to put an end to that dreadful noise. It seemed dreadful to see the great beast lying there, powerless to move and yet powerless to die, and not even to be able to finish him. I sent back for my small rifle and poured shot after shot into his heart and down his throat. They seemed to make <u>no impression.</u> The tortured gasps continued as steadily as the <u>ticking of a clock.</u>

Here's a final excerpt, taken from "Who Killed King Kong?" by X. J. Kennedy:

Intentionally or not, the producers of *King Kong* encourage this identification by <u>etching</u> the character of Kong with keen sympathy. For the ape is a figure in a tradition familiar to moviegoers: the tradition of the <u>pitiable monster.</u> We think of Lon Chaney in the role of Quasimodo, of Karloff in the original *Frankenstein.* As we watch the Frankenstein monster's <u>fumbling and disastrous</u> attempts to befriend a flower-picking child, <u>our sympathies are enlisted</u> with the monster in his <u>impenetrable loneliness.</u> And so with Kong. As he roars in his chains, while barkers sell tickets to <u>boobs</u> who <u>gape</u> at him, we perhaps feel something more deep than <u>pathos.</u> We begin to sense something of the problem that engaged Eugene O'Neill in *The Hairy Ape:* the dilemma of a displaced animal spirit forced to live in a jungle built by machines.

...etching...

...pitiable monster...

...fumbling and disastrous...

...impenetrable loneliness...
...boobs...gape...
...pathos...

All these samples show writers that are supurb at drawing pictures for the reader. Whether it is a rather intellectual essay, like Kennedy's on King Kong, or a rough-and-tumble lark like Guthrie's, or a multi-level description like Orwell's, the principle remains the same. **They all use specific, concrete words, and they use them vigorously to draw pictures for the reader.**

APPLICATION

Pick out the words that contribute to the vividness of the passages below.

A

When my son and I arrived at the pigyard, armed with a small bottle of castor oil and a length of clothesline, the pig had emerged from his house and was standing in the middle of his yard, listlessly. He gave us a slim greeting. I could see that he felt uncomfortable and uncertain. I had brought the clothesline thinking I'd have to tie him (the pig weighed more than a hundred pounds) but we never used it. My son reached down, grabbed both front legs, upset him quickly, and when he opened his mouth to scream I turned the oil into his throat—a pink, corrugated area I had never seen before. I had just time to read the label while the neck of the bottle was in his mouth. It said Puretest.

The screams, slightly muffled by oil, were pitched in the hysterically high range of pig-sound, as though torture were being carried out, but they didn't last long: it was all over rather suddenly, and, his legs released, the pig righted himself.

In the upset position the corners of his mouth had been turned down, giving him a frowning expression. Back on his feet again, he regained the set smile that a pig wears even in sickness. He stood his ground, sucking slightly at the residue of oil; a few drops leaked out of his lips while his wicked eyes, shaded by their coy little lashes, turned on me in disgust and hatred. I scratched him gently with oily fingers and he remained quiet, as though trying to recall the satisfaction of being scratched when in health, and seeming to rehearse in his mind the indignity to which he had just been subjected. I noticed, as I stood there, four or five small dark spots on his back near the tail end, reddish brown in color, each about the size of a housefly. I could not make out what they were. They did not look troublesome but at the same time they did not look like mere surface bruises or chafe marks. Rather they seemed blemishes of internal origin. His stiff white bristles almost completely hid them and I had to part the bristles with my fingers to get a good look.

—E. B. White

B

Little Stevie Cauthen sat down in the jockey quarters and peeled off his hot pink riding silks.

"Where's my roses?" Cauthen asked.

A moment later, the 18-year-old jockey, with the angelic face of a choirboy, clutched a giant bouquet of longstem roses to his thin, bare chest and ceremoniously began handing out the flowers, one by one, to other jockeys in the room.

"Here you go," Cauthen said, in his soft, girlish voice. He reached out and offered a rose to 57-year-old Bobby Baird, Cauthen's chronological counterpoint in the Kentucky Derby. Baird was touched by the gesture. His eyes began to mist.

It was a private, poignant postscript to the drama that had just unfolded moments earlier at fabled old Churchill Downs, where for the last 104 years men have chased after stardust, riches and a measure of immortality.

Cauthen realized that dream Saturday in his very first Derby run, riding Affirmed to a 1⅓-length win over late-charging Alydar.

Baird, in contrast, has devoted 40 years of his life as a jockey but never even come close to winning America's most celebrated thoroughbred horse race known romantically as the Run for the Roses. And with his career in the home stretch, he probably won't get another chance, either.

But Steve Cauthen, still too young to buy a mint julep, has everything ahead of him, for years to come.

Cauthen clearly demonstrated a poise and savvy beyond his teenage years as he avoided being squeezed out on the first turn and then held off late charges by Believe It and Affirmed's chief rival, Alydar.

Bobbing like a pink blossom aboard his big chestnut steed, Cauthen held Affirmed in reserve for six furlongs as Sensitive Prince broke fast and angled sharply in front of the field from his far outside position.

Affirmed then moved up boldly on the second turn, relinquished the lead briefly a quarter mile out and then ran away from Believe It, keeping onrushing Alydar at bay.

Cauthen was well in command of the situation long before he ever reached the gate for this prestigious horse race that puts a premium on speed and courage and heart.

—David Casstevens

APPLICATIONS FOR YOUR OWN WRITING

Getting punch in your writing probably comes down to three simple things:

1 Replace vague, general words with specific, exact words
2 Cut out every word you don't absolutely need
3 Use action verbs

These three will just about do it. If you revise your words with these principles in mind, you will have *power* and *punch* in your writing. Here are some specific examples that illustrate the three principles:

1 Replace Vague Words With Specific, Concrete Words   Look at the difference in these sentences:

VAGUE: The landscape is very varied.
SPECIFIC: The landscape changes from high, old mountains in the east to flat, horse-raising country in the middle to river-bottom delta land in the west.

VAGUE: The people living in the housing project are diverse.
SPECIFIC: The people living in the housing project come from ten different countries on four different continents.

VAGUE: The pizza was great.
SPECIFIC: The pizza started with a crust made of fresh-baked dough on which was piled a layer of cheddar cheese, ground beef, mushrooms, anchovies, sliced meatballs, sausage, baloney, pepper, onions, green pepper, and finally another layer of cheese: mozzarella.

Whenever you supply a specific for a general word, you will add power and punch to what you write.

REDUNDANCIES

If you describe an object as red in color and round in shape, you're really nailing it down, taking no chance on being misunderstood. But you're also betraying insecurity and will bore your reader to tears. This kind of writing lacks crispness. It's limp.

The following list gives examples of redundancies that should be avoided. The words in parentheses are the portion of the phrase that can (and should) be omitted without risk of weakening it or changing its meaning.

Because (of the fact that)
The maximum (possible) amount
A range (all the way) from
A (time) interval or period
An (innumerable) number of
(Final) climax
(Capping) the climax
Assemble (together)
Connect (together)
Add (together)
Connect (up)
Fuse (together)
Square (in shape)
Few (in number)
Big (in size)
Adequate (enough)
(Entirely) completed
Atop (of)
Inside (of)
All (of)
(And) moreover
This (same) program
Equally (as) willing
The same (identical) meaning
Throughout (the whole of)
Bisect (into two parts)
Halved (in two parts)
(Most) unique
Bald (-headed) man

The modern man (of today)
(Every) now and then
Total effect of (all) this
Mutual advantage (of both)
(Surrounding) circumstances
Endorse (on the back)
They are (both) alike
Favorable condition for warping
   (to occur)
Necessary (requisite)
(True) facts
(Successful) achievements
Recoil (back)
Repeat (again)
Return (back)
Each (and every)
Thus (as a result)
Continue (on)
Termed (as)
Blue (in color)
(Still) persists
Might (possibly)
(As) yet
(But) nevertheless
The pregnant Chinese (woman)
(As to) whether
2 P.M. (in the afternoon)
(New) beginners

— Ernst Jacobi

2 Cut Out Every Word You Don't Absolutely Need   Save your reader time and energy; cut out the flab. Make your writing lean. **There is nothing that will steal your power sooner than a lot of extra, flabby words that the reader has to wade through and climb around and over to get to your message.** See the difference for yourself:

Fat: There are many people alive in the world today who are living strange and unusual lives.
Lean: Many people live strange lives.

Fat: Modern men and women of today are both alike in similar ways; they repeat again and again their messages after they have already said them once.
Lean: Both men and women tend to repeat their messages.

Fat: Because of the fact that I don't have any money and am therefore flat and broke, I don't go inside a restaurant.
Lean: Because I don't have any money, I don't go inside a restaurant.

BUREAUCRATIC PHRASES AND ALTERNATIVES

Bureaucratic	Direct
by means of	by
in the event of	if
along the lines of	like, as
with the result that	
designed so that	so that
in order to	
with a view toward	
for the purpose of	to
for the reason that	
on the grounds that	because, since
on the basis of	
in connection with	
in relation to, with regard to,	about
with respect to, in the matter of	

—Ernst Jacobi

The words in parentheses are stereotyped business jargon—chatter that should be eliminated.

(This is to inform you that) Mr. Broadbeam will call on you at your office (as) soon (as possible).

(We are pleased to direct your attention to) paragraph 8 (which) indicates that . . .

Please (feel free to) write (to this office) if you (find yourself in) need (of) additional details.

(Data obtained during) flight tests indicate that . . .

—Ernst Jacobi

---

3 Use Action Verbs Most texts take a completely unyielding stand against passive verbs. That's because students often use the passive voice to avoid taking a stand about anything, or because business and technical writing is made characterless and flavorless because of excessive use of passive constructions. Occasionally, though, the passive is useful to the writer—as when a cause or agent is unknown. However, for now it will probably do more good to take the traditional stand *against* passive verbs —and then later allow them into writing in just—and only—the places where they actually are appropriate.

Let your reader *see* what is happening. Passive verb forms kill writing, and nobody knows "who dunnit." It's a classic way of concealing the evidence or hiding the responsibility, but it usually makes for downright dull reading.

Here are some examples of action verbs that let the reader see *exactly* what is happening.

He *moved* toward us.

leaped	loped	crept
slouched	trotted	crawled
jumped	paced	scooted
stumbled	staggered	barged
ambled	lurched	exploded
sauntered	fell	shot
jogged	strolled	whizzed
dashed	jigged	oozed
reeled	moseyed	marched
lurched	flew	strutted
sprinted	dragged	crawfished

PASSIVE: The music was heard late at night. (Who heard it?)
ACTIVE: The landlord heard the music late at night. (Oh!)

PASSIVE: The missing funds were looked for. (Who did the looking?)
ACTIVE: The bank janitor looked for the missing funds. (Ah ha!)

As you revise for *specifics, lean sentences,* and *active verb forms,* you will put punch in your writing that will very likely cause your readers to remember for a long time what you had to say. *Give it to them!*

VITIATED VERBS

A particularly undesirable by-product of the passive voice is the use of vitiated, or debased, verbs. A vitiated verb is one that has been turned into a noun but continues to take the place of the verb by appearing in combination with an auxiliary or some other "weak" verb. Examples:

Vitiated	Active/Strong
An indication of . . . is provided by . . .	The . . . indicates that . . .
Repayment will be made . . .	We will repay . . .
Consideration is given to . . .	We are considering . . .
Make an adjustment of . . .	Adjust . . .
An evaluation has been made . . .	We have evaluated . . .
The writer has an appreciation of . . .	We appreciate/like . . .
An inclination is shown by . . .	. . . inclines
The operation was performed . . .	The doctor operated . . .
Attribution of the remarks was made to . . .	He attributed the remarks to . . .
An investigation has been undertaken of . . .	We have investigated/studied . . .
A positive rating was arrived at by . . .	We rated . . . positive because . . .
An analysis has been made of . . .	We have analyzed . . .
A report has been released by . . .	XYZ has reported that . . .
Emphasis should be placed on . . .	. . . should be emphasized
An improvement has been made in . . .	. . . has been improved

Verbs are the muscles and sinews of language. They move your sentences forward and make your words flow. Each time you change a verb into a noun you slow your cadence and lower the pressure. You break your stride when you vitiate verbs.

— Ernst Jacobi

APPLICATION

Each of the sentences below contains problems in word use. Identify the problem and revise the sentence to correct it.

1 The air smelled good, the trees looked nice, the breeze was just right, and we felt great.

2 Exercise is something that should be tried by everyone.

3 In my estimation, the requirement of additional classrooms is an unwise move undertaken by the school board.

4 It is expected by most of the members of the community that the abandonment of the drive to retain the trees will be detrimental to the city.

5 The old house on the corner was in sad need of repair: the porch was falling, most of windows were broken, the paint was peeling all over, the roof looked terrible.

6 The Congress's insistence on backing up the unfair demands by the President only resulted in the creation of an atmosphere of resentment and mistrust among the voters.

7 It was agreed by everyone that a good time was enjoyed at the great movie last night.

JACK AND JILL TURN LEGAL

"JACK AND JILL"

Accident Report

Jack and Jill	The party of the first part hereinafter known as Jack . . . and . . . The party of the second part hereinafter known as Jill . . .
Went up the hill	Ascended or caused to be ascended an elevation of undetermined height and degree of slope, hereinafter referred to as "hill."
To fetch a pail of water.	Whose purpose it was to obtain, attain, procure, secure, or otherwise, gain acquisition to, by any and/or all means available to them, a receptacle or container, hereinafter known as "pail," suitable for the transport of a liquid whose chemical properties shall be limited to hydrogen and oxygen, the proportions of which shall not be less than or exceed two parts for the first mentioned element and one part

Jack fell down	for the latter. Such combination will hereinafter be called "water." On the occasion stated above, it has been established beyond reasonable doubt that Jack did plunge, tumble, topple, or otherwise be caused to lose his footing in a manner that caused his body to be thrust into a downward direction. As a direct result of these combined
And broke his crown	circumstances, Jack suffered fractures and contusions of his cranial regions.
And Jill came tumbling after.	Jill, whether due to Jack's misfortune or not, was known to also tumble in similar fashion after Jack. (Whether the term, "after," shall be interpreted in a spatial or time passage sense, has not been determined.)

—*Don Sandburg*

DISSECTING SHEET

In order to drive home the necessity for looking at your paper *after* you have finished examining it for surface errors, structural weaknesses, and lack of polish, we present a checklist that we call a DISSECTING SHEET. It has been used with students for several years now, and many of them have said this was one of the most useful things we ever taught them.

The dissecting sheet works this way:

You examine your paper just as you would a cat in biology. Where are the bones? How are the parts of the skeleton connected? What has happened here? What occurs when you do this, that? **You will be taking your paper apart and putting it back together again.** And the questions all cover the major areas for improvement that we have been encountering in years of teaching. You will want to fill out a Dissecting Sheet for everything you write, and as you become more familiar with it, you will learn how to adapt it for any kind of writing—a business letter, a scientific report, etc. It is your authors' gift to you. Use it any way you can. Change it as you like. If it helps you learn to complete a writing project, we are happy.

"You know, Rio," Papa nodded half without knowing it, "it takes a better guitar-picker to know what not to do than it takes to bang and wham out all over the place."
—Woody Guthrie

DISSECTING THE ANIMAL

Now is the time for you to take a *good* look at the essay you have written. Look at its anatomy. Find its parts. See if there are any broken bones—or any bones at all. You know the constraints present when anyone tries to communicate by writing, so now is the time to check to see if you have done everything possible to get your message to the reader. By filling in the questions below, you will see if your writing "works."

1 Recall the communication chart in the Shaping section (or look at it again). Remember, there is the idea in the person's head on the left that has to travel across all those spaces and get into the other person's head on the right.

WHAT IS THE IDEA IN YOUR PAPER THAT WAS IN YOUR HEAD THAT YOU NOW WANT TO GET INTO YOUR READER'S HEAD?

2 Read your first two sentences. (Remember, you have about that much space to get and keep your reader's attention.) Would *you* read past these two sentences? Mark the appropriate box below:

_____ first two sentences extremely interesting; I can hardly wait to read on.

_____ first two sentences OK, and I'm mainly counting on my reader's good will.

_____ first two sentences crummy. I wouldn't read another word.

3 Look at your opening paragraph. Do you have any pronouns in it? (Not that there's anything especially wrong with pronouns, but they often signal that generalizations have been made, and generalizations *unless specifically planned by a writer* are often death to your message.) If you have any pronouns, write them here. If not, write *none*.

4 Do you use any words like *people, everyone, society,* etc.? If so, what specific purpose do these words serve? (These words often signal non-person writing, no personal interest in the subject.) If you used none of these words, write *none* here.

5 Have you been *very* clear in your opening paragraph to state exactly the message you are taking the trouble to write to another person? Write the sentence here that comes directly from your paper showing your purpose in writing the paper. (If this isn't in the first paragraph, tell where it is and how it happened to be in that place. If the purpose of your paper is found in more than one sentence, write as many of the sentences from the paper as are necessary to show what the purpose is.)

6 What is the connection between your first and second paragraphs?

7 Read over the rest of your paper. How many separate points do you make in order to get your message across? List them here:

1.

2.

3.

4.

5.

(If you made more than five, you probably tried to cover too much territory in a single writing; people usually do not remember over five pieces of information at one time.)

8 For each point you made, there should be several sentences following that point explaining it, illustrating it, describing it, analyzing it, defining it, developing it in some way. Take each point you made and answer the following questions about it:

POINT: (write it again here).

How many sentences are connected with this point to develop it? _____

Is this point alone in a paragraph, or is it among other points in the same

paragraph? _____ _____

If it is with other points, why is it? Because the points all go together in one paragraph? Because there weren't enough sentences about the point?

What method of development did you use to explain the point to your

reader? _____

When you left this point and went to the next, did you connect the two in any way? Explain in detail:

Write your second point here:

How many sentences did you use to develop it? _____
How is this point connected to the one above it and the one below it?

Look at all the other points in your paper and answer these same questions about them.

9 It's hard to make a point to a reader if you don't use concrete examples. Read your paper and find 8 examples of very graphic, concrete word pictures. (If you can't find that many, pick out the ones you can find. If you don't have eight, put some more in before you turn the paper in.)

1.

2.

3.

4.

5.

6.

7.

8.

10 Pick out two things you *really* like in your paper and write them here:

11 How did you end the paper?

12 Would a reader feel *psychological closure* at the end of the paper? How did you provide this?

13 On a scale of 1 to 10, with 10 being the highest, how successful do you guess you were in getting your idea into another person's head?

14 Check appropriate boxes below (as many as apply):

_____ I spent the equivalent amount of time on this paper that I usually spend studying for a major exam.

_____ I wrote this paper at the last minute.

_____ I revised this paper.

_____ I liked what I wrote about.

_____ I took this assignment seriously.

_____ I wish I were a thousand miles from here on vacation.

WRITING ASSIGNMENT: THE EXPLORATORY ESSAY

If you have ever explored a cave, you know that you go into it with no expectations whatsoever—just the adventure of what you might find when you get inside. The whole point of the expedition is to *explore*, not to look for a specific thing or have a firm agenda about what you are going to do and when. To enjoy exploring a cave, you don't have to discover hidden treasure, a lost tribe, or the secret to the world's energy crisis. You just enjoy the not knowing when you start and the knowing when you stop. You enjoy the *act* of *exploring*.

Writing an exploratory essay is very much like exploring a cave. You just look at a subject from all sides—go into all the nooks and crannies, follow the paths that open up as you explore—just to discover. You are saying to your readers when you write an exploratory essay, "Have you ever thought of this topic this way?" or "Hey, look at what is going on here!" or "Let's see what we can find out about this subject by looking at it with no preconceived ideas or set opinions."

A good exploratory essay, then, does these things:

1 The essay discusses more than one way to look at the subject.
2 The writer sets out to explore the subject, not take a definite stand on it or have an answer about it at the beginning.
3 The writer allows the *readers* to explore the subject with her or him—gives the readers the feeling that they are moving right along with the writer in seeing what can be said about the topic or subject. The writer generates thoughts for the readers to consider and leaves the readers with a chance to keep on thinking about the subject.

To Explore:
To investigate systematically; to examine; to search into or range over (a country for the purpose of discovery).

Read the following samples of exploratory essays. See what discoveries, approaches, possibilities these writers wanted to share with you. Do these essays meet the requirements of a good exploratory essay? Be ready to discuss your answers in class.

Three Days to See

In this first essay, Helen Keller explores what she would like to see if she were given just 3 days of sight.

If I were the president of a university I should establish a compulsory course in "How To Use Your Eyes." The professor would try to show his pupils how they could add joy to their lives by really seeing what passes unnoticed before them. He would try to awake their dormant and sluggish faculties.

Perhaps I can best illustrate by imagining what I should most like to see if I were given the use of my eyes, say, for just three days. And while I am imagining, suppose you, too, set your mind to work on the problem of how you would use your own eyes if you had only three more days to see. If with the oncoming darkness of the third night you knew that the sun would never rise for you again, how would you spend those three precious intervening days? What would you most want to let your gaze rest upon?

I, naturally, should want most to see the things which have become dear to me through my years of darkness. You, too, would want to let your eyes rest long on the things that have become dear to you so that you could take the memory of them with you into the night that loomed before you.

If, by some miracle, I were granted three seeing days, to be followed by a relapse into darkness, I should divide the period into three parts.

On the first day, I should want to see the people whose kindness and gentleness and companionship have made my life worth living. First I should like to gaze long upon the face of my dear teacher, Mrs. Anne Sullivan Macy, who came to me when I was a child and opened the outer world to me. I should want not merely to see the outline of her face, so that I could cherish it in my memory, but to study that face and find in it the living evidence of the sympathetic tenderness and patience with which she accomplished the difficult task of my education. I should like to see in her eyes that strength of character which has enabled her to stand firm in the face of difficulties, and that compassion for all humanity which she has revealed to me so often.

I do not know what it is to see into the heart of a friend through that "window of the soul," the eye. I can only "see" through my fingertips the outline of a face. I can detect laughter, sorrow, and many other obvious emotions. I know my friends from the feel of their faces. But I cannot really picture their personalities by touch. I know their personalities, of course, through other means, through the thoughts they express to me, through whatever of their actions are revealed to me. But I am denied that deeper understanding of them which I am sure would come through sight of them, through watching their reactions to various expressed thoughts and circumstances, through noting the immediate and fleeting reactions of their eyes and countenance.

Friends who are near to me I know well, because through the months and years they reveal themselves to me in all their phases; but of casual friends I have only an incomplete impression, an impression gained from a handclasp, from spoken words which I take from their lips with my fingertips, or which they tap into the palm of my hand.

How much easier, how much more satisfying it is for you who can see to grasp quickly the essential qualities of another person by watching the subtleties of expression, the quiver of a muscle, the flutter of a hand. But does it ever occur to you to use your sight to see into the inner nature of a friend or acquaintance? Do not most of you seeing people grasp casually the outward features of a face and let it go at that?

For instance, can you describe accurately the faces of five good friends? Some of you can, but many cannot. As an experiment, I have questioned husbands of long standing about the color of their wives' eyes, and often they express embarrassed confusion and admit that they do not know. And, incidentally, it is a chronic complaint of wives that their husbands do not notice new dresses, new hats, and changes in household arrangements.

The eyes of seeing persons soon become accustomed to the routine of their surroundings, and they actually see only the startling and spectacular. But even in viewing the most spectacular sights the eyes are lazy. Court records reveal every day how inaccurately "eyewitnesses" see. A given event will be "seen" in several different ways by as many witnesses. Some see more than others, but few see everything that is within the range of their vision.

Oh, the things that I should see if I had the power of sight for just three days!

The first day would be a busy one. I should call to me all my dear friends and look long into their faces, imprinting upon my mind the outward evidences of the beauty that is within them. I should let my eyes rest, too, on the face of a baby, so that I could catch a vision of the eager, innocent beauty which precedes the individual's consciousness of the conflicts which life develops.

And I should like to look into the loyal, trusting eyes of my dogs—the grave, canny little Scottie, Darkie, and the stalwart, understanding Great Dane, Helga, whose warm, tender, and playful friendships are so comforting to me.

On that busy first day I should also view the small simple things of my home. I want to see the warm colors in the rugs under my feet, the pictures on the walls, the intimate trifles that transform a house into home. My eyes would rest respectfully on the books in raised type which I have read, but they would be more eagerly interested in the printed books which seeing people can read, for during the long night of my life the books I have read and those which have been read to me have built themselves into a great shining lighthouse, revealing to me the deepest channels of human life and the human spirit.

In the afternoon of that first seeing day, I should take a long walk in the woods and intoxicate my eyes on the beauties of the world of Nature, trying desperately to absorb in a few hours the vast splendor which is constantly unfolding itself to those who can see. On the way home from my woodland jaunt my path would lie near a farm so that I might see the patient horses plowing in the field (perhaps I should see only a tractor!) and the serene content of men living close to the soil. And I should pray for the glory of a colorful sunset.

When dusk had fallen, I should experience the double delight of being able to see by artificial light, which the genius of man has created to extend the power of his sight when Nature decrees darkness.

In the night of that first day of sight, I should not be able to sleep, so full would be my mind of the memories of the day.

The next day—the second day of sight—I should arise with the dawn and see the thrilling miracle by which night is transformed into day. I should behold with awe the magnificent panorama of light with which the sun awakens the sleeping earth.

This day I should devote to a hasty glimpse of the world, past and present. I should want to see the pageant of man's progress, the kaleidoscope of the ages. How can so much be compressed into one day? Through the museums, of course. Often I have visited the New York Museum of Natural History to touch with my hands many of the objects there exhibited, but I have longed to see with my eyes the condensed history of the earth and its inhabitants displayed there—animals and the races of men pictured in their native environment; gigantic carcasses of dinosaurs and mastodons which roamed the earth long before man appeared, with his tiny stature and powerful brain, to conquer the animal kingdom; realistic presentations of the processes of evolution in animals, in man, and in the implements which man has used to fashion for himself a secure home on this planet; and a thousand and one other aspects of natural history.

I wonder how many readers of this article have viewed this panorama of the face of living things as pictured in that inspiring museum. Many, of course, have not had the opportunity, but I am sure that many who *have* had the opportunity have not made use of it. There, indeed, is a place to use your eyes. You who see can spend many fruitful days there, but I, with my imaginary three days of sight, could only take a hasty glimpse, and pass on.

My next stop would be the Metropolitan Museum of Art, for just as the Museum of Natural History reveals the material aspects of the world, so does the Metropolitan show the myriad facets of the human spirit. Throughout the history of humanity the urge to artistic expression has been almost as powerful as the urge for food, shelter, and procreation. And here, in the vast chambers of the Metropolitan Museum, is unfolded before me the spirit of Egypt, Greece, and Rome, as expressed in their art. I know well through my hands the sculptured gods and goddesses of the ancient Nile-land. I have felt copies of Parthenon friezes, and I have sensed the rhythmic beauty of charging Athenian warriors. Apollos and Venuses and the Winged Victory of Samothrace are friends of my fingertips. The gnarled, bearded features of Homer are dear to me, for he, too, knew blindness.

My hands have lingered upon the living marble of Roman sculpture as well as that of later generations. I have passed my hands over a plaster cast of Michelangelo's inspiring and heroic Moses; I have sensed the power of Rodin; I have been awed by the devoted spirit of Gothic wood carving. These arts which can be touched have meaning for me, but even they were meant to be seen rather than felt, and I can only guess at the beauty which remains hidden from me. I can admire the simple lines of a Greek vase, but its figured decorations are lost to me.

So on this, my second day of sight, I should try to probe into the soul of man through his art. The things I knew through touch I should now see. More splendid still, the whole magnificent world of painting would be opened to me, from the Italian Primitives, with their serene religious devotion, to the Moderns, with their feverish visions. I should look deep into the canvases of Raphael, Leonardo da Vinci, Titian, Rembrandt. I should want to feast my eyes upon the warm colors of Veronese, study the mysteries of El Greco, catch a new vision of Nature from Corot. Oh, there is so much rich meaning and beauty in the art of the ages for you who have eyes to see!

Upon my short visit to this temple of art I should not be able to review a fraction of that great world of art which is open to you. I should be able to get only a superficial impression. Artists tell me that for a deep and true appreciation of art one must educate the eye. One must learn through experience to weigh the merits of line, of composition, of form and color. If I had eyes, how happily would I embark upon so fascinating a study! Yet I am told that, to many of you who have eyes to see, the world of art is a dark night, unexplored and unilluminated.

It would be with extreme reluctance that I should leave the Metropolitan Museum, which contains the key to beauty—a beauty so neglected. Seeing persons, however, do not need a Metropolitan to find this key to beauty. The same key lies waiting in smaller museums, and in books on the shelves of even small libraries. But naturally, in my limited time of imaginary sight, I should choose the place where the key unlocks the greatest treasures in the shortest time.

The evening of my second day of sight I should spend at a theater or at the movies. Even now I often attend theatrical performances of all sorts, but the action of the play must be spelled into my hand by a companion. But how I should like to see with my own eyes the fascinating figure of Hamlet, or the gusty Falstaff amid colorful Elizabethan trappings! How I should like to follow each movement of the graceful Hamlet, each strut of the hearty Falstaff! And since I could see only one play, I should be confronted by the many-horned dilemma, for there are scores of plays I should want to see. You who have eyes can see any you like. How many of you, I wonder, when you gaze at a play, a movie, or any spectacle, realize and give thanks for the miracle of sight which enables you to enjoy its color, grace, and movement?

I cannot enjoy the beauty of rhythmic movement except in a sphere restricted to the touch of my hands. I can vision only dimly the grace of a Pavlova, although I know something of the delight of rhythm, for often I can sense the beat of music as it vibrates through the floor. I can well imagine that cadenced motion must be one of the most pleasing sights in the world. I have been able to gather something of this by tracing with my fingers the lines in sculptured marble; if this static grace can be so lovely, how much more acute must be the thrill of seeing grace in motion.

One of my dearest memories is of the time when Joseph Jefferson allowed me to touch his face and hands as he went through some of the gestures and speeches of his beloved Rip Van Winkle. I was able to catch thus a meager glimpse of the world of drama, and I shall never forget the delight of that moment. But, oh, how much I must miss, and how much pleasure you seeing ones can derive from watching and hearing the interplay of speech and movement in the unfolding of a dramatic performance! If I could see only one play, I should know how to picture in my mind the action of a hundred plays which I have read or had transferred to me through the medium of the manual alphabet.

So, through the evening of my second imaginary day of sight, the great figures of dramatic literature would crowd sleep from my eyes.

The following morning, I should again greet the dawn, anxious to discover new delights, for I am sure that, for those who have eyes which really see, the dawn of each day must be a perpetually new revelation of beauty.

This, according to the terms of my imagined miracle, is to be my third and last day of sight. I shall have no time to waste in regrets or longings; there is too much to see. The first day I devoted to my friends, animate and inanimate. The second revealed to me the history of man and Nature. Today I shall spend in the workaday world of the present, amid the haunts of men going about the business of life. And where can one find so many activities and conditions of men as in New York? So the city becomes my destination.

I start from my home in the quiet little suburb of Forest Hills, Long Island. Here, surrounded by green lawns, trees, and flowers, are neat little houses, happy with the voices and movements of wives and children, havens of peaceful rest for men who toil in the city. I drive across the lacy structure of steel which spans the East River, and I get a new and startling vision of the power and ingenuity of the mind of man. Busy boats chug and scurry about the river — racy speedboats, stolid, snorting tugs. If I had long days of sight ahead, I should spend many of them watching the delightful activity upon the river.

I look ahead, and before me rise the fantastic towers of New York, a city that seems to have stepped from the pages of a fairy story. What an awe-inspiring sight, these glittering spires, these vast banks of stone and steel—structures such as the gods might build for themselves! This animated picture is a part of the lives of millions of people every day. How many, I wonder, give it so much as a second glance? Very few, I fear. Their eyes are blind to this magnificent sight because it is so familiar to them.

I hurry to the top of one of those gigantic structures, the Empire State Building, for there, a short time ago, I "saw" the city below through the eyes of my secretary. I am anxious to compare my fancy with reality. I am sure I should not be disappointed in the panorama spread out before me, for to me it would be a vision of another world.

Now I begin my rounds of the city. First, I stand at a busy corner, merely looking at people, trying by sight of them to understand something of their lives. I see smiles, and I am happy. I see determination, and I am proud. I see suffering, and I am compassionate.

I stroll down Fifth Avenue. I throw my eyes out of focus so that I see no particular object but only a seething kaleidoscope of color. I am certain that the colors of women's dresses moving in a throng must be a gorgeous spectacle of which I should never tire. But perhaps if I had sight I should be like most other women—too interested in styles and the cut of individual dresses to give much attention to the splendor of color in the mass. And I am convinced, too, that I should become an inveterate window shopper, for it must be a delight to the eye to view the myriad articles of beauty on display.

From Fifth Avenue I make a tour of the city—to Park Avenue, to the slums, to factories, to parks where children play. I take a stay-at-home trip abroad by visiting the foreign quarters. Always my eyes are open wide to all the sights of both happiness and misery so that I may probe deep and add to my understanding of how people work and live. My heart is full of the images of people and things. My eye passes lightly over no single trifle; it strives to touch and hold closely each thing its gaze rests upon. Some sights are pleasant, filling the heart with happiness; but some are miserably pathetic. To these latter I do not shut my eyes, for they, too, are part of life. To close the eye on them is to close the heart and mind.

My third day of sight is drawing to an end. Perhaps there are many serious pursuits to which I should devote the few remaining hours, but I am afraid that on the evening of that last day I should again run away to the theater, to a hilariously funny play, so that I might appreciate the overtones of comedy in the human spirit.

At midnight my temporary respite from blindness would cease, and permanent night would close in on me again. Naturally in those three short days I should not have seen all I wanted to see. Only when darkness had again descended upon me should I realize how much I had left unseen. But my mind would be so crowded with glorious memories that I should have little time for regrets. Thereafter the touch of every object would bring a glowing memory of how that object looked.

Perhaps this short outline of how I should spend three days of sight does not agree with the program you would set for yourself if you knew that you were about to be stricken blind. I am, however, sure that if you actually faced that fate your eyes would open to things you had never seen before, storing up memories for the long night ahead. You would use your eyes as never before. Everything you saw would become dear to you. Your eyes would touch and embrace every object that came within your range of vision. Then, at last, you would really see, and a new world of beauty would open itself before you.

I who am blind can give one hint to those who see—one admonition to those who would make full use of the gift of sight: Use your eyes as if tomorrow you would be stricken blind. And the same method can be applied to the other senses. Hear the music of voices, the song of a bird, the mighty strains of an orchestra, as if you would be stricken deaf tomorrow. Touch each object you want to touch as if tomorrow your tactile sense would fail. Smell the perfume of flowers, taste with relish each morsel, as if tomorrow you could never smell and taste again. Make the most of every sense; glory in all the facets of pleasure and beauty which the world reveals to you through the several means of contact which Nature provides. But of all the senses, I am sure that sight must be the most delightful.

Questions but No Answers on the Incident of the Hurled Ashtray

Nora Ephron explores what she thinks about an incident that occurred in a restaurant in London. This is a superb example of an exploratory essay in which the writer clearly does not have an opinion, clearly has not made up her mind about a subject, and just lets the reader go with her as she explores the issue at hand.

I once heard a swell story about Gary Cooper. The person I heard the story from did this terrific Gary Cooper imitation, and it may be that when I tell you the story (which I am about to), it will lose something in print. It may lose everything, in fact. But enough. The story was that Gary Cooper was in a London restaurant at a large table of friends. He was sitting in a low chair, with his back to the rest of the room, so no one in the restaurant even knew that he was tall, much less that he was Gary Cooper. Across the way was a group of Teddy boys (this episode took place long long ago, you see), and they were all misbehaving and making nasty remarks about a woman at Cooper's table. Cooper turned around to give them his best mean-and-threatening stare, but they went right on. Finally he got up, very very slowly, so slowly that it took almost a minute for him to go from this short person in a low chair to a ten-foot-tall man with Gary Cooper's head on top of his shoulders. He loped over to the table of Teddy boys, looked down at them, and said, "Wouldja mind sayin' that agin?" The men were utterly cowed and left the restaurant shortly thereafter.

Well, you had to be there.

I thought of Gary Cooper and his way with words the other day. Longingly. Because in the mail, from an editor of *New York* magazine, came an excerpt from a book by Michael Korda called *Male Chauvinism: How It Works* (Random House). I have no idea whether Korda's book is any good at all, but the excerpt was fascinating, a sort of reverse-twist update of Francis Macomber, as well as a pathetic contrast to the Gary Cooper story. It seems that Korda, his wife, and another woman were having dinner in a London restaurant recently. Across the way was a table of drunks doing sensitive things like sniggering and leering and throwing bread balls at Mrs. Korda, who is a looker. Her back was to them, and she refused to acknowledge their presence, instead apparently choosing to let the flying bread balls bounce off her back onto the floor. Then, one of the men sent over a waiter with a silver tray. On it was a printed card, the kind you can buy in novelty shops, which read: "I want to sleep with you! Tick off your favorite love position from the list below, and return this card with your telephone number. . . ." Korda tore up the card before his wife could even see it, and then, consumed with rage, he picked up an ashtray and threw it at the man who had sent the card. A fracas ensued, and before long, Korda, his wife, and their woman friend were out on the street. Mrs. Korda was furious.

"If you ever do that again," she screamed, "I'll leave you! Do you think I couldn't have handled that, or ignored it? Did I ask you to come to my defense against some poor stupid drunk? You didn't even think, you just reacted like a male chauvinist. You leapt up to defend *your* woman, *your* honor, you made me seem cheap and foolish and powerless. . . . God Almighty, can't you see it was none of your business! Can't you understand how it makes me feel? I don't mind being hassled by some drunk, I can take that, but to be treated like a chattel, to be robbed of any right to decide for myself whether I'd been insulted, or how badly, to have you react for me because I'm *your* woman . . . that's really sickening, it's like being a slave." Korda repeats the story (his wife's diatribe is even longer in the original version) and then, in a *mea culpa* that is only too reminiscent of the sort that used to appear in 1960s books by white liberals about blacks, he concludes that his wife is doubtless right, that men do tend to treat women merely as appendages of themselves.

Before printing the article, *New York* asked several couples—including my husband and me—what our reaction was to what happened, and what we would have done under the circumstances. My initial reaction to the entire business was that no one ever sends me notes like that in restaurants. I sent that off to the editor, but a few days later I got to thinking about the story, and it began to seem to me that the episode just might be a distillation of everything that has happened to men and women as a result of the women's movement, and if not that, at least a way to write about etiquette after the revolution, and if not that, nothing at all. Pulled as I was by these three possibilities, I told the story over dinner to four friends and asked for their reaction. The first, a man, said that he thought Mrs. Korda was completely right. The second, a woman, said she thought Korda's behavior was totally understandable. The third, a man said that both parties had behaved badly. The fourth, my friend Martha, said it was the second most boring thing she had ever heard, the most boring being a story I had just told her about a fight my college roommate had with a cabdriver at Kennedy Airport.

In any case, before any serious discussion of the incident of the hurled ashtray, I would like to raise some questions for which I have no answers. I raise them simply because if that story were fed into a computer, the only possible response it could make is We Do Not Have Sufficient Information to Make an Evaluation. For example:

Do the Kordas have a good marriage?

Was the heat working in their London hotel room the night of the fracas?

Was it raining out?

What did the second woman at the table look like? Was she as pretty as Mrs. Korda? Was she ugly? Was part of Michael Korda's reaction—and his desire to assert possession of his wife—the result of the possibility that he suspected the drunks thought he was with someone funny-looking?

What kind of a tacky restaurant is it where a waiter delivers a dirty message on a silver tray?

What about a woman who ignores flying bread balls? Wasn't her husband justified in thinking she would be no more interested in novelty cards?

Did Michael Korda pay the check before or after throwing the ashtray? Did he tip the standard 15 percent?

Since the incident occurs in London, a city notorious for its rampant homoerotic behavior, and since the table of drunks was all male, isn't it possible that the printed card was in fact intended not for Mrs. Korda but for Michael? In which case how should we now view his response, if at all?

There might be those who would raise questions about the ashtray itself: was it a big, heavy ashtray, these people might ask, or a dinky little round one? Was it glass or was it plastic? These questions are irrelevant.

In the absence of answers to any of the above, I would nonetheless like to offer some random musings. First, I think it is absurd for Mrs. Korda to think that she and she alone was involved in the incident. Yes, it might have been nice had her husband consulted her; and yes, it would have been even nicer had he turned out to be Gary Cooper, or failing that, Dave DeBusschere, or even Howard Cosell—anyone but this suave flinger of ashtrays he turned out to be. But the fact remains that the men at the table *were* insulting Korda, and disturbing his dinner, as well as hers. Their insult was childish and Korda's reaction was ludicrous, but Mrs. Korda matched them all by reducing a complicated and rather interesting emotional situation to a tedious set of movement platitudes.

Beyond that—and the Kordas quite aside, because God Almighty (as Mrs. Korda might put it) knows what it is they are into—I wonder whether there is any response a man could make in that situation which would not disappoint a feminist. Yes, I want to be treated as an equal and not as an appendage or possession or spare rib, but I also want to be taken care of. Isn't any man sitting at a table with someone like me damned whatever he does? If the drunks in question are simply fools, conventioneers with funny paper hats, I suppose that a possible reaction would be utter cool. But if they were truly insulting and disturbing, some response does seem called for. Some wild and permanent gesture of size. But on whose part? And what should it consist of? And how tall do you have to be to bring it off? And where is the point that a mild show of strength becomes crude macho vulgarity; where does reserve veer off into passivity?

Like almost every other question in this column, I have no positive answer. But I think that if I ever found myself in a similar situation, and if it was truly demeaning, I would prefer that my husband handle it. My husband informs me, after some consideration, that the Gary Cooper approach would not work. But he could, for example, call over the captain and complain discreetly, perhaps even ask that our table be moved. He could hire a band of aging Teddy boys to find out where the drunks were staying and short-sheet all their beds. Or—and I think I prefer this—he could produce, from his jacket pocket, a printed card from a novelty shop reading: "I'm terribly sorry, but as you can see by looking at our dinner companion, my wife and I have other plans."

I'm going out to have those cards made up right now.

Fling

In this exploratory essay, a student, Karen Davis, plays with the word fling. *Her instructor challenged her to take the single word and see what kind of essay would finally emerge after she thought about the subject for a while. This is the result of her exploration.*

CONTEXT: *Written as an imitation of an Art Buchwald newspaper column*

AUDIENCE: *The general reader of newspapers*

I just came to a profound realization about the English language. No, the idea didn't just walk up and tap me on the shoulder; well, in a way I guess it did. But it didn't walk up by itself—somebody sent it.

The idea is this: There are certain words that we all know (we can pronounce, spell, and even define them) although we never say, write, read, see, hear, taste, or smell them. Take, for example, the word *fling*.

Now the person who sent this idea to me was a teacher who suggested that I write a paper on *fling*. We all know about teachers and their suggestions for papers. Well, this was, by far, the weirdest suggestion I have met yet.

After struggling with, "What in the world am I going to say about *fling*," I realized what a non-word *fling* is. I felt the tap on my shoulder.

Just think about it a while. Would you stroll over to a friend and say, "I'm having a *fling*"? Or would you approach a friend and say, "I'd love to have a *fling* with you"? How about "I think I'll *fling* my coat on that chair"? Or "I bet you can't *fling* that frisbee this far"? It's just one of those words that never comes to mind.

As a matter of fact, I can't think of one single place where I could go to find the word *fling*. (Oh sure, I could find it in a dictionary, but that's cheating.) What book, magazine, store, ball park, joint, place, gang of people could I go to and be sure to find or hear the word *fling?* I can't think of a single place. Unless maybe it's a group of actresses. They always seem to be flinging themselves in distress somewhere—onto couches, into beds, over cliffs. . . .

Maybe that's it. Maybe the word is just too dramatic for normal people, too simple for snooty people, and too useless for scientists and such. That's fine. But why do all us simple, everyday people even *know* the word?

I've got it. Remember in first grade doing those drills—ring, sing, ping, sting, ding, king, wing, *fling*. I just bet that's how it all got started. I don't use *ping* or *ding* very often either.

Now that I think about it, I probably even thought fling was an O.K. word for a little while. Until seventh grade. If there's one thing that will make a word useless and not O.K. it's an unusual conjugation. You know, like *fling*. I'm still not sure if it's fling, flang, flung or what. That type of thing can make any word disappear real fast, if it's too hard to use.

I wonder how long it will be before another profound realization is flung (flinged? flanged?) at me?

Writing Your Own Exploratory Essay

1. CONTEXTS
Choose one of the following contexts for your own exploratory essay. Write your context and audience at the top of your first page.

A

You've just been elected to the House of Representatives from your Congressional District. While in high school, you were very active in student council—you never held an elected office but you served on many committees and were famous for keeping the student body informed of the council's projects and getting their support. Now, twenty-five years later, you have been asked to give the keynote address to your state's association of student councils. At a time when school administrations and students themselves are questioning the worth of student government, high school students, council sponsors, teachers, and administrators have come to hear your speech. Write the speech you would give to this audience. Remember that the speech is merely exploratory—you don't want to tell all schools what they should do because you don't know about every situation and don't feel qualified— you're just exploring the value of your past experiences to you and the possibilities for modern-day student councils.

B

Your state legislature is considering raising the legal drinking age from eighteen to twenty-one. The editor of your school newspaper isn't sure whether this move would be good or bad. As a matter of fact, restrictions from the administration wouldn't allow the school newspaper to print an article which takes a stand on this particular issue. As a reporter, you get the assignment to write an article for the newspaper exploring the pros and cons of raising the legal drinking age. Remember, your audience is the readers of your newspaper who want to know how this issue could affect them and the school administrators will also be reading

to make sure you're totally objective. (And don't forget those businesses that advertise in the paper who sell alcoholic beverages!)

C

Your best friend is really disturbed. He's living at home and is in his third semester at the local community college. He's passed all of his courses but he's not sure what he wants to get a degree in or what he wants to do. He just wrote you a letter asking what you think he ought to do. He's considering joining the Navy or continuing in college. You're hesitant to give advice. You went away to the state university and have had different experiences than he has. But you've got to answer the letter because you want this friend to know that you're really concerned. You decide that the best thing to do is to write a letter that explores the possibilities of the Navy and college, but that's all you do. You don't want to say which is better or worse because you honestly don't know. Write the letter.

D

You've just won the *Reader's Digest* Sweepstakes for $100,000. The editor of the magazine has asked you to write an article exploring what you can do with this money. The editor is planning a special May issue on "After Graduation: What Next" and is interested in your article for this issue. Many graduates say, "If I only had the money," and your approach on what to do when you get the money will add a different twist to this issue.

2. CREATING

If you can't decide which context to choose, try looping the contexts to see what emerges. When you've chosen your context, do one of the three creating techniques to get ideas for your essay. Since the exploratory essay is looking at a subject from different angles, cubing might seem a natural technique to you. Or since it's totally objective, classical invention with its matter-of-fact approach might feel right for you. The only thing you have to do right now, however, is to generate ideas for your essay. Choose your technique and enjoy creating for at least forty-five minutes.

3. SHAPING

A. Make your preliminary agreements. Evaluate your exact audience in terms of your specific purpose.
B. Write a thesis statement aimed at that audience. Check the thesis against the checkpoints. Be sure you have something to say.
C. Select and use only those ideas that explore your thesis for your audience. If an idea doesn't fit the purpose *and* the audience, don't use it.
D. Do a Bare Bones outline after your trial draft.
E. Read your paper out loud to somebody. Find a different person and have him or her read your paper out loud to you. Are you hearing what you thought you said? Is it interesting? Clear? Easy to follow?

4. COMPLETING

On this essay you will have a chance to do a complete revision: for flow, for energy, and for punch. Since the subject matter itself won't require so much thought—say, the way an evaluation essay might—you can afford to spend a little extra time on the revisions. Take time to polish this essay. See what you can do with replacement of words, with combinations of sentences, with flair in the use of function paragraphs. Read the essay aloud to several people and get their reactions. If it is possible, let the essay cool for several days before you look at it again; many refinements will just jump out at you if the words are cold enough for you to approach them with fresh eyes. Give this essay a thorough going over in the Completing Stage. When you are happy with the revisions—or when time runs out, whichever occurs first—put the essay in good form, check for correctness, and pass along to your readers, knowing that you have done the best job possible.

FINAL CONSIDERATIONS

You have now done your final revising. *You have revised for flow*—to see that the thought runs smoothly and continuously throughout the essay. *You have revised for energy*—putting sentences in the best order possible, changing phrases to get the emphasis on just the right thing, cutting words to have the writing lean and to the point. *You have revised for punch*—using words that produce pictures for the reader and giving the exact word to capture an elusive thought. Though you could probably tinker with the essay indefinitely, improving the style or being just a centimeter more exact (writers almost never feel that they are *really* through), you know that at this point the writing contains a message that is stated clearly and directed specifically toward your reader. You are now ready to EDIT the paper and make the final copy to send to the reader.

EDITING

It is at this point that you start looking for errors and mistakes, for it is absolutely in your own best interest to make the paper perfect. Wouldn't it be terrible to have done all this work—made all these revisions and rough drafts—and then leave careless errors in the writing that will cause your reader to think you are a sloppy writer? Very likely the mistakes and errors in your writing will fall into one of a very few categories. And although it's true that there are really hundreds of possibilities, you've eliminated most of them by the careful three-stage process you've gone through. This means that, thanks to your good and careful work, most likely the errors will be one of these:

MOST LIKELY PLACES TO LOOK FOR ERRORS

1 Misspelled words (or typing errors or handwriting errors).
2 Apostrophes left out or put in the wrong place.
3 Punctuation errors and omissions—particularly commas left out or in the wrong place.
4 Sentence fragments.
5 Run-together sentences.

When you think about it, that isn't a very long list to have to check on. Of course, you may have a long history with any of those errors— perhaps extending back to elementary school days. So we suggest two things: First, study the information in the Handbook section that applies to your particular errors and **learn the principles once and for all.** Chances are almost nil that these principles will change in your lifetime, so once you learn them, that's it. *Learn the rules and you'll never have to learn them again.* The second recommendation is to **read the paper out loud to someone else.** This small thing—reading the paper out loud—could actually be the secret to finding errors and mistakes in your work before you turn it in for final evaluation. You can just about be certain that if you stumble over something when you are reading it, there *is* something there to fix. Countless times students, when they are

SUGGESTIONS:
1 Learn the rules *you* need to know.
2 Read your paper *out loud* to somebody else.

reading their papers out loud to other members of the class, are overheard to say something like "Oh, I left part of that sentence out" or "I didn't say what I thought I did or meant to say there; I'll fix it before I turn it in." Reading out loud will catch a lot of your mistakes.

The third thing you can do is **have someone else proofread your paper for you.** It is *very* difficult for the person who has written a paper to see mistakes in it. For one thing, the eye compensates for letters left out or words missing, and your brain will just fill in the blanks. Since you, the writer, *know* what you are saying, the words don't actually have to be there on the page for you to *think* them as you read. Also, you may not know certain principles of correctness (like commas or apostrophes) and it may take you a few weeks to learn these rules. In the meantime, your papers have to be evaluated. So get someone who is good at catching errors to go over your paper with you before you turn it in.

Finally, the most important thing we can say about mistakes and errors in your writing is **BE AWARE.** Experience repeatedly shows that the problem isn't that students *can't learn* these things—it is just that they are not *conscious* of them. They don't realize how important the completing stage is in the writing process. They don't know that they create their own failure by being inconsiderate and passing on mistakes and errors that the reader has to cope with—something that the reader isn't willing to do. (The reader's word to you, the writer, is "That falls into *your* territory. *You* get it cleaned up and right if you want *me* to take *my* time to read it.") So, many writers are just plain *unaware,* and that is their downfall. **If you will just be *aware*—awake and conscious—of the lurking problems you *might* have with grammar mistakes, spelling errors, etc., you will be ahead of about half of all the people who are studying how to write.**

MANUSCRIPT FORM

When you have checked your paper for errors and oversights, you are ready to write or type the very final copy for presentation to the reader. *Now you want to think about the way the writing is going to look on the page.* Be alert to this! As in editing, don't let carelessness or laziness cause you to do a half-way job. Nobody would spend hours building a beautiful walnut bookcase and then display it at a craft fair with sawdust and garbage all over it. **The way your paper *looks* will have a considerable psychological effect on the reader.** And while a good-looking paper with no content won't get you anywhere, a paper with excellent content but a sloppy appearance usually won't either. You can't win *either* way on this one. It has to be *both.* Good content + good appearance = success with reader.

The total is equal to the *sum* of its parts. Period! Parts alone don't make it.

Whether your paper is handwritten or typewritten, there are some conventions that you should always observe:

1. **Make your paper as neat as possible.** Erase carefully, and when-

ever possible, use correction fluid instead of an eraser. Correction fluid is especially good for long corrections.

2. **Use one side of the paper only.**

3. **Use standard size (8″ × 10½″ or 8½″ × 11″) ruled paper if you are handwriting, or 8½″ × 11″ unruled paper if you are typing.** Do not use legal size, colored, or spiral-notebook paper or cheap typing paper.

4. **Always number your pages.**

Making a Handwritten Paper As Attractive As Possible:

1. **Always use a black or blue ball-point pen.** Do not use felt-tip markers; they tend to make your writing too bold and unattractive. Never use pencil for the final copy. It suggests that the paper is not yet in final form.

2. **Write neatly and legibly.** Remember that if your reader doesn't understand your writing, he or she is not likely to pay attention to your message. If double spacing makes your handwriting easier to read, then double space—but make sure your teacher doesn't object to this.

3. **If you have a title for the writing, put it on the top line of the first page.** Skip at least one line, preferably two or three, before beginning the text of your paper. If you don't have a title, begin on the second or third line of the page.

4. **Follow the margin on the left side of the paper and leave at least a half-inch margin on the right. Don't write on the last line of the page.** Your words should neither bleed off the right nor fall off the bottom edge of the page.

How to Make a Typewritten Paper Look Professional:

1. **Always double space when you type.** Single spacing is difficult to read.

2. **Use good quality paper.** It is difficult to read material typed on cheap typing paper or onionskin paper. Do not use erasable bond. Its finish, which makes erasures easy, also makes smudging more likely. Besides, unless you erase very carefully and professionally, erasures

will still be noticeable and will often be messy. If you plan to type most of your papers, invest in several hundred sheets of good-quality typing paper bought at a book or office supply store, not at the local grocery store.

3. **Use a good black or blue ribbon.** Change your ribbon when it begins to look faint. A paper typed using a worn-out ribbon is difficult to read. Do not use italics or script characters except for special effects. See that the type in your typewriter is clean.

4. **Leave at least one-inch margins all around.** If you will bind your paper in a folder, the left margin should be slightly wider to avoid making that side of the page look cramped once it is in the folder. The top margin on the first page should always be about two inches. Type the title; then triple space before beginning the body of the paper.

How foolish it is to court disaster by not taking into account every *psychological* as well as rhetorical aspect of how a written message gets from the writer to the reader. Errors and sloppy appearance are so easy to fix that they should *never* be the cause of a person's failing to get your message. *Don't let it happen.* Value your message and your time too much! Play by every "rule" in the book that contributes to your writing being a success.

The important thing once again—in editing as well as in anything else—is **THINK OF YOUR READER.** Let everything about your writing—appearance, correctness, message, form—contribute to the message's *getting across.*

WRITING ASSIGNMENT: THE ASSERTION-WITH-PROOF ESSAY

Assert:
To state positively with great confidence.

Proof:
Facts, examples, information so certain or convincing as to demonstrate the validity of a conclusion beyond reasonable doubt.

We all know somebody whom we can always count on to be making loud assertions, but who usually is just blowing off steam: there's no proof behind the declarations. Of course, as you saw in the personal viewpoint essay, there are occasions when a writer is expected to give her or his opinion and is not expected to substantiate that opinion in any way at all. No proof is required because the writer has clearly been given the opportunity to just sound off. Unless you are writing for one of these distinct occasions when a personal viewpoint essay is appropriate, however, you need to back up all your assertions with proof that will convince your readers that you are right. Sometimes that proof will be documentation from research; sometimes it will be carefully developed and logical discussion; sometimes it will be examples that the readers can check if they so desire. The stronger the proof, the quicker your assertion will be accepted by the reader.

As you look over the assertion-with-proof essays that follow, you will discover that the most convincing and well-written ones have these characteristics:

1 The assertion is clearly stated early in the essay.
2 The proof follows quickly and is obviously in support of the assertion.
3 The proof consists of facts, examples, information that the readers can check or of discussion so logical and convincing that the readers accept it without argument.
4 There is *sufficient* proof cited to convince the reader.

Ask yourself these questions as you read the assertion-with-proof essays below. Be ready to discuss your answers in class.

—Where does the assertion appear in the essay?
—What kind of proof does the writer cite?
—Is the proof convincing?

READINGS:

Running Can Decrease Heart Attacks

In this assertion-with-proof essay, Peter Wood cites evidence that runners are less likely to have a heart attack than persons who do not run. Are you convinced by his proof?

Though it is a rather undistinguished town of some 45,000 souls, Framingham, Mass., is of increasing importance to runners. Many will recognize it as the seven-mile point on the Boston Marathon course. More importantly, though, it is the site of a long-range health study, and what this study has revealed about cholesterol and the heart is having far-reaching impact on runners.

About 20 years ago, the U.S. Government funded a "prospective" health study in Framingham. A prospective investigation focuses on a large and representative group of people. They initially undergo various tests and complete questionnaires after which the investigators wait around to see who gets sick or dies of what and when. From this monumental study, we know that people who have high blood pressure, smoke cigarettes and are overweight are considerably more likely to develop heart disease than lean nonsmokers with normal blood pressures. And those with high blood cholesterol levels are more likely to suffer heart attacks later on than those with lower levels. And so the Framingham study became the cornerstone of the belief that high cholesterol is dangerous and has led thousands of physicians to counsel millions of patients: "Get your cholesterol down."

For many years the theory of what constituted "risk factors" for heart attack remained the same: high blood pressure, smoking, excess weight and high blood cholesterol. Runners scored pretty well on the first three, being characteristically normotensive, nonsmoking and lean. But cholesterol? There was little evidence to suggest that runners showed much advantage here. And so it remained until 1975 when the awareness of a new risk factor, high density lipoprotein, rose spectacularly, like a comet in the epidemiological sky. To see how this relates to Framingham, cholesterol and runners, we need to make a brief excursion into physiology.

There are two fatty substances that our bodies need and make, and which are important in any discussion of heart disease: cholesterol and triglycerides. Cholesterol is a vital part of our cell walls and is the raw material from which we make bile acids and the sex hormones.

Triglycerides are a compact form of energy, stored in our fat tissue. We need to move these two materials about the body, but there is a problem: The great transport system of the body — the blood — is largely water, while cholesterol and triglycerides do not dissolve in water. Nature has solved this problem by packaging cholesterol and triglycerides together with protein as minute particles called "lipoproteins."

To understand what cholesterol is doing to our arteries, and what our "cholesterol level" really means, we have to appreciate that cholesterol comes packaged in three different forms or families of lipoprotein particles. All these particles are minute (you need an electron microscope to see them), but some are bigger than others. They are classified by their *density*. The largest and least dense are the very low density lipoproteins, or VLDL. Next come the middle-sized low density lipoproteins, or LDL, and finally, the small high density lipoproteins, or HDL. All three particles contain protein.

The large VLDL carry most of the triglycerides, so a high blood triglyceride level means a high VLDL level. On the other hand, cholesterol is carried by both LDL and HDL particles, so that a high blood cholesterol can mean a high LDL, a high HDL or both. A small amount of cholesterol is also carried in the VLDL particles, but we will forget this for the sake of simplicity.

None of this would matter to most of us if these particles had no effect on our health, or if they all had the same effect. But recent medical research has shown clearly that the three particles have different effects. The health consequences of high levels of VLDL are not very clear, but the available evidence suggests low levels are preferable. The middle-sized LDL particles have a longer and more sobering medical history. It has for many years been known that high levels of LDL particles in the blood are associated with (and probably cause) hardening of the arteries (atherosclerosis) and eventually heart attacks. When LDL concentrations are extremely high, as in a rare inherited disease called homozygous familial hypercholesterolemia, the sufferer (if untreated) typically dies in his early 20s of heart attack. So all of us would prefer relatively low levels of LDL.

Finally there is HDL, the smallest and most dense cholesterol-carrying particle. For many years the level of these particles was measured in experiments and the results filed and forgotten. It wasn't clear where they fit into the picture. Then, in 1975, two brothers, Miller and Miller, in England, pulled together a number of lines of evidence indicating that *high* levels of HDL seemed to be associated with *fewer* heart attacks.

• Women (with much less heart disease than men) have *lower* than average HDL levels.

• Populations with high heart attack rates (for instance, the Scots) tend to have *low* average HDLs; those with low rates (Jamaican farmers, Greenlander Eskimos) have *high* average HDLs.

• Heart attack victims turn out to have *lower* than average HDL levels.

• Laboratory animals that are traditionally resistant to experimental heart attack, such as the rat and the dog, have high HDL levels and low LDL levels in their blood.

The evidence continues to come in and the "HDL hypothesis" has become a favorite subject of discussion in heart disease research circles.

It is an unusual risk factor because the more of it you have, the better a so-called "negative risk factor." At present it is not proven that low HDL levels *cause* atherosclerosis and heart attacks. But there is evidence that LDL may lead to trouble, and HDL may help to prevent it. Try to imagine billions of these tiny lipoprotein particles—"large VLDL, intermediate LDL and small HDL—rushing through our blood system, jostling the larger red blood cells, constantly bombarding the inner walls of our arteries, driven relentlessly on by the beating heart. According to current thinking, some of the LDL particles penetrate the inner walls of the arteries and deposit their cholesterol, which over the years leads to atherosclerosis and (if the coronary arteries of the heart are affected) heart attacks. This is much more likely to occur if the concentration of LDL particles in blood is generally high over many years. The HDL particles, on the other hand, are pictured as scavengers, constantly scouring the inner artery walls and picking up the potentially damaging cholesterol to be returned to the liver for removal in the bile, via the stool. With this model in mind we can see why high LDL is bad for hearts, while high HDL is probably beneficial.

A final point to remember is that cholesterol riding on the three types of lipoprotein particles adds up to the familiar "total cholesterol count." We can see how a total cholesterol value is hiding a good deal of information. For instance, two people with identical total cholesterol counts of 220 milligrams might turn out to have very different lipoprotein make-ups:

	SUBJECT A	SUBJECT B
VLDL	25 mg	25 mg
LDL	120 mg	170 mg
HDL	75 mg	25 mg
	220 mg	220 mg

Clearly, the *risk* of heart attack is considerably greater for subject B than for subject A, because of the lower HDL levels and higher LDL levels.

As the HDL story was unfolding, my Stanford co-workers, Drs. Bill Haskell and John Farquahar and I were looking at the lipoproteins of groups of male and female runners aged 35-59. To qualify as a "runner," each participant needed to have run at least 15 miles per week on average for the past year. The men reported an average of 40 miles run per week, the women 35 miles. We compared 41 male runners and 43 female runners with larger numbers of typical men and women of similar age selected randomly from towns in Northern California. These controls were generally quite sedentary in their habits. The runners had slightly lower total cholesterol levels, but the differences were hardly exciting for either sex. Looking at the villainous LDL, we found the levels to be gratifyingly lower in the runners. And finally we examined the "good guys," the HDL. Levels were much higher in the runners than in the sedentary control groups. Thus, the pattern of lipoproteins in the runners predicts a considerably lower-than-average risk of developing heart disease.

In recent years the Framingham study, under Dr. William Castelli, has been looking at the future health consequences of high and low HDL levels. Dr. Castelli believes that the single most powerful predictor of risk of heart disease that we can get from blood measurements is the ratio: Total Cholesterol/Cholesterol in HDL.

The Framingham researchers compared the frequency of heart disease at various Total Cholesterol/HDL ratios. They found that the higher the ratio, and thus the lower the HDL, the greater the heart disease rate. The following table shows how the risk of developing heart disease varies with this ratio, and also where the middle-aged male runners and sedentary males in our Stanford study fit in.

GROUP	
Framingham males with:	TOTAL CHOLESTEROL
	HDL-CHOLESTEROL
Twice average risk of heart disease	9.6
Average risk of heart disease	5.0
Half average risk of heart disease	3.4
Stanford male runners	3.1
Stanford male controls	4.9

It is clear from these figures that our male sedentary group had much the same score (4.9) as that of Framingham males with average risk of heart disease. But our male runners' score of 3.1 was comparable to that of the "half average risk" group in the Framingham study. The women runners were also well placed, with less than half the risk of average Framingham women. Of course, women (runners or not) show much lower heart disease figures than men of similar age. A fascinating aspect of these results is that the lipoprotein pattern shown by the running men (high HDL, low LDL) is very similar to that generally shown by women. So running appears to convert the male cholesterol pattern to that of the female, which is beneficial from the heart disease point of view.

There are a number of other factors which could explain our findings, but we have ruled out most of them. For instance, runners are predictably quite lean, in contrast to the rather alarming frequency of obesity in this country. (I weigh 125 pounds—if I were "average" for my height, age and sex, I should weigh 175.) The current feeling among researchers is that the leanness of active individuals contributes to, but does not entirely explain, the excellent lipoprotein status of runners. If we could study a large group of lean but sedentary individuals, or a group of fat, long-time runners, we could investigate this question fully; but as you can imagine, such groups are hard to find! It is also true that runners seldom smoke, so it is possible that not smoking raises HDL. The Framingham study found that smokers have lower HDLs than non-smokers, but this may be because the nonsmokers tend to be more active.

Finally, the possibility remains that runners eat differently from sedentary people. Some recent work of ours has shed light on this possibility. After looking at diet records completed by runners and sedentary controls we conclude that runners (at least, our 35-59 year olds) eat much the same as everyone else—the same proportions of fat, carbohydrate, protein, cholesterol and so on. The exception is caloric intake. Runners consume more calories because they burn more.

Many researchers now say that diet can play a role in raising or lowering LDL levels, but that eating patterns have little effect on HDL levels. This means that exercise, and particularly running, may be the key to raising HDL levels. Incidentally, alcohol appears to raise HDL levels in blood, which brings joy to many drinkers' hearts. But in our study at Stanford, runners consumed alcohol at the same rate as the controls on a per-1000 calorie basis. Thus, the large differences we detected in HDL are associated with running, not drinking.

A final, often asked question is: "Established runners certainly seem to have a good lipoprotein pattern, but does this mean that a sedentary person who adopts an exercise program will undergo the favorable changes?" A considerable amount of work is in progress on this important health question, including a one-year training study in initially sedentary men that our group is conducting at Stanford. Some completed studies show that running does indeed produce such changes, while others contradict this. We need to learn more about the necessary intensity and duration of training before we can give a final answer.

To summarize, recent studies have shown that runners possess a characteristic blood lipoprotein pattern that is now known to be strongly associated with lower risk of developing heart disease and heart attack. This happy situation is on top of the great health benefits already conferred on runners because they are lean nonsmokers with excellent cardiovascular fitness. Once again, the runner appears to be doing the right thing.

La Causa

Felipe V. Ponce, Jr., explains in this essay the cause of the Chicano, or Mexican-American, movement and the direction in which it is going. His assertion is a personal one, and he also gives proof through example and fact.

There is presently a major movement in this country. A movement most of us in the Midwest know little if anything about. It has been coming for centuries, it has been on the conscience of Americans for decades and it is upon us today. The movement is the Chicano movement; its people are Chicanos, Mexican-Americans.

When I have the chance to talk with my fellow students, I like to talk with them about Chicanos and "La Causa," the Cause, because many of us are unaware of the existence of this movement and its people. Many of us don't know of America's second largest minority of nine million Mexican-Americans. Many of us simply gape as we drive down a highway and see fifty or sixty Mexicans stooped over picking tomatoes in a field. Many of us simply gape as we drive through a barrio, a Mexican slum, in northwest Indiana and see substandard living conditions. Many of us simply gape in our Sociology 161 and 163 classes when our "knowledgeable" professor goes on and on about Blacks and anti-Semitism, and it never occurs to us that they're not the only ones who have problems. Everything is not either Black or White, there's a little bit of brown in between. But many of us continue to gape and nothing registers.

I am very much aware of and involved with the movement, first, because I'm a Chicano and, second, because I, like you, have a vital stake in the future of this country. I, like you, must have an awareness of the social ripples around us today which will be tomorrow's waves of action.

There are other reasons why this movement should be understood. If you're interested in politics, nine million people are hard to ignore. If you're interested in social problems, nine million people are hard to ignore. If you're interested in business, a market of nine million people is hard to ignore.

The history of today's Chicano dates back to the time of the Aztecs and other sixteenth-century Indian tribes. They were noble lords of a culture that was one of the high points of civilization. Along came the Spaniards, Christians who looted, murdered, and raped, and for their crimes were promptly knighted. Spaniard and Indian joined and the Mexican was born.

Mexicans in the United States have come through two ways; annexation and immigration. In 1848 most of what we know as the West was taken over by the United States. This included the five states where most Chicanos live today: California, Arizona, Colorado, New Mexico, and Texas. The Mexicans living in these areas became United States citizens whether they wanted to or not. Although there had been immigration, since that time the numbers of Mexicans entering the country were small until the 1900s. Between 1910 and 1930 there was a large influx from Mexico. People were attracted by agriculture, the booming railroad industry, and the industrial paradise of the North. My family, for instance, is fairly typical in the pattern we followed. First wetbacks, illegal entrants, then entering legally, we lived in southern Texas for a few years before we moved to East Chicago. There my father found work in the steel mills.

As I said before, most Chicanos live in the Southwest. One interesting fact is that Los Angeles has the largest concentrated population of Mexicans anywhere, surpassed only by Mexico City itself. In Los Angeles there are almost one million Chicanos. It is known by observation that thousands of Mexicans live in the urban centers in such states as Kansas, Illinois, Indiana, and Michigan to name a few. For instance, in my home town of East Chicago, which has a population of 45,000, there are approximately 14,000 Chicanos.

The problems that we face in the Southwest and throughout the United States are many. There are inequities in education, in employment, in housing — three of the most important necessities in our society. Chicanos average 3.9 years less education than Anglo or white Americans — 1.6 years less than Blacks. In Texas, for example, 80 percent of Chicano students drop out before they graduate from high school. Yet he is expected to obtain an education despite de facto segregated schools or classes, inferior school buildings, and unfair testing procedures. When a rural Chicano student in southern Texas takes an achievement test, it is usually a test based on the reality of Evanston, Illinois, or New Rochelle, New York, rather than Crystal City, Texas, or Oxnard, California. Also the absence of bilingual instructors and the presence of teachers with negative attitudes toward their students help reinforce the secondary status of Mexican students.

Chicanos throughout the Southwest are generally not considered for higher paying jobs or certain job categories and in some cases are not considered for employment at all. Discrimination takes a variety of not-so-obvious forms such as irrelevant testing, unfairness in promotion, and unequal pay. Most Chicanos, especially the older people, do not have the means to challenge these practices and many are unaware of their right to do so.

The U.S. Commission on Civil Rights has extensively documented the fact that there is serious discrimination against Mexicans in the administration of justice, especially in the areas of police brutality, illegal search, and exclusion from juries. On the community level, regular city services such as water, electricity, garbage removal are often lacking in the barrios.

Two major influences created the process that is now known as the Chicano Movement. The first was the growing urbanization that accompanied the mechanization of farming. The second was the development of the California Grape Strike. The California farm workers' strike, led by Cesar Chavez, has served as catalyst in forming the current Chicano movement. Much of the rhetoric and symbolic language of the grape strike has been incorporated into the movement. "La Causa" once meant the cause of the strike and grape boycott. Now "La Causa" means the cause of the entire political-economic movement. The grape strike further demonstrated what unified group action could achieve.

Leadership on a national level has yet to develop. The person who comes closest to filling the need is Cesar Chavez. However, many urban Chicanos identify him with rural problems only and feel that his approach is too moderate. Two other persons come closer to providing leadership for less patient Chicanos. They are Reis Tijerina of New Mexico, and Corky Gonzales of Colorado. I personally feel that Cesar Chavez has the potential to lead the movement on a large scale. He has the ability to attract and develop wide support from many groups whereas Reis and Corky appeal mainly to the young and to the militant. Although Reis and Corky do not have the stature of Cesar, they are probably closer to the feelings of many Chicanos.

Hopefully, you should begin to understand why many of us don't see ourselves as typical Americans and why we don't embrace the culture and social standards of the middle class. For many of us it is impossible; and for others of us it is undesirable. Too often doing so means negation of a long, rich, and truly beautiful cultural heritage. We accept Mexico for what it is—our cultural homeland—and similarly we accept this country for what it is—the place where we must live our day-to-day existence. We do not believe we must become Anglicized in order to take part in this society. Rather we intend to improve America for our people without giving up our unique cultural background. The name Chicano has helped us come together and has given our movement strength.

The Chicano Movement is here. "La Raza" or "Our People" are organizing and petitioning for their rights. The nine million people who became citizens of this country willingly or unwillingly are no longer willing to accept the inequities in education, employment, and housing which have been part of our lives. We are reevaluating our culture and realizing that it is a thing to be preserved, indeed treasured. In short, we are coming to grips with our reality and a strong sense of unity is developing across the nation. La Causa is growing in momentum and its people, the Chicanos, are growing in pride, dignity, and determination.

Tears Can Be Crucial to Your Physical/Emotional Health

Barbara Lang Stern makes a fascinating assertion in this essay. Do you agree with her when you have finished reading the article?

Do you let yourself go and cry from time to time? Or do you almost always hold back your tears? Chances are you've heard or read that crying is a healthy emotional release, but did you know it might help to prevent certain physical illnesses as well?

"All of us have two systems of tearing," says Stephen E. Bloomfield, M.D., clinical assistant professor in ophthalmology at New York Hospital-Cornell Medical Center. "There is, first of all, a constant flow of tears which is produced by tiny glands in the conjunctiva or lining inside the lids of the eye. This basic tearing creates a film that's very much like a soap bubble in the sense that it can be compressed and stretched by the eyelids without breaking or getting holes in it. The tear film does the vital job of keeping the cornea moist. If the cornea dries, it will get erosions or little abrasions that can be very painful. Eventually, if there is severe drying, vision will be impaired because the cornea will become opaque.

"The second back-up system involves the lachrimal gland located at the outer corner of the eye. This good-sized gland can put out a lot of tears in response to irritants such as fumes, smoke, or foreign bodies in the eye. This reflex tearing is the eye's automatic response to *any* kind of adverse stimulus. For instance, wind and heat cause faster evaporation of the cornea's normal tear film. The lachrimal gland responds by producing extra moisture, and you may have 'teary' eyes on an exceptionally windy day. The lachrimal gland also produces the tears you may cry when your feelings are touched.

"Most people don't realize how fascinating and complex a tear is. It's made up of three different types of products—water, mucus, and fat—in the proper proportions to keep the tear film flexible and intact. Tears also contain sugar and protein, which nourish the cornea, as well as a bacteria-destroying enzyme known as lysozyme, which effectively protects the eye against infection by a lot of organisms that we're constantly exposed to."

Clearly, tears play a crucial role in the health of our eyes; but what about their benefit to our overall well-being?

Psychologists have long known that, whenever we have strong emotions that we hold in or deny, one way or another our unexpressed feelings show up. Sometimes they appear as substitute emotions: if we aren't able to let out our anger, we may get depressed. Feelings may manifest themselves through all kinds of behavior. One of the most familiar is the way we show restlessness or impatience by tapping a foot or drumming our fingers. Often, our strong unexpressed emotions can result in physical illnesses ranging from headaches, ulcers, and digestive problems to high blood pressure, insomnia, skin rashes, and many other conditions.

Tears represent an acknowledgment and expression of many of our feelings such as grief, sorrow, frustration, fear, helplessness, and sometimes relief or joy. Some people find that crying helps them to understand their emotions by making them more conscious of how they feel.

Furthermore, there is evidence to suggest that withholding tears can cause specific problems, while releasing them can end the difficulty.

"Asthma patients often are afraid to cry," says Walter A. Stewart, M.D., psychoanalyst, teacher, and author, "yet they will frequently abort an asthmatic attack if they do begin to shed tears. It's also been widely noticed that people who don't cry often catch a great many colds; but, once they become able to weep, their susceptibility to colds disappears."

"One reason you might have more colds if you hold back tears is that, when you're under stress, your body puts out steroids which affect your immune system and reduce your resistance to disease," Dr. Bloomfield comments.

In an intriguing book, *Your Mind Can Stop the Common Cold* (Peter Wyden), Lucy Freeman attempts to explain more specifically the connection between unshed tears and catching colds. She suggests in part that, when you feel like crying, one of the changes that takes place is your nose's becoming engorged or congested with blood. If you go ahead and weep, tears drain through your nasal tear ducts, easing your nose. But, if you suppress your tears, the nose nonetheless "becomes engorged and stays engorged as it awaits tears that never flow," writes Freeman.

"This prolonged engorgement weakens the resistance of the nose, either against invading viruses or viruses that reside in the nose in moderate numbers as protective organisms but that, when the nose has to overexert itself and falls into a weakened condition, multiply and cause an infection that the whole body is then forced to fight."

For this and other reasons, Freeman concludes that "when you catch a cold, you may have a hidden wish to weep."

As children, many of us were encouraged by our parents *not* to cry. Yet today, we're revising our opinion of what constitutes weakness. Acknowledging that you feel pain and weeping may take more strength or courage than pretending that the hurt doesn't exist. And revealing your emotions to someone else often means being willing to take a risk.

Of course, there are times when you'll decide it's inappropriate to cry. You'll want to consider the impact it will have on others as well as on you. So you may choose to suppress your tears in front of a frightened child or perhaps a rival or boss. Yet at the right time, with the right person, tears may be a sign of trust or intimacy, of readiness to share your deeper needs and feelings with another. Letting yourself cry can be a step toward greater physical and emotional well-being.

Moby Dick *and* Jaws: *Man's Fear of the Depths of the Sea*

In this essay written by a student, Beatrice Egle, the writer asserts that Melville's story and Benchley's story, which became a film, both appeal to people because we are all afraid of the sea.

CONTEXT: *This essay was written as a classroom assignment. The writer was given only a single word, depth, and told to write an essay on that subject. This assertion-with-proof paper was the final result.*

AUDIENCE: *Classmates and professor.*

The superficial similarities between *Moby Dick* and *Jaws* are obvious even to modern lay readers who have only heard about Melville's story. Both Moby Dick and the man-eating shark are white. Both terrorize man because of the death and destruction they cause. Both evade their hunters with an ease that threatens man's supposed dominance over creatures of the land and sea. Despite the aesthetic difference in the two works, the urge to compare them is irresistible because the similarities are not merely superficial. The appeal of Melville's and Benchley's stories is based on their ability to dramatize man's terror of the depths of the sea.

The terror inspired by Moby Dick and the great white shark is only partially due to their destructiveness. They terrorize man, in large part, because they are creatures of the unfathomable depths of the sea. Even today, when photography and deep-sea diving equipment enable scientists to study the ocean's depths, the area remains a mystery. The musical accompaniment to television specials on the depths of the ocean is always music that inspires awe. The region is always dark. Dangerous creatures lurk at every turn. And man remains an intruder despite his artificial light and underwater laboratories.

Man's inability to discover the secrets of the depths of the ocean is precisely what makes Moby Dick and the great white shark such terrible creatures. Their domain remains unfathomable to man, and when they invade man's territory, he can neither understand them nor control their mindless actions. They inspire fear because they come from a region that is unknowable to man and they constantly remind of his limitations.

Melville and Benchley reveal, perhaps unconsciously, man's tendency to deify what he does not understand. The depths of the sea can be seen as the opposite of Heaven. We have made height the dwelling of God — whether he is a merciful, fatherlike God or an anthropomorphic god like the Olympian Zeus. If good dwells in Heaven, then evil must dwell in the depths of the earth or of the sea. So Moby Dick and the great white shark are both symbols and manifestations of evil. And quite unconsciously, Melville's and Benchley's characters deify these creatures.

It is easy to see how that deification occurs. Moby Dick and the great white shark are powerful; they mirror God's omnipotence with the difference that their omnipotence is vile and destructive. In fact, it is their mindless destruction that makes Moby Dick and the great white shark deific. Despite Ahab's frenzied attribution of motives to Moby Dick, we know that the whale is guided only by instinct. His destruction of the *Pequod* is as purposeless and unmotivated as are the shark's attacks on swimmers. It is this obliviousness to man's world that makes Moby Dick and the great white shark deific. Unlike our Judeo-Christian God or the Greco-Roman gods, they cannot be appeased or praised. They can only be feared, and fear figures into the worship of any god.

Ultimately, the mystery and the terror that surround the white whale and the great white shark is the mystery that surrounds the depths of the sea. Man fears what he does not understand, and that fear can unconsciously turn into deification. As long as the depths of the sea remain unfathomable to man, stories like *Moby Dick* and *Jaws* will continue to appeal to — and to terrorize — readers.

Writing Your Own
Assertion-With-Proof Essay

CONTEXTS

A

You are the parent of a small child; the two of you have just returned from the grocery store where he did nothing but whine and cry for the latest junk food cereal that was advertised on the Saturday morning cartoons. You know this cereal is coated with sugar and is not good for children, and, finally, you have had enough. You sit down and write an assertion-with-proof essay that you plan to mail to the network president. This essay will center on what you believe television commercials are doing to children. You plan also to send a copy of the essay to your local newspaper.

B

You are a senator who recently voted for an arms treaty that will result in the closing of a factory and the loss of hundreds of jobs in your district. Your constituents are furious with you for your vote, which they see as having cost them money and jobs. However, you feel morally justified for your vote and are firm in your conviction. Write an open letter asserting your convictions and reasons for voting as you did. This letter will appear in the monthly newsletter to your constituents who live in a middle-class urban area. These constituents depend either directly or indirectly on defense contracts for local factories for their livelihood.

C

You are a newly appointed football coach at a local high school. You are surprised to learn that the previous coach used pain-killing drugs to enable the better players to play even when injured. You know this is illegal and dangerous to the young men on your team. You make the decision that under no circumstances will you administer pain killers to a player. You must prepare an essay that will appear in the newspaper, be read in the locker room, and be posted on the school bulletin board. You want no doubt as to your position and the reasons for it. Your football team is composed of teenage boys from a rural community whose major interest is "winning" football.

D

You and your friend have always done things together, even crazy things like cutting classes and pulling pranks. Now your friend has started smoking and wants you to try it. You have strong feelings against smoking and vow that you will never join your friend. In fact, you are so upset about your friend's new habit that you decide to write an assertion-with-proof essay for your school newspaper in which you give your reasons for thinking that young people should not smoke.

E

Martin Luther turned history around the day he wrote down a list of statements telling exactly where he stood on matters of religion and nailed it to the front of the church door. Imagine that you have just had a blowout with your parents (or children). You are really steamed. You decide to write your own assertion of your rights in the family. You know, however, that you must use proof, also, to back up your assertion, else your parents (or children) won't read past the first line. You plan to leave the essay on the kitchen table so that it absolutely cannot be ignored.

F

You are an avid television watcher. In fact, you absolutely love television. Everywhere you go these days it seems as though someone is talking about how bad television watching is for you and how people ought to stop watching it. Finally, you decide to speak your piece. Your friend edits the little magazine that is put in all the stores, motels, etc., in town to be taken free of charge by anyone who wants a copy. She often runs a short essay by some local person; last week's topic was "How to Build a Tree House," which a friend of yours wrote. You call the editor and ask her if she will take your essay on the value of television. She says she'll be happy to—that it ought to make lively reading. So, you sit down and write the assertion-with-proof essay in which you declare that television watching is a good thing to do.

G

Go to the library and get evidence, facts about, information on some subject you are interested in learning about. Then, with your instructor, plan a context for an assertion-with-proof essay that will be based on your work in the library.

H

Write an assertion-with-proof essay on some book, poem, play, or movie you have recently read or seen. Work with your instructor on the context and audience for the essay.

WRITING ASSIGNMENT: PERSONAL VIEWPOINT ESSAY

There are occasions when a writer gets to *sound off*, to give an opinion that does not have to be supported, documented, or even explained. Some of the forms personal viewpoint essays take are editorials, guest columns, speeches, and special assignments when the writer is asked to respond to a particular issue, subject, or the like. Sometimes the personal viewpoint is important because of the writer, who may be a celebrity, famous government official, or newsworthy personality. Sometimes the personal viewpoint is important because the writer represents a large or definite segment of society and is, in effect, speaking for them. Other times the personal viewpoint is important because the writer is an editor of the magazine or newspaper in which the piece appears, and the personal viewpoint can give readers a fix on the slant of the magazine or newspaper itself. Other times the personal viewpoint is important just because the writer has a real flair for writing, is terribly amusing, or so capable of saying what everybody is thinking but couldn't say so well.

A personal viewpoint essay has no particular form. It is merely the writer's opinion, pure and simple. The writer does not have to explain carefully why he or she believes this particular thing or thinks this particular way, and the reader does not have to do any more than take the essay or leave it. Personal viewpoint essays are usually very interesting to read, however, because they almost always carry the stamp of the writer's personality prominently.

In the readings that follow, decide why each personal viewpoint included here is worth the reader's time. Be able to discuss your answers in class.

READINGS:

Why I Left The U.S. and Why I Am Returning

In this personal viewpoint statement, Eldridge Cleaver discusses his reasons for leaving and returning to America, personal statements about his views on America and the American political system.

I am often asked why I want to return to the United States. This question never fails to bowl me over, and I find it impossible to answer. I also feel that it is an improper question. In fact, most people who ask are not really interested in that question. What they actually want to know is what will I do if they allow me to return.

I always take the opportunity to explain why I left in the first place. Lots of people believe I left because I preferred to go live in a Communist country, and that now, several years and many Communist countries later, I find the grass not greener on the Communist side of the fence. So now, here I stand, locked outside the gates of the paradise I once scorned, begging to be let back in. Let me clarify.

On April 6, 1968, two days after Dr. Martin Luther King, Jr., was assassinated, there was a gun battle between members of the Black Panther Party and the Oakland Police Department. Bobby Hutton was killed. Warren Wells and I received gunshot wounds. Two policemen were wounded. Eight party members, myself included, were arrested in the area of the gunfight.

After I received emergency treatment, guards from the California Department of Corrections transported me directly to San Quentin State Prison, in the spirit of "Oh, boy, we got you now!" It seemed obvious to them that I had violated my parole. I, along with the others, was indicted by an Alameda County Grand Jury. And although bail was set on all of us, the Corrections Department refused to allow me to go free on bail, claiming jurisdiction over me as a parole violator.

I pleaded not guilty. Without a trial or hearing of any sort, the prison authorities were prejudging my case, declaring me guilty, and, in effect, sentencing me to prison. My attorneys filed a petition for a writ of habeas corpus. A hearing was held before Chief Judge Raymond J. Sherwin of the Solano County Superior Court.

Judge Sherwin ordered me free on bail. I quote . . . from his decision:

The record here is that though the petitioner was arrested and his parole cancelled more than two months ago, hearings before the Adult Authority [the state parole board for male felons] have not even been scheduled.

There is nothing to indicate why it was deemed necessary to cancel his parole before his trial on the pending criminal charges of which he is presumed innocent.

It has to be stressed that the uncontradicted evidence presented to this Court indicated that the petitioner had been a model parolee. The peril to his parole status stemmed from no failure of personal rehabilitation, but from his undue eloquence in pursuing political goals, goals which were offensive to many of his contemporaries.

Not only was there absence of cause for the cancellation of parole, it was the product of a type of pressure unbecoming, to say the least, to the law enforcement paraphernalia of this state.

Judge Sherwin's decision exploded like a bomb inside California legal, political and police circles, because it missed the whole point: From Governor Ronald Reagan down, the politicians wanted me silenced, and here Judge Sherwin was talking about due process of law!

People who supported my fight for my rights posted $50,000 bail, and I was free.

The law-enforcement paraphernalia was not stopped by Judge Sherwin's condemnation, and the Adult Authority moved swiftly to have his ruling reversed in the Appellate Court. The court refused to examine the facts at issue in the case and instead simply affirmed the arbitrary power of the Adult Authority to revoke parole. Because of a technicality in court procedure, the ruling ordering me returned to prison could not become effective for sixty days. I was due to surrender on November 27. That day, I was in Montreal. That was seven years ago.

History shows that when the American political system is blocked and significant segments of the population are unable to have their will brought to bear on the decision-making process, you can count upon the American people to revolt, to take it out into the streets, in the spirit of the Boston Tea Party.

During the 1960's, the chips were down in a fateful way, uniting the upsurge of black Americans against the oppressive features of the system, and the gargantuan popular opposition to the Indochina wars. It was left to the Nixon Administration to bring the issues to a head. In the end, the system rejected President Nixon and reaffirmed its own basic principles.

A fabulous new era of progress is opening up to the world, and coping with all of the problems unleashed by Watergate has opened up a creative era for American democracy. I believe that every American, regardless of his politics, has a duty to re-examine some of his beliefs.

This is particularly true of those active at both extremes of the political spectrum. Those of us who developed a psychology of opposition must take a pause and sum up our experiences. We must recognize that in a sense we are playing in a brand new ball game. The slogans of yesterday will not get us through the tasks at hand. I believe that for America to deal with problems posed on the world level, a fundamental reorientation in the relationship between the American people is absolutely necessary.

We can not afford to refight battles that have already been either won or lost. If Richard Nixon and his friends had accepted the verdict of the people in 1960, rejecting him at the polls, the nation would have been spared the debacle of Watergate. But the truth is that nations do get the leaders they deserve.

With all of its faults, the American political system is the freest and most democratic in the world. The system needs to be improved, with democracy spread to all areas of life, particularly the economic. All of these changes must be conducted through our established institutions, and people with grievances must find political methods for obtaining redress.

Each generation subjects the world it inherits to severe criticism. I think that my generation has been more critical than most, and for good reason. At the same time, at the end of the critical process, we should arrive at some conclusions. We should have discovered which values are worth conserving. It is the beginning of another fight, the fight to defend those values from the blind excesses of our fellows who are still caught up in the critical process. It is my hope to make a positive contribution in this regard.

Rewards of Living a Solitary Life

In this personal statement May Sarton, the novelist and poet, argues that living alone brings many rewards.

The other day an acquaintance of mine, a gregarious and charming man, told me he had found himself unexpectedly alone in New York for an hour or two between appointments. He went to the Whitney and spent the "empty" time looking at things in solitary bliss. For him it proved to be a shock nearly as great as falling in love to discover that he could enjoy himself so much alone.

What had he been afraid of, I asked myself? That, suddenly alone, he would discover that he bored himself, or that there was, quite simply, no self there to meet? But having taken the plunge, he is now on the brink of adventure; he is about to be launched into his own inner space, space as immense, unexplored and sometimes frightening as outer space to the astronaut.

His every perception will come to him with a new freshness and, for a time, seem startlingly original. For anyone who can see things for himself with a naked eye becomes, for a moment or two, something of a genius.

With another human being present vision becomes double vision, inevitably. We are busy wondering, what does my companion see or think of this, and what do I think of it? The original impact gets lost, or diffused.

"Music I heard with you was more than music." Exactly. And therefore music *itself* can only be heard alone. Solitude is the salt of personhood. It brings out the authentic flavor of every experience.

"Alone one is never lonely: the spirit adventures, waking/In a quiet garden, in a cool house, abiding single there."

Loneliness is most acutely felt with other people, for with others, even with a lover sometimes, we suffer from our differences, differences of taste, temperament, mood. Human intercourse often demands that we soften the edge of perception, or withdraw at the very instant of personal truth for fear of hurting, or of being inappropriately present, which is to say naked, in a social situation. Alone we can afford to be wholly whatever we are, and to feel whatever we feel absolutely. That is a great luxury!

For me the most interesting thing about a solitary life, and mine has been that for the last twenty years, is that it becomes increasingly rewarding. When I can wake up and watch the sun rise over the ocean, as I do most days, and know that I have an entire day ahead, uninterrupted, in which to write a few pages, take a walk with my dog, lie down in the afternoon for a long think (why does one think better in a horizontal position?), read and listen to music, I am flooded with happiness.

I am lonely only when I am overtired, when I have worked too long without a break, when for the time being I feel empty and need filling up. And I am lonely sometimes when I come back home after a lecture trip, when I have seen a lot of people and talked a lot, and am full to the brim with experience that needs to be sorted out.

Then for a little while the house feels huge and empty, and I wonder where my self is hiding. It has to be recaptured slowly by watering the plants, perhaps, and looking again at each one as though it were a person, by feeding the two cats, by cooking a meal.

It takes a while, as I watch the surf blowing up in fountains at the end of the field, but the moment comes when the world falls away, and the self emerges again from the deep unconscious, bringing back all I have recently experienced to be explored and slowly understood, when I can converse again with my own hidden powers, and so grow, and so be renewed, till death do us part.

Women in Leadership Roles

This is the Editor's Page from U.S. News and World Report *for May 2, 1979. Marvin Stone gives his personal opinion that women have become a significant addition to the leadership pool.*

In Britain, a woman is at the helm, as Prime Minister. In Chicago, the machine's candidate for mayor took a beating. A woman did it, and went on to take the reins of the nation's second-biggest city.

Women, in fact, are now the mayors of a good handful of America's large cities. And they are found in increasing numbers at every level of local government.

These reports illustrate a speedup in women's achievement of leadership roles in politics. The year 1979 is confirming a big change in the social structure of the English-speaking world, and the nature of that change deserves examination.

James MacGregor Burns, a student of the qualities of leadership, has this to say in his book by that title: "In some cultures, . . . women are cut off from power positions as well as from the steppingstones and access routes that reach toward leadership. . . . The male bias is reflected in the false conception of leadership as mere command or control.

"As leadership comes properly to be seen as a process of leaders engaging and mobilizing the human needs and aspirations of followers, women will be more readily recognized as leaders and men will change their own leadership styles."

We would like to think that women have a special human quality to bring to politics, and in all probability they do. But the main thing the British Tories' Margaret Thatcher and Chicago's Jane Byrne seem likely to demonstrate is simply that women have the same leadership capabilities as men.

Prime Minister Thatcher—the "Iron Lady"—did indeed come up through a succession of jobs that entailed contact with the people. But it did not take any special rapport for a Conservative to see that Britons grew fatigued of their meager lives, that the lords sickened of being taxed out of their castles, that the umbrella brigade was losing its incentive to achieve. Thatcher hammered away in the style for which she is known, and earned her place.

It was much the same in Chicago. Michael Bilandic drew the Democratic machine's O.K. to succeed himself. But he had bitterly offended Byrne. It's true that she capitalized on public anger at corruption and the irritation of householders when neither snow nor garbage was removed. She herself, however, was a product of the machine and a right-hand person of the late Richard Daley. The notable thing she did was to get in the ring with the men and punch them out for the Democratic nomination—and then go on to capture the mayoralty.

But that's not the whole story. The fact is that women in the United States already are treading Burns's "steppingstones and access routes," and in rising numbers. They appear as county commissioners, members of township councils, mayors, and state-cabinet and executive officials.

More than 10 percent of the nation's state legislators now are women. There are two women governors—Ella Grasso in Connecticut and Dixy Lee Ray in Washington. And the roster of female lieutenant governors has risen from zero to six since 1974. In addition to the two women in the federal cabinet, close to 20 percent of President Carter's political appointees have been women—a record.

Thus the 1978 elections, declares the National Women's Political Caucus, created a reservoir of women officeholders "to draw on for future congressional, vice-presidential and presidential candidates."

The Center for the American Woman and Politics, at Rutgers, the state university of New Jersey, finds that "women are more likely than men to consider themselves above average in responsiveness to constituents."

Whether this is a realistic assessment or not, women have become a significant addition to the leadership pool. It is a welcome occurrence, for they are needed.

Dear Ms. Wood

In late 1978 an advertisement appeared in New York Magazine *in which a Ms. Pamela Wood was quoted as saying that nobody reads an English theme except English teachers. Russell Norris, a freshman English student who was just finishing his first semester in a composition class, took issue with Ms. Wood's assertion and wrote this letter, which he later mailed to each of his classmates in the writing course.*

Dear Ms. Wood:

I am currently enrolled at a major university as a freshman in a freshman English course. I read your quote, "The only people who are generous enough to read English themes are English teachers," right before my final exam and decided to respond to it for my last paper in the course. I think your quote is only true of some English themes in some English classes. Personally, I can say this because I love to read English themes, and I am *not* an English teacher.

Before I came here to college, I attended a small, private, highly accredited secondary school in a major city. During the four years I spent there, your quote would have held true: I hated every English theme I ever wrote or read. Now, however, after a semester away at college, my writing has changed drastically, mostly due to the efforts of my teacher, 24 classmate teachers, and me.

In high school I was taught the old introduction, 3 points, conclusion, whup, slap, bummo instant English paper theme method. Usually these themes were on some boring subject, so unimportant to me that sitting here I can't remember even one of the topics I ever wrote on. But during the last 3 months, I have learned more about *real* writing and giving some kind of value to the reader than I learned the rest of my life up till now. In my class there are 24 people plus one full-time teacher. But, in a way, we are all teachers, because we help each other almost as much as the real teacher helps us. For instance, at the start of every class period, we do a thing called foregrounds. We go around the room, everyone stating his or her name and exactly what's on his or her mind at that particular instant. It helps everyone to relax and also lets the teacher know when someone might be a little preoccupied with another test. It lets everyone get to know each other a little better. Another thing we do is to help each other very much on each paper. We are never allowed to turn in a paper unless we have read it to at least two of our classmates. Usually we deal with contexts, zinger openings, concentrating on hearing a person's voice in the writing, and looking for word pictures, along with promise and delivery units. I don't believe your quote would hold true, then, for anyone in our class because we all enjoy helping each other on our themes. We feel cheated if we *don't* get to hear what each other writes.

Now, I realize that I've only just begun to write. For the past 4 years, I've only been putting down on paper what I thought the teacher wanted to hear, not what I wanted to talk about. But if you can write on something you like or know about, something that *you're an insider on,* then I guarantee, along with my English teacher, that your writing will take on a new and clearer perspective. And once people learn to communicate on something they like, the easier it is, then, for them to make themselves write on what they don't like.

I agree that some English themes are not too easy to read—because I have written a lot like this. But chances are that the people who write essays that only an English teacher would be generous enough to read haven't been exposed to the same ideas I or my classmates have. After this course I now believe I could write on anything. I've learned to put my emphasis on giving the reader value, on writing on a subject in a way that it will be public rather than private, and on sounding like myself instead of some anonymous non-person. I am looking forward to the day when your quote will be totally unfounded. But as it stands—and until my teacher can get her message across to the rest of the world—I will be ahead on the road to writing really well.

Sincerely yours,
Russell Norris

Writing Your Own Personal Viewpoint Essay

CONTEXTS

A

You are a person who really enjoys going to the movies, especially western films. It is the anniversary of the death of John Wayne, and you have been asked to write a personal viewpoint essay on what John Wayne represented to you and how you feel about his place in movie history. There has never been a time when you didn't "know" John Wayne, and you are thrilled to have this opportunity to give your personal viewpoint on the great man. Write the essay that will appear in the film column of your local paper.

B

You are an elderly man who has lived alone for ten years. Your only companion has been a small dog which you raised from a pup. This dog has been with you for eight years. Your house is being purchased by the state because a new freeway is going through; you are going to live in a government-subsidized apartment. Unfortunately, there is a rule that no pets are allowed. You have argued to no avail with the authorities, so you are going to have to give up your pet. You aren't going to do so, however, without a final word on the subject! You sit down and write an essay to send to the American Association of Retired Person's monthly magazine. Your subject: the right of persons to make their own decisions about whether or not they have pets. Write the essay you are going to send in.

C

You are sitting in the stands, watching a great football game. Suddenly, a fight breaks out on the field. Both benches empty, and soon overanxious fans are climbing onto the playing surface to get their two shots in. Of course, the game is delayed twenty minutes while officials try to pull struggling fans off the field. You are mad as you can be over the interruption in the game, and as soon as you get home you sit down and write a sound-off editorial and send it to the local citizens' page in your newspaper. Write the personal viewpoint essay you will send.

D

You're late for class. You sprint out to your car, fire up the engine, and careen out of your driveway onto the highway. Wham! Suddenly you are in a line of traffic that is moving only ten miles an hour. The cars are backed up for miles, and you can see in the distance the cause: a line of protestors blocking the road. At first you fret. Then you fume. Finally, you remember that you are going to be writing a personal viewpoint essay in class today. So, you start planning how to state your views: that groups that use ways of calling attention to their causes which also affect other people are wrong. Write the essay that resulted from this experience.

E

You have just been assigned some personal viewpoint essays to read in class. One of them made you so mad that you can't wait to pick up your own pen and start writing. You want the instructor to let you read it to the class (and perhaps even give them copies) as another viewpoint on one of the subjects they were assigned to read. Write the essay you want your classmates to hear.

WRITING ASSIGNMENT: THE PERSUASION ESSAY

All of us have ideas or beliefs that we hold valuable. Whether it's a profound idea about how people should prepare for the afterlife or simply a fervent wish that our friends would go see a movie we just enjoyed, the usual result of strong feeling is that we want others to share that feeling and do something to show they share it. Since we usually can't force people to believe as we do, we must often persuade them; and since their response is important to us, we want to know the best ways to do that persuading.

"Will you marry me?"

"May I have the job?"

"Would you like to start a family?"

"Do you think I should join the army?"

If you think you may ever require an answer to questions like these, you need persuasive skills. If the answers to such questions would make a difference in your life, you would do well to find out how to get the right ones. To learn these skills, we will write a persuasion essay. The purpose of this essay will be *to cause the readers to do, think, or believe something different* after reading our words. In the assertion-with-proof essay, your aim was to make a strong statement and back it up, but your aim did not extend to causing the reader to *act upon* your words. In the persuasion essay, however, your intention *is* to cause your reader to act upon your words.

A good persuasion essay will have these characteristics:

1 The readers will know immediately what the writer wants them to do, believe, or the like.

2 The writer indicates that he or she knows the subject extremely well.

3 The writer is aware of the reader's needs and appeals to those needs.

4 The writer will anticipate what will appeal to the reader and choose language appropriate to that tone.

5 The writer will not attempt to effect numerous changes in the reader all at once, but will concentrate on one area of change.

6 The writer will make clear what the readers should do as a result of reading the essay.

In the selections below, pay special attention to what method the writer uses to persuade the reader to act. Be able to discuss these readings in class.

READINGS:

The Case for the ROTC

E. K. Dortmund attempts to give readers enough information, facts they might not already know, and logical argument to convince them to support the ROTC.

The Reserve Officers Training Corps is going through hard times. It is caught in a barrage of scorn and skepticism: from the high ridge of academia has come sporadic, but effective, sniping; Congress, wooed by the hoary notion of a professional army, considers setting trip-wires in its path; and, wherever bands of activists for Pure Democracy pitch their camps, songs of abolition continue to fill the air. In short, ROTC is in trouble. It deserves, at the very least, then, a careful look and perhaps even a murmur of encouragement.

ROTC emerged from a deep, yet salutary, confusion—since colonial times, American society was unclear about the type of military apparatus it should have. Should it be professional and national, or should it be amateur and local? In a republic, was the part-time citizen soldier, of necessity, preferable to the full-time warrior? At the Constitutional Convention in 1787, the decision was reached to adopt both of Mars' henchmen. Although, in time, this would cause much disparity in military training, leadership, and equipment, and spawn new plagues of pork-barrel politics, most Americans at the end of the 18th century viewed the compromise as sensible. Buttressed by the principle of civilian control of the military, the Constitutional compromise seemed to guarantee that what had tyrannized ancient and contemporary societies so regularly—the usurpation of civil power by an unchecked and undiluted warrior class—now was reduced to an improbable happening in the new American republic's shining future.

So it was that, by the early 19th century, the military structure comprised both regular armed forces and national units. The latter organizations harbored the idea of a reserve force tightly affiliated with the separate states. The notion of a national reserve force as a component of, and a direct supplement to, the regular army and naval forces ran counter to the powerful ideology of States' Rights, which insisted not only that the national military bureaucracy—a necessary evil—be kept as small as possible, but that the control of national defense reflect the sovereignties of the separate states.

This strong view, shared by all the states before 1860, continued to dominate the South during the Civil War. The Southern military command remained loyal to the claims of state militia and local guard units. In contrast, Lincoln and the North undercut the tradition of local military controls for the Frankensteinian benefits of a central command; and, as much as anything, this decision to organize the war effort sealed the Confederacy's doom. Clearly, one of the key consequences of the Civil War was a disturbing alteration of the American republic's

18th-century military structure. Thus, it was no small matter when, in 1866, Congress decreed that, of the U.S. Army's 45 infantry regiments, four should constitute a national, but limited-duty, "Veterans Reserve Corps," comprising only men wounded in action. This reserve organization was important because it signified the beginning of the end of exclusive local control of reserve forces, and yet it testified to the persistence of the idea that a reserve military organization, aside from the economies involved, was a legacy not to be spurned.

For the modern reserve organization, the significant date is 1908, when Congress created the Medical Reserve Corps of the Army. This unit was expanded by national legislation in 1912, 1916, 1920, and by additional Congressional action until it assumed its present full personality as the U.S. Army Reserve. It served as the model for the subsequent Naval, Air Force, Marine, and Coast Guard reserve programs.

In all of this, one problem excited special interest: What kind of officer corps should America create and tolerate? Should it be a private club of professionals, trained only in military classrooms? The answer was to leaven a small national officer corps with part-time officers drawn from state militia and guard organizations. The latter could be either the aristocratic patrician or the village go-getter, but, in either case, the conduct of war was not to be the exclusive privilege of a narrowly trained elite divorced from republican society and civilian values. From this tradition, ROTC, which since World War II has been a major source of officers for the armed forces, emerged.

Its exact and unassuming moment of birth was in 1819, when the American Literary, Scientific, and Military Academy was founded in Vermont (now Norwich University). Other than West Point, this was the first institution of higher learning to prescribe military studies as a part of the collegiate curriculum. It was followed by other military colleges and academies, and eventually by a system of Federal support for colleges that agreed to include military science and tactics in their curricula. This latter development was spurred by the Army's need for a steady supply of trained officers during the Civil War. (The passage of the Morrill Land Grant Act in 1862 provided that tracts of Federal land be given to the states for the support and maintenance of at least one college where the main teaching emphasis would be placed upon agriculture, military tactics, and mechanical arts. The act clearly required the offering of courses in military affairs.) Then, in response to World War I, the National Defense Act of 1916 regularized and formalized the program by creating the Army ROTC as the framework for the program in the schools. The Navy and Air Force programs began in 1926 and 1946, respectively.

Currently, ROTC operates as a four-year offering in nine military colleges and nearly 300 civilian colleges and universities. Under the ROTC Vitalization Act of 1964, two-year programs for students unable to participate in ROTC during their freshman and sophomore years are also available. By 1965, just before ROTC came under heavy critical fire, about 12,000 college graduates annually were granted Reserve Commissions as second lieutenants upon completion of their ROTC programs conducted by Regular Army officers. Usually 10% or so of the students were designated "distinguished military graduates" and given permanent appointments in the Regular Army. The extraordinary result was that, since World War II, the vast majority of second lieutenants and nearly half of all officers regardless of grade on active duty in the U.S. Army were ROTC graduates.

This, then, was the situation when the war in Vietnam careened out of reason in 1965. For all the complaining about its operation, ROTC seemed to serve the nation's best interests. No great claim was made for its merits, but no serious criticism came its way either. Citizens' manifestoes demanding its abolition were nonexistent. If anything, in the 1950's, ROTC was viewed like a pair of yellow brogans—faintly comic, but sturdy and useful.

Up to a point, of course, criticism was deserved, even when indulged in by regular officers notorious for their knee-jerk anti-ROTC bias. If some complaints had been made, wary friends of ROTC might have spared it much future grief. To begin with, ROTC was academically often farcical. Throughout the nation, faculty, students, and administrations viewed ROTC with the same guilty indulgence as they viewed the academic shenanigans of varsity athletic programs. Furthermore, ROTC now and again served questionable academic purposes. For example, units became not the agencies for studying military history, tactics, and technology, very reputable subjects (far more reputable, surely, than classes in football theory), but the mouthpieces for Cold War propaganda. The Korean War helped fuel this propaganda; the Eisenhower years exploited it; the Kennedy repertory company, while pretending to be amused by it, fell confused victim to it. Directly reflecting all of this, ROTC, by the middle 1960's, was less a program in military tactics than one which preached the monolithic menace of international communism. It had become something of an embarrassment to the academic community.

Other complaints scored points as well. From the taxpayer's view, the post-World War II ROTC was rather a boondoggle. College and university students uninterested in military life enlisted in ROTC for the few dollars tendered during its junior and senior years. In addition, ROTC served as a dodge from the draft and sheltered certain students from reserve call-ups. Moreover, in many an athletic factory, the ROTC classroom was packed with slumbrous football players hunting easy academic credits and protection against too low a grade point average. Clearly, the armed forces were going to receive into their ranks a curious flock of indifferent, self-indulgent, and incompetent officers. The question a few citizens and academicians asked was simple: What was the good in all this? The answer was, they felt, pretty obvious—there wasn't much good in it. Still, no need to fuss too much. Like Congress, ROTC was suspect, but worth tolerating.

And so it was until the White House ordered, in 1965, massive troop increases in South Vietnam and extensive bombing in North Vietnam. Then, the attacks against ROTC became more numerous, more serious, and more successful. Led now by students and younger faculty outraged by what they deemed America's brutal use of imperial power in Asia, colleges and universities suddenly looked upon the ROTC units as invitations to riot. Generally, the intensified arguments against ROTC obeyed the following high-minded pattern: ROTC has no place on the campus because it is alien to the nature and purpose of higher education; it indoctrinates rather than frees the mind; the content of its courses is uncivilized; and it is designed to train one to war against humans. (And this simple fact must mean that ROTC surely has no home in any Catholic or Christian university.) The presence of ROTC, a government agency which pays students not to think candidly, threatens to twist the university into becoming the servant of narrow national interest. The university has a nobler purpose—it must be a "republic of virtue" and it must be universal in its ultimate loyalty. In removing, by force if necessary, ROTC from the university, one could detach the university from America's most heartless and curiously stupid war—the abomination of Vietnam.

The consequence of such impassioned outbursts was that, on many a campus, ROTC began to retreat. Student governments, administrative boards, and faculty councils cooperated to remove the buttons of its academic standing. In 1969, the Yale faculty took academic credit from ROTC courses, and officers commanding ROTC units were stripped of their professorial rank; thus, at Yale and other institutions, ROTC became just another extracurricular affair, and a highly unpopular one at that. At Princeton, ROTC was banned altogether; at the University of Oregon, students and concerned faculty wished to vote ROTC out. By the spring of 1970, enrollment had dropped noticeably in units throughout the nation. Then came demands from liberal "realists" for the creation of a professional army with an elite officer corps—better that than the university ever again serving the dubious interests of the military.

During the peak of this attack against ROTC, few voices were raised in its defense. Its lukewarm friends easily were intimidated. The university community and the nation at large, thus, were not reminded of a homely truth: as a reflection of America's 18th- and 19th-centuries' concern for curbing both the national budget and militarism, ROTC is, like the older reserve corps, simply a program designed to attract and maintain a substantial number of well-informed, civilian-oriented officers in the armed forces. Surely, it is only common sense to recruit officers as broadly as possible from all segments of the society to insure that the military bureaucracy, which, after all, is here to stay, is made as trustworthy as possible by constantly subverting its anti-civilian and anti-democratic propensities. In an imperfect world, ROTC remains, to its modest credit, what it was supposed to be from the outset—a hedge against the Prussian mentality.

Rather surprisingly, there are signs that this conventional wisdom is being heeded once again. No doubt for reasons both practical and enlightened, ROTC programs are springing to life again. At Princeton, ROTC returned to campus in January, 1972, as an extracurricular activity; and recently, by a narrow margin, the Faculty Senate of the University of Oregon voted retention of the school's ROTC program. If, in 1969-70, 15 schools asked that ROTC be withdrawn, in 1972-73 ROTC was represented by more units and on more campuses than ever before, although the total enrollment is still far below, perhaps by 50%, the ripe enrollment years of 1965-69.

This proliferation is the partial consequence of $65,000,000 in ROTC scholarships and subsidies made available for the 1971-72 college year. Financially pinched schools are now as quick to spot ROTC's merits as a few years ago, they were prepared to see its perniciousness. In addition, for 1973–74, the Army, Navy, and Air Force are offering more than 6,000 new ROTC scholarships. The Army, for example, is offering 1,000 four-year, full-tuition scholarships, which can be used at almost 300 colleges and universities. The scholarships cover the full cost of tuition, books, laboratory fees, and other educational expenses. They also provide an initial travel allowance from home to school, and pay an allowance of $100 a month for up to 10 months of the school year.

One unpublicized feature of ROTC's present revival is that many new programs are at black colleges. Hence, ROTC helps not only to subsidize black schools, but also to insure an increasing number of black officers in the officer corps—a beneficial and truly radical state of affairs, one the white middle-class activists of the late 1960's failed to imagine.

The upshot is that June, 1972, saw the ROTC programs produce nearly 15,000 new officers. Thus, ROTC is still the largest single source of newly commissioned officers. In the era of Vietnam, the service academies graduated only three per cent of the officers needed to lead our armed forces. ROTC and Officer's Candidate Schools produced the rest, and at a much lower cost to the brooding taxpayer. (In 1971–72, it cost the government $169,000,000 to graduate 2,800 academy officers, while ROTC commissioned nearly 15,000 officers for only $65,000,000.)

The facts encourage me to murmur, "ROTC, Right On," and, in a more didactic vein, to argue that ROTC should be preserved, if for no other reason than this one: it is one of the last, faint reminders of our lost republican ideals. Rather than strengthening a democratic society, the attack on higher education's ROTC programs further weakens that society by undercutting one of the few public agencies which help to insert civilian values—as banal as they may be—into the military establishment. Jefferson's 18th-century judgment that military instruction as a part of collegiate instruction insures national safety, thus, still is worth considering in the 1970's for the rich sound of its sturdy, double-edged good sense.

Letter from Birmingham Jail

Martin Luther King, Jr., wrote one of the most effective pieces of persuasion we have in the twentieth century when he asked his fellow clergymen to support his efforts to bring fairness and justice to his people, the blacks.

My Dear Fellow Clergymen:

While confined here in the Birmingham city jail, I came across your recent statement calling my present activities "unwise and untimely." Seldom do I pause to answer criticism of my work and ideas. If I sought to answer all the criticisms that cross my desk, my secretaries would have little time for anything other than such correspondence in the course of the day, and I would have no time for constructive work. But since I feel that you are men of genuine good will and that your criticisms are sincerely set forth, I want to try to answer your statement in what I hope will be patient and reasonable terms.

I think I should indicate why I am here in Birmingham, since you have been influenced by the view which argues against "outsiders coming in." I have the honor of serving as president of the Southern Christian Leadership Conference, an organization operating in every southern state, with headquarters in Atlanta, Georgia. We have some eighty-five affiliated organizations across the South, and one of them is the Alabama Christian Movement for Human Rights. Frequently we share staff, educational, and financial resources with our affiliates. Several months ago the affiliate here in Birmingham asked us to be on call to engage in a nonviolent direct-action program if such were deemed necessary. We readily consented, and when the hour came we lived up to our promise. So I, along with several members of my staff, am here because I was invited here. I am here because I have organizational ties here.

But more basically, I am in Birmingham because injustice is here. Just as the prophets of the eighth century B.C. left their villages and carried their "thus saith the Lord" far beyond the boundaries of their home towns, and just as the Apostle Paul left his village of Tarsus and carried the gospel of Jesus Christ to the far corners of the Greco-Roman world, so am I compelled to carry the gospel of freedom beyond my own home town. Like Paul, I must constantly respond to the Macedonian call for aid.

Moreover, I am cognizant of the interrelatedness of all communities and states. I cannot sit idly by in Atlanta and not be concerned about what happens in Birmingham. Injustice anywhere is a threat to justice everywhere. We are caught in an inescapable network of mutuality, tied in a single garment of destiny. Whatever affects one directly, affects all indirectly. Never again can we afford to live with the narrow, provincial, "outside agitator" idea. Anyone who lives inside the United States can never be considered an outsider anywhere within its bounds.

You deplore the demonstrations taking place in Birmingham. But your statement, I am sorry to say, fails to express a similar concern for the conditions that brought about the demonstrations. I am sure that none of you would want to rest content with the superficial kind of social analysis that deals merely with effects and does not grapple with underlying causes. It is unfortunate that demonstrations are taking place in Birmingham, but it is even more unfortunate that the city's white power structure left the Negro community with no alternative.

In any nonviolent campaign there are four basic steps: collection of the facts to determine whether injustices exist; negotiation; self-purification; and direct action. We have gone through all these steps in Birmingham. There can be no gainsaying the fact that racial injustice engulfs this community. Birmingham is probably the most thoroughly segregated city in the United States. Its ugly record of brutality is widely known. Negroes have experienced grossly unjust treatment in courts. There have been more unsolved bombings of Negro homes and churches in Birmingham than in any other city in the nation. These are the hard, brutal facts of the case. On the basis of these conditions, Negro leaders sought to negotiate with the city fathers. But the latter consistently refused to engage in good-faith negotiation.

Then, last September, came the opportunity to talk with leaders of Birmingham's economic community. In the course of the negotiations, certain promises were made by the merchants—for example, to remove the stores' humiliating racial signs. On the basis of these promises, the Reverend Fred Shuttlesworth and the leaders of the Alabama Christian Movement for Human Rights agreed to a moratorium on all demonstrations. As the weeks and months went by, we realized that we were the victims of a broken promise. A few signs, briefly removed, returned; the others remained.

As in so many past experiences, our hopes had been blasted, and the shadow of deep disappointment settled upon us. We had no alternative except to prepare for direct action, whereby we would present our very bodies as means of laying our case before the conscience of the local and the national community. Mindful of the difficulties involved, we decided to undertake a process of self-purification. We began a series of workshops on nonviolence, and we repeatedly asked ourselves: "Are you able to accept blows without retaliating?" "Are you able to endure the ordeal of jail?" We decided to schedule our direct-action program for the Easter season, realizing that except for Christmas, this is the main shopping period of the year. Knowing that a strong economic-withdrawal program would be the by-product of direct action, we felt that this would be the best time to bring pressure to bear on the merchants for the needed change.

Then it occurred to us that Birmingham's mayoral election was coming up in March, and we speedily decided to postpone action until after election day. When we discovered that the Commissioner of Public Safety, Eugene "Bull" Connor, had piled up enough votes to be in the run-off, we decided again to postpone action until the day after the run-off so that the demonstrations could not be used to cloud the issues. Like many others, we waited to see Mr. Connor defeated, and to this end we endured postponement after postponement. Having aided in this community need, we felt that our direct-action program could be delayed no longer.

You may well ask, "Why direct action? Why sit-ins, marches, and so forth? Isn't negotiation a better path?" You are quite right in calling for negotiation. Indeed, this is the very purpose of direct action. Nonviolent direct action seeks to create such a crisis and foster such a tension that a community which has constantly refused to negotiate is forced to confront the issue. It seeks so to dramatize the issue that it can no longer be ignored. My citing the creation of tension as part of the work of the nonviolent-resister may sound rather shocking. But I must confess that I am not afraid of the word "tension." I have earnestly opposed violent tension, but there is a type of constructive, nonviolent tension which is necessary for growth. Just as Socrates felt that it was necessary to create a tension in the mind so that individuals could rise from the bondage of myths and half-truths to the unfettered realm of creative analysis and objective appraisal, so must we see the need for nonviolent gadflies to create the kind of tension in society that will help men rise from the dark depths of prejudice and racism to the majestic heights of understanding and brotherhood.

The purpose of our direct-action program is to create a situation so crisis-packed that it will inevitably open the door to negotiation. I therefore concur with you in your call for negotiation. Too long has our beloved Southland been bogged down in a tragic effort to live in monologue rather than dialogue.

One of the basic points in your statement is that the action that I and my associates have taken in Birmingham is untimely. Some have asked: "Why didn't you give the new city administration time to act?" The only answer that I can give to this query is that the new Birmingham administration must be prodded about as much as the outgoing one, before it will act. We are sadly mistaken if we feel that the election of Albert Boutwell as mayor will bring the millennium to Birmingham. While Mr. Boutwell is a much more gentle person than Mr. Connor, they are both segregationists, dedicated to maintenance of the status quo. I have hoped that Mr. Boutwell will be reasonable enough to see the futility of massive resistance to desegregation. But he will not see this without pressure from devotees of civil rights. My friends, I must say to you that we have not made a single gain in civil rights without determined legal and nonviolent pressure. Lamentably, it is an historical fact that privileged groups seldom give up their privileges voluntarily. Individuals may see the moral light and voluntarily give up their unjust posture; but, as Reinhold Niebuhr has reminded us, groups tend to be more immoral than individuals.

We know through painful experience that freedom is never voluntarily given by the oppressor; it must be demanded by the oppressed. Frankly, I have yet to engage in a direct-action campaign that was "well timed" in the view of those who have not suffered unduly from the disease of segregation. For years now I have heard the word "Wait!" It rings in the ear of every Negro with piercing familiarity. This "Wait" has almost always meant "Never." We must come to see, with one of our distinguished jurists, that "justice too long delayed is justice denied."

We have waited for more than 340 years for our constitutional and God-given rights. The nations of Asia and Africa are moving with jet-like speed toward gaining political independence, but we still creep at horse-and-buggy pace toward gaining a cup of coffee at a lunch counter. Perhaps it is easy for those who have never felt the stinging darts of segregation to say, "Wait." But when you have seen vicious mobs lynch your mothers and fathers at will and drown your sisters and brothers at whim; when you have seen hate-filled policemen curse, kick, and even kill your black brothers and sisters; when you see the vast majority of your twenty million Negro brothers smothering in an airtight cage of poverty in the midst of an affluent society; when you suddenly find your tongue twisted and your speech stammering as you seek to explain to your six-year-old daughter why she can't go to the public amusement park that has just been advertised on television, and see tears welling up in her eyes when she is told that Funtown is closed to colored children, and see ominous clouds of inferiority beginning to form in her little mental sky, and see her beginning to distort her personality by developing an unconscious bitterness toward white people; when you have to concoct an answer for a five-year-old son who is asking, "Daddy, why do white people treat colored people so mean?"; when you take a cross-country drive and find it necessary to sleep night after night in the uncomfortable corners of your automobile because no motel will accept you; when you are humiliated day in and day out by nagging signs reading "white" and "colored"; when your first name becomes "nigger," your middle name becomes "boy" (however old you are) and your last name becomes "John," and your wife and mother are never given the respected title "Mrs."; when you are harried by day and haunted by night by the fact that you are a Negro, living constantly at tiptoe stance, never quite knowing what to expect next, and are plagued with inner fears and outer resentments; when you are forever fighting a degenerating sense of "nobodiness"—then you will understand why we find it difficult to wait. There comes a time when the cup of endurance runs over, and men are no longer willing to be plunged into the abyss of despair. I hope, sirs, you can understand our legitimate and unavoidable impatience.

You can express a great deal of anxiety over our willingness to break laws. This is certainly a legitimate concern. Since we so diligently urge people to obey the Supreme Court's decision of 1954 outlawing segregation in the public schools, at first glance it may seem rather paradoxical for us consciously to break laws. One may well ask: "How can you advocate breaking some laws and obeying others?" The answer lies in the fact that there are two types of laws: just and unjust. I would be the first to advocate obeying just laws. One has not only a legal but a moral responsibility to obey just laws. Conversely, one has a moral responsibility to disobey unjust laws. I would agree with St. Augustine that "an unjust law is no law at all."

Now, what is the difference between the two? How does one determine whether a law is just or unjust? A just law is a man-made code that squares with the moral law or the law of God. An unjust law is a code that is out of harmony with the moral law. To put it in the terms of St. Thomas Aquinas: An unjust law is a human law that is not rooted in eternal law and natural law. Any law that uplifts human personality is just. Any law that degrades human personality is unjust. All segregation statutes are unjust because segregation distorts the soul and damages the personality. It gives the segregator a false sense of superiority and the segregated a false sense of inferiority. Segregation, to use the terminology of the Jewish philosopher Martin Buber, substitutes an "I-it" relationship for an "I-thou" relationship and ends up relegating persons to the status of things. Hence segregation is not only politically, economically, and sociologically unsound, it is morally wrong and sinful. Paul Tillich has said that sin is separation. Is not segregation an existential expression of man's tragic separation, his awful estrangement, his terrible sinfulness? Thus it is that I can urge men to obey the 1954 decision of the Supreme Court, for it is morally right; and I can urge them to disobey segregation ordinances, for they are morally wrong.

Let us consider a more concrete example of just and unjust laws. An unjust law is a code that a numerical or power majority group compels a minority group to obey but does not make binding on itself. This is *difference* made legal. By the same token, a just law is a code that a majority compels a minority to follow and that it is willing to follow itself. This is *sameness* made legal.

Let me give another explanation. A law is unjust if it is inflicted on a minority that, as a result of being denied the right to vote, had no part in enacting or devising the law. Who can say that the legislature of Alabama which set up that state's segregation laws was democratically elected? Throughout Alabama all sorts of devious methods are used to prevent Negroes from becoming registered voters, and there are some counties in which, even though Negroes constitute a majority of the population, not a single Negro is registered. Can any law enacted under such circumstances be considered democratically structured?

Sometimes a law is just on its face and unjust in its application. For instance, I have been arrested on a charge of parading without a permit. Now, there is nothing wrong in having an ordinance which requires a permit for a parade. But such an ordinance becomes unjust when it is used to maintain segregation and to deny citizens the First-Amendment privilege of peaceful assembly and protest.

I hope you are able to see the distinction I am trying to point out. In no sense do I advocate evading or defying the law, as would the rabid segregationist. That would lead to anarchy. One who breaks an unjust law must do so openly, lovingly, and with a willingness to accept the penalty. I submit that an individual who breaks a law that conscience tells him is unjust, and who willingly accepts the penalty of imprisonment in order to arouse the conscience of the community over its injustice, is in reality expressing the highest respect for law.

Of course, there is nothing new about this kind of civil disobedience. It was evidenced sublimely in the refusal of Shadrach, Meshach, and Abednego to obey the laws of Nebuchadnezzar, on the ground that a higher moral law was at stake. It was practiced superbly by the early Christians, who were willing to face hungry lions and the excruciating pain of chopping blocks rather than submit to certain unjust laws of the Roman Empire. To a degree, academic freedom is a reality today because Socrates practiced civil disobedience. In our own nation, the Boston Tea Party represented a massive act of civil disobedience.

We should never forget that everything Adolf Hitler did in Germany was "legal" and everything the Hungarian freedom fighters did in Hungary was "illegal." It was "illegal" to aid and comfort a Jew in Hitler's Germany. Even so, I am sure that, had I lived in Germany at the time, I would have aided and comforted my Jewish brothers. If today I lived in a Communist country where certain principles dear to the Christian faith are suppressed, I would openly advocate disobeying that country's anti-religious laws.

I must make two honest confessions to you, my Christian and Jewish brothers. First, I must confess that over the past few years I have been gravely disappointed with the white moderate. I have almost reached the regrettable conclusion that the Negro's great stumbling block in his stride toward freedom is not the White Citizen's Counciler or the Ku Klux Klanner, but the white moderate, who is more devoted to "order" than to justice; who prefers a negative peace which is the absence of tension to a positive peace which is the presence of justice; who constantly says, "I agree with you in the goal you seek, but I cannot agree with your methods of direct action"; who paternalistically believes he can set the timetable for another man's freedom; who lives by a mythical concept of time and who constantly advises the Negro to wait for a "more convenient season." Shallow understanding from people of good will is more frustrating than absolute misunderstanding from people of ill will. Lukewarm acceptance is much more bewildering than outright rejection.

I had hoped that the white moderate would understand that law and order exist for the purpose of establishing justice and that when they fail in this purpose they become the dangerously structured dams that block the flow of social progress. I had hoped that the white moderate would understand that the present tension in the South is a necessary phase of the transition from an obnoxious negative peace, in which the Negro passively accepted his unjust plight, to a substantive and positive peace, in which all men will respect the dignity and worth of human personality. Actually, we who engage in nonviolent direct action are not the creators of tension. We merely bring to the surface the hidden tension that is already alive. We bring it out in the open, where it can be seen and dealt with. Like a boil that can never be cured so long as it is covered up but must be opened with all its ugliness to the natural medicines of air and light, injustice must be exposed, with all the tension its exposure creates, to the light of human conscience and the air of national opinion, before it can be cured.

In your statement you assert that our actions, even though peaceful, must be condemned because they precipitate violence. But is this a logical assertion? Isn't this like condemning a robbed man because his possession of money precipitated the evil act of robbery? Isn't this like condemning Socrates because his unswerving commitment to truth and his philosophical inquiries precipitated the act by the misguided populace in which they made him drink hemlock? Isn't this like condemning Jesus because his unique God-consciousness and never-ceasing devotion to God's will precipitated the evil act of crucifixion? We must come to see that, as the federal courts have consistently affirmed, it is wrong to urge an individual to cease his efforts to gain his basic constitutional rights because the quest may precipitate violence. Society must protect the robbed and punish the robber.

I had also hoped that the white moderate would reject the myth concerning time in relation to the struggle for freedom. I have just received a letter from a white brother in Texas. He writes: "All Christians know that the colored people will receive equal rights eventually, but it is possible that you are in too great a religious hurry. It has taken Christianity almost two thousand years to accomplish what it has. The teachings of Christ take time to come to earth." Such an attitude stems from a tragic misconception of time, from the strangely irrational notion that there is something in the very flow of time that will inevitably cure all ills. Actually, time itself is neutral; it can be used either destructively or constructively. More and more I feel that the people of ill will have used time much more effectively than have the people of good will. We will have to repent in this generation not merely for the hateful words and actions of the bad people, but for the appalling silence of the good people. Human progress never rolls in on wheels of inevitability; it comes through the tireless efforts of men willing to be co-workers with God, and without this hard work, time itself becomes an ally of the forces of social stagnation. We must use time creatively, in the knowledge that the time is always ripe to do right. Now is the time to make real the promise of democracy and transform our pending national elegy into a creative psalm of brotherhood. Now is the time to lift our national policy from the quicksand of racial injustice to the solid rock of human dignity.

You speak of our activity in Birmingham as extreme. At first I was rather disappointed that fellow clergymen would see my nonviolent efforts as those of an extremist. I began thinking about the fact that I stand in the middle of two opposing forces in the Negro community.

One is a force of complacency, made up in part of Negroes who, as a result of long years of oppression, are so drained of self-respect and a sense of "somebodiness" that they have adjusted to segregation; and in part of a few middle-class Negroes who, because of a degree of academic and economic security and because in some ways they profit by segregation, have become insensitive to the problems of the masses. The other force is one of bitterness and hatred, and it comes perilously close to advocating violence. It is expressed in the various black nationalist groups that are springing up across the nation, the largest and best-known being Elijah Muhammad's Muslim movement. Nourished by the Negro's frustration over the continued existence of racial discrimination, this movement is made up of people who have lost faith in America, who have absolutely repudiated Christianity, and who have concluded that the white man is an incorrigible "devil."

I have tried to stand between these two forces, saying that we need emulate neither the "do-nothingism" of the complacent nor the hatred and despair of the black nationalist. For there is the more excellent way of love and nonviolent protest. I am grateful to God that, through the influence of the Negro church, the way of nonviolence became an integral part of our struggle.

If this philosophy had not emerged, by now many streets of the South would, I am convinced, be flowing with blood. And I am further convinced that if our white brothers dismiss as "rabble-rousers" and "outside agitators" those of us who employ nonviolent direct action, and if they refuse to support our nonviolent efforts, millions of Negroes will, out of frustration and despair, seek solace and security in black-nationalist ideologies—a development that would inevitably lead to a frightening racial nightmare.

Oppressed people cannot remain oppressed forever. The yearning for freedom eventually manifests itself, and that is what has happened to the American Negro. Something within has reminded him of his birthright of freedom, and something without has reminded him that it can be gained. Consciously or unconsciously, he has been caught up by the *Zeitgeist,* and with his black brothers of Africa and his brown and yellow brothers of Asia, South America, and the Caribbean, the United States Negro is moving with a sense of great urgency toward the promised land of racial justice. If one recognizes this vital urge that has engulfed the Negro community, one should readily understand why public demonstrations are taking place. The Negro has many pent-up resentments and latent frustrations, and he must release them. So let him march; let him make prayer pilgrimages to the city hall; let him go on freedom rides—and try to understand why he must do so. If his repressed emotions are not released in nonviolent ways, they will seek expression through violence; this is not a threat but a fact of history. So I have not said to my people, "Get rid of your discontent." Rather, I have tried to say that this normal and healthy discontent can be channeled into the creative outlet of nonviolent direct action. And now this approach is being termed extremist.

But though I was initially disappointed at being categorized as an extremist, as I continued to think about the matter I gradually gained a measure of satisfaction from the label. Was not Jesus an extremist for love: "Love your enemies, bless them that curse you, do good to them that hate you, and pray for them which despitefully use you, and persecute you." Was not Amos an extremist for justice: "Let justice roll down like waters and righteousness like an ever-flowing stream." Was not Paul an extremist for the Christian gospel: "I bear in my body the marks of the Lord Jesus." Was not Martin Luther an extremist: "Here I stand; I cannot do otherwise, so help me God." And John Bunyan: "I will stay in jail to the end of my days before I make a butchery of my conscience." And Abraham Lincoln: "This nation cannot survive half slave and half free." And Thomas Jefferson: "We hold these truths to be self-evident, that all men are created equal. . . ." So the question is not whether we will be extremists, but what kind of extremists we will be. Will we be extremists for hate or for love? Will we be extremists for the preservation of injustice or for the extension of justice? In that dramatic scene on Calvary's hill three men were crucified. We must never forget that all three were crucified for the same crime—the crime of extremism. Two were extremists for immorality, and thus fell below their environment. The other, Jesus Christ, was an extremist for love, truth, and goodness, and thereby rose above his environment. Perhaps the South, the nation, and the world are in dire need of creative extremists.

I had hoped that the white moderate would see this need. Perhaps I was too optimistic; perhaps I expected too much. I suppose I should have realized that few members of the oppressor race can understand the deep groans and passionate yearnings of the oppressed race, and still fewer have the vision to see that injustice must be rooted out by strong, persistent, and determined action. I am thankful, however, that some of our white brothers in the South have grasped the meaning of this social revolution and committed themselves to it. They are still all too few in quantity, but they are big in quality. Some—such as Ralph McGill, Lillian Smith, Harry Golden, James McBride Dabbs, Ann Braden, and Sarah Patton Boyle—have written about our struggle in eloquent and prophetic terms. Others have marched with us down nameless streets of the South. They have languished in filthy, roach-infested jails, suffering the abuse and brutality of policemen who view them as "dirty nigger-lovers." Unlike so many of their moderate brothers and sisters, they have recognized the urgency of the moment and sensed the need for powerful "action" antidotes to combat the disease of segregation.

Let me take note of my other major disappointment. I have been so greatly disappointed with the white church and its leadership. Of course, there are some notable exceptions. I am not unmindful of the fact that each of you has taken some significant stands on this issue. I commend you, Reverend Stallings, for your Christian stand on this past Sunday, in welcoming Negroes to your worship service on a nonsegregated basis. I commend the Catholic leaders of this state for integrating Spring Hill College several years ago.

But despite these notable exceptions, I must honestly reiterate that I have been disappointed with the church. I do not say this as one of those negative critics who can always find something wrong with the church. I say this as a minister of the gospel, who loves the church; who was nurtured in its bosom; who has been sustained by its spiritual blessings and who will remain true to it as long as the cord of life shall lengthen.

When I was suddenly catapulted into the leadership of the bus protest in Montgomery, Alabama, a few years ago, I felt we would be supported by the white church. I felt that the white ministers, priests, and rabbis of the South would be among our strongest allies. Instead, some have been outright opponents, refusing to understand the freedom movement and misrepresenting its leaders; all too many others have been more cautious than courageous and have remained silent behind the anesthetizing security of stained-glass windows.

In spite of my shattered dreams, I came to Birmingham with the hope that the white religious leadership of this community would see the justice of our cause and, with deep moral concern, would serve as the channel through which our just grievances could reach the power structure. I had hoped that each of you would understand. But again I have been disappointed.

There was a time when the church was very powerful—in the time when the early Christians rejoiced at being deemed worthy to suffer for what they believed. In those days the church was not merely a thermometer that recorded the ideas and principles of popular opinion; it was a thermostat that transformed the mores of society. Whenever the early Christians entered a town, the people in power became disturbed and immediately sought to convict the Christians for being "disturbers of the peace" and "outside agitators." But the Christians pressed on, in the conviction that they were "a colony of heaven," called to obey God rather than man. Small in number, they were big in commitment. They were too God-intoxicated to be "astronomically intimidated." By their effort and example they brought an end to such ancient evils as infanticide and gladiatorial contests.

Things are different now. So often the contemporary church is a weak, ineffectual voice with an uncertain sound. So often it is an arch-defender of the status quo. Far from being disturbed by the presence of the church, the power structure of the average community is consoled by the church's silent—and often even vocal—sanction of things as they are.

But the judgment of God is upon the church as never before. If today's church does not recapture the sacrificial spirit of the early church, it will lose its authenticity, forfeit the loyalty of millions, and be dismissed as an irrelevant social club with no meaning for the twentieth century. Every day I meet young people whose disappointment with the church has turned into outright disgust.

Perhaps I have once again been too optimistic. Is organized religion too inextricably bound to the status quo to save our nation and the world? Perhaps I must turn my faith to the inner spiritual church, the church within the church, as the true *ekklesia* and the hope of the world. But again I am thankful to God that some noble souls from the ranks of organized religion have broken loose from the paralyzing chains of conformity and joined us as active partners in the struggle for freedom. They have left their secure congregations and walked the streets of Albany, Georgia, with us. They have gone down the highways of the South on torturous rides for freedom. Yes, they have gone to jail with us. Some have been dismissed from their churches, have lost the support of their bishops and fellow ministers. But they have acted in the faith that right defeated is stronger than evil triumphant. Their witness has been the spiritual salt that has preserved the true meaning of the gospel in these troubled times. They have carved a tunnel of hope through the dark mountain of disappointment.

I hope the church as a whole will meet the challenge of this decisive hour. But even if the church does not come to the aid of justice, I have no despair about the future. I have no fear about the outcome of our struggle in Birmingham, even if our motives are at present misunderstood. We will reach the goal of freedom in Birmingham and all over the nation, because the goal of America is freedom. Abused and scorned though we may be, our destiny is tied up with America's destiny. Before the Pilgrims landed at Plymouth, we were here. Before the pen of Jefferson etched the majestic words of the Declaration of Independence across the pages of history, we were here. For more than two centuries our forebears labored in this country without wages; they made cotton king; they built the homes of their masters while suffering gross injustice and shameful humiliation—and yet out of a bottomless vitality they continued to thrive and develop. If the inexpressible cruelties of slavery could not stop us, the opposition we now face will surely fail. We will win our freedom because the sacred heritage of our nation and the eternal will of God are embodied in our echoing demands.

Before closing I feel impelled to mention one other point in your statement that has troubled me profoundly. You warmly commended the Birmingham police force for keeping "order" and "preventing violence." I doubt that you would have so warmly commended the police force if you had seen its dogs sinking their teeth into unarmed, nonviolent Negroes. I doubt that you would so quickly commend the policemen if you were to observe their ugly and inhumane treatment of Negroes here in the city jail; if you were to watch them push and curse old Negro women and young Negro girls; if you were to see them slap and kick old Negro men and young boys; if you were to observe them, as they did on two occasions, refuse to give us food because we wanted to sing our grace together. I cannot join you in your praise of the Birmingham police department.

It is true that the police have exercised a degree of discipline in handling the demonstrators. In this sense they have conducted themselves rather "nonviolently" in public. But for what purpose? To preserve the evil system of segregation. Over the past few years I have consistently preached that nonviolence demands that the means we use must be as pure as the ends we seek. I have tried to make clear that it is wrong to use immoral means to attain moral ends. But now I must affirm that it is just as wrong, or perhaps even more so, to use moral means to preserve immoral ends. Perhaps Mr. Connor and his policemen have been rather nonviolent in public, as was Chief Pritchett in Albany, Georgia, but they have used the moral means of nonviolence to maintain the immoral end of racial injustice. As T. S. Eliot has said, "The last temptation is the greatest treason: To do the right deed for the wrong reason."

I wish you had commended the Negro sit-inners and demonstrators of Birmingham for their sublime courage, their willingness to suffer, and their amazing discipline in the midst of great provocation. One day the South will recognize its real heroes. They will be the James Merediths, with the noble sense of purpose that enables them to face jeering and hostile mobs, and with the agonizing loneliness that characterizes the life of the pioneer. They will be old, oppressed, battered Negro women, symbolized in a seventy-two-year-old woman in Montgomery, Alabama, who rose up with a sense of dignity and with her people decided not to ride segregated buses, and who responded with ungrammatical profundity to one who inquired about her weariness: "My feets is tired, but my soul is at rest." They will be the young high school and college students, the young ministers of the gospel and a host of their elders, courageously and nonviolently sitting in at lunch counters and willingly going to jail for conscience' sake. One day the South will know that when these disinherited children of God sat down at lunch counters, they were in reality standing up for what is best in the American dream and for the most sacred values in our Judaeo-Christian heritage, thereby bringing our nation back to those great wells of democracy which were dug deep by the founding fathers in their formulation of the Constitution and the Declaration of Independence.

Never before have I written so long a letter. I'm afraid it is much too long to take your precious time. I can assure you that it would have been much shorter if I had been writing from a comfortable desk, but what else can one do when he is alone in a narrow jail cell, other than write long letters, think long thoughts, and pray long prayers?

If I have said anything in this letter that overstates the truth and indicates an unreasonable impatience, I beg you to forgive me. If I have said anything that understates the truth and indicates my having a patience that allows me to settle for anything less than brotherhood, I beg God to forgive me.

I hope this letter finds you strong in the faith. I also hope that circumstances will soon make it possible for me to meet each of you, not as an integrationist or a civil-rights leader but as a fellow clergyman and a Christian brother. Let us all hope that the dark clouds of racial prejudice will soon pass away and the deep fog of misunderstanding will be lifted from our fear-drenched communities, and in some not too distant tomorrow the radiant stars of love and brotherhood will shine over our great nation with all their scintillating beauty.

Yours for the cause of Peace and Brotherhood,
Martin Luther King, Jr.

A Young Minister to His Church

In this letter of persuasion, written by a student in an English class, a fictional young minister persuades his congregation to treat a minority people, the Chicanos or Mexican Americans, with fairness and love.

Gentlemen:

You knew when you hired me that I am twenty-six years old, have a wife and a new son and that I just graduated from the seminary. Let me tell you some other things about me. I made a C in the conjugation of Hebrew verbs. I don't know how to tell when wheat is "in the dough." I busted a pipe on the church's hot water heater trying to fix it. I'm looking forward to learning a lot of things. One thing I do know is that when we have hold of love, God said we should share it. I've seen a lot of love demonstrated since I've been here. I've seen people helping each other work cattle and keeping each other's kids and making quilts together and taking sick folks to the doctor. I want us to think about extending that love.

Since I've been here, I've heard a lot of statements like these:

"_____ are lazy" (except for the laborers)

"_____ drink too much"

"_____ don't know how to plan for the future"

"_____ won't tell the truth"

"_____ steal"

"_____ have too many kids"

These ideas seem to be believed for two reasons: (1) they were taught to us by our parents, and (2) they have, in fact, been true about many of these people we know personally. May I tell you something I learned when I studied history? *These characteristics have always been shown by people who don't control their own lives.*

Your community has just lived through some history. In the last few years things have happened that have caused _____ to see themselves in a different way, and from now on they're going to behave differently. Our church stands right now in a position to direct them toward brotherhood and community spirit or, by what we do or don't do in the next few years, cause hostility. What we decide to do may determine whether our children will be able to raise their families in this country. You have seen how much harm can be done by a few people preaching hate and hostility; why don't we see how much healing we can get out of tolerance and love?

I don't have in mind a campaign to see how many ____ we can corral into our worship services or a raid on the Catholic church. In fact, I'm not talking about an organized program of any kind. I'm talking about a feeling that God really meant it when He said, "There is no difference between the Jew and the Greek." As the spiritual leaders of this town, you can make that feeling happen.

I'm putting this in a letter to you for two reasons. First, I am very serious about this. The Christian conscience cannot ignore the circumstances we are living with. Second, I want you to do what may seem like a strange thing. I want you to read [this letter] every day between now and next Sunday. Discuss it with each other every day, if possible. Notice if what you say and feel changes any during the week.

I will appreciate hearing your comments next Sunday. I hope you will begin to think of ways our church can present itself as a spiritual welcome to everybody in our town.

(Signed)

Writing Your Own Persuasion Essay

1. CONTEXTS

A

Your brother, who is young, progressive, and well qualified, is running for the state legislature, and you have agreed to seek support for him among your peers. In a short, informal essay, persuade the members of your class, your church group, or the people with whom you work to vote for your brother.

B

You are a young woman with several small children to support. In an effort to better yourself, you want to enroll in the local university. However, the school does not provide day-care facilities, and you cannot afford the private ones.

Write a letter to the chancellor, who has denied such petitions in the past, in which you persuade him to take the steps necessary to establish such facilities and convince him that the measure will be advantageous to the school.

C

You are working in a library to pay your way through school. The part of the job that you like best is going to the local elementary school to talk with the fourth graders about reading. You want *all* of them to love to read. This will be your third time to visit them, and you think hard about something new to say that will really *persuade* the children to read more. Write the essay that will be the background of your presentation.

D

Your father is headstrong and refuses to get a physical examination. It is true that he is seemingly very healthy, but at his age, you would feel better if he got a checkup at least once a year, if for no other reason than just maintaining his good health. Write the letter that will persuade your father to go get his yearly physical.

E

You have just bought a bright red previously owned Chevette. You were given a warranty that certified that the car was guaranteed for six months. Unfortunately, you have had nothing but trouble—the air conditioning fluid blew out, the carburetor stuck, and the electron emission fouled up. The last time it broke down thirty-five miles from the nearest telephone, and you had to go to enormous trouble to get a wrecker, get to the repair shop, and get your car back again. What is worse is that dealer who sold you the car now claims that the warranty does not include the things that have since broken down. You are furious—you happen to love the car and want it repaired and in good order, and at no expense to you. You plan to write to the state Consumer Protection Agency reporting this dealer and asking that the agency investigate him and see that your warranty is honored. Write the letter you will send.

PRACTICAL APPLICATIONS

OUTLINE

HOW TO APPLY CREATING, SHAPING,
AND COMPLETING TO ALL WRITING SITUATIONS

PURPOSE

In applying the writing process, you will:

Learn to adapt the stages of Creating, Shaping, and Completing to different types of writing

Get practice in various kinds of writing that you will likely do after you are out of school

Experience the relationship between writing and research

Learn to write speeches

Discover the secret to doing well on essay examinations

Practice writing skills which you can use in getting a job and doing well on that job after you are hired

Learn how to write about literature

Learn to keep a journal

WRITING THE RESEARCH PAPER

You've just heard that one of the major requirements of a course you are taking is a research paper, and you groan. You *know* what hard work that kind of writing is. Probably the first thing you think of is how difficult the footnotes are to type and how many hours it takes to find the material in the library. Well, cheer up: much of the misery can be taken out of the activity for you. What you will need, and what you are about to be shown, is a *system*—a system that moves step by step, making the paper a manageable task. This chapter will teach you a system that should work for all the research projects you will ever need to do.

But: *Why does doing a research paper seem like such a job?*

Several things account for it, which, summed up, come to this: *while* you are having to exercise all the ordinary and regular skills involved in the writing process—getting ideas, deciding about audience, shaping, revising, completing—you are also having to exercise several *new* nonwriting skills simultaneously. And it is this load-on-load that makes it seem like so much work.

SOMETHING OLD, SOMETHING NEW . . .

What are the nonwriting skills that you have to master in order to do a good research paper?

1 First of all, the *Creating Stage* for a research paper is different from the *Creating Stage* in other kinds of writing. The creating techniques that you have learned to use—cubing, looping, classical invention, and others—all call for information and knowledge that you already possess. When you did the creating technique, you pulled out this old information—or discovered new thoughts that emerged from the interaction of facts, experiences, and information that you had already possessed.

With the research paper, however, it's different. To do your initial creating for this kind of writing, you do not begin with what you already know. You actually begin by putting information *into* your head, not taking it out. This new information is then used some days or weeks later when you are planning and writing the paper itself. *The assumption is that you don't already possess a lot of knowledge or information on the subject of your paper.* (If you did, there wouldn't be much need to research the topic; it would be mostly a waste of time.) **The idea in *research* paper writing is that you must gather new information from outside sources *before* you can have anything to say on the subject.** Going to the library is actually *the creating technique* for this kind of writing. You may, of course, loop or cube some part of the new information later in a secondary creating activity, but the first step to finding an idea in this case is to go find out what other people have said on the subject.

And here's the rub.

This new creating technique requires a skill that you haven't had to use in other essays: *how to find material in the library*—before you can use the material. They are two separate operations. Learning how to use the library, then, is an extra thing to master (very valuable, of course, but still *extra*), so it is no wonder that you feel from the very start that doing a research paper is more work.

2 Another "extra" in research paper writing is learning **how to take notes, how to incorporate these notes into the body of an essay,** and **how to give credit for the information.** Again, this is a skill you haven't had to exercise in most of the other writing you have done. And without question, it is tedious. Deciding when to give credit to an author and when not to requires a lot of thought. Getting the paragraphs based on your notes to sound like coherent, flowing sentences instead of separate items from your notecards requires a lot of rewriting. But these skills of notetaking, incorporating notes into your own writing,

and documenting notes correctly are essential to an acceptable research paper. So, that's another skill to learn—on top of all the skills necessary in the writing process itself.

3 Finally, there's the *form* of the paper itself. **All the outside sources must be documented in footnotes and collected in a bibliography,** and knowing how to cite and to type footnotes and bibliography is a big job. Anyone who has ever typed too far down on the page and run out of space for the footnotes or who has forgotten to indent the second line of the bibliography when about one-third way down the page knows the frustration that the *form* of a research paper can bring. This, then, is a third nonwriting skill that you have to know how to do.

To do a good research paper, therefore, you have to have a large number of skills—some writing skills, some nonwriting.

WRITING SKILLS	NONWRITING SKILLS
Finding an angle or thesis	Learning how to use the library
Writing to a particular audience	Learning how to take notes
Fully developing the points	Learning how to incorporate notes into an essay
Shaping the essay for the reader	Learning how to document
Revising	Learning proper research paper forms
Editing and correcting	

Is it any wonder, then, that the project looks big?

But, you may say, if it's all this much work why do it? Is *anything* worth that much time and effort? Here are some reasons that may help you answer *yes* to your own question.

1 Learning to use the library is a skill which will stay with you for life. And it is a skill transferable to any kind of research you will ever want to do.

2 Once you learn the system for notetaking, citing information, and documenting sources, you'll know it for good. And the same system that you learn now will work when you do research projects for your company, when you look up legal briefs for an appearance in court, or when you search for the latest information on the income tax laws in order to beat an IRS audit.

3 Learning correct documentation form really means simply learning where to look something up. (It's *never* anything you have to memorize.) Getting practice in how to do it right is really nothing more than a matter of following the accepted practices in order to make reading your research paper as easy as possible. Good documentation also serves the readers by letting them know what books, articles, and other matter they could read if they wanted to know more about your subject.

4 Finally, however, more than any of these reasons the thing that makes the research paper worth doing is the sheer power it gives to

you: *personal power*. Here you are: Here's a subject:

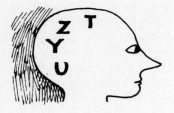

You know something about *U, Y, Z* and *T*, but you don't know anything about *X*. With research paper know-how, however, you can go into the library and learn about *X*. You come out smarter.

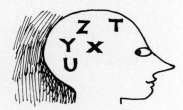

You now *contain X* and, above all, you can *communicate X* to someone else! This means that if you know how to use the library, how to take notes, how to document, you can find out anything you want to know—*anything!* There is *no* worldly knowledge that can be kept from you. And that is power—the power to be knowledgeable, to find out anything you want to know on your own, and to be able to communicate this to other human beings—for the rest of your life. You may never have to do a formal research paper again (although you also may, depending on how you decide to make your living and fortune), but you *will* have opportunity after opportunity to use the skills you learn in this process *to your advantage*.

WATCHING A RESEARCH PAPER BEING WRITTEN

Recalling those public television specials where families like the Louds were filmed as they went about their day-to-day lives, we are going to do something quite similar in this chapter. We shall be following a student as she writes her research paper for her freshman English class. Without having her before us on television, we shall nevertheless have her diary, notecards, bibliography, and several pieces of the information she used for the final paper. *By following her progress, you can learn how to write a research paper yourself.* All we need to know to follow Karen's work is that her teacher assigned the topics in the English class, and Karen's was this: *Do research on the book TOM JONES and the movie TOM JONES. Write a research paper based on a topic which surfaces when you do your reading in the library.* Of course, the instructor gave more information in class when the assignment was made, but this is basically what Karen had to go on as she began the work. As we follow her progress, Karen's diary appears in italics and our remarks on the progress she is making appear in regular type.

February 1.   I just can't believe it. This is the absolute pits. A research paper on Tom Jones. *Who cares about* Tom Jones? *English teachers, I guess. That's why he gave us such a useless assignment. I've never even seen the movie so* how can I compare it to the book? Come to think of it, I've never even read all the book. We were supposed to read it last year in senior English, but I never finished. 400 pages is just too long. I read* Cliff Notes *instead.*

I don't know where in the world I'll find time to do research. Teachers seem to think that their class is the only one. Well, I happen to be taking 12 hours besides English, and it's time everybody realized that.

The only research paper I've ever written was in high school, and that was on golf. I chose that topic because Dad had a million Golf *magazines on the floor behind his chair. So I just used a couple of those, one encyclopedia, and a dictionary as my sources.*

I'll never find anything in this school's library. I think they organized it for the graduate students. I do well to find the xerox machine.

What does Karen's first diary entry tell us?

——that she is very confused about the topic assigned to her by the teacher; it is about something she knows nothing about. She just hasn't realized yet that *she's not expected to know anything about it.* Right now all she feels is confused.

——that she feels she has no time. This is a normal reaction to a project she doesn't think she can do anyway.

——that she has no skills in research paper writing. She knows that the one term paper she did in high school was just a get-by situation. And she's very worried because she has no real experience or know-how.

——finally, that she feels lost in the library. Even if it does have everything she needs, she doesn't know how to find it.

What would be the best advice for Karen? It would go something like this:

1 **You need to realize that librarians are professionals.** They know everything there is to know about the library, and *they expect to be asked for help.* People doing research almost never use these professionals enough. Don't wait until you have a question. Go to the librarian just as soon as you are ready to begin the research paper. Tell him or her what you are working on and that you will be asking for assistance when you

need it. Establish contact by this courtesy visit and become known to the people who can help you the most in your work.

2 Begin early. So many of the problems in doing a research paper come about because much or everything is left to the last minute. You may discover that the library has to borrow books for you from another library or that a book you need is already checked out, so leave time for things like this. Also, remember the rule of thumb that *an activity probably takes three times the amount of time you think it will.* Plan for this. So don't underestimate the amount of time it will take to write the paper itself and type it. *Begin early!*

3 Begin the project in a treasure-hunt frame of mind. Approach the library as though it were a field where some fantastic treasure was buried that you were going to discover and get to keep. Be willing to be surprised. And realize that everything is there that you are going to need to know. It may not look at first as though anything is there on your subject. (When did you ever find treasure placed right out in the open?) The topic may be listed under something you hadn't thought of; the library may have separate collections or divisions you don't know about; the topic may be included in a bigger subject. Ask the librarian before you waste much time at all. There will not be a chance that there is *nothing* on your subject. It will be there, and with time you will find it.

You may, on the other hand, be overwhelmed by how much material you *do* find. There may seem to be two hundred times more material and information than you could ever use. In that case, ask a librarian where it would be best to start. If you approach the project with the frame of mind of "There's no telling what I might find!" or "Wonder what I will learn about this that I never knew existed before?" you will get pleasure out of the act of finding information even in the midst of all the seeming pain.

4 Don't worry at this point about the topic. Your first visits to the library are *exploratory* anyway, and as you read and take notes you will get clearer on what possibilities there are in your topic. Just hold on to the comforting fact that you aren't *supposed* to know anything about it at this point.

February 4.   Tom Jones is worse than my little brother. At least brothers go to sleep sometimes. Tom Jones just haunts me and follows me day and night. I'm honestly afraid to go to the library. I don't even know where to start. I don't even have a topic yet, except the general idea of the assignment.

I finally confessed to the prof that I'd never seen the movie, and he wasn't even surprised. He said that didn't matter because he wanted me to research what other people thought about it. I've got to get to the library.

I didn't even know when the thing came out. He said in the early '60s. I guess that is someplace to start.

February 5.   I feel relieved. I just found out that we don't need a topic until after we go to the library and read a bunch of stuff.

I've got to get to the library.
Heaven help me!

Karen is stalling for time. She's worrying and not working. The only thing to do is to plunge in—to get over to that library and start looking. If she doesn't do that soon, she won't have enough time when she does start, and she will see all her nervous fears realized. She'll actually create her failure! Here is good advice for her:

1 Go to the bookstore and load up on supplies.
2 Get 3 × 5 notecards for the bibliography sources (why not some color—they come in blue and pink and green and yellow—something that will cheer you up as you work).
3 Get 4 × 6 or 5 × 7 notecards for the notes themselves. (Again, go for color!)
4 Stock up on a handful of strong rubber bands to hold the cards together. If you really have the money, buy one of those bright plastic boxes to hold your cards. Again, the more ample and cheerful your work tools, the better you will feel.
5 Get several ballpoint pens and reserve them just for your research project.

The mere buying of these supplies will move Karen one step closer to the library. She will feel that she has *done something* about the assignment, and that's a great first step. She will also be prepared when she does go to the library.

February 7.   I finally did it. I took my new supplies and went to the library. The most familiar thing I saw when I got in there was the card catalog, so I decided to start there. And I actually found something!

First I looked for the subject Tom Jones *and couldn't find it. Then I looked under Henry Fielding, the author, and found a heading, "The History of Tom Jones." (I didn't even know that was the name of the book.) I was really excited to see 4 books that I thought I could use even though I wasn't familiar with the titles.*

Next, I thought I'd see what the encyclopedia had to say. The librarian showed me a weird one that was divided into two parts—the Encyclopedia Brittanica. *She said look at the Macropedia for details, so that's where I looked. It said Fielding was pretty controversial. I xeroxed that page just in case of an emergency.*

After that I asked the librarian where I could find out exactly when the movie came out, since I am supposed to do something about the movie and the book. She showed me a book called Film Facts, *and it has all the scoop on films. It said—under* Tom Jones, *of course—that the movie was produced in 1962. Progress! So I took my 4 books on the novel and wrote down the name of* Film Facts *and the page the information was on, and decided to call it a night. I figured I had found enough for one evening.*

Going to the card catalog first was a smart thing for Karen to do; she did find four books listed there. What she missed, however, was something very important on the card—a notice that one of the books had a *bibliography* included.

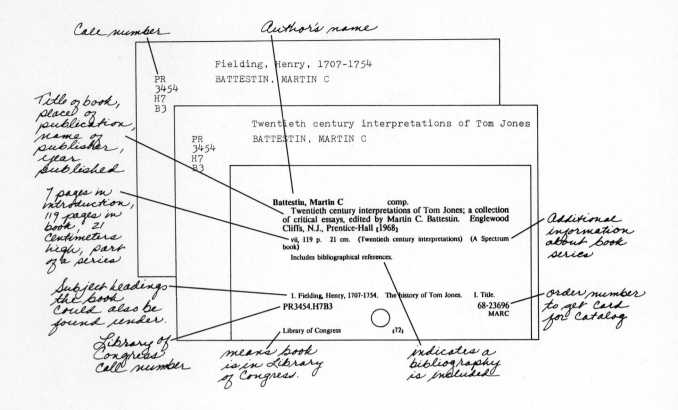

Call number

Author's name

Title of book, place of publication, name of publisher, year published

7 pages in introduction, 119 pages in book, 21 centimeters high, part of a series

Subject headings the book could also be found under.

Library of Congress Call number

means book is in Library of Congress.

indicates a bibliography is included

Additional information about book series

order number to get card for catalog

```
          Fielding, Henry, 1707-1754
PR        BATTESTIN, MARTIN C
3454
H7
B3
```

```
          Twentieth century interpretations of Tom Jones
PR        BATTESTIN, MARTIN C
3454
H7
B3
```

```
Battestin, Martin C                    comp.
    Twentieth century interpretations of Tom Jones; a collection
of critical essays, edited by Martin C. Battestin.    Englewood
Cliffs, N.J., Prentice-Hall [1968]

    vii, 119 p.  21 cm.  (Twentieth century interpretations)  (A Spectrum
book)

    Includes bibliographical references.


    1. Fielding, Henry, 1707-1754.  The history of Tom Jones.    I. Title.
PR3454.H7B3                                          68-23696
                                                        MARC

Library of Congress            [72]
```

She didn't see, then, that this particular book included a list of other books on the same subject. If she had noticed this, she could have turned to that list at once and had a large number of additional sources for her research without looking a bit further. It would have been a real short-cut. So our advice to her would be to **read the card carefully to see if the book cited can lead you to other books.**

Karen also has a lead on this card that she may not have noticed. **Near the bottom are** *subject headings* **that tell where to look in the Subject Catalog** (she's looking now in the Author Catalog). If she will go to the Subject Catalog and look under Henry Fielding or *The History of Tom Jones,* she will probably find several more sources very quickly. The subject card would look like the author card except that it would have a designation at the top of it saying what the book is about. (And a third way she might find the book listed is under its title, as on the title card.) *The clues are all there;* Karen just must be able to read them. If she can, she'll be able to find everything she needs and fast.

Another thing Karen needed to start doing immediately was to make her bibliography cards. Every time she finds a source, she should write down every piece of information she would need to find that book again or to cite it in her paper when it gets written. **Making bibliography cards (using 3 × 5 cards)** *fully* **and** *correctly* **will be one of the biggest time**

savers of the whole project. If everything doesn't get written down, Karen will have to go back to the library later for the date of publication or the publisher or some other piece of information that she needs but neglected to write down. Here is how a bibliography card for a book should look:

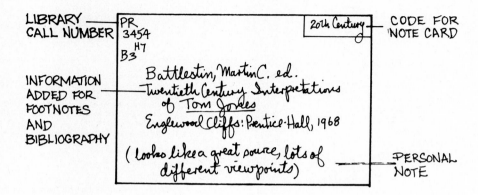

The bibliography card for Karen's encyclopedia article should look like this:

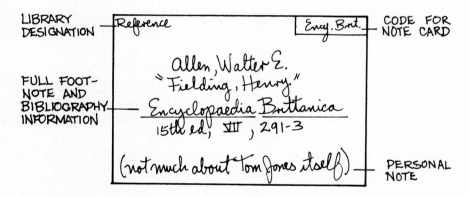

If she makes a bibliography card for every source *as she goes along,* Karen will make her job of looking for material and documenting the paper much easier and hassle-free. Even though it takes a little time, it will save *enormous* time in the long run.

> A stitch in time saves nine.

February 9. I looked through those 4 books, and they look as though they are written for graduate school research. Am I supposed to be a genius when I'm a freshman? There's only one of the 4 that I can even begin to read. And boring! Ugh!

  Back to the library. Why don't people write stuff that we can read?

February 10. This is really discouraging. I went to the Reader's Guide *to find magazine articles about the movie—that's where the librarian said to look. I looked* under "Tom Jones," "film," "Henry Fielding," and didn't find a single thing. "Tom Jones" wasn't even listed, and "Film" and "Fielding" didn't have anything about Tom Jones. I absolutely hate this.

I guess I'll go back to the librarian and ask more questions.

February 11. The librarian suggested I go to the Reader's Guide, *which lists magazine articles, for the years around the time the movie "Tom Jones" came out. I had been looking in this year's* Reader's Guide. *When I went to 1961–63, I did find some entries, although I don't know yet how much they will help me.*

Subject headings

FILM adaptations
Bookmakers. il Newsweek 61:73 Ja 14 '63
Not by the book; film treatment of Advise and consent. H. Koningsberger. il Horizon 4:116-18 My '62
Rights and permissions. P. Nathan. See issues of Publishers weekly
Swifty the great. il Time 79:54-5 F 2 '62
When a book becomes a movie. J. M. Culkin. il Sr Schol 81:24T-26T O 10 '62

FILM censorship. See Moving picture censorship

FILM critics. See Critics

FILM dryers. See Photography—Apparatus and supplies

FILM festival, Cannes. See Cannes international film festival

FILM festivals. See Moving picture exhibits

FILM racks. See Photography—Apparatus and supplies

FILM speeds. See Photography—Exposure

Title of article, author, has pictures, found in Senior Scholastic magazine, Vol. 81 pages 24-26, October 10, 1962

FIELD trips. Nature study. See Nature study
FIELDING, Gabriel
To be continued. M. Cosman. Commonweal 75:78-9 O 13 '61
Uses of fear. Harper 224:92-5 F '62
FIELDING, Henry
Henry Fielding's pieceable animal. H. K. Miller. Sat R 44:36-7 Ag 5 '61
FIELDING, Marian
Bite back at insect bites. McCalls 88:154B Ag '61
FIELDING, Waldo L. and Benjamin, Lois
Medical case against natural childbirth. McCalls 89:106-7+ Je '62
FIELDS, Ann
Pueblo sketches; poem. Poetry 99:158-9 D '61

About author

Appears in Saturday Review Vol. 44, pages 36-7 August 5, 1961

February 14. I've finally had a real breakthrough. The listings in the Reader's Guide *helped some. The real progress came, though, when the librarian suggested I look in the* New York Times Index *to get newspaper reviews of the film. I didn't even know we had old newspapers in the library! They are all on microfilm, something else I had never used before. I am learning a lot!*

When I looked in the New York Times Index *under* Tom Jones, *there was nothing. Fielding, Henry—nothing. Motion Pictures—Hallelujah! I found it. Right there under motion picture reviews,* Tom Jones—*4 articles. I got the microfilm (sounds like real detective work) from the librarian and found out the library could make copies for me from the microfilm. I got copies of all 4 articles. I feel so much better. People in the 60s loved the movie, and I'm even starting to like it better myself. With these 4 articles from the newspaper and the magazine articles I found under* Tom Jones, *I ought to have something to work with!*

Critic at Large

'Tom Jones' Film Version Is a Reminder to Reread Fielding Masterpiece

By BROOKS ATKINSON

AFTER roaring with delight at an early showing of the motion picture "Tom Jones," some of us thought we should reread the original Henry Fielding novel.

For it appeared that none of us had read it after having passed without honor in school. "Tom Jones" shares with "Don Quixote" the distinction of being the least read masterpiece in fiction—less read than "War And Peace," which is equally loquacious.

There was another reason for rereading "Tom Jones." In the last scene of the film that John Osborne has made from the novel, Tom is pictured as riding in a tumbrel through the streets of London on the way to the scaffold. None of us could remember such a macabre episode in the novel. For a very good reason: there is none. After taking the reader through more than 1,100 pages of adventure and buffoonry, Fielding delivers Tom from prison with an excess of unction and sentimentality. The last pages are saturated in glucose—most of the characters undergoing transports of affection for good Mr. Allworthy and abasing themselves on their knees before him.

●

The procession to the gibbet in the film is therefore unauthorized. But no complaints are being registered here. For Mr. Osborne and Tony Richardson, the director, have captured in 135 minutes of film the comic hubbub of a very long novel. Since their pell-mell conclusion puts screen excitement ahead of Fielding's realism, the academicians will have to brand the film "a flawed masterpiece," which is the polite equivalent of a sorrowful shake of the head. But Fielding's maudlin last pages are also flaws in his masterpiece. Let's not quibble over the taste of one scene in a rousing screenplay that is notable for its comic freshness.

To 18th-century readers the Fielding novel must have been as refreshing as the film is to us. Both the novel and the film give cant a good thwacking. In one of his entertaining fireside chats with the reader, Fielding scorns literary piety: "There are [sic] a set of religious, or rather moral writers, who teach that virtue is the certain road to happiness, and vice to misery, in this world. A very wholesome and comfortable doctrine, and to which we have but one objection, namely, that it is not true." A Bow Street magistrate, Fielding dealt every day in the realities of human nature.

●

Samuel Richardson, author of "Pamela" and "Clarissa Harlowe," knew to whom Fielding was referring. No doubt that is why he said that "the virtues of Fielding's heroes are the vices of a truly good man." And that is why Dr. Johnson, an impenitent moralist, adhered to Richardson. To Boswell's assertion that Fielding drew very natural pictures of human life, Dr. Johnson retorted: "Why, Sir, it is a very low life. Richardson used to say that had he not known who Fielding was he should believed he was an ostler."

Tom Jones is no profligate. He is a cavalier young man who lacks common sense. He is more like Squire Booby in "Joseph Andrews" than the obscure Mr. Summer who begot him unlawfully on the severe person of Mr. Allworthy's maiden sister. Tom's ludicrous adventures in a recognizable British landscape are in the comic tradition of Shakespeare, whom Fielding adored; and of Dickens, who carried on the same humorous extravagance in the next century.

Except in the witty prologue, there is nothing immaculate in Mr. Richardson's film. It is full of the sweat, farm-yard grunts, the recklessness, tippling and bawdiness of 18th-century England. Obviously, Mr. Richardson, his writer and his actors had a good time putting their film together. That's only fair. Fielding had a good time writing his novel.

There are a couple of things we'd say to Karen here. First of all, she's doing great in her detective work. We applaud her for not being afraid to go back to the librarian when she needs assistance, and she deserves praise for not giving up when she gets discouraged.

However, **she should begin** *now* **to take notes** instead of paying so much money to have things xeroxed. She's probably doing this for a feeling of security, but it isn't necessary and it isn't an efficient use of her time. She could glance at the articles in the *New York Times* and jot down anything she thought she might be able to use later. Of course, she doesn't know her exact topic yet, and that may be why she is collecting everything rather than making notes. If she began making notes, however, she would get into the subject matter of her topic much sooner (instead of merely having a pile of books and xeroxed copies stacked up). She would be clearer about exactly what she wanted to write about. Also, Karen may not always find herself in a library that has the expensive machines for copying microfilm. She needs to begin making notes *now*, particularly with short pieces like newspaper and magazine articles.

Here is the best advice about taking notes:

1 Use 4 × 6 notecards.
2 In the upper right-hand corner write the code words—last name of author, name of encyclopedia, etc.—from the bibliography card so that you will know what the source was for the information.
3 At the beginning of the note, write the page number of the source. (This is *critical* because you have to be able to footnote the exact page. Don't get caught in the library at midnight the day before the paper is due looking for page numbers!) As soon as the page in your source changes, write the new number immediately on the notecard, even if you are in the middle of a line.
4 Write the information in your own words. If you feel something *must* be stated just as the writer put it, copy it word for word and put quotation marks around it.
5 Number the notecard at the bottom for your own purposes. You'll probably drop the notecards a hundred times while you are doing the

BIBLIOGRAPHY CARD

> ATKINSON
>
> ATKINSON, BROOKS
> "Critic at Large: Tom Jones film version is a reminder to reread Fielding masterpiece."
> New York Times, November 8, 1963.
> section 6, page 20, columns 4-5
> (looks like great source)

```
┌─────────────────────────────────────────────┐
│ COMPARING BOOK AND MOVIE        ATKINSON     │
│                                              │
│ PAGE 28 " To 18th century                    │
│ readers the Fielding novel                   │
│ must have been as refreshing                 │
│ as the film is to us."                       │
│                                              │
│                                              │
│                      1                       │
└─────────────────────────────────────────────┘
```

```
┌─────────────────────────────────────────────┐
│ REAL LIFE IN BOOK AND MOVIE     ATKINSON     │
│                                              │
│ P.28 Both the book and the movie catch       │
│ the fun of life. They both show              │
│ that vice can be fun too, even though         │
│ it is usually virtue that people             │
│ praise. People like the story be-            │
│ cause it shows real human nature.            │
│                                              │
│                      2                       │
└─────────────────────────────────────────────┘
```

paper, and it takes hours to get them back in order if they aren't numbered.

6 When you have finished with one notecard, write a word or two at the top of the left-hand side which can be your index for the card—some words that tell you what the subject of that notecard is. This will help you when you start to sort the cards later.

February 21.   I've read most of the material now that I got from the library, but I still don't have any idea what I am going to write on. I definitely don't want to write the usual boring paper that puts everybody to sleep. There must be something interesting about Tom Jones to make so many people want to read and see him.

That quote from Atkinson about people in the 18th century being as refreshed by the book as people in 1960 were by the film is the only thing that has seemed to have any promise at all for a topic. I thought about writing a paper that compared the reactions of the 18th-century general public to the movie. I don't really think I've got the material to do that, though. The only 18th-century reactions that I have found are mostly literary and don't mention much about the general public at all. Maybe the general public didn't read. They must have read the book, though, or at least have known a lot about it because the big scholars didn't care much for it, and I figure somebody had to like it to make it popular.

February 22. I've decided that 3/4 of the work in doing research is thinking. My brain has never worked this hard in my life. It's such a relief to come up with ideas and to find material, but it hurts. I don't think there's been one hour since I got this assignment that I haven't thought about Tom. I will be so glad when it's over, and I can think about something else for a while. I have a feeling that after I get my paper all thought out and come up with a definite idea most of the work will be over.

Karen is absolutely right about the importance of *thinking* in the research paper process. Right now—after finding and reading as much material as she can and taking preliminary notes—she is at that point where writers usually sit down to begin their essay. She has completed that first nonwriting task of locating material in the library, and now she is ready to do the first stage of the actual writing process—creating or finding an idea.

The best advice for Karen at this point would be to do some of the creating techniques she learned earlier—*looping, cubing, classical invention.* She has put new information into her head, and now she can see what her own mind will do with this new knowledge. (That alone will be a pleasant thing for Karen to observe.) She could probably save herself a lot of worry and fretting if she did a few creating exercises at this point. Very likely some good ideas would emerge as possibilities for a focus for the paper. And doing creating activities would be a welcome break from the close reading she has been doing. They would also be a way to collect her thoughts and just see where things stand at this point.

February 23. I'm still toying with that idea of people being refreshed in the 18th century just as they were in the 20th. What is there about Tom Jones *that would make it fun for people living so many years apart? I went back to the encyclopedia to see if I could find anything on 18th-century England. I looked in Britannica and could find only very factual information—nothing I could compare to the 1960s. So I looked in the card catalog under the subject heading of Great Britain "Social Conditions and Customs—18th Century." The number of books was overwhelming, but I copied down several call numbers. By the time I finished I didn't feel like climbing all those stairs, so I just checked out one book that was on the first floor. I glanced at the introduction and read ". . . the conflicts and tensions of 1760 are identical with those of 1960." Maybe this is it! I think I'll read the whole book.*

There are a couple of things to notice here. One is that Karen is still playing with the idea that came after she read one sentence in the film review in the *New York Times,* an idea that fascinates her and yet that came from a very small piece of information. The point to notice is that you will never know when an idea will strike you—or from what source. It doesn't take a long piece of material to give you a thought, and you cannot set up "getting the thought." It just happens when it does. *The thing you have to do is keep moving.* It's like those four kinds of luck mentioned in the *Creating Section* of this book—**if you stay in motion, something will finally turn up.** (Remember the quote, "The dog that trots about finds the bone"? That's what Karen has done, and the idea that seems to stick with her came unexpectedly and unplanned.)

The second thing to notice is that luck was at play again in the one book Karen checked out the day she was tired. She had found so many, a lot were on other floors of the library, and she went for the one closest at hand—one that she wouldn't have to climb stairs to get. And *that* book turned out to have some information on just the thing she had been thinking about. There is no need to pretend that this kind of luck doesn't come to the aid of your research paper project. Sometimes just good fortune will cause you to put your hands on exactly the right thing. (Other times the greatest good will and effort in the world doesn't seem to turn up anything.) Serendipity plays a part, too: you will be looking for one thing and find another; it all falls within the territory of your research. And be certain of this: in the end, if you look enough and stick with your research, any "bad luck" you might be having will do a fade-out.

February 24. The name of that book I found on the first floor was The Augustan Vision. *I couldn't figure out why it was listed in the card catalog under 18th century. But then I looked in the introduction to the book and it said that this book is about the entire 18th century. The librarian suggested that I look up "Augustan Age" in the* Glossary of Literary Terms, *and I learned that it was an ancient period but that the same name was used for the first 45 years of the 18th century or the entire century. Why can't everybody just decide on a term for this period and make everybody use it? I'm really tired of coming across twelve different terms every time I open a book, just to discover that all the terms stand for the same thing. This is getting* very *exhausting. Already I've had to look up a million things in source books. I think I might qualify as a literary scholar if I live through this.*

No wonder people who do this for a living seem so strange....

Frustrated again—and we can see why. But information is almost never in a concise package; it comes in bits and pieces, chaotic and squirmy. It's understandable why Karen is tired.

February 26. I can't believe I hadn't thought of this before! In the middle of the night last night, I realized that maybe I ought to check out the book Tom Jones *since I was doing research on it. What a stupid thing to miss. Well, I got a copy, and that was the smartest thing I've done yet. Not only did I get a copy of the book, but I got one that has all sorts of good stuff in the back. It has parts of papers and letters that people in Fielding's day wrote right after they had read the book, regular and normal people. That's just what I needed. And, as I suspected, they loved the book.*

This is definitely a breakthrough. I feel encouraged.

You have to ask, "Why in the world didn't she think of that sooner?"

Well, just because she didn't! Your own mind doesn't always progress orderly and smoothly during the thinking process, and often it will be working for you when you are unaware that anything is going on. It's been said that the best thing to do with a question on a test that you can't answer is to "put the question on the back burner," meaning to put it out of your conscious mind and let the subconscious work on it for a while. Evidently, Karen's subconscious mind was working for her and threw up a very important suggestion when she was least suspecting it. That's why it is very smart to *trust yourself* (provided, of course, that you are doing the necessary leg-work) and not get frantic. *Good ideas will come.*

February 27. Good luck strikes again! When I was looking over my notes, I realized that I had never looked under "Motion Pictures" in the Reader's Guide. *I went back and looked in the 1963 book and, sure enough, I found 7 articles listed in* Life, Time, Newsweek, Saturday Review, *and other magazines. This is a* major *breakthrough!*

I had to look in this machine in the library to find out where the magazines were (I think it's called the microfish — *more detective work). I copied the call numbers and found the magazines. It was so neat to look through those old magazines and find the articles. I noticed that JFK was killed and that Viet Nam was going full force; this made me start thinking about what might have been going on in England when* Tom Jones *came out. I don't know much history, but I do know that in the 1770s England had a skirmish going on — in America. I wonder if I could find out something about conditions, events, concerns in England in the 18th century and in America in the 1960s. That might give me a clue to why people liked the book then and people like the movie now. That might make an interesting paper. I can find stuff on the 1960s — that's no problem. But I wonder where I can find stuff on the 18th century. I guess I'll go back to the encyclopedia, card catalog, and librarian.*

I'm so glad to have those articles.

It's good to watch Karen actually get excited over her ideas. She is now thinking about something she probably has never thought about before and is actually cooking up a "problem" that could become the focus for her paper: *what is there about the book and the movie that gives people of both centuries so much pleasure?* She's definitely making progress.

February 28. I have been reading a little in that book The Augustan Vision, *and I'm discovering some interesting things. The author tells how few people were financially supporting the entire population in England, how the sexes were trying to get their roles defined, how there was a growing movement toward humanitarianism. Well, if that doesn't describe movements going on today that began or got stronger in the 1960s, I don't know what does. There are obvious differences, of course, between the two centuries (like not so much mechanization, knowledge, etc., in 1700s), but the* conflicts *and* tensions *seem to be based on similar feelings. Maybe these conflicts and tensions made people need to lose themselves in a hilariously funny novel or movie.*

Cross index

finally, entries on Tom Jones itself!

Voilà!

I can see the paper developing!

March 1.   I am so relieved to have a topic. I just decided for certain that I would write the reasons the book and movie were both popular, and when I decided on that for sure, I ran out of my room, down the hall, down the stairs, and out the door. I thought I deserved some fresh air, and I felt so light and happy. I feel like most of my work is over, although I haven't written one word of the paper yet.

Karen has finished a big chunk of the work — using the library to best advantage for finding material she needs and deciding on a *more specific* topic to base her paper on. She is ready now to begin the *Shaping Stage* of the writing process.

March 3.   I just went out and bought a new pen. I've discovered that I have to take more notes. I don't have enough on the exact thing I am going to write about.

I do have the sources, though, so it's just a matter of doing some more reading and notetaking. I am hoping the new pen will inspire me. I'm just not inspired to finish up. Everybody else is gone. The TV's off, and I'm sitting here having to take more notes.

March 6. I've just looked over all my notes to get ready to do the first draft of my paper. I turned out to have plenty of material, although I was afraid for a while that I would not find enough to say. I've got more cards than I can probably use. When I look at the cards, I can definitely see a concrete pattern emerging from my notes. Tom *the book and* Tom *the movie both laugh at and, in a sense, attack social institutions — like the Church and philosophers, the family and marriage, the military, social rank and class, and roles of sexes. It seems that in the 18th century, like in the 1960s, there was a general current of questioning these institutions and re-evaluating and changing some of them. These tensions, which sometimes came out in politics, made both cultures ready to read or view a story of an ordinary person who didn't blindly uphold all these institutions as sacred and absolutely perfect. This is what I am going to try to show in my paper.*

When I first got this research paper assignment, I never dreamed that I'd learn this much or be able to make such comparisons. I really feel smart. I really am learning, although I wouldn't admit it to my English prof!

The thoughts are jelling. Karen is beginning to make some sense out of all she has read. She now knows what the thesis for her research paper will be, and she can now write the first draft to see just how she can state and prove that thesis. As it turns out, Karen is writing the kind of research paper that *makes a statement and then proves it,* like the *assertion* essay you wrote earlier. Other people in her class are probably writing other types of research papers. Some may be doing a *problem and solution* research project, in which they state clearly some major problem and then use outside sources to find the solutions to this problem. Others may be doing a *report-type* research paper, where they merely set out to give the facts about some topic. Actually, a *research paper* could serve most of the purposes of the *essays* you have written earlier in this text; the difference is that outside information would be used instead of what you already knew.

March 5. I think I'm really beginning to see what research is all about. I didn't really do any research on that golf paper last year. It's one thing to talk *about some topic and another to* read *about a topic, come up with an idea based on the reading, and support that idea with details from the outside sources. The process of reading and gathering and organizing information to help an audience understand my ideas is really getting clear.*

I still think it is a dumb topic; I'd much rather be learning about something more useful. I was hoping to write a paper that I could use later on in other classes.

I really had a scare in class today. The teacher said something about "credibility of sources." Good Lord, what next? I don't even know what that means, much less whether or not I did it. This is just all one big pain. Anyway, I talked to him afterwards and found out that he meant that our sources had to be by reputable people. I don't even know these 18th-century people! He glanced over my bibliography cards and said my sources were credible. What a relief! What in the world would I have done if they weren't?

March 6. I just started trying to write my second draft. I did one, just going through my notecards very fast and trying to prove my thesis. Now I need to see what needs to be done to make the paper really stand up. Before I did my first draft, I divided my notecards into piles and then went from one pile to another as I wrote the paper. Now I see, though, that some things should come before others, etc. I was getting very confused, and then I came up with a brilliant plan. I wrote a real sketchy outline for my paper that looks like this:

    1. Establish mutual praise
       A. Movie.
       B. Book.
    2. Why?
       Book and movie did same thing—dealt with institutions in satirical form.
    3. Briefly, why 2 centuries' audiences enjoyed these attacks:
       18th,
       20th.
    4. Conclude that producer saw similarities between societies' attitudes and capitalized on this to produce an important movie of this century.

This might even be the germ of my final outline that I include with the research paper itself. At any rate, it can serve as a guide for me as I do the second draft.

March 7. When I read over my second draft today, I saw that I need to give a slightly different slant to my groups. I think now they will look like this when I do the final version of the paper.

    1. Movie and book both well received by audiences.
    2. Both dealt with life.
    3. Both examine society and deal with issues of the day (reflect attitudes).
    4. That's what makes Fielding last two centuries.

I AM AN ABSOLUTE GENIUS!!!

March 10. I'm in a state of shock. Writing the final version of my paper wasn't nearly as hard as I thought it would be. The biggest trouble I had was working in my quotes and outside information into my own sentences. The first version sounded just like my notecards strung along together. I even laughed to myself and thought, "I might as well just give the notecards to the teacher." But this last time I reworded things, added a lot of transition sentences to get from one point to another, and tried to paraphrase most everything. I got a little mixed up about whether to put a footnote in or not, and I'm still not sure about all that. But I think I've got it in pretty good shape.

Unbelievable—the end is in sight. All I've got to do now is type the paper in its final form, do the footnotes and the bibliography, type the outline, and get it ready to hand in! I really feel good.

Tom Jones Lives a Long Life

By

Karen Brinkley

English 103

Professor Cowan

March 15, 1979

Tom Jones Lives a Long Life   *Title of research paper*

Optional Heading

OUTLINE

Thesis: There are several reasons why <u>Tom Jones</u> was
         interesting to audiences who lived 200 years
         apart.

Point the paper explains

I.   Introduction: <u>Tom Jones</u>'s Success in Two Centuries

      A. Twentieth-Century Movie

      B: Eighteenth-Century Novel

II.   Explanation: Life as a Subject

Topic Outline

      A. Eighteenth-Century Concern

      B. Twentieth-Century Concern

III. Reason: Society as an Issue

      A. Eighteenth-Century Hypocrisies and Issues

      B. Twentieth-Century Hypocrisies and Issues

IV.   Conclusion: Lasting Success as a Masterpiece

Tom Jones Lives a Long Life

Opening establishes popularity of movie in the 20th Century

"Most of the critical excitement last week centered on 'Tom Jones,'" one American movie critic wrote in October *Corresponds to Outline I A* 1963, "the brilliant and bawdy film of the Henry Fielding novel. . . . And it well should have been, for this rare rendering of the classic of 18th-century English literature . . . is a wonderfully energetic and entertaining film, one of the most completely antic that has ever been brought to the screen."[1] Another 20th-century critic agrees: "We are, in fact, still very much in the midst of the 'Fielding revival' . . . , one sign of which has been the brilliant success of the recent film Tom Jones."[2] Readers in 18th-century England were as excited about the book Tom Jones as moviegoers in 20th-century America were about the film. Brooks Atkinson, a critic for the New York Times, guessed that "to 18th-century readers the Fielding novel must have been as refreshing as the film is to us."[3] According to *Transition Sentence* popular opinion in 18th-century England, Atkinson's guess was correct.

This ¶ establishes the popularity of the book in the 18th Century

A 1751 anonymous reader called Tom Jones "on the whole . . . the most lively book ever published."[4] Two thousand copies were printed in its first edition and were sold *Corresponds to Outline I B* before the announced date of publication (February 10, 1749). This was "perhaps an unheard of case."[5] By the end of February, the second issue of 1,500 copies came out, and by the end of the year 6,500 copies had been printed. The book was "in every Hand, from the beardless Youth, up to the hoary Hairs of Age."[6] Boswell, a famous writer in the 18th century, said, "'Tom Jones' has stood the test of publick opinion with such success, as to have established its great merit. . . ."[7] Captain Lewis Thomas, a soldier in Fielding's day, agreed: "I am just got up from a very Amazing entertainment; to use a Metaphore in the Foundling, I have been these four days past a fellow traveller of Henry Fielding's, and a very agreeable Journey I have had."[8]

Transition paragraph

Thesis of Essay

Obviously, then, the readers in 18th-century England enjoyed Henry Fielding's book Tom Jones as much as 20th-century Americans enjoyed the film version. When I discovered this idea while doing research on the novel and the film, I began to wonder what a work could have that would make its topic so interesting to audiences two centuries apart in time.

These next 3 ¶'s establish that Tom Jones is about life

Corresponds to Outline IIA & B

Very simply stated, "Life is the subject matter of the writer of fiction . . . ,"[9] and this concern for life is one of the main reasons for Tom Jones's continued success. George Saintsbury called Tom Jones "an epic of life--not indeed of the highest, the rarest, the most impassioned of life's scenes and phases, but of the healthy average life of the average natural man. . . ."[10] The character Tom

Jones was described in Life magazine as "one of the most engaging unheroic heroes in all English literature,"[11] and another source said "Tom Jones appears . . . as a kind of Everyman striving toward maturity against his own weaknesses and the pressures of a hostile world."[12] Since Tom Jones the novel and Tom Jones the movie are both concerned with ordinary people and everyday life, both have managed to captivate their audiences.

Some 18th-century critics disliked Tom Jones because it dealt with ordinary life; they thought "the 'lowness' of his themes--his preoccupation with the adventures . . . of footmen and foundlings, of country wenches and Mayfair demi-reps" was damaging.[13] A 20th-century critic, however, thinks these qualities are exactly what appeals to 20th-century Americans--"Fielding's wit and hearty good humor and, above all, his tolerant humanity . . . seem . . . congenial to us," he says.[14]

Corresponds to Outline II A & B

In addition, the Encyclopaedia Britannica states that Fielding is remembered today because of his concern for human weaknesses and morality.[15] Another source praises Fielding because he "described for the first time in English a real man."[16] And this idea of a real man in a "country viewed through the wryly critical eyes of a man who knew too well the hypocrisies of his people and his age" is

Corresponds to Outline II A & B

exactly what appealed to 20th-century viewers.[17] The movie
presents a view of 18th-century England that most 20th-
century viewers were not used to seeing; one critical review
described it as "a great, sprawling boisterous film that is
out to unbutton the elegant embroidered waistcoat . . . and
show it dirty, cruel, yahooish, leching, and guzzling, as
well as stylish."[18]

Transition sentence

Because Fielding not only dealt with life but also with
the hypocrisies of society, his subject matter appealed to
people in the 18th and 20th centuries. Pat Rogers, in his
book The Augustan Vision, states that whenever a society

The next 3 ¶s discuss society in 18 century England

Corresponds to III A

becomes confident and politically stable, it will begin
thinking about inward problems--"questions of personal
identity and private relationships."[19] This is what people
in Fielding's time and the 1960s did. A census taken in the
1700s showed that a large portion of England was living in
poverty; yet, generally speaking, it was described as "a
period of prosperity with relatively few bad years."[20]
England's economy was boosted and the population somewhat
redistributed. People started to read at an earlier age
because of the charity school movements; an increase in
manufactured goods left housewives with more time to read;
and more people on the lower social scale--footmen, appren-
tices, waiting-maids--were learning to read.[21] Overall,

England was advancing intellectually and scientifically.[22]

The people of Fielding's day found a new liberalism because of the increase in education. Rogers said "whatever is, is right" became the "watchword of a whole optimistic philosophy."[23] As I have already stated, the public was very interested in humanity. Five new public hospitals were built in one decade, and the very rigid social classes were beginning to break down. Sons of the aristocracy were going into business; men with land married girls with money, and business became the fashionable thing among nobility.[24] Many social institutions that were once sacred were being re-evaluated.

Marriage was one such institution. As seen in Tom Jones, fewer and fewer couples were quietly accepting the marriage arranged for them by their parents. On the other hand, although Tom loves Sophia, he felt free "indulging in the pleasures of the flesh with any woman who was good-looking and facile."[25] There was also a growing interest in determining and rearranging roles for men and women. Women had freedom with leisure time and property that pre-vious generations did not have. Although women did not have careers, the ones with property had a secure status without having to marry. Advances were being made.[26]

To people in the 18th century, possessions meant

Transition sentence

security, and the loss of possessions greatly threatened "social identity."[27] After glancing through several magazines printed at the time the movie <u>Tom Jones</u> was released, I discovered that the society of the 1960s was not too different.

The next 6 ¶s discuss society in America in the 1960s

Americans in the 1960s were concerned with improving the lot of humanity. In November of 1963 <u>Life</u> magazine ran a series of articles on the plight of the American Negro, *Corresponds to III B* and Congress was passing laws and making rulings to help them. Just as social classes were breaking down in the 18th century, minorities were gaining more fair treatment in the 1960s.

The women's liberation movement also grew and gained recognition in the 1960s. Betty Friedan gained popularity as she battled for her sex against the "feminine mystique."[28] Women were advancing in the 18th and 20th centuries.

Scientists made life a bit easier for people in the 1960s, too. The new interest in space brought many advancements to households, and great strides were made in medicine. One article of October 1963 in <u>Life</u> reported that scientists were closing in on the secret of life with the new research in DNA.

Perhaps the two biggest issues in the 1960s compare to major events in 18th-century England. In the 1960s, America was involved in the Viet Nam war, a war that proved to be as humiliating for Americans as was England's war of the 18th century. In 1776, England lost one of her colonies and marked the war off as a minor skirmish, but the country felt humiliated to be defeated by such a small, powerless group of people. Americans' dissatisfaction in the 1960s over the Viet Nam conflict was evident in all magazines and newspapers of the decade. Some aspect of the Viet Nam war was the lead article for _Life_ magazine almost every other week in early 1963.

The only event that affected America more than Viet Nam in 1963 was the assassination of President Kennedy. Eighteenth-century England was also concerned with the murder of Charles I. A sermon delivered in that century said that the murder of Charles I was worse than Christ's death since Charles (unlike Christ) was an anointed king.[29] When I read the pages and pages of articles written about President Kennedy after his death, I got the feeling that Americans felt the same way about his murder.[30]

Since Americans in the 1960s were concerned about humanity and trying to question and improve their social institutions, they, like the people of 18th-century England, were ready to laugh at a book and movie that satirized these institutions. The film was called "a social satire written

in blood with a broadaxe" since the producer "sharpens the
author's satire to a cruel point."[31] In the movie, scenes
of the slums were brief but vivid and vicious. This sort
of scene, mixed in with hilarious scenes in the countryside,
gave the audience an opportunity to laugh at the hypocrisies
of people and society, yet they could not forget that something had to be done to end such hypocrisy.

Begins conclusion here

Corresponds to Outline IV

"Certainly Henry Fielding's novel contains all the
elements necessary for a good movie," one critic said. "It
has lovers' misunderstandings, it deals with the very rich,
it has comedy, chases, action, sex."[32] But it has much more
that has made the tale able to endure two centuries.

In the novel, Fielding wrote: "I have endeavoured in
the Following History to laugh Mankind out of their favourite Follies and Vices."[33] This statement is the worth of

Reinforces thesis of paper

the tale. "Two centuries have passed," *Time* magazine
states; "Mankind still has its favourite Vices; and Novelist
Henry Fielding's sprawling, brawling masterpiece still
stands as the greatest comic novel in the language."[34]
Because mankind has its vices and people in 18th-century
England as well as 20th-century America were concerned with
correcting those vices, Tom Jones appealed to audiences
separated by centuries in time.

Frederick Hilles, a Fielding critic, quotes a character

Final remarks bringing paper to a close from a play who is standing in front of Fielding's tomb. He says to himself:

> Perhaps it was worth dying in your forties if two
> hundred years later you were the only non-
> contemporary novelist who could be read with un-
> affected interest, the only one who never had to
> be apologised for or excused on the grounds of
> changing taste.[35]

That must be the mark of a true masterpiece--one that stands

the test of time.

ENDNOTES

[1] Bosley Crowther, "Cinematic 'Tom Jones': Fielding's Classic Novel Made into Great Film," _New York Times_, Oct. 13, 1963, Sec. 8, p. 1, col. 6.

[2] _Twentieth-Century Interpretations of Tom Jones: A Collection of Critical Essays_, ed. Martin C. Battestin (Englewood Cliffs, N.J.: Prentice-Hall, 1968), p. 2.

[3] Brooks Atkinson, "Critic at Large: 'Tom Jones' Film Version Is a Reminder to Reread Fielding Masterpiece," _New York Times_, Nov. 8, 1963, Sec. 6, p. 28, cols. 4-6.

[4] Ian Watt, "Fielding as Novelist: Tom Jones," _Twentieth-Century Interpretations of Tom Jones: A Collection of Critical Essays_, ed. Martin C. Battestin (Englewood Cliffs, N.J.: Prentice-Hall, 1968), pp. 19-32.

[5] _Twentieth_ . . . , p. 8.

[6] Ibid.

[7] "From Boswell's Life of Johnson," _Henry Fielding's Tom Jones_, ed. Sheridan Baker (New York: W. W. Norton, 1973), p. 787.

[8] Lewis Thomas, "A Very Amazing Entertainment," _Henry Fielding's Tom Jones_, ed. Sheridan Baker (New York: W. W. Norton, 1973), p. 773.

[9] Henry Fielding, _The History of Tom Jones A Foundling_, ed. Somerset Maugham (Philadelphia: The John C. Winston Company, 1948), p. xv.

[10] Ibid., p. xxvi.

[11] "Tom Jones Wins in a Romp," _Life_, Oct. 11, 1963, p. 120.

[12] _Twentieth_ . . . , p. 15.

[13] Ibid., p. 1.

[14] Ibid., p. 2.

[15] Walter E. Allen, "Fielding, Henry," _Encyclopaedia Britannica_, 15th ed., VII, 292.

[16]Maugham, p. xxii.

[17]Arthur Knight, "SR Goes to the Movies: Richardson's England," Saturday Review, Oct. 5, 1963, p. 52.

[18]"The Current Cinema," New Yorker, Sept. 7, 1963, p. 98.

[19]Pat Rogers, The Augustan Vision (New York: Barnes & Noble, 1974), p. 87.

[20]Ibid., p. 11.

[21]Ibid., p. 85.

[22]Ibid., p. 8.

[23]Ibid., p. 9.

[24]Ibid., p. 11.

[25]Maugham, p. xxiii.

[26]Rogers, pp. 87-90.

[27]Ibid., pp. 99-100.

[28]In November 1963, Life magazine began a series of articles on Betty Friedan's attack on what she called the feminine mystique.

[29]Rogers, p. 9.

[30]Almost all November and December 1963 issues of Life, Time, Newsweek, etc. were devoted almost entirely to JFK.

[31]"Cinema: John Bull in His Barnyard," Time, Oct. 18, 1963, p. 117.

[32]Knight, p. 52.

[33]Fielding, p. 1.

[34]"Cinema . . . ," p. 117.

[35]Frederick W. Hilles, "Art and Artifice in Tom Jones," Henry Fielding's Tom Jones, ed. Sheridan Baker (New York: W. W. Norton, 1973), p. 917.

BIBLIOGRAPHY

Allen, Walter E. "Fielding, Henry." Encyclopaedia Britannica.. 15th ed., VII, 291-3.

Atkinson, Brooks. "Critic at Large: 'Tom Jones' Film Version Is a Reminder to Reread Fielding Masterpiece." New York Times, Nov. 8, 1963, Sec. 6, p. 28, cols. 4-5.

"Cinema: John Bull in His Barnyard." Time, Oct. 18, 1963, p. 117.

Crowther, Bosley. "Cinematic 'Tom Jones': Fielding's Classic Novel Made into Great Film." New York Times, Oct. 13, 1963, Sec. 8, p. 1, col. 6.

"The Current Cinema." New Yorker, Sept. 7, 1963, p. 98.

Fielding, Henry. The History of Tom Jones a Foundling. Ed. Somerset Maugham. Philadelphia: The John C. Winston Company, 1948.

"From Boswell's Life of Johnson." Henry Fielding's Tom Jones. Ed. Sheridan Baker. New York: W. W. Norton, 1973, pp. 786-7.

Hilles, Frederick W. "Art and Artifice in Tom Jones." Henry Fielding's Tom Jones. Ed. Sheridan Baker. New York: W. W. Norton, 1973, pp. 916-32.

Knight, Arthur. "SR Goes to the Movies: Richardson's England." Saturday Review, Oct. 5, 1963, p. 52.

Rogers, Pat. The Augustan Vision. New York: Barnes & Noble, 1974.

Thomas, Lewis. "A Very Amazing Entertainment." Henry Fielding's Tom Jones. Ed. Sheridan Baker. New York: W. W. Norton, 1973, pp. 773-4.

"'Tom Jones' Wins in a Romp." Life, Oct. 11, 1963, pp. 120-5.

Twentieth-Century Interpretations of Tom Jones: A Collection of Critical Essays. Ed. Martin C. Battestin. Englewood Cliffs, N.J.: Prentice-Hall, 1968.

Watt, Ian. "Fielding as Novelist: Tom Jones." Twentieth-Century Interpretations of Tom Jones: A Collection of Critical Essays. Ed. Martin C. Battestin. Englewood Cliffs, N.J.: Prentice-Hall, 1968, pp. 19-32.

March 15. The paper is written, footnoted, bibliographied, proofread—ready to turn in. Now I'm really nervous.

I feel good that I was able to write on a different topic.

I feel good that I learned something about research. I know I will use it later.

I feel good that the actual final paper wasn't as hard to write as I thought.

I feel good to be rid of Tom Jones *forever!*

I just hope the prof feels good.

THE ABC'S OF USEFUL INFORMATION IN WRITING A RESEARCH PAPER

A

Abbreviations found in sources

anon. Anonymous

b. Born

bibliog. Bibliography

c. *(circa)* About a certain date; indicates an approximation of the date

cf. *(confer)* Compare or see

col. Column

d. Died

diss. Dissertation

ed. Edited by or edition

e.g. For example

et al. *(et alii)* And others

f or **ff.** One or more pages following the page already cited

ibid *(ibidem)* In the same work already cited

i.e. In other words

infra See below for further discussion

l. or **ll.** Line or lines

loc. cit. *(loco citato)* In the passage cited earlier

MS. Manuscript

n. fn. Note, footnote

N. B. Take special notice

op. cit. *(opere citato)* In the work cited previously

p. or **pp.** Page or pages

passim From various places in a work cited

rev. Revised

see Means to look under some other word or in some other place

ser. Series

supra Mentioned above

viz. Namely

vol. or **vols.** Volume or volumes

Almanacs   See *Reference Material*

Atlases   See *Reference Material*

Audience   The research paper you write in this course will probably be the one with the most "classroom" context of all the essays you have written in the course. In real life, however, the audience for a research paper would be the company you work for, the committee you belong to, or the periodical you are writing for. Then you would adapt your material, writing style, vocabulary, etc., to that particular audience. For this first research paper—which is a practice run and a learning situation—you will probably do best to *think about a general reader like yourself as your audience.* **The main things you should strive for are** *(a)* **clearness,** *(b)* **coherence,** *(c)* **smoothness,** *(d)* **interest for the general reader,** and *(e)* **accuracy.** Later, after you have learned the mechanics of research paper writing, you can adapt your work to a more *specific* audience and purpose.

B

Bibliographies and Library Guides   See *Reference Material*

Bibliography Cards
1 Use 3 × 5 index cards.
2 Copy the library call number in the upper left-hand corner of the card.
3 Write a code for the card in the upper right-hand corner to use on your notecards for identification of source.
4 Write author's name, last name first.
5 On next line write complete title of book.
6 On next line write city where the book was published, name of publisher, and year published.
7 For other sources, such as encyclopedia articles, magazine articles, etc., put the information on the bibliography card as shown under *Bibliography Form.*
8 At the bottom of the card in parentheses write a note to yourself about the potential usefulness of the book.

Bibliography Form   See *Footnote and Bibliography Form*

Biographical References   See *Reference Material*

Booklists   See *Reference Material*

C

Cards See *Notecards* and *Bibliography Cards*

Choosing a Subject See *Subject*

Copying See *Plagiarism*

D

The Dewey Decimal System of Book Classification

000 General Works	500 Pure Sciences
100 Philosophy	600 Technology
200 Religion	700 The Arts
300 Social Sciences	800 Literature
400 Language	900 History

Dictionaries See *Reference Material*

E

Encyclopedias (general) See *Reference Material*

Encyclopedias (specialized) See *Reference Material*

Endnotes See *Footnotes/Endnotes/Notes*

F

Footnote and Bibliography Form Typing footnotes and bibliographical entries is frustrating and time-consuming. The rules that govern mechanics and punctuation in these seem arbitrary and illogical. The fact that there is no definitive way to do this makes the whole process of documentation seem ridiculously detailed. Different areas of study (e.g. psychology) have their own style for documentation, so what you learn in your English class may be entirely wrong for a paper for chemistry, math, or history. To a certain extent, then, mechanics and punctuation in documentation *are* arbitrary—but they are never illogical. Each discipline can defend the logic behind its documentation system: one may strive for simplicity, another for brevity, another for completeness. The system you use in your English class is one that aims at completeness and clarity.

Because documentation is so detailed and meticulous, you may be tempted to think of the Notes and Bibliography pages as insignificant parts of your paper. Actually, these pages are very important. They provide a reader with all the information needed in order to consult —if he or she wants to—the sources you have used in your paper. This is why punctuation and mechanics are so important in documentation. A reader must be able to determine from your documentation whether the source is a book, an article in a book or journal, a newspaper, and so on. The conventions of punctuation and mechanics that you observe in documentation tell your reader these things.

The notes, which may appear at the bottom of the page (footnotes) or at the end of the paper on a sheet titled *Notes*, document your use of borrowed material. **They include the author's name, the title of the work you are referring to, publication information, and the page number for the specific reference.** All this information must be punctuated in some way and must conform to standard conventions if it is to be useful to your reader. Study this sample footnote, paying close attention to the *mechanics* that govern its form:

Superscript number matches note number in the text

First line indented

Author's name in regular order

Comma after author's name

Publication information enclosed in parentheses

[1]Leon V. Sigal, <u>Reporters</u> <u>and</u> <u>Officials</u> (Lexington, Mass.: D. C. Heath & Co., 1973), p. 11.

Name of state abbreviated

Colon follows place of publication

Comma separates publisher and copyright date

Comma follows publication information

Entry ends with a period

The bibliography, which is usually the last page of your paper, lists in alphabetical order all the sources you directly cite in your paper.

Each bibliographical entry presents the same information as a corresponding footnote, but in a slightly different form.

First line not indented

Period after author's name even when there is no initial

Last name first

Period after the title

Sigal, Leon V. Reporters and Officials. Lexington, Mass.:

D. C. Heath & Co., 1973.

Colon after place of publication

Comma between publisher and date of publication

Period at end of note; no specific pages cited

"Hanging" indentation -- all lines after first are indented

Punctuation and form change slightly for other kinds of materials—articles, newspaper stories, essays, government documents—but the basic conventions remain the same.

The following examples illustrate the proper form for the most common footnotes and bibliographical entries. The footnote form *(F)* and the bibliographical form *(B)* are given together to help you compare the differences between the two.

BOOKS
One author
F: [1]Lewis Thomas, *The Lives of a Cell: Notes of a Biology Watcher* (New York: Bantam Books, 1974), p. 4.
B: Thomas, Lewis. *The Lives of a Cell: Notes of a Biology Watcher*. New York: Bantam Books, 1974.

Two or three authors
F: [2]Arthur Shulman and Roger Youman, *The Television Years* (New York: Popular Library, 1973), p. 90.

B: Shulman, Arthur, and Roger Youman. *The Television Years.* New York: Popular Library, 1973.

Three or more authors

F: [3]Robert E. Burns et al., *Episodes in American History* (Lexington, Mass.: Ginn and Co., 1973), pp. 103–105.

B: Burns, Robert E., et al. *Episodes in American History.* Lexington, Mass.: Ginn and Co., 1973.

No author cited

F: [4]*Protect Your Pet Against Heartworm Disease* (Princeton, N.J.: American Cyanamid Co., 1975), p. 78.

B: *Protect Your Pet Against Heartworm Disease.* Princeton, N.J.: American Cyanamid Co., 1975.

Editors

F: [5]*Leukemia,* Frederick Gunz and Albert G. Baikie, eds. (New York: Grune & Stratton, 1974), p. 137.

B: *Leukemia.* Gunz, Frederick, and Albert G. Baikie, eds. New York: Grune & Stratton, 1974.

Editions

F: [6]Harold L. Nelson and Dwight L. Teeter, Jr., *Law of Mass Communications: Freedom and Control of Print and Broadcast Media,* 2nd ed. (Mineola, N.Y.: Foundation Press, 1973), p. 92.

B: Nelson, Harold L., and Dwight L. Teeter, Jr. *Law of Mass Communications: Freedom and Control of Print and Broadcast Media.* 2nd ed. Mineola, N.Y.: Foundation Press, 1973.

More than one volume

F: [7]Jay B. Hubbell, *American Life in Literature* (New York: Harper & Brothers, 1949), II, 53.

B: Hubbell, Jay B. *American Life in Literature.* 2 vols. New York: Harper & Brothers, 1949.

Essay or chapter from book

F: [8]Nancy McLaurin, "Pfeiffer College Undergraduate Curriculum," *Options for the Teaching of English: The Undergraduate Curriculum,* ed. Elizabeth Wooten Cowan (New York: The Modern Language Association, 1975), pp. 70–76.

B: McLaurin, Nancy. "Pfeiffer College Undergraduate Curriculum." *Options for the Teaching of English: The Undergraduate Curriculum.* Ed. Elizabeth Wooten Cowan. New York: The Modern Language Association, 1975, pp. 70–76.

Translation

F: [9]Homer, *The Odyssey,* trans. Robert Fitzgerald (London: Panther Books Ltd., 1971), p. 101.

B: Homer. *The Odyssey.* Trans. Robert Fitzgerald. London: Panther
Books Ltd., 1971.

Book in series
F: [10]C. V. Wedgwood, *The World of Rubens.* Time-Life Library of
Art (New York: Time Inc., 1967), p. 123.
B: Wedgwood, C. V. *The World of Rubens.* Time-Life Library of Art.
New York: Time Inc., 1967.

Articles signed and unsigned in encyclopedia
F: [11]Walter E. Allen, "Fielding, Henry," *Encyclopaedia Britannica,*
15th ed., VII, 292.
B: Allen, Walter E. "Fielding, Henry." *Encyclopaedia Britannica.* 15th
ed., VII, 291–3.
F: [12]"Japan," *The Random House Encyclopedia,* 1977, 1210.
B: "Japan." *The Random House Encyclopedia.* 1977, 1210.

Article in journal
F: [13]Michael Zeilik, "The Birth of Massive Stars," *Scientific American,*
238 (April 1978), 113.
B: Zeilek, Michael. "The Birth of Massive Stars." *Scientific American,*
238 (April 1978), 110–18.

Article from weekly magazine
F: [14]"Battered Child," *Newsweek,* June 30, 1968, p. 68.
B: "Battered Child." *Newsweek,* June 30, 1968, p. 68.

Review
F: [15]Stanley Kanfer, "The Shocking Entertainer," rev. of *Mencken: A
Study of His Thought,* by Charles A. Fecher, *Time,* May 29, 1978,
p. 98.
B: Kanfer, Stanley. "The Shocking Entertainer." Review of *Mencken:
A Study of His Thought,* by Charles A. Fecher. *Time,* May 29, 1978,
pp. 98, 100.

Newspaper article signed and unsigned
F: [16]Karen Rogus, "Elderly 'Cannot Live on Bread Alone'; They
Need Hot Lunches," *Houston Chronicle,* June 4, 1978, Sec. 4, p. 3.
B: Rogus, Karen. "Elderly 'Cannot Live on Bread Alone'; They Need
Hot Lunches." *Houston Chronicle,* June 4, 1978, Sec. 4, p. 3.
F: [17]"VFW Hospital Volunteers Honored," *Walla Walla Union-
Bulletin,* October 15, 1978, Section B, p. 11, cols. 1–5.
B: "VFW Hospital Volunteers Honored." *Walla Walla Union-Bulletin,*
October 15, 1978, Section B, p. 11, cols. 1–5.

Footnotes Endnotes Notes Footnotes can be given in two places: the
notes can appear at the bottom of the page where the footnote numbers
themselves appear (the origin of the term *foot* note—at the foot of the

page) or they can appear all together at the end of the research paper. When they appear together at the end, the page on which they appear is titled *Notes* or *Endnotes* (coming at the end of the paper instead of the foot of each page). Either term is correct; the choice is up to you. Putting the footnotes at the bottom of each page is somewhat more convenient for the reader but much less convenient for the typist. The placement of notes at the end of the paper seems to be the more prevalent practice today. Your instructor will tell you which placement he or she prefers.

FOOTNOTES FOR WORKS PREVIOUSLY CITED

In the past the Latin terms ibid, loc. cit., and op. cit. were used when a reference that had already been mentioned was mentioned again. Increasingly, now, however, a short form of the first citation is being used because it is much clearer for the reader and easier for the writer.

Here are the short forms to follow:

1 If a source has already been cited and it is the only one by that particular author used in the research paper, merely repeat the author's name and the page number for the footnote.
[18]Kanfer, p. 100.

2 If the author wrote more than one of the sources you are using, you would cite the author's name and the name of the particular source you are quoting.
[19]Kanfer, "The Shocking Entertainer," p. 100.

3 If the source has no author, merely cite it the second time by title.
[20]*Protect Your Pet Against Heartworm Disease*, p. 74.
(You may also write Protect Your Pet . . . or Protect . . . instead of the full title, if desired. Check with instructor for preference.)

4 When you cite a source that you have just used (and have written some of your own thoughts in between), you may use the short word Ibid. to indicate that the material you are now footnoting is from the exact same place as the previous footnote.
[21]Kanfer, p. 100.
[22]Ibid.

5 If the page has changed, but the information is from the same source as the previous footnote, you can cite it this way.
[23]Kanfer, p. 100.
[24]Ibid., p. 98.

Check with your instructor to see what form is preferred for citation of second footnotes.

I

Indexes   See *Reference Material*

L

The Library of Congress System of Book Classification

A	General Works
B	Philosophy, psychology, religion
C	Auxiliary Sciences of History
D	History: General and old world
E & F	History: Americas
G	Geography, anthropology, recreation
H	Social sciences
J	Political Sciences
K	Law
L	Education
M	Music
N	Fine Arts
P	Language and literature
R	Medicine
S	Agriculture, forestry, plant and animal industry
T	Engineering and Technology
U	Military Science
V	Naval Science
Z	Bibliography and Library Science

M

Manuscript Format

1 Always double space.
2 Always indent paragraphs 5 spaces.
3 Complete research paper will consist of the following:
   a. Title page
   b. Outline of the paper
   c. Body of the paper, each page after the first numbered
   d. Footnotes or endnotes
   e. Bibliography of all sources used in the paper
4 Keep your notecards and bibliography cards; the instructor may call for these so that she or he can trace the development of your paper.
5 If you have long quotations, single-space them and indent 8 spaces from the left-hand margin. If you have new paragraphs in the quotation, indent them 3 additional spaces.

Notecards

1 Put notes on 4 × 6 cards.
2 On each notecard put the code from the bibliography card to identify the exact source of the information.
3 Write in your own words unless there is something you feel you *must* have exactly in the author's words.
4 Put the page number from the source on the card immediately when you begin taking notes. If the page number changes while you are writing, put the new page number down immediately, even if it is in the middle of the line. This will let you know precisely where your information came from.
5 Put a word on the top left-hand side of the card identifying the subject on that card.
6 Number your notecards so you can keep them in order.
7 Don't write in pencil. You'll be handling the cards so much that the writing is likely to get smeared unless it is in ink.
8 Don't put information from two different sources on the same card.
9 If you are quoting and leave out any words, use dots (called ellipses . . .) to show where you've omitted anything in the quotation.
10 Don't abbreviate. You're likely to forget the abbreviation by the time you get back to it.
11 Write where you can read it. Don't get in such a hurry that your notes are indecipherable when you return to them.

Notes   See *Footnotes/Endnotes/Notes*

Outline

DEFINITION.

A topic outline is made of words or short phrases. A sentence outline is made of complete sentences. The choice of which to use depends on how much specific information the writer wants to include in the outline.

DESCRIPTION.

Most outlines have 3 or 4 types of headings. Capital Roman numerals indicate the main divisions of the outline. Capital letters indicate the subparts of these main divisions. Arabic numerals indicate the breakdown of the information listed under the second-level headings. Lower-case letters indicate parts of the third-level heading.

```
I.
   A.
      1.
      2.
   B.
II.
   A.
   B.
   C.
III.
   A.
   B.
IV.
   A.
   B.
      1.
      2.
      3.
   C.
      1.
         a.
         b.
      2.
```

RULES.

1 If you have a I, you must have a II; if an *A*, then a *B*, and so on. A single level of heading cannot appear by itself.

2 The wordings of the headings of levels of the same type should be parallel. (I should be worded like II and II like III, for instance.)

3 One level can have subdivisions in one section of the outline and no subdivisions in another section. This occurs because there is sometimes much to say about one topic and little or nothing to say about another. The outline, of course, shows the points made in the paper. And if there are no points under a particular heading, nothing will appear there in the outline.

4 Capitalization of words in topic outlines is done two ways:

   A Only the first word of each line is capitalized unless a word is a proper noun.

   B Every word in the outline is capitalized except for prepositions, articles (a, an, the), and conjunctions appearing in the middle of a line.

   The choice is up to the writer.

5 No punctuation is needed after any head, no matter what level.

6 A period is placed after each Roman numeral, capital letter, Arabic numerals and lower-case letters in the outline.

7 Heads of the same level appear even with each other in the outline.

8 Double-space between headings in the outline.

P

Paraphrase **To *paraphrase* means to put in your own words.** Here is a paragraph quoted from the *Encyclopaedia Britannica* followed by a paraphrase of the information.

QUOTE

The History of Tom Jones, a Foundling was published on February 28, 1749. With its great comic gusto, vast gallery of characters, and contrasted scenes of high and low life in London and the provinces, it has always been the most popular of his works. The reading of this work is essential both for an understanding of 18th-century England and for its revelation of the generosity and charity of Fielding's view of humanity.

PARAPHRASE

Three things made Henry Fielding's novel, *The History of Tom Jones, a Foundling,* published on February 28, 1749, popular. The book is full of blustering humor, there are a large number of characters in the novel, and Fielding gives pictures of upper-class and lower-class everyday activities in England. When you read this book, you can see Fielding's attitude toward all people, rich and poor, especially how much he understood human nature.[1]

Notice that even though this quote has been completely paraphrased, it is still footnoted, because all the *ideas* came from this source.

Plagiarism To *plagiarize* means to take someone else's words and/or ideas and put them into your writing as though they were yours. Some people deliberately steal other writers' work, but much plagiarism in students' research papers occurs through carelessness, uncertainty, or ignorance. Some simple rules will help you know how to avoid plagiarism.

1 Always put quotation marks around any direct statement from someone else's work. Also give a footnote for this quotation.

2 Footnote any paraphrase of another writer's ideas or statements.

3 Footnote any thoughts you got from a specific source in your reading.

4 Footnote any material, ideas, thoughts, etc., you got from your reading that can't be described as general knowledge.

5 Footnote any summary (even if in your own words) of a discussion from one of your sources.

6 Footnote any charts, graphs, tables, etc., made by others or any you make with others' information.

ORIGINAL VERSION, QUOTED DIRECTLY FROM SOURCE:

Two plausible explanations exist for the Anasazi departure from a homeland where life was full and complete: either life had ceased to be good and they were starved out, or they were driven out by someone else. There are strong indications that a severe drought extended over the plateau from 1276 to 1299, and quite possibly the Anasazi found agriculture as they had come to depend on it impossible. There are subtle inconsistencies to the theory, however, that tend to impeach its universality, giving rise to the second possibility. Wandering Shoshonean hunters—raiders by nature—had begun to roam the plateau somewhat earlier, and given the fortresslike quality of most Anasazi pueblos and cliff dwellings, it seems possible that these raiders had begun to make part, or most, of their living by preying on the vulnerable fields of the agriculturists. If this was the case, the Anasazi would in time be forced out. Whatever the answer, and it may be a combination of both, the Anasazi departed to other regions.

—Donald C. Pike

STUDENT VERSION 1:

Nobody really knows why the Anasazi, the cliffdwellers, left their homes, but two possible reasons are given. The drought of 1276–1299 may have destroyed agriculture as the Anasazi had come to depend upon it. The Shoshonean hunters, raiders by nature, may have also begun preying on the vulnerable fields and crops of the Indians. No one knows for sure, but these two explanations, perhaps even in combination, may explain the abandoned cliff dwellings.

Remarks: The writer has clearly plagiarized. Here are the reasons this is true:
1 The writer uses information that is not common knowledge, information she got from reading the original paragraph, and yet she does not footnote it.
2 The writer uses many of the author's exact words and phrases—steals them, in fact—and she does not mention that the words and phrases are not hers. Even though she does use some of her own words occasionally, she owes credit to the author for the knowledge in the paragraph itself and for the author's direct words.

STUDENT VERSION 2:

Authorities often give two explanations for the departure of the Anasazi from their homeland. Either they were starved out, or they were driven out. There was a drought from 1276 to 1299, and it is possible that this drought affected the farming drastically.[1] Also, there was a roaming band of raiders, the Shoshonean, who may have attacked the Anasazi.[2] Whatever the answer, and maybe it was a combination of both the drought and the invaders, the Anasazi departed to other places.

Remarks: The student is still plagiarizing. Even though she footnotes the two facts, she is still passing off many of the author's words as though they were hers. Just footnoting the two facts does not give the student the license to use the author's phrases and words without giving credit.

STUDENT VERSION 3:

Anybody who has ever seen or read about the Indian cliff dwellings is perplexed by the question, why did the Anasazi leave? Their homes were very advanced in structure and design. They had good farms. There are two explanations generally given. The Indians may have left because of a severe drought that occurred in 1276–1299.[1] They may also have been forced out by the Shoshonean, a tribe of raiders.[2] Nobody really knows for sure. Whatever the reason—whether it was the drought, the invaders, or a combination of both—the Anasazi left their homes, and all that remains there now are the magnificent cliff dwellings that fascinate and intrigue everybody who sees them.[3]

> *Remarks: Finally, the student has stopped plagiarizing. The first two sentences could be considered general knowledge or conclusions she came to after her preliminary general reading, therefore not attributable to any particular source. She clearly footnotes the two reasons given by Donald Pike in the original paragraph. And she even footnotes her last sentence because she has used Pike's idea that the reason might be a combination of both. Even though she has used her own words in that last paragraph, she gives credit to the author's idea because she didn't know it until she read it from him.*

Q

Quotations   See *Reference Material.*

R

Reference Material

ATLASES, YEARBOOKS, AND ALMANACS
Atlas of World History, Rand McNally, 1970
Britannica Atlas: Geography Edition, 1974
The CBS News Almanac, 1976–present
Demographic Yearbook, 1949–present
Facts on File, 1940–present
The Geographical Digest, 1963
Information Please Almanac, 1947–present
National Geographic Atlas of the World, 1975
The Negro Almanac, 1967–present
The New Cambridge Modern History, 1970
The New York Times Atlas of the World, 1972
The Oxford Bible Atlas, 1974
Rand McNally Commercial Atlas and Marketing Guide, 1876–present
The Statesman's Yearbook, 1864–present
Statistical Abstract of the United States, 1878–present
The Times Atlas of the World: Comprehensive Edition, 1971
Webster's New Geographical Dictionary, rev. ed., 1977
The World Almanac and Book of Facts, 1868–present
Yearbook of the United Nations, 1947–present
Yearbook of World Affairs, 1947–present

BIOGRAPHICAL REFERENCES
Biography Index, 1946–present
Chambers's Biographical Dictionary, 1978

Contemporary Authors: A Bio-bibliographical Guide to Current Authors and Their Works, 1967–present
Dictionary of American Biography, 10 vols. & supplements, 1944–1974
Dictionary of National Biography, 22 vols. & supplements, 1882–1953
Directory of American Scholars, 7th ed., 4 vols., 1978
International Who's Who, 1935–present
Twentieth Century Authors, 1942, supplement (1955)
Webster's Biographical Dictionary, 1972
Who's Who (Great Britain), 1897–present
Who's Who in America, 1899–present
Who's Who in [. . .] (Regions such as West, East, South, Midwest, etc., and professions such as theatre, football, jazz, insurance, etc.)
Who's Who of American Women, 1958–present

BIBLIOGRAPHIES AND LIBRARY GUIDES

Basic Reference Sources: An Introduction to Materials and Methods, Louis Shores, Chicago, American Library Association, 1954
Bibliographic Index: A Cumulative Bibliography of Bibliographies, New York, H. W. Wilson Co., 1937–present
Bibliography of Agriculture, Washington, U. S. National Agricultural Library, 1942–present
Guide to Reference Books, Eugene P. Sheehy, Chicago, American Library Association, 9th ed., 1976
Guide to the Use of Books and Libraries, Jean K. Gates, New York, McGraw-Hill, 3rd ed., 1974
Historical Abstracts: Bibliography of the World's Periodical Literature, Eric H. Boehm, ed., Santa Barbara, Clio Press, 1955–present
MLA International Bibliography of Books and Articles on the Modern Languages and Literatures, MLA, New York, 1922–present
The Modern Researcher, Jacques Barzun and Henry F. Graff, New York, Harcourt, rev. ed., 1970
The New Cambridge Bibliography of English Literature, George Watson, ed., Cambridge University Press, 4 vols., 1969–74
The New York Times Guide to Reference Materials, Mona McCormick, New York, Popular Library, 1978
Reference Books: A Brief Guide, Baltimore, Enoch Pratt Free Library, 7th ed., 1970
Science Reference Sources, Frances B. Jenkins, Cambridge, MIT Press, 5th ed., 1969
Sources of Information in the Social Sciences: A Guide to the Literature, Carl M. White et al., eds., Chicago, American Library Association, 2nd ed., 1973
The Use of Books and Libraries, Minneapolis, University of Minnesota, 10 vols., 1933–1963
A World Bibliography of Bibliographies, Theodore A. Besterman, Lausanne, Societas Bibliographica, 4th ed., 5 vols., 1965
Year's Work in English Studies, London, English Association, 1919–present

BOOKLISTS

Books in Print, 1948–present. All books currently in print in U. S. Author and title.

Cumulative Book Index, 1898–present. Author, subject, and title index of all books printed in English.

Paperbound Books in Print, 1955–present. All books in U. S. printed in paperback.

Subject Guide to Books in Print, 1957–present. All books currently in print in U. S. by subject.

DICTIONARIES

The American Heritage Dictionary, 1970

The Basic Dictionary of Science, Macmillan, 1966

Dictionary of American Slang, 2nd ed., 1975

Dictionary of the Bible, John L. McKenzie, Macmillan, 1965

Dictionary of Geological Terms, 1962

Grove's Dictionary of Music and Musicians, 5th ed., 9 vols. and supplement, 1955

The Interpreter's Dictionary of the Bible, 4 vols., 1962

McGraw-Hill Dictionary of Modern Economics, 1973

McGraw-Hill Dictionary of Scientific and Technical Terms, 2nd ed., 1978

The Oxford English Dictionary, 12 vols. and supplement, 1933

The Random House Dictionary of the English Language (Unabridged Edition), 1970

Roget's International Thesaurus, 1962

Webster's Third New International Dictionary of the English Language, 1966

ENCYCLOPEDIAS (GENERAL)

Chambers's Encyclopedia, 15 vols., 1973

Collier's Encyclopedia, 24 vols., 1977

Encyclopaedia Britannica, 30 vols., 1978

Encyclopedia Americana, 30 vols., 1978

New Columbia Encyclopedia, 4th ed., 1975

The Random House Encyclopedia, 1977

ENCYCLOPEDIAS (SPECIALIZED)

Cassell's Encyclopaedia of World Literature, rev. ed., 1973

Encyclopaedia of Banking and Finance, 7th rev. ed., 1973

Encyclopaedia of Religion and Ethics, 13 vols., 1908–1927

Encyclopedia of American History, 5th ed., 1976

The Encyclopedia of the Biological Sciences, 2nd ed., 1970

The Encyclopedia of Education, 10 vols., 1971

Encyclopedia of Educational Research, 4th ed., 1969

Encyclopedia of Painting, Bernard S. Myers, ed., 1955

The Encyclopedia of Philosophy, 4 vols., 1973

The Encyclopedia of Physics, Robert M. Besancon, ed., 2nd ed., 1974

Encyclopedia of Psychology, H. J. Eysenck et al., eds., 3 vols., 1972

Encyclopedia of World Art, 15 vols., 1959–1968

An Encyclopedia of World History, 5th ed., 1972
International Encyclopedia of the Social Sciences, 17 vols., 1967
The Larousse Encyclopedia of World Geography, 1965
McGraw-Hill Encyclopedia of Science and Technology, 4th ed., 1977
The Mythology of All Races, 13 vols., 1932
The Negro in American History, 3 vols., 1972
The New Catholic Encyclopedia, 15 vols., 1967
New Larousse Encyclopedia of Mythology, 1974
The Oxford Companion to American History, 1966
The Oxford Companion to Music, 1970
The Reader's Encyclopedia, William R. Benet, ed., 2nd ed., 1965
The Reader's Encyclopedia of World Drama, 1969
Universal Jewish Encyclopedia and Readers Guide, 11 vols., 1944
Van Nostrand's Scientific Encyclopedia, 5th ed., 1976

INDEXES (GENERAL)

Book Review Digest, 1905–present. Summarizes reviews of books from a large number of periodicals. Gives critical reception of books reviewed.

Humanities Index, 1974–present. Periodical articles about the humanities. Author and subject entries. (See *Social Sciences and Humanities Index* for 1965–1974. See *International Index to Periodicals* for 1907–1965.)

New York Times Index, 1851–present. Subject index in alphabetical order. Includes abstracts of newspaper articles. Every article appearing in this newspaper will be included by subject in the index.

Nineteenth Century Readers' Guide, 1890–1899. Periodicals for the last ten years of the 1800s.

Poole's Index to Periodical Literature, 1802–1906. Indexed by subject. Author index in supplemental volume.

Readers' Guide to Periodical Literature, 1900–present. An excellent guide for general purpose reading. Lists articles from a broad range of periodicals. Entries by author, subject and cross listing. Most articles appearing in this index written for general public.

Social Sciences Index, 1974–present. Periodical articles in the social sciences. Indexed by author and subject. (See *Social Sciences and Humanities Index* for 1965–1974 and *International Index to Periodicals* for 1907–1965.)

INDEXES (SPECIALIZED)

Accountants Index, 1921–present. Author and subject index of books, pamphlets, and periodical articles.

Applied Science and Technology Index, 1958–present. Subject index. (Before 1958, see *Industrial Arts Index*.)

Architectural Periodicals Index, 1972–present. Covers architecture and allied arts, constructional technology, design, landscape, etc. Indexed by subject and architect/project.

The Art Index, 1929–present. By author and subject. Indexes periodicals and museum bulletins.

Biographical Dictionaries Master Index, Gale Research Co., 1975. Subject index. Guide to *Who's Who* and collective biographies.

Biography Index, 1946–present. Indexes information about people, dead and alive. Indexed by biographee and profession.

Biological Abstracts, 1926–present. References, abstracts, and indexes to world's life sciences research literature. Indexed by subject, author, and keyword.

Biological and Agricultural Index, 1964–present. Subject index to periodicals in these and related fields.

Business Periodicals Index, 1958–present. Subject index. Covers many fields such as accounting, economics, advertising, public relations, etc.

Chemical Abstracts, 1907–present. Index to periodical articles, papers, conferences. Indexed by subject, keyword, author.

Congressional Information Service Index to Publications of the United States Congress, 1970–present. Lists all written material from Senate and Congress.

Dramatic Index, 1909–1949. Articles on theatre and plays.

Education Index, 1929–present. Indexed by author and subject. Articles in magazines, books, and other sources discussing the entire field of education.

Engineering Index, 1906–present. Subject index. Includes reports of technical societies, government agencies, laboratories, as well as engineering periodicals.

Essay and General Literature Index, 1900–present. Essays and articles which have appeared in books.

Film Literature Index, 1973–present. Indexed by title of movie and by director.

Index of Economic Articles, 1961–present. Subject and author indexes. (For 1886–1965, see *Index of Economic Journals*.)

Index to London Times, 1906–present. By subject.

The Monthly Catalog of the United States Government, 1898–present. Lists all government publications by title, date, and purpose. States availability of material.

Music Index, 1949–present. By subject and author.

The Newspaper Index, 1972–present. Subject listings from *The Chicago Tribune, The Los Angeles Times, The New Orleans Times-Picayune*, and *The Washington Post*.

Nuclear Science Abstracts, 1947–present. Indexed by personal author, corporate author, and report number.

The Philosopher's Index, 1967–present. By subject and author. Includes American and foreign periodicals and journals.

Psychological Abstracts, 1927–present. Author and subject indexes.

Public Affairs Information Service Bulletin, 1915–present. Subject index for areas such as government, international relations, economics, etc.

Religion Index, 1977–present. Indexed by author and subject. Index of book reviews by author. (See *Index to Religious Periodical Literature* for 1949–1976.)

Television News Index and Abstracts, 1972–present. Indexes subject by topic, institution, and personality.

Theatre, Film and Television Biographies Master Index, Gale Research Co., 1979. Subject index to biographical sketches of people in performing arts found in biographical directories and dictionaries.

Ulrich's International Periodicals Directory, new editions periodically. Lists all periodicals available in various fields.

Vertical File Index, 1932–present. Subject and title. Includes pamphlets, leaflets, mimeographed materials, etc.

QUOTATIONS

Familiar Quotations, John Bartlett, 14th ed., 1968
Dictionary of Quotations, Bergen Evans, 1968
The Oxford Dictionary of Quotations, 2nd ed., 1953
The Home Book of Quotations, Classical and Modern, 10th ed., 1967

S

Second Footnotes   See *Footnotes for works previously cited*

Subject   Topics are often assigned in freshman English classes. If you are not given a specific subject, however, here are some things to remember when you choose what you want to research.

1 Choose a subject that you actually have some interest in. You are going to be spending a *lot* of time reading and writing about this subject. It would be really smart, therefore, to choose something that you would actually like to find out about. You might have a brainstorming session with some classmates to see what areas might turn up that you're interested in. You might also ask yourself questions like these to find out what you might enjoy researching:

a In my spare time I do _____ .

One question I've often had about this is _____ .

b Every time I read about _____ , I wonder _____ .

c One of the biggest problems in my town (church, club, school) right now is _____ . I would like to find out _____ about this.

d I've often heard people say _____ , but I've never understood the reasons behind it or heard an explanation of it.

e When the technological (engineering, scientific) breakthrough of _____ occurred, I was flabbergasted. I absolutely could not understand how they did it.

f I'd like to know the latest news (facts, information, research) on _____ . What *is* the current state of knowledge about this?

g I'd like to know the pro's and con's of the controversial subject _____ .

2 Be sure your subject is something that *can* be answered by research. For instance, don't pick a subject that would require only common knowledge or your own experience. This wouldn't be research, and doing research is the purpose of this writing project. Also, don't pick a subject that can't be answered because it is so speculative — for example, *Who Was the Best President of the United States?*

3 Be sure the subject is something that you can handle in a relatively short period of time. You aren't going to be writing a thesis or dissertation or a book — just a single research paper. Avoid a subject like *The History and Development of Solar Energy* and choose a more specific area like *Solar Energy for the Home*. Be as narrow and specific as possible.

4 Choose a subject that is compatible with one of these purposes for writing:
a To make an assertion and back it up with proof from your reading.
b To state a problem and give the solution.
c To report on the current situation, state of development, new knowledge in the area.
d To answer an important question about the topic.

If your paper has a purpose (like the essays you have been writing), it will have a focus from the very start, and you will be much happier, because you'll have a direction in which you are going — a reason for writing. That will be a big relief.

APPLICATION

1   After answering the questions under Choosing a Subject (Number 1), make a list of subjects that you might be interested in having as the topic for your research paper.

2   Examine the following subjects. Mark *G* for *Good* if you think the topic meets the requirements for a good subject. Mark *NG* for *Not Good* if the topics don't meet the requirements.
a. Who was the better poet — Robert Frost or Carl Sandburg?
b. The problem of crowded freeways.
c. The causes of the energy crisis.
d. Vitamins as a controversial subject.
e. How did the world begin?
f. What is the big bang creation theory?
g. Ways to make a car run more efficiently.
h. Vitamin C will make a person healthy.
i. Good places for vacations.
j. Television violence is bad for children.
k. Explanation of inflation.
l. Ways to invest money.
m. State of churchgoing in the 1980s.

3   These are some subjects students want to use for their research papers. What purposes do the subjects seem to fit best? Mark *A* for *Assertion*, *P/S* for *Problem/Solution*, *R* for *Report on Current Situation*, and *Q* for *Question Answering*.

_____ 1. Advancement of blacks in government jobs.

_____ 2. Achievements of minority groups in the history of the West.

_____ 3. Mass-transit systems for metropolitan areas.

_____ 4. Trends in church attendance.

_____ 5. Role of diet in treating cancer.

_____ 6. Explanation for American fascination with football.

4   Look at the following subjects. What would be two or three likely sources for information on them?
a. Benefits of jogging.
b. Solar energy for homes.
c. Jane Fonda.
d. Vegetarian diets.
e. Problems in the Social Security System.
f. How holograms are made.
g. Reviews of the movie *Star Wars.*
h. World hunger.
i. Recent political developments in Spain.
j. The speaker, occasion, and circumstance when these words were spoken: "I shall return."
k. Rodeos in America.

5   Choose four of these subjects, go to the library, and find three books, articles, or references that you would read if you were going to do a research project on the topics. Make bibliography cards for each source.

6   Go to the library and locate two indexes in the reference section that are not listed under *Reference Material* in this text. Write down the names of the indexes and a brief summary of what they contain.

7   Read the article on the devil wind (Information Essay section). Then read the notes below. Mark *I* for *Incorrect* if the writer has plagiarized, footnoted unnecessarily, or misquoted. Mark *C* for *Correct* if the note needs no footnote, has been documented correctly, and is quoted accurately.

_____ 1. Dust devils are generally more powerful than over 25 percent of all the tornadoes that occur in the world.

_____ 2. Professor T. Theodore Fuijita has said that "a strong dust devil is generally more powerful than over one-fourth of all tornadoes that occur in the world."[1]

_____ 3. Dust devils are most common where there are hot temperatures, dry surfaces, and a lot of loose soil.

_____ 4. Dust devils are caused by cool air rising and hitting a layer of warm air, creating thermals.[2]

_____ 5. Dust devils can be very dangerous.[3]

_____ 6. Most of the damage caused by tornadoes comes from the "mini-funnels" inside the big funnel.

_____ 7. Dust devils and tornadoes both have little funnels inside big funnels.[4]

_____ 8. Dust devils can occur in bathtubs when the plug is pulled.[5]

_____ 9. In 1902 a dust devil destroyed a stable and carried the roof several hundred feet away.

_____ 10. Dust devils can have as many as 12 to 16 little funnels inside the big wind.[6]

_____ 11. Suction vortices may be the explanation for a tornado hitting one building and destroying it while not touching the building right next to it.[7]

_____ 12. Tornadoes are dangerous.

8 Read these paragraphs and then make ten notecards for them just as you would if you had come across the material in your reading for your own research paper.

The Anasazi tradition itself can be divided into two parts: the earlier Basket Maker and the later Pueblo. The Basket Makers have been traced back in the San Juan region to about the time of Christ. They were so named, logically enough, because of the fine basketry they produced and because they had none of the pottery researchers had found in other, chronologically later archaeological sites. Many of the early Basket Makers lived in caves, although in some areas they began to build pithouses, a trend that would grow and spread. The pithouses were shallow, saucerlike dwellings, walled and roofed with a combination of logs and mud mortar. Until about A.D. 500 the Basket Makers moved within the San Juan region, dividing their time between hunting and cultivating a yellow flint corn.

About the year 500 changes began to appear in the Basket Maker pattern of life. The modifications were not abrupt but evolutionary and varied in time from place to place throughout the San Juan, but generally speaking, the mood of change was upon the Basket Makers about this time. In the broadest terms, they were becoming more sedentary; a greater dependence on agriculture was developing; pithouses were deepened and more permanently constructed to accommodate domestic activities and family ceremonies; and they began to build the circular, subterranean ceremonial structures that would become rigidly formalized as great kivas. They also began to make pottery, a skill apparently learned from neighbors to the south.

Toward the end of this period, nearing A.D. 700, they began to show signs of a dramatic cultural advancement. The bow and arrow made its appearance, displacing the less efficient atlatl and spear. Cotton weaving was introduced, and full-grooved axes suddenly were in use. All were signs of contact with other peoples, but the rapid acceptance of the new ways indicated that the Anasazi had an adaptable, inquisitive, and thoroughly dynamic culture.

The accomplishments of the Basket Maker Anasazi were extraordinary, but about A.D. 700 they began a transition in building techniques that earned them a new name, Pueblo, and changed the architectural modes of their Southwest neighbors. The Pueblo Anasazi built in stone and masonry, rising up to build on the surface and reserving subterranean structures for ceremonial purposes. Rapidly developing their skills as masons, the Anasazi first built a few contiguous rooms and later elaborated the style into multistoried warrens of rooms and plazas that served as cities.

Whatever the stimulus for all the change and growth, whether it came from within or without, the Anasazi multiplied the refinements in their cultural pattern dramatically during the ensuing centuries. Between about 900 and 1100, they began building some of their most impressive dwellings, raised pottery craftsmanship and decoration to hitherto unknown levels, indulged in a variety of craft arts, devoted a compelling amount of energy to religion and the construction of enormous kivas, and saw their influence spread across the entire Southwest, with certain tendrils of their culture reaching as far as southwest Texas and Nevada. Their culture spread almost intact into the Upper Rio Grande region and with slight modifications poured down over the Mogollon Rim to the mountains and deserts of central and southern Arizona to become the Sinagua and later Salado.

For two hundred years following this phenomenal florescence, the Anasazi consolidated their gains and settled down to enjoy the good life they had wrought. From roughly A.D. 1100 to 1300, the largest Pueblos were built, pottery in its most advanced forms was crafted, and the Anasazi lifeway seemed established. Some might argue that it had ceased to grow and that a culture which does not grow must necessarily begin to die. The question is largely moot, though, because before 1300 the Anasazi began to leave their homes—in some cases a full century before that date—until by 1300 the once great cities of the plateau were silent and vacant, drying in the Southwest winds like the husk of some long dead insect, retaining form but lacking the essence of a once active life.

—*Donald Pike*

9 Turn Karen Brinkley's topic outline on *Tom Jones* into a sentence outline after you have read the research paper following it.

10 Arrange each of the items below in the appropriate footnote and bibliography form.

1. A book edited by S. H. Frost, M. P. Weiss, and J. B. Saunders.
   Title: *Reefs and Related Carbonates: Ecology and Sedimentology.*
   Publisher: American Association of Petroleum Geologists.
   Place of publication: Tulsa, Oklahoma.
   Date of publication: 1977.
   Reference from p. 276.

2. Author: Allan G. Cameron and Brian A. Fox.
   Title: *Food Science: A Chemical Approach.*
   Publisher: University of London Press.
   Place of publication: London.
   Date of publication: 1970.
   Reference from pp. 150–151.

3. Author: Carol T. Nadelson.
   Title: "The Woman Physician."
   Journal: *Journal of Medical Education.*
   Publication information: vol. 47, March 1972, pp. 176–183.
   Reference from p. 176.

4. Author: William Strunk and E. B. White.
   Title: *The Elements of Style.*
   Edition: second.
   Publisher: The Macmillan Company.
   Place of publication: New York.
   Date of publication: 1972.
   Reference from pp. 27–28.

5. Author: Robert E. Ornstein.
   Title: *The Psychology of Consciousness.*
   Publisher: W. H. Freeman and Company.
   Place of publication: San Francisco.
   Date of publication: 1972.
   Reference from pp. 129–30.

6. Author: David Viscott.
   Title: *How to Live with Another Person.*
   Publisher: Arbor House.
   Place of publication: New York.
   Date of publication: 1974.
   Reference from pp. 48–49.

7. Author: Joseph Fletcher.
   Title: "The New Religious Morality."
   Editors: A. K. Bierman and James A. Gould.
   Book: *Philosophy for a New Generation.*
   Publisher: The Macmillan Company.
   Place of publication: New York.
   Date of publication: 1970.
   Page numbers: 178–187.
   Reference from p. 180.

8. Title: "Hill Defends State's Death Penalty Statute."
   Author: none given.
   Newspaper: *Houston Chronicle.*
   Date of publication: March 31, 1976.
   Page: p. 1 and p. 4 in Section 1.

9. Author: Leo Bogart.
   Title: *The Age of Television.*
   Edition: second.
   Publisher: Frederick Ungar Publishing Company.
   Place of publication: New York.
   Date of publication: 1956.
   Reference from p. 99.

10. Author: Robert Keathly.
    Title: "The Hornet's Nest at Langly."
    Newspaper: *The Wall Street Journal.*
    Date of publication: February 11, 1976.
    Page: 16.

THE TOP 20: QUESTIONS TO ASK ABOUT YOUR RESEARCH PAPER

GENERAL

1 Is the paper interesting and easy to read even if the subject is unfamiliar?
2 Have I given some of my own thoughts, ideas, or opinions in addition to the information I got from my sources?

TITLE

3 Does the title arouse curiosity and accurately reflect the content of the paper?

OUTLINE

4 Is the outline in proper form?
5 Does the outline reflect the actual organization of the paper?

THESIS STATEMENT

6 Is the thesis of the paper clear to the reader at the very start?
7 Does the thesis statement limit and focus the paper as well as illustrate the purpose of the paper?
8 Does the thesis statement do one of the following: *(a)* clearly state the assertion to be proven in the paper, *(b)* present the problem that the paper is going to concentrate on and suggest the solutions to be given, *(c)* set a context for the report of current conditions on the subject, *(d)* pose the question that the essay sets out to answer—?

DEVELOPMENT AND ORGANIZATION

9 Does everything in the paper relate to the thesis?
10 Is there a logical order in the development of the paper?
11 Are all the main points adequately supported with quotes and references? Are they fully developed?

CONCLUSION

12 Does the final paragraph or two pull the paper together by giving the reader a sense of completeness and closure? Is the thesis reviewed, summarized, or referred back to?

MECHANICS

13 Do you have transitions connecting the sections of the essay?
14 Are there any spelling errors?
15 Did you punctuate correctly?
16 Did you use accepted grammatical forms?

DOCUMENTATION

17 Is there any plagiarism?
18 Have you integrated your research material into the essay so that it doesn't sound like a paste-up job of your notecards? Did you use enough sources?
19 Are the footnotes in proper form? Is there a bibliography entry for each source cited in a footnote?
20 Is the bibliography in correct form?

WRITING ABOUT LITERATURE

When you begin to write about literature, you are, as in research paper writing, moving into an area that demands two separate sets of skills: *You have to know how to read and interpret literature,* and *you have to know how to write.* Reading and interpreting literature is something you have likely done extensively in class before you were asked to write an essay about a story, poem, or play. A brief review, then, of the elements of fiction, drama, and poetry can form the background for a hard look at what to *do* with these elements of literature when you must write an essay about them. This chapter will show you how to bring together your knowledge about reading literature and your ability to write.

REVIEW OF ELEMENTS OF FICTION AND DRAMA

The elements of fiction and drama fall into five groups ranging from the simple to the complex. Each of these groups represents a way to approach a story or a play when you are writing about it. Here are the five groups:

1 Setting
 Plot   *Facts plus significance*
 Character

2 *Development*
Contrasts
Tensions/conflicts   *Internal movement plus significance*
Resolutions

3 *Point of view*
Form   *Author's craft plus significance*
Tone/mood

4 *Theme*   *Meaning plus significance*

5 *Context in history*
Context in genre   *External placement plus significance*
Context in author's work

These elements move from the more elementary to the most abstract or comprehensive. They are all ways in which you can approach a piece of literature for an essay.

1 Setting
    Plot   **Fact plus significance**
    Character

These three are absolutely essential to any work of fiction or drama. They are almost the first things you become aware of as you read a story or novel or as you read or watch a play.

Setting: *Where* does it take place? City or village or plains or mountains? In a hospital, a hunting lodge, aboard a luxury liner, or in a ghetto basement? *It has to happen somewhere,* and the setting can be very important to the action. Often what happens is at least *connected* to the setting, if not actually *caused* by it. (At times a setting can serve as a backdrop for the action of the story or play, but even then it is somehow related to what goes on.) Further, the setting is also the *time* that the story or play happens. *When* does it occur? Is it contemporary, set in the future, or placed in the past? Is it contemporary for the author but not the reader? Are the issues that the play or story takes up issues that concern us today? **Where and *when*, then, are the crucial elements of any general description of the setting.**

Plot: *What* happens? A plot summary is a simple recapitulation of the action, a quick telling of the main events or happenings. Does the hero or heroine emerge victorious? Does the protagonist avenge the death of the loved one? Does the hunter kill the bear? Plot can be defined as *the sequence of happenings in the story.* **The author sets up particular events, circumstances, or actions that carry the story along.** The plot is the author's vehicle for doing whatever he or she wants to accomplish in the story or play.

Character: *Who* is the play or story about? What kind of person is the main character? If there is more than one main character, which one seems most important and why? How are they alike? different? Who are the minor characters? How do they contribute to the plot? For example, do they ring the doorbell at the crucial moment, bring in the necessary message, interrupt the lovers, provide comic relief, comment wisely on what is happening or about to happen? Sometimes minor characters are present just to advance the plot; they may also be present in order to contrast with the main characters—to be particularly silly (and thus show how wise the main character is) or thoughtful (and thus show how foolish the main character is). When you describe a character, you have to talk about more than the physical characteristics: *characters are the sum total of how they look, think, feel, and act.* **Character is revealed in the story or play by what the characters do, what they say, how they look, what the writer tells you about them, and what others in the story or play say about them.** A person attempting to get a fix on any character will have to look at all these aspects to get the complete picture.

2 **Development
Contrasts
Tensions/conflict   Internal movement plus significance
Resolutions**

These elements of fiction and drama have to do with the way the story or play *moves,* the way they are *dynamic.* Looking at these elements can be one of the best ways to understand the story or play and is therefore very rewarding as a method of interpretation.

Development: Consider two things here: *development of the plot* and *development of the characters.* **For plot, what changes happen?** For example, you tend to expect certain things to happen from the way the story or play begins; sometimes they don't turn out that way, and we call these changes *developments of the plot.* Maybe the king has already won two tremendous victories and is looking for a third, but treachery from a trusted lieutenant causes the defeat of his armies and the loss of his kingdom.

For character development, perhaps a person who has acted mostly out of impetuosity and impulse learns from sad experience to be more thoughtful about major decisions. This **change in the character** can be the way the author makes one of the most important points in the story or play. The change in a character will make her or him appear more human, more lifelike. Characters that don't change in a story, especially if they play any major role, don't seem real; in fact, they are called *stock characters* because they just stay the stereotyped way they are. The development of plot and character is often what makes a story or play really interesting. **For the reader, noticing how the plot or character changes and getting at the significance of this—what does it mean, what does it say—is to get at the very heart of the piece of literature.**

Contrast: **What sorts of contrasts has the author presented?** Perhaps the main character has been raised in luxury but has experienced a reversal that makes her learn what it is like to live in dire poverty. The contrast between her two lifestyles will surely be worth considering. Or perhaps there is a contrast between the way a parent behaves (like a bully and braggart) and the way a child behaves (in a different manner). Perhaps there is a contrast between one character's ability to reason and another's. Between one's courage and another's cowardice. Between one's zest for adventure and another's preference for the ordinary. Or a contrast between the setting at the beginning and the setting at the end; or contrast between setting and circumstances (for example, an elegant casino and glittering appearance of people contrasted with their despair and compulsion as they gamble).

Tension/Conflict: What gives the story its *suspense*, its *energy?* Is the heroine pitted against an antagonist (human against human)? Is the hero trying to survive in the desert or on a storm-tossed sea (human against nature)? Or is the main character attempting to overcome years of indecisiveness in order to make one final emphatic gesture or decisive act (human against herself or himself)? Is the conflict between the heroine's strict upbringing and a new opportunity for personal freedom? The hero's dreams and his abilities? Between opportunity for profit and knowledge that it would be to take unfair and illegal advantage of people who are unable to defend themselves? **Look for tension and conflict, and you can be sure that you are looking for something very important at the heart of the story.**

Resolution: How does it all work out? How is the tension or conflict dealt with finally? Does the heroine win, lose, or draw? Does virtue triumph over evil? Conscience over profit? Is the hero destroyed or exalted? **See how it all winds up, and you'll be seeing what the author meant you to learn or experience from reading the story or play.**

3 Point of View
    Form   **Author's craft plus significance**
    Tone/Mood

With these elements you move from *what happens* in the story or play to *how the author writes* the piece of literature. These elements can be very illuminating as additional statements of what the story or play "means." This is true because **the author will have deliberately chosen to use the point of view, the form, and the tone for specific purposes in whatever he or she is writing.** These elements are a bit less obvious, perhaps, from the ones in groups 1 and 2, yet *they almost always influence a reader's response and cause certain reactions.* The ability to identify and discuss the significance of these elements will take you a long way toward being a mature and sophisticated reader of literature and writer about literature.

Point of View: Whose eyes and mind are you seeing the story through? No two people, of course, ever see life exactly the same way, so **it is very important for a reader to determine who is telling the story and how much the author lets·the reader know.** The story may be told by an omniscient voice that knows everything or by one of the characters in the story that only knows what he or she knows. The author may not be in evidence at all but may let an "I" in the story be the spokesperson. The point of view may also be like a camera, with the actions being seen or people's words being heard but no voice or character commenting on them. No matter which point of view an author chooses, *that point of view is used for a purpose* and figuring this out can be an excellent means of interpreting the story.

Point of view in drama is usually objective, like the camera. There is no comment or interpretation done by the dramatist except through certain characters' words or actions. At times, however, a playwright will let a character explain something directly to the audience — Hamlet with his soliloquies or the narrator in *The Glass Menagerie* — and we can get a particular point of view from these utterances. The play may also, on occasion, be completely from a character's point of view, and we see only what the character sees rather than what an objective camera would record, as in the modern drama *Da*.

Identifying the point of view and determining what that particular point of view contributes to the story or play lets you, the reader, see into the complexities of the author's craft and thus figure out his or her purpose or aim. It's one more way to get meaning from the thing you have read or seen.

Form: Does the tale move in a direct line from start to finish, or are there many switches in time and location? For example, *The Three Little Pigs* moves in straight chronological time, with heightening drama building up from the conflict between the wolf and the pigs to the climax of the final tension between the wolf and the one pig left. *Oedipus Rex*, on the other hand, has a very complex structure with foreshadowing, with elements emerging from the past and being superimposed on the present, with missing bits of information introduced here and there.

Predictable movement — *introduction* (setting and characters), *conflict* (when/over what), *complication* or *reversal* (something unexpected happens or turns up), and *resolution* (it comes to an end somehow) — usually means that the *form* is not being emphasized by the author. But unusual twists may mean that the author is also making a statement with the form of the play or story, and if you, as a reader, can figure out what this might be, you have another way of knowing what it all means. In *The Glass Menagerie* and *Death of a Salesman*, for instance, the form of the plays — the use of slides on a screen, the use of *space* to identify *time* — actually assists the dramatists in saying what they want to say. Taking careful note of these forms lends an additional layer of meaning to the work.

Tone/Mood: Is the story playful, sincere, grotesque, hair-raising, giddy, somber? Are you cheered up by reading it, or depressed when you put it down? Do you want to think about it for a while afterward, or do you at once forget about it? What *feeling* does the work produce?

The tone or mood lets you know how the author wants you to feel about the subject and can actually set up or foreshadow what is going to happen next. Nobody reading the opening of Edgar Allan Poe's "The Fall of the House of Usher" can fail to realize that something eerie is about to happen; the tone tells all. The tone of the movie *The Deerhunter* —established with the first shots on the screen—sets up the viewer for the dreariness and ordinariness that are part of what the director gets across. With the tone the writer lets you know what he or she wants you to make of what you are reading or seeing. As such, it is an extremely valuable statement about the author's viewpoint and position. *The tone reveals purpose.*

4 Theme   Meaning plus significance

A theme in a story or a play works just like a thesis sentence in an expository essay: **it is the main idea, the central statement, that the writer wants to get across.** It is the insight the writer wants to share, the point she or he wants to make. If you can identify the theme, you will know what the story or play "means." Usually, a theme will be a comment on life, a particular viewpoint on a subject, or perhaps a statement about human beings. A story or play will have a theme when the writer's intention is to tell what he or she thinks is a truth or an accurate picture of life.

A theme is not a moral. Morals preach; *themes reveal.* Morals are statements about what is right and what is wrong. Themes are any insight an author has about life, any generalizations she or he wishes to make. The theme in *Death of a Salesman* is not some moralistic dictum such as "It's bad to lie." Rather, the theme is a very complex statement about the damage of living in unreality, the effects of roads not taken, and the influences that shape character and produce integrity or the lack of it. This is a much more complicated insight than the simple moral and is much closer to the "meaning" in the play. The theme in "The Lottery" is not a moral such as "People are cruel and should not be trusted." The theme has to do with Shirley Jackson's views on tradition and custom and the power they have in life. Any temptation to reduce a theme to a moral is a temptation to see only a small fraction of the meaning of the story or the play.

You will never see the theme stated baldly and flatly. Therefore, **you have to piece together the theme from careful study of such elements as the character development, the conflicts, resolutions, tone, point of view.** A composite picture of these elements will reveal the theme, the main statement, that the author wrote the work to say.

5 Context in History
Context in Genre
Context in Author's Work

External placement plus significance

A final way a reader can study a piece of literature is by placing it in a larger context that will shed some light on the story or play from the outside. This requires a thorough knowledge of the background of the work, a comprehensive understanding of the forms particular kinds (genres) of literature take, or an inclusive familiarity with other things the author has written. If a reader has this broad knowledge, **a particular story or play can take on** *additional meaning* **because it is placed in a larger context.**

Context in History: Knowing the times in which a story or play was written can sometimes add a dimension to understanding it. When you look at Arthur Miller's *The Crucible* and realize that its historical context was the time of the McCarthy hearings in this country, you may be able to get an even firmer fix on Miller's theme. Knowing that Samuel Richardson wanted to be a preacher but that his family was too poor for him to go to school helps explain his purpose in writing *Clarissa;* he wanted to instruct as well as delight. Being able to put Mary Wollstonecraft Shelley's novel *Frankenstein* into its historical context of the Industrial Revolution and the rise of science in England helps explain her motivation for writing. Knowing historical context, then, can add to your understanding of a novel or play and provide a more complete view of the work in its time.

Context in Genre: *Genre* is the term used for the categories that a piece of literature fits into as a result of its form. The main categories are *fiction* (novel and short story), *poetry,* and *drama.* Each of these categories has certain distinct characteristics. Drama, for instance, is written in dialogue, is written to be performed, and has acts and scenes and stage directions. Poetry has a particular form on a page, employs elements such as rhythm, stanzas, rhyme, images, etc., in a way peculiar to itself.

When a work is studied in the context of its genre, it is compared with, contrasted to, or discussed in the light of other pieces of literature in the same category. You might, for instance, study Emily Dickinson's poetry by comparing it to Ann Taylor's to see how much Dickinson has departed from early tradition. The form of Virginia Woolf's novels could be contrasted with Fanny Burney's to see what changes had come in the forms of fiction over the centuries. Seeing how a work *departs* from the traditions of the genre, *modifies* them, or *ignores* them can be a clue to the meaning and intention of the author.

Context in Author's Work: Looking at a work as part of the whole group of things the author has written can be revealing. Knowing Richard Brautigan's early book *Trout Fishing in America,* for instance, provides a comparison and preparation for a later novel, *The Abortion.*

Reading all of Eugene O'Neill's plays lets you know how his themes changed or remained the same, how his characters developed over time, how his form varied or didn't. Being able to put a single work into the larger context of other things written provides much more to say about the story or poem being discussed.

REVIEW OF ELEMENTS OF POETRY

What is there to talk about in an essay on poetry? What does a person need to know about poems before sitting down to write about them? Looking into a house from different windows gives a different perspective with each glimpse, and in the same way a reader can look at a poem from different angles and in different ways, which, when summed up, help bring understanding and insight into what it all means. A quick review of some of the basic elements of poetry will remind you of the various ways you can study a poem; each of them can be a focus for your interpretation and writing.

1 Definition
2 Imagery
3 Compactness
4 Meaning
5 Structure and Form

1 DEFINITION

Many have tried to define poetry—but it's rather as Louis Armstrong said about jazz: if you have to ask what it is, you'll probably never find out. Yet we keep trying. Someone has said that poetry is those words that, heard by a man while shaving, would cause him to nick himself. Another person, groping for a definition, said that poems were words that did not go all the way across the page from the left-hand margin to the right! Robert Frost said that "like a piece of ice on a hot stove, the poem must ride on its own melting." What all these attempts to catch the meaning of the word *poetry* illustrate is how elusive a definition of the word really is.

But the truth of the matter is that in essence we all know what poetry is, and we've known since we were children. Our first brush with the *elements* of poetry probably came with nursery games and rhymes. This early introduction to verse and its elements was a beginning for our response to poetry itself. There's a natural and innate satisfaction that we human beings get from the rhythm, sound, emotional impact of words made into poems. What a poem *can* do is actually cause us to *experience*. We are struck by the impact. We live the experience. And that's probably the best definition there is—that poetry, when it's good and when we are really turned on by it, is highly concentrated experience and feeling conveyed through words. *Poetry aims at producing in readers the experience of experience, thereby intensifying and making richer and fuller their lives.*

2 IMAGERY

Remember the old adage, "A picture is worth a thousand words"? You've probably experienced this when someone was trying to tell you about a place visited and then in exasperation said, "Oh, wait a minute. I've got some pictures we made on the trip. I'll just show you. That way you can see what I mean."

Writers, however, don't have this option, and poets are even more limited than prose writers in finding a way to let the reader "see" what they are talking about. A prose writer can use a lot of examples and detailed discussion to get the picture across, but a poet has much less space. Not being able to depend upon a snapshot or a painting and having little room to elaborate, poets must do *everything* with words and space. To produce pictures for the reader, then, they use images—more or less concrete, descriptive words or phrases that appeal to our senses. These images then work like an alarm clock to wake up our senses. See how Shakespeare wakes up our eyes with these pictures in words of winter in England:

> When icicles hang by the wall
>   And Dick the shepherd blows his nail,
> And Tom brings logs into the hall,
>   And milk comes frozen home in pail

And here Gary Snyder wakes up our eyes, hands, noses, mouths, and emotional responses with this poem:

AFTER WORK

> The shack and a few trees
> float in the blowing fog
>
> I pull out your blouse,
> warm my cold hands
>   on your breasts.
> you laugh and shudder
> peeling garlic by the
>   hot iron stove.
> bring in the axe, the rake,
> the wood

we'll lean on the wall
against each other
stew simmering on the fire
as it grows dark
     drinking wine.

In the images in this stanza of a poem called "Town Fire," Greg Kuzma puts the reader on the scene.

The policeman on the corner is directing traffic.
He has a bright pink thumb
which looks like a bright pink clothespin.
He waves it in the air,
and when he waves it over his shoulder
he points down a long empty street.
This is where the reporters will park.
This is where they will scribble in notebooks
NEWS OF THE FIRE.

The images in these poems create the *experience* for you. Instead of merely being told about a thing, you are there!

3 COMPACTNESS

Mark Twain once said that to instruct a mule, first hit it between the eyes with a two-by-four. At times we feel that this is what a poem has done to us. The way so much is said in so little space almost stuns us. In this haiku we are struck by the impact of so few words.

SPRING SCENE

On the temple bell
     Has settled, and is fast asleep
     A butterfly.
          —Anonymous

Poets make every word count. The lines are, in the words of a student, "lean, mean, and muscle-ly." Wordiness puts people to sleep in the best of circumstances, and poets won't have us be asleep. They will make and remake a poem until every word carries as much meaning as it possibly can.

In this poem by Gwendolyn Brooks, you can see how much is said with so few words.

WE REAL COOL

The Pool Players. Seven at the Golden Shovel.

We real cool. We
Left school. We

Lurk late. We
Strike straight. We

Sing sin. We
Thin gin. We

Jazz June. We
Die soon.

One of the ways poets achieve this compactness is through the use of figures of speech, words, or groups of words that add dimensions of meaning because of the associations the reader is able to make. Here is another stanza of Greg Kuzma's poem, "Town Fire," that gives meaning through the use of figures of speech.

The fire hose is a big gray spaghetti.
It is plugged into a fire hydrant
that looks like
a man standing in high-waisted pants
with his thumbs sticking through his belt loops.
The fire, usually nearby,
looks like red silk
drawn out of windows
as if by electric fans.
The house, which is "on fire"
resembles a nutmeg sherbet.
Calls ring in the air, FIRE FIRE,
WATER, WATER. LADDERS LADDERS.
And then there is the circle of
the fire trucks.

Emily Dickinson uses metaphor to compare a train to a horse in lines like these:

I like to see it lap the miles,
And lick the valleys up,
And stop to feed itself at tanks;

And then, prodigious, step
. . . .

This compactness in poetry creates experience for the reader because the meaning of the poem is not lost in a welter of words. Of course the reader must pay strict attention to every word, but this is richly rewarded by the much greater feeling extracted from the poem.

4 MEANING

"I don't like poetry," someone will say, "because I can never figure out what it means." People often feel this way because they are looking for some kind of meaning that can be summed up in a sentence or two and understood by the logical mind. Some poems—and good ones—do have this kind of meaning, of course. Look, for instance, at this example:

FIRST FIG

My candle burns at both ends;
    It will not last the night;
But ah, my foes, and oh, my friends—
    It gives a lovely light!
               —*Edna St. Vincent Millay*

Other poems, however, do not have a meaning that can be reduced to simple statements. **The *real*, or *total*, meaning of a poem is not what it says but the *experience* that it expresses.** The "meaning" of a poem is just what the poem communicates by simply *being*. Archibald MacLeish probably said it best:

ARS POETICA

A poem should be palpable and mute
As a globed fruit,

Dumb
As old medallions to the thumb,

Silent as the sleeve-worn stone
Of casement ledges where the moss has grown—

A poem should be wordless
As the flight of birds.

A poem should be motionless in time
As the moon climbs,

Leaving, as the moon releases
Twig by twig the night-entangled trees,

Leaving, as the moon behind the winter leaves,
Memory by memory the mind—

A poem should be motionless in time
As the moon climbs.

A poem should be equal to:
Not true.

For all the history of grief
An empty doorway and a maple leaf.

For love
The leaning grasses and two lights above the sea—

A poem should not mean
But be.

Here are two poems whose meaning could not be summarized in a sentence or two. Their total meaning is the very experience of the poems themselves.

THE RED WHEELBARROW

so much depends
upon

a red wheel
barrow

glazed with rain
water

beside the white
chickens.
—*William Carlos Williams*

LUNCH

The joy is simple and perfect:
to have a single nectarine

cut in four on a plate on a table.
The afternoon like a wall

thrust up to heaven, shining
and clear. Nothing

in the soft, scented dark
but the plate, the form

the hands at rest silently.
                              —*Paul Christensen*

5 STRUCTURE AND FORM

The original Greek word that *poetry* came from meant *to make,* and poets
do make something: they make the experience recur or occur for the
reader and they literally make the poem itself that creates this experience. By building their poems deliberately and carefully, poets achieve
the magic that is bigger than the poems themselves: the impact on the
reader. Just studying the way poets build a poem—the structure and
form—won't get at the magic of the poetry itself, but it will increase your
awareness of *how* the poet came to achieve the magic. The structure and
form of poems are made up of things like repetition of words, balance,
parallels, rhythm, stanza or line form, rhyme (or the absence of it), and
words that carry their meaning in their sound. These structural elements contribute to what the poem "means." Once you begin to see the
structure—perhaps the movement of the idea or the development of the
thought through repetition or the establishing of contrasting elements—
for the rest of the poem you can watch the motion. And this gives
pleasure.

In "Naming the Parts" the whole point of the poem is made by the
play of *naming the parts of a gun* against *the presence of flowers and bees in the
garden outside.* Seeing the structure move back and forth between the
two is to catch the experience the poet wants you to have.

NAMING THE PARTS

Today we have naming of parts. Yesterday,
We had daily cleaning. And tomorrow morning,
We shall have what to do after firing. But today,
Today we have naming of parts. Japonica
Glistens like coral in all of the neighboring gardens,
    And today we have naming of parts.

This is the lower sling swivel. And this
Is the upper sling swivel, whose use you will see,
When you are given your slings. And this is the piling swivel,
Which in your case you have not got. The branches
Hold in the gardens their silent, eloquent gestures,
   Which in our case we have not got.

This is the safety-catch, which is always released
With an easy flick of the thumb. And please do not let me
See anyone using his finger. You can do it quite easy
If you have any strength in your thumb. The blossoms
Are fragile and motionless, never letting anyone see
   Any of them using their finger.

And this you can see is the bolt. The purpose of this
Is to open the breech, as you see. We can slide it
Rapidly backwards and forwards: we call this
Easing the spring. And rapidly backwards and forwards
The early bees are assaulting and fumbling the flowers:
   They call it easing the Spring.

They call it easing the Spring: it is perfectly easy
If you have any strength in your thumb: like the bolt,
And the breech, and the cocking-piece, and the point of balance,
Which in our case we have not got; and the almond-blossom
Silent in all of the gardens and the bees going backwards and
      forwards,
   For today we have naming of parts.
                                                    —*Henry Reed*

   In Mari Evans's poem "I Am a Black Woman," the repetition of the single word *humming* and the placement of that word in the first stanza contribute enormously to the experience of that stanza. Notice, then, that the second stanza has a different form, lines that run fast after each other, breathless, without punctuation to break the end of each line. Finally, the third stanza has still a different form, one that contributes to the statement the poet is making as she ends the poem. *The form and structure of this poem are definitely a significant part of the experience of the poem itself.*

I AM A BLACK WOMAN

   I am a black woman
   the music of my song
   some sweet arpeggio of tears

is written in a minor key
and I
can be heard humming in the night
can be heard
                    humming
in the night

I saw my mate leap screaming to the sea
And I/with these hands/cupped the lifebreath
from my issue in the canebrake
I lost Nat's swinging body in a rain of tears
and heard my son scream all the way from Anzio
for Peace he never knew. . . . I
learned Da Nang and Pork Chop Hill
in anguish
Now my nostrils know the gas
and these trigger tire/d fingers
seek the softness in my warrior's beard

I
am a black woman
tall as a cypress
strong
beyond all definition still
defying place
and time
and circumstance
    assailed
        impervious
            indestructible
Look
    on me and be
renewed.

In this beautiful poem from Ecclesiastes, repetition and balance are the structural devices that create the power of the lines:

To everything there is a season,
And a time to every purpose under the heaven:
A time to be born, and a time to die;
A time to plant, and a time to pluck up that which is planted;
A time to kill, and a time to heal;
A time to break down, and a time to build up;
A time to weep, and a time to laugh;
A time to mourn, and a time to dance . . .
                    3:1–4, Authorized (King James) Version.

There are further insights possible when you look for structure among the rhythms and end-rhymes, alliterations, and other devices of the poet's craft. You can really appreciate a beautiful cabinet without knowing all about the elements of carpentry and woodworking and finishing, yet when you learn about things like dove-tail joints and drawer-glides, you have an even deeper appreciation. The same is true of learning about the structure of poems. You will experience more profoundly and directly what each poem wants you to know.

HOW TO WRITE ABOUT FICTION, DRAMA, AND POETRY

THE CREATING STAGE

The first step in writing any good essay on literature is to have the skills of reading and interpreting that we have just been examining. If these elements are part of your fund of knowledge when you sit down to look at a poem, story, or play, you won't have to sit there drawing a complete blank, not knowing where in the world to begin.

Probably the best way to get ideas on what to say is to do a *Creating Stage* which is a modification of the classical invention technique you practiced earlier in this book. *Ask yourself a lot of questions.* Of course, no amount of probing or stimulating your thoughts can produce something to say about literature if you have never thought about literature. Nothing, unfortunately, will substitute for *knowing*. But if you do know in general what to look for when you read literature, asking yourself questions as you sit down to write will give you ideas that can become the point of your paper. *You don't need a lot of technical know-how.* In fact, if you just know how to look at a poem, story, or play, you have enough background to do excellent work. With that background you can use questions like a checklist to see what comes up that you would enjoy writing about.

BAKER'S DOZEN: QUESTIONS TO ASK YOURSELF ABOUT FICTION

1 Is there anything particularly unusual about the setting? Does the setting itself serve as a "character" in the story? How significant is time in the story? How is the setting presented?

2 What is interesting about the major character(s)? How does the major character change? How is character in the story revealed — by author's comments, by other's remarks in the story, by things the character does and says?

3 What is the point of view? How would the story be different if it were

told from another point of view? Does the point of view shift? If so, what is gained/lost by this shift?

4 What insight does the author give in this story? How is the theme revealed? What is my reaction/response to this theme? Is this theme universally true? Can I compare this theme to one in another piece of fiction?

5 What makes the story "good"? What are its strengths? What are its weaknesses? Will this story last?

6 What do I know about the author's other writing? Can I say anything about this story by comparing it to stories written in other times in history? Do I know anything about the historical context of the story? Is there anything about the time when it was written that would illuminate the author's purpose? Can I discuss the way this piece of fiction is like/unlike other pieces of fiction? Can I compare/contrast this story with another one written by the same author? Do I know how this story was received by the public? by critics?

7 What is the conflict in the story? How is this conflict revealed? How is the conflict resolved? Is this resolution believable?

8 Is there anything unusual about the way the story is written? Are there a lot of flashbacks? If so, of what value are they in the story? Can I say anything about the author's style? Is there anything different about the form—say, drawings, interspersed as in a Vonnegut novel or sentences run together as in Faulkner's work? If so, what is there to say about this form? Are there any motifs that recur throughout the story—water, nature, clocks, gardens, bouquets, snakes, etc.? If so, can I trace any development in these? Or can I relate them to the theme/conflict/tension in the story? Does the author do anything unusual with words? Is there anything special to say about the language?

9 Are there two types of people, two views of life, two opposing philosophies contrasted in the story? If so, how are these related to the theme? How are they revealed? Can I compare/contrast two characters and relate this to the meaning of the story?

10 How does the author establish the tone of the book? How does this tone relate to the conflict? the theme? the resolution? the characters? Does the tone change in the story? If so, what does this change contribute to the story?

11 Is the theme of the story a criticism of society? institutions in society? government? people? Is the theme a celebration of life? an affirmation of the good? Is the theme a warning? A concern?

12 What is the most important development that occurs in this story? What is significant about that?

13 Is this story believable? What makes it realistic? What makes it a fantasy? If it is a fantasy, can it also be "true"? If it is realistic, can it also be "false"? What makes the story believable or unbelievable?

THREE × THREE: QUESTIONS TO ASK YOURSELF ABOUT POETRY

1 What is there to say about the way this poem looks on the page?
2 Are figures of speech present in this poem? If so, how do they contribute to the total meaning of the poem?
3 Are there any particular words that, if studied carefully, would illuminate the meaning of the poem? What can be said about the compactness of this poem?
4 What are the strong images in the poem? How do these images relate to the experience of the poem?
5 Who is the speaker in this poem? What is the speaker like? What lines/words in the poem reveal the character of the speaker? Who is being spoken to in the poem?
6 Is there any significant repetition in this poem? Balance? If so, what can I say about their importance to the poem?
7 How does the title relate to the rest of the poem?
8 What is the mood in the poem? The rhythm? How are these revealed and what do they add to the total meaning of the poem?
9 What does this poem *mean* (in the total sense of meaning)? What is the experience of the poem? What moves me about this poem?

PLUS FIVE: QUESTIONS TO ASK YOURSELF ABOUT DRAMA

Many of the questions about fiction can also be asked when you are going to write about a play, since both drama and fiction concern themselves with character, plot, setting, conflict, resolution, context in history, genre, and author's works, point of view, tone, and theme. There are some additional questions, however, that you can ask that relate to the form and structure unique to drama. You have the previous fiction questions, then, plus these five:

1 How soon does the dramatist reveal the plot, conflict, and major characters? Specifically, how are these revealed? Is there anything important to say about this?
2 What specific speech(es) in this play reveal the theme? What can be gained by analyzing this speech in detail?
3 What scenes/dialogues/speeches in the play set up the rising action of the plot, the climax, and the falling action? What does looking at these do to help you understand the play?
4 Are the main characters tragic or comic? Are they realistic? In what ways do they act like all human beings? What explains how they came to be how they are? Do they represent any universal truth about human nature?
5 How is the play staged? What do the stage directions add to my understanding of the play? Why do particular characters leave the stage

when they do? Is there a telephone ring or a letter delivery? What do these allow the dramatist to reveal to the audience? In what other ways could this same thing have been revealed? Why do the acts break when they do? What is the function of each scene in an act?

The purpose of these questions in the *Creating Stage* is not for you to sit down and write detailed answers to them. They are not a quiz. They can serve, however, as reminders of the many alternatives and perspectives you have when you read and interpret literature.

THE SHAPING STAGE

The first step in the *Shaping Stage* of an essay on literature is the formulation of a *purpose* and a *thesis*. Most likely you will be writing to *explain*, to *inform*, or to *assert* (although you may also write to give a personal viewpoint if the assignment allows that, or you may write to argue and persuade the reader). The purpose and the thesis, of course, are so integrally related that it is impossible to talk about one without the other. **The thesis will be the main idea, point, assertion you make in the essay,** the thing that everything else in the essay hangs on.

Suppose you have just read *Macbeth* and during the *Creating Stage* you find out that you would really like to discuss the theme of the play. Your thesis might be *The theme of* Macbeth *is revealed through the actions of Macbeth himself.* With this thesis, then, you would begin an *assertion* essay that would contain proof or substantiation that you were right in your interpretation.

The audience for whom you are writing when you do a literary essay is usually a nonaudience, in the real sense of *audience*. With most classroom assignments in literature, you are usually writing to the teacher (and perhaps your classmates) because one purpose of the essay (like tests) is to show that you know information—in this case, elements of fiction, drama, or poetry—and have the skill of interpretation, and can also write. So a literature essay will usually be an academic assignment rather than an outside context assignment. You will need, therefore, to write for the "general reader," and imagine that the teacher is enough like you to enjoy reading the kind of writing you yourself enjoy. Take into account the things that are true for all readers, what they respond to, what they don't.

There are real-life contexts, of course, that can serve as the reason for your essay. Reviews appear all the time in magazines and newspapers. Articles are written for journals. If you should place your essay into a *particular* situation context, be certain that you take into account the nature of your *specific* audience. For instance, if you were discussing a new novel for a monthly book club meeting, you could make certain assumptions about that audience—such as that they had read the book or heard about it, that they liked literature—and if you were giving the review as part of Library Week activities at a downtown civic club breakfast meeting, you would have to make crucial adjustments in your tone, content, and purpose.

Perhaps the most important thing you need to remember about the development of the essay is to fill it up with *details*. Don't skimp. Use example after example, reference after reference. Absolutely show your reader what you mean. If you are informing the reader about general characteristics of science fiction as a genre, spell these out. Illustrate each characteristic copiously. Even give quotations to back up your statements. Interpreting literature is a *thoughtful* act, and readers need as much information as you can possibly give them so that they will have something to think about.

THE COMPLETING STAGE

The *Completing Stage* of a literature essay differs little from the completing stage of any piece of writing. **You want the essay to be free of all errors. You want it to flow smoothly from one point to the next. You will want to add concrete details when you revise during the completing stage if you have been too abstract.** The same general principles about sentence variety, punctuation, grammar, paragraph development, etc., hold in the essays on literature as in any other. Do the best job you possibly can to make a perfect presentation of the ideas you have worked so hard to come up with and to get across to someone else.

APPLICATION

1 Here is a student academic essay written in response to a classroom assignment to pick a short story and discuss some significant literary element in it. The student chose the short story "What We Don't Know Hurts Us" and decided to discuss conflict in the main character as the focus for the paper. Be ready to discuss this essay in class.

CONFLICT IN CHARACTER IN "WHAT WE DON'T KNOW HURTS US"

Charles Dudley, the protagonist in Mark Schorer's "What We Don't Know Hurts Us," has just bought a run-down house that he neither chose for himself nor wanted to buy. He is not happy with the purchase, but then neither is he happy with many other situations in his life. His idea of the good way to live is very different from the way he is obliged to live in his present circumstances. "To own something was, to that extent, to be owned, and he did not like the feel. His idea of a good way to live was in a duplex apartment owned by someone else, in Charles

River Square, or, better than that but always less likely, in a duplex apartment owned by someone else, on the East River. *He connected happiness with a certain luxury, and, probably, sexuality with elegance and freedom"* (italics added). Charles has neither luxury, elegance, nor freedom in his present environment. The things that surround him are not the things he would like to have surround him. Everything he has or sees is less than perfect because it is measured by his dream fantasies.

After becoming frustrated with the unmanageable vegetation that he is trying to uproot, Charles throws down his mattock and dives through the thicket into the clearing. Looking up he sees Josephine, his wife, "sitting on the railing of the balcony onto which the french doors of their bedroom opened." This bedroom setting could be very romantic—even elegant and luxurious as his fantasy demands. But not in Charles's life. His wife is not wearing a soft negligee and beckoning him to leave his work, as she does in his dream. Instead, in her pose on the balcony, she is as opposite to his idea of sexuality and happiness as she could be. "She was holding a dust mop, and a tea towel was wrapped around her head, and her face seemed pallid and without character, as it always did to Charles when she neglected to wear lipstick." To show his disgust at the disparity between his dream and the reality, Charles merely snorts instead of replying to Josephine's question when she calls to him. What he sees is not what he would like to see.

Even things in nature are, like Charles, not free from pressure of outside forces. The pepper tree that he has freed from the overgrowth had "delicate, drooping branches and . . . long gray tendrils that hung down from the branches to the ground." But even this sensuous product of nature is robbed of its beauty. "A big branch of the eucalyptus at the very edge of the property had forced the top of the pepper tree to grow out almost horizontally from the main portion of its trunk." How does Charles accept this unique formation? Certainly not as Josephine, who remarks, "It's charming, like a Japanese print." Instead, with his usual feeling of frustration over things that are not as they should be, he sputters, "Look at the damned thing!"

The trees that Charles is struggling to uproot are fakes. "As a tree it was a total fraud, and in spite of the nuisance of its numbers, and of its feminine air of lofty self-importance, it was, with its shallow roots in this loose soil, very vulnerable to attack. Charles beat away at it in an angry frenzy, as if he were overwhelming, after a long struggle, some bitter foe." The conflict that this man feels because he does not have the kind of life that he would like to have is generalized to make him see other things as being the predicament itself. If he cannot attack his own situation, he surely can attack the fraudulent trees.

Charles's newly purchased house is not what many newly purchased houses are. In the first place, he sees it as an imitation of something and despises it for this imitation. "I certainly never wanted to own a miserable, half-ruined imitation of a Swiss chalet. . . ." His unhappiness goes even further, however, and is associated with the disorderly and unkempt appearance of the house while it is being remodeled. "An electrician had torn away a good deal of plaster and lathing, and a carpenter had ripped out some bookshelves and ugly mantels and taken down most of a wall between the dining room and a useless hallway, but neither had returned, and painters, plasterers, paper hangers had not yet come at all. . . . The result was that the house was almost fantastically disordered and bleak and squalid, and while Josephine managed to keep an even temper under these conditions, Charles, who found them very trying, did not." Even his newly purchased house has to be worked over, changed, and redone before it can begin to be elegant and luxurious and correspond to his dream.

So the conflict is evident. The husband and father desires freedom, luxury, and elegance, yet instead feels trapped in a miserable environment. He has, in reality (as he sees it) a yard full of fraudulent trees and "neglected vegetation . . . which had a disgusting, acrid odor," an exotic pepper tree which has an abnormal top, a wife who wears tea towels and goes without lipstick, and a house that is unlivable. Conflict figures heavily in the story because Charles, who sees only through this screen of his dream, finds life distorted in general. A pathetic incident involving his young son startles him into an awareness that perhaps the conflict he feels is not as significant as he may have thought it was. He comes to think that there may be more to life than what can be measured by his fantasy standards of luxury, elegance, and freedom.

2   Here is an academic essay a student wrote in response to a poetry essay assignment: "Write an essay in which you discuss language or structure in a poem as each contributes to the meaning and experience of the poem." The essay discusses the language in Robert Frost's "The Telephone," and it received the grade of *B*. Read the poem and then the essay. See whether you can determine why this paper received the evaluation that it did. Be ready to discuss this in class.

THE TELEPHONE

'When I was just as far as I could walk
From here today,
There was an hour
All still
When leaning with my head against a flower
I heard you talk.
Don't say I didn't, for I heard you say—
You spoke from that flower on the windowsill—
Do you remember what it was you said?

'First tell me what it was you thought you heard.'

'Having found the flower and driven a bee away,
I leaned my head,
And holding by the stalk,
I listened and I thought I caught the word—
What was it? Did you call me by my name?
Or did you say—
Someone said "Come"—I heard it as I bowed.'

'I may have thought as much, but not aloud.'

'Well, so I came.'

LANGUAGE OF INDIRECTION IN "THE TELEPHONE"

Robert Frost uses *language of indirection* in "The Telephone" to reveal attitudes and character traits of the speakers. The speakers' response to nature, their sentiment for each other, and their willingness to be playful and childlike are never openly discussed, but they are all revealed through the indirect language that Frost uses in the poem.

The "I" of the poem, in the first stanza, describes an experience that had occurred earlier in the day:

When I was just as far as I could walk
From here today
There was an hour
All still
When leaning with my head against flower
I heard you talk.

"Leaning with my head against a flower" reveals much that this speaker does not openly express. A person might pick a flower, lie in a bed of flowers, or intently study a flower—but to *lean against* a flower is a strange act. This speaker may feel that nature—a flower—can support, refresh, and provide rest. When the speaker was physically exhausted (for the speaker had gone as far from the house as was possible that day), the flower was a means of renewing strength for walking back. A touch of tenderness is also expressed in this leaning, as one person will lean on another in moments of emotional closeness. Although the speaker never directly states this close affinity to, and relationship with, nature, they are implied in the indirection of the word *lean* itself.

The speaker sees nature not only as a support and a resting place, but also as a means of communication, an instrument that transmits the voice of someone at home. "When . . . against a flower/I heard you talk." The flower is the speaker's personal receiver, a private telephone.

It transmits the voice of a friend or loved one just as the manufactured coiled wire and the invented talking box do for most people.

This use of the flower reveals the speaker's playfulness. He or she does not seem to be embarrassed at calling a flower a telephone. It also reveals a willingness to *not* be mechanical and scientific. The speaker's thinking is not subject to restraints that bind more literal minds. The speaker can be as original as a child.

The reply of the person at the house when the speaker asks if words had actually been spoken shows the closeness of the two. The one at home says, "First tell me what it was you thought you heard." This person was able to understand immediately what the walker had experienced that day. She or he does not rebuke the walker for having such "foolish" thoughts about a flower; there is no ridicule of the playfulness or the sensitivity. The person at home falls into the walker's mood because they know each other well and can be close in their thoughts. Any antagonism or friction between these two would have destroyed this moment that they are sharing. The person at the house is able to be in the same frame of mind as the walker and to understand the association of nature with their friendship or love.

Finally, a third statement of indirect language is found in these lines:

I listened and I thought I caught the word —
. . . I heard it as I bowed.

The speaker *bowed* to catch the flower's communication, a position that shows humility, but also a cramped position which a person unaccustomed to responding to nature this way would find rather uncomfortable. It is a posture that must be assumed with conscious effort. It also suggests a quiet and reverent attitude. The speaker is conveying both a description of conscious effort and a sense of sacredness, which are involved in using nature as a means of communication.

3   The following informal essay was written as a response to a class assignment that asked students to discuss the drama *Oedipus Rex* from the standpoint of its theme. They were to discuss this theme and show how it was common to human beings in general — that is, they were to identify the theme and then relate it to their own lives. Here is what one student wrote. Read it and be ready to discuss in class your evaluation of his work.

THEME IN OEDIPUS REX

In all good tragedies the main character must finally face up to the truth at the end of the play. In the drama *Oedipus Rex*, by Sophocles,

Oedipus is enlightened at the end and comes into ownership of the truth.

Oedipus' character is a big factor in his confronting the truth. Sophocles developed many aspects of Oedipus' character through the play, including his rashness in killing his father, his anger in his talks with Tiresias, and his pride, which caused him to believe he could go beyond the god's predictions. Although these aspects of his character are quite important in developing the theme, Oedipus' determination to find the truth is what really causes him to confront his own life. This determination made him strive forward even when his wife and mother, Jocasta, begged him to stop searching.

Although Oedipus' character was a big factor in his finding the truth, other hints and other characters were just as important. One of the main sources of truth in the play is Tiresias. I was very moved by one of Tiresias' lines during his argument with Oedipus. Oedipus asks Tiresias if he can go on with the terrible accusations against him. Tiresias replied that he can if the truth has power. This same line came back to give me extra power a few weeks ago in church. The gospel dealt with the disciples discussing the resurrection of Christ. The line so powerful to me came from one of the disciples as he said, "How can you kill the author of truth?" Truth cannot be destroyed, and it is in the end that truth unravels the events in Oedipus' life.

Several hints throughout the play not only build up the theme but finally cause Oedipus to face the truth. He first begins to get worried when Jocasta tells him that her husband was killed at a crossroads, for Oedipus knows that he killed a man at the crossroads. The messenger and shepherd also reveal to Oedipus that Polytus and Merope were not his real parents and that he is the son of Jocasta. Oedipus could then clearly see that the predictions that he would sleep with his mother and kill his father had come true.

After the realization, Oedipus accepts the fact that he has sinned and accepts responsibility for his actions, realizing that his innocent motives do not exempt him from his sins. The value in this play is revealed in the theme—that what finally matters is having ownership of the truth. As I read Oedipus I got deeply involved with the man and his problems. I watched him go from great heights as the savior of the city to the absolute lowest point. At the end I felt relieved that the truth had finally come out; but more than this, I was relieved of the pity and fear I had built up inside myself. In the play, the city was relieved of the blight on the land, and the power of truth finally overcame the mask that Oedipus was hiding behind. The power and beauty of that "rebirth" for Oedipus is also quite powerful to me more now than ever as a result of my sister's giving birth to a beautiful, clean little baby girl. I realized that the rebirth of a person can also be that powerful. As one throws off the junk and idealized self-image, one can indeed be born again to a rich and rewarding and aware life.

WRITING ESSAY TESTS

THE CREATING STAGE

By now you are probably accustomed, when approaching a writing assignment, to think first: "The *Creating Stage*—how can I find something to say?" **The *Creating Stage* for writing *essay answers* is actually a *Recovery Stage* and depends for its success on retrieving what you have put into your mind** while studying. The very purpose of the test is to determine whether you have learned a certain thing in class, to see if you can discuss important concepts covered in class. Your instructor is setting up a situation where you can prove that you *have* learned and *what* it is you've learned. This means that *the method of creating you use will be one that lets you recall the information you have studied*. No amount of cubing or looping and the like will give you material for an answer that you haven't already put into your mind.

Probably the creating technique that works best here is a traditional one—in fact, *the question itself may give you a hint:*
— *compare* and *contrast* the economic systems of Russia and America
— *describe* the life cycle of the tomato
— *analyze* the . . .
There really isn't a lot of "free creating" necessary. You either know something to say on the subject or you don't.

But let's assume that you *have* studied—what can you do next?

Probably the best thing to do is to **make a list of the main points you can think of at once on the question.** (Tests don't give you much time to "create," unlike the privacy of your own home.) This is a time when a quick outline or a list will probably be in order. You aren't really writing in this case to know what you *think* on a subject or to find out something you *didn't* know you knew. Your aim is to draw out/remember what you have recently put into your head and make applications from this material.

Next, **put this list of points in the margin of your test paper** so that you can see it from time to time as you write the answer. (Also, your instructor will be able to see the list if you run out of time and see where you had planned to go with the answer.)

Yes, the *Creating Stage* is very short in writing an essay test answer and very closely tied to how much studying you have done. The *Creating Stage* will probably be as simple as *making a list of what you remember*— the points you want to cover.

THE SHAPING STAGE

This is the critical step in writing an essay answer. There are several givens you can be almost certain of:

1 The instructor will be bored reading the tests.
2 The instructor will get very tired reading the tests.
3 The instructor will already *know everything* in the answer and will just be trying to determine whether you know it.

Writing essay test answers is really a rather limited type of communication process. Instead of trying, as the writer, to get the reader's attention, you can count—to a certain extent—on having the reader's attention! Instructors are after all paid to read the tests, and they are usually very conscientious about doing that. Contrast this situation to other writing times when you don't know whether the reader will continue to read or not. You can, however, depend on the good will of your instructor in reading your essay answers to the end.

You *can't* count, however, on the instructor's not getting tired or bored or confused or persuaded that you don't know a thing (all affecting your grade). So the Shaping Stage is extremely important in the presentation of your answer. You should have these objectives:

1 To prove immediately that you know the material.
2 To be very clear.
3 To be as specific as possible.
4 To come across as an individual and a (rather) distinct personality.

What the instructor wants to know from your test answers is not the *information* itself—she or he already knows this—but rather whether *you* know the information. This isn't communication in the real sense of the word, but it is in its way a kind of communication, one that you as a student need to be expert in.

In shaping essay answers, begin immediately with a sentence that tells the instructor what you are going to discuss. *This will be the topic sentence or thesis sentence of your answer.* (In fact, your entire answer will probably be one long topic sentence paragraph or a series of topic sentence paragraphs.)

You need not begin the answer with the same kind of lead-in, attention-getting opening you use in essays when you have to attract your reader's attention away from whatever he or she has been thinking about.

What is paramount here is the *subject matter*. The instructor is by and large uninterested—at this time particularly—in your personality or individuality except as that plays off the subject matter. The instructor *is* interested in knowing that you know the material, so you must make that clear immediately.

The next thing you must do in the essay answer is to give the information. If you can put it in a series of three to five points, give these swiftly and clearly. Then for each point give an example or two. Your instructor wants to know whether you know the material and whether you understand it. *Be specific.* Quote as many facts, give as many examples, as you can in the time allowed.

WHAT TO DO IF YOU THINK OF A NEW POINT WHILE WRITING

As you know from the creating activities you have done, writing itself often generates new ideas, retrieves information you had forgotten, and stirs up, in general, your thinking apparatus. If this happens while you are writing an essay test answer, *put a quick note to yourself in the margin* (you can scratch it out later) and after you've finished the point you're making, look for a minute at your list and think where your new point might fit best. **The important thing is not to run off with the new thought in the middle of what you are saying when you think of the new point.** Instructors are no different from other humans—they like order. They, like the readers of your essays, need to be able to see where you are going. Rambling answers will confuse and perhaps even annoy your instructor. Keep him or her happy and calm! Having a definite *order* to your answer, where you clearly go from one point to another, is a huge step in this direction.

THE COMPLETING STAGE

The way your answer *looks* on the paper will be very important in your instructor's grading. Remember these facts of life:
1 The instructor will have many papers to grade.
2 The instructor will already know the material.
3 The instructor likes order.
4 The instructor will respond much more favorably to neatness and correctness.

Be realistic. If a reader has to squint to read your writing, you're the loser. If the words are misspelled, this can irritate your instructor immediately. *Do everything in favor of yourself that you possibly can.* Save yourself enough time to look over the paper:
1 Be neat.
2 Write legibly.
3 Check spelling.
4 Be sure you have complete sentences.
5 Read over what you've written to be sure that it makes sense. Is a word left out? too many words put in? Did you write one word when you meant another?

You will defeat your own purpose if you write frantically to the last minute and don't leave yourself enough time to look over the answer. You can do more by checking the answer than by giving one more point.

WHAT TO DO IF YOU DON'T KNOW THE ANSWER

Never leave a question blank. Even if you don't know specifics for an answer, **write something.** Two things can serve as sources of answers: (1) loop writing on class discussions, and (2) points you know about other things that might be applicable to the question.

If you cannot remember a single thing from the text on the subject, loop writing may provide you with something to say. Decide how much time you have to spend on the question and divide that by thirds. *Plan to loop for the first third. Loop on class discussions.* (Then use the other two thirds of the time to write the answer.)

I remember the professor saying . . .

I remember being in class and . . .

When you've finished the looping, look it over and spot as many points as you can that were made in class that you might somehow relate to the question. You may not be able to develop these points from textual material fully, but you can give *examples* that *you* make up. **The important things to remember are not to panic, to stir up your thinking by writing, to pick out some points from class discussion that you can apply, and to organize these well.**

Even if an answer isn't absolutely applicable to the question, you will get some points very likely for writing an organized response. This is better than getting nothing.

SUMMARY

This pattern may not feel right at first but do it anyway:

1 **Take time to plan** *before* **you write.** Even if everyone around you is writing furiously, make a list of what you are going to say *before* you start writing.

2 **Write in an orderly fashion.** Think of your points distinctly one by one, and if you think of a new idea, put it in deliberately, not randomly.

3 **Finish in time to look over the answer.** You may find this difficult because of the temptation to write to the very end. But remember, the instructor doesn't want to know *everything* you know. If you select from what you know and present this selection in an orderly fashion, you'll get the grade you want.

4 **Be in charge yourself.** Don't let the test situation panic you or control you. Be calm, or you'll probably forget even the few facts that you think you do know. An essay test situation is simply a time for you to show your instructor something that he or she expects you to know. Be sure to take advantage of this opportunity. Organize; and write with the instructor in mind.

APPLICATION

1   Here are two examples of essay examination answers that received a grade of *A* from the instructor. Read them and be able to discuss why you think the instructor liked them.

EXAM QUESTION: *Discuss the use of the pointed arch in Gothic architecture.*
STUDENT'S ANSWER:

1. List made by student before beginning answer (appears in margin of test paper):

Pointed Arch

1. Allowed irregular spaces to be covered
     Example: *a* Rhomboidal bays of ambulatory
                      b Polygonal chapels of French Chevet
                      c Polygonal chapter-houses of England
2. Made possible use of ribs
     Example: *a* St. Denis Abbey Church
                      b Cathedral of Canterbury
                      c Cathedral of Salisbury
3. Made possible rectangular bays
     Example: *a* Church of Sainte Chapelle
                      b Cathedral at Amiens

2.   The answer itself:

The use of the pointed arch had a great significance to Gothic architecture. The first and most important task it accomplished was allowing an irregular area to be covered by arches and vaults. The round arch required a square vaulting bay, but the pointed arch with its extreme flexibility allowed almost any shape that was necessary. The arch allowed the steepness of the arches to vary, and this let the builders adapt the shape to whatever design might be included in the blueprint. Examples of irregular areas covered by this method are the rhomboidal bays of the ambulatory, the polygonal chapels of the French Chevet, and the polygonal chapter-houses of England.

The second achievement of the pointed arch was the making possible of an intricate system of vaulting ribs which served both structural and aesthetic purposes. The idea of the Gothic builder was to make a vault like a skeleton by use of the projecting ribs. Examples of the use of ribs can be seen in all Gothic cathedrals. Three such examples are the St. Denis Abbey church, the Cathedral of Canterbury, and the Cathedral of Salisbury.

Last, the pointed arch also made possible the rectangular as opposed to the square bay. This caused the total weight of the building to be distributed over twice as many points. The horizontal divisions, or bays, that were once present are then lost causing the eye to see the church nave as one smooth continuous aisle, as seen in the Church of Sainte Chapelle in Paris or the Cathedral at Amiens.

These three uses of the pointed arch were very important because they allowed Gothic architects to achieve the structural and aesthetic qualities that Gothic architecture is noted for.

EXAM QUESTION: *How did the Peloponnesian War affect Greece?*
STUDENT'S ANSWER:

1. List made in margin of test before writing answer:

    1. Ended 404 B.C.
    2. Defeated Athens
    3. Left Greece powerless
    4. Sparta & Thebes (2nd half of 4th century B.C.)
    5. States lost liberty to Philip of Macedon
    6. Life structure changed
    7. The individualism approach to life was taught
    8. Independence of city-state relationship lessened
    9. Final effect of Greek civilization spreading around the world

2. The answer itself:

Greece was affected by the Peloponnesian War in several ways. First, Greece was left defenseless and weak after the defeat of Athens. This weakness allowed Sparta and later Thebes to control Greece. As a result, in the latter half of the fourth century B.C., Greek states lost their liberty to Philip of Macedon.

Second, with this loss of liberty, the entire structure of Greek life was changed. The original balance between the city-state and individual was destroyed. Basic simple views concerning man and the state were changed into political and social upset and turmoil. The attitudes about life changed and became more self-centered and individualistic.

Third, as a result of this individualism, the state-individual relationship soon dissolved. Greek attitude also changed, leading to the search for knowledge of the world. Through this search, the Greeks experienced a time of human discovery.

Finally, it is easy to say that the Peloponnesian War was a powerful influence on the developments in Greece. But even though the country was adversely affected, in the long run and in a round-about way, the Peloponnesian War caused Greek civilization to spread around the known world. This was because Philip of Macedon's son was Alexander the Great, and everybody knows about his conquering the world. In this conquering, he took Greek civilization with him.

2 Here are two examination questions written by other students. Read each and write or discuss the strengths and weaknesses of the answers.

EXAM QUESTION: *Explain why the oceans are not filled in and the earth isn't a slush on the surface.*

STUDENT'S ANSWER:

1. List made before answering:

> *a* Subduction
> *b* Plate tectonics
> *c* Deposition
> *d* Erosion

2. The answer itself:

With all the sediment from erosion flowing into the oceans, how come the oceans are not filled in and the earth surface a slush pot?

One reason is the simple idea called subduction. Subduction is a simple idea; the sheet of rock from one area is going or being forced under another. Along the west coast of South America this is evident. The Andes Mountains are a side effect of this.

Second, the way these rock plates can be explained is an idea called plate tectonics. This idea states that there are rockplates on the surface of the earth, and they are constantly colliding and something has to give. The Himalayas are a good example.

A third reason to examine is the fact that all around you are deposition of material from erosion and volcanic activity, not to mention thrust of mountains over time. Rivers are constantly flowing with large amounts of sediment. The Amazon River. The island of Hawaii is a volcanic mountain. You can see the accumulation, but the disappearance is not quite so apparent.

Fourthly, erosion is happening at an unbelievable rate. With all this erosion, the oceans should be filled in. Take the Mississippi River for instance. In the last one thousand years it has built up a seven kilometer river delta. If you multiply this by one thousand times for the whole earth and take into account the depths, the oceans should have been filled in at least twenty-five million years ago. Subduction is the best guess.

EXAM QUESTION: *List four major engineering achievements prior to the twentieth century and discuss their importance.*

STUDENT'S ANSWER (no list made):

The first major engineering project was the irrigation system. This idea enabled the Egyptians to farm many miles of nonproductive land. Secondly, and just as important, was the building of roads. The Romans built roads mainly for communication, not transportation. Their army was constantly changing, and roads were vital to their success. The third development was the refinement of steel. This was a significant step to modern engineering, since it allowed production of machinery. The fourth design was a result of refinement of steel. It was the invention of the steam engine. This was very useful since it gave man an alternative energy source to slavery.

HOW TO WRITE ESSAY EXAM ANSWERS

1 Read the question carefully to see what approach to take. Almost every question reveals this.
2 Make a quick list or outline of the points you want to make *before* you start writing your actual answer.
3 Make it the aim of your answer to communicate to the instructor that you know the material.
4 Have a straightforward thesis or topic sentence that lets the instructor know exactly what you are going to say.
5 Be very orderly; go from point to point in a specific order.
6 Give a lot of details, examples, and illustrations. Fill your answer up with specifics.
7 Write from class discussions and personal experience if you can't think of specific information from your textbook or the instructor's remarks.

WRITING SPEECHES

YOU AS A SPEECH MAKER

You may look at the title of this chapter and say, *I'm never going to give any speeches; why should I study this?* The truth is, though, that you will probably give a lot of "speeches" in your life. Even if the speeches aren't formal affairs in front of audiences of thousands, you will be many times in your life *up in front of the public talking for a period of time about your ideas or thoughts.*

What are some of these occasions when you might give a speech? Perhaps it will be the short talks you will give around a conference table when you are trying to get your co-workers to accept *your* recommendations. Maybe the progress report you will deliver to your group in a company or firm, to a corporate Board of Directors, or to your office staff. Speeches before the city council about roads or taxes. Talks before the school board. Speeches when you are running for a seat in city government. Guest speaking engagements when you are invited to a local civic club to discuss some activity or situation that you are ex-

> Speech: Public ordering of private awareness for social interaction.
> —Dominic LaRusso

pert in; speeches at church; speeches at conventions; short talks for panel discussions; addresses to your professional society; talks to the local high school or the local press. The times you are going to be talking in public can surprise—and please—you.

You should know how to prepare a speech consummately well. In fact, one of the most frequent uses to which you may put the writing skills you are learning in this course will be preparing speeches and talks. This chapter will show how the writing of essays and the writing of speeches differ, and it will show you how to adapt your knowledge of the stages of the writing process to the preparation of speeches and talks.

ANALYZING THE AUDIENCE

You will, of course, when you deliver your speech experience the advantages of being able to *see* your audience and of being able to use extra *nonverbal* means to get your points across—tone of voice, gestures, head movements, shift of body, pauses, silence, etc. However, you will also experience the difference between delivering your ideas orally and having them on paper for a reader. Your audience will *not* be able to slow down the way readers would if they got confused or tired. Audiences *can't* look back up at the sentences a few paragraphs before—as readers can—to see what you said there that relates to what you are saying now. Audiences *can't* stop to think about a point you've just made before going on to the next part of the essay. Because these things are true, there are certain things that you must think about when you write your speech that will let you assist the audience in overcoming some of these drawbacks to public speaking situations.

You have been aware, from the very beginning of the discussion of writing essays, of the importance of knowing *who your audience* are so that you can make the choices appropriate to them. At times, however, in written papers you could not know who you were going to have as an audience, and you had to write for that fictitious "general reader." You do have the great advantage in preparing a speech of knowing much more specifically to whom you are going to be talking. You will also know the *occasion* of the speech and the *purpose* for it.

Since you are in the lucky position of knowing a lot about the people to whom you will be talking, take full advantage of this and **assess everything you possibly can about the audience.** (See Checklist for a Speech.) Otherwise, you may have the best prepared written text in the world, and it will fall flat because it doesn't fit the audience.

PLANNING THE SPEECH

After you have a full picture of your audience, you are ready to start planning the speech. **You need to determine what your subject and your purpose are going to be.** Are you going to try to persuade? to inform? to explain? to entertain? to inspire? to get the audience to act on a particular thing, to *do* something? You may, of course, be given a general subject by the person or group who invites you, or the occasion for the speech itself may suggest the subject matter and/or the purpose. If neither of these is the case, however, and you are given complete freedom on the subject and the purpose, you will find that doing a creating activity like looping is a very valuable way to come up with something you want to say. Just write something like "What do I want to talk about and why?" at the top of a sheet of paper and start looping. Very likely you will see your subject and your purpose emerge.

When you make a final decision about your subject, be sure to think about things like: why will the audience be interested? will the subject be appropriate to the occasion? if the subject is something I know a lot about, can I narrow it down and limit it to an area that I can easily handle in the time I will have to talk?

WRITING THE SPEECH

How will the actual writing of the speech differ from the way you have been writing essays? It won't in many areas. Many of the things you learned about shaping essays hold true for writing speeches. You'll still want to have an attention-getting opening. You'll still need to tell your audience very soon what your purpose and thesis are. You will want to develop your points fully with vivid details and probably several personal examples. (One of the advantages of the public speaking situation is that you have an opportunity to have the audience experience *you* as a *person* in a much greater way than the reader can, so take full advantage of this. It is the *humanness* of the situation that the audience will remember long after they have forgotten your literal message.) You will also, as in writing, want to give a sense of completion at the end.

There are ways, however, that the writing of your speech will differ quite a bit from the writing of essays. Most of these differences have to do with one of these four areas: the *level of simplicity,* the *evidence of the structure,* the *kind of language,* and the *amount of direct address.* Let's look at each of these four areas to see how they appear in good speech writing.

1 **A good speech is simple to understand.**
Since your audience can't return to the words if they forget a point you've already made and since they are in an environment where many things will vie for their attention—people's coughs, the climate, the outside noise, the room decorations, and many others—you cannot expect them to stick with you while you give some complex, convoluted line of thought. You should, therefore, have a very clear message, simple to understand, and illustrated with an abundance of examples, facts, personal experiences, stories, and the like. Remember at all times that your listeners have to be able to follow you. So keep the thesis and its support as simple as you possibly can.

2 A good speech has a very evident structure.

You have options about just how openly you show your reader the "bones" of your essay. You might say, for instance, something like this in a paragraph:

Excessive eating is caused by three things. First, there is physical cause. . . . Second, there is emotional cause. . . . Third, there is personal cause. . . .

This paragraph clearly shows all its "bones." *The outline of the writer's thoughts is very visible.*

Contrast that paragraph with this one:

Excessive eating can't be traced to any one cause. Some people eat too much because they have physical problems such as thyroid gland that doesn't function properly or a metabolism rate that is abnormally low. Other people over-eat because they have emotional problems that they attempt to combat with food. People also eat excessively because they have food as a hobby; they read about it, love the taste of it, experiment with cooking it, appreciate it in its finest forms, and . . .

You do not see the "bones" of this paragraph as clearly as you did in the previous paragraph. The same basic structure is there, but it is incorporated into the paragraph itself in the second example, whereas it stands out in the first. In writing, you make the choice about how much of your structure "shows" based on your purpose in writing, your own style and personal preferences, and your audience. You aim for absolute clarity, and you still have options on how to achieve that clarity.

THE SPEECH OF THE DAY

George T. Delacorte, an 85-year-old publisher, recently gave New York City a fourth fountain. This one was in front of City Hall. On the day the fountain was presented to the mayor of the city, this is the speech George Delacorte gave:

> Here's my speech. The fountain is
> my speech. The tulips are my speech.
> The grass and trees are my speech.
> And that's what I have to say to you.

From *New Yorker*, May 14, 1979, p. 33.

In writing a speech, however, you *must* make your structure clearly evident. The listener's mind will wander no matter how well you speak. The listener's mind won't be able to hang on to all your previous points without being reminded. They won't have anything to follow except your verbal roadmap. "I'll give you three examples . . ." "Here's my first point . . ." "I've now given two of my three examples. The third one is . . ." "Remember that I've said . . ." "Last, I . . ." You should also repeat or sum up any main points of your speech more than once. Again, this is necessary because (1) you have no way of knowing whether the listeners heard you the first time, (2) the listeners may have heard you but have already forgotten the point, and (3) the listeners may have heard the point but dismissed it because they didn't think it was important. Just as you used *signal* and *transition* words to assist a reader in getting from one point to another in your essays, you have to provide this same kind of roadmap in a speech, but in much greater detail. Be sure to include these in your rough draft of the speech as you write.

3 **A good speech uses informal language.** Words used in speeches are usually more informal than those used in writing. This informality shows up in things like the use of contractions (*I'll* instead of *I will*), use of personal pronouns, shorter sentences, pieces of sentences instead of complete sentences, more questions, and more repetition of words. When you write your speech, you should use words that sound like *conversation* and that sound like *you* when you say them.

Informal language will also appear in the humor and light tone that you will use occasionally in the speech in order to give the listeners a chance to have a breathing spell. When you've just been pushing one of the most serious points in your speech, give the audience a little relief. Tell a humorous story or change language to a lighter tone.

4 **A good speech contains many direct addresses to the audience.** Bring the audience into your speech. When you're speaking, say things like, "I'm sure you all remember. . . ." This will give the audience a chance to shake their heads, smile approval or frown disapproval. "Your president has told me that your organization. . . ." This lets them know that you have been interested enough to ask about them before the speech. "If you have ever . . . you will enjoy my next point. . . ." "Have you ever seen. . . ." These will create a connection between you and the audience. Direct addresses like this make the speech a talk *to* and *with* some other people, not a talk *at* them. Act as though you are in a conversational situation. Using direct addresses will help you do this.

DELIVERING THE SPEECH

Since you are going to be delivering the speech instead of handing it to a reader, you won't have to do the usual completing activity that you do when you write essays. In fact, the written version of the speech should stay at home when you go to deliver the talk. **Take only notes so that you actually talk with the audience.** There's no greater insult than for an audience to be read to; it's the height of arrogance and pomposity. Don't ever do it. *Your completing stage for a speech will occur when you deliver it.*

ANALYZING SPEECHES

Let's look now at a speech to see how it was written.

CHECKLIST FOR A SPEECH

1 What is the name of the group?
2 What is the day and date of the speech?
3 What time does the speech start?
4 How long will I be given to speak?
5 What time should I arrive at the place?
6 Where will I give the speech?
7 Who is the contact person who invited me or who will meet me there?
8 Why did the group invite me?
9 What is the subject of my speech?
10 What are the seating and speaking arrangements?
11 Will there be alcohol and/or food?
12 Are there a podium and microphone?
13 Are there a chalkboard, chalk, erasers?
14 Are the people grouped close together?
15 Will I see the location before I speak?
16 How many people will be in the audience?
17 Where will they come from?
18 What will they believe about relevant subjects (e.g. God, religions, violence, patriotism, etc.)?
19 How do they make their living?
20 What will be their ages?
21 What will they already know about my subject?
22 Why will they be gathered together?
23 What other groups, clubs, etc., will they belong to?
24 Will there be both men and women present?
25 Why was I invited?
26 What method of persuasion is most likely to influence them?
27 What will they know about me?
28 What will be my status with them?
29 Will there be other speakers?
30 What are the group's successes and problems?
31 Will there be people I know in the audience?
32 What will be my purpose?
33 What will be my thesis—the target I aim for in giving the talk?
34 What will be my goal?
35 What are the intended results of my speech—what will it look like when the goal is reached?

The speech is identified as to speaker, occasion, and audience. Notice especially the four areas discussed earlier: simplicity, evidence of structure, informal language, and direct addresses to the audience.

Watch, also, for clear statements of the purpose and the thesis in the speech.

SPEECH 1

SPEAKER: *Congresswoman Catherine May.*

OCCASION: *Luncheon meeting of American Agricultural Editors Association.*

AUDIENCE: *Editors of agriculture magazines, newsletters, articles, etc.*

SPECIAL INFORMATION: *Congresswoman May was a member of the Agriculture Committee, House of Representatives.*

The American Farmer

Ladies and gentlemen, I'm pleased and honored to have this opportunity to share some thoughts with you on the farmer-consumer relationship. But, first, I would like to digress just a little and read you a very timely and relevant article from the Boston *Herald Traveler* which was brought to the attention of our House Agriculture Committee by none other than the Secretary of Agriculture in one of our sessions a few weeks ago.

Purpose of Speech

Even though many of you may be familiar with it by now, I'm going to read it anyway because it wears so well.

Humor

"Harvard's main administration building, University Hall, often the target of student radicals, was once again the site of a student protest this week.

"This time, however, the protestors were from neither Africa or SDS, but from AGRO, the Harvard agrarian society.

"About a dozen student farmers staged the demonstration to present a list of 19 demands to the Harvard administration.

"Dressed in overalls, and chanting, "Hoe, Hoe, Hoe the row—drop them books, there's hay to mow," a parody of an SDS slogan, the AGRO's marched around Harvard Yard distributing carrots to passersby.

"Some of the students carried signs reading, 'Have you thanked a farmer today?'—'We're all soil brothers under the skin,' and "Iowa is bigger than all New England.'

"Addressing an enthusiastic crowd of about 100 from the steps of Widener Library, the leaders called on Harvard to establish an agricultural studies program for 'them students which feel a kinship with the soil.'"

"Represent AGRO fairly by placing a chicken on the student-faculty disciplinary committee; establish a scholarship fund for 'poor peasants' to be paid for by planting Harvard Yard to cactus in the fall and rice in the spring.

"Sever all official relations with the U.S. Department of Agriculture because of that agency's role in 'suppression and persecution' of U.S. farmers.

"Appoint as its next president Dewey Burchak, Mayor of Big Sag, Montana.

"A spokesman said that the demands were 'unnegotiable mostly, except for a couple, which are unnegotiable, a little,' and warned of a possible 'peasant revolt' if the demands were not met by sundown.

"After the demonstration, the crowd dispersed peacefully. Only one injury was reported. Jim Trott, of Ft. Benton, Montana, and leader of AGRO, bit himself on the lip while reading the demands to a crowd in the Yard."

I don't know that there is any profound significance in this parody of student protest, but I find it quite refreshing that, despite all our problems, some of us—especially our young people—are able to retain that one personal characteristic so essential to maintaining perspective—a sense of humor.

I want to talk with you today, though, about another kind of protest—the protest over rising food prices. This serious and continuing phenomenon of our times is, in large part, a reflection of bewilderment and confusion on the part of the consumer—a bewilderment and confusion which all too often seems to result in a finger of blame being pointed to the producer of our food supply.

Farmers, too, are concerned about that widening spread between the basic price at the farm and what it becomes when the consumer fills her shopping cart many miles and many processing steps away. But, the farmer still has not been able to get his story across—the message that he is, indeed, the consumers' *real* protector.

And, it is crucial to the farmer that this message be understood, for he is more vulnerable today to the outrage of this Nation's consumers than he ever has been in the past. In this age of growing interdependence, in this country where east and west coast are neighbors, he is more susceptible to their whims and fancies, to their demands for specific quality and variety, to their boycotts, and to the legislation enacted by their representatives in Congress. In this time of diminishing political strength for agriculture, it is vital that farmers inform their customers as to just who they are, what they are, and what their contribution to our society actually amounts to. And, just as it is important for all segments of our society to listen to each other, it is incumbent upon consumers—housewives—that they listen, objectively and responsibly, to what their suppliers of food and fiber are trying to tell them.

So, what are farmers really trying to say? They are saying, for one thing, that they have done more than any other group to keep consumer food prices down—to keep food a bargain! They are saying that they have, over the years, dramatically increased their efficiency and productivity in the face of spiraling production costs and static prices. They are saying that the two indisputable, primary forces behind mounting food costs are inflation and consumer demand for convenience foods. Let's take a look at some of the factors which have combined to create these forces.

Marketing costs have skyrocketed in the last few years at every step in the process from raw material on the farm to the finished product in the kitchen. They have been accentuated greatly by a switch of buying habits. The lesser priced items needing preparation at home are largely being replaced by the "instant" convenience products which reflect pyramiding labor input.

Support: facts, statistics, specific examples

Disregarding for the moment the fact that more than 25 percent of the market basket contains items other than food, let's examine some of the valid examples for the upward surge of retail prices.

The facts show that our fondness for highly processed snacks has increased by 68 percent over a decade ago. Although this may seem to be a minor item in the family food budget, it actually has taken on more than a minor role.

More examples

Potatoes can be cited as an example of this trend, although by no means is this item unusual. For whole potatoes, farmers receive from one and one-half cents a pound up to three cents—depending upon area and supply situation. At the supermarket, potato chips sell for well over one dollar a pound, and instant mashed potatoes would run seventy-four cents per pound.

Of course, the comparison between three cents for potatoes at the farm and seventy-four cents for instant potatoes at the supermarket must be qualified, for dehydration saves on retail weight. But, labor and machinery required to peel, cut, cook, package and deliver the light-weight containers, unavoidably drives prices upward immensely.

According to current USDA figures, an average of sixty percent of retail food costs come from marketing expenses.

The spread between the farm value and retail continues to widen, increasing 1.2 percent more in the first quarter of this year than in the same three months of 1969. In the past 10 years it has increased more than twenty percent.

Structure: summarizes point just made

While the price spread between farm and consumer does not tell all of the inflation story, it does reveal that farm prices have remained relatively static while the costs of operating a farm and farmer living costs have skyrocketed. Operation input is well over 100 percent more than fifteen years ago.

Food price increases are actually far down the list of contributors to the rising cost of living. A recent survey in 39 metropolitan areas across the country for the 1967–69 period showed taxes to be the fastest growing cost factor in the family budget—and the survey measured only *direct* taxes, not those added on indirectly to the cost of every item or service purchased. Next to taxes, the big increases included: Social Security taxes, insurance and contributions—13 to 15 percent; medical care—14 percent; clothing and personal care—11 percent. Higher food prices came along with an 8 to 9 percent boost; transportation added 8 percent; and housing costs moved up 5 to 6 percent.

Now, let's look again at food costs and the reasons for their increases.

Milk is a commodity which has fewer add-on costs at the processing level than most others. Pasteurizing and packaging are the major steps connecting producer with consumer. It is not changed in structure when sold as fresh milk, and therefore should be more of a bargain than where many labor steps are required—for example, to change cereals from a kernel of grain to a breakfast food or to snacks. Final price of the cereal or snack could be 49 cents or more, for which the farmer might receive two or three cents.

In the Federal Trade Commission study and economic report made in 1966 on bread and milk prices, it was shown that the hourly return in five dairy areas for the farmers themselves ran from 84 cents an hour down to 30 cents. At the same time, dairy plant employees were receiving $2.20 to .84. This explains why, for a long period of time, thousands of dairy owners were forced to quit business. Fortunately for consumers, the rapid decline of dairies has now halted as dairymen are establishing a more solid economic footing for themselves in most sections.

Bringing the milk situation up-to-date from the 1966 study, we can explore recent developments in New York. Employees of the milk processing plants and the truck drivers negotiated a $35 weekly wage boost last November, and office workers in those plants were raised $25 per week.

Milk is selling in New York City supermarkets for between 58 and 60 cents per half gallon—a rise of 2 cents to 4 cents. Producers of the milk obtained about one-half cent more for that half gallon.

It would appear from this price spread that the retailer obtained a lion's share of the increase, but this is not so. The many costs in between gobbled up most of that difference.

I do not want to belabor all the various costs involved, but, as an example, transportation cost increases are having a significant impact on the price of milk as well as other food items. Wages, maintenance, taxes, licenses and scores of other items are forcing railroads and trucking companies to increase charges from 6 to 10 percent yearly.

Looking further into labor costs on the food bill, the USDA reports that employees of food marketing establishments earned an average of $2.82 per hour in August of last year. That's 6 percent more than in August, 1968, and nearly double the hourly earnings in 1965.

The same trend can be seen in the food manufacturing industry. These wage earners received an average of $2.93 in August last year—nearly 6 percent higher than the year before.

And, in the wholesale food trade, hourly earnings averaged $3.10 per hour in that same month—again, 6 percent more than a year earlier.

Structure: what she is going to talk about

Example

Structure: what she is doing with this point

Structure: repeats point so listener will really get it

Structure: where the speech is going now

Facts, statistics, illustrations, example

Employees of retail food stores averaged $2.54 in the same period, or 6.7 percent more than in August, 1968. And, in some areas, further increases since that time have raised food store wages even higher.

The USDA has also compared rising costs of food in relationship to labor, and has found that direct labor costs *per unit of food* at the market has moved up some 26 percent in the past ten years, although overall labor costs rose some 58 percent. This means that considerable efficiency has been gained at all producer, marketing, wholesale and retail levels. Had this not been the case, food prices would probably have risen considerably more.

Turning to the farm itself, production per man-hour in agriculture since 1950 has increased at a rate more than double that of all non-farm industry. Between 1957–59 and 1969, per man-hour out-put on the farm increased some 83 percent.

Structure: where the speech is going now

It's worthwhile, I think, to pursue this point of efficiency just a bit further. In a recent article in the *Wall Street Journal*, which I'm sure many of you saw, Norman Fischer outlined the major role played by genetics in increasing production efficiency and holding down the cost of food. In the last quarter century, he pointed out, U.S. farmers have used new genetic technology to double the average milk production of each dairy cow; halve the time and the amount of food needed to produce a broiler chicken; reduced by three months the time needed to produce a market-weight turkey; sharply boosted a layer hen's egg output; and shortened the time needed to bring beef cattle and hogs to market, with less feed and more red meat per carcass. In just the last dozen years, he noted, livestock scientists have increased the amount of ham and loin in hogs by more than 20 percent, the equivalent of adding an extra ham to every porker.

Structure: emphasizes point so listener will get it

However, the new genetics, like every other field of human endeavor, has its failures as well as its successes. On the same day the *Journal* article appeared, a small item in the *National Observer* reported that an experiment to develop featherless chickens didn't come off so well.

The theory was that such chickens would save the energy normally used to grow feathers, and therefore the chickens would be bigger and would lay larger eggs. It didn't work, the *Observer* noted, the featherless chickens ate more than their feathered friends, laid fewer eggs, were susceptible to ulcers, and used a lot of energy trying to keep warm. And, when fried, they taste just like regular chickens.

Light tone

Well, featherless chickens notwithstanding, it is this kind of research and applied technology which, among other factors, has helped to provide consumers with food which has risen in cost much less than other consumer goods.

One farmworker now produces food and fiber for himself and *forty-four* other people. Only ten years ago that figure was twenty-four, and in 1949 it was just fourteen. In other words, one hour of farm labor now produces nearly seven times as much food and other crops as it did in 1919–21.

This is a record of which we can all be proud — and thankful, for the direct result is that the average American family currently is spending only 16.5 percent of its income after taxes for food. A year ago this figure was 17 percent, and 20 years ago it was 22 percent. In Western Europe, incidentally, the average family has to put out approximately 25 percent of their disposable income for food, while in the Soviet Union the portion is almost 50 percent, and in Asia it is estimated at 75 percent.

Structure: restates point made earlier

And yet, while the American consumer reaps the benefit of this efficiency, the farmer faces higher costs and lower profit margins. Since 1949, the national income has shown an increase of 255 percent. But farm income, while up, is only up 18 percent.

Structure: restates thesis in another form

The ability of American agriculture to feed and clothe the 300 million or more people who will inhabit the United States by the year 2000 can be assured only if the farmer receives a return sufficient to use efficient modern equipment, meet his labor costs, and use necessary fertilizers and other aids. In other words, we have to pay 1970 prices for what he needs in 1970 to go on farming. And few people realize that a minimum investment of $100,000 is necessary just to acquire the land and machinery and other items to farm efficiently, and almost $200,000 is necessary to provide an income to house, feed, and clothe a family of four and provide an education for two children.

Structure: tells where speech is going now

Turning again to food prices, it really is difficult to see where costs affecting the price of foods at the retail stores could be eliminated or reduced in any appreciable degree. Built-in escalators seem to exist, either by virtue of the inflation spiral or by demand of the housewife. Even packaging, which may seem a candidate for such cost cutting, is often determined in considerable degree by housewife preference.

Example

The huge shopping centers are another factor, representing multimillion dollar investments, but which are demanded by shoppers because of their convenience. Regular store rentals based upon today's soaring construction and maintenance costs, and upon land values, plus perhaps a 5 percent assessment on gross sales by the shopping center owner for promotion and other purposes represents an additional cost burden which must be reckoned in the ultimate consumer prices.

Structure: repeats something she has already said

I mentioned taxes as a direct major item for our families, running well ahead of food increases. That is just part of the story. Taxes and interest rates are heavy contributors to the costs of food marketing, but are often overlooked as a factor. Farmers, of course, have generally been forced to absorb the constantly burgeoning taxes on each phase of their operation. Unlike other businesses, they cannot pass on these extra costs since they have little or no control over the price they receive at the marketplace.

Example

Some time ago, I saw an estimate that over 50 percent of the retail price of a loaf of bread is actually fixed by taxes of one kind or another. This was based on taxes in fractions of pennies added on at every stage of production, from the equipment used in planting and harvesting of the wheat to the final taxes on packages and trucks delivering the bread to the shelves of the retail store and the final destination—the consumer's table.

Trading stamps and other "giveaway" gimmicks have proven to be no small items in food costs. These often add two percent or more to the retail selling price, yet many stores have learned they must offer them or lose out in the battle for the consumer dollar.

Looking at the "big picture" of America's food bill, the facts show that of the $60.6 billion difference between the amount farmers received for food products in 1968 and the amount consumers paid, labor costs accounted for $27.3 billion. Other major components were packaging—$7 billion; transportation—$4.6 billion; and corporate profits *before* taxes—$3.6 billion.

Statistics

Although profits are often blamed for rising prices and expenditures for food, they obviously are a relatively small percentage of total marketing costs. Net profits of leading retail food chains average a little over one percent of sales, declining generally during the past few years. Net profits for food manufacturers in 1969 averaged about 2.5 percent of sales.

The trend in profits throughout the food industry has been downward at nearly all levels. The 1966 Federal Trade Commission report set up initial data, as did the report that same year of the National Commission on Food Marketing, of which I was a member, and subsequent follow-ups reveal little change in the profit pattern.

As we move into this new decade, we are all hopeful, of course, that inflation as a factor in rising food costs can be eliminated, or at least brought into some reasonable kind of control. Even if this is accomplished, however, it doesn't mean that food prices will be stabilized, for as housewives demand more and more of the convenience foods, more fancy packaging, more extras, it is simply going to mean more cost.

Begins to bring speech to a close

So, even without inflation, food prices will continue to be an issue—an issue with which farmers and the food industry in general are going to have to come to grips.

We cannot solve our problems by making any one sector of our economy a scapegoat, but I am becoming increasingly concerned over the developing conditions which lend themselves to making a scapegoat of the farmer. As I said earlier, farmers are more vulnerable now than ever before, both politically and economically. Out of 435 members of the House, only 31 are from districts which have 25 percent or more of their people on farms. Only 83 have as much as 15 percent of their people living on farms. And, 21 states don't have a single district in which as many as 15 percent of the people are farm people.

Structure: restates thesis

It is obvious that agriculture must have the help and understanding of urban America, not only to obtain passage—and funding—of needed legislation, but also to keep from becoming the object of punitive "food price" politics.

It's going to take, among other things, an increased awareness among farmers and their organizations of urban needs and problems—an increased realization that the problems of the cities and urban areas are also theirs, and that they must cooperate to find solutions.

Farmers also need to understand better the value of positive public relations—and I don't mean that in the "Madison Avenue" sense. I mean that the farmer must make use of every available opportunity to let his city cousin know exactly what he is doing for him—that food is a bargain, and that farmers are making every effort to keep it that way.

And, as I mentioned earlier, consumers are going to have to face up more to their responsibilities to the farmer—the responsibility of looking beyond the price tag to understand a little better where their food actually came from before it got into the can, and the how and why of its cost and availability.

And you, as agricultural editors, play a major role in this communication process between agricultural and urban America. You have a very heavy responsibility here of which I know you are keenly aware. But it doesn't lie just on your shoulders, either. Every form of news media must share this responsibility, as well as those of us in Congress, in government and in other areas where thoughts may be expressed and facts presented which may influence the opinions of others. It is up to all of us to understand our responsibilities here, and to fulfill them as objectively and as effectively as we can.

Thank you.

APPLICATION

1 Choose one of these contexts and write a speech. The speaker in each case will be you.

1 Occasion: High School Sports Banquet
Award Night Ceremony.
Audience: All players and participants in men's and women's athletics at high school; parents of award winners; coaches; dates of athletes; some faculty.
Special information: You were an athlete at this high school, and now as a college student you have been invited back to give the banquet address.

2 Occasion: Monthly meeting of Displaced Homemakers.
Audience: A group of about 25 women who are recently widowed or divorced.
Special information: These women are interested in enrolling in college, although most of them are very frightened. Their ages range from 30 to 67. Displaced Homemakers is a government sponsored organization that works to assist these women in making new lives for themselves. Most of them have never been employed outside the home. You

have been invited to speak to them about what they can expect when they get into college.

3 Occasion: Monthly meeting of local hobby club.
  Audience: A group of about 40 adults who share the same interest in a particular hobby.
  Special information: You are known for your expertness in the hobby this club is organized to promote. You have been invited to come talk with them about your own experience in the hobby; they hope to learn from, and be inspired by, you.

4 Occasion: Annual convention of your religious organization.
  Audience: Leaders in the organizations and members of the church, synagogue, etc.
  Special information: This is the special meeting during the annual convention when a layperson—someone not a spiritual leader or of the clergy—is honored by being requested to address the group of about 500 people. You are to discuss ways laypersons can get more involved in, and participate more in the work of, the church.

5 Occasion: Specially called meeting of the heads of departments in your business to discuss specific problems in the company and how they might be solved.
  Audience: All heads of departments, men and women, ages 30–64, about 10 in all.
  Special information: You are an executive trainee in this company. Your boss really liked one of your ideas on how to solve a nagging problem the company has and has asked you to come to the special meeting of department heads to present your ideas. This is a great opportunity for you to make good.

BUSINESS WRITING

INTRODUCTION: WRITING FOR THE WORLD OF WORK

What marks the difference between *business* writing and the rest of the kinds of writing in the world? Well, *purpose*, for one thing. The purpose of business is to make a profit, and, therefore, **we can think of business writing as being** *specifically* **related to buying or selling, dealing in commodities and services.** Business writing asks, *How much does it cost? How much will it save? How much will it earn?*

FEATURES OF BUSINESS WRITING

Tone   If there is a single quality that sets apart this particular style of writing, that quality is *tone.* One of the conscious choices writers have is what roles they will assume in a piece of public writing, and this text has everywhere emphasized how important it is for you as a writer to be genuine, not to sound "put on" or "artificial" or to adopt some kind of prefabricated cardboard model of how everybody "should" come on. Your question, then, is how you can be genuine and still put on a special costume for a special role.

The right tone for business writing is "businesslike": crisp, efficient, orderly—sounding like someone who means business, who can really get the job done. To present that aspect of yourself doesn't require putting on any kind of mask or concealing your true qualities—not at all. It does mean using the "composing" process in order to pull together exactly the presentation you mean to make, in exactly the same way that you'd pose for a studio portrait in a different way than you'd pose for a snapshot during a picnic. **What you want to do is show the strongest, most efficient side of yourself: serious, dependable, confident, capable, and effective.**

Now, how does that get expressed in the actual writing? If you keep in mind *the image of yourself that you intend to present,* and *the purpose of the writing*—to communicate information, data, in the least complicated, most direct, most accessible form possible—then you'll quickly pick up on what's involved. The following is an excerpt from a student essay on how to make crepes. The three paragraphs show the writer's personality in an engaging, personable way. In first reading them, limit your attention to that fact alone. Then see what changes are necessary to give the same message a business tone.

Some people pronounce "crepe" to rhyme with pep, and others pronounce it so that it rhymes with drape. No matter how it is pronounced, it is a delicious "envelope" for almost any filling and for any age individual who enjoys a variety of foods. Crepes have a long and international history. The origin of the crepe is not certain. It is thought to have evolved over centuries from a simple flour and water mixture flattened and baked over fire to hold food. A crepe is a perfect way to appeal to children's meals, dinner for one or two, and for those "what-shall-we-have nights." It is to provide instructions on how to make a beef crepe with a cheese sauce that this paper is written.

Before I explain the detailed procedure on how to make this particular crepe, I shall give a better insight to what a crepe really is. A crepe is sometimes compared to a pancake in that it is made from the same type of ingredients. The crepe is actually the outer surroundings but the combination of the crepe and the filling would be considered the entree. There are numerous ways which crepes can be used including a party appetizer, main course, dessert, or do it yourself hors d'oeuvres.

In explaining the preparation of this recipe, there are three steps which include the batter, cooking of the crepe, and the filling and rolling of the crepe. I will separate each different part into a new paragraph for clearer understanding.

—Vicki Tatum

Clearly the writer is being charming—almost chatty—certainly informal and rather leisurely. All that might be perfectly appropriate for an "essay" approach, but different aspects of the writer's personality need to be highlighted for business writing. To make the writing more businesslike, we can remove the uncertainty in the first paragraph (rephrase "origin is not certain") and make the wording more direct (rework the last sentence in that paragraph). In the second paragraph, taking the "I" out will also give it some distance, and rewriting in order to make the flow constant and direct will also help (take out the "backing up" of "Before I . . . I'll give a better insight into . . ."). In the third paragraph, cutting down unnecessary words and removing "I" will do the trick. Here's how the "businesslike" version would appear:

BUSINESSLIKE TONE:
Purposeful
Systematic
Efficient
Earnest
Methodical

The "crepe," whether rhymed with *pep* or *drape,* is a delicious envelope for almost any filling. Although the origin is not known, the crepe is thought to have evolved over centuries from a simple flour and water mixture flattened and baked over fire then wrapped around other food. It is somewhat like a pancake, being made from the same basic ingredients. Although "crepe" refers only to the outer wrapping, the word has come to refer to combinations of wrap and filling.

Crepes can be made in a variety of ways and served for numerous occasions: party appetizer, main course, or dessert. This paper gives instructions for making a beef crepe with cheese sauce.

This recipe has three steps:
> preparation of the batter
> cooking the crepe
> filling and rolling the crepe.

Step one: Preparing the Batter.
The proportions of flour, eggs, and liquid can be varied to produce . . .

What makes the tone of the second distinctively more businesslike? Removing the "I" so as to keep the writer's "personality" in the background, rewriting to heighten the degree of certainty, and causing the ideas to be more organized and the writing less wordy and more direct.

Also, the use of an indented list for the three steps and subheads to identify the sections that cover each of the steps—all these contribute to the tone.

Here's another example, this time from a student who got himself so far out of the picture that he forgot that there was anyone out there he was writing to. Because he is a finance major, he assumes everyone else knows what he already knows. He winds up with a paragraph that fails to communicate—that is, doesn't get knowledge from one person to another. If you already understand it, you'll do fine. If you're looking forward to being informed, to having your understanding enlarged, you'll be disappointed. Here's the sample:

A particular recession's characteristics will vary slightly between themselves, but all produce a temporary yet radical change in our economy. While government budget deficits tend to widen and tax revenues drop, trade deficits tend to disappear altogether.

A reader has to know in advance what a recession is in order to start off with any understanding at all and presumably will also need to know what a recession's "characteristics" may be. Furthermore, the reader needs to know how "temporary" is temporary—a day, six months, ten years? and how "radical" is radical—millions bankrupt and out of work, or an unemployment increase of 2 percent? So **tone is also related to audience, and must be appropriate to the level of understanding possessed by the reader.** If this passage is directed to someone who already understands it, there's really no point in writing it—they already know what it has to say. If it's written to the ordinary consumer in order to explain the causes and characteristics of recessions, then it will take a lot more work.

Here's a final example of tone that doesn't work, taken from a student paper intended to analyze hydroponics (growing plants in a soilless culture) as a possible investment area for a large nonagricultural corporation. His purpose is to look into this new area and determine whether the corporation should or should not put money into further research or in actual acquisition of hydroponics facilities. In this passage, you can see how overloaded and sluggish the sentences are. The use of jargon, passive voice, and the level of abstractness produce writing so thick that it dulls the reader's wits and makes the flow of ideas all but impossible. Here's the excerpt:

Kannaco faces the decision of whether or not to continue investing in agriculture. To continue with agricultural operations, which were beneficial to the company in the past, would mean developing a method that would eliminate or control the uneconomical facts of the present. To do this, and in the process raise the quality of the product that will

> "Good writers are those who keep the language efficient. That is, keep it accurate, keep it clear."
> —Ezra Pound

demand a higher market price, suddenly brings agricultural investments back into the realm of serious consideration and acceptance.

Phew! This is a *perfect* example of what *not* to do. The tone is inflated, the writing is wordy and repetitious, and the thoughts are buried beneath tons of fat. No doubt the writer assumed that this was the way business writing sounded and so "put on" that same sound. However, see how the message can sound businesslike but at the same time give off energy and crispness:

If Kannaco is to continue investing in agriculture, new proposals will be needed which eliminate or control the factors that have recently made such investments unprofitable. A proposal with that kind of control, and with a quality product that demands a high market price, would be worth Kannaco's serious consideration.

That's about half the length, and four times as lively. What's involved, aside from changing the writing, is waking up to the fact that writing is written *to* somebody, *for some reason.* **Bring that *reason* to the foreground and you can almost automatically see how to handle *tone*.** Obviously, as this last example shows, the point is *not* to be artificial or to put on some kind of act. The point is to be businesslike and to do whatever you can in your writing that will heighten that businesslike effect.

Accessibility   The second feature of business writing is its *accessibility. Everything is peeled away that could possibly interfere with the message, slow it down, or conceal it.* It is open, easy to get.

As you have seen, the tone of business writing contributes to accessibility. This means **keeping sentences short and direct** rather than long and complex, **using familiar words** rather than exotic ones (*use* rather than *utilize*, for example), **avoiding unnecessary words,** and **avoiding jargon.** Writers often reach for such heavy phrasing because they want to sound impressive. What happens, in fact, is that the reader is pushed into insensibility by such swollen phraseology. Strunk and White's advice is, "Eschew obfuscation." It's their way of spoofing the very thing they're criticizing. They could have said, "Be clear."

A version of jargon is the buzzword — something that will automatically tingle the reader. In fact, buzzwords are artificial technical language, and while they seem to lend great weight to an utterance, they actually are almost totally meaningless. To demonstrate just how empty and arbitrary buzzwords can be, Gerald Cohen devised *Dial-A-Buzzword* — three dials that rotate independently and produce automatic combinations that, in Shakespeare's words, "are full of sound and fury, signifying nothing."

GERALD COHEN'S DIAL-A-BUZZWORD offers you a thousand impressive three-word combinations. Write your next proposal or technical manual in half the time.

Directions:

1. Turn the dials to line up the words.
2. Select the most pleasing 3-word combinations.
3. Join the selected combinations into sentences.

THE BEST WORD	
LONG, HEAVY, FORMAL WORDS	**EVERYDAY WORDS**
abate, abatement	drop, decrease, cut down
behest	request
cognizant	aware
delineate	draw, describe
facilitate	ease, help
germane	relevant

hiatus	gap, interval
impair	weaken, damage, hurt
multitudinous	many
nadir	low point
obviate	prevent, do away with
palpable	obvious, visible, clear
remuneration	pay
terminate	end
vicissitude	change
wherewithal	means

From Thomas E. Pearsall and Donald H. Cunningham, *How to Write for the World of Work* (New York: Holt, Rinehart & Winston, 1978), pp. 90–91.

Accuracy   Business writing always deals with information that matters, that has consequences. Therefore *accuracy* matters—a great deal. A simple business letter illustrates the point completely.

SAMPLE LETTER: ORDER

```
                                    1401 Marble Hill
                                    Newton, Pennsylvania 99222
                                    October 10, 1979

        Denver Auto Parts
        16 Chambers Place
        Denver, Colorado 22446

        Dear Sir,

        Please send me the following parts from your September catalog:

            one rear window gasket seal, part #3320756   (page 27)  $19.75

            one "handy-jack" hydraulic lift, #740        (page 3)    98.00

            one VW Specialties Catalog                   (page 50)    3.95

                                            TOTAL:  $121.70

        Enclosed is my check for the full amount.  Please ship my order

        as soon as possible to the address above.

                                    Sincerely,

                                    André Worth Vergara
                                    André Worth Vergara
```

See how many opportunities there are for accuracy to make a difference? In the return address or the name or address of the dealer; in the description of the parts or the page or price or number; in the arithmetic. Any error in any item might mean a delay, or an overcharge, or unnecessary correspondence back and forth to clear up the matter.

It goes without saying that technical writing must be accurate, or else it is completely valueless. What good is a document reporting the interchange patterns on a proposed freeway which misses the real location by 50 miles, a progress report that inaccurately reports the amount of work completed so far, a description of a tool or process that leaves out an essential part of step—? Not much.

Format   Because the message is so important, and because its accessibility is so important, there are several special devices of *format,* or presentation, that assist the writer in being accurate and complete and assist the reader in finding exactly the information sought. The sample letter on the previous page, a simple order, shows several of these format conventions.

As you can see, the whole letter has a kind of block form, and each block contains certain information. Because that convention (or agreement) always works that way, the reader doesn't have to look all through the letter to find, say, the return address: it's always in block #1. Here's a diagram of a STANDARD BLOCK LETTER, and the kinds of information it always contains in each block.

You'll notice that the return address (1) and the close, signature, and typed name (7, 8, 9) are lined up together, and that the address, greeting, and body all line up together (2, 3, 4, 5, 6). Each block is separated from the others by double spaces except for the signature (8), which appears in the 4 spaces between (7) and (9).

Each of those blocks serves the writer: you can expect to find in each block its appropriate piece of information and check to see that it is clear and accurate. And it serves the reader because *every* letter will be in that form and so he/she doesn't need to start from scratch every time the mail comes through the slot in the door. It simplifies the task for everybody.

Business writing also has an advantage over "essay" writing in that **steps or pieces or parts or stages can be** *itemized:* **indented and listed directly.** In the sample order letter, the three items being ordered get special emphasis by being placed prominently on the page. They really stand out for the reader—and the writer, too, can readily double-check numbers, figures, descriptions, and dates. The same information could be placed in regular paragraph form, but itemizing allows it to be grasped fully and immediately.

Appearance   The *appearance* of business writing is slightly different from *format.* Appearance has to do with attention to such matters as details of margins at the top and bottom, the way a letter is placed on a page with proper balance on all sides, using a new typewriter ribbon (or black or blue ink if a letter is handwritten), and being free from foolish spelling or punctuation errors and also from smudges, strikeovers, and crossed-out words. *Appearance is visually what tone is verbally.*

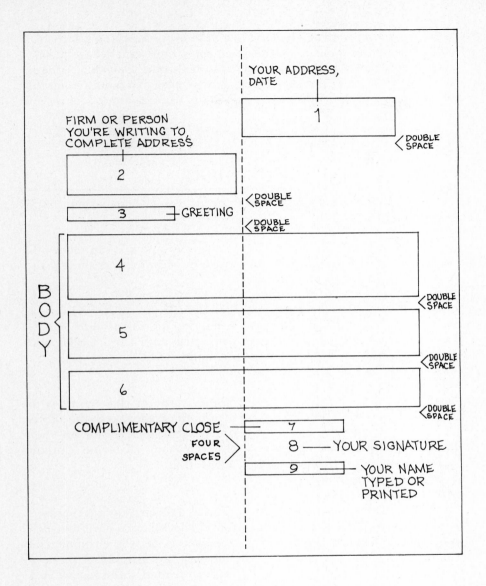

It is the overall impression that greets the eye, quite apart from whatever is written. And depending on the writer's care, it can create the initial impression of someone who is businesslike, orderly, and in control of matters, or it can suggest some kind of strolling disaster area. If it's a riot of smudges, strikeovers, cross-outs, and spelling errors, it won't get far in the business world, no matter *what* the content is about. *First impressions do count, so you can expect to have business writing judged by its appearance.*

Obviously, you won't be turning in a business proposal on a Big Chief tablet, written in pencil. At the same time, you want to avoid lilac-colored initialed stationery with sandalwood aroma, pens that write in shocking pink (in addition to all felt-tipped pens), and handwriting full of curlicues and flourishes. *Over*doing it will work as much against you as *under*doing it.

APPLICATION

1   Revise the following sentences to remove wordiness, jargon, buzz-words.

A

In relationship to development of fruit, studies have shown and actual practice proved that some crops will divert all their attention in the form of water and nutrients into the enlargement of the ripening fruit, and to supply excess water to the plant can mean the difference in producing small or large fruit.

B

Large corporations are able to invest large amounts of capital into a project because money is available in large corporations or is easily obtained from financial institutions alert for investment opportunities.

C

Implementation of this overall operative factor will almost guarantee multiple interactive criteria and will certainly systematize these performance areas.

D

In conclusion, I would like to wind up this paper by making this final point at the end, namely, that management creates an environment where people can efficiently reach or accomplish desired goals.

E

Bicycles that are neglected can be needlessly difficult to ride or they can cause expensive breakdowns or injury to the rider.

F

The purpose of this report is to inform the reader about the effects of television advertising on your children and what one can do about it.

G

Federal agencies have recognized that children have a hard time distinguishing between commercial and program material. A number of documented studies show that children under 8 years of age have difficulty comprehending the difference. They watch commercials just the way they watch programs.

H

The air was filled with enthusiastic awe. The film mesmerized the audience with skydivers plummeting from great heights, performing aerial acrobatics and complex formations with the agility and finesse of a ballerina. After the film, candidates with fists full of legal tender, impatiently queued, wondering if they would make this week's first jump course.

2 Make the presentation of this information more effective by changing it from narrative form to itemized format.

A

All parachutes have four major parts: (1) The canopy, a nylon air retarding device, displaces the skydiver's weight over approximately two hundred square feet and allows a descent at a slower rate of speed. Most circular canopies have twenty-eight "gores," or pie-shaped panels, sewn together to form a hemisphere. (2) The harness, strapped onto the skydiver, makes it virtually impossible for the jumper to be separated from the rest of the parachute. (3) A container holds the canopy until the jumper pulls the ripcord. (4) Suspension lines, usually seven hundred fifty pound test nylon material, connect the canopy to the harness.

B

Steel storage bins come in 6, 7, 8, and 9-ton sizes. They cost $54,000 for the 6-ton size, and $108,000 for each of the 7, 8, and 9-ton sizes. Steel flat warehouses come in the same sizes. They cost $25,600 for the 6-ton size, $29,000 for the 7-ton size, $34,100 for the 8-ton size, and $38,400 for the 9-ton size.

C

Several factors have caused the rise in the cost of owning a new home. Property taxes have gone up, and so has insurance. Building costs have gone up. Mortgage costs have also increased. Utilities are also higher than they used to be.

3 Write to a real firm and order three or more items. Use the complete block form of letter. Itemize the things you are ordering, and specify serial numbers and prices. If you are ordering from a catalogue, cite the date and page. Make the layout of the letter really work for you.

BUSINESS LETTERS

THE "YOU" ATTITUDE

Compare these two statements:

1 "We are proud to open our new store, our third in Savannah."
2 "We are happy to open a new store in your neighborhood to serve you better."

The first is no doubt true—people have good cause to be proud of opening a new store, especially if it's their third. But that statement comes from the position of the *writer*—not the *reader*. We're glad they are proud—but what's that to us? The second, however, has the YOU ATTITUDE. Their happiness (not pride) is about being in *your* neighborhood, and the store is there to serve *you* (not to add another store to the chain). This difference is what is called the *"you" attitude*.

Of course there's no simple cure-all technique for business writing, and using the word *you* every third line would be as artificial, and as foolish, as using buzzwords or inflated diction. But the point is to **think in terms of the reader's benefit** and then **write in such a way that the reader's benefit is emphasized and highlighted.** *What are the reader's needs, concerns, interests?*

One of the experts in writing with the *"you" attitude* is L. L. Bean, the famous catalog company in Freeport, Maine. Less skillful people might have said something like, "Shoulder satchel. Leather-like vinyl has a distinct fashion stripe. Three separate compartments hold equipment and clothes. Adjustable straps with harness hook hardware. Can be used for many purposes. Size $15 \times 10 \times 5$. Made in Korea. $14.99." In fact, if you read a lot of mail-order catalogues, some of them are not much more effective than that. But not Bean's. Here's their version:

"DO IT 'CAUSE I SAY SO"

"DO IT 'CAUSE YOU'LL ENJOY IT"

THE YOU ATTITUDE

Bean's Tackle Bags

Designed to meet the requirements of fishermen for a strong, lightweight shoulder bag, large enough to carry necessary tackle, raingear, lunch, etc., yet small enough to carry conveniently. Serves equally well for canoeing gear and camera equipment.

Made from heavy, double texture, waterproof duck with leather reinforcing. Has two outside pockets as shown. Adjustable 2" heavy web shoulder strap detaches at one end, permits fastening bag to canoe or boat thwart. Two sizes:

Regular: Size 15"x5¼"x9½" high. Wt., 1 lb. 14 oz.
6861P Regular Tackle Bag, $19.50 postpaid.
Large: Size 20"x5½"x12" high. Wt., 2 lbs. 12 oz.
6844P Large Tackle Bag, $25.50 postpaid.

It almost reads like poetry, the way it stirs up responses in the reader. "Designed to meet the requirements of fishermen" suggests, right off, that they are speaking to a special audience and know exactly who that audience is, what they think about tackle bags, and what they value: "strong, lightweight . . . large enough to carry necessary tackle, raingear, lunch, etc. . . ." And the specific details (not just *tackle*, but *necessary* tackle) reassure you that they know what they are talking about. So do the details about the material and workmanship; and, to help the reader visualize it even more powerfully, there is the added detail about "fastening bag to canoe or boat thwart." The material is presented clearly, vividly, from the point of view of the reader.

REQUESTS

In a sense, *requests* and *orders* are similar in that both ask somebody to do something. Yet someone sending in an order is, in effect, merely responding to an invitation—an announcement, or an advertisement, or even a visit or call from a salesperson. A *request*, though, is usually something you generate on your own because of something you need or want. For example, it's not uncommon for students, doing research projects, to write to government agencies for special information. Most of us have had occasion to ask someone else for advice—a professor, a friend, an expert. When we handle requests in letter form, there are a few simple considerations that help things move along smoothly.

Be Clear and Specific   You won't get far writing to the state highway department and asking for "information about highways in this state." *What* about highways do you want to know? How the reduced speed rate has affected fatalities? What the plans are to finish paving that new stretch of Interstate? How many state parks are served by major highways? **The more specific and precise you can be, the more likely you are to get what you want.** If you're doing a research paper on oil production, you could, if you wanted to, write Exxon and say, "Please tell me about oil production." Your chances are much improved, though, if you are more specific: "Please send me whatever public information you have about the environmental impact of offshore drilling."

Encourage Response   Just because you ask doesn't mean that those you ask will oblige you with an answer. A request that's clear, specific, and polite will help to "enroll" them in your project, cause them to be sympathetic and to lend a hand. Other ways of encouraging response are by *telling who you are* and by *explaining how you'll use the information you're requesting.* **The more "real" you are for them and the more understandable your request, the more likely they are to do what you're asking them to do.**

REQUESTS:
(1) Be clear and specific.
(2) Encourage an answer.

Page 544 contains an example that will show you these elements in action. The requests are *clear* and *specific*, the writer *identifies herself* and *explains her purpose in writing* and *tells how the information will be used.*

No model will serve any and all occasions, but with some alterations, this one will do pretty well. Here's the outline form:

paragraph 1: identifies writer and project.

paragraph 2: establishes that writer is not merely idle (she has already researched the library, for example); justifies the request (the additional information will add to the material already gathered); tells what will be done with the information; offers to share a copy.

paragraph 3: tells how many questions there are (*four*, not "a few"); presents the questions in numbered, itemized form; asks clear, specific questions.

SAMPLE REQUEST

Dear Ms. Elk:

    I am a sophomore education/psychology major at the University of Nevada and am writing a paper for one of my classes on the effect of TV commercials on children under 6.

    I've had excellent luck with my library research, and now I want to add current information from our local TV stations, like Channel 3. I will share my report with other members of my class and I've written to the local TV magazine to see if they might publish all or part of it. I would of course be pleased to send you a copy if you would like to have one.

    Would you please spend a few minutes answering these four questions?

1. Is there a person on your staff in charge of ads for children's programs? If so, could I please have the name?

2. Is there a network policy about the kind, number, subject, or treatment of commercials for children's programs? If so, may I have a copy?

3. Are there criteria that you at Channel 3 have developed (perhaps in addition to the network's) covering children's commercials?

4. Is there anything you think I should know about children's commercials--any studies or guidelines or data which I haven't asked about? If so, would you please let me know what they are (and if available, please send me copies).

    My paper is due in five weeks, so I would appreciate your response as soon as possible. Thank you for your assistance in this matter.

                             Sincerely,

paragraph 4: says when the material is needed;
             acknowledges the reader's assistance.

It's clear, complete, forthright, and polite. There's no guarantee that an answer will be forthcoming, but there's certainly a good chance — if the letter has anything to do with it.

RESPONSES

Here is an excellent opportunity to practice the *"you" attitude*. It's also one of the areas of business writing where you can do as much *creating* as you do *shaping* and *completing*. Not only is it a chance to communicate directly with a customer, employer or employee — it's also an opportunity to cement a friendly, cordial and bonding relationship.

How to Say "Yes"   Compare these two responses:

1 POST CARD

```
                                507 McAvelly Place
                                Gay, Nebraska

Dear Member:

        We received your check and order form.
Your membership card and T-shirt will be
mailed in a few weeks.  We appreciate your
business.

                Sincerely yours,


                Runners and Walkers, Inc.
```

Dear Member,

        HERE IT IS! YOUR WORLD RUNNERS PACKET.

    We understand the anticipation that has been building
while you have been waiting for your World Runners packet.
Please accept our apologies for its delay.

    As a member of World Runners, you have joined a network
of aligned individuals who share the satisfaction of a common
physical fitness activity -- running, as well as a deep desire
and commitment to ending hunger on our planet in this century.

    World Runners started as little more than a good idea on
September 12, 1978, and has grown steadily to become one of the
larger running clubs in this country, with a membership exceeding
1600 people, from 41 states and 15 countries. World Runners'
ability to expand into a viable and influential club is directly
related to your willingness to share the club with your friends.

    On April 16, 1979, Landon Carter (Founder of World Runners)
spearheaded a team of forty World Runners who competed in the
renowned Boston Marathon. Thousands of people participated in
raising over $620,000.00 in pledges. April 16, 1979 proved to
be the largest Hunger Project enrollment event in the history of
the Hunger Project.

    World Runners was generated out of a desire to provide a
form, through which people who run can express their commitment
to end hunger. We are inspired by the initiative many members
have actively taken in using World Runners as a way of expressing their personal commitment to the end of hunger and starvation. Thank You.

                YOU MAKE A DIFFERENCE

    As a member, you can expect to be kept abreast of upcoming
World Runners' events, as well as information about what people
are doing in the area of communicating the end of hunger and
starvation, through running.

                    (continued)

1735 Franklin Street · San Francisco, California 94109 · (415) 441-3774

The enclosed letters sent in by members of the club ex-
emplify the inspiration and spirit of the club, and we are
privileged to share them with you. (See additional pages)

Wear your World Runners T-shirt and pin, display your
bumpersticker and decal, and allow them to be an outward expression of your commitment to having hunger end.

Notes: 1. If you have previously received any of the items
            normally sent in a members packet (i.e. T-shirt),
            it will not be included in this packet.

        2. First washing of your shirt should be done in cold
            salt water to avoid the possibility of shrinkage.

        3. Please note our current address:
            World Runners, 1735 Franklin Street, San Francisco,
            California 94109 (415) 441-3774

It is a privilege to be on the same team with you. Keep running
and carrying the message.

                              With Love,

                              Duffy Herman & Lal Stoller

You might ask, "Why give all the information in that long letter? They knew all that before they joined the organization, didn't they?" Probably most people who join an organization know what they are joining, so that's a fair guess. But for one thing, it lets the new member get a *renewed sense of the purpose of the organization.* For another, it lets the new member see that *it is the member's own club:* "Wear your World Runners T-shirt and pin, display your bumpersticker and decal. . . ." It renews and reaffirms the relationship, and clearly indicates the writers' intention to continue it.

You can say "thanks" and let it go at that, or you can sit down, do some creating, and compose a response that practically creates a celebration, marks an occasion, and—for certain—keeps the reader in mind and is written for his/her point of view.

An excellent "second sale" letter happens to come from a small bakery in Corsicana, Texas—along with a color brochure describing their fruitcakes and an order blank. Although the brochure describes the fruitcakes themselves, what does this letter gain by describing the company's history and the celebrities who stayed in the "elite private hotel" on the second floor over the bakery?

From the end of world hunger to fruitcake may seem an impossible leap of the mind, but both letters are responses—the first to a membership check, the second as a follow-up to an earlier order for fruitcake. But the bonding between you and the letter writer are the same in both. The first reminds you what a fine purpose the organization has; the second tells you about the glorious past of the original bakery. The first bridges to the new member: "YOU MAKE A DIFFERENCE," the second makes a transition from the past to the present in paragraph 11, and develops the *"you" attitude* in paragraph 12. The final SPECIAL NOTE in the fruitcake letter gives the product one last boost: it's economical!

When you're giving a "yes" response, it pays to do enough creating to produce a strong—and maybe even original—*"you" attitude* that will strengthen the relationship and contribute to further good feelings.

The same principle holds when you're simply announcing good news: **put the good news in the most prominent place in the letter—right out front.** If there are details, they can follow.

Congratulations: You've just won our annual Anniversary Sale-A-Bration drawing!

I'm pleased to inform you that you have been accepted to graduate school at State University.

Let me be the first to congratulate you on your promotion.

You'll make a wonderful supervisor.

COLLIN STREET BAKERY

P.O. Box 79   Corsicana, Texas 75110
Area Code 214-874-6511
Cable: Fruitcakes

L. William McNutt, Jr.
John Crawford
Norman E. Shaw

Dear Friend:

We're proud of our freshly baked world famous DeLUXE FRUIT CAKES and convenient mail order gift service, and we'd like very much for you to give us a try this year.

A lot of nice words and awards have fortunately come our way over the last 81 years. But, you can find out all about these things for yourself in the enclosed color brochure.

Right now though — perhaps you'd enjoy reading a little bit of Bakery history and some interesting facts — not often printed.

. . . The year is 1896. The place — a primitive kitchen-store on Collin Street — in a small central Texas town (50 miles south of Dallas) called Corsicana. The skilled young German baker — AUGUST "GUS" WEIDMANN — just off the boat which brought him from Wiesbaden, has formed a partnership with a dashing, rather flamboyant young businessman named TOM McELWEE. Tom's marketing and promotional flair was already aimed at Weidmann's wonderful and delicious "white fruit cake" — recently named the Original DeLUXE.

Ten prosperous years pass. A grand new Collin Street Bakery goes up on 6th Avenue. The legend of the DeLUXE is ready to take wing.

Having wealth, drive and a worshipful wonder of celebrities, Tom McElwee turns the new Bakery's entire second floor into an elite private hotel . . . (just two blocks away a young fellow named CONRAD HILTON was running the Beaton Hotel). Then, the doors are thrown open to welcome the touring stars of opera, vaudeville, theatre and sports.

549

Among the Bakery's many guests are listed ENRICO CARUSO, WILL ROGERS (WILL, JR. dedicated our present facilities in 1965), TOM MIX (his wonder horse TONY was, however, quartered in the stable behind the hotel), JOHN J. McGRAW of the New York Giants, and heavy weight boxer "GENTLEMAN" JIM CORBETT.

In fact, it was JOHN RINGLING and his touring circus troopers who brought Collin Street Bakery its first big Christmas order! These freshly baked cakes were destined to be handed out during these talented entertainers' travels — both here and abroad; therefore bringing the DeLUXE its first real taste of international acclaim.

Yes indeed, world-wide acceptance started back then — and now has increased to the extent DeLUXE was shipped into 158 foreign lands last year. And, as a matter of record, satisfied Bakery customers reside in 131 of these countries.

Today, we successors to the departed Mr. Weidmann and Mr. McElwee have made certain nothing fundamental in our personal service and product quality will ever change. Gus' famous recipe (which today hangs on his weather beaten clip board near our ovens), is still followed to the letter — including the part of that original formula which calls for an unalterable 27% (by weight) of the crispiest, freshest pecans available on the market.

Just as in the old days — (and this to us is most important) all cakes are baked to order. This simply means they're never baked ahead and stored — as are so many of the food products nowadays.

The DeLUXE you and your friends will enjoy cannot be duplicated in flavor and honest culinary beauty under any other trade name on earth. And, incidentally, the DeLUXE can only be purchased direct from our 81 year old bakery. So you see — your family, friends and business associates will never see it displayed or offered for sale on any store shelf. It is exclusive and unique and a most welcomed traditionally American gift.

Remember, you won't risk anything because we definitely believe in and stand behind our time-honored policy of immediate cash refund or fresh cake replacement — if ever there's the slightest question as to quality or safe and sound delivery.

It's real easy to order — just refer to the brochure and order blank. And, whether it's one gift or a hundred — we'll take care of all the details. Believe me, you and those on your gift list will be glad you chose DeLUXE as your holiday remembrance.

Best wishes from Corsicana.

John Crawford

JC/xm

P.S. Please send check or money order to cover your first purchase. Then, we'll handle all future business on an open account basis. Thanks.

SPECIAL NOTE: Since the price of a DeLUXE does include delivery to all 50 states, all U. S. possessions, Puerto Rico and APO-FPO addresses — it's got to be one of the most economical quality gifts around today!

Available the Year Around · Unconditionally Guaranteed

551

Even such a simple event as an announcement can also be the occasion for a "second sale" approach, an approach that will lead to future good relationships. Once you know that, you'll be able to figure out your own applications for each situation. The more you take advantage of such occasions, the more effective you'll become at business writing.

When it's necessary to say *no* in a letter, it's usually advisable to be particularly careful to have a *positive* tone. *You don't want to appear negative or hostile, nor do you want to appear indifferent.* You wouldn't say, for example,

"I received your so-called letter about your silly complaint."

Even if the letter was strongly written—even if it made you furious—you still want to keep your response calm. What you hope is that you can somehow handle the situation. If you cannot, you can at least avoid aggravating it. Say instead,

"Thank you for your letter of May 23rd about your new Arctic air conditioner."

So **the first principle of saying** *no* **in a letter is to keep the tone calm and positive.**

The second principle is to **avoid saying** *no* **until you've covered all the facts and reasons for refusing.** That way, you can show that you do indeed have facts and reasons, and that you've considered them thoughtfully. That arrangement will help the reader to keep an open mind about it, too, since he or she will have to read through the letter to find your answer. And if you think about it, putting the refusal first and then following it with the reasons may make it seem as though you made up your mind first, then thought up the reasons.

Here is a sample that follows the principles quite well:

SAMPLE RESPONSE: "NO"

Dear Mr. Medici,

We received your letter and your Truebuilt clock-radio model number 3220. Our shop test showed that the clock did, indeed, make the grinding noise you describe in your letter. The problem appears to be a worn gear.

As you know, at Truebuilt we stand behind our work, and we are completely devoted to customer satisfaction. Your clock-radio model 3220 is a fine product, and once the gear is replaced, it should give satisfactory service for many years to come.

In your letter, you request that we repair the clock at our own expense, and we would be happy to do so if the item were under warranty. But because we have no record of your having registered this radio with us, nor is there a sales receipt from you showing date of purchase, we feel you will understand why we cannot agree to repair it at our own expense.

However, we would be pleased to do the repair for you at our regular shop rate. We estimate the repair at about $7.00, which is the lowest cost that will permit us to do a satisfactory job. Our specially-trained repairmen can quickly have the clock-radio in tip-top shape. Or, if you prefer, we can return the radio to you as is.

Please let us know what you'd like us to do. We look forward to serving you and to making your Truebuilt clock-radio a continuing source of satisfaction to you.

Sincerely,

The first paragraph establishes receipt of the clock-radio and the accompanying letter and gives agreement about the problem. Paragraph 2 develops the "second sale" approach, reminding the customer about Truebuilt's integrity and concern about its products. Only in paragraph 3 does the letter indicate refusal—and even there it presents the reasons carefully first and even avoids the word *refuse*. Paragraph 4 suggests an alternative—Truebuilt will repair the clock for a nominal amount. The closing paragraph sounds a cooperative note and stresses the customer's satisfaction. Mr. Medici may or may not continue on good terms with Truebuilt, but he's much more likely to than if he had gotten back a letter saying something like:

```
Dear Customer:
    You were in error to return the Truebuilt clock
radio to us.  We do not repair any appliance which is
not under warranty.  Our records show that you did not
register the radio and that, therefore, we are not
obligated to repair it.
                            Sincerely,
```

JOB APPLICATIONS AND RÉSUMÉS

When you're applying for jobs, you have two valuable tools: the letter of application and the résumé. Both have become well established over the years, so that there is an *expected form* to them, an *expected tone, appearance, order*. Yet because they are, in effect, devices by which you advertise yourself, it's very useful to look beneath the surface of the forms, to spend some extra time developing material that can be sorted into either the résumé or the application or both, and some time in working up the final appearance so that the letter will support the résumé, the résumé will back up the letter—and both will do the job for you that you want them to do: present you to the world of work as someone who is qualified, attractive, and definitely worth hiring.

Audience   Imagine the person who will be getting your letter — seated behind a desk piled high with incoming mail. Imagine, next, the first form letter — unimaginative, automatic, mechanical-sounding — then the second, the third, and so on to maybe the one hundred ninety-ninth. Imagine the boredom and the wearisomeness of it all. The reader just cannot stand one more form letter. But *she opens yours!* Ah-ha! It's original, personal, sparkling, scintillating. It has, of course, all the expected conventional material and information, but in addition to that, it carries your own unmistakable stamp, ring, quality.

   This vignette may be a bit dramatic, but it happens often enough to be a fair representation of reality. And it does demonstrate that even in such a potentially impersonal information-moving situation as a job application letter, *your ability to come up with an attractive presentation may provide just the edge that gets you past all those others.*

Point: **It is to your advantage to get on top of the conventions of any set piece of business writing, and then to go *beyond* them.**

Conventions of the Job Application Letter   By the time you've read through the early sections of this chapter, you already know a lot about the conventions of business writing in general. What about the conventions of the job application letter?

   At the fundamental level, there are three parts:

1 **What do you want to say?**
        I want this job.
        I'm qualified for it.
        You'd be well off to hire me.

MESSAGE

2 **Whom are you saying it to?**
        Someone who does the actual hiring.
        Someone who screens applicants but
            doesn't do the actual hiring.

AUDIENCE

3 **What do you want out of it?**
        I want my letter to look better than
            the others.
        I want to establish my qualifications.
        I want this job offered to me.

PURPOSE

The way to say "I want this job" is to simply say that, although you can do some creating processes and come up with something a bit more individualized and effective. The way to say "I'm qualified" is by giving evidence (or information) about three areas of your life: school, work, and activities. You send all this to a real person (and take care to treat

JOB APPLICATION LETTER:
Highlights your qualifications, emphasizes particular achievements and abilities.

RÉSUMÉ:
Gives, in outline form, the data about your education, work experience, and activities that will be of interest to an employer.

DO CREATING *ON:*
I want this job.
I'm qualified.
You should hire me.
I'm writing to ———— .

the person like a person, not a wall.) And you make your letter presentable by adhering to the conventions of shaping and completing (all of which is covered in the pages that follow).

But first, it is important to be clear about the areas in which you are going to develop information, and to understand that any *creating* you do will produce material usable in *both* letter and résumé, thus serving double duty.

CREATING

I Want This Job Since forthrightness is often taken by business as a sign of virtue, *come right out with it.* Once you are clear that you want the job, you needn't feel self-conscious saying so.

Notice that reference is to *this* job, not *the* job or *a* job; it's important to sharpen the focus. You're writing to a *particular company* in a *specific location* with a *unique product* — so don't tell them that you'd like to find *some* work *somewhere.*

Here are four creating activities for I WANT THIS JOB.

1 **Make lists of all the reasons you can think of for wanting *this* job.**
Write as fast as you can for 3 to 5 minutes, and don't stop. Produce as many reasons as you can. Don't worry whether the reasons are good. You are writing to get the ideas flowing, to make original and strong connections.

REASON: You probably have reasons right now — *but everybody else probably has the same reasons, especially if they concern salary, location, and promotion.* So it's worth a few minutes to do some creating here. At the end you may still come up with the same old three — salary, location, and promotion — but even so, there's a greater chance that you'll have a special way of expressing it that is particularly your own — and that will help your letter to stand apart from the crowd.

2 **List everything you can think of about *this* job.**
Again, write as fast as you can for 3 to 5 minutes.

REASON: This activity helps get the job itself clearly focused and will help you both to see what skills, knowledge, and attitudes it requires and to relate your own qualifications to it very specifically.

3 **Ask all the questions you can think of about this job.**
REASON: You're turning up information from a different point of view; you'll discover information about both you and the job that you can use later.

4 Do cubing on *this* job.

>Move swiftly through the cubing activities.
>
>REASON: This formal procedure will ensure that you examine the job from at least 6 more points of view—and will produce more and different information.

I'm Qualified for This Job   Everyone who applies for the job will claim to be qualified; what's wanted is some *evidence* of this qualification. The three most common areas of qualification, usually, are *education, work experience,* and *interests.* Since almost every other letter will have a wooden, mechanical recitation on these points, your task is twofold: to **come up with *your* qualifications** and to **present them interestingly, even arrestingly.** That's a tall order, since the "rules" governing applications are a bit restrictive, with expected information in the expected places and in more or less the expected formats. Again, though, *creating* processes will help.

1 Do *cubing* on *my qualifications for this job.*

>Move around your own qualifications as you go through the six steps: *defining, comparing, associating, describing, analyzing,* and *arguing.*
>
>Begin to get "out of your own skin" a little, to see yourself as someone else would see you.
>
>REASON: This develops a sense of how you look as a candidate—how others see your strengths.

2 Do *looping* on *I'm qualified for this job.*

>Let this different process bring up different areas, resources, awarenesses.
>
>Some repetition is natural, but keep looking for new material to emerge.
>
>REASON: You keep adding to the pile of ways in which you're qualified for *this* job.

3 Review your life, like a movie, swiftly (about 10 minutes) and jot down every event that might have any bearing on your qualifications for this job.

>Consider family activities, interests, projects.
>
>Any travel? Adventures? Inventions? Scrapes?
>
>What sorts of things did you do? How do others relate to you? What do you never do?
>
>REASON: This develops a bank of *interests* you can draw on later.

You'd Be Well Off to Hire Me   Whenever we get to this spot in our own letters, we get a sinking feeling; after all, there are so many other applicants—who in the world would possibly want to hire *us!* But once again, *creating* processes come to the rescue.

1 List all the things you might be able to do for the company if you had *this* job.

> List *all* of them, and don't worry about whether they are "good" or "bad."
>
> Include foolish ones ("I can keep a chair warm; I can lick envelopes").
>
> REASON: You see yourself from the company's viewpoint and develop an impressive list so that it actually begins to seem as though they *would* be well off to hire you.

2 Complete this sentence at least 20 times (35 is even better): "On this job, I intend to . . ."

> Think of all the things you really mean to do on that job.
>
> REASON: You clarify your intention to be serviceable on this job, and you'll begin to see the value you really do offer.

Now that you've done enough to be limber and to have the juices flowing nicely, here is a final assortment of things to make lists about. Spend 10 or 15 minutes on each of these—*they are much more specific than the earlier creating activities*—and they'll very likely provide superinformation for the rough draft of your letter and résumé.

1 List all the *jobs* you've ever had, whether you were paid or not.

> What kinds of tasks did you do? What regular chores? Where did you help out? What did you do there? How would that relate to what you might do on *this* job?

2 List all the times you've taken any *initiative*, taken the lead.

> Were you captain at team sports? Leader in organized activities—Scouts, Kiwanis, Bluebirds, Businesswomen of America?
> Think of childhood.
> Grade school.
> High school.
> College.

3 List all the times you've been *successful*.

> What did you win? What awards? What acknowledgements? Prizes? Ribbons? Medals? Certificates?
> What records did you break? Contests?
> What do you really do well that everybody knows about?
> What do you do really well that few people know about?

4 List all the things you like to do.

> How do you like to spend your time?
> What hobbies? Trips? Interests? What gives you pleasure when you spend time at it? What do you enjoy finding out about?

When you finish these creating activities, you have a *lot* of material. Some of it will be pretty worthless, some of it may be something you never would have thought of before, and some of it—much, probably—will be very useful indeed, once it is sorted out.

SHAPING

I'm Writing to _____

You've developed plenty of material so far, and you can sort it into the three basic groups: *education, work, interests.* The next question is: *what do you keep and what do you discard?*

To deal with that question, begin with a sense of audience. Remember that somewhere, on the other end of the mail route, there's a real person, sitting at a desk, holding a letter-opener, about to slit your—envelope. **The clearer you can visualize that person, the greater your chances of surviving the operation.** Having a specific person in mind will help you to (1) select and order the material at hand and (2) get the tone that will be most effective for that particular person.

Whom are you writing to? Essentially, it comes down to two types:

1 Someone who does the actual hiring
2 Someone who screens all the incoming mail and then passes a few along for the "hiring" person to consider.

Unless you're writing directly to the head of the laboratory, the owner of the store, the foreman at the cannery, chances are that you won't be writing to the person who does the hiring. Instead, you'll be writing to a "screening person"—someone whose job it is to keep nearly everyone out (and thus to save the time of the person who will actually offer the job). Large corporations, businesses, and industries will almost always have a personnel department—and if they do, you can be sure you'll be writing to the screening person. For the screening person, you'll need to be more distant, professional, cool, controlled. For the hiring person, you can probably afford to show a bit more personality, be a bit more direct and affable.

First Paragraph: Make It Hook and Hold

The first paragraph is the place to display your best and brightest credentials. It is probably *the* paragraph, of the whole letter, that counts the heaviest. To get it off to a fast start, be sure it contains everything it should: how you found out about this job (and which one you're applying for if there is more than one); your "hook"—the particular connection or claim, edge, or leverage you have that other applicants don't; and an instant, thumbnail summary of your qualifications.

That first paragraph establishes who you are—and remember that a busy reader may very well take the short-cut of deciding everything on that one paragraph. You have four to seven lines to put forward your

FIRST PARAGRAPH:

How you heard;
which job;
your "hook";
your qualifications.

strongest (1) **reasons for wanting this job,** (2) **qualifications for this job,** (3) **connections with this job.**

You'll want to sort through those piles very carefully now—but don't take more than about 20 minutes.

The usual order for presenting this information is:
> **how you heard about the job**
> **which job you're applying for**
> **your "hook"**
> **your qualifications.**

However, there's no hard and fast rule about this. You can vary that order to put your own case most strongly. If you heard about the job from an influential person, put that information out early. If your training is particularly thorough, mention that right away. If your experience is especially rich, then that's what you want to put first. Here are some sample first paragraphs. In them you can see the effect of audience awareness and a sample of the varieties of hooks and presentations. These writers are all successful in writing first paragraphs that connect them to the job in a way that the reader will recognize and regard as special.

SAMPLE APPLICATION LETTERS: FIRST PARAGRAPH

SAMPLE 1:
Mention a Name

In a conversation with Mr. Charles Thompson on March 12, I learned that several positions will be available for junior auditors this September. I am very interested in working in this position with Ernst & Ernst because of the excellent fringe benefits offered and the opportunities for advancement.

SAMPLE 2:
Response to Ad, Specific Job

I am writing in response to your ad in Monday's *Hartford Chronicle* announcing the opening for a degreed accountant with banking experience.

SAMPLE 3:
Mention a Name and Education

During Eastern Transmission Company's recent orientation meeting at Howard University, your personnel director, Mr. Crockett, expressed a need for graduates with a B.B.A. degree in accounting. I will receive this degree in May, and am interested in the accounting experience that your company would provide.

SAMPLE 4:
Personal Contact, Name, Education

I spoke to you at our last AIFD meeting, and you suggested I write and apply for part time work this summer and next fall. Jim Johnson, my major professor, and I both felt that working in your florist shop would give me the experience I need to compete for the better design jobs after graduation.

SAMPLE 5:
Name and Experience

Mr. J. B. Lee, one of your business associates, informed me of a job opening in your firm this summer. Working in Denver the last few summers, I have heard of your reputable marketing department and am very interested in filling the vacant position.

Last summer I worked in the Information Systems department of your company under the supervision of Walt Arp. As a Computing Science major at the University of Wisconsin, I had basic understanding of computer systems and a knowledge of Fortran and PL/I languages. While I was working at Michigan-Wisconsin, Mr. Arp instructed me in the COBOL language and seemed very pleased with the programs I was able to produce as a result of his instruction. I would like to work for your firm again this summer and would prefer to work in Mr. Arp's division if possible.

SAMPLE 6:
***Everything!* Mentions Work, Person, Education, Experience, Plans**

If you are writing directly to the person doing the hiring, you are a bit freer to play up why you are applying for *this* job. If you know something favorable about the person, the job, the company, the product/services, work it in *if appropriate*. It's always legitimate to acknowledge a person or a laboratory or firm for their actual accomplishments, but it's more appropriate to do that to the person doing the hiring than to the person doing the screening. The first is more likely to respond than will the latter.

Paragraph on Education For the body of the letter—after the introduction—you'll probably **give one paragraph to each group of qualifications:** a paragraph on education, another on work, and a third on interests. Of course your *Data Sheet* will carry the full details: schools, degrees, courses, places where you worked, dates—all that. So all you want to do in the paragraph on education is to give the highlights, emphasize the points you want the reader to be sure to get.

If you have taken any courses that are particularly relevant to this job, mention them. If you've had many courses related to this job, select only those that are most likely to make the best impression. And be sure to mention them by name, not by course number. *History 205* hardly tells anybody anything; *Colonial American History* tells a good deal more. If the relationship between the course and the job isn't completely obvious, explain the connection: "Because of the course in Colonial American History that I took last semester, I have developed a particular interest in working as a gunsmith at Williamsburg this summer."

If you have done special research projects in the area or related areas, mention them. Be sure to include any honors or awards, any distinctions that might demonstrate your particular qualities. Field trips? Work with a distinguished professor? Whatever it is, get it into this paragraph if it is connected to school and relevant to this job.

EDUCATION

courses
research
honors
awards
distinctions
field trips
teachers

SAMPLE PARAGRAPHS: EDUCATION

I am majoring in poultry science and have taken several courses in basic agriculture economics, breeding, feeding, and marketing. As part of my program, I served an internship at a broiler production farm similar to yours. My résumé (enclosed) contains more details about my education

SAMPLE 1:
Connects Coursework to Job Application

and special training. I'm sure you will see that I am well qualified to work for your company.

SAMPLE 2:
Handles Problem of What to Say When You Haven't Yet Had Many Courses.

As a sophomore marketing major at Rutgers, I have begun to sample courses in theory, research, methodology, and techniques. I look forward to continuing my education, and in the meantime am looking for opportunities to apply my formal education to actual business situations. My association with your firm could prove a valuable experience for both of us.

Notice that this student might have said something to the effect that, "Since I'm only a sophomore, I haven't really gotten into the course-work very deeply yet." However, keeping the *"you" attitude* here, she has managed to write about her education as a series of opportunities, most of which lie before her. A nice job, and a model for converting a liability (little education) into an asset. The forthright desire to apply the education right away and the determination to give value combine to carry it off.

SAMPLE 3:
Lists Courses by Title Selects 3 Titles From the Many He Might Have Mentioned

In my academic program I have concentrated on financial accounting, with a strong emphasis in oil and gas accounting. Specific courses I have taken that relate to your industry are:

Accounting Problems: Oil and Gas Accounting

Advanced Accounting

Accounting Theory

These courses and others have provided me with a strong background in business.

Paragraph on Work   Your work experience is evidence for the qualities that you hope to convince the reader you possess—qualities of employability. Any job—babysitting or pumping gas, volunteer nursing or carrying newspapers—shows that you are willing to hang in there day after day, steady and reliable. If you're a middle-aged adult, with many jobs over the years, you may need more than a paragraph to do justice to your career. If you've moved through a series of jobs to positions of increasing responsibility, say so. If you earned recognition or set performance records unusual for a person of your age and experience, don't keep it a secret.

Most applicants will *say* they have certain qualities; you want to be sure to give *evidence* for *your* claims. Probably your creating activities have produced plenty of material, even though you may not actually have had a job that paid. If you haven't had a regular job, discuss the kinds of things you did do—help out in the lawnmower repair shop, tend the neighborhood grocery, run a Kool-Aid stand, start up a kind of day-care school for little kids in your apartment building, and so on. Consider *anything* that might be related to work—activities, attitudes—

anything. **If you think it demonstrates the qualities you know you have of reliability, tenacity, and imagination — or whatever you think will be especially attractive in a candidate for *this* job — *mention it!*** Of course you don't want to be completely ridiculous about it, so use your own good sense, too. And if you truly have absolutely nothing to say about work experience, you may want to leave this area blank and concentrate your energies in other directions. Probably, though, if you take a close look at those piles of generated material, you will find several concrete examples of the qualities you think will make you desirable as an employee, and you should probably put them into your letter.

As in the education paragraph, **be sure to arrange the material in some sensible order.** A jumbled hodge-podge won't do the job for you, won't impress the reader. Orderliness will. List the details chronologically, or in some other way that makes sense. Perhaps you'll want to give time jobs. Perhaps you'll point out how managing a twelve-member family calls for budgeting, planning, and organizing of a kind very similar to the skills you'll need for the job you're applying for. Whatever order you choose, be conscious that you *are* choosing.

SAMPLE PARAGRAPHS: WORK

My previous employment by Gulf Oil will allow me to start this job already understanding the computer system and able to operate at top efficiency. I have already completed Gulf's orientation courses and the JCL course given to new employees in Gulf's Computer Department, so I am familiar with your computer system.

As my résumé shows, I have worked part-time and summers all through high school and my first two years of college. All these jobs were in the field of retail selling and have provided me with a fairly wide background, so that I can quickly adapt to special kinds of selling. My performance was consistently in the top 20 percent for salespeople in similar areas, and I won three sales contests and was recognized at the annual Hupley's Incentive Banquet.

For the past three summers, I have been employed by the M. David Lowe Personnel Agency. As a "temporary," I was exposed to a wide variety of jobs including receptionist to a Japanese steel company, receptionist to an advertising agency, law firm secretary, and mail sorter/deliverer for a major oil company. I learned how to rapidly adapt to the frequently changing job requirements of temporary work.

As my résumé shows, I was married shortly after high school and have spent the last 15 years successfully managing a family of six. This has involved:

> careful financial planning: organizing categories, establishing priorities, balancing income, outgo, and savings;
> efficient management of time, scheduling, sequencing of activities;

WORK
jobs
responsibilities
positions
helping out
experiences
similarities

SAMPLE 1:
Previous Work with Same Firm

SAMPLE 2:
Previous Similar Work, Mentions Résumé

SAMPLE 3:
Shows Advantages of Part-Time Work

SAMPLE 4:
Emphasizes Background Related to Job Skills

supervision of education of four children; raising funds for PTA, managing two School Board campaigns.

These experiences, plus considerable skill in interpersonal relations, have prepared me to make a significant contribution in marketing Isen Household Products.

This last sample shows what can be done when a person is determined to find background experiences that do, indeed, prepare him/her to make a significant contribution.

Paragraph on Interests/Activities Finally, **if you have any outside activities that might also be of interest** or **accomplishments not connected with either school or work, group those together.** If you are writing to a screening person, you might want to leave this information for the résumé. If you're writing directly to the hiring person, it is more likely that you'd want to include it. Information about activities is almost always included on a résumé sheet; it is optional in the letter of application.

If, for example, you have an uncommonly large stamp collection, you might mention it; acquiring and arranging and keeping track of so much detail might well demonstrate exactly the qualities the employer is looking for. If you run five miles a day, rain or shine, that's probably evidence of a strong will and a healthy constitution. Being politically active or deeply religious may or may not help; keep in mind whom you're writing to and consider what the reaction might be. If you're good at team sports, chances are you'll be considered a good candidate for membership in the firm; if you're a voracious reader, chances are you'll be thought to have some potential as a researcher. If you love to work with numbers or solve problems or lead Girl Scout troops, that may be worth mentioning too. Just go ahead and sort through everything in the *activities and interests* pile. Whatever you come up with, be sure to relate it to *this* job.

SAMPLE PARAGRAPHS: INTERESTS/ACTIVITIES

SAMPLE 1:
Job-related Activity, Personal Contact

In addition to my coursework, I am also involved in several extracurricular activities. I am active in the Marketing Society and have arranged for guest speakers to address our group. I also belong to the Century Singers, a choral group at this college. Through this organization, I met Ms. Bradley and assisted her in implementing the promotion efforts for this year's spring concert.

SAMPLE 2:
Job-related Activity

As you know, I am a member of AIFD, Student FTD, and California State Florists' Association. I have also worked with student floral concessions in the Floriculture club and this has taught me many sales methods and basic skills. I have participated in the California Allied Florists' design contest and scored well on my arrangement.

I enjoy both group and individual activities. In high school I was a member of the Plano Wildcat Marching Band, the concert band, the German Club, and the National Honor Society. At Clark College I have been active in jogging—20 to 30 miles a week—and have been treasurer of the Snow Ski Club for three terms.

SAMPLE 3:
General Activities

Conclusions   With the body of the letter taken care of, you can now wrap the whole thing up. **Your conclusion is the final image you leave with your reader,** so you should take almost as much care with it as you did with your introduction. Keep it brief and crisp. Close with a snappy recapitulation of WHY THIS JOB and YOUR QUALIFICATIONS and YOUR DESIRE FOR THE JOB. Then ask for a specific date for an interview or a response. Many applicants close weakly by saying they are "available" for an interview (who cares?) or that they "hope" they hear (who wants to waste away on hope?) or else they thank the reader for spending time with this letter (as though the letter weren't worth the time). Asking for a specific date for the interview is professional. It sounds strong, assured, and puts the burden on the reader *to respond.* Here are three examples of effective conclusions, each asking directly for an interview:

SAMPLE PARAGRAPHS: CONCLUSIONS

I would like to meet with you the week after final exams, May 12–May 19, if that is convenient. I can be reached after 5:00 at 846-3010 or at work at 845-1031. If I am not there, leave a message and I will return your call. I am looking forward to hearing from you.

SAMPLE 1:
Phone

Sincerely,

I am very interested in discussing your summer job vacancy with you and will be in Chicago May 5. I would like to make an appointment for 2:00 P.M. and can be contacted at (613) 845-6256. I will be looking forward to hearing from you.

SAMPLE 2:
Phone
(Notice that "can be reached" is not as effective as the paragraph above.)

Sincerely,

I will be visiting San Francisco Friday, May 4, and have made plans to visit your office between 8 and 11 A.M. Will you be available to talk with me then? I am looking forward to meeting you and your staff.

SAMPLE 3:
Time, Place, Date

Sincerely,

I will be employed by Mr. G. A. Fitzgerald, of your department, during this summer (May 14–August 25). I would like to meet with you sometime during the last two weeks of May to discuss the job openings in the Systems Operation division and how my experience and education can benefit your department.

SAMPLE 4:
Benefit to Employer

Yours very truly,

COMPLETING

Once you have the content and form taken care of, give your draft a final going-over. Check that the balanced phrases are in parallel construction. Check for spelling, punctuation, capitalization, and other such mechanical errors. Check for odd or awkward phrases too. Be careful to eliminate "hoping," being "available," or thanking the reader for considering such a weak and unworthy candidate as your humble self. Be sure the addressee's name is spelled correctly. If you don't have the name already, the campus placement office can help you find it. Check the dates, the zip codes, and the punctuation for greeting and closing. Are there good clear indentions for the new paragraphs (5 spaces) or a double space between them? Is the conclusion strongly stated? Did you remember to type your name and leave room for the signature too?

When you've finished checking, your rough draft will probably really *look* rough. Rather than go straight to the finished copy, you may want to type the draft once more, this time to see how the margins will look, how the letter will balance on the page. With a clean "rough" draft in front of you, you won't have to make any decisions—or guesses—while you're typing the final copy.

Because the occasion is important (you *want* that job), you must be sure to **give the letter the best appearance you can.** Be sure the ribbon is fresh—crisp and black is what's wanted here. If you're not a very good typist, find somebody who is. This letter should be clean all the way through, with no typos, erasures, strikeovers, or dabs of correction fluid. One campus newspaper advertises some typists who say, "You don't pay for any page with a typo. We guarantee our work." That's the kind of typist you're looking for.

Be sure to use good quality paper, too. The *appearance* of your letter gives off messages a mile wide. Are you flimsy dime-store stock or high quality bond? Are you crisp and clear or gray and faded? Are you right on target, complete and accurate, or are you covered with erasures, strikeovers, and paint-outs? Take pains to make the *appearance* of the letter say what you want it to say about you. You wouldn't appear for an interview with hunks of your hair whacked out and wearing sneakers with a toe or two peeping loose. So don't present a letter that looks like that either. Let it express the competent, attractive, dynamic **you.**

With a carefully developed message, a clear purpose, a real audience, and an attractive appearance, your letter will represent you powerfully and effectively—just the way you want it to.

SAMPLE LETTERS OF APPLICATION

Here are three sample letters of application. Each is well done; together they offer a modest range of variations while expressing their writers' particular qualities.

CHECKLIST FOR COMPLETING

Mechanics: names, dates, zip codes, punctuation.

Completeness: introduction, body, conclusion.

Style: tone positive and strong, phrases clear and natural, parallelism OK.

Appearance: layout on page, margins, typing, paper.

Return address

P. O. Box 8499
Richland Terrace
Digby, Georgia 30205

Internal address

Mr. Robert Pennington, Supervisor
Davidson's Personnel Department
817 Round Street
Atlanta, Georgia 30307

Dear Mr. Pennington: *Salutation*

Mentions name, which job, and education

Kim Bradley, Assistant Buyer of the Home Appliances department in your downtown store, referred your name to me. While conducting a tour of her department on January 15, Ms. Bradley informed me of Davidson's summer intern program for college students pursuing business degrees. As I live in the Atlanta area from May to September and am a marketing major at the University of Georgia, I would like to become an intern for Davidson's during those summer months.

work

For the past three summers, I have been employed by the M. David Lowe Personnel Agency. As a temporary, I was exposed to a wide variety of jobs including receptionist to a Japanese steel company, receptionist to an advertising agency, law firm secretary, and mail sorter/deliverer for a major oil company. I learned how to adapt rapidly to the frequently changing job requirements of temporary work.

Activities

Currently, I am taking marketing courses concerning consumer behavior, promotion, and retailing. My extra-curricular activities include membership in the Century Singers, a choral group at the University of Georgia. Through this organization, I met Ms. Bradley and assisted her in implementing the promotion efforts for the 1978 spring concert.

résumé

The enclosed résumé will give you further information about my education and will provide a list of references.

Conclusion

I will be in Atlanta from May 14 to May 23. Would it be possible for me to interview with you or another member of the personnel management on May 16? Prior to those dates, I can be reached by mail or by phoning 404-789-3333.

Sincerely, *Close*

Signature

Martha E. Schutt

Typed name

567

404 James Street
San Diego, California 94567
April 24, 1980

Ms. Amilde Hadden
Beautiful Flowers, Inc.
890 University Drive
San Diego, California 94566

Dear Ms. Hadden:

Personal contact

    I spoke to you at our last AIFD meeting, and you suggested I write and apply for part-time work this summer and next fall. Jim Johnson and I both felt that working in your shop would give me the experience I need to compete for the better design jobs after graduation.

Activities

    I have participated in many different activities in school which give me good qualifications to work for you. As you know, I am a member of AIFD, Student FTD, and California State Florists' Association. I have also worked with student floral concessions in the Floriculture Club, and this has taught me many basic skills and sales methods. I have competed in the California Allied Florists' design contest and scored high on my arrangement.

Employer

    I am currently working in the admissions and records department of San Diego Community College, and this job has given me the public relations experience which is so important in the retail florist shop. I have spoken to my boss, Mr. Dave Workman, and he said that although he hates to lose a worker with three years of experience, he is enthusiastic about my getting a job related to my field of study. Feel free to contact him if there are any questions about my experience or work capabilities.

Conclusion

    I would like to meet with you the week after final exams, May 12-May 19, if that is convenient. I can be reached after 5:00 at 932-4567 or at work at 932-7654. If I am not at the number when you call, please leave a message; I will return your call. I am looking forward to hearing from you.

Sincerely,

Kara O'Connor

Enc: résumé

324 N. Washington Street
Batavia, Illinois 61606
(606) 876-3211

April 21, 1980

Mr. Denis Bedar, Analyst Manager
Control Data Corporation
8585 North DeKalb, #444
Chicago, Illinois 60616

Dear Mr. Bedar:

   I am a junior technical communications major at the University of Illinois. One of your analysts, Mr. Mike Tittle, has suggested I write to you for summer employment as a programmer and applications analyst. Mr. Tittle and I first became associated three years ago when he was an analyst for United Computing Systems and I was a UCS client.

   I have three years of practical work experience in computing, in addition to my college work. I know how to tie into networks and communications systems and have taught remote telecommunications and systems languages. I plan to continue working in the computing field after my graduation in December 1980.

   I have enclosed a résumé which gives more detailed information about my education and work experience as well as names of people who will provide references for me

   I will be in Chicago on Friday, May 4, and have made plans to visit your office between 8 and 11 a.m. Will you be available to talk with me then?

   I am looking forward to meeting you and your staff.

                    Sincerely,

                    Kay L. Wallace

encl.

RÉSUMÉ

It will probably be good news and somewhat of a relief to learn that your data sheet is much, much less demanding than the letter of application. For one thing, there's almost no more "creating" to go through. For another, practically all you do is fill in the boxes, correctly, of course, but no more than that.

A résumé in fact has only two qualities: accuracy of information and aesthetic appeal.

The first of these—accuracy of information—is all but completely taken care of through the writing you've already done for the application letter. The aesthetic appeal is handled through carefully doing shaping work on the form provided—that is, *don't try to get it all right the first time.* Use the first draft to get the material logged in accurately and the second draft to experiment with layout. When you're satisfied that the information is complete and accurate and the layout is accessible and crisp, then you're ready for the final draft that makes it all look so polished.

How, then, *should* it look—and what *does* go into a data sheet? Take a look at the attached model—that's faster than a long essay of explanation.

Résumé: Model 1

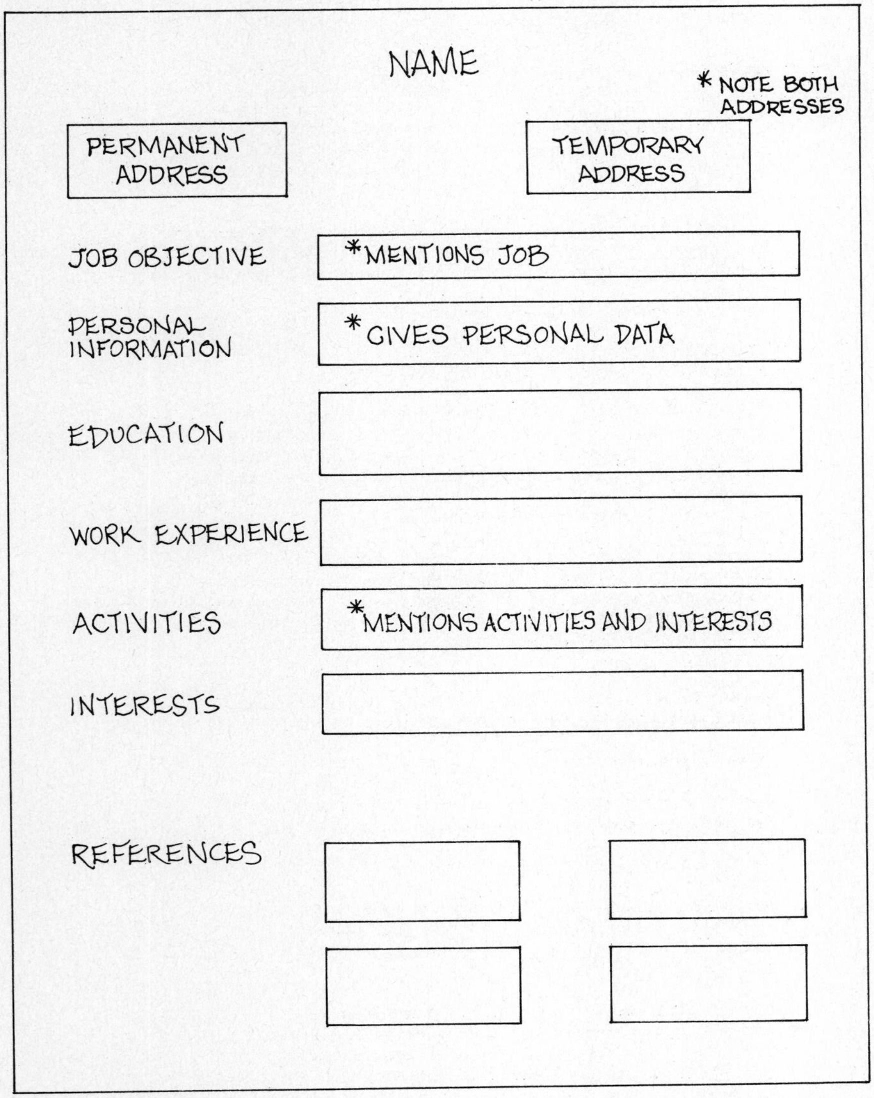

As this diagram shows, there is nothing mysterious or difficult about the résumé sheet. The subheads show the reader where to find the crucial information. All you need to do is take care to place the information in an attractive arrangement visually. What follows is a résumé sheet worked out on this model.

James R. White

Permanent Address

1507 17th Street
Plano, Texas 75074
Telephone: 214-423-3326

Temporary Address

1602 Finfeather # 28
Bryan, Texas 77801
Telephone: 713-822-6252

JOB OBJECTIVE	A position of responsibility in the Controller's or Treasurer's office of a large oil company, with eventually qualifying for general management positions.
PERSONAL	Age 23, single, excellent health.
EDUCATION	Plano High School, Plano, Texas Graduated 18 out of a class of 456
	Texas A&M University, College Station, Texas Candidate for B.B.A. degree in May 1979, with a 3.0 average. Majored in accounting (emphasizing financial accounting) with courses in marketing, finance, management, business analysis, and economics. Received Dean's list honors for 3 semesters.
PREVIOUS EMPLOYMENT	Framed houses for seven consecutive summers from 1971. Supervised work crew in 1977. Subcontracted sheetrock and roofing work myself in 1976 and 1977. Worked as full time cashier and stocker for The Kroger Company while a senior in high school.
ACTIVITIES	Plano High School Member of the Plano Wildcat Marching Band, concert band, German Club, and National Honor Society.
	Texas A&M University 3 term treasurer of the TAMU Sport Parachute Club. Member of TAMU Accounting Society, Snow Ski Club, Pre-Vet Society, and the Brazos Valley Corvette Club.
INTERESTS	Jogging, skydiving, current events

REFERENCES

Dr. Allen Bizzel
Accounting Department
Texas A&M University
College Station, TX 77843

John W. Harris, D.V.M.
P. O. Box 1628
Bryan, TX 77801

Dr. Sid McDaniel
Entomology Department
Texas A&M University
College Station, TX 77843

Dr. Tom Oxner
Accounting Department
Texas A&M University
College Station, TX 77843

Here is a second model together with a completed résumé. What is important for you to remember is that there are a variety of models. You have the choice of many, so just locate a résumé style that pleases you and follow that model.

Résumé: Model 2

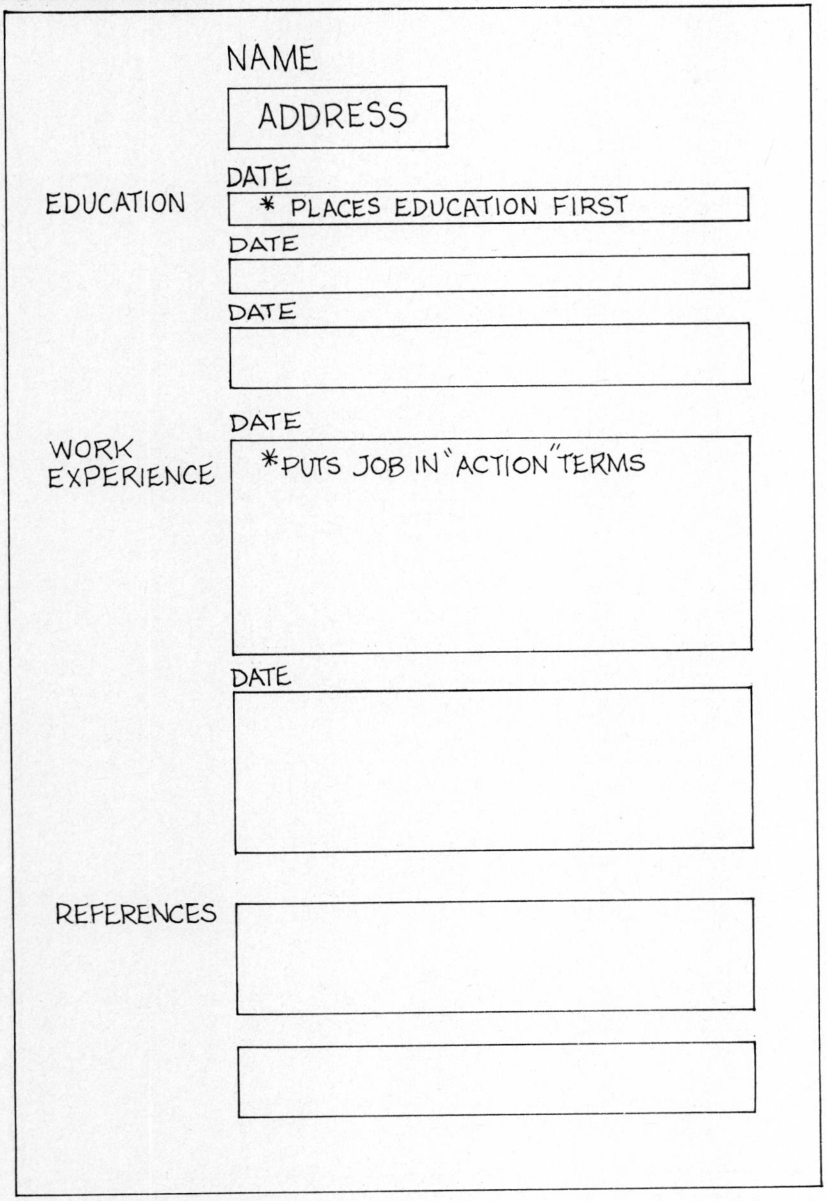

NAME

ADDRESS

EDUCATION

DATE

* PLACES EDUCATION FIRST

DATE

DATE

WORK EXPERIENCE

DATE

*PUTS JOB IN "ACTION" TERMS

DATE

REFERENCES

RÉSUMÉ

BARBARA WALKER
201 Lee Street
Walla Walla, Washington 99362

Education
1972-75:
Walla Walla High School
Graduated May 1975.

1975-77:
Walla Walla Community College
Graduated with A.A. degree, June 1977.

1977-79:
University of Washington, Seattle
Graduated with B.B.A. in Accounting, August 1979.
Passed CPA Examination, November 1979.

Work Experience
1978-present:
Seattle Student Finance Center
--Handle daily deposits ranging from $2,000 to
  $50,000.
--Verify checks written against the accounts.
--Post transactions electronically and manually.
--Balance all transactions at end of each day.
--Assist in preparation of monthly financial
  statements.
--Train new workers.

1977-June to September and December:
Accounting Assistant at Reserve Equipment
Company, Olympia, Washington
--Prepared employee payroll checks.
--Reconciled monthly bank statements.
--Performed duties of Accounts Payable Clerk.
--Filed and answered telephones.
--Posted and balanced various ledgers of
  parent company and its subsidiaries.

References
Sue Young, Supervisor
Seattle Student Finance Center
P. O. Box Z
Seattle, Washington 99330

Jan Moore
Reserve Equipment Company
40 N. Bledsoe Avenue
Olympia, Washington 99345

What, then, is there to know about résumé sheets?

1 All of them look pretty much alike, and yours will need to look like the rest of them.

2 People reviewing them will expect information to be organized in the standard way so that they can easily and quickly find what they want to know.

3 They are used as a quick reference, and they'll probably be used during the interview also.

And that's pretty much it. Once you know the basic formats, you have some latitude, so long as you keep the design clean and uncluttered. The basics about education and work experience must be there, with your name and address, and two to four references. Information about health and marriage, interests, and activities is optional.

Try to keep your sheet all on one page. Busy people don't want to be bothered with more than one page, so edit it down to that size if you possibly can and still do justice to your qualifications. Sometimes you can get more information by adjusting the layout — narrower margins will give you more information per line, for example, and lists that run in a double column take up less space than a single column stretching down the page with white space going to waste on both sides.

If your résumé sheet begins to look cluttered, edit out some of the details. Remember that it is supposed to be a mere outline that gives only the most basic facts of your life — the facts an employer might find useful in deciding whether to hire you. And remember that the résumé sheet has a copartner in the letter of application. The résumé gives the bare essential; the application letter highlights and emphasizes, points up and interprets. The two go together; divide the responsibilities between them. Team them up, and score.

APPLICATION

1 Write a letter of request for something you actually want to receive. Be sure to encourage an answer to your letter. Getting the item or information, of course, will be the greatest test of the effectiveness of your request. You may actually create the company's sending the information or item very quickly if you put the right kind of encouragement into the request letter.

2 Imagine that you are president of a company that sells hiking gear. You have just received an order from a customer for a down jacket. You run your business according to the "you" attitude, and you intend to have this customer order something again. Write a response letter that makes the customer feel really thanked and which will bring another order at some time in the future to your company.

3 Write a response letter in which you must tell a customer *no*. Aim at the same time to keep the customer's good will. Use the "you" attitude.

4 Write a job application letter and a résumé sheet.

a Aim for a job you'd really like to have: a part-time job while you are in school, a summer job, or a full-time job you might pursue when you graduate.

b Do appropriate *creating* activities on your reasons for wanting the job and your qualifications for it.

c Arrange your information in groups labeled EDUCATION, WORK EXPERIENCE, INTERESTS/ACTIVITIES.

d With your audience in mind, select the details you will use.

e Do a rough draft for order, completeness, and appearance.

f Do a completed, final version.

WRITING A JOURNAL

Most of the writing you do for this class and others will be, in final form, an essay. That kind of writing demands that your thoughts be put in clear, logical order and be expressed in clear, well-considered sentences. In short, it requires finished, polished, ordered, deliberate work. Furthermore, almost every writing assignment that you get in later years will have the same requirements. Given that fact, what justification can there be for a chapter on journal writing in a text on college writing?

There are four good reasons for writing regularly in a journal, and all of them contribute significantly to your skill, range, control, ease, and strength as a writer. First, **your journal provides a rich resource that you can draw on when you're writing your essays**—a treasure trove of topics, subjects, observations, thoughts, and expressions. Ross Winterowd calls this aspect of journal writing "catching the shadow of an idea and recording it so it won't get lost." Second, because you make regular entries in it, **a journal gives you regular and frequent opportunity to practice the writing skills you're acquiring.** In writing, as in so many other activities, the more you practice the more proficient you become. Third, **keeping a journal will sharpen your senses.** You become alert to sensations, sights, sounds, tastes, smells, images, dreams, wishes, gripes, conversations—because you're deliberately looking, consciously seeking material that you'd enjoy putting into your journal. Looking for material, you begin to pay attention to things that before would have just slipped by. And as you record your observations, you reinforce the habit of being observant. Fourth, and best of all, **a journal is a source and record of your growth as a writer and as a person.** It contains a record of significant moments in your life. Rereading it is like flipping through a photograph album, except better, because a journal gives you much more than just the glossy image. And because journal writing encourages you to look for significances, the very seeking in turn provides for your outward expansion and growth.

IT'S __NOT__ YOUR GRADE SCHOOL DIARY

How exactly does a journal work, anyhow? You may be remembering the diary you tried keeping in grade school, the one that recorded the date and weather and the fact that you went to school on schooldays and "played" on the weekends. How is a journal different from that?

Nearly all grade school diaries merely tell what happened—it rained or it didn't, you got kissed or you didn't. A journal may also contain those events, but it gets much more into the events, how they looked, smelled, sounded, tasted, felt. *It does its best to capture the things themselves; and it gets at the significance of the things.* Journal writing develops a special state of mind, or attitude. You develop, cultivate, encourage a quiet thoughtfulness. Rather than simply say that such-and-such happened, you begin to really think about it—find out what, exactly, is meaningful about it.

Sometimes it can merely catch a moment out of your day, but a moment intensely observed. This example will help make this clear. Last week after a sudden light rain, one of your authors, Greg, wrote about this experience:

> Lovely, pale-green, almost white, just-barely-green butterfly looking like a nervous leaf—looking so much like a leaf that you wonder why it's folding in the middle. It's gotten wet, caught in a quick summer rain. I think it can't fly because it's wet and its wings are too heavy. Such a delicate thing, to be undone by a drop or two of water. I see why butterflies are symbols of beauty *and* impermanence. On the ground, among brown fallen leaves and under new bright light-green leaves. I'm glad I saw it.

When that passage was later reread, it conferred great pleasure. In the fourth grade, this same writer might have written, "I saw a butterfly today." That's the difference. In the Foreword to *Essays of E. B. White,* the author writes:

The essayist is a self-liberated man, sustained by the childish belief that everything he thinks about, everything that happens to him, is of general interest. He is a fellow who thoroughly enjoys his work, just as people who take bird walks enjoy theirs. Each new excursion of the essayist, each new "attempt," differs from the last and takes him into new country. This delights him.

It's that sense of delight, that everything is interesting—that's the attitude that your journal can develop in you. And while the essayist needs to be concerned about whether his or her writing *is* of "general" interest, the journal-keeper need be on the lookout only for those things that are *personally* interesting. For after all, the journal is primarily for the journal-writer; it is primarily a matter of personal interest and preference. More about this later.

ACCUMULATING A RICH RESOURCE

As you use the journal to develop your capacity to observe, to respond, to catch the wonder and joy and marvelousness of life, you don't need to *do* anything with it. You just let the observations accumulate. Sometimes you simply record an event and use it as an excuse to flex your language and contact something real—as in the butterfly passage above—an excuse to become observant and thoughtful. If that turns out to be something that you later want to work up into an essay, fine. If you can take a piece of it—an image, phrase, insight, comparison—and use that bit in an essay, more power to you. Some entries will seem to have more "essay potential" than others. What's important, though, for you as writer is that *you are getting into the habit of linking writing to thinking.* You'll also have a pile of written thoughts that you can draw upon, depart from, develop. And if you've been one of those who have always churned out the un-thought-out 500-word theme, you'll appreciate the advance here.

One way of becoming a person who *has* something to say is to **notice how language can put you in contact with a thing—or how it prevents contact.** For example, think of all the words and expressions for *rain* that country people are likely to have, and how few city people are likely to have. If *rain* is the only word for it, it's clear that language is not providing much contact. Anthropologists report that Eskimos have nearly 30 words for *snow*, that desert nomads have more than 20 words for *sandstorm*, and Trobriand Islanders have more than 40 words for *sweet potato*. Well, if you're an Eskimo, a desert nomad, or a Trobriander, you pretty well grow up without much noticing that variety, the way a fish grows up without noticing that it's in water. However, there can be moments of noticing, and those moments can start the insight rolling.

One way we use language to dismiss a thing, to box it up and ship it off, is to oversimplify the thing. "That's just a penny." "That's just a

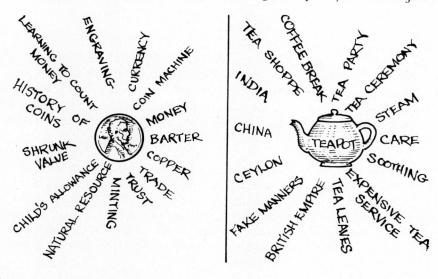

teapot." The *journal attitude* invites you to notice when words are being used to stop thought, to take something for granted, to dismiss it. Then you can break through those dull, dismissing boxes and discover the riches within. **Break through by thinking of all the *other* words there might be for that thing. Think of all the possible significances that thing might have for you, for someone else in your time, for someone in the past, for someone in the future.** You'll see yourself having quite a lot to say, interesting things, things only *you* could have come up with, things that will help other people get in contact with experience, life, existence, significance, wonder.

Or **break through by *really seeing* what you're only looking at.** That is, go beyond mere looking at it, and experience it fully, openly, as it really is.

JOURNAL WRITING AND ESSAY WRITING

Journal writing differs from essay writing because there is much less composing. There's almost no concern whatever about selecting, ordering, arranging, fitting the writing to the audience. Journal writing is much freer, and many people find it more fun because there's no censorship. **There's no one way it *has* to be—and there are no rules.** It can be any length on any subject, as serious or as silly as you want. It doesn't even have to be in sentences; sentence fragments, or lists of words, will do as well. You can draw in your journal, too, doodle and sketch away if you want to.

There's simply the pleasure of developing, the joy of discovery, the satisfaction of working out the significance of something, for yourself. Journal writing gives you a quiet place to withdraw to, where you can **get in touch with yourself,** give yourself a breathing spell—just you and your journal in your corner of the world.

Journal writing is also a way of keeping your writing loose, fluent, and free from self-consciousness. The rhythms and conventions of private writing are much different from those of public writing, usually—so **let your journal writing be natural, *your* way of doing it.**

Journal writing will automatically stimulate ideas and *serve as a "file" or "reference desk"* where good ideas are kept. Often good ideas can be developed into powerful and effective essays—but the journal serves perfectly well, even if *none* of the entries finds its way into any of your formal writing: the journal develops facility with thinking and writing. And it is also its own reward; there's *no obligation* to do anything with the journal except to enjoy it (and, of course, write in it regularly). That alone will produce amazing results and is worth the time and effort even if there weren't other benefits (and, of course, there *are* other benefits).

To accumulate a rich
resource

To record (and stimulate)
personal growth

To sharpen powers of
observation

ACCUMULATING

Now that you know what is meant by *journal* and the *journal attitude*, here are some specific activities you can do in your journal, grouped according to the kind of proficiency each develops—accumulating a rich resource of ideas, sharpening powers of observation, and recording (and stimulating) personal growth. The fourth proficiency, practicing writing, is obviously a part of each of the other three. There may be other overlapping, too; this list of activities can only scratch the surface of possible ways of writing in your journal. Feel free to follow your own inclinations and use these suggestions as pump-priming. You'll discover your own natural modifications and will want to extend these activities as you go along.

APPLICATION

ACCUMULATING

Read through all these activities to get your creative juices flowing. If, while you're reading, you feel like writing, fine. *Stop reading and start writing!* When you've finished writing, come back and finish the reading.

1   Record some bit of overheard talk or something you have read. Think about why it had some impact on you. Then cultivate the *journal attitude* by exploring some of the ways this bit is meaningful to you.

2   When you notice a resemblance between two things, write it in your journal. You can even do the comparison game by thinking of the most unlikely pair of things that you can think of: a brick and a banana, a flea and an elephant, a toaster and a pencil, a piece of yarn and a telephone. Or take two very similar things—two nickles, two cheerleaders, two drummers, two blades of grass—and list all the differences you can think of. The point of the game is to go *beyond* the obvious, so that when it gets hard, it gets good.

3   Describe a picture that has special meaning for you. A photo of your grandfather in front of his workbench, your mother with her hands held as she always holds them, two friends with arms around each other's shoulders. Maybe a snapshot that catches your brother looking thoughtful, your sister in a baseball uniform, somebody looking through a window or standing in line. Describe the picture in a way that explains what it means to you.

You can do the same for a painting, a billboard, poster, song, dance program, movie, sculpture, trophy, pottery, etc.

4 Write a letter to someone you don't know—maybe someone famous or dead or both. What would you say to Steve Martin? to Winston Churchill? to Attila the Hun? to Florence Nightingale? Hellen Keller? Joan of Arc? Shakespeare? Amy Carter? Coretta King? Oral Roberts? Pope John Paul II? Tell the person whatever you want to. Admire, sympathize, scold—whatever.

5 Write about something you've changed your mind about. As we live, our attitudes change. Tell what you used to think about something, what happened to change your mind, or what happened when you realized you no longer thought the old way about it, and what you think now. Perhaps something like a political party, or something you used to collect—stamps, dolls, model cars—that doesn't seem interesting or worthwhile now. Perhaps your attitude toward some food that you used to eat but don't eat now, or vice-versa. Perhaps your attitude toward people who lived in a certain place or dressed or spoke in a certain way.

6 Write about something you used to love as a child. Marbles? Cars? Doing tricks with a yo-yo? Skipping rope? Riding a trike? Playing dolls? Splashing in rain puddles? Eating popsicles in the summer? Building a snowman? Tell how good it used to be.

7 Describe an experience that was a turning point for you. We all have lots of these; think of one and tell what happened. Perhaps it was the day you finally knew you could swim, the time you realized your parents' relationship to each other, the time when you knew you really belonged, the time you discovered you were a small fish in a big pond. Write about (a) what happened and (b) what you realized.

Here's an example by Anaïs Nin from her *Diary: 1931–1934:*

There was a meeting of psychoanalysts, and there were seven of us in the train going to Long Beach.

The long, sad boardwalk, with its scraping noise of feet on wood. Crowds. Discord between sea and voices, voices screeching like owls, discord between the colorlessness of the sea and the crude raw colors of movie advertisements, between the smell of hot dogs and the smell of fish, angry flying clouds and grit of sand. The crowd walking, chewing, the wind stirring up dyed hair, the salt so bitter in the bite of the wind on the lips, bold houses which should have been hiding, exposing diseased façades, open-jawed shops with loud-speakers deriding the hiss of the sea, announcing the sale of furniture, of horoscopes, of dolls. The long boardwalk, gritty to walk upon, a fair of monsters exposed without charge, faces of owls, rictuses of walruses, the eyes of sting rays. A hotel which looked like a penitentiary on the outside and like a brothel inside, all red and gold. The sea was there, its rhythm broken by radios blaring. The vast dining room where everyone had passed, no one had passed, all bearing names on their lapels. Conventions. The sea cannot enter. Dusty curtains are drawn, and there are too many waiters, too many signs on the doors, too many bells, too many mirrors, rugs, cigar butts in vases filled with sand. The sea was concealed and silenced.

It was that day, at a dinner, with a tag on my shoulder, that I discovered I did not belong to the world of psychoanalysis. My game was always exposed. At the door there is always a ticket collector asking: "Is it real? Are you real? Are you a psychoanalyst?" They always know I am a fraud. They do not take me in. It seemed to me that day that all of them were examining fragments which should never have been separated except in a laboratory. I was not a scientist. I was seeking a form of life which would be continuous like a symphony. The key word was the sea. It was this oceanic life which was being put in bottles and labeled. Underneath my feet, moving restlessly beneath the very floor of the hotel, was the sea, and my nature which would never amalgamate with analysis in any permanent marriage. I could not hear the discussion. I was listening for the sea's roar and pulse.

It was that day I realized once more that I was a writer, and only a writer, a writer and not a psychoanalyst.

I was ready to return home and write a novel.

A few days later I sailed for home. When I left, New York was covered with fog. I could only hear the ship's sirens.

SHARPENING

Journals are a lot of things, including a record of your perceptions and sensations. Writing is the kind of activity that can cause you to see the world with fresh eyes—look closer and sharper and clearer. It can make you more aware of each sense, and that awareness will in turn expand your range of perception and response.

In a way, developing the senses is merely extending the *journal attitude;* it is simply another area to be aware of and thoughtful about. And it will provide lots of new material to write about, too. For example, if one day you're sitting and wondering what to write for your journal entry and you see an ant walking across your table, you can either dismiss that ("Oh, that's just an ant"), as sometimes language dismisses things, or you can focus your attention on observing the ant—not just looking at it, but really *seeing* it in full detail. How large is it? How is its body shaped? How many legs? Does it have antennae? Where are they located, exactly? How does it walk—what is the pattern of movement with the legs? Does it go along at a steady pace or in a series of darting movements? Does it keep to the same direction, or move here and there? What happens when it comes to an obstacle (your pencil, your paper, your finger)? What color is it? What exactly is it doing? How long have you observed it? What happened between when you first "saw" it and when you began to *observe* it? All that can make for really interesting writing.

Strangely enough, there is considerable evidence that people live most of their lives in their heads talking to themselves about things they remember from the past or things they imagine. Cultivating awareness of the senses, ability to observe and respond to what is right here and right now, is a way of getting in touch with reality and will give great energy, a sense of well-being, and a sense of importance and excitement to "ordinary" moments. These are *sharpening* activities, and they are a way of waking you up and making your senses really work for you.

We must learn to reawaken and keep ourselves awake, not by mechanical aids, but by an infinite expectation of the dawn, which does not forsake us in our soundest sleep.
— Thoreau

Most of us are awake to our senses about 1/24 of the time—if that much. Yet if we couldn't screen things out we could hardly concentrate on any single thing, and certainly we would be too distracted to get anything accomplished. Yet how refreshed and energized we feel when we do wake up for that fifteen minutes!

The following activities offer specific directions of things to do that help you wake up the other 23/24 of the time—things that will probably give you a sense of alertness and excitement, awareness and aliveness. You can look on these as minivacations if you like, or simply as interesting experiments. Or you can think of them simply as exercises. However you approach them, though, you'll have your awareness tweaked during the activity, and chances are excellent that you'll have flashes later when what you did in the activities resurfaces with a new application to a new experience.

APPLICATION

SHARPENING SEEING

1 Look at something you don't understand—a circuit diagram, a topographical map, a complicated machine (sewing machine, car engine). Notice what you *see* when you look at it. Then have someone who knows about it explain it to you. *Now* what do you see?

2 Look at the pattern of the cross section of a lemon, apple, orange, cucumber, tomato, grapefruit. Note the patterns carefully, then put the object out of sight and draw it from memory. When you've finished your drawing, get the object out and look again. Then write about the difference between looking at a thing and observing it.

3 Draw some familiar object from memory: a deodorant tube, lamp, telephone, housekey. When you've finished drawing it from memory, put that drawing aside. Then, with the object in front of you, draw from direct observation. When you finish the second drawing, get everything out of sight—things, drawings—and make a third drawing, again from memory. What did you "learn"?

4 Write about seeing something (or somebody) for the first time. When you become aware of something for the first time, what do you notice? After a while, do you notice different things—that is, does your attention shift to other visual qualities? Do some things matter more in the beginning than they do later on? ("The first time we saw a huge Texas sunset behind the campus watertower, it almost literally took our breath away; later, though it remained spectacular, it no longer had the power to stop us in our tracks. And the more familiar we became with the sky, the more our seeing shifted from the sky to the things on the ground: the walks, buildings, trees, grass.")

APPLICATION

SHARPENING HEARING

1 Watch TV with the sound off. What do you notice different?

2 Watch TV with the sound on but the picture blacked out. Again, what happens?

3 Why do people take portable radios to the beach, to the mountains?

4 Neon lights, traffic, talk in a lunchroom, machines in a laundromat—what rhythms are there?

5 What memories of sounds do you have? (Creak of a wicker chair, creak in floor, way a door slams, early morning farm sounds, street sounds, sounds of familiar footsteps coming upstairs.)

6 What can you hear when it's "quiet"?

7 What can you hear when it's "noisy"?

APPLICATION

SHARPENING SMELL

1 Try tasting something while you're holding your nose.

2 Really smell something *before* you taste it—coffee, dried fruit, sliced tomato, pizza. Get right down on it and sniff! Pick out all the smells that you can separate. Really enjoy the experience of smelling your food. *Then* taste it. Well?

3 Think of places that have special smells. "This smells like a cabin ought to smell." "I don't like the way this hotel smells." Woods, wood-yards, gymnasiums, locker rooms, poolhalls, perfume counters, basketball courts, clothing stores, candy shops, leather stores, hayfields, tobacco barns, bakeries. How far away can you pick up that first whiff? As you approach? Through the door?

4 Think of things that have special smells. Your father's chair smelled different from your mother's. Closets? Bureau drawers? Attics? Trunks? Old books? Cedar chests? How do they smell? What special associations do they have?

5 What smells are associated with certain days: Christmas, Hanukkah, 4th of July, Labor Day, family reunion, picnic, Thanksgiving, birthday.

6 Did you ever get used to a smell, take it for granted, and be surprised by it later? For example, a whiff of sagebrush that reminded you of a place you visited as a child. The smell of wet dirt after a rain. The smell of the factory in town. Apples on the ground. Neighborhood grocery store. What smells trigger memories?

APPLICATION

SHARPENING TASTE

1 Buy something new to eat at the grocery store, something brand new to you. Bring it home and eat it. Describe the experience. Order a brand-new dish at a new restaurant. When you get home, describe that ordering/eating/tasting experience.

2 Discuss tasting something new at somebody's house—chili? raki? taramosalata? grits? pheasant? venison? rabbit? strawberry cake? Did you know it was new before you tasted it? How did you feel about trying it? (Does that keep you from trying new things?)

3 Discuss something *you* really like to taste—a particular flavor of ice cream, steak fixed a special way, fresh creamed corn, omelettes, hot spiced sausage.

4 Taste memories. Remember the taste of wood tongue depressors? Cafeteria silverware? Library paste? Crayons? Remember something you used to taste long ago—a table top, doorknob, water faucet—and let the memories flow from that remembered taste. Cinnamon toothpicks, chlorine pool water, grass stems, a yellow pencil, an eraser.

APPLICATION

SHARPENING TOUCH

1 What exactly is the difference in feeling between sandpaper and a feather?

2 People like to rub old coins, an old watch, a worn medal, or a new shiny bolt. What accounts for the satisfaction we get from touching such things?

3 Consider things that you dislike touching. Make a list. Get some friends to make a list. How many items appear on *many* lists? How many appear on only one or two? What does that suggest about where we develop our preferences about touching things?

4 Round up a golf ball, a marble, a ping-pong ball, and a steel ball bearing. Carefully explore them by touch — any two of them, or all four. Consider such things as density and temperature, as well as rough/smooth, heavy/light, etc.

5 What can you feel with your feet? Put on wet shoes. Stand barefoot on a cold floor, on a carpet, on gravel, on boards, on grass.

6 Compare a dry leaf to a live one. Experiment with the touch of each: veins, stem, tissue. Experience the pliability, the brittleness, the definition of the separate parts.

USE THE JOURNAL TO RECORD (AND STIMULATE) PERSONAL GROWTH

Someone once compared life to a river, starting out at a spring or a trickle at the edge of a snowfield, becoming larger and deeper as more currents feed in, joining larger currents still, moving swiftly sometimes, slowly sometimes, with occasional shallow spots, rapids, snags — but always in motion, always changing. One reason journal writing is so pleasurable and so important is that you are able to mark your path, chart where you've been, what you were doing at a particular time, what you thought. *It is a record of the path your life takes, a record of your progress.* You experience the pleasure of saying things on paper, expanding yourself, taking measure. Looking back you see how life passes on, how all things work out, how everything is just a spot in the entire continuum.

In that sense, everything you write in your journal serves to capture and reflect one person's unique way of seeing the world. So no matter what you write about, it will give you a sense of history and perspective about your life. Whatever you choose to put in there is a picture of you simply because it is something that *you* chose out of all the welter of stuff there is out there in the world. Rereading your journal, you can probably make some interesting discoveries about your life from those things alone even if you said nothing else, made no remarks about them. (On the TV program "60 Minutes," experts claimed the ability to reconstruct your life from just your checkbook!) So a journal, even if it's limited to objective events, can be a chart of where you were in your personal growth at a particular time.

Yet there are other activities that are particularly effective in themselves for providing stretching, growth. Writing dialogues will enlarge your point of view by imagining what another person might say from his or her position. Writing about critical situations lets you consider various consequences and prepare for eventualities. Watching for areas of growth helps to produce those areas of growth. For example, if the

> I went to the woods because I wished to live deliberately, . . .
> — Thoreau

journal directions ask you to write about something new that you have just learned, you become aware of how much you do learn or how much you don't. Either way, focusing your attention on your growth produces awareness of growth, and that in turn promotes further growth.

Also, *your struggle for self-expression is a struggle for style.* One of the "records" your journal will provide is a track of the development of your many and various styles. Activities that encourage this are also stretching, developing activities, just as those that express the self result in adjustment to, or reconciliation with, some situation. And getting things "off your mind" is a way of clearing up your mind for other things—and that too facilitates the flow.

What's at stake for you as writer is that the use of language is one of the most important means of expression that a human being possesses with which to construct the self. The self is always defined by its doing something to achieve its intentions. Humans use language to achieve the projects that they value. What's significant about journal writing is that there is a personal stake in it for the writer. The focus is on you, the writer. It is you who dominate this writing, and it is by this writing that you achieve new aspects of your individuality. In the discovery of self is the discovery of style, and vice-versa. But by translating self into written language, you objectify the self, put it outside your head and onto paper; you "stop the river" at that place. You look at the river from a fresh viewpoint, imagining how someone else might view it; you see it from above the surface and below, from before and after. This translation of experience for yourself alone is of course a preliminary for the translation of experience for others. *Private writing is a valuable prelude to public writing.*

APPLICATION

TO RECORD (AND STIMULATE) PERSONAL GROWTH

1 Record something important to you. Begin it by writing, "Right now what's important to me is _____." Then explain what it is and the ways it is important.

READ A JOURNAL TODAY:

Pepys
George Sand
Samuel Johnson
Ninn
Anne Frank
Lewis & Clark
Holt
Coleridge
Terkel

2 How do you feel in different kinds of weather? When you're aware of particularly strong reactions to weather—say, after five days of rain—write about that. Is it too hot, too cold, too wet, too dry? For what? Does your attitude toward the weather have anything to do with the rest of your life—for example, are you more likely to gripe about the weather if you have a big test coming up or you're having a squabble with somebody important? Check it out.

3 Experiment with feeling a new way about the weather. If you always hate the rain, see if you can find *anything* at all to like about it. Even to be happy about. You can't control the weather, but maybe you can learn really to enjoy all of it.

4 Prepare for a critical situation that is likely to happen fairly soon. Imagine exactly what will happen and write a description of it. List all the possible outcomes and figure out what you'll do about each. When you've finished writing about it, how do you feel about that situation?

5 On a day you feel really down and energyless, write about that. Really get into it, and be as specific as you can about exactly how you feel; get all the details you can — how your body feels, how the world looks, how you look at the rest of the world. When you finish writing that description, see if you still feel the same.

6 Next time your inner voice says, "No you can't, you're not strong enough, smart enough, good-looking enough," etc., write a dialogue between you and the little voice in which you argue back. Really put that little voice in its place. Do this activity as often as you like — that little voice has had free reign for possibly your whole life, and it deserves a lot of answering.

7 Learn five new things every day for a week. At the end of each day list the five things. At the end of the week, look over your lists. What can you say about the things you learned? What did you learn from doing the activity? Did you let anyone know about what you were doing? What was the reaction? What did you say? What would you say now? Would you do it again? Why or why not?

8 Tell the truth. Do it for every situation. Do not lie, fudge, fib, weasel, prevaricate, or bend the truth, nor tell even a little white lie. Tell the truth. At the end of each day, record incidents that made this activity easy or hard, frustrating or rewarding. At the end of the week, write whether telling the truth helps or hinders your growth. What is the truth about telling the truth?

9 For a week, keep every agreement you make. Absolutely. If that means you don't have time to sleep, don't sleep. If that means you have to cut down the number of things you try to get done, cut them down. If that means you have to miss a meal or two, miss them. After a week of keeping your agreements, how is your life running?

10 Respond to what you read. Copy it, comment on it, criticize it, praise it.

17 THINGS TO DO IN A JOURNAL

Walter Clark, University of Michigan

1 Copy poems, sentences, paragraphs, graffiti, cemetery road signs, sayings.
2 Write first drafts of letters.
3 Write about how hard, irritating, absurd, impossible, it is to write in a journal.
4 Make word associations.
5 Note things from classes and reading that catch your fancy.
6 Make pen or pencil sketches (draw a leaf).
7 Describe things. What is the color of a pine trunk?
8 Describe people. (What do they do? What are they aware of? What *would* they do in specific situations? What do they seem to feel? What do you feel about them?)
9 *Where* are you?
10 Search for questions.
11 Explain the difference between living in the town and living in the country. (Where are *they*?)
12 Explain the difference between having an education and making an education.
13 Tell lies.
14 Record: dreams, weather, drinks, replies you made or should have, intentions.
15 Give commands!
16 List books you want to read later.
17 Write "Kilroy was here."

THE HANDBOOK

PARTS OF SPEECH

Why should you know what a part of speech is? If you had never learned that a noun is the name of a person, place, thing, or idea, wouldn't you still be able to speak and write English? You certainly would. You would have learned (internalized) the rules for making English sentences and for using English words just by listening to others speak. But even a person who has never studied grammar formally can tell you that only certain words can occur in certain positions in a sentence. When you study parts of speech, you learn why this is so.

Words are assigned to a specific part of speech according to the functions they perform in a sentence. While many function as the same part of speech in every sentence (for example, *the, beside, of, Susan, he*), most may function as several parts of speech. Look at this list of words: *arm, finger, table, position*. Most of us would readily agree that they are all nouns since they all name things. But in actual use they can be several parts of speech, as these sentences illustrate:

Armed with a yellow pad and a dozen sharp pencils, Mike decided to begin his theme.

Mom plans to buy an *arm*chair for Dad.

She *fingered* the imported silk blouse longingly.

Pass me another *finger* sandwich.

After a fruitless three-hour meeting, the frustrated committee voted to *table* the motion.

I found an antique *table* lamp at the auction yesterday.

Resigned to an afternoon of studying, she *positioned* herself under the oak.

The administration has issued *position* papers on a number of issues.

If you were to insist that each of the words above could be used only as a noun simply because it names an object, you would give up some creative uses of the words. Understanding the function that each part of speech performs can help you use words imaginatively and purposefully. This is why studying parts of speech is valuable. To know how to use English creatively, you must understand how words work together to create meaning.

In studying parts of speech, you study the internal structure of English, and studying the internal structure of anything helps you understand the whole much better. Those who understand what goes on under the hood of a car understand why a car runs smoothly, why it won't start sometimes, why it jerks strangely. Those who know how to sew understand what's wrong with a garment when "it just doesn't fit right." The same is true of words: knowing something about parts of speech enables you to see why a sentence doesn't sound right—and it helps you fix it so that it does sound right.

Words in English are classified into eight parts of speech: noun, pronoun, verb, adverb, adjective, preposition, conjunction, and interjection.

NOUN

Although this is not a complete definition, a noun names a person, place, thing, or idea. Nouns can be divided into two broad categories: proper nouns and common nouns.

1 A proper noun names a specific person, place, thing, or idea:

William Shakespeare	The Netherlands
Robert Redford	Saturn
The Queen Mary	the Revolutionary War
Chicago	the Washington Monument
King Tut	the Sphinx

Proper nouns are always capitalized.

2 A common noun names a person, place, thing, or idea that is one of many others in a class. Most nouns are common.

girl	railroad	pillar	universe	assumption
toy	honesty	sky	mind	development

Notice that these nouns name very different things. Is *honesty* a naming word in the same way *toy* is? What does *development* name?

Clearly, nouns can be very different from each other. To help us identify the differences among them, we can assign *features* to nouns.

Noun Features

1 Nouns may be abstract or concrete. Abstract nouns name ideas, events, and other things that are intangible:

joy	Civil War	category	manner
growth	Christianity	marriage	motherhood

Concrete nouns name things that are tangible, that can be touched, felt, seen, or experienced in some way:

pen   woman   sofa   house   head   dog

2 Nouns may be human or non-human:

man	Art Buchwald	girl	waiter
nurse	Trigger	Cleopatra	elephant

3 Nouns may be masculine or feminine:

lion	daughter	gander
tigress	widow	widower

4 Nouns may be animate or inanimate. Animate nouns name living things:

ameoba   animal   goldfish   engineer   teacher

Inanimate nouns name nonliving things:

rock   ocean   chair   mountain   water   cloud

These features are important because they restrict the kinds of words that nouns may combine with to form meaningful sentences. Certain verbs must have animate nouns, others only abstract nouns, and so on. When you ignore the features of a noun, you may produce the kind of sentence that teachers label *awk,* like the following one:

Any person absent on the final day of class would have meant that the end-of-school party could not be held.

This sentence is awkward because the verb—*would have meant*—should take an abstract, nonhuman subject instead of the concrete, human *person.* Revision should clear up the problem:

Even one person's absence would have meant that the end-of-school party could not be held.

Now the abstract subject *absence* fits the verb.

Noun Functions

Nouns have two basic functions in sentences: they may be subjects or objects. As a subject, a noun announces the topic of a sentence or a clause. In the sentences below, the nouns that function as subjects are underlined:

When the sudden <u>rainstorm</u> ended, the <u>swimmers</u> returned to the lake.

The <u>president</u> will make an important foreign-policy statement to-night.

The <u>desk</u> occupies most of my office.

As an object, a noun completes the meaning of a verb or verbal (verbals will be discussed in detail under *verbs*) or it joins with a preposition to form a prepositional phrase. The nouns used as objects are underlined in these sentences:

OBJECT OF THE VERB: I finally finished my <u>term paper</u> at 3:00 A.M.
The president vetoed the <u>tax reform bill</u>.

OBJECT OF A VERBAL: Typing that <u>paper</u> was hard work.
I still plan to write a <u>book</u> someday.

OBJECT OF A PREPOSITION: During its last <u>session</u>, Congress gave itself a raise.
I asked the movers to place the couch against the <u>wall</u> in the <u>living room</u>.

Noun Identifiers

Nouns can be made *plural*, and they can be made *possessive*. (There are some exceptions, but this is a general rule.) Nouns are usually made plural by adding *s* or *es*: taco/tacos; beach/beaches; radio/radios

Some nouns are irregular, and their plurals are exceptions: ox/oxen; foot/feet; knife/knives

Usually, a noun is made possessive by adding an apostrophe and an *s*: *'s*
fire/fire's warmth   writer/writer's desk

Making a noun possessive is one of the hardest things for beginning writers to get right. You have to decide if the noun is going to be plural possessive or singular possessive (this merely means that you have to know if you are talking about one thing/person or more than one). The placement of the apostrophe in the possessive depends on whether the word is singular or plural.

The lady's coat (singular possessive) The ladies' coats (plural possessive)

APPLICATION

1   Pick out the nouns in the following passage and describe their function in the sentences.

People in Oregon can get fresh shrimp almost any time of the year. They can also get salmon, tuna, and oysters. Prices will be highest in January-March. Most markets will prepare the fresh fish for you, and some markets will even dry or can the fish if you have no way to preserve it at home. The old fishing villages along the coast are some of the best sources for seafood and fish.

2   Identify the nouns in the following sentences:

1 Skylab Watch is something I hope I never have to worry about again.

2 Worry will give you ulcers.

3 Her manner suggested that she was tired.

4 The combination of peaches and strawberries was a delicious concoction.

5 The lions' manes made beautiful patterns on the zoo sidewalk.

PRONOUNS

Pronouns are usually defined as noun substitutes because they frequently replace nouns mentioned earlier in a sentence or in a previous sentence. As noun substitutes, pronouns are important in reducing redundancy in sentences. Look at this sentence, for example:

John broke his leg as he was climbing down the mountain.

We know that each pronoun refers to *John,* but it would be frustrating and redundant to rename John each time we refer to him:

John broke John's leg as John was climbing down the mountain.

One of the most important functions of the pronoun, then, is to make communication more efficient by eliminating unnecessary repetition of nouns.

Pronouns are considered noun substitutes for another reason: they perform the same functions nouns do. They serve as subjects of sentences and clauses or as objects of verbs and prepositions.

This is my favorite book.   (subject)

I refuse to go to that class one more time.   (subject)

I explained to *him* why *I* was not going.   (subject of sentence & clause and object of preposition)

You don't mean *that,* do you?   (object of the verb)

My jeans are different from *those.*   (object of preposition)

Because of their close relationship to nouns, pronouns could be considered a kind of noun, and many grammarians and linguists classify them as nouns. However, they perform so many functions that they must be considered a separate part of speech which can be broken down further.

Personal Pronouns: I, you, he, she, it, we, they, me, him, her, us, them
These occur in the same positions as nouns, but notice that the form of the pronoun changes with its function in the sentence. If it is used as a subject, the *nominative* form is used:

I answered the telephone when *you* called.

They plan to move into the new house across the street.

But when the personal pronoun serves as an object, the *objective* form is used:

I will accompany *them* on the trip to New Mexico.

Tell *us* all about the trip.

Mary will take the trip with John and *me.*

Possessive Pronouns: my, mine, his, her, hers, its, our, ours, your, yours, their, theirs

As indicators of ownership or possession, these pronouns function just as possessive nouns do. Essentially, they modify the nouns with which they appear:

> his books, our time, my story

Reflexive Pronouns: myself, himself, herself, itself, yourself, ourselves, themselves

Reflexive pronouns occur *only* when a noun and pronoun or two pronouns in the same simple sentence or clause clearly refer to the same antecedent. This is why the pronoun is called reflexive: it is grammatically and semantically bound to the noun or pronoun it refers to. These sentences illustrate that reflexive pronouns must refer to a noun or pronoun in the same simple sentence:

> Mary considers Mary a good person. → Mary considers herself a good person.
>
> Johnny's mother had warned Johnny to behave Johnny's self before she spanked him. → Johnny's mother had warned him to behave himself before she spanked him.

Reflexive pronouns may also be used as *intensive pronouns* to provide emphasis to a noun or pronoun:

> Joan herself wrote the short story.
>
> We painted the house ourselves.
>
> I myself did all the work.
>
> The boys themselves did all the cooking.

Notice that in each case, the intensive pronoun could be omitted without detracting from the meaning of the sentence—*Joan wrote the short story.* It simply makes the noun emphatic.

Relative Pronouns: who, whose, whom, which, that, when, where, wherever

This set of pronouns replaces the noun in a relative clause. Like all other pronouns, relative pronouns are *referents;* that is, there is always a noun to which the pronoun refers:

> The dress *which* I worked on yesterday is still not finished.
>
> The street *where* Joan lives is hard to find.
>
> I remember the man *who* told me how to get there.

In the first sentence, *which* refers to *dress;* in the second, *where* refers to *street,* and in the third, *who* refers to *man.* Notice that the relative pronoun is always the first word in the relative clause.

Demonstrative Pronouns: this, that, these, those

Demonstrative pronouns function as nouns or as modifiers.

NOUNS: *This* is not what I had in mind when I suggested we have a party.

What did she mean by *that?*
Which of *those* did you want?
These are the best shoes I've ever owned.

Notice that demonstrative pronouns are somewhat vague when they are used as nouns. Out of context, you don't know what any of these pronouns refers to. In the context of longer passages of speech or writing, demonstrative pronouns always refer to a specific noun.

MODIFIERS: *Those* flowers are the freshest ones in the shop.
These women have not failed to turn in any papers on time all semester.
If you like exciting mysteries, read *this* book.

Interrogative Pronouns: who, which, what, whom, whose

Interrogative pronouns are used in questions to represent the information that is unknown.

Who is the woman you were talking to?
Whom do you plan to go home with?
What are you writing your term paper on?
Which boys were caught in the department head's office?

Like relative pronouns, interrogative pronouns always appear at the beginning of the clause or sentence since it is the unknown information that is the focus of the sentence. Unlike relative pronouns, however, the referent for these pronouns is unknown.

Indefinite Pronouns: each, everyone, anybody, either, some, somebody, one, no one, several, everybody, any, all

Indefinite pronouns may function as nouns or as modifiers:

NOUNS: Give me three copies of *each.* (object of preposition)
Some say she's the best chemistry teacher in the school. (subject)
No one came to the party. (subject)
Anybody can answer that. (subject)

Indefinite pronouns have no specific antecedent, but they are pronouns because they clearly function as noun substitutes. This set of pronouns is useful when specificity is not important to the meaning of the sentence.

MODIFIERS: *Several* boys were caught in the dean's office late last night.
One girl said she hated reading *all* the novels.
They ordered *several* cases of soft drinks for the picnic.

APPLICATION

Identify the pronouns in the following sentences:

1   Our house will have a glass dining room.

2   Several men asked if the car's electrical system has its own self-correcting mechanism.

3   Whoever has been here is not here now.

4   The place that I saw the little red fox was right over by the fence.

5   That was it.

6   Ours is not the best set of clubs, but they work fairly well.

7   David considers himself a good musician.

8   Their time was short; we asked them if they would begin the program at once.

9   Those bright red rain boots are just what I want. Do you have any?

10   Either of them will be OK, but I prefer the one that nobody has ever used at all.

VERBS

The verb may be considered the heart of the sentence because it contributes to and affects meaning more than any other element in the sentence. It determines the number of nouns needed to make a sentence meaningful. It determines the time and the quality of the action. It sometimes focuses the reader's attention on a particular part of the sentence. So when we talk about the verb, it is not enough to define it as an action word. We must study the verb as a unit in itself to see how it differs from other parts of speech, and we must also study it as one of the elements of a sentence to understand how it contributes to communication.

Verbs in English have four principal parts that form the basis of the tense system: present, past, perfect, present participle. Tense refers to the way we indicate *when* an action occurs. In English, we really have only two tenses, past and present, but we can add helping verbs and modals (to be discussed below) to make the time and quality of the action more specific and to give the illusion that there are more than two tenses.

Verbs may be *regular* or *irregular* depending on how the principal parts are formed. In regular verbs, the past and perfect are formed by adding *-ed* to the present:

Present	Past	Perfect	Present Participle
dress	dressed	dressed	dressing
cross	crossed	crossed	crossing
pass	passed	passed	passing
alert	alerted	alerted	alerting

In irregular verbs, the past and perfect sometimes show changes in the main vowel, and sometimes, the past and perfect forms are entirely different from the present:

Present	Past	Perfect	Present Participle
go	went	gone	going
lie	lay	lain	lying

Present	Past	Perfect	Present Participle
write	wrote	written	writing
do	did	done	doing
is	was/were	been	being

Principal parts are important in understanding how time (tense) is expressed by the verb. *Present* expresses action going on right now:

I *pass* by his house every day.

Tom *is* sick today.

The past expresses completed action:

He *crossed* the street without looking.

Mary *wrote* me a long letter.

The perfect also expresses past action, but the addition of *have* as a helping verb changes the *aspect* (quality) of the past action. Helping verbs will be discussed in more detail under *Auxiliary*.

He *has done* all he can do.

I *have crossed* that street many times.

The present participle is used with a form of *be* to convey the sense of continuing action or future action:

John *is going* home with me.

She *is* upstairs *dressing* for her important job interview.

The Auxiliary (helping verb)

As the sentences above show, the principal parts alone allow only limited distinctions of time and quality of action. To increase the range of action expressed by the verb, we use auxiliaries—special verbs that work with the main verb of a sentence. We have two kinds of auxiliaries in English: helping verbs and modals.

Helping verbs are forms of *have* and *be* used with the perfect and with the present participle to change the quality rather than the time of the action. Notice how a helping verb changes the quality of the past action in these sentences:

PAST: I saw all I wanted to see at the museum.

PAST PERFECT: I had seen all I wanted to see, so I went home.

PRESENT PERFECT: Since I have seen all of these exhibits before, I will skip the museum tour.

Similarly, the addition of *be* to the present participle changes the *aspect* of the action:

Since she moved to Dallas, she is writing home twice a week.

We are now passing by the capitol.

Helping verbs can be used together to further qualify the verb:

Jack has been watching TV for three hours.

The meaning of the verb *has been watching* is quite different from the simple past—John *watched* TV for three hours. The expanded meaning occurs when we combine the perfect (*have* + perfect) and the progressive (*be* + present participle).

Modals are special kinds of verbs used with any of the principal parts to express the mode of the action. The modal indicates whether action is possible, permitted, required, or desired. The list of modals is short:

can	may	must	will	shall
could	might	ought	would	should

Things to remember about modals:

1 Modals always appear before the main verb:

I *can* finish this tonight if I hurry.

He *will* call me when he's ready.

2 When modals are used with helping verbs, the perfect or progressive markers (*-ed* or *-ing*) follow the modal:

He could have *been* a good writer if he had tried.

You should have been *studying* instead of sleeping.

3 Modals must be used with other verbs; a modal alone does not express action. Try writing a sentence using only *shall* or *might* as the verb. You can't because by leaving out the verb, you leave out the heart of the sentence.

Certainly, there are times when modals appear alone:

Mary asked me if I was going to her party. I said I *might* if I finished all my work by then.

In context, we realize that *go* is the understood verb in the second sentence. Only when the context is understood do modals appear alone.

When we consider the possibilities allowed through combinations of principal parts, helping verbs, and modals, we see the versatility of English verbs:

He writes home every week.

Until this month, he had been writing home every week.

He has written more letters in two months than I have in two years.

We should write home more often.

I will write my parents tomorrow.

If I'm too busy, I may write the next day.

I must have been writing my paper in the library when you called.

Notice that the combinations reveal a rigid ordering of the main verb, helping verbs, and modals. The modals and helping verbs are optional, but when they are used, they must be ordered like this:

1	2	3	4
(modal)	(have + perfect)	(be + present participle)	verb

One may be used without the other, but the order must remain the same:

(modal)		(be + present participle)	verb
will		be	writing

(modal)	(have + perfect)		verb
could	have	written	

(modal)			verb
may			write

(have + perfect)	verb
had	written

(be + present participle)	verb
are	writing

Notice that only the first word in the verb phrase indicates tense:

PRESENT PERFECT: have written
PAST PERFECT: had been writing
PAST PERFECT: could have been writing

You can never have two indicators of time as these ungrammatical verb groups have:

could had written
can are writing

You recognize the ungrammaticality of these verbs because you know that in English only the first verb element indicates tense. This is one of the rules of English syntax.

APPLICATION

Describe the verbs in the following sentences as fully as you can. Indicate the tense and the kind of auxiliary in each.

1   They are playing in the new stadium.

2   The paper, marked the way it was, seemed to be what upset her.

3   We could have seen the moon if we had moved over just a few feet.

4   Have you looked for your watch under that vase which Mother just moved?

5   The walls are full of pictures which were painted by famous people.

6   Some people see little reason to add up their check balance each week, but I find that it is absolutely necessary if I am to keep up with how much money I have.

7   Various changes in the weather caused the vines to ripen more slowly; therefore, this was not a good year for wine.

8   When you see what I have put on your desk, you will jump for joy.

9   We have already priced the land and found that it is not reasonable.

10   Do you foresee any drying up of the wells in this vicinity?

Subject-Verb-Complement Combinations

One of the most important functions of the verb is to indicate the number of nouns needed to complete the meaning of a sentence. We know that there must always be a noun to function as the subject for the verb, but some verbs require one noun, two nouns, or an adjective as a complement (completer of the action). These verb-noun combinations are classified as intransitive, transitive, or linking.

1 When an action verb is complete without a complement, it is an intransitive verb.

> I was talking with my mother on the telephone.
> Our congressman voted against the bill.
> To get my exercise, I walk to school every day.

2 When an action verb requires a noun or nouns to complete its meaning, it is a transitive verb.

> He hit *the ball* farther than he ever had before.
> The president will almost certainly veto *the bill*.

The noun following the verb in these sentences is a direct object, but some verbs take an indirect object as well as a direct object:

>   IO   DO
> My mother taught me the alphabet when I was three.

>   IO   DO
> He gave me a beautiful corsage.

To test for an indirect object, simply reword it as a prepositional phrase that indicates at whom the action of the sentence is directed:

> My mother taught the alphabet *to me*.
> He gave a beautiful corsage *to me*.

A small group of verbs requires two objects, a direct object and an objective complement which may be either a noun or an adjective:

> In the last election, the American voters elected a Democrat *president*.
> Mary considered Tom *a bore*.
> We painted the hall *red*.

3 When the complement renames or modifies the subject, the verb is a linking verb. We have two kinds of linking verbs in English: *be* verbs and verbs that deal with the senses or with states of being. What makes the complement of a linking verb different from the complement of a transitive verb is that it may be a noun (predicate nominative) or an adjective (predicate adjective). Furthermore, this complement carries most of the meaning in a sentence whose verb is a linking verb. The function of the linking verb is to show identity between the subject of the complement, so the verb itself carries little meaning and conveys little or no action. Notice how important the underlined complements are to the meaning of these sentences. *Be* as a linking verb:

> Mary was *sick* today.
> The truth is *that I just didn't have time to do it*.
> Truth is *evasive*.

Note the underlined complements of the linking verbs:

> The heroine remained *unmarried*.
> She became *despondent* when her lover died.
> Professor Smith's clothes always look *wrinkled*.
> In his baggy pants and narrow ties, he seems *unconcerned* about style.
> I feel *awkward* every time I talk to him.

APPLICATION

Identify the verbs in the following passage as transitive, intransitive, or linking. Pick out the complements for the transitive and linking verbs.

Just past the area known as Lasseter's Country, heavy clouds began to bustle over the horizon. Down it came. It rained cats and dogs. It rained elephants and whales, and it hailed. Within an hour the track was a running river and we were all drenched, though the camels soon grew accustomed to the flapping of their orange raincoats.

Camels have feet like bald tires. They simply cannot cope with mud, and leading them over precariously slippery patches is painful and exhausting to both driver and animal. In the midst of the storm Dookie, my best boy, my wonder camel, who was last in line, suddenly sat down with a thud and snapped his noseline.

I went back to him and tried to get him up. He refused. I shouted at him and had to kick the poor beast until he groaned to his feet. To my horror I saw that he was limping. It looked as if the trip was over.

From *National Geographic* (May 1978), p. 589.

Active and Passive Voice

One way to provide focus in a sentence is to change the usual subject-verb-complement order. With an action verb, the subject functions as the doer of the action and the complement as the receiver of the action:

Bill (doer) threw (verb) the ball (receiver) powerfully to the second-baseman.

As my teacher looked over my paper, I revised several paragraphs.

The policemen chased the boys for two blocks.

Ordinarily, the doer is the focus of the sentence because he or she appears before the verb and the complement, but when you want to change the focus, you may change the *active* sentence into a *passive* sentence by putting the receiver of the action in the subject position:

The ball was thrown powerfully by Bill to the second-baseman.

The boys were chased for two blocks by the policemen.

The change from active to passive voice is a variation of the regular order of the sentence. The formula for this change is simple:

1 Transform the subject of the sentence into the agent of the action by rewriting it as a *by* prepositional phrase: by Bill, by the policemen.
2 Move the direct object (the receiver of the action) into the subject position.
3 Rewrite the verb using a form of *be (was, were, is, are)* and the perfect principal part: threw → was thrown, chased → were chased.

APPLICATION

Pick out the passive and active verbs in the following passage.

Some "inborn" defects—some defects that are the direct consequence of an individual's genetic makeup as it was fixed at the moment of conception—are said to be of *recessive* determination. By a recessive defect is meant one that is caused by, to put it crudely, a "bad" gene that must be present in both the gametes that unite to form a fertilized egg, i.e., in both spermatozoon and egg cell, not just in one or the other. If the bad gene is present in only one of the gametes, the individual that grows out of its fusion with the other is said to be a *carrier* (technically, a heterozygote).

Recessive defects are individually rather rare — their frequency is of the order of one in ten thousand — but collectively they are most important. Among them are, for example, phenylketonuria, a congenital inability to handle a certain dietary constituent, the amino acid phenylalanine, a constituent of many proteins; galactosaemia, another inborn biochemical deficiency, the victims of which cannot cope metabolically with galactose, an immediate derivative of milk sugar; and, more common than either, fibrocystic disease of the pancreas, believed to be the symptom of a generalized disorder of mucus-secreting cells. All three are caused by particular single genetic defects; but their secondary consequences are manifold and deep-seated. The phenylketonuric baby is on the way to becoming an imbecile. The victim of galactosaemia may become blind through cataract and be mentally retarded.

Verbals

Although the verb usually functions as the predicate of a sentence, certain verb forms can serve as nouns and adjectives and adverbs. When a verb functions as a different part of speech, it is called a *verbal*. We have three kinds of verbals in English: *participles, gerunds,* and *infinitives.*

A participle is a verb used as an adjective. You can recognize participles when you note the use of the perfect form or the *-ing* form of a verb to modify some noun or pronoun in the sentence. In each of these sentences, the underlined phrases are participles that modify the noun serving as the subject:

The *evaporating* mist made the morning seem muggy.

Walking through the street, Tom could see the damage the flood had done.

The *tired* man trudged in to his last job interview.

A gerund is a verb used as a noun. You can recognize a gerund when you notice an *-ing* form (the same as the present-participle form) of a verb used in a position generally filled by a noun:

Studying makes me sleepy.

Going to the lake and spending the day fishing is my idea of a good time.

An infinitive is formed by adding *to* to the present verb form. Infinitives function as nouns, adjectives, or adverbs.

NOUN: *To quit* now would be unwise.

               He plans *to read* the novel tonight.

ADJECTIVE: The best way *to write* is to isolate yourself from all distractions.

ADVERB: He is eating heavier meals *to gain* weight.

               To sleep comfortably and soundly, drink warm milk before going to bed.

As these sentences illustrate, verbals may be either single words — *evaporating, studying, to quit* — or phrases that include an object or an adverb—*to gain weight, to read the novel, walking through the street, to sleep soundly and comfortably, going to the lake.*

APPLICATION

Identify the verbals in the following sentences as gerunds, participles, or infinitives. For each verbal, explain its function in the sentence and identify its object where there is one.

1 Concentrating on your subject is the most important component of studying.

2 I begin to read hurriedly so that I can finish.

3 To avoid this, I usually take breaks while studying.

4 Approaching the area, we again dismounted and began to cautiously search the area by foot.

5 Conforming can be harmful if it causes someone to lower his own standards.

6 To be a hero, one must drastically change the flow of history and the lives of all that come into contact with him.

7 Being accustomed to buzzards and occasional hawks, we failed to pay it much mind until it started making low sweeps over the sheep.

8 Focusing on the bird, we realized it was a bald eagle.

9 The capacity to manipulate the genes of living things certainly represents an ethical crisis.

10 To succeed in college you must be willing to devote much time to studying.

ADJECTIVES

Adjectives are modifying words. Their function is to restrict the meaning of a noun by making it more specific, by describing it, or by indicating its characteristics. By adding adjectives to a noun, you make the subject more specific, which is desirable because the amount of information conveyed to a reader is increased.

Modification occurs on the level of words, phrases, and clauses:

the *healthy* girl (word)
the girl *with the rosy cheeks* (prepositional phrase)
the girl *who sat in the dentist's office* (clause)
the house *where I live* (clause)

Single-word adjectives usually occur before the nouns they modify:

the red bird the ugly house rush-hour traffic
the trickling stream the eccentric, old professor

Adjective phrases and clauses occur after the nouns they modify:

the tropical bird *with the brilliant red and blue feathers*

the eccentric old professor *whose clothes seemed at least 10 years old*
rush-hour traffic *that wastes several hours of a worker's day*
Predicate adjectives occur after *to be* verbs and linking verbs:

    The meal was *delicious.*   I feel *fine* today.

    His clothes look *wrinkled.*   She remained *despondent.*

Although there are many words that we automatically qualify as adjectives—*fast, correct, brown, first, pretty, ugly, high*—the English language allows us to form adjectives in several ways.

Adjectival endings may be added to other parts of speech:

-y	sticky	gummy	sunny	chewy
-ful	beautiful	bountiful	colorful	awful
-ive	vindictive	instructive	conducive	restive
-al	verbal	colonial	proverbial	herbal
-ic	ironic	economic	metallic	gastric

Sometimes other parts of speech serve as adjectives without an added ending:

    college textbook   *wall* hanging

    food processor   *desk* top

    lawn mower   *lawn* chair

Frequently, when other parts of speech, especially nouns, are used as modifiers, the words tend to be perceived as a single unit. For instance, in the following phrases and in most of those above, it is difficult to determine whether the structure is an adjective plus noun or simply a compound noun:

    lawn mower   brick wall   china closet

In either case, the phrases were originally formed by joining a noun used as an adjective to another noun in a modifying relationship.

As you saw in the discussion on verbs, participles are verb forms used as adjectives:

    the *grieving* parents   the *condemned* prisoner

    the *tired* man   the *assigned* essay

    the paint *peeling* off the walls   the clothes looked *wrinkled*

The degree of modification can be altered through comparative and superlative forms:

    the tallest boy   the older brother   the happiest girl

    a most fortunate incident   the more appropriate answer

Adjectives are important in writing because of the effect they have on style and meaning. They qualify and restrict the meaning of nouns, but they can also make reading tedious. Think of all the books you have read in which the author gets involved in lengthy descriptive passages. When we are in a hurry to get on with the story, we frequently skim over these "colorful" passages. However, we can't arbitrarily claim that adjectives make writing good or bad. The effectiveness of adjectives depends on the writer's purpose.

In newspaper writing, for instance, adjectives are considered undesirable. The goal in news reporting is objectivity, and descriptive words detract from objectivity. Journalists concerned primarily with conveying information limit their use of adjectives so as to keep their own impressions out of the objective news account. Notice how the writer of the wire story below limits the use of adjectives:

The world's first "test-tube baby," delivered by Caesarean section a week early because of a threat of blood poisoning, is in excellent condition, her doctors said Wednesday.

Gynecologist Patrick Steptoe assured a news conference that the 5-pound, 12-ounce daughter of Mrs. Lesley Brown, 30, was in excellent condition despite the mild emergency that led to the decision to operate. She was born at 11:47 P.M. Tuesday night at Oldham General Hospital.

However, when objectivity is not as important, adjectives contribute to the vividness of the writing:

From the luscious coolness of a freshly cut watermelon to the fragrance of an abundant blueberry bush, the pleasures of summer fruits abound. This is the season to savor perfectly ripened peaches, sweet but slightly tart raspberries, the richness and color of a bunch of green grapes, and delectably juicy cherries — each taste a fond reminder of one's first encounter with these memorable flavors.

From *Gourmet* (August 1978), p. 30.

Adjectives may be the most misunderstood part of speech. When writing is dull and colorless, an easy remedy seems to be to add adjectives. But, sometimes, adjectives add nothing to writing. If adjectives are vague or general—good, great, wonderful—writing is no more vivid than it is without the modification. Adjectives, then, should be used carefully, deliberately, and consciously. In themselves, adjectives are neither good nor bad. It is only in context that they are useful and effective.

ADVERBS

Adverbs, like adjectives, are modifying words, phrases, or clauses. They add specificity to the action in a sentence when they modify verbs, but they can also modify adjectives and other adverbs. The following sentences show the variety of functions and positions that adverbs (or phrases and clauses serving as adverbs) can take:

Finally, my mother agreed to let me go.

Fortunately, she also agreed to help me pay for my expenses.

We were scheduled to meet *in the park.*

During the party, they threw me *in the pool.*

I learned much about literature *when I took Professor Smith's course.*

To lose weight, I plan to stop eating desserts.

She didn't let her son ride the roller coaster *because she thought it was unsafe.*

These sentences show that adverbs may occur in many different positions in a sentence. Frequently, when an adverb occurs at the beginning, it is called a *sentence modifier* because it modifies the whole sentence rather than the verb alone. Notice the difference between the use of *finally* and *fortunately* in the sentences above. An adverb that modifies the verb can be moved closer to the verb without making the sentence sound awkward, but the sentence adverb sounds best in initial position:

My mother *finally* agreed to let me go.

She also *fortunately* agreed to help me pay my expenses.

Fortunately, the sentence modifier, sounds most natural in initial position, but *finally,* which modifies the verb, may be moved to different positions without creating awkwardness. The sentence adverb comments on the action conveyed by the entire sentence.

Sentence adverbs also occur as transitional words, as in the following example:

The wedding was scheduled to take place in her grandfather's garden. The reception, *however,* was to be held at the most elegant hotel in the city.

However links the two sentences by pointing back to the previous sentence and by signaling to the reader that the second sentence is a contrast to the first. This type of sentence adverb is a conjunctive adverb.

The examples above also show that adverbs may occur as words, phrases, or clauses. For the writer, this fact means an additional resource in conveying meaning and information to the reader. The writer's choice of a particular level reflects the specificity she or he wants to convey. Notice how each level adds specificity to the meaning of this sentence:

My brother plans to work in an oil field   tomorrow.

during summer vacation.

as soon as school is out.

Adverb Forms

Adverbs occur in a variety of forms. Many words are considered adverbs simply because they convey the sense of time or place:

still   now   today   only   there   south

But adverbs may be formed by adding *-ly* to an adjective. These are generally adverbs of manner because they tell how something is done:

quickly   slowly   convincingly   colorfully   hopefully

Like adjectives, adverbs also express degree through comparative and superlative forms:

most convincingly   more slowly   liveliest   lonelier

Finally, there are some adverbs which modify other verbs and adjectives by intensifying their meaning rather than by modifying them. Appropriately, these are called *intensifiers.* The words in italics in the following sentences are intensifiers:

We read the chapter *fairly* quickly.
Everyone agrees that she is a *very* pretty girl.
He is *somewhat* reluctant to talk about his past.
I'm *quite* sure I won't be able to devote *too* much time to this.

APPLICATION

Pick out all the adverbs in the following sentences indicating what they modify and identifying them as single word, phrasal, or clausal adverbs or as intensifiers.

1 A miniature study of Japanese loanwords will also be made.

2 There are quite a large number of borrowed words in our language.

3 When he first went to France communicating was rather difficult.

4 To finish research on time, he plans to spend most of the weekend in the library.

5 Unfortunately, our teacher did not curve the test grades.

6 My chemistry professor plans to drop our lowest grade to reduce the effect of our bad grades.

7 He was up all night studying for the exam. However, he's sure he failed it anyway.

8 By planning your time carefully, you might be able to go camping and to finish your paper this weekend.

9 It is hard to think independently and to act individually in our society.

10 As they approached the town, they could begin to see the damage the tornado had done.

PREPOSITIONS

Prepositions are words or groups of words that indicate relationships between the object of the preposition and some other word(s) in the sentence. Prepositions function as indicators of time, place, cause, manner, agency, association, or other relationships. Usually, prepositions occur in phrases that function as adverbs or adjectives, as the following sentences illustrate:

Tom lives *by* a noisy freeway.
She sat *beside* me *at* the movies.
In the summer, I'll be working full time *at* our local drugstore.
To me, a summer job is a good way to prepare *for* a fulltime job *after* graduation.
In spite of her mother's refusal, Jane went anyway.

When the object of the preposition is separated from the preposition, the sentence may end in a preposition. For many people, this construction is one of the worst grammatical sins in the English language. There is really no logical reason for claiming that it is incorrect to end a sentence with a preposition. We hear and use sentences like these all the time:

> Who are you going to the party *with?*
>
> Who are you mailing that *to?*
>
> That's something I won't put *up with.*

Notice how stiff the sentences sound if they are revised to avoid the preposition at the end:

> With whom are you going to the party?
>
> To whom are you mailing that?
>
> That's something with which I won't put up.

The objection to ending sentences with a preposition is that it makes the sentence sound informal and casual. Ending a sentence with a preposition is not a grammatical but a stylistic matter.

Verb Particles

Certain prepositions have become so closely associated with certain verbs that the verb and preposition form a verb unit:

> Would you *look up* this word for me?
>
> *Call* me *up* when you want to talk.
>
> I can't *make out* what number this is.
>
> We took three prospective buyers to *look over* the property.

In these sentences, *up, out, over* don't function as ordinary prepositions because they don't link an object noun to another part of the sentence. The prepositions are merely bound to the verb in such a way that they change its meaning. *Look* is quite different from *look up, make* is quite different from *make out,* and *look* is quite different from *look over.* Prepositions that are part of the verb are called verb *particles.*

However, not all prepositions that seem to be bound to the verb are particles. In the sentence we looked at above—*That's something I won't put up with*—*put up* is not a verb plus particle; it is an idiom, a frozen expression of the language. A true particle can be separated from the verb without affecting the verb-particle bond and without affecting meaning:

> I *looked* the number *up.*
>
> They spent three hours in *looking* the property *over.*

CONJUNCTIONS

Conjunctions join words, phrases, and clauses. *Coordinating conjunctions* join grammatically equal elements:

> *Mary* and *her teacher* met to discuss her grades.
>
> They argued *politely* but *earnestly.*
>
> *She tried to get her grade changed,* but *Dr. Allen refused to do it.*
>
> I love to sit on the patio *early in the morning* and *late in the evening.*

Notice that in each of the sentences, the conjunction joins elements of the same grammatical rank: two nouns, two adverbs, two independent clauses, two prepositional phrases.

There are only a few words that function as coordinating conjunctions:

    and   but   for   or   nor   (sometimes *so* and *yet*)

When coordinating conjunctions occur in pairs, they are called *correlative conjunctions:*

> *Neither* Tom *nor* Mary is going.
>
> *Not only* did he fail his chemistry test, *but* he *also* missed the deadline for turning in his English paper.

Correlative conjunctions include *either . . . or, neither . . . nor, not only . . . but also, both . . . and, not . . . but.*

Subordinating conjunctions join unequal elements. In fact, the function of these conjunctions is to show a dependent relationship between two clauses:

> *Because I was late three times,* I was penalized one letter grade.
>
> *Although I worked hard to make the canoe waterproof,* it flooded *when we were in the middle of the lake.*

Subordinating conjunctions are important in making writing more efficient, for they enable the writer to condense thoughts expressed in separate sentences into a single sentence that shows how the thoughts are related. They express relationships of time, place, cause, opposition, similarity, contrast, addition. Furthermore, the occurrence of a subordinating conjunction is a clue that the clause following it must be linked to an independent clause. Therefore, knowing that subordinating conjunctions signal dependence should help you recognize and avoid sentence fragments.

The following are some of the words that function as subordinating conjunctions:

after	when	whenever	until
although	because	wherever	unless
as	so (that)	while	through
as if	before	though	when
if	how	even though	that (when introducing noun clauses)

Conjunctive Adverb:

> He had studied until 2 A.M. However, when he saw the test, he realized he hadn't studied enough.

In this sentence, *however* does not indicate a grammatical relationship between the two sentences. It is not necessary to make the sentence grammatical, and it could be left without affecting the fundamental meaning. Conjunctive adverbs are communication aids; they make logical (not grammatical) relationships between sentences that would be only implicit otherwise. They are aids to coherence.

APPLICATION

Identify the conjunctions in the following sentences as coordinating or subordinating or as conjunctive adverbs.

1   Political upheaval means that the issues must be dealt with and that someone must rise to the occasion to decide upon these issues.

2   Although many will disagree with this opinion, I believe that the Supreme Court should hold a place today as one of the few respected and concerned institutions in our country.

3   Indeed, what history truly shows, if one can but see it, is that heroes also have that special inner quality that sets them apart from the rest of mankind, that makes them glow with an inner glory all their own.

4   History shows that real heroes are not merely brave or courageous, for bravery can be feigned and courage taken from a bottle.

5   Most of the boys seem to know that what they are doing is wrong, but they are too engrossed in their affairs to try to set themselves on the right path.

6   If I am reading or studying an assignment, I try to concentrate very hard on it. Sometimes, though, this is hard when I am reading or studying for a long period of time.

INTERJECTIONS

When you interject something, you interrupt the usual flow of a thought or sentence or conversation. That is exactly what interjections do—they interrupt the usual grammatical flow of the sentence. Interjections are not grammatically bound to the sentences they appear in, but they do add expressions of surprise, emotion, or anger. In the following sentences, the interjections are italicized. Notice that the commas set them off from the rest of the sentence both grammatically and semantically.

> *Oh,* I didn't know you were waiting for me.
> *Good grief,* Charlie Brown, won't you ever learn?
> *Alas,* I was doomed to fail my first college math course.

Interjections should be used sparingly in writing. Although they emphasize speech effectively, they sometimes seem overdramatic, archaic, or out of place in writing.

SENTENCE ERRORS

After you've gotten your words down in the order and shape you want them to be in, you must take time to make sure your sentences are also in correct form. You've already seen that sentences are governed by rules, some of which are very rigid. We say "rigid" because when those rules are broken, the effectiveness of your message may be affected. Checking over your sentences to catch careless syntactical and grammatical errors is an important part of the completing stage. You want to ensure that your reader gets your message without any distractions from awkwardly constructed sentences. What follows is an examination of some common errors that crop up in everybody's writing.

SYNTAX ERRORS

Agreement

Rules of agreement affect the relationship between subject and verb and between pronoun and antecedent. Agreement simply means that a singular subject must have a singular verb and that a pronoun must match its antecedent (the word it refers to) in number (singular or plural), in gender (masculine, feminine, or neuter) and in person (first, second, or third). Usually, agreement occurs automatically when you speak and write. For example, when you say, "John likes to have doughnuts for breakfast," you know that since *John* is a singular noun, the verb must be singular too. However, if you had said, "My roommate and I like to have doughnuts for breakfast," you would have used a plural verb, *like,* to match the compound subject, *my roommate and I.*

Problems in agreement between subject and verb occur when it's not clear whether the subject is plural or singular. Notice how subtle agreement errors can be:

The chef's salad and the baked chicken looks good.

At first, the sentence sounds correct. The sentence communicates your message, but in writing, it's hard to overlook that compound subject — chef's salad *and* baked chicken. The verb should be plural — *look* — to agree with the plural subject.

Compound subjects joined by *or* and *nor* often cause agreement problems:

Neither John nor my brother are going to camp this summer.

The sentence sounds acceptable, but the conjunctions *nor* and *or* suggest singularity: not *both,* but one or the other is going. The verb, therefore, must be singular:

Neither John nor my brother is going to camp this summer.

Indefinite pronouns — *each, every, any, anybody, one* — cause similar agreement problems, especially when there is a prepositional phrase between the subject and verb:

Each of the boys want to try out for the team.

Only one of the chairs need to be reupholstered.

What has happened in these sentences is that the object of the preposition has influenced the verb choice. *Boys* and *chairs* are so close to the verb that they seem to be plural subjects. To avoid this error, simply remember that *each, none, any,* and other indefinite pronouns are singular.

Prepositional phrases affect other kinds of subjects as well:

The decreasing number of college students have been attributed to the declining birth rate over the past twenty years.

If you take out that prepositional phrase, you notice that the subject—*decreasing number*—is singular, so the verb should be *has been attributed.*

Agreement also affects pronoun reference. Remember that a pronoun is a noun substitute. Usually, the sentence contains a noun to which the pronoun refers, and the pronoun must reflect the grammatical features of that noun. If the noun is plural, the pronoun must be plural; if it is feminine, the pronoun must be feminine. Most of the time, pronoun agreement presents no problems, but some sentence constructions make pronoun agreement difficult to achieve. As in subject-verb agreement, indefinite pronouns cause problems here too:

Everybody finished *their* themes in 50 minutes.

Someone left *their* umbrella here.

Does *everyone* want *their* coffee in the living room?

You hear constructions like this all the time. There is really no problem in communicating meaning; the problem is grammatical. Indefinite pronouns like *everybody, anyone, anybody, someone, no one, one, each* are always singular, so they must be matched by singular pronouns. Since speech is much less rigid than writing, pronoun agreement is not distracting then. However, in writing, communication is much more formalized, and lack of pronoun agreement may distract the reader. To achieve agreement in each of these sentences, *their* should be replaced with *his* or *her.*

Pronouns cause problems in sentences for one other reason. Sometimes, it's not clear what the antecedent of the pronoun is. Remember: a pronoun must refer to a specific noun. Sometimes, however, you may be misled by a word or phrase that appears to be an antecedent but actually isn't:

The *Swiss* have not been at war for many years. *It* is a neutral country.

It clearly refers to *Switzerland,* but notice that the only possible antecedent is *Swiss.* To correct this, you would rewrite the sentence as follows:

Switzerland has not been at war for many years. It is a neutral country.

In this sentence, notice how the writer easily makes a pronoun reference error:

He was opposed to gun control because he felt every citizen should have one for self-defense.

Any reader would know that *one* is a substitute for *gun,* but the antecedent is *gun control.* Again, revision is necessary to correct the error:

He was opposed to gun control because he felt every citizen should be allowed to own firearms for self-defense.

APPLICATION

1 Rewrite or correct the following sentences so that each subject agrees with each verb.

1 I knew there was very few thieves, and I was thoroughly convinced those thieves weren't going to have a key to my room.
2 I think knowledge and good sense does not have to be obtained from a university.
3 Virtue and conscience is totally up to the individual himself.
4 A person's pride in achievement and his desire to live to enjoy these achievements is a good reason for capital punishment to be instituted.
5 In this atomic age, the lives of millions rests in the hands of a very small minority.
6 The huge size and appetite of the eagle also causes many people to feel threatened by these birds.

2 Rewrite the following sentences so that there is agreement between each pronoun and its antecedent.

1 This is possibly where a college could say they help round us out emotionally. They try to provide human activities that touch us deeply.
2 Very soon, people are either going to have to change their views on what colleges are for or colleges will change it for them.
3 In Newman's *Idea of a University*, he is first stating how a gentleman is an object of the university.
4 In Cuba today, Castro is the dominating factor in the Cuban way of life and their politics.
5 A person who would take it upon himself to deprive someone of life and happiness would get what they deserve: the death penalty.
6 Even if anyone had read it, they would not have been able to relate to it.
7 It depends on who has power and how they choose to manipulate the public.
8 A person would be very dull if they knew only facts and figures without having a personality formed from personal experiences.
9 If a criminal knew that he would receive capital punishment for committing murder, they might think twice before committing such an act.
10 Because of its widespread use, man has formed theories pertaining to alcoholics.

Predication

Faulty predication, a mismatch between the subject and the verb and the object, is a common sentence error. The subject, verb, and complement not only have to be grammatically compatible but also have to fit together logically. This error is hard to detect. Even though something seems to be wrong with the sentence when you read it, the meaning may come across anyway. In the following sentences, you can understand what the writer means, but the subject-verb-object relationship is illogical in each.

> Any person absent on the final day of classes would have meant that the end-of-school picnic could not be held.

Here, the subject-verb base is *person would have meant*. The relationship is illogical because *person* is a concrete noun, but the verb and noun clause complement clearly call for an abstract subject. The sentence should be rewritten:

> Any person's *absence* would have meant that the end-of-school picnic could not be held.

In this sentence, a superfluous *about* causes faulty predication:

> The subject of his talk was about employment after graduation.

What has happened in this sentence is that the meaning of *subject*—what something is about—and the prepositional phrase *of his talk* have merged to produce an awkward sentence. You can say *The subject of his talk was employment* or *His talk was about employment,* but not both, as the original sentence does.

Some errors in predication occur when an adverb phrase is forced to function as a noun phrase:

> An allegory is where characters symbolize virtues and vices.
> The reason I'm not going is because I don't like the girl who is hosting the party.

Frequently, the verb *be (is, was, were, am)* signals equality between the noun and the complement, so the complement must be grammatically equivalent to the noun. These sentences should be rewritten so that a noun or noun clause after *is* shows equivalency between the subject and the complement:

> An *allegory* is a *story* in which characters symbolize virtues and vices.
> The reason I'm not going is *that I don't like the girl who is giving the party.*

Sometimes the subject-verb relationship is simply illogical:

> When air fares are reduced, there will no longer be so many cars driving people to vacation spots.

The actual subject is *cars* and the verb is *will be driving*. The verb needs a human subject rather than an inanimate one:

> There will no longer be so many people driving cars to vacation spots.

or

> There will no longer be so many cars driven to vacation spots.

APPLICATION

Correct the predication errors in the following sentences:

1   The oil produced by Middle East countries has developed to be the heartbeat of the United States industrial machine.

2 To charge someone with the title of hero is a very daring and challenging label.

3 Just because there are no definitely outstanding figures in the political arena does not mean that our age is one without heroes.

4 The best part of the wave is usually when you take off and make your initial drop.

5 Life for me, as compared to life before I came to college, has really made me a more responsible person.

6 On the other hand is the creationist, who believes that the universe and all things in it were created by a vast, omniscient being.

7 It was because of the way the pipes looked last night that caused the fire marshall to declare the cause of the fire to be due to a buildup of a natural gas leak.

8 The first reason for this doubt is because of uncertain facts.

9 Another way most students change when coming to a college or university is culturally.

10 My purpose for witnessing this natural drama was that I am a professional hunter.

11 The only method for determining the heroes of today's society is by viewing the acts that possibly contain vitality on a scale of their future impact.

12 To call someone a hero is the result of personal views and attitudes toward the particular individual.

Modification

Modification, one of the means of expanding the basic sentence pattern, sometimes causes sentence errors. It should always be clear to the reader what sentence element a modifier refers to. As in most sentence errors, there may be no great loss of meaning when misplaced modifiers occur, but the resulting awkwardness or ambiguity may distract the reader or may create an unintentionally comical sentence. Most sentences with misplaced modifiers can be corrected through slight revision.

DANGLING PARTICIPLE: Having many heroic qualities, George Washington's life was colored by a handful of fables.
The problem here is that the participial phrase modifies *George Washington* instead of the subject *life*. Revision can correct the error:

> Having many heroic qualities, George Washington lived a life colored by a handful of fables.

INTRODUCTORY PHRASE: Through the use of polls, it is evident that the majority of the American public doubts the findings of the Warren Commission.

The problem here is that the introductory adverbial phrase *doesn't seem to go with any part of the sentence*. Again, slight revision can correct the sentence:

> Through the use of polls, we have learned that the majority of the American public doubts the findings of the Warren Commission.

PREPOSITIONAL PHRASE: We have, for example, men who have done something that most of us will never do, such as the astronauts, Arctic explorers, mountain climbers.

Here, the reader is led to expect examples of what it is that most of us will never *do*. Instead, it modifies *men* which occurs much earlier in the sentence. To avoid this sort of awkwardness, the sentence should be rewritten so that the prepositional phrase is closer to the word it modifies or so that it accurately modifies the word it follows:

> We have men such as the astronauts, Arctic explorers, mountain climbers, who have done something that most of us will never do.

or

> We have men who have done something that most of us will never do, such as journey to outer space, explore the Arctic, climb mountains.

To avoid errors in modification, always place the modifier as close as possible to the word it modifies. And you should always make sure that there is a word to be modified. Your goal in effective modification, as in all parts of writing, should be *to make your meaning and intention clear to the reader,* so you shouldn't force your readers to decipher your meaning or to correct mentally the sentences they are reading.

APPLICATION

Rewrite the following sentences to correct faulty modification.

1 Deeply upset, Ann's overwrought condition caused her to achieve a low score on the college entrance exam.

2 Among the examples used by the author, he remarked that although many of his teachers were spinsters, he didn't turn out to be a spinster.

3 While taking the lab test, an assistant grader approached one of my friends and attempted to take up her paper.

4 Being computer tests, the student does not receive his answer sheet or a copy of the questions.

5 Coming from an all-girl high school, the adjustment to a co-educational college has been a very big one.

Parallelism

The key to effective parallelism is the matching of grammatical parallelism with logical parallelism. When those parts don't match, we have the problem of faulty parallelism. Your thoughts may fit together nicely and the repetition available through parallelism may provide the emphasis you want, but unless the parallel elements are grammatically parallel, the pattern is more distracting than it is emphatic.

Notice how grammatical and logical parallelism combine effectively in this sentence:

> A university turns out people who have matured greatly, who have respect for others, and who have developed great responsibility.

The parallel relative clauses modifying people are the heart of the sentence. Each clause describes the kind of person a university turns out, thereby creating logical parallelism. Grammatical parallelism is achieved by repeating the relative pronoun *who* and similar predicates in each clause (*respect* is not a verb; it is a predicate adjective, but it still reinforces the pattern since the verb in that clause is *have*):

> *who have matured* greatly
> *who have respect* for others
> *who have developed* great responsibility

Such parallelism in form and content has a pleasing effect on the reader. Unfortunately, when there is parallelism in content but not in form, the effect is not as pleasing.

Problems in parallelism can usually be traced to faulty coordination between the elements that are supposed to be parallel. Remember, coordination and parallelism link grammatically equivalent sentence elements. When the coordinated parts are not grammatically equal, the sentence sounds awkward:

> He admired Mary's arrangement of yellow roses and daisies on the piano and how she had brightened the room with smaller arrangements.

Here, the writer has coordinated a noun—*arrangement*—with a noun clause—*how she had brightened the room*. The sentence should be revised so that both elements are nouns or noun clauses:

> He admired the arrangement of yellow roses and daisies on the piano and the smaller arrangements that brightened the room.

or

> He admired how Mary had arranged the yellow roses and daisies on the piano and how she had brightened the room with smaller arrangements.

Faulty parallelism is a serious sentence error because it can be very distracting. The pattern sets up expectations for the reader, who anticipates that parallelism in thought will match parallelism in grammatical structure. If a parallel series starts with one grammatical category and shifts to another, the effect of parallelism is destroyed, and the reader is disappointed.

APPLICATION

Rewrite the following sentences to correct faulty parallelism.

1   There are many deep considerations to be made, like your new found responsibilities, your goals and aims, and how your partner is going to fit into them, and making sure that the real reason for marriage is not to be an escape.

2   Egoistic suicide occurs in a society where interpersonal relationships are few, unsubstantial, and tend to be utilitarian.

3   I have seen individuals who respect their rights and the rights of others misused, slandered, their room vandalized, and labeled as two-percenters.

4   The essay is intended to make known to the female why conditions exist between men and women and possible ways that these conditions could be improved.

5   I would like to explain in more detail the two types of hunters, the pleasures of hunting, and how some of the laws are set.

6   Most of these students have their own ideas of what they want to be and can stand on their own two feet.

7   I am going to college for three reasons: the first being that it seems like the thing to do, the second being that my parents wanted me to go and the third because of the chance of being wealthy and having a comfortable life.

8   Colleges and universities are places where people should learn about life and how to function in life and deal with the real world.

9   A university should be a place where students receive a degree only through years of hard studying and because they deserve it.

10   A degree should not carry the meaning of a passport to wealth and power, but that the person who earned it is qualified to take a chance at wealth and a comfortable life.

PUNCTUATION ERRORS

Some sentence errors occur when you fail to use punctuation marks to indicate relationships between sentences. You will see later that punctuation is a system for marking sentences so that the reader can follow the writer's thought, stopping and pausing in the appropriate places. When these marks are missing or when they are misused, meaning may be lost or misunderstood.

Comma Splice
A comma splice occurs when you join two independent clauses with a comma:

As a child, the alcoholic did not learn the things a child needs to learn, thus his life was destined to go bad.

Remember that an independent clause demands a punctuation mark that signals completion, so independent clauses should always end in a period, a semicolon, or a comma.

You can correct a comma splice in one of the following ways:

1 Rewrite the sentence as two independent sentences:

As a child, the alcoholic did not learn the things a child needs to learn. Thus, his life was destined to go bad.

2 Assuming the ideas of the sentences are closely related, replace the comma with a semicolon:

As a child, the alcoholic did not learn the things a child needs to learn; thus, his life was destined to go bad.

3 Make one sentence dependent on the other through subordination:

Since the alcoholic did not learn as a child the things children need to know, his life was destined to go bad.

4 Join the independent clauses with the appropriate coordinating conjunction:

As a child, the alcoholic did not learn the things a child needs to learn, and so his life was destined to go bad.

A comma splice is a serious punctuation error for two reasons: (1) it suggests that you are unable to distinguish between independent clauses, which should be marked with a period or semicolon, and dependent clauses, which may be marked with a comma, and (2) it sends the reader conflicting signals. The comma signals only a pause, but the s-v-c pattern of the two independent clauses signals completion and indicates a need for terminal punctuation.

APPLICATION

Pick out the comma splices in the following sentences and rewrite each sentence correctly.

1 A man with a higher education has a good opinion about himself, therefore other people have a good opinion about him.

2 She has a rare talent, it is to inspire anyone with the least interest to do anything to keep on trying.

3 Knowing the basics in their chosen field gives students a head start when they enter a job, otherwise they would have a hard time getting started.

4 She is always smiling and joking, even when she is tired, she always seems to have compassion for others and a ready smile.

5 Common sense cannot be deduced, this a trait learned through actual living experiences.

6 It is often said that mankind should not live in the past, but make the most of and live in the present, this is practically impossible to accomplish.

7 It is now the time since we know who the enemy is, we must begin a movement of reform before we lose our identity.

8 A university is not a place in which nonfunctioning people go in and functioning people come out, it is more of an awakening period.

9 Now guess what happened to me, well, some call it sea sickness and I had it bad.

Run-on Sentences

Run-on sentences (or fused sentences) are much like comma splices except that in this kind of error, all punctuation is omitted between the independent clauses:

> Universities are an important part of our world for it is their teaching of our children that should someday bring about a better world.

A run-on sentence misleads the reader. With no period or semicolon to mark the end of one sentence, she reads the attached sentence as if it were part of the first one. When she discovers the writer's mistake, she must reread the sentences, mentally inserting the needed punctuation.

Run-on sentences send loud signals to the reader. They suggest that the writer is a careless editor, and they reveal the writer's failure to indicate closure in a sentence through appropriate terminal punctuation.

You can correct run-on sentences in several ways:

1 Rewrite the run-on sentence as two separate sentences:

> Universities are an important part of our world. It is their teaching of our children that should someday bring about a better world.

2 Insert a semicolon between the fused sentences if the two sentences are closely related in content:

> Universities are an important part of our world; it is their teaching of our children that should someday bring about a better world.

If the sentences are joined by a coordinating conjunction, they must be separated by a comma:

> Universities are an important part of our world, for it is their teaching of our children that should someday bring about a better world.

3 Use subordination to make one sentence dependent on the other:

> Universities are an important part of our world since their teaching of our children may someday bring about a better world.

APPLICATION

Explain why the following sentences are run-on sentences. Rewrite each correctly.

1 The author believes that the job of a university is to teach students knowledge and philosophy he also believes that the knowledge and

philosophy they learn are later mistaken for virtue and conscientiousness.

2 Don't get the wrong impression Jeff is not a troublemaker he is genuinely sorry for the trouble we have gotten into and will never make that mistake again.

3 Some days I'll start to clean to the extent of clearing a pathway to my bed I'm usually in a cleaning mood but don't really have the energy.

4 This shows what a brave dog he was yet two nights later he was frightened by our counselor's guitar.

Fragments

A fragment is the opposite of a run-on sentence: a run-on sentence occurs when two sentences are run together without punctuation, but a fragment occurs when part of a sentence is punctuated as a complete sentence.

Fragments may suggest to the reader that the writer does not know the difference between a complete sentence and a clause or a phrase. Usually, this isn't the problem, though. When you write your first draft, fragments slip in unnoticed during the pressure of composition. Your thoughts are coming fast, and you don't take time to consciously make each sentence perfect and grammatical the first time you write it. That's perfectly all right—for the first draft. During the completing stage you should catch and correct fragments.

Look at the sentences below. Try to figure out how the fragment occurred.

Many people look down on conformity. They see those who are always following blindly as fools who are too scared to think for themselves. Perhaps not having to think is why they conform. That and the fact that there is safety in numbers.

The last sentence is a fragment. It probably occurred when the writer got so caught up in getting her thoughts down that she didn't notice the grammatical form of her sentence. You could correct this fragment in several ways.

1 Link it to the previous sentence:

> Perhaps not having to think is why they conform, or perhaps they feel there is safety in numbers.

or

> Perhaps not having to think is why they conform—that, and the fact that there is safety in numbers.

2 Make it a complete sentence:

> Perhaps not having to think is why they conform. The feeling that there is safety in numbers may also explain why people conform.

Although you should try to get rid of fragments in your writing, you should know that they are not always grammatical errors. Frequently, writers use fragments intentionally for emphasis, as an afterthought, or as a transitional device. The following passages are from an article in which a writer describes his impressions and his memories as he comes back home to care for his dying mother. Notice that the fragments are necessary to create the illusion that the writer is allowing us to look into his mind:

For his mother is, in fact, near death, though lingering, and that is why he has spent three restless weeks in her house—a thousand miles west of his own, in a suburban town on the Hudson. Waiting. A duty.

John wonders if *he* has somehow contrived to bring his mother there. A figment, perhaps, a tilt of the mind.

He thinks, too, of how often and how far during his stay he has stumbled into the past. The house is full of things that, as he prowled it, have brought him memories or surprises. A rag doll, his mother's childhood confidante, now worn and burst at the seams, with only one button eye left. His father's telescope, the larger lens still cracked. John's own doing. And, oddly, a medal presented by the Italian government to one Professor George Niles, in March of 1922.

From Robert Henderson, "Colloquy," *The New Yorker*, July 17, 1978, p. 25.

Intentional fragments are okay. It is the accidental ones that disturb the reader and that you want to be sure to get rid of during editing and proofreading.

APPLICATION

Explain why the fragments in the following passages are errors. Rewrite each to correct the error.

1 The ironic tone comes from an exaggerated description of the female stereotype. Using ridiculous images of women bedecked in all sorts of jewels, tottering around on sidewalks, and girls melting with joyous gratitude over a box of cheap chocolates.

2 For those who are happy with the way things are, conformity is an asset. If people think as they do, things won't change. Their happiness is secure. Conformity can also be against those who oppose change. For instance, if a new view catches on. One by one people gradually accept it, not questioning it.

3 They see in each other the security which they so desire but cannot see what the price is for that security. The price being the responsibilities and commitments of marriage.

4 Students should know about the government and what has made it last for 200 years. Because it is very easy to criticize things you know nothing about.

5 Many people are successful without being an alumnus of some college or university. The key word here being success.

6 Thinking that the camera was rolling, I executed my part with great vigor. Vigorous enough that I suffered a minor head injury when I jumped off a ten-foot cliff in pursuit of the villain.

7 What we need in a realistic sense is to provide a more meaningful challenge to life. Also to simplify our lives to the point that we can regress to elementary math and the wheel.

8 The only reason I would attend a private university would be because of the curriculum it offered. For example, if the state university did not have a degree plan that I wanted to pursue or courses I wanted to take.

Apostrophes

One of the most common errors in the work of beginning writers is the omission of the apostrophe or the placing of it incorrectly. An apostrophe is always required to show that something belongs to someone or something else: to show possession.

The faculty's decisions	(The decisions of the faculty)
My favorite aunt's house	(The house of my favorite aunt)
The plot's twists and turns	(The twists and turns of the plot)
The travelers' routes	(The routes of the travelers)

Usually, you can check to see if an apostrophe is needed by turning the phrase around and seeing if *of the* can be substituted. Don't leave this apostrophe out.

Even when an apostrophe is inserted in students' writing, that apostrophe is often put in the wrong place. This error usually occurs because the word is plural and the apostrophe is placed as though it were single or vice versa. A good rule of thumb to remember is this:

If a word is singular, you add the apostrophe and *then* the s: boat's motor
time's way
of passing
oven's heat

(The exception would be if the singular word ended in an *s;* you would then have the option to just add an apostrophe: Janis' room. You won't be wrong, however, to go ahead and put the apostrophe and the *s;* and as long as you are in the least doubt, do this for all singular words showing possession.)

If a word is plural, be sure that you have already made it plural, and *then* add an apostrophe.

Singular	Plural	Plural Possessive
boy	boys	boys'
friend	friends	friends'

If the plural of a word does not end in an *s*, add both the apostrophe and the *s*.

Singular	Plural	Plural Possessive
child	children	children's

Finally, watch *its* and *it's*. Remember: if you write *it's*, you mean *it is*, so read the sentence to see if *it is* fits:

It's my time for a rest. (It is my time for a rest.)

If *it is* won't fit, the word should be spelled *its*—with *no* apostrophe. Its fur was so soft. (You see that you could not read this It is fur . . .)

So, remember: *It's* equals *It is*.

Its means possession.

Application

Put the apostrophe in correctly in these sentences:

1 Rachels peach cobbler is superb; its the best I've ever tasted, in fact.
2 The boys teachers said they should be rewarded for their work.
3 We bought a Little Playmate and its size is perfect for our purposes.
4 The calves hooves struck the mud and made prints.
5 The temperatures range was from 40–65 in one day.

Change the following words to the form requested:

1 Tailor to plural possessive
2 Cascade to single possessive
3 Wife to plural possessive
4 Label to plural possessive
5 Box to plural possessive
6 Box to singular possessive
7 Lady to singular possessive
8 Lady to plural possessive
9 Finger to singular possessive
10 Child to plural possessive

DICTION AND STYLE

Diction is an elusive term. It appears in the margins of your themes, marking everything from poor use of passive voice to the use of a word in an inappropriate context. For our purposes, we'll think of diction as the conscious choice of words to achieve a desired end.

Style, too, is something hard to pin down. It's something like a person's signature or way of dressing. (You've been in a store and said to someone with you, "That outfit looks just like you." You were able to do that because you intuitively knew the person's "style.") Style is a part of our writing, whether we realize it or not—whether it is "boring/bland" style or "high/flowery" style or something in between. What we are able to do, however, as we progress in our writing is play with our style— deliberately alerting it to fit the voice we are using and the audience to which we are writing (though we are suspicious of just *how* much one can play with one's own style without the writing sounding false and artificial). At any rate, your style is determined, usually without your being conscious of it, by how long your sentences are, what level and kind of words you use, what pattern your sentences take, etc.

We're just going to discuss *style* and *diction* in general, believing that as you learn to write, you will develop an appropriate style and use appropriate words simply because you are going to be writing in real situations for real people. When your message is something you want to deliver and you know to whom you are delivering it, your style and diction will almost automatically be appropriate. Until, however, you have had more practice, you may want to study *diction* and *style* deliberately, just to see what you can learn.

Diction is an important consideration in editing because word choice influences style and tone. The words you choose determine whether your style is formal, informal, or colloquial.

To understand how words create style, you need to know a little bit about the history of our language. English had borrowed heavily from languages all over the world, but especially from Latin and Greek and from French. English developed from the languages of the Germanic tribes that invaded England and Scotland between A.D. 450 and 800. The ordinary words of our language—prepositions, articles, and basic nouns and verbs such as *man, woman, wife, bread, ride, give, sleep*—can be traced to the languages of these tribes. Linguists refer to these everyday words as the Anglo-Saxon core of the language. After the Norman invasion of 1066, a large body of French words was borrowed. In general, this French influence refined the English language. For example, English speakers began to make distinctions between meat served at the table (French) and the animal from which it came (Anglo-Saxon): *cow* and *beef, pig* and *pork, lamb* and *mutton.* The large body of borrowings from Greek and Latin entered the language through the influence of scholars. Latin was the language of scholarship until the Renaissance, so books were written in Latin and all serious scholarship was conducted in Latin. Consequently, words from Latin and Greek were used then as they are now to add dignity and formality to writing. Words like *fortitude, abdomen, resuscitate, transition* began to appear as synonyms for their more homely Germanic counterparts. That was the beginning of style through diction.

In the list below, notice the difference among Anglo-Saxon, French, and Latin words of approximately the same meaning:

Anglo-Saxon	French	Latin
begin	commence	initiate
end	finish	conclude
kingly	royal	regal
time	age	epoch

Style becomes more formal as you shift from Germanic to French to Latin words. Familiarity with these levels of diction should help you become more flexible in your writing. You don't have to be a word scholar in order to write effectively, but you should know why one word seems more formal than another. Also, you should realize that impressive, formal words may not always be right for the message you are trying to convey. If *heart attack* fits your context, don't try to make your writing more impressive by using *cardiac arrest* instead.

Besides levels of diction, several other techniques affect the formality of your writing. Using first-person and second-person pronouns always reduces formality. Referring to yourself as *I* and to the reader as *you* always makes your writing less formal, and frequently it is the mark of a colloquial or a conversational style. However, you must be careful not to misuse the first- and second-person points of view so that your tone becomes inappropriately "chatty."

The deliberate use of passive voice instead of active, as you will see later, is another technique for making writing formal. And the use of abstract words rather than concrete words also contributes to formality.

As you read this passage by Henry Boettinger, notice how the level of diction and the other techniques we've discussed affect style:

Ideas are not truly alive if they remain locked in a single mind. Our need to transfer them to others forces us to consider why and where we want them to go, and how we want them to get there. This demands orientation toward the audience. "Audience" in its narrow sense, of course, assumes a *hearing* of the message. While the human voice is the most powerful method of communication, we will use "audience" in the broader sense, as the group aimed at regardless of the form used. Our objective is to get an idea accepted, and usually a mixture of methods—letters, memos, or reports as well as talks, conferences, and formal presentations—will be necessary if the idea is to have more than a trivial impact. The same principles and approaches are applicable to all forms, and the over-all play should use whatever combination best does the job. We will go into the strategy and tactics involved in some depth later.

You are correct if you think that the diction and style here are informal, perhaps almost casual. But can you explain how the author achieves that effect? First, notice that he uses first person: "our need," "forces us to consider why and where we want them to go," "we will use," "our objective." However, notice also that overall the tone is not casual; there is no indication of "chumminess" or colloquialness. The writer uses first person to refer to himself and to writers in general, not to establish chumminess with the reader. The result is a friendly, yet business-like tone. Notice also that all the sentences are in the active voice, giving the passage vitality and contributing to the informal effect. Finally, the level of diction is informal; there is a mixture of Anglo-Saxon and Latin and Greek words.

Let's analyze a second passage, this by Frank Smith:

Reading is an act of communication in which information is transferred from a transmitter to a receiver, whether the reader is a scholar deciphering a medieval text or a child identifying a single letter on a blackboard. Because of this basic nature of reading, there are insights to be gained from the study of theories of communication and information; there are concepts that are particularly useful for the construction of a theory of reading, and a terminology that can be employed to increase the clarity of its expression.

The present chapter will be particularly relevant to the following aspects of reading: reading is not a passive activity—the reader must make an active contribution if he is to acquire the available information. All information acquisition in reading, from the identification of individual letters of words to the comprehension of entire passages, can be regarded as the reduction of uncertainty. Skilled reading utilizes redundancy—of information from a variety of sources—so that, for example, knowledge of the world and of language will reduce the need for visual information from the printed page.

One of the first things you probably noticed about this passage is the abundance of words that end in -ion. These are abstract nouns that refer to ideas and intangible things: *information, communication, construction, expression, contribution, acquisition, identification.* There is nothing wrong with using -ion words, but overreliance on them leads to overreliance on the passive voice (abstract nouns and passive voice tend to occur together) and to consistent use of weak verbs such as *is, are, will be,* (and remember that the verb is the heart of the sentence). The result is abstract writing that is sometimes difficult for the reader to understand.

A second notable thing about this passage is the frequent use of passive voice: "information is transferred," "insights to be gained," "a terminology that can be employed," "all information acquisition can be regarded." Frequent use of the passive voice contributes to formality and frequently to unnecessary abstractness in thought.

Finally, the third person point of view contributes to the formality of the passage. There is neither a perceptible writer nor a specific intended reader. Both writer and reader remain unspecified and distant from each other because of the use of the third person.

These analyses should not be taken as suggestions that one kind of diction or one particular style is always superior to all others. By studying the passages closely, we can understand a little better how writers use words to create certain effects. The main consideration that makes one kind of diction appropriate and another entirely wrong is the author's purpose.

APPLICATION

1 In the passages below identify the words and techniques that contribute to informality, formality, or colloquialness.

A

Writers are driven by a compulsion to put some part of themselves on paper, and yet they don't just write what comes naturally. They sit down to commit an act of literature, and the self who emerges on paper is a far stiffer person than the one who sat down. The problem is to find the real man or woman behind all the tension.

For ultimately, the product that any writer has to sell is not his subject, but who he is. I often find myself reading with interest about a topic that I never thought would interest me — some unusual scientific quest, for instance. What holds me is the enthusiasm of the writer for his field. How was he drawn into it? What emotional baggage did he bring along? How did it change his life? It is not necessary to want to spend a year alone at Walden Pond to become deeply involved with the man who did.

This is the personal transaction that is at the heart of good nonfiction writing. Out of it come two of the most important qualities that this book will go in search of: humanity and warmth. Good writing has an aliveness that keeps the reader reading from one paragraph to the next, and it's not a question of gimmick to "personalize" the author. It's a question of using the English language in a way that will achieve the greatest strength and the least clutter.

—*William Zinsser*

B

How is aim determined? Obviously, it is partly determined by the cultural context and the situational context in both of which the text of the discourse is a part. This means, of course, that the intent of the author of the text partially determines the aim of the discourse.

But it would be dangerous to adduce author intent as the main criterion of the aim of a discourse, for often a discourse does not achieve the author's intent — "That's not what I meant at all," says the character in Eliot's "Prufrock." And again we may not have the author's intent available to use in recorded form; or, especially in propaganda and literature the expressed "intent" of the author may not at all be the real intent. The fallacy of judging the intent of a work by the intent of the author has been called the "intentional fallacy."

—*James Kinneavy*

2 Read through the following passage selecting from each pair of words the one which fits the level of diction of the entire passage. Explain why one word is more appropriate than the other.

Ours is an (age, era) without heroes—and, when we say this, we suddenly realize how (greatly, spectacularly) the world has changed in a (lifetime, generation). Most of us grew up in a time of towering (personalities, figures). For better or for worse, great men seemed to (rule, dominate) our lives and control our (destiny, future). In the United States we had Theodore Roosevelt, Woodrow Wilson, Franklin Roosevelt. In Great Britain, there were Lloyd George and Winston Churchill. In other (countries, nations) there were Lenin, Stalin, Hitler, Mussolini, Clemenceau, Gandhi, Kemal, Sun Yat-sen. Outside of politics there were Einstein, Freud, Keynes. Some of these great men (influenced, changed) the world for good, some for evil; but whether for good or for evil, the fact that each had not died at birth made a difference to everyone who lived after them.

Today no one (bestrides, walks) our narrow world like a (colossus, giant); we have no giants who play roles that one can imagine no one else playing in their (stead, place). There are a few figures on the (margin, edge) of uniqueness, perhaps: Adenauer, Nehru, Tito, De Gaulle, Chiang Kai-shek, Mao Tse-tung. But there seems to be none in the epic (style, stature) of those mighty figures of our recent past who (seized, grabbed) history with both hands and gave it an (imprint, mark), even a direction, which it otherwise might not have had. As De Gaulle himself (said, remarked) on hearing of Stalin's death, "The age of giants is over." Whatever one thought, whether one (admired, liked) or (detested, hated) Roosevelt or Churchill, Stalin or Hitler, one felt the (sheer, plain) weight of such men on one's own (existence, life). We have no (comparable, similar) pressures today. Other men could be in the places of the leaders of America or Russia or Britain or Italy without any change in the (course, way) of history. Why ours should be an age without heroes, and whether this (condition, state) is good or bad for us and for civilization, are (topics, subjects) worthy of (investigation, questioning).

CONNOTATION AND DENOTATION

Diction helps to determine style because of the denotation and connotation of words. Denotation is the objective, nonemotional, "dictionary" meaning of a word. For concrete words, denotation can be paired to an object in the real world. For instance, the word *chair* brings to mind the image of a specific object: a dining room chair, the chair by your desk, or perhaps your favorite lounge chair.

Connotation is the emotional or intellectual reaction elicited by a word. Many words suggest certain feelings that are entirely separate from the denotative meaning. For example, *cotton candy* has a specific denotation for most people: the fluffy, whipped, sugary candy you buy at carnivals and circuses. But the connotation may vary significantly from one person to the next. For one person, *cotton candy* may carry favorable connotations; he may think of how much fun he has had at carnivals and fairs, and cotton candy symbolizes that fun. For another person, the connotations may be negative; she may associate cotton candy with the frightful experience of getting lost at a county fair when she was only five years old.

Despite these private associations, connotation is a valuable resource for the writer because many words carry universal connotations. You can be relatively certain that these words arouse similar emotional responses in the majority of your readers. Recently, such words as *Vietnam, Watergate, pardon,* have usually elicited negative responses. Other words that are almost certain to arouse strong negative or positive reactions are *gay, Anita Bryant, ERA, busing, abortion, taxes.* Because we've seen them consistently in a particular context, most of these words have lost their denotative meaning. When readers encounter these words, they think of the associations they make rather than of the denotation. Thus, when he reads or hears the word *Vietnam,* he won't just think of the country in the Far East, but he'll also think of war, killing, refugees, government mistakes. Similarly, *gay* has become so closely associated with homosexuals that we can no longer use the word to denote happiness or lightheartedness.

It is not just these special words that carry connotations. Many of the ordinary words we use every day carry strong connotations, and you can use these associations to fulfill your purpose in writing, to create a certain tone, and to elicit specific responses from your reader.

In the following passage, notice how Germaine Greer uses the connotations of verbs to create a reaction against what she calls the female stereotype:

In that mysterious dimension where the body meets the soul the stereotype is born and has her being. She is more body than soul, more soul than mind. To her belongs all that is beautiful, even the very word beauty itself. All that exists, exists to beautify her.

The sun shines only to *burnish* her skin and *gild* her hair; the wind blows only to whip up the color in her cheeks; the sea *strives* to bathe her; flowers *die gladly* so that her skin may *luxuriate* in their essence. She is the crown of creation, the masterpiece. The depths of the sea are *ransacked* for pearl and coral to deck her; the *bowels of the earth* are *laid open* that she might wear gold, sapphires, diamonds and rubies. *Baby* seals are *battered* with staves, unborn lambs *ripped* from their mothers' wombs, millions of moles, muskrats, squirrels, minks, ermines, foxes, beavers, chinchillas, ocelots, lynxes, and other *small and lovely creatures* die *untimely deaths* that she might have furs. Egrets, ostriches and peacocks, butterflies and beetles *yield* her their plumage. Men *risk* their lives hunting leopards for her coats, and crocodiles for her handbags and shoes. Millions of silkworms *offer* her their yellow labors; even the seamstresses roll seams and whip lace by hand, so that she might be clad in the best that money can buy.

The effectiveness of this passage depends on the universal connotations aroused by the italicized words and phrases. Through the effect of connotation, the tone moves from mild irony—"sun shines only to burnish her skin and gild her hair"; "flowers die gladly"—to a highly critical tone—"the depths of the sea are ransacked"; the bowels of the earth are laid open"; "baby seals are battered." Had the writer used words with milder connotations, the irony and the strength of the passage would be reduced:

the sun shines only to tan her skin and make her hair shine

the depths of the sea are explored

>   the depths of the earth are mined
>   young seals are harvested

Although connotation can help you slant your meaning to achieve the rhetorical effect you want, inappropriate connotation can destroy the effect you want. For example, in this sentence, the writer has used *subject* without thinking of its negative connotations:

>   Going to a large university subjects a student to a variety of cultural,
>   social, and intellectual experiences.

The verb *subjects* implies that one is doing something against one's will, but the tone of the sentence doesn't reinforce that connotation. Perhaps the writer meant

>   Going to a large university allows the student many opportunities
>   for cultural, social, and intellectual growth.

As you revise your paper, make sure the connotations of your words fit in with the tone you are trying to convey.

Be careful when you go to a thesaurus to find a suitable synonym. Although the synonyms under each entry share a basic meaning, the connotations may vary so greatly that one word cannot be substituted for another. For example, *average, commonplace, ordinary, mediocre,* and *typical* all mean about the same thing, but they can't be used interchangeably. Saying someone is an *average* student is quite different from saying he is a *mediocre, ordinary,* or *typical* student. *Mediocre* suggests inferiority, while *ordinary* and *typical* suggest there is nothing extraordinary about the student. The denotation of *commonplace* makes it inappropriate for describing a person; the word usually describes inanimate, abstract nouns such as *occurrence* or *event.*

Don't substitute synonyms indiscriminately. If you do use a thesaurus, make sure you know the denotation and the connotations of the words you are dealing with.

APPLICATION

1   Analyze a series of magazine ads on a single object; for instance, luxury cars, economy cars, low tar and nicotine cigarettes, regular cigarettes, televisions, liquor, soft drinks. Be prepared to discuss orally or in writing your observations about the ad writers' use of connotation.

2   Study each group of words below. Look up those whose meaning or connotation you are not sure of. Explain what the words in each group have in common and how they differ especially in connotation. For each group, write a paragraph illustrating the appropriate denotation and connotation of the words.

a   objective, neutral, fair, unbiased, indifferent
b   hard-working, devoted, fanatical, obsessed
c   study, look over, scrutinize, examine, analyze
d   exhibit, show, illustrate, flaunt
e   proclaim, announce, tell, reveal, blurt out
f   use, exploit, employ, utilize

VIVID WRITING

As you revise and edit your paper, strive to make your writing as vivid as you can. Your task as a writer is to make it as easy as possible for a reader to understand your message, and one way to do this is to choose your words carefully and deliberately. Much mediocre writing can be improved merely by working at making it more vivid. "Vivid" writing shouldn't be confused with descriptive writing characterized by abundant adjectives and adverbs. Certainly, effective use of modifiers makes writing vivid, but vividness can be achieved in other ways: by using concrete rather than abstract diction, by limiting the use of the passive voice, and by using figurative language.

Concrete and Abstract Diction

Being concrete is one of the most difficult tasks that faces an inexperienced writer. As speakers, we are conditioned to communicate abstractly. When we speak to others, much of the time we are not primarily interested in conveying specific information. We are more interested in the simple social contact we enjoy through conversation. Think about the conversations you have each day. How many of them involve the exchange of vital, specific information? Most of your conversations are small talk, aren't they? It makes no difference whether you are discussing a movie, a professor, a date, or a personal problem, your conversations tend to be more social than informative, so being specific and concrete is a secondary concern. In the conversation below, what are the speaker's intentions? Are they exchanging information or merely being social?

Phil: Hey Stan, how's it going?

Stan: Okay, Phil. How're things with you?

Phil: I just got through the hardest chemistry test anyone ever took.

Stan: Yea? Who do you have this semester? White?

Phil: Yea. How'd you guess?

Stan: Oh, I've heard about him.

Phil: I think he's out to flunk two-thirds of the class.

Stan: Well, maybe you'll end up in the lucky one-third. See you later; I've gotta go to history.

If you analyze the conversation, you'll see that very little concrete information has been exchanged: Stan learns that Phil just had a chemistry test and that Professor White is his teacher. Phil learns that Stan is on his way to history class. Everything else is general and abstract. What does "how's it going" mean? What does Stan mean by "okay"? What makes the test the hardest anyone ever had? Interestingly, the answers to these questions aren't important. In fact, if we were to insist on specificity in every ordinary conversation, the purpose of those conversations — social contact — would be defeated. Generality characterizes most of our casual speech, but we accept that because we aren't looking for specificity then.

Unfortunately, generality also characterizes much of the writing produced by beginning and inexperienced writers.

To understand why vividness is important in writing you need to understand that words function differently in speech and in writing. Speech is not always social, but it is always ephemeral. The words are uttered, and if your mind doesn't register the meaning of the sounds, the message is gone forever. Fortunately, when the meaning doesn't register, you can approach the speaker—whether he is a friend you are having a conversation with, a teacher lecturing to your class, or a boss explaining your duties—and ask for clarification of the message. Writing, on the other hand, is permanent, so we depend on written words to convey and preserve our most important communications. With this permanence goes a great responsibility—the need to be exact. When you have only a text—something in writing—before you, you cannot turn to the writer and ask for clarification as you can when communication is oral. This is why concreteness is so important in writing. Concreteness enables a reader to form a mental image of the information you are trying to convey to him, and he won't be able to do this if your diction is consistently abstract and vague.

Abstractness creeps into writing in several ways. You may have a tendency to use words like *situation, reason, thing, aspect, experience,* which may convey little or no meaning. Usually, these are "filler" words, used when a more precise word evades the writer. Abstract diction also occurs when too many *be* verbs are used. *Is, was, am, were,* and other forms of *be* are meaningless; they merely link the subject to the predicate noun or predicate adjective. The more you use *be* verbs, the less vigorous and less concrete your writing is. Many times, an overabundance of *be* verbs goes along with a tendency to use abstract nouns as the subject of the sentence. Remember that the features of the noun used as the subject determine the verb which may be used. An abstract noun—like *reason, situation, aspect*—cannot take an active verb that expresses action concretely and vigorously. When you don't control all of these tendencies toward abstraction, you produce sentences like the following:

> Although many factors have to be postulated in order to account adequately for the attainment of reading behavior, the formation and use of concepts are, in fact, related to a significant portion of the variance in each subsystem of reading.

Notice that the subject—*factors*—is an abstract noun, forcing the writer to use a passive verb—*have to be postulated.* An abundance of abstract nouns through the rest of the sentence—*attainment, formation, use, concepts, portion, variance, subsystem*—confuses the reader and makes it almost impossible to understand the writer's meaning. If you are frustrated by this sentence, keep it in mind as you revise your own writing. Watch for sentences like this one:

> The reason that most freshmen are unhappy during their first month at college is that they are away from home for the first time and are trying to adapt to a different kind of school environment all at the same time.

Rewrite it to make it less wordy and more concrete:

> During their first month at college, many freshmen feel confused as they adjust to being on their own for the first time and to going to class when they choose.

Examine carefully any sentence that begins "the reason . . . is because," "there is," "it is." The abstract subjects in these constructions tend to make sentences wordy and sometimes awkward, as this sentence shows:

> The abundance of women at our university campus is responsible for the empty men's dorms on weekend nights.

Revision reduces wordiness and abstractness:

> The two-to-one female-male ratio at our university ensures that nearly all the men can have dates on weekends.

To say that all abstraction is wrong would be to deprive ourselves of a valuable linguistic resource. We need abstract words because we think in abstractions. In fact, many linguists and psychologists point out that our thought moves from the specific to the abstract and the general. For instance, we have words to refer abstractly and generally to classes made up of specific members. The term *mammal* refers to everything from man to whales. *Dog* refers to the most pampered toy poodle as well as to the most homely mutt. *Canine* refers to wolves as well as to domesticated dogs. Here, abstractness makes communication efficient since the words *mammal, dog,* and *canine* bring to mind the qualities that link the creatures in each class.

However, abstractness can interfere with communication when it is used carelessly. If a word like *dog,* which has a concrete referent in the real world, can confuse a reader, think about what might happen with words that have no concrete referents: *beauty, liberty, freedom, situation, information.* These words are necessary for our communication; otherwise, they wouldn't be in the language. But they should be used carefully. There should be no doubt in the reader's mind about their meaning. The writer whose primary goal is to communicate with readers avoids using abstract words indiscriminately. Realizing that abstract words increase the possibility of misunderstanding, you either explain the abstract word through a concrete example or you replace it with a concrete noun, verb, or adjective.

APPLICATION

1 Abstraction and vagueness will be no problem if you choose concrete and specific nouns, verbs, and adjectives. The following passage describes the famous ballerina Anna Pavlova. Notice how Agnes de Mille uses exact verbs and precise adjectives to form our image of the dancer.

As her *little bird body* revealed itself on the scene, either immobile in *trembling mystery* or tense in the *incredible arc* which was her lift, her instep stretched ahead in an arch never before seen, the tiny bones of her hands in *ceaseless vibration,* her face *radiant,* diamonds *glittering* under her dark hair, her little waist *encased* in silk, the great tutu *balancing, quickening* and *flashing* over her *beating, flashing, quivering* legs, every man and woman sat forward, every pulse quickened. She never appeared to rest static, some part of her *trembled, vibrated, beat like a heart.* Before our *dazzled* eyes, she *flashed* with the *sudden sweetness* of a hummingbird in action too quick for understanding by our gross utilitarian standards, in action sensed rather than seen. The movie cameras of her day could not record her *allegro.* Her feet and hands *photographed* as a blur.

2   As you work at making your writing vivid, avoid the following words. Usually, they only approximate your meaning because their denotation is rather general. Search instead for nouns, verbs, and adjectives that say exactly what you intend.

a lot	great	lots of	phase	terrible
aspect	interesting	matter	pretty	terrific
factor	item	nature	provide	thing
fine	large	nice	several	variety
			situation	various

In the sentences below, identify vague words that detract from precision in meaning. Explain how each sentence might be improved.

1 Jones Hall is really a nice dorm; I love it there. And my suitemates and roommates are really supernice. I had pretty good luck for just pot luck.
2 You should see all the construction work they are doing on campus. It sure makes everything a hassle.
3 This a great place to attend school.
4 All my teachers are real nice and they really seem like good teachers. They also appear to be very understanding.
5 I went to see "The Other Side of the Mountain" about the skier. It's the kind of movie I'll never forget. I keep wondering what I would have done had it been me.
6 You wouldn't believe the changes going on here. They tore everything up and built new stuff.
7 The author showed a small town in Minnesota and its people through the use of both irony and satire.
8 Hunting has a moral issue, especially when it is viewed as a sport.

3   The following paragraphs from a student paper represent a good attempt at writing vividly. Notice the specificity of the adjectives and verbs. Notice, also, however, that the writer tends to use the weak verb *have.* Revise the passage applying what you've learned about exact diction.

    The two young men had hired a small motorboat and were on their way to experience some of the wonders—physically and emotionally—of the ocean. They had no real knowledge of the sea, except for the small pieces of information they had picked up from novels and the stories they had heard old fishermen recite; but they were sensible people with good brains. What could possibly go wrong?

As the boat raced through the thick green waves toward the horizon the boys sat rigidly at the back. One of them had his hand tightly clenched to the tiller but was not guiding the boat in any particular direction. The wind tore through the youths' tangled hair, and slapped viciously at their faces, but the excitement had such a hard grip on their hearts it was impossible to even consider slowing down. The boat continued further and further as if it were trying to reach the horizon; but as it got nearer, the horizon tormentingly slid out of their reach.

Suddenly a huge wave hit both of the boys full in the face. The blow was so fierce it jerked their heads back and caused them to lose control of the boat. It spun around wildly for a split second and then the engine coughed twice and died. The two boys looked at each other with panic on their faces, and then one began to laugh and the other immediately joined him. They were shocked at how completely absorbed they had been in the speed of their craft, but they were scared of showing their feelings.

Figurative Language

Figurative language is one of the best ways of making your writing concrete and vivid. Unfortunately, it is also one of a writer's least used and most misused resources. Most of us shy away from figurative language; it is the language that poets use. It *does* characterize poetic language, but it is not exclusively the language of poetry. We shouldn't be intimidated by figurative language. It is really nothing more than the use of a word or phrase in a transferred sense. This means that the expression is to be taken in a figurative rather than a literal sense. We use figurative language every day to make our speech more specific and more vivid: he lost his temper, his temper flared, he was beside himself with grief, her enthusiasm overflowed, her laughter was contagious. If you think of the literal meaning of these expressions, the sentences in which they occur may seem absurd. Figurative language involves a transfer of meaning; you transfer the usual meaning of a word—*contagious, flare, lose*—to a different context. The result is a sentence that communicates vividly, concretely, and efficiently. It's far more effective to say "her laughter was contagious" than "she was laughing so much that everyone felt like laughing too."

Notice that figurative language rests on the power of connotation. "Contagious" carries negative connotations when it refers to a disease, but in this figurative sense, the writer is only interested in the qualities that suggest "catching." In contrast, you wouldn't want to say "her laughter was infectious" because the connotations of infectious are overwhelmingly negative.

Figurative language can make your writing lively, interesting, and concrete, but don't force yourself to use it. If you do, you will be using it to embellish and decorate rather than to make concrete. If a simile (a comparison using *like* or *as*) or a metaphor (an implied comparison) occurs naturally to you, use it, but don't strain your mental energies trying to come up with good metaphors. Notice how naturally and effectively figurative language fits into this sentence:

Perhaps a sentence is so excessively cluttered that the reader, hacking his way through the verbiage, simply doesn't know what it means.

The writer intends to be humorous by comparing a reader to a person hacking his way through a dense jungle or forest, and that image is appropriate to his light tone.

Keep these guidelines in mind when you use figurative language:

1 Avoid trite metaphors such as "tower of strength," "beacon of hope."
2 Make sure the metaphor fits the style and tone of the rest of your writing.

Figurative language that clashes with the subject and tone of a piece of writing distracts the reader.

APPLICATION

Discuss the appropriateness of the figurative language in these passages:

A

She ascended to her old position at the top, where the red coals of the perishing fire greeted her like living eyes in the corpse of day. There she stood still, around her stretching the vast night atmosphere, whose incomplete darkness in comparison with the total darkness of the heath below it might have represented a venial sin beside a mortal sin.

B

A row of tall, varnished case-clocks from the interior of a clockmaker's shop joined in one after another just as the shutters were enclosing them, like a row of actors delivering their final speeches before the fall of the curtain.

C

From the decaying embers no appreciable beams now radiated, except when a more than usually smart gust brushed over their faces and raised a fitful glow which came and went like the blush of a girl.

D

Finally in April we all talked Grandpa into going to a specialist in Houston. Their diagnosis was cancer. They said that it was out of control and that there was nothing they could do but to keep him as comfortable as possible. Grandpa had always been a symbol of strength in our family, so this news hit us like a ton of bricks.

Trite Diction

Vividness in writing is reduced by trite diction. Trite phrases and clichés were once fresh and original, but they have lost their vividness through overuse. Trite expressions slip into our speech very easily.

When we're talking and an exact expression evades us, we reach for the nearest cliché. But remember that oral speech is much more general than writing, so triteness in casual speech is not a problem. In writing, however, triteness is something to avoid. One writer has described clichés as blank checks that a writer gives to the reader hoping the reader will fill in the meaning himself. Trite diction has a lulling effect on the reader. Since the expressions are familiar to everyone, the reader exerts less effort in following the writer's thoughts. Furthermore, since the expressions are predictable and overused, the reader may conclude that the thought is also unoriginal.

Avoid such clichés and trite expressions as:

out of the horse's mouth	rude awakening
pretty as a picture	nip in the bud
whistling in the dark	apple of his eye
well-rounded education	can't judge a book by its cover
in this day and time	fresh as a daisy
in the nick of time	blind as a bat
giant step	easy as pie

APPLICATION

1   In the following passage, trite expressions are underlined. Substitute fresher more precise expressions for each.

In America today people are stumbling around in the darkness of National uncertainty, due to a lack of national heroes. Our country has been torn asunder internally by international policies made by our government. Americans need a man who is extremely self-confident and powerful, one who can pull them out of the despair of lack of leadership; such a man would deserve the name of hero.

In these troubled times America's national leaders are deathly afraid of offending popular opinion. They are trying to please everyone all of the time. Thus, our leaders act just as confused and mystified as the masses.

What has happened to America's leading figures to make them act in such an insane fashion? Simply stated, America has lost the determination and drive which propelled it forward in our earlier years. Americans have seen their most powerful men held up as criminals for the whole world to see. Americans have witnessed a spirit-breaking defeat in warfare, and these circumstances have beaten America down to its knees, and its leaders lack the drive to reorient it.

2   Trite diction is not always the result of using clichés. Sometimes triteness is due to the use of nouns and verbs or nouns and adjectives in well-worn combinations. In the following sentences, the underlined words are examples of these combinations:

1 The sun was glaring down on all our greased bodies and giving us the most professional tan we had ever had. The water was refreshingly

cool and a gorgeous shade of blue. All good things must end, and we decided to go to our rooms, clean up, and enjoy some night life.

2 While the figures are staggering, there are still a few ways to soften the college tuition crunch.

In the passage below, identify clichés and trite expressions. Rewrite the paragraphs, substituting original expressions for the trite ones.

When it comes to unforgettable characters, Alan Jones takes the cake. Alan is my best friend and can usually get us into some pretty wild circumstances. He is about five foot nine, with wide shoulders and slim build. Alan is a tad bit vain about himself, but I guess everyone is nowadays. I am not sure how we met each other, but it was a few years back and really not of significant importance. We were both the same type people: silly, easy-going, and mischievous. Alone, each of us was like a firecracker without a fuse, docile, yet together we were like an acetylene torch to dynamite. Alan played baseball in high school and coached a little league team after classes.

Passive Voice

In studying about sentences, you learned that the passive voice provides the writer an alternative to the usual s-v-c pattern. The passive voice, you recall, changes the order of the sentence parts. Thus, an active sentence—A speeding car struck a student on his way to school this morning—becomes

A student on his way to school was struck by a speeding car this morning.

Notice, however, that it isn't just word order that has changed. Although the message of the sentence remains the same, the focus is different in each. In the active sentence, the speeding car is the focus; in the passive sentence, the student becomes the focus. This capacity for varying focus makes passive voice a resource to writers.

Unfortunately, many writers misuse and overuse passive voice. Passive voice also involves changing an active subject—*speeding car*—into a prepositional phrase of agency—*by a speeding car*. Sometimes, though, the agent can be omitted to create an impersonal tone:

Students are asked to proceed to the gym immediately after lunch.

Who does the asking? Presumably, the principal, but the statement seems far more authoritative if the agent is omitted than it does when the agent is retained:

Students are asked *by the principal* to proceed to the gym immediately after lunch.

In this next sentence, the passive voice is used without the phrase of agency:

It is believed that the world will suffer massive food shortages this century.

Here, the passive voice might have been used for one of the following reasons:

1 The writer is the one who believes that we will suffer food shortages, but to create an aura of authority and to sound impressive, he avoids a personal reference in an active sentence:

> *I believe* that the world will suffer massive food shortages this century.

2 It could be that demographers or farmers are the ones who have predicted the shortage, but by leaving out the agent—it is believed *by demographers* or *by farmers*—the information in the sentence seems absolute and factual rather than speculative.

When it is used consciously to create a desired effect as in the sentences above, the passive voice is a valuable resource in writing. However, the passive voice is frequently used carelessly and indiscriminately, contributing to wordiness and reducing vividness. A passive sentence usually requires more words than an active sentence:

ACTIVE: The president asked Congress to carefully consider the results of the bill before overriding his veto. (16 words)

PASSIVE: Congress was asked by the president to consider carefully the results of the bill before overriding his veto. (18 words)

Certainly two additional words will not make your writing excessively wordy, but when sentence after sentence is passive, the extra words add up.

Another effect of using the passive voice is a reduction in vividness. Remember that the verb is the heart of the sentence. Passive verbs are formed by combining a form of *to be* with the past participle—*was* asked, *is* expected, *will be* hired—and *to be* is a colorless, empty verb. It merely links; it shows no action. So, unless you are deliberately using a passive voice to focus on the complement rather than on the subject, strive to make your writing vigorous and direct by preferring active verbs.

Finally, passive voice can make your writing awkward. In the following sentence, the writer's attempt to be impersonal by avoiding a second-person pronoun and his inadequate focus on *difference* contribute to the awkwardness of the sentence:

> The difference between your insurance benefits and your hospital bill will be required to be paid upon discharge.

Rewriting the sentence with a different focus eliminates the awkwardness and wordiness:

> Upon discharge, you will be required to pay the difference between your insurance benefits and your hospital bill.

> The difference between your insurance benefits and your hospital bill must be paid upon discharge.

As you edit your papers, question the appropriateness of every passive verb. Could the information in that sentence be conveyed more directly and more naturally in the active voice? If it can be, then revise the sentence.

APPLICATION

Explain how the use of passive voice makes these sentences awkward. Rewrite each to make it more vivid.

1   By this definition, it can be seen that heroes are very influential in American society today.

2   Technology is pointed out by the author as being one of the basic causes of the schizoid condition.

3   The topic is taken very seriously by the writer and the persona that she uses (which is both serious and full of resentment) expresses her seriousness.

4   But a stand was taken by him, and whether he is right or wrong, this fact cannot be ignored.

5   Through the activities of Sir Thomas More, it is seen that in order to live in society a person has to give up part of himself.

PROBLEMS OF DICTION AND STYLE TO GET RID OF IN REVISION

As you revise, be on the lookout for three major causes of wordiness: deadwood, redundancy, and circumlocution.

DEADWOOD
Deadwood is any word or expression that contributes nothing to your meaning and is therefore superfluous. This sentence is full of deadwood:

> Because of the fact that America's oil reserves are slowly running out, it is to be expected that the country will have to find other methods of supplying energy.

"Because of the fact that" and "it is to be expected" are examples of deadwood. They can be scratched out without detracting from the meaning:

> Because America's oil reserves are slowly running out, the country will have to find other methods of supplying energy.

Whenever you find one of the following phrases in your writing, scratch it out. In most cases, your sentence will survive without it, and usually it will be a much clearer sentence than it was before:

> due to the fact that
> it happened that
> there are/is

Deadwood also occurs when you use more words than necessary. Notice how each of these expressions can be trimmed down to a single word or to a shorter phrase:

make an attempt to	try
reach a decision	decide

Clutter is the disease of American writing. We are a society strangling in unnecessary words, circular constructions, pompous frills and meaningless jargon. Our national tendency is to inflate and thereby sound important.
— William Zinsser

it is the belief of	believes
is in the process of being	is being
the question as to whether	whether
in a hasty manner	hastily
owing to the fact that	since/because
in spite of the fact that	though/although/despite
the fact that I had arrived	my arrival
the fact that he had not succeeded	his failure
of great importance	important
in connection with	with

For beginning writers, deadwood is hard to detect and difficult to get rid of. Those empty phrases and superfluous words seem to make writing more impressive. Truly impressive writing communicates cleanly, directly, and efficiently. Deadwood works against efficient communication.

REDUNDANCY

Redundancy also leads to wordiness. Redundancy—unnecessary repetition—occurs when words are used carelessly and thoughtlessly. When a person refers to a "new innovation" he is not listening to what he is saying. *Innovation* already means "new," so the phrase is redundant. Watch for phrases that show needless repetition of the same meaning in two words:

fellow colleague	colleague
surrounding environment	environment
impending failure that will eventually occur	impending failure
carelessly discarded litter	litter
necessary prerequisite	prerequisite
long in size	long
blue in color	blue
of an indefinite nature	indefinite
by means of	by

Circumlocution

Circumlocution—the deliberate use of roundabout expressions—creates wordiness and obscurity. Again, the objective of writers who use circumlocutions is to sound impressive, not to communicate efficiently and directly. Ironically, when you recognize circumlocutions in a piece of writing, you are struck not by its impressiveness, but by its absurdity. In the passage below, circumlocutions are underlined. Notice how they obscure meaning and make communication difficult.

(1) As silent tears flowed down my cheeks in diamond-filled rivulets, I reflected on the presumptuous attitudes of society's "young adults." (2) Of course, generalization during a period of severe depression is opted for, and I consider myself no failure!

(3) It appeared to me that the feelings of humans aged eleven to nineteen towards the humans that had survived on this planet for the longest number of

years ranged from bothersome to useless. (4) Sporting a different opinion, and allowed to exclude myself from this degrading category for the sole reason that I was the inventor of the horrible thought, I began to defend this misconception possessed by the multitudes.

(5) My attitude, I must admit, ran the gamut from bothersome to surprisingly capable and extremely helpful, so I cannot debate the reasoning behind the depicting of "old people" as bothersome. (6) In order to clear my records, I must reveal that I consider almost every age of our species bothersome! (7) I believe that to be a predominant human characteristic, perhaps even a prerequisite!

The writer reveals other problems—the use of trite diction and errors in denotation, but circumlocution is the problem that interferes with communication the most. The roundabout expressions confuse the reader. Sentence (3) is particularly obscure. It seems that it is the feelings of young people that are bothersome and useless, but it becomes clear later that "bothersome and useless" refers to older people. In sentence (4), circumlocutions reverse the author's intended meaning. The writer says he will *defend* the misconception when he actually means that he will prove it wrong.

By rewriting the circumlocutions as direct expressions, the writer's message becomes clearer, shorter, and much easier to understand:

As I sat crying, I reflected on the presumptuous attitudes of young people. We all tend to generalize when we are depressed, and that's what I was doing then. As I saw it, teenagers consider older people bothersome and useless. I, of course, excluded myself from this generalization, and I tried to prove that prevalent attitudes toward older people were founded on misconceptions.

I believe older people can be productive, but I admit that I sometimes consider them bothersome. I cannot defend that attitude; however, I consider people of almost any age bothersome, and I think most people feel this way at one time or another.

Wordiness that results from using circumlocutions, redundancy, and deadwood can be difficult to get rid of. Writing is hard work, and many writers are reluctant to scratch out a single word that represents the effort behind their writing. Don't let yourself make that mistake. Remember that the quality of communication is more important than the quantity of composition. Think of words as a resource too valuable to waste. Write as if you had to pay for each word you put down on the page so that using unnecessary words is like wasting money. To avoid wordiness you don't have to go to the extreme of making your writing telegraphic. Simply train yourself to question the function of every word in your writing, and scratch out any word that doesn't add to your meaning.

APPLICATION

1   The following passage illustrates how wordiness reduces the impact of writing. Read it and try to identify the writer's problems; then read the analysis below.

(1) The writer of the passage which is the subject of this essay has the opinion that today is an "age without heroes." (2) I personally feel that he is in error. (3) There are several reasons why I feel that the author of the passage is wrong in his assumptions.

(4) The first reason for which I disagree with him is his faulty definition of a hero. (5) He puts forth the idea that a hero is anyone who has done something famous or has affected the world so strongly that his name becomes an important part of history. (6) Some of his heroes are Hitler, Mussolini, and Mao. (7) These men are famous for their misuse of power and the amount of misery that they have caused other people. (8) Just because a person exerts a tremendous influence on other people does not make him a hero.

ANALYSIS:

In sentence (1), the clause "which is the subject of this essay" is superfluous. The reader can assume that since the writer is referring to the passage, it is the subject of the essay. "Has the opinion" should be reduced to "believes." Sentences (2) and (3) are repetitious; notice that the idea of sentence (2) is repeated in (3). "There are several reasons why" and "of the passage in question" are deadwood and should be edited out. In sentence (4), sentence structure, an abstract noun plus a *to be* verb, leads to wordiness. The verb in sentence (5), "puts forth the idea," can be reduced to "suggests." Sentences (6) and (7) could be combined to reduce wordiness since they deal with the same subject. In sentence (8), the colloquial construction "just because . . . does not . . ." contributes to wordiness.

Several other problems contribute to wordiness. The writer's references to himself, "I personally feel," "the first reason for which I disagree," are not necessary since the reader can assume the essay represents the writer's opinion. There is nothing wrong with using the first person; the problem here is that the writer has allowed personal reference to take the place of strong verbs that would present his views more effectively.

The constant references to the passage on which the essay is based also contribute to wordiness. If the author and the title are available, they should be used in the first reference. If they aren't, the writer should devise a way to write about the ideas in the passage without referring to it as "the passage in question."

As you read the revision, explain what has been done to reduce wordiness and increase efficiency in communication.

REVISION:

The writer believes that today is an "age without heroes." For several reasons, he is wrong. First, I disagree with his definition of a hero. He suggests that a hero is anyone who has done something famous or has affected the world so strongly that his name becomes an important part of history. Some of his heroes—Hitler, Mussolini, and Mao—are famous for their misuse of power and for the amount of misery they caused. A person does not become a hero simply by exerting a tremendous influence on other people.

2 Read the following passage, identifying problems in inexact diction and wordiness. Revise it to make it more precise and less wordy.

The choice of a particular university is very important in a student's college career. Prospective college students select a university by considering many factors. Every student has decided on certain qualities his or her university must possess. To some students distance is an important aspect of their choice. They want to be close to home, far away from home, or just far enough so they will have some independence. Others view reputation as a vital factor. The college may have to be in the "Ivy League" class. Others may want to attend a private, religious university. Still others want the college of their choice to be well known academically. All of these factors are considered to a certain degree in making a decision concerning which university to attend.

3 Rewrite the following sentences to reduce wordiness. Explain what causes wordiness in each.

1 The writer's diction in this first part is so that it creates a distance between the reader and writer.
2 Princess Lea is trusting from the beginning of Luke.
3 In our ultra-modern society of today, it is increasingly difficult to maintain the friendly easygoing outlook on life that was prevalent in the past.
4 The style in this essay is very effective in achieving the purpose of the writer.
5 One point that is often overlooked by many is the fact that Lee had given most of his slaves their freedom before the outbreak of the War Between the States.
6 A third reason which makes Howard Roark and his society a dream is the fact that nothing can keep him from achieving his goal.
7 In the late 1800s a scientist of some esteem put forth and had published a copy of what he believed to be an explanation of the origin of man—the scientist of course was Charles Darwin.
8 It is a common misconception among the feline owners of the world that the Siamese breed of cats is, without exception, the most unfriendly of their kind. My self owning an example of living proof, I can readily disprove this common belief. My Siamese cat, Kohlou by name, is undoubtedly one of the most affectionate animals I have ever seen.
9 The first thought which comes to mind is one of shock.

10 Agronomists are very certain that there will soon be a food crisis. Many things are being discovered to help ease food shortages, such as polypropylene. However, it is difficult to carry out plans or to get the richer nations to help develop the poorer ones.

11 When people begin their lives as children, they are very heavily influenced by their parents.

Jargon

Notice in the quotation at the beginning of this section that the author cites meaningless jargon as one of our writing problems. *Jargon* sometimes refers to the vocabulary characteristic of a particular group; for example, medical jargon, educational jargon, legal jargon. In this sense, the word carries no negative connotations. It merely refers to the set of words that professional or social groups use to communicate among themselves efficiently. In a different sense, jargon is a problem in writing. Anytime a writer is more interested in impressing the reader than in communicating effectively, his writing may be labeled jargon.

No single problem turns writing into jargon. Instead the problem is really an accumulation of problems—wordiness, pretentiousness, abstractness, overuse of the passive voice—but the biggest problem is the motivation in using jargon. Usually, it reflects an attempt to make trivial ideas seem important.

No one deliberately sets out to produce jargon. Writers use jargon for several reasons. They confuse quantity with quality, so they think more words and bigger words are the key to good writing. Sometimes, self-consciousness may lead a writer to use jargon. Remember: writing is permanent, and once words are down on paper, they become public and are subject to criticism or praise. Consequently, many writers use jargon to sound intelligent and impressive. Ironically, jargon produces bad writing, and readers who recognize jargon realize that the writer is insecure and pompous rather than intelligent and impressive.

You can avoid jargon by remembering that the object of writing is communication. Because it obscures meaning, jargon interferes with communication. The following guidelines, based on what we've discussed about effective use of words, should help you avoid the problems that contribute to jargon:

1 Make your writing as clear and as straightforward as possible. Avoid "big" words and pretentious language simply to impress your reader. Be merciless in editing your writing. Strike out any word that adds nothing to your meaning, regardless of how impressive the meaningless phrase seems. Remember the term for meaningless phrases: DEADWOOD.

2 Strive to make your writing vivid. Whenever possible replace *is* and other *to be* verbs with a stronger verb. Avoid too many abstract nouns (*-tion* and *-ment* endings). Remember: these nouns can frequently be replaced by a verb to make a stronger sentence.

3 Be natural. Don't avoid a first-person pronoun simply because you fear it may make your writing too casual. Don't use the third person

(*one, a person, the student*) in an attempt to sound impersonal. Don't rely on passive voice as a means of sounding impressive.

APPLICATION

The following passage is a good example of jargon; identify the problems that characterize it as jargon and then rewrite it.

Perhaps the most significant development of the Industrial Revolution (aside, of course, from the revolution itself) was the beginning of awareness in some individuals of the less favorable ramifications of technology. This awareness, although negligible at first, eventually became the vital factor in the prevention of world self-destruction through unbridled technological advances. Fortunately, vigilance against the cerebrean nature of our scientific age continues to serve as a bulwark against problems which could increase severely in magnitude (e.g. the ecological balance or nuclear weapons) as time progresses.

In addition to the material problems of a technical society, there are difficulties of wider and far more abstract scope. These difficulties are evidenced most graphically by examination of technological advance in terms of the response and development of the individual. It is to be suspected (without much doubt) that previous decades of near-obsession with technology, frequently for its own sake, have resulted in a society which is over-oriented toward a systematic approach to its problems. In fact, the primary ill of modern society could well be expressed as its continuous attempt to adopt a rigid set of formulae and apply them, in toto and without exception, to human beings. Such a denial of "human variability" is, of course, a mistake, and can, as pointed out, lead only to disaster. Yet, society continues to career, without apparent suspicion, toward a point from which there may well be no return.

ERRORS IN DICTION AND STYLE

The problems we've been considering—wordiness, jargon, redundancy, abstractness—are not errors. You should avoid them because they reduce the impact of your writing and sometimes confuse your message for the reader. However, there are some problems in diction that we do consider errors because they involve mistakes in meaning, context, and associations.

Wrong Denotation

You've already learned that denotation of a word is its dictionary meaning. Sometimes, when writers get in a hurry or use words carelessly, they misuse the denotation of a word. For example, a sports announcer covering a college football game may describe the beginning of the game as "a bombastic opening." If you look in a dictionary, you'll find that no meaning of *bombastic* fits the context. *Bombastic* means "high-sounding, high-flown, pretentious," a meaning that has nothing to do with the opening of a football game. Clearly, the announcer has made a mistake.

He wanted a strong word to describe the opening minutes of the game, a word that conveyed excitement, unexpectedness of the underdog's surprise touchdown. No doubt, he chose *bombastic*, thinking that it was somehow related to the meaning of *bomb*.

Probably no other error makes you look as foolish before your reader as an error in denotation. You can avoid making these embarrassing errors by understanding why they occur:

1 When a writer attempts to use a new, unfamiliar word that she may have heard before, she may use it in the wrong context. This is what happened to the announcer.

2 Sometimes a writer inadvertently uses a word similar in sound to the one he wants:

> They faced the *aspect* of spending a night in the woods.

The correct word is *prospect.*

3 Some errors in denotation occur when a writer confuses homophones:

> Our football team should *fair* better this season than it did last year.

The correct word is *fare.*

Errors of this kind are hard to detect since they occur as you transfer an oral expression into writing, but you can avoid wrong denotation by being a careful listener, by using a new word only when you are positive you have used it correctly, and by reading carefully so that you learn to use words like *bombastic, aspect, fare* in the correct contexts.

Unidiomatic Expressions

All languages have certain groupings of words that native speakers recognize as idiomatic expressions. This means that throughout the development of the language certain words have been used together consistently so that they now form an idiom, a unit of speech that is what linguists call "frozen." This means that only certain words can be used in the expression; if the words are changed, the phrase loses its idiomatic quality and frequently its meaning as well.

If idiomatic expressions are familiar to native speakers of a language, you might expect an English speaker to use idioms correctly and effectively. Frequently, however, carelessness in speaking or writing leads to the use of unidiomatic expressions as in the following sentence:

> The senator *agreed to* the proposal for a compromise, but when the bill was rewritten, he *disagreed to* most of the points.

"Agree with," "agree to," and "disagree with" are idiomatic expressions, but "disagree to" is unidiomatic.

A similar error is the misuse of direction in meaning. When you read a sentence like

> I have a very inadequate feeling when I think about writing this book,

it makes sense superficially. However, if you think about what the sentence says, you'll see that the expression is awkward. What the writer means is not that the feeling is inadequate but that he feels inadequate. This is what we mean by direction in meaning. The meaning of *inadequate* can point to the subject *I*, but not to the complement *feeling*. The adjective *inadequate* can modify a concrete, human noun but not an abstract noun. The problem occurs when a writer attempts to change the order of a commonly used phrase such as "I feel inadequate."

To avoid making these mistakes in writing and in speaking, listen carefully to how other people use words. Also, don't try to vary your style by changing the direction of a phrase like *feel inadequate* by separating the words in an idiom.

Mixed Metaphors

You've already seen that figurative language makes writing vivid and concrete. However, when a metaphor is misused, the result is an error in diction. Metaphors and many other figures of speech are based on analogy. This means that there must be some basis of comparison between the literal and figurative meanings you are trying to convey. Furthermore, that comparison must be appropriate and consistent throughout the unit of writing in which the metaphor occurs. When you introduce incompatible images to describe a single idea or object, you produce a mixed metaphor. Notice how the figurative language in this sentence creates conflicting images:

> Men, I'm asking you to put your shoulders to the wheel and help bail us out of this financial quagmire.

The speaker has given the reader the opportunity to visualize a ludicrous image: workers with their shoulders to the wheel simultaneously in a sinking boat and in a quagmire.

A mixed metaphor is an error in diction because it defeats the purpose of figurative language. It causes the reader to laugh at the image or at the writer rather than to see the point more clearly. It obscures meaning by distracting the reader through an unintended comical or incongruous image. Therefore, when you use figurative language, make sure that it clarifies rather than obscures your message and that the image you present is consistent at least through the sentence in which it appears.

APPLICATION

The following sentences contain errors in diction. Identify the problem in each and explain how it can be corrected.

1 During the midwinter months the ducks have their complete foliage; therefore you must have decoys that look lifelike.

2 The college student needs to accomplish the correct approach to studying or will certainly suffer the consequences.

3 After the reader notices these unmistakable words, his curiosity is aroused enough to pursue their significance.

4 Now she is susceptible in believing the hidden messages of the ad.

5 Catching fish is not the primary role of fishing; having fun is.

6 In today's processed world, people develop traits of materialistic dependency and selfishness.

7 Because sight was his weakest interpretation of what was happening around him, the snake used his ears to lock in on his goal.

8 The majority of the reading public does not realize that there are a number of subtle tricks exploited by the advertiser.

9 The choice of which college at which I would pursue my further education was slow in forming but quick to harden.

10 With skyscrapers, busy streets, and many people, the country family was in for a lot of new experiences when they moved to a big city.

11 The baked potato melted in my mouth and slowly drifted down my throat.

12 The degree of work one puts in will determine the amount of money he will receive.

13 The reader is drawn to the advertisement because certain promises await him at the flick of a cigarette.

14 There are three beautiful models garnished in beautiful fur coats to attract the reader.

15 He realizes that this comely scenery which has overcome him has simple and common words.

16 In America, a nation of superfluous people, the external pressures become so important that the inner wants and needs of the soul fall by the wayside.

17 There were over 25 calls reporting broken water pipes in the city. "We hardly ever get calls like this," explained the utilities workman, "but we've had a mirage of them today."

18 We would talk about the problems of the world and Barney in his bass and usually very intelligible speech would begin to exclaim the uselessness of war, his hate for communism, his sincere religious views, and his concern over the ever-present political problems of our country.

USAGE

This episode between Linus and Sally illustrates one of the greatest misconceptions about grammar. Sally is frustrated because in his zeal to correct her grammar, Linus has overlooked her question, has ignored her message. Unfortunately, people do this all the time: they let grammatical errors, both significant and insignificant, block communication. Consequently, many students claim that they hate writing—or that they can't write—because they find it impossible to try to communicate with a reader who is more concerned about correctness than with the writer's message.

Just how important are grammar rules? Why do we have rules if they seem to interfere with communication?

To answer these questions, we must define grammar more precisely, and we must distinguish between grammar and usage. Grammar is the systematic description of a language on the levels of sound (phonology), words (meaning or semantics), and sentences (syntax). When we talk about parts of speech, or subject-verb-complement patterns, we are talking about grammar. Grammar does not include pronouncements about what is right and wrong. It merely describes how it is that speakers put sounds together to make words and how they combine words to make sentences.

Well, then, where did people get the notion that grammar should dictate correctness? To answer this question, we need to go back to the eighteenth century when grammar books first began to appear in great numbers in England and Colonial America. At that time, the English language had been affected by many, many developments that occurred over hundreds of years:

1 English had evolved from Old English, the foreign-looking language spoken from A.D. 449 to 1100, to Middle English (1100–1500), which was heavily influenced by French borrowings after the Norman Invasion of England in 1066. By 1500, through a number of sound changes in vowels, changes that occurred simply through the blending of dialects and through increased communication among people from different parts of England, English had evolved to Modern English. However, it was still quite different from English as we know it today; you can see these differences in Shakespeare's plays, even though you can still understand the language.

2 The printing press had been introduced in England in 1477, making it necessary to standardize spelling and sentence structure. With the wider distribution of printed material, more and more people were reading and writing, so it was necessary to establish rules and conventions so that communication would be possible.

3 Social and economic classes began to change, and soon more and more people were becoming members of the upper class through wealth attained in commercial pursuits. This meant that education (especially reading and writing) must become more widespread.

It was inevitable that the language would change through all these things, but to keep it from changing for the worse, self-declared grammarians began writing grammar books. It was at that time that the notion that change deteriorates a language first appeared. It was also then that some of the more illogical rules of our language first were formulated. The rule prohibiting double negatives was made by a mathematician and the one prohibiting a preposition at the end of a sentence by Latin scholars. By the eighteenth century, grammar had become *prescriptive* rather than descriptive. The authors of early grammar books felt that it was their duty to tell people (to prescribe) how to speak correctly and to condemn arbitrarily certain linguistic practices as incorrect. Their primary motivation was to protect the English language from further deterioration.

Since then, grammarians have realized that *usage* determines acceptability and appropriateness in language. Usage is the way ordinary people actually talk and use the language. If people throughout the country use *ain't* to mean *are/am not*, grammar books and dictionaries must *recognize* its occurrence; recognizing the occurrence of a certain linguistic form is quite different from accepting it as correct in all contexts.

Determining when a particular form is correct and when it is not is the reason we study usage in school. Formal study of our language makes us sensitive to appropriateness and context. Even though *ain't* is used throughout the country by many classes of people, it may not always be right to say *ain't* instead of *are not*.

Usage actually covers two different things. First, it deals with functional varieties of the language—with slang, colloquialisms, and casual, formal, and informal styles. Almost any variety of English is acceptable in the appropriate context. Look at this passage from the opening of Mark Twain's *Huckleberry Finn:*

You don't know about me without you have read a book by the name of *The Adventures of Tom Sawyer,* but that ain't no matter. That book was made by Mr. Mark Twain and he told the truth, mainly. There was things which he stretched, but mainly he told the truth. That is nothing. I never seen anybody but lied one time or another, without it was Aunt Polly or the widow, or maybe Mary. Aunt Polly—Tom's Aunt Polly, she is—and Mary and the Widow Douglas is all told about in that book, which is mostly a true book, with some stretchers as I said before.

No one will deny that Huck has used incorrect grammar and slang throughout this passage. Yet, many people consider this one of the greatest books in American literature. Why do we accept Huck's (or Twain's) incorrect grammar and usage? Because we recognize that Twain was manipulating language to create realism, to make his readers see Huck as an uneducated, naive boy. In writing, then, the writer's purpose has much to do with determining what is acceptable and appropriate.

A second concern of usage is to explain why certain words are frequently misused. Similarities in spelling and meaning often lead to confusion of words like *affect* and *effect, allusion* and *illusion.* Usage also covers stubborn grammatical problems like the appropriate use of *who* and *whom.* Later in this chapter there is a list of words that present usage problems with explanations on how to use those words correctly.

DIALECTAL VARIETIES OF ENGLISH

One problem that often comes under the heading of usage is the appropriateness of dialectal varieties of English. The problem is serious because of the social and political implications of saying that one dialect should be preferred to all others.

A dialect is a variety of a language spoken by a particular group of people bound by political, social, economic, professional, or geographic ties. Some of the most familiar dialects of English are Black English, Appalachian dialect, and Southern dialect. However, dialects of sorts also exist among professional and occupational groups, such as doctors, educators, lawyers, and construction workers; all have their own varieties of language characterized by words, ideas, and attitudes unfamiliar to people outside their groups.

Dealing with dialectal varieties of English in the schools and in society is a problem because of the implication that certain dialects are "non-standard" and therefore inappropriate for all situations. Many educators believe that it is the responsibility of the English teacher to eradicate nonstandard dialects and to teach all students to use standard English because it is understood by more people and is appropriate in a wider variety of situations. Unfortunately, no matter how noble the intentions of educators are, the implication that nonstandard dialects are inferior to standard English still remains.

One observation that might help reduce the problem created by dialectal varieties of English is the recognition that dialects represent oral language. Nonstandard dialects appear inferior when they are written because they reflect pronunciations and sentence patterns quite different from standard written English. Writing is an artificial form of communication because it represents an attempt to put speech on paper. Consequently, there are codes (rules) that apply to written language that don't apply to speech.

In writing, dialectal varieties are valuable in fulfilling the writer's purpose, as we have seen in Mark Twain's creation of Huck's character. However, Twain's use of nonstandard dialect was conscious and deliberate. It is only when dialectal varieties are used in inappropriate contexts that they are considered wrong—but notice, it is the *use* of the dialect, not the *dialect itself,* that is inappropriate.

The failure to recognize the oral nature of dialects and the reluctance to admit that nonstandard dialects are appropriate in some situations have made the issue of nonstandard English a political and social problem. It won't be solved until more people—including politicians, educators, and laymen—understand that there are no absolutes in the use of language. Grammatical correctness and dialectal appropriateness is determined by the situation, and the situation includes such variables as context, the writer's intentions, and the makeup of the audience.

GLOSSARY OF USAGE.

accept, except   Easily confused because of similar spelling and pronunciation. *Accept* is a verb meaning *to receive. Except* is a preposition meaning *with the exclusion of.* (*Except* can also be a verb meaning to leave out.)

> No applications will be accepted after November 15 except those delayed through the mail.

adapt, adopt   Two distinct, different verbs. *Adapt* means *to change something to fit a new purpose:*

> He adapted his beliefs about reincarnation to her religious beliefs.

Adopt means *to accept something as one's own without change:*

> He adopted Mary's beliefs about life after death.

advice, advise   Both refer to helping someone with a difficult decision or a problem. *Advice* is a noun; *advise* is a verb:

> His advice was to take the course now.
> He advised me to take the course now.

affect, effect   Frequently confused because of similar spelling and meaning. *Affect* is a verb meaning *to influence:*

> I'm not sure how this new drug will affect you.

Effect is a noun meaning *a result:*

> The most common effect is dizziness.

affective, effective   Easily confused. *Effective* means *producing the intended result:*

> The drug was effective in getting rid of his cold.

Affective is a technical, psychological term for *emotional:*

> Educators claim that the affective domain influences a student's learning process.

ain't   Controversial. Generally considered nonstandard but used by many educated speakers in casual speech. Inappropriate in formal writing and in classroom writing, unless it is deliberately used to create a particular stylistic effect.

all ready, already   *All ready* is an adjective phrase meaning *everything is ready:*

> We were all ready to go on the trip when we discovered the transmission was about to fail.

Already is an adverb meaning *by this time* or *prior to some designated time:*

> Have you done your assignment already?

all right, alright   Should be two words. The one-word form is incorrect.

allusion, illusion Frequently confused and misused. *Allusion* is a reference; *illusion* is a deceptive impression:

> It is frustrating to read something filled with allusions that I don't recognize.
>
> He had the illusion that I was going to type his 10-page paper.

alot should be two words—*a lot.* Colloquial; should be avoided in formal and in classroom writing.

among, between *Between* refers to two items; *among,* to at least three:

> She couldn't decide between her new red dress and her favorite blue dress.
>
> The new teacher had expected to find more than ten *A* students among all five of her classes.

amount, number Frequently misused. *Number* is used with enumerated, countable items; *amount* refers to a total quantity not considered in units:

> The amount of homework I have each night is increasing.
>
> The number of assignments in my English class is more than I expected.

as, like *As* is a conjunction, so it should introduce a clause. *Like* is a preposition:

> She didn't clean up her room as I asked her to.
>
> I want a pair of jeans like Mary's.

bad, badly Frequently misused. *Bad* is an adjective, *badly,* an adverb:

Incorrect: I feel badly about forgetting to call you.
Should be: I feel bad about forgetting to call you.
Correct: He performed badly in his recital.

being as, being that colloquial expressions; use *because* or *since* instead:

Avoid: Being as I may be late. . . .
Better: Since I may be late. . . .

beside, besides Both are prepositions. *Beside* means at the side of; *besides* means in addition:

> He sat down beside her.
>
> He doesn't have much to do tonight besides his homework.

but that, but what colloquial expressions that should be avoided in writing. They are redundant; use *that* alone:

> There is no question but that he'll go.

Rewrite as: There is no question that he'll go.

can, may *Can* expresses ability or power; *may* refers to permission, opportunity, or willingness:

> They can finish that tonight if they hurry.
>
> They may not be able to finish that tonight.

can't help but Colloquial expression acceptable in speech but not in writing.

Avoid: I can't help but worry about him.
Write: I can't help worrying about him.

cite, sight, site   Easy to confuse in meaning and spelling. *Site* refers to a building or a piece of land. *Sight* refers to landmarks or things to see. *Cite* means to quote as an authority or example:

Construction sites usually detract from the attractiveness of the surrounding area.
Did you see all the sights in London?
She cited Professor Green's book as the source of her ideas.

continual, continuous   *Continual* means recurring at intervals; *continuous* means uninterrupted:

This afternoon, it rained continuously for two hours.
We've been unable to have our picnic because of the continual rain this summer.

convince, persuade   *Convince* means to win agreement; *persuade* means to move to action:

I convinced John that the movie was worth watching.
I persuaded John to go see the movie with me.

could of   Incorrect form that shows interference from speech.

Mary could of called last night if she had known you were here.
Should be: Mary could have called last night if she had known you were here.

devise, device   *Devise* is a verb; *device,* a noun:

I must devise a way of getting out of here by midnight.
This device is supposed to cut down the phone bill.

different from, different than   The correct grammatical form is *different from,* but *different than* is appropriate in some cases:

These jeans are different from the ones I ordered.
It tasted different than I had expected.

enthuse, enthused   Back formation from *enthusiastic.* Widely used, but many grammarians and English teachers still object that it is colloquial.

farther, further   *Farther* is an adverb referring to literal distance; *further* refers to distance only figuratively:

They had discussed the problem in two four-hour meetings. Further discussion was postponed to give the committee a chance to rest.
We hadn't driven to the cabin in years. Today, it seemed farther out of town than it did when I was a child.

fewer, less   *Fewer* is used in comparing quantities that can be counted separately. *Less* is used in comparisons involving amounts or quantities that aren't enumerated:

I have fewer clothes than she has.
The Joneses make less money than we do.

good, well   Ordinarily, *good* is an adjective: This pie tastes *good*. And *well* is an adverb: He did the work well.
But the words are interchangeable when they refer to the state of one's health:

> Aren't you feeling good?
> Aren't you feeling well?

hopefully   A sentence adverb used much as *fortunately* is used:

> Fortunately, the war ended before too much destruction occurred.
> Hopefully, the war will end before many lives are lost.

However, many object that *hopefully* means "I hope that" or "It is hoped that," and they argue that those phrases should be used instead of the adverb. Its use is widespread, although it should probably be restricted to speech and informal writing.

imply, infer   Confused frequently because both deal with judgments about what others say. *Imply* refers to what a statement means:

> Your criticism implies that the book is not worth reading.

Infer means to take an implication; it refers to a judgment made by a speaker or a listener:

> From your criticism, I infer that it would be a waste of time to read that book.

irregardless   Common in speech, but a nonstandard variant of *regardless*. Logically, the two negative affixes—*ir-* and *-less*—should not occur in one word.

its, it's   *Its*, the possessive pronoun, requires no apostrophe. *It's*, a contraction for *it is*, requires an apostrophe.

lend, loan   Purists and traditionalists frown on using *loan* as a verb, but it is used frequently in speech:

> Would you loan me a quarter?

Use *lend* in writing.

lie, lay   Verbs related in meaning; frequently confused because of an overlap in their principal parts: *Lie* is an intransitive verb meaning to recline; *lay* is a transitive verb meaning *to place* or *set down*. They share the same form for the past principal part of *lie* and the present of *lay:*

PRESENT	PAST	PERFECT
lie	lay	lain
lay	laid	laid

Use them in the following senses:

> I want to lie down when I get home. Yesterday, I lay in bed until 9 o'clock. I haven't lain in bed that late for a long time.
> Please lay the book on the table carefully. Yesterday, you laid it on the edge and it fell off. I should have laid it down myself.

loose, lose *Loose* is an adjective meaning *unrestrained* or a verb meaning *to unfasten. Lose* is a verb meaning *to misplace.* They are confused because of their similar spelling.

> My bicycle chain is loose.
> If I don't tighten it, I'll probably lose it.

lots, lots of Colloquial expressions which should be avoided in writing.

may be, maybe *May be* is a verb form: an auxiliary + verb *be. Maybe* is an adverb:

> He may be going to New York soon.
> Maybe he's going sooner than he thinks.

myself Should be used only as a reflexive pronoun, never as a substitute for *I* or *me:*

> Wrong: If you want a ride, call either John or myself.
> Should be: If you want a ride, call either John or me.

prejudice, prejudiced Use these words carefully. If you use it as a participle, make sure the *d* appears

> The defendant feared the jury would be prejudiced against him.

principal, principle Homophones frequently confused. As a noun, *principal* means *a leader* or *chief* or *head;* as an adjective it means *main:*

> My brother will play the principal character in the school play.
> His principal was pleased with the drama coach's choice.

Principle is a noun that means *theory, concept,* or *rule:*

> The law of diminishing utility is one of the principles you study in an economics class.

proved, proven Commonly used interchangeably as the past participle and perfect forms of *prove. Proven* may be used as an adjective (past participle) but not as the perfect form. The correct perfect form is *proved.*

> After working five hours, he has finally proved his algebra problem.
> My grandmother claims this is a proven remedy for colds. [*proved* would be inappropriate here].

raise, rise *Raise* is a transitive verb meaning *to lift up; rise* is intransitive and means *to get or go up:*

> He raised the box above his head.
> I saw it rise above his head.

real, really Common in colloquial speech, but should be avoided in writing when used as intensifiers. *Real* may be used in formal writing to mean *actual* or *true* punctuation.

sensual, sensuous Frequently confused. *Sensual* means *carnal,* or having to do with sex, as in *sensual thrill. Sensuous* refers to the senses:

> The baby was delighted by sensuous impressions.

set, sit Verbs sometimes confused. *Set* is transitive and means *to put something down*. *Sit* is intransitive and means *to occupy a place by sitting.*

> Set the book on the table.
> He invited me to sit by him.

shall, will Many people still claim that *shall* is the only correct form to use with the first-person pronoun: I shall go to town tomorrow. However, it sounds too formal, and it bears connotations of commands or prophecy:

> Thou shalt not steal.
> I shall return.

Will is appropriate in most contexts, although in questions, *shall* can be used without too much formality: Shall I join you?

should of Incorrect form due to interference from speech. The correct form is *should have.*

unique Means one of a kind but is frequently used in the sense of "unusual" or "rare."

> Going to Europe was a unique experience.

The objection to the use of *unique* is that its "original" meaning has been lost or obscured through overuse.

used to Be sure the *d* is there. Since *d* and *t* merge when you use the phrase in speech, it's easy to forget that *used* is a past participle or a past form and must end in *d:*

> He used to run four miles every day.
> He is not used to getting up so early.

who, which, that Relative pronouns frequently used interchangeably. *Which* and *that* should refer to inanimate or animate, nonhuman objects; *who* should be used when referring to persons.

who, whom Relative pronouns frequently used interchangeably. *Who* should be used when the relative pronoun is the subject of the clause, *whom* when it is the object:

> the young man who will marry my sister
> the young man whom my sister will marry

would of Incorrect form that reveals interference from speech. The correct form is *would have.*

PUNCTUATION

Punctuation can be one of the most difficult and frustrating parts of editing. The rules that govern this part of writing sometimes seem arbitrary, and that makes it difficult to use punctuation correctly. However, when we study punctuation, we discover that it is as systematized as syntax. Furthermore, we realize that punctuation marks are very important in indicating the writer's purpose.

Correct punctuation is effective punctuation. We can't deny that there are rules to tell us where commas should go and when colons should be used, but punctuation is more than the mechanical application of those rules. We can approach punctuation on two levels: on a mechanical level and on a functional level.

On the mechanical level, punctuation is a series of rules that are applied automatically, almost mindlessly, when certain conditions occur in sentences. All your life, you've heard rules like the following:

Place a comma before the coordinating conjunction in a compound sentence.

Use commas to set off nonrestrictive clauses.

A mechanical approach to punctuation is fine, if you can remember what terms like "compound sentence" and "nonrestrictive" clause mean; but you may not remember them. That is when a functional approach may be more rational.

On the functional level, punctuation is a system in which marks and symbols signal to the reader the writer's intentions about how a sentence should be interpreted. In speech, you "punctuate" your sentences with pauses, rises in voice pitch, intonation, modulations in speed of utterance, facial gestures, hand motions. In writing, punctuation compensates for the absence of these visual and vocal clues to meaning. Commas, periods, semicolons, dashes, parentheses, underlining, and other marks of punctuation help the reader follow your train of thought. Effective use of punctuation tells the reader much about your intentions in your sentences. Punctuation, then, is primarily for the reader. The more you write, the more you will discover that punctuation marks can work for you in directing your reader how to read in the same way that a conductor's baton directs an orchestra when it plays a piece. This personal and somewhat intuitive use of punctuation, however, will come only after you know the basic "rules" of punctuation so well that they are second nature for you. So master the few standard rules and then let yourself learn to enjoy really *using* punctuation to your advantage.

ELEMENTS OF PUNCTUATION

ELEMENT PERIOD	FUNCTION	EXAMPLES
	A period indicates a full stop at the end of a sentence.	Boysenberry ice cream is good.
■	A period is used with an indirect question instead of a question mark.	She asked if I liked the opera.
	A period is used after an *acceptable* sentence fragment.	Did you enjoy the festival? Very much.
	A period always goes inside the quotation marks.	"Daffodils often grow on hills." That was the statement made by the horticulturist.

ELEMENT	FUNCTION	EXAMPLES
	Use periods after initials in names.	John F. Kennedy, Dr. E. K. Hambrick
	Use periods between dollars and cents.	$54.98
	Use periods with abbreviations.	Inc., Ms., M.D.

	Use periods following the numbers or letters in lists or outlines.	I.
		   A.
		   B.

COMMA

,

A comma can link, enclose, separate, and show omissions.

To link:
Place a comma before a coordinating conjunction *(and, but, or, nor, for, so, yet)* when it combines two sentences (independent clauses).

The tacos were good, and the sangria was even better.

(Some handbooks suggest that the comma can be omitted if the sentences are short, if there is no complicated punctuation in them, and if the sentences won't be misread. You will always be safe, however, if you insert the comma. This will obviate your having to make an individual decision each time.)

To separate:
Commas separate introductory elements from the rest of the sentence.

During the first game of the series, we had four runs, six hits, and no errors.
Finally, I'm finished.
Yes, I know I'm excited.

The comma may be omitted if the introductory clause or phrase is short and does not cause confusion without the mark of punctuation. You will never be wrong, however, to insert the comma.

When you go I will go.

Commas separate items in a series.

Cigarettes harm your lungs, my lungs, and everybody's lungs.
I learned how to be a leader, how to take orders, how to control my temper, and how to work with others.
I ate the big, juicy, wormless, delicious red apple.

The comma before the final item in a series is optional.

We had stories to tell of Indian pueblos, spicy food and hot summer nights.

No comma is needed if all items in a series are joined by *and.*

We saw Porsches and Jaguars and Mercedes Benzs on the lot.

ELEMENT	FUNCTION	EXAMPLES
	A comma joins two coordinate modifiers. (To identify coordinate modifiers, see if they can be switched and the meaning stays the same.)	Her romantic, optimistic view of life encouraged us.
	A comma separates a nonrestrictive element that comes at the end of the the sentence.	They all like the fall of the year, especially if they are in the mountains.
COLON ■ ■	A colon is a punctuation mark of anticipation that halts the reader, then connects the first statement to the following one.	
	A colon can connect a series or list to the sentence.	I have four classes: math, biology English, and history.
	A colon can link one statement to another to develop, illustrate, explain, or amplify it. When used in this way, the colon can even link two sentences.	Any large cafeteria can have two related problems: it must fix enough food but not too much, and it must keep the food from spoiling.
	A colon can introduce a stacked list.	The following courses will be offered in the fall: Math 103 Math 209 Math 308 Math 104 Math 210 Math 309
	A colon adds emphasis to a phrase that completes a sentence.	Only one thing can make me happy: a new camera.
	Colons can separate chapters and verses as well as hours and minutes.	Genesis 1:1 9:30 A.M.
	In proportions, colons mean ratios.	$8:4 = 12:x$
	A colon can follow salutations in letters.	Dear Sir: Dear Karma: Dear Ms. Geoffry:
	When using colons with quotations, capitalize the first letter of the first word of the quotation if the quote originally began with a capital letter.	The sign stated: "No shoes, no shirt, no service."
	A colon always goes outside quotation marks.	These are qualities he calls "good": wine, women, and song.
	If you quote a statement that ends with a colon, drop the colon and add ellipses.	"Any large cafeteria can have two related problems . . .," an author contends.
QUESTION MARK ?	Use a question mark at the end of a sentence that asks a question.	What do you think you're doing?

ELEMENT	FUNCTION	EXAMPLES
	With quotations, when the writer who is doing the quoting is asking the question, the question mark goes outside of the quotation marks.	Did she say, "I wouldn't marry you if my life depended on it"?
	When the quotation is a question, the question mark goes inside the quotation marks.	She asked, "What do you think you're doing?"
SEMICOLON	A semicolon can join two sentences that are close in meaning. It indicates a greater pause than a comma but not as great a pause as a period. Semicolons can also add clarity to involved sentences.	
	Place a semicolon to join closely related sentences.	I want to go; he doesn't.
	Use a semicolon to join closely related sentences combined with a conjunctive adverb.	I want to go; however, he doesn't.
	Use the semicolon to divide series in sentences that have several series.	This year I'm taking math, English, weightlifting, and biology; next year I'm taking history, chemistry, drafting, and swimming.
	Use a semicolon to separate sentences joined by a coordinating conjunction if the sentences already have commas.	In most cases, I would order steak, baked potato, and salad; but today I think I'll order fish.
EXCLAMATION POINT	Exclamation points are used at the end of sentences to show surprise, anger, or emphasis.	She's married! Hell, no, I'm not giving in! I'll never do that again!
QUOTATION MARKS " "	Quotation marks enclose direct repetition of words.	
	When you quote anything word for word from another source, enclose those words in quotation marks.	The report said, "Too many high school graduates are going to college."
	If a quotation is longer than five lines, indent all of the lines of the quotation five spaces from the left margin, single-spaced. Don't use quotation marks with indented quotations.	

	If a quotation is more than one paragraph (and it is not indented because it's not more than five lines), put quotation marks at the beginning of every paragraph but at the end of only the last paragraph.	"I can't pay the rent; I can't pay the rent.
		   "My kids are hungry.
		   "My house is cold.
		   "My husband left me.
		   "I can't pay the rent."

ELEMENT	FUNCTION	EXAMPLES
	If you have a quotation within a quotation, use single quotation marks (the apostrophe key on a typewriter) on the inside quote.	Regan asked, "Did I hear him say 'Get lost'?"
	Use quotation marks to indicate titles of short stories, magazine and newspaper articles, songs, and television programs.	"The Death of a Salesman" "Captain Kangaroo" "Grease"
	Always put periods and commas inside closing quotation marks.	"The Death of a Salesman," "Grease." He said, "I'll go."
	Always put colons and semicolons outside closing quotation marks.	The hero said, "I'll pay the rent"; that surprised me. These are my favorite "classes": lunchtime, study hall, and rest period.
	For all other punctuation: If the punctuation is a part of the quotation, place it inside the quotation marks; if the punctuation is not a part of the quotation, place it outside the marks.	
	See *question marks*.	
	Words used in a special way or words to which the writer wants to draw attention for some reason are put in quotation marks.	"Teasing" your hair is bad for it.
APOSTROPHE **,**	Use the apostrophe to show possession, to mark the place where letters are omitted, and to indicate the plural of numbers and letters.	
	Possession: An apostrophe is used with an *s* to form the possessive case of some nouns.	Barbara's lifestyle
	With compound nouns, the last noun takes the possessive to show that they both own something.	Quick Draw and Huckleberry's capers
	When each noun possesses something (individually), then both nouns are possessive.	Jack's and Jill's pails
	With singular nouns that end in *s*, you can form the possessive by adding only an apostrophe or by adding an apostrophe and an *s*.	a waitress' job, an actress' costume a waitress's job, an actress's costume
	Use only an apostrophe for plural nouns that end in *s*.	a secretaries' meeting, students' reports

ELEMENT	FUNCTION	EXAMPLES
	Add only an apostrophe to nouns that end in multiple consecutive *s* sounds.	Charles' tricks, Jesus' parables
	Don't use an apostrophe with possessive pronouns.	yours, its, his, ours, whose, theirs
	Omission: An apostrophe marks where letters or numbers have been left out of a word or date.	I'm, I'll, can't, back in '43
	Plurals: Apostrophes indicate the plural of numbers.	6's, 70's, seven 1,000's
	An apostrophe with an *s* can show the plural of a word as a word.	You had seventeen *you's* in that paragraph.
	If a term is all capital letters or ends in a capital letter, you don't need an apostrophe for the plural.	I'll have six B.A.s before it's all over. Eight ADDs are enough for that computer program.

DASH

	When typing, use two hypens (--) to indicate a dash.	
	A dash can indicate a sharp turn in thought.	That marks the end of that class—unless I failed the last test.
	A dash can add emphasis to a pause.	I'll get the job done—after I take another break.
	Dashes can set off an explanatory series or an appositive series.	Two of the applicants—Steve and Lisa—will be offered jobs.
	Dashes can add emphasis to a parenthetical element (an item inserted in the sentence that isn't essential to meaning).	Only one person—you—can control what you say.

PARENS (PARENTHESES)

( )

	Recently we discovered that the punctuation marks were called parens and the information inside the parens, along with the parens, was called parenthesis. This news is not earth-shattering, but it is interesting.	
	Parens suggest a closeness between the writer and the reader and imply that you two know something that the rest of the world might not know. Parenthetical information is played-down and de-emphasized: it may not be essential to a sentence, but it may be interesting or helpful to the reader.	Many American presidents (for example, Dwight Eisenhower) were military leaders. CUNY (City University of New York) offers a variety of programs.

ELEMENT	FUNCTION	EXAMPLES
	Punctuation:	
	Parenthetical material does not affect the punctuation of a sentence. If a parenthetical clause comes at the end of a sentence, for example, the period to end the sentence would go outside the parens.	I like some history courses (American), but hate others (ancient Greek).
	When numbering a series of items in a sentence, use two parens, not one.	I'll eat (1) potatoes, (2) meat, (3) carrots, and (4) gravy.
	When a complete sentence is parenthetical, the end punctuation goes inside the parens.	I want to know (You can tell me if you want to.) what I've got to do to improve.
	If you have an item that you need to set off with parens inside of a parenthetical idea, use brackets.	I want to know (You can tell me [if you want to].) . . . .
ELLIPSIS ● ● ●	Ellipsis is a punctuation mark that shows you've left out some words.	
	When you quote only part of a statement, insert ellipsis to show where you've left the information out.	"Work . . . is the privilege of all citizens," the politician explained.
	It's not fair to leave any important information out of a quotation or to pull words from a quotation and change the meaning.	
BRACKET ( )	Brackets are used to set off material that is your own inside quotation marks which surround someone else's words.	"The trio [Kingston Trio] will appear at the Bottom Mark Sunday, November 12," read the announcement in the paper.
VIRGULE/SLASH /	A virgule or slash is used to separate two things which belong together as choices or to separate lines of poetry that have been run together.	Do you know the either/or rule? Roses are red/Violets are blue/Sugar is sweet/And so are you.

APPLICATION

1   Discuss the appropriateness of the punctuation marks in the following passage.

I first took up the piano when I was five, in the late 1940's. The town in which I lived, a small Georgia town of about 5000 people, had very few music teachers; but the one I had was as good, I thought, as any you might find in a big city. She was unusual in that she assigned us "sheet music" to play almost as soon as we learned how to put our hands on the keys. I remember, with pleasure, my first piece of sheet music (I think I even remember the color: blue); it was "A Snowy Day." I was just a wee thing and, naturally, couldn't reach the pedals. I used only one hand, but I played with enthusiasm. Fortunately, people were just happy to see a little girl like me up there at all—so nobody laughed at the simplicity of what I played. When I got off that stool, I felt as proud as I did fifteen years later when I was chosen to play "Star Dust" at my college senior banquet!

2   Fill in the blanks in the sentences below with appropriate punctuation marks. Be able to explain your reason for each choice. In some sentences, several marks may be used to perform the same function.

1 A university is one of the most important institutions in the world today__ with universities__ we all have a chance to succeed.
2 The appeal of the editorial is essentially apolitical__ it is not a cry for socialism but a cry for charity.
3 The doctor is forced to leave his town and everyone he knows__ but he cannot be stripped of his most valuable possession__ his courage.
4 The motivation must come from within__ if a person is depending on someone else for her motivation__ the chances are very good that her motivation will never come.
5 The bare facts are pitiable enough__ his ragged clothes, his poor health, and the freezing weather.
6 He must be able to justify all of his own actions__ since he will be practically__ if not totally__ alone in his convictions.
7 A university education fuels the one fire that is common in all of those who are successful__ the burning desire to learn.
8 Self-motivation is most evident in someone doing something she enjoys doing__ therefore__ it is important to choose a field of study that one finds interesting.
9 People enjoy receiving gifts__ education is one of the best gifts a person can give herself.
10 If we do not alleviate it__ poverty will surely destroy us all__ if not physically__ then spiritually.

3   Decide if the following phrases and clauses are restrictive or nonrestrictive and punctuate them accordingly.

1 My brother who just graduated from law school has gotten a job.
2 Time and again I've seen people many of whom I would never see again become very involved with me in what I was doing.
3 The park which I have often sat in really needs a renovation.
4 If they her mother and father knew what was happening, they would be thrilled.
5 Do you think as you look back on it that the decision was good?

6 What can be said they wanted to know about the situation?
7 The men and boys who had just arrived found the camp very much to their liking.
8 The face of the clock which was brown with white numbers was beautiful.
9 To do that job was a task which everybody dreaded.
10 The dish to be prepared correctly requires a particular kind of onion.

4   Put the apostrophe in the correct places in these sentences.

1 Its true that that persons hat is the funniest Ive ever seen.
2 The childrens playroom is painted orange and yellow.
3 Their parents reactions were not surprising.
4 Give everything its due.
5 Wherever you go, its not going to be home.
6 Her friends summer plans are still up in the air.
7 Tommies chickens are laying eight to twelve eggs a day.
8 Thats amazing.
9 That is Malcolms or Freds motorbike.
10 Her mother-in-laws plane arrived right on time.

5   Punctuate the following sentences:

1 Wherever you go whatever you do remember me.
2 In the dim twilight of the evening the stars peeked out and we said hello.
3 If not watched carefully misplaced modifiers are likely to squint dangle become misplaced or otherwise behave badly.
4 Youll feel like giving them a good shake and sending them to bed without supper.
5 Sadly they put the flag at half mast.
6 Here are your color choices blue white pink purple and red.
7 My choice is for the tall glass her choice is for the short one.
8 When you see them and they see you what will you do?
9 Whatever else happens I will be at the party on time I really want to see everybody arrive.
10 Stop and see the caves whatever you do.
11 The rocks of the desert desert refers to an arid place where plants must accommodate themselves take on the colors of the sky the sand the plants and the animals.
12 When they go I will go.
13 What can I do asked the young woman who had joined the group.
14 Three fourths of all people on the ship had never seen the May 14 1976 edition of the paper.
15 China Syndrome is a movie that reminds people of Three Mile Island.

6 Punctuate this letter.

Dear Wilson

I know you wont believe this but I am finally writing a letter I have gotten settled you wouldnt believe what that has taken and really like this place. I think you will too when you come. Probably the most unique thing about it is the countryside how it looks how it feels how it just takes you in. Coming from the Northwest the way I did I didnt know that I would be living among some of the tallest trees in North America I asked someone the other day why the trees were so tall and she said I think its because these are first growth trees I dont believe they have ever been cut There has to be some explanation because Ive never seen anything like it I want you your parents and all my friends to see the place

I have already met a lot of people many have dropped by the house to say hello. Among the nicest customs of the place is the bringing of token presents to newcomers. Ive gotten fresh peaches a half a watermelon some fresh bass from the creek and people havent stopped bringing things yet I am already thinking about buying a freezer which I have never owned before just to take advantage of the great foodstuff grown in these parts

When you see Peggy tell her that even though she told me how much I would like this place I wasnt prepared for my response The thing she told me which really sticks in my mind was that she also had made a long move from one part of the country to another and the move although it had been hard had really been stimulating and beneficial. As you might imagine I have been using her as a model

Among the things I would like for you to do for me there are these see if I left my bike lock in the old garage on that nail on the right hand side of the door call Jeremy and ask him to mail my tennis shoes which I left on the back porch after we went swimming and find out if the post office has started forwarding my mail.

And if you want me to do anything for you in this beautiful part of the country like checking to see if the corn is in yet or getting you some beautiful river rocks for a fireplace or signing up for a hike up Mt LeConte just let me know I do want you to know that in spite of my pleasure at being in my new place I miss you and all my friends there I really want to keep in touch I am getting a telephone tomorrow my number will be 615 332 5475 Call me as soon as you can

                        Sincerely
                        Edna

SPELLING

Spelling errors are among the most difficult errors to detect when you are editing your work. In detecting punctuation errors and sentence-structure problems, you at least know when an error is likely to occur, and you can train yourself to watch for it. For instance, you can watch for structures that might lead to comma faults. But how are you supposed to know whether you've misspelled a word? Many textbooks suggest that you check every word you are not sure of. If you think that advice is illogical, you're right. It is based on the assumption that we can intuitively guess which words may be spelled incorrectly. Sometimes, that is true. That advice works with difficult words or with words that you are so uncertain about that you can't even attempt to spell them. But it's not just difficult words that are misspelled. It is the everyday, ordinary words that are misspelled most frequently. Unfortunately, misspelling often reflects carelessness or a failure to observe usage rules. When you spell *all right a-l-r-i-g-h-t* or the possessive pronoun *their t-h-e-r-e*, the problem is not really spelling—it is usage. Misspelling difficult words and misspelling words because of a failure to observe rules are two extremes of the spelling problem; fortunately, both are relatively easy to correct. You can find difficult words in the dictionary, and you can check the usage section of most grammar textbooks for the others.

The spelling errors that are most troublesome and most difficult to correct are those that you don't suspect are errors. When you spell *aggravate a-g-g-r-i-v-a-t-e* or *separate s-e-p-e-r-a-t-e*, the words slip right by in proofreading because it doesn't occur to you that you might have misspelled them. Don't expect your reader to be understanding and to say, "Oh well. He probably doesn't know that *aggravate* is spelled with an *a* not an *i*." No! What the reader will say is, "What a dummy! Everyone knows that *aggravate* is spelled with an *a* not an *i*!"

The reader's reaction to spelling errors is the strongest argument for learning to spell correctly. Misspelling, like punctuation and syntax errors, distracts the reader. How can you expect the readers to hear and accept your message when your misspellings are making more noise than they can ignore?

You may think it's a little late to be learning how to spell. After all, you may think, if you didn't learn to spell correctly in twelve years of schooling, you certainly won't learn in one or two semesters of college English. You *can*, however, learn to spell now, despite past failures, if you approach the problem methodically.

First, you should understand why some spelling errors occur.

1 When you experience the pressure of writing, you sometimes omit, add, or substitute letters in words that you know how to spell. In the rush of writing down your thoughts, words, sounds, and letters get jumbled up as your brain sends signals to your hand. So, you write *it* instead of *is*, *then* instead of *than*, *to* instead of *the*. Errors like these are comparable to typos on the typewriter. Fortunately, you can catch every one of these errors when you proofread. They should jump right out at you.

2 Homophones—words that sound alike or nearly alike but have different meanings and spellings—are another common cause of spelling errors. Again, you know that *weather* and *whether* mean entirely differ-

ent things; yet occasionally you write a sentence like this:

> My decision on weather to go to our local junior college or the state university was one of the most difficult in my life.

Even though the error is explainable, it is not excusable. Readers have no patience with writers who make careless mistakes like this. Your reliability and authority as a writer suffer when you habitually confuse homophones. Train yourself to be sensitive to homophones. Study this list of words that are frequently confused, and don't let your hand write one down when you intend the other:

are — our	led — lead
forth — fourth	loose — lose
past — passed	whether — weather
where — wear — were	principle — principal
foreward — forward	capital — capitol
conscious — conscience	sight — site — cite
hear — here	

3 When you confuse words like *accept — except, affect — effect, allusion — illusion,* the problem is more than just a simple confusion of homophones. There is more than misspelling involved here. To use these words correctly, you must learn the distinctions in meaning which make one member of these pairs entirely inappropriate in the wrong context. The usage section will help you distinguish between pairs like the following:

accept — except	allusion — illusion
affect — effect	advice — advise
access — excess	adapt — adopt

4 Finally, there are those words that cause spelling errors simply because, for some reason, they are difficult to spell. You may have heard people say that inconsistencies in spelling and pronunciation make English a hard language to learn as a second language. To a certain extent this is true. Imagine what it must be like for a non-English speaker to learn to spell *rough, though,* and *fought,* where *ough* is pronounced differently in each. Native speakers are plagued by similar problems:

a Distinctions between   -ent, -ant — dependent, existent, dominant
-al, -el, -le — barrel, battle, nobel, noble, political
-ly, -ally — basically, publicly, politically
-able, -ible — acceptable, permissible, excitable, eligible

b Indistinct vowels in

privilege	definite	separate	grammar	sponsor
primitive	sacrifice	pursue	calendar	divine

Unfortunately, there is no trick to help you remember which is the correct spelling. However, it is unlikely that you misspell every one of these, so make a special effort to learn those that do give you trouble. Don't guess at the spelling. If you're not sure whether the word is spelled *insoluable* or *insoluble,* take a few minutes to look it up.

COMMONLY MISSPELLED WORDS

accept, except	environment	personal, personnel
access, excess	equipped, equipment	perform
accommodation	euphemism,	precede
acknowledgment	euphuism	presence, presents
adapt, adopt	exceed	principal, principle
affect, effect	excite	privilege
all together,	existence	proceed
altogether	fare, fair	prophecy, prophesy
altar, alter	formally, formerly	quiet, quite
angel, angle	forth, fourth	receive
believe	forty	referring
benefited	grammar	respectively, respect-
berth, birth	guarantee	fully
born, borne	hear, here	right, rite
calendar	holy, wholly	schedule
capital, capitol	hungry	separate
censor, censure	instance, instants	similar
choice, choose, chose	irrelevant, irreverent	sophomore
cite, sight, site	it's, its	staid, stayed
coarse, course	judgment	stationary, stationery
complement,	knew, new	success
compliment	know, no	suit, suite
congratulations	laboratory	superintendent
council, counsel	later, latter	than, then
counselor	lead, led	their, there, they're
dairy, diary	loose, lose	threw, through
decent, descent	luxurious	to, too, two
definite	maintain, mainte-	vain, vane, vein
description	nance	weak, week
desert, dessert	moral, morale	weather, whether
dining, dinning	ninety	who's, whose
dyeing, dying	occasion	worse, worst
elicit, illicit	occurred	writing
emigrant, immigrant	past, passed	

Final advice to help you improve your spelling:
1 Notice the kinds of spelling errors you make habitually. Keep a list of the words that are marked as misspelled in your graded papers. Learn to spell them correctly, and resolve that you won't make that error again. There is no excuse for misspelling *separate, receive, achieve, definite* more than once.

2 When you read, pay attention to the spelling of unusual words or words that you use in speech all the time but rarely in writing—for instance, *facetious*.

3 Learn the spelling rules that will clear up habitual errors.

SPELLING RULES

Despite the inconsistencies in English spelling, there are some rules that show spelling isn't as haphazard as it sometimes seems to be. You should learn these, not simply because they are rules, but because they can help you avoid errors that distract your reader's attention away from your message.

-ie/-ei

If you don't already know this rule, memorize it and use it:

> *I* before *e*
> Except after *c*
> Or when sounded as *a*
> As in *neighbor* or *weigh*

Unfortunately, there are many exceptions to this rule—*weird, leisure, height, foreign*—but it's helpful in remembering the spelling of many commonly misspelled words—*receive, deceive, achieve.*

FINAL e + SUFFIX

a When the suffix begins with a vowel, drop the final *e:*

stare + ing	staring
note + able	notable

Except when the word ends in *-ce/-ge:* courageous, singeing, noticeable, knowledgeable.

b When the suffix begins with a consonant, keep the final *e:* wasteful, shameful, likeness, engagement, pavement, careful.

Important exceptions: abridgment, judgment, argument, acknowledgment.

FINAL CONSONANTS

a When a suffix beginning with a vowel is added to short words or short accented syllables ending in a consonant, double the final consonant:

defe*rr*al	bu*gg*ed	handica*pp*ed
fi*tt*ed	sti*rr*ing	begi*nn*ing

b If the final syllable ends in a consonant but is not accented, don't double the final consonant:

bigoted	riveter	murderer

c When a suffix beginning with a consonant is added to a word ending in a consonant, the final consonant is not doubled:

deferment   fitness   capful

FINAL y + SUFFIX
Change *y* to *i*, except when the suffix is *-ing:*

beautiful   satisfied   But: flying
                               dying
died   lied   satisfying

FINAL c + SUFFIX THAT BEGINS WITH A VOWEL
Change *c* to *ck:*

picnicking   trafficked
panicky   frolicking

There are many more rules of English spelling, but these are the ones that will help you prevent the misspellings that occur most frequently.

APPLICATION

1 There is at least one misspelled word in each of the following sentences. Find the misspellings and indicate why they are misspelled. Also, check the pronunciation.

1 Higher incomes yield more social priveledges and better success in our society.
2 The coyote is the subject of many legonds atributing to him various abilitys.
3 The coyote ganed the image of the sneeky, cunning killer because he is extreamly smart.
4 It is necessary to clerify what the author means by equality.
5 Thinking independantly is the very thing that brings Winston to his downfall.
6 This generally results when there is a drought, a suvere winter, or the ocassional lean year, when through no explainable reason there is an extream lack of wild game.

2 Choose the correct spelling for each of the following words.

1 separate, seperate
2 definately, definitely
3 judgement, judgment
4 privilege, privelege
5 devide, divide
6 embarass, embarrass
7 pronounciation, pronunciation
8 memento, momento
9 fourty, forty
10 oposition, opposition
11 grammar, grammer
12 acheive, achieve
13 calender, calendar
14 preceed, precede
15 occurance, occurrence
16 arguement, argument

17 existant, existent
18 similiar, similar
19 writting, writing

20 recieve, receive
21 professor, proffessor
22 aggrivation, aggravation

MECHANICS

Mechanics are rules that standardize certain things in writing. In some cases they function as signals to the reader; but, in most cases, mechanics are simply conventions that standardize things like capitalization, the use of numbers, and abbreviations.

Some mechanics rules are easier to remember than others. The rules that deal with punctuation may be easier to remember than those for using numbers. Fortunately, you don't have to memorize any of these rules. You can find them quickly in this book and in most books about writing. It is important that you observe these rules, though, because readers expect you to observe conventions even on things that don't substantially affect your message.

CAPITALIZATION

1 Capitalize the first word of every sentence.

2 Capitalize proper nouns:

<u>Names of Persons</u>
James Frank Harper
Herman Melville
Jesus Christ
Ronald Nelson

<u>Names of Places</u>
Washington, D.C.
Luxembourg

<u>Events and Periods</u>
the Civil War
the Stone Age
the Renaissance

<u>Monuments, Museums, Buildings, etc.</u>
the Smithsonian Institute
the Library of Congress
the Lincoln Memorial
American Buddhist Academy

<u>Names of Vessels</u>
The *U.S.S. Constitution*
Apollo 8
Old Ironsides

3 Capitalize names of deities:

Jehovah   Krishna   Jupiter

4 Capitalize titles before and after names:

Dr. John Smith
Mrs. Jack McHenry
Ms. Carol Roberts
Capt. John Smith

Professor Barbara Walker
the Rev. Bill Baker
Susan O'Casey, Ph.D.
Queen Elizabeth II

5 Capitalize the first word and all other words except prepositions,

conjunctions, and articles in the titles of literary works, movies, and works of art:

The Catcher in the Rye	*Star Wars*
For Whom the Bell Tolls	*Romeo and Juliet*
the *Mona Lisa*	"Ode to a Nightingale"

6 Capitalize names of recognized groups and organizations:

Republicans	Christian Science
Democrats	Daughters of the American Revolution
Jaycees	National Organization for Women

7 Capitalize *specific* course names:

Math 130   Psychology 441

8 Capitalize directions when they refer to specific geographical areas:

Gone with the Wind is set in the South.
She's from *West* Texas.

9 Avoid unnecessary capitalization:

I am taking a *history* course this semester.
Dallas is *northwest* of Houston.
They consider themselves members of the *upper class.*
John will be a *senior* next year.

ABBREVIATIONS AND SYMBOLS

You should use abbreviations and symbols sparingly and carefully in your writing. There are few abbreviations and symbols that are acceptable for the kind of writing you do in an English class, but if you notice the writing you are exposed to every day—newspapers, magazines, textbooks—you will see that abbreviations and symbols are rarely used there too. In general, writers avoid abbreviations because they make writing seem casual and unpolished. That's why you should avoid abbreviations like *dept., apt., Mon., assoc.,* in the context of your writing. Don't write:

I have an appointment with the head of the math dept. tomorrow.

In some cases, abbreviations are permissible. The following guidelines should help you use abbreviations properly:

1 Abbreviate titles when they are part of a name: Mrs. Emma Curtis Hopkins, Dr. James Smith, Lt. Col. James T. Anderson.

2 Organizations that are more commonly known by initials than by the full name may be abbreviated: AFL-CIO, NASA, NATO, SALT, OSHA, NOW. When you are not sure whether your audience will recognize the acronym, be sure you write out the whole name the first time you refer to it; you can use the initials for subsequent references.

3 Abbreviate the names of states only when they are part of an address. If you are referring to Fresno, California, in the text of your paper, do not write Fresno, Calif.

4 Latin abbreviations—etc., e.g., i.e.—are permissible in most writing.

5 Other acceptable abbreviations include the following: A.M., P.M., A.D., B.C., rpm, mph.

6 Many abbreviations have become common through everyday use: TV, CB, hi-fi, stereo, C.O.D. Use them only if they fit the tone of the particular piece you are writing.

7 Use the dollar sign ($) only for exact sums or for estimates of very large sums—$4.83, $1.6 billion—but write "about three dollars."

8 Do not use the ampersand (&) as a substitute for *and* in your writing unless it is part of an organization's name, as in Harper & Row.

9 Spell out percent (%) and cents (¢):

The survey shows that only 9.6 *percent* of all college freshmen are financially independent.

The price of ground beef has gone up 50 *cents* a pound in one month.

NUMBERS

Figures used in the text of your writing should be spelled out most of the time. Follow these guidelines for using numerals correctly:

1 Spell out numbers from one to ten. In very formal writing, spell out all two-digit numbers.

We have to read *five* books this semester; we may choose from a list of *25* novels.

2 Use figures to indicate exact sums, time, large figures, dates: 2:30 A.M., $8.65, 203,431, 1961, 500 B.C.

3 Avoid beginning a sentence with a figure. If you can't rewrite the sentence so the figure is not at the beginning, then spell out the number.

Avoid: 1963 marked the beginning of an important era in American life.

Rewrite: In 1963, Americans began an important era in politics.

4 Numbers from 21 to 99 are hyphenated when spelled out: thirty-five, ninety-seven. Make sure you learn how to spell these: forty (not fourty), ninety (not ninty).

ITALICS

Indicate italics in handwritten and typed work by means of underlining. Use italics in the following instances:

1 to indicate foreign words: writ of *habeas corpus, in absentia.*

2 to indicate emphasis: What do you mean *he* did it?

It was Tom, *not* Bob, who wrote the winning essay.

3 to refer to words as words: *Penultimate* is one of my favorite words, but I hardly ever get to use it.

4 to indicate titles of literary works, works of art, movies, ships: *The Queen Mary, The Agony and the Ecstasy, Starry Night.*

APOSTROPHE

The apostrophe may be considered a mark of punctuation. What distinguishes it from other marks discussed under punctuation is that it is used to punctuate single words while commas, semicolons, periods, and colons are used to punctuate sentences. It is a difficult mark to use correctly consistently because it has no equivalent in speech. Commas and periods are comparable to pauses in speech, but there is no oral equivalent for the apostrophe. Consequently, this mark is easy to omit or misplace. Fortunately, the rules for using the apostrophe are few and are relatively uncomplicated:

1 Use an apostrophe in contractions to indicate that letters have been omitted:

haven't   doesn't   she's   we'll

2 Use an apostrophe and *s* to indicate possession: Tom's car, this week's menu, the boy's illness. Remember that in forming plural possessives, the apostrophe goes after the *s:* the students' unrest, our professors' homes, two weeks' notice. Also remember that irregular plurals form the possessive just as if they were singular: children's clothes, women's lib. Words that end in *s* may be punctuated as possessives in two ways: Mr. Jones' car or Mr. Jones's car. Choose the form that you feel most comfortable with or—practically speaking—that your teacher prefers. Finally, remember that no apostrophe is required for possessive pronouns: his, theirs, ours, yours. *It's* means *it is;* the possessive pronoun *its* requires no apostrophe.

3 Use an apostrophe to indicate the plural of symbols, letters, and words:

You have too many *but's* in this sentence.
John Henry Newman and Thomas Carlyle lived in the *1800's.*
The *d's* in your typewritten work are hard to see.

HYPHEN

The hyphen is another mark of punctuation that applies to words rather than to whole sentences. (Make sure you do not confuse the hyphen with the dash. On the typewriter, the dash is formed by striking the hyphen key twice. In regular handwriting, you can simply make the dash longer than the hyphen.)

The hyphen has two main uses: it indicates compounds and word division.

1 Use a hyphen between parts of compound words: all-night, quasi-governmental, attorney-general, son-in-law. Compound adjectives are usually hyphenated: fire-breathing dragon, hard-hearted professor, blood-thirsty beast. If you are not sure whether a compound should be hyphenated, check the dictionary.

2 Use a hyphen with the following prefixes:
  a Hyphenate words formed from a prefix and a proper noun: all-American, anti-Soviet.
  b Hyphenate to avoid two identical vowels next to each other: re-entry, anti-intellectual.
  c Hyphenate prefixed words to distinguish them from words spelled the same but without the hyphen: re-create/recreate, redress/re-dress, re-cover/recover.

3 Hyphenate to indicate word division at the end of a line, but observe these guidelines:
  a Do not divide words of one syllable like *forced, though, calmed.*
  b Do not separate a suffix or syllable of less than three letters (*-ed, -le*) or a one-letter prefix or syllable (*a-, e-, o-*).
  c Separate hyphenated words (*sister-in-law, well-known, semi-retired*) only at the hyphen.
  d Do not divide a word on the last line of a page.

QUOTATION MARKS

1 Use quotation marks to indicate that you are employing someone else's exact words. Always use quotation marks when you directly quote a source in a research paper:

As James Cashin states, accounting, in the broad sense, is "a systematic recording of business transactions, their summarization and the interpretation of the summaries."

2 Use quotation marks when writing dialogue:
  "Well, do you want to go?" I asked Paul.
  "Only if we can get back by 6 o'clock," he answered.

3 Use quotation marks when you intentionally use a word in a novel way or when you want pointedly to indicate sarcasm, irony, or humor:
  In one of his poems, e. e. Cummings writes about "manunkind."
  To make her "new dress," she simply altered her sister's old prom gown.

4 Observe the following guidelines in punctuating quotations:
  a When a quotation ends in a period, question mark, or comma, place the mark *inside* the quotation marks:

Man's basic problem, according to anthropologist Don White, is "his inability to willingly live peaceably with other members of his species."

At a crucial point in the story, the main character asks, "What does life mean? What does anything mean?"

The best position for your hands on the steering wheel is not the 10 o'clock and 2 o'clock position, but the 9 o'clock and 3 o'clock position. "You have more control and your arms will be less likely to tire," explains the driving instructor.

b Semicolons and colons are placed outside the quotation marks:

Not everyone goes to college to "find his or her role in life"; many students simply expect to have a good time, learning something only incidentally.

I think there are several things we can label "all-American": our universal desire to better our social status through each generation, our need to replace objects when they begin to seem out-of-style or old-fashioned, and our never-ending effort to gain more leisure time.

c When a question mark or an exclamation point is not part of the quotation, it goes outside the quotation marks. Periods, however, are always placed inside the quotation marks:

I can't believe he actually said "yes"!
What would you do if I said, "I don't care"?

EDITING — THE FINAL STAGES

The activity of editing a piece of writing for presentation to a reader encompasses many things. It includes stylistic revision, reorganization of material, proofreading for errors in spelling, syntax, word choice, and simply looking over your paper to catch careless errors. In a writing class, your paper undergoes two kinds of editing. First, you edit the paper to make your writing as good as you possibly can before you submit it for a grade. Then, as your teacher grades it, he or she edits it to show you how to improve your writing next time. Both kinds of editing are made easier if you have a set of symbols to indicate the changes that need to be made.

As you work with your rough drafts, you may find the following symbols helpful in noting problems in your writing:

? a passage seems unclear

ss sentence seems awkward

∂ delete a word, sentence, or passage

✳ insertion needed for further explanation or similar reason

The point in using these symbols is to allow you to mark your errors and weak points as you note them without taking time to correct them then. As you revise your paper, you need to see it as a whole, and you'll never be able to do this if you are constantly correcting errors and making changes as you read it. These symbols allow you to read through your whole paper, marking places for revision or correction quickly and briefly.

Once your rough draft is complete, you will find it helpful to read it aloud to yourself or to a friend before typing it or writing it in final form. This oral reading will help you pick out sentences that sound awkward and spot unnecessary repetition that may not have been evident as you read through silently. You then experience the paper as a whole rather than as a series of sentences and paragraphs.

As you read your paper orally, you will get an idea of how a reader will react to it. You will give yourself the opportunity to see your paper as a piece of communication rather than as a classroom assignment that must be grammatically perfect.

Revision should continue even through this oral reading. Certainly, it should not be necessary to make extensive changes now, but you may find you can still make minor improvements. Writing can actually be improved with every rereading. Use your editing symbols to mark any changes you want to make as you read aloud.

Don't underestimate the importance of this oral reading. Once you do it, you will find that it will become a vital step in your revision process. If you've never read a paper to yourself or to a friend before, the first time you do it, you may feel awkward, but keep trying until this oral reading helps you see your writing as actual communication.

PROOFREADING

At this point, your paper should be in final form, ready to turn in. **Read it one more time to catch careless errors.** This sort of editing is called *proofreading*. At this stage, you are looking only for typographical errors, omitted letters or words, sometimes even omitted sentences, misspellings, incorrect punctuation, and similar minor errors. Use the following symbols to indicate to yourself or to your typist the necessary change:

capitalization needed

no capitalization

insert comma

insert semicolon

insert period

$\mathscr{e}$ delete

$\mathcal{C}$ close up

$\wedge$ insert a word or sentence

$\#$ insert a space

$\mathcal{U}$ transpose letters

THE TEACHER'S CORRECTION SYMBOLS AND COMMENTS

When you get your graded paper back, you'll notice that your teacher has his or her own set of symbols to mark the problems in your paper. The following list may help you interpret the symbols and abbreviations in the margins of your papers:

awk a favorite comment for many teachers. It may mean anything from awkward sentence structure to illogical statement. If you don't understand what it means, ask your teacher to explain.

ab word should not be abbreviated. Spell it out.

agr faulty subject-verb agreement

choppy too many short sentences

coh paragraph or sentence lacks coherence

colloq inappropriate use of a colloquial expression

coor coordination needed or ineffective coordination

CF comma fault, a necessary comma has been omitted

CS comma splice, two complete sentences joined only with a comma

D diction, incorrect word or inappropriate word choice

DM dangling modifier

frag sentence fragment

good idea, sentence structure, etc. is especially good, perhaps even impressive

paral faulty parallelism

pass ineffective or unnecessary use of passive voice

pron. ref. pronoun does not agree with antecedent or antecedent is not clear

¶ paragraph needed

No ¶ no paragraph needed

rep awkward or unnecessary repetition

run-on run-on sentence, two sentences linked without any punctuation

p incorrect punctuation

sp spelling

SS something is wrong with sentence structure

sub subordination needed or ineffective subordination

t incorrect or inappropriate verb tense

trans transition needed or ineffective transition

trite expression is trite; should be replaced with an original one

U paragraph or sentence lacks unity

usage faulty or inappropriate usage

wordy sentence or passage is wordy

APPLICATION

1 Passage *A* shows how editing symbols can be used in revision. Study the passage carefully, then edit passage *B*.

A

In the passage from ~~John Henry Newman's book~~, The Idea
of a University, ∧Newman says that∧ most people believe that universities turn students
into ideal gentlemen, ~~through most the people's eyes.~~ But
only the close observer can tell that the university student
is ~~a fake~~, not∧ a gentleman, but ~~one~~ who has all the ~~outside~~ external
qualities of a gentleman and not the inner qualities of
virtue and conscientiousness. ~~Since this passage was
written in the mid eighteen hundreds~~, Newman could have
been right about the universities ~~then~~, but ~~looking at the
universities now~~, I believe that over all the university is
a ~~very~~ good institution for those who seek a higher
education.

To me∧ the university ~~is a place where I can go~~ represents a way to
fulfill my dream in life. ~~Granted~~, However the university is not
for everyone--just those who want it. ∧ Someone who wants to be a carpenter,
a construction worker∧ or a farmer∧ may have no reason to attend a
universit~~ies~~y, but ∧ an aspiring a docter, scientist, businessman,∧ or teacher

has
~~all~~ ~~have~~ to continue ~~their~~ education in universities, which *make / smoother transition to idea of expense* sometimes can be expensive.

a university education
Because ~~going to universities~~ is expensive, I believe

the students who attend are ~~very~~ serious about their studies

are not concerned
and grades, and ~~less serious~~ about making a good impression

on
~~to~~ the professor or instructor. Of course, there are some

students who attend college to have fun, to get married, or

these form
even just to get away from home, but I feel ~~this~~ a very

small minority.

~~As I said before~~ the majority of the students ~~who~~ attend

college ~~do so~~ because they want a higher education in a

certain field. Most ~~of these students~~ have their own ideas

they would like to think and act independently.
of what they want to be, and (can stand on their own two feet.) ?

If you agree that today's student seeks independence,
~~Agreeing with the proceeding statement~~, you would have *to* believe

he   *can*
that ~~the majority of students~~ ~~would~~ not be influenced by ~~their~~

proffessors or instructors enough to become one of Newman's

false
students of ~~fake~~ virtue and conscientiousness.

B

John Newman in his *The Idea of a University* believes that regardless of how much knowledge and philosophy you fill a man with; he is still human and his emotions will appear even when his mind has been filled with unemotional, logical knowledge. Newman wants his reader to realize that college does not change a persons personality. Yes, it does help to cultivate the mind, but it does not and cannot change a human beings feelings. The passionate side of us, (if strong enough) will always win out over the logical side of us. Personally I agree with Newman that college is a place of education. I think that college should offer a wide variety of knowledge for students to take advantage of, and to create a few social activities so the passionate side of us can expand as well as the knowledgable side of us.

Universities today should offer career oriented subjects for students to study. For example, I myself am interested in Electrical Engineering. The college I am attending offers this subject of study. I plan to take advantage of the knowledge that it will give me of electrical components. I certainly don't expect it to give me some overwhelming emotional feelings. Double E was not created to help the emotional side of me expand also. Personally I think that is my own problem not Electrical Engineerings.

2   The following sentences contain the kinds of errors you should catch in proofreading. Identify the error in each and explain how to correct it.

1 Sit down and ask yourself what is really unbearable, civilizations constant demands, or its hectic pace.
2 The small town offers many things not offered in a large city such as: a closer relation to nature, hunting and fishing, knowledge of farming, perhaps closer family ties, and much more room.
3 Procrastination is my major weekness.
4 There was nothing the doctors could do but to keep him as comfortable as possible.
5 A university opens up an opportunity for a student to use his or her own mind.
6 When students graduate, they should be able to discuss intelligibly any number of areas concerning our society—how it works, what it was, and the possible directions it might be taking.
7 These problems can generally be solved by considerate and understanding teachers.
8 It was certainly a courageous thing to do.
9 The desire to learn brought this person to the university today, and that same desire will send her out to success in society tomorrow.
10 Thus the early Greeks had an understanding of power and its effects on man.

A.B.C. GUIDE TO CORRECTING YOUR WRITING

THE ITEM . . .	EXPLAINED . . .	AND IN ACTION ! ! !
a/an	Use *a* before words that begin with a consonant and *an* before words that begin with a vowel (a, e, i, o, u). Words beginning with pronounced *h* take *a;* words with the *h* not pronounced take *an.*	a bartender, a juggler, a Fiat; an onion, an obnoxious oaf; a humble team; an hour.
abbreviations and symbols	Abbreviate titles when they are part of a name.	Mr. Ralph Switzer, Dr. Penny Rupley, Lt. Col. Samuel T. Anderson
	Abbreviate organizations that are more commonly known by their initials than by their full name.	AFL-CIO, NASA, NATO, SALT, OSHA, NOW
	Abbreviate the names of states only when they are part of an address.	I live in Fresno, California. Box 683, Fresno, Calif.
	Abbreviate Latin terms used in writing.	etc., e.g., i.e.
	Other abbreviations are acceptable in writing.	A.M., P.M., A.D., B.C., rpm, mph.
	Some abbreviations are common in everyday use. Use them in your writing if they fit the tone of your paper; if not, spell the words out.	TV, CB, hi-fi, stereo, C.O.D.
	Use the dollar sign only for exact sums or for estimates of very large sums.	$4.83, $1.6 billion, about three dollars
	Avoid & (ampersand—the symbol for *and*) in formal writing unless it's a part of a company's name.	Julius and Susan . . . . Harper & Row
	Spell out percent (%) and cents (¢).	The survey shows that only 9.6 percent of all college freshmen are financially independent. The price of ground beef has gone up 50 cents a pound in nine months.
above/below	Sounds too legal in phrases like *the above reasons, the ideas listed above,* and *in view of the above.* If you can, substitute a word or phrase like *therefore, because of these reasons, for these reasons,* etc. The same is true for *below.*	
absolute/absolutely	Because these words are used so often, they have lost some of their punch.	

THE ITEM . . .	EXPLAINED . . .	AND IN ACTION ! ! !
	Instead of *I am absolutely exhausted, I am exhausted* sounds more confident and sincere.	
accept/except	*Accept* is a verb meaning *to receive.* *Except* is a preposition meaning *with the exclusion of.*	I *accept* your explanation. *Except* for the fact that she can't type, she'd make a good secretary.
access/excess	*Access* means *approach* or *permission.* *Excess* means *more than the usual or specified amount.*	I don't have *access* to the record. An *excess* of money is one thing I'll never have.
active voice/passive voice	Active voice is what you consider as the normal order for words in a sentence. The subject does the action, the verb states the action, and the complement receives the action.	She hit the ball. The president called the meeting to order. I smashed the desk with my bare hands. (Active voice)
	Passive voice is a rearrangement of this regular sentence order. More often than not, the passive voice is awkward and lacks punch. The only time the passive voice is better than the active voice in writing is when whatever is receiving the action is more important than whatever is doing the action. In the passive voice, the subject of the sentence is the receiver of the action, the verb is a form of *be* and the past participle, and the complement is the doer of the action.	The ball was hit by her. The meeting was called to order by the president. The desk was smashed (by me) with my bare hands. (Awkward Passive) The concert was cancelled. The bill was passed. The thief was apprehended. (Acceptable Passive)
	To change a sentence from the passive to the active, take the complement of the passive and make it the subject of your new sentence. Then the subject will perform the action, not receive it.	From: The report was submitted by the committee: To: The committee submitted the report.
A.D.	A.D. means *in the year of our Lord* and should always be written before the date.	A.D. 1982
adapt/adopt	*Adapt* means *to change something to fit a new purpose.* *Adopt* means *to accept something as one's own without change.*	Shawn *adapted* his old dance steps to the disco beat. We *adopted* the neighborhood's stray dog and named it Useless.
adjective	Adjectives are modifying words. They make nouns more specific, describe them, or indicate their characteristics. Adjectives also expand the basic sentence pattern by changing a noun and verb combination to a subject and predicate combination.	

THE ITEM . . .	EXPLAINED . . .	AND IN ACTION ! ! !

Adjectives can be words,
phrases,
or clauses.

the *healthy* girl
the girl *with the rosy cheeks*
the girl *that I despise*

Single word adjectives are usually before
the nouns they modify.

the *red* nose, the *ugly* statue,
the *eccentric, old* professor

Adjective phrases and clauses are usually
after the nouns they modify.

the devil *with the blue dress*
rush-hour traffic *which drives me mad*

Predicate adjectives occur after linking
verbs.

The meal was *delicious*. I feel *fine*.
His brain is *wrinkled*.

To form adjectives:

1　Add an adjectival ending to another
　　part of speech.
　　　-y　　stick, gum, sun, chew
　　　-ful　beauty, bounty, color
　　　-ive　vindicate, instruct, conduct
　　　-al　 verb, colony, proverb
　　　-ic　 irony, economy, metal

sticky, gummy, sunny, chewy
beautiful, bountiful, colorful
vindictive, instructive, conducive
verbal, colonial, proverbial
ironic, economic, metallic

2　Use other parts of speech as adjectives
　　without added endings.
　　Nouns:
　　　food, desk
　　　lawn, college
　　Verb Forms:
　　　grieving
　　　tired
　　　condemned
　　　assigned

food processor, *desk* top
lawn mower, *college* textbook

grieving parents
the *tired* man
the *condemned* prisoner
the *assigned* essay

Adjectives may be the most misunderstood
part of speech. When our writing is dull
and colorless, we're tempted to add a lot
of adjectives to liven it up. But sometimes adjectives add nothing to writing.
If they are vague or general—*good, great,
wonderful*—they don't make the writing
more exciting. Use adjectives carefully,
deliberately, and consciously. In themselves, adjectives aren't good or bad.
How we use them makes the difference.

admit/confess

Admit is not quite as serious as *confess*. A
confession is considered legally binding.
We might *admit* that we could be wrong,
but we're not going to *confess* anything
until we're certain we're wrong.

I *admit* that you could be right.
I'll never *confess* to stealing that popsicle.

adopt/adapt

See *adapt*.

THE ITEM . . .	EXPLAINED . . .	AND IN ACTION ! ! !

adverb

Adverbs are modifying words. They can make the action in a sentence more specific or they can add detail by modifying adjectives and other adverbs.

Finally, my dad agreed to let me go.
We met *in the park*.
I couldn't sleep *because I heard noises*.

Adverbs can be used anywhere in a sentence, but they should be close to the word they're modifying.

The reception, *however*, was at home.

Adverbs can be
words,
phrases,
or clauses.

My brother will work *this summer*.
I will work *during summer vacation*.
She'll work *as soon as school ends*.

Adverb forms include:

1 Words of time or place

still, now, today, only, there, south

2 Adjectives with -ly ending added
quick, slow, convincing, colorful, hopeful

quickly, slowly, convincingly, colorfully, hopefully

3 Intensifiers (words that intensify other words rather than just modify them).
fairly
very
somewhat
quite, too

We read the chapter *fairly* quickly.
I am very *irritated*.
Evidently, you are *somewhat* confused.
I'm *quite* sure she won't be *too* upset.

advice/advise

Advice is a noun.

Advise is a verb.

Her *advice* was good, but it wasn't what I wanted to hear.
She *advised* me well, but I didn't want to listen.

affect/effect

Affect is a verb that means to influence.

Effect is a noun that means a result.

I'm not sure how this new drug will *affect* you.
The *effect* of that loss will never be known.

afraid/frightened/scared

You're *afraid* of a danger that lasts for some time;
you're *frightened* or *scared* by an instant or immediate danger.

I'm *afraid* of having to speak.
The thought of going into that old cemetery at night *scares* me half to death.

again/back

If you use these after words that begin with *re-*, you're just repeating yourself and wasting ink. Instead of *resume again*, just say *resume*.

aggravate

You can only aggravate a condition that is already bad, so avoid using *aggravate* in sentences like *That aggravates me* when

THE ITEM . . .	EXPLAINED . . .	AND IN ACTION ! ! !
	you mean that something annoys or irritates you.	
aggression	*Aggression* is a hostile act and should be singular. Try not to use the word to mean *hostilities* as in *She has to get control of her aggressions.*	Chinese *aggression* was evident in the latest offensive.
agreement	*Agreement* simply means that a singular subject must have a singular verb and a singular pronoun that functions as an object must refer to a singular noun that functions as an object. The same is true for plural verbs and pronouns.	
	Usually, agreement occurs naturally when you speak and write. For example, when you say, "John likes to have doughnuts for breakfast," you know that since John is a singular noun, the verb must be singular, too. And when you say, "Give the test to her," you know that *her* refers to a singular noun acting as an object.	
	See also *pronoun reference, subject-verb agreement,* and *subject-verb-object agreement.*	
ain't	The use of *ain't* is controversial. Yes, it's used by many educated speakers in casual conversation. However, it's not appropriate in formal and classroom writing unless it's deliberately used for a particular effect.	
all/all of	Use *all of* only when referring to items that you could actually count. If you're not referring to items that could be counted, use *all.*	*All of* the fish were active. *All* I wanted was some peace and quiet.
all . . . not	Statements with *all . . . not* are often not clear. *All the bums in the world are not worth saving* leaves the reader confused. Does this say that none of the bums, or only some of them, are worth saving? Try using *not all* when you mean only *some.*	
all right	*All right* is always two words. Alright isn't correct.	

THE ITEM . . .	EXPLAINED . . .	AND IN ACTION ! ! !
all that	Avoid *all that* in sentences like *I didn't care all that much.*	
all together/altogether	*All together* means everybody is together. *Altogether* means entirely.	We were *all together* at the party. She is *altogether* too snobbish.
allusion/illusion	*Allusion* means a reference. *Illusion* means deceptive impression.	I certainly didn't recognize those *allusions* to the Bible. The magician's *illusions* fooled me.
almost/most	*Almost* means nearly. *Most* is used to draw comparisons. Don't shorten *almost* to *most* when you mean nearly as in *I like most everybody.*	
already/all ready	*Already* is an adverb that means *by this time* or *prior to* (some designated time). *All ready* is an adjective phrase that means *everything is ready.*	Have you finished those jalapeños *already*? We were *all ready* to go to the concert when we discovered that the car had a flat tire.
among/between	*Among* refers to at least three items. *Between* refers to two items.	I never expected to find you *among* this group of people. He couldn't decide *between* playing football and studying sociology.
angry/mad	See *mad.*	
ante-/anti-	*Ante-* means before. *Anti-* means against.	ante-bellum, antecedent anti-establishment, antisocial
anybody/any body nobody/no body somebody/some body	*Anybody, nobody,* and *somebody* are all indefinite pronouns. *Any body, no body,* and *some body* are adjectives and nouns paired together.	*Nobody* will ever know what I've gone through. *No body* was found after the crash.
anyways	Use anyway, not *anyways.*	She won't go anyway.
anywheres	Use anywhere, not *anywheres.*	I can't find it *anywhere.*
apprehend/comprehend	*Apprehend* means to recognize the meaning of something. *Comprehend* means to understand thoroughly. It usually takes longer to *comprehend* something than it does to *apprehend* it.	I hope I *apprehend* what you're saying. No matter how long you wait, I'll never *comprehend* the law of the why.
apt/liable/likely	*Apt* usually denotes a habitual tendency. *Liable* usually means *susceptible* in an undesirable sense.	Our team is *apt* to lose. I'm *liable* to lose my temper any minute.

THE ITEM . . .	EXPLAINED . . .	AND IN ACTION ! ! !
	Likely means apparently qualified.	He was voted Most *Likely* to Succeed.
area/field/subject	Try not to overuse these words as in *Her hardest courses are in the field of economics.* Say *Her hardest courses are in economics* instead.	
argue/quarrel	*Argue* has an extra meaning; in an argument, you're usually trying to give reasons or evidence for a case. A *quarrel* is usually just a complaint.	
around	Not all people think it's all right to use *around* when you mean *approximately.* To be safe, say *about* three minutes or *approximately* three minutes.	
as/like	*As* is a conjunction, so it will introduce a clause. *Like* is a preposition.	They didn't do their homework *as* I asked them to. I want a pair of jeans *like* Mary's.
as/such as	You can't substitute *as* when you mean *such as.* Instead of saying *I love all green vegetables as broccoli, spinach, and turnips,* say *such as broccoli.* . . .	
as far as . . . is concerned	Whenever you want to use this idea, be sure to complete the statement. Don't just say *As far as homework, I have too much.* Say *As far as homework is concerned, I have too much.*	
as good as/as much as	Don't use these phrases to mean *practically* as in *She as good as ordered me to say it.*	
as if/as though	Both of these phrases are accepted.	
aspect	*Aspect* literally means a position facing a particular direction. Try not to use the word when you mean view in general because the word loses some of its meaning and most of its punch.	After I considered what you said, I could see a new *aspect.*
assure/ensure/insure	*Assure* means to promise. *Ensure* and *insure* both mean the same thing: to guarantee or make sure. Because *insure* reminds us of insurance, some writers use it only in that sense and use *ensure* to mean *make sure* in other senses.	She assured me she'd be here. I *ensured* my job security when I got tenure. He insured his personal property for $100,000.00.

THE ITEM . . .	EXPLAINED . . .	AND IN ACTION ! ! !
at the same time that	When all you mean is *while*, don't waste so many words and so much space by saying *at the same time that!*	
at this (that) point in time	This phrase is just a wordy way of saying *now (then)*.	
author	Author should be used as a noun. Some people say *She authored seven plays*, but *She wrote seven plays* sounds better.	
auxiliary verb	See *verb*.	
average/mean/median	To find an *average*, divide the sum of two or more quantities by the number of quantities. *Mean* is the midpoint in figures. *Median* is the middle number in a sequence of numbers.	The average of 8, 12, and 4 is 8 (24 divided by 3). The *mean* of 10 and 30 is 20. The *median* of the series 1, 3, 5, 7, 9 is 5.
awake/wake	Use *awake* when you mean to become awake and *wake* when you intend to wake somebody else up.	I'm *awake!* Don't *wake* me up!
aware/conscious	*Aware* usually refers to circumstances or happenings. *Conscious* usually refers to your own feelings.	I'm *aware* that the game starts at 7. I *consciously* made the decision.
awhile/a while	*Awhile* is an adverb. *A while* is a noun plus the article *a*	I laughed *awhile* then I cried *awhile*. I laughed for *a while*.
back/again	See *again*.	
background	Try not to overuse this word when you actually mean reason. *Background* is a contrast to *foreground* and should be used as such.	
bad/badly	*Bad* is an adjective. *Badly* is an adverb.	I feel *bad* about forgetting you. He performed *badly* last night.
balance	See *emphasis*.	
basically/on the basis of	These words are often used when they add nothing to the sentence. Try leaving them out. We were judged *on the basis of* appearance.	We were judged on appearance.

THE ITEM . . .	EXPLAINED . . .	AND IN ACTION ! ! !
	The chair is *basically* sound.	The chair is sound.
B.C.	B.C. means *before Christ* and should come after the date.	1060 B.C.
being	*Being* can often be eliminated from a sentence when it's not a part of the main verb. With the majority of the vote *being* neither for or against, the bill will probably be dropped.	With the majority of the vote neither for or against, the bill will . . . .
being as/being that	Avoid using these phrases when you mean *because* or *since*. *Being as* she's always late	Because she's always late . . . .
below	See *above*.	
bemused	*Bemused* means *bewildered*, not *amused*.	
beside/besides	*Beside* means *at the side of*. *Besides* means *in addition*.	I sat down *beside* her. I'll have three tacos *besides* the order of enchiladas, guacamole, rice, tamales, re-fried beans, and tortillas.
better than	Don't use *better than* when you mean *more than*.	
between/among	See *among*.	
between each/ between every	Since between deals with two things, you don't need to add *each* or *every* to it. I slept *between each* nap.	I slept *between* naps.
between you and I	Since between is a preposition here, you need to say *between you and me*. *Between you and I* isn't correct.	
bi-/semi-	*Bi-* means twice. Biannually means twice a year. *Semi-* means half. Semiannually means every two years.	
bored	You are either *bored by* or *bored with*, not *bored of*.	
born/borne	*Born* refers to birth. *Borne* refers to carrying.	I was *born* November 10, 1952. I've *borne* this burden long enough.

THE ITEM . . .	EXPLAINED . . .	AND IN ACTION ! ! !
both	Avoid pairing *both* with words like *alike, together,* etc.; that just repeats the same idea. Use *and,* not *as well as,* to connect two words with *both.*	*Both* Rita and I want to learn to ski.
breakdown	Try not to use *breakdown* when you mean an analysis or a listing of items.	
bring/carry/take	*Bring* means *to transport something so that it is nearer.* *Carry* means *to transport something in any direction.* *Take* means *to transport something so that it is farther away.*	*Bring* me that paper. *Carry* that coin with you everywhere. *Take* this book back to the library.
bunch/crowd	Use *bunch* when referring to things. Use *crowd* for people or animals.	You're in a *bunch* of thorns. You look like you're in a *crowd* of elephants.
burglar/robber/thief	A *burglar* steals things by breaking and entering. A *robber* steals money by harming or threatening a person. A *thief* steals things when the victim doesn't know what's happening. A corporate executive could be a thief without actually breaking and entering or threatening or physically harming the victim.	
but however/ but nevertheless/ but yet	All of these phrases add nothing to a sentence because there is no need for two transitions when one will do just as much. I want to go, *but yet* I want to stay.	I want to go, *yet* I want to stay. I want to go, *but* I want to stay.
but that/but what	These phrases are also unnecessary. Try *that* instead. There's no question *but that* we'll win.	There's no question *that* we'll win.
can/may	*Can* refers to an ability or power. *May* refers to permission, opportunity, or willingness.	They *can* finish that article tonight if they hurry. They *may* not finish — ever.
can not/cannot	Unless you want to emphasize *not,* use *cannot.*	

THE ITEM . . .	EXPLAINED . . .	AND IN ACTION ! ! !
capitalization	Capitalize the first word of every sentence.	
	Capitalize proper nouns: persons, places, things, events and periods, and sailing (air and sea) vessels.	Jane Fonda, Pip, John the Baptist Luckenbach, Texas, Washington, D. C. Mount Rushmore, the Library of Congress Civil War, Stone Age, Renaissance *U. S. S. Coral Sea, Apollo 8, Old Ironsides*
	Capitalize names of deities.	Jupiter, Jehovah, Krishna
	Capitalize titles before and after names.	Dr. I. M. Sominex, Rev. Bill Baker, Sue Young, Adventurer
	Capitalize the first word and all other words except prepositions, conjunctions, and articles in the titles of literary works, movies, songs, and works of art.	*The Catcher in the Rye,* "Hunger Artist," the *Mona Lisa, The Park, Star Wars, Saturday Night Fever*
	Capitalize the names of recognized groups and organizations.	Republican, Democrat, Jaycees, Christian, Daughters of the American Revolution, National Organization for Women
	Capitalize *specific* course names.	Math 130, Psychology 441
	Capitalize directions when they refer to a specific geographical area.	*Gone with the Wind* is set in the South.
	Avoid unnecessary capitalization.	I'm taking a *history* course now. Renton is *northwest* of Seattle. They consider their group to be *upper class.* I hope to be a *senior* next year.
carry	See *bring.*	
case/instance	Often these words are used when they're not needed. Who was involved *in the instance* of the car theft?	Who was involved in the car theft?
cause/reason	A *cause* makes something happen or produces an effect. A *reason* is a statement of explanation or justification.	The *cause* of death is not known. The *reason* I failed that test? — I didn't study.
cause is due to	In case you feel an urge to use this clause — don't. It's wordy and does nothing for your sentence.	
censor/censure	A *censor* is a person who decides if something will be allowed.	The *censor* won't let such words be used on the radio.

THE ITEM . . .	EXPLAINED . . .	AND IN ACTION ! ! !
	A *censure* is the criticism of that thing.	The administration heaped *censure* on our broadcast.
center around	*Center on* or *center upon* sounds more accurate.	
character	Don't use this word needlessly. She was *of a generous character.*	She was generous.
childish/childlike	Both of these words mean the same thing. *Childish*, however, is associated with bad qualities.	Her *childlike* innocence is refreshing. You're acting so *childish!*
cite/sight/site	*Cite* means to quote an authority or example. *Sight* refers to landmarks or things to see as well as vision.	He *cited* the coaches' instructions as the reasons for his success. Did you see all the *sights* in South Dakota? I hope he regains his *sight* after the surgery.
	Site refers to buildings or a piece of land.	Construction *sites* are dangerous.
clause	A *clause* is a group of related words, including a subject and verb, which acts together as one part of speech. Although it has a subject and a verb, a *clause* does not always stand as an independent sentence; it may depend on another sentence for meaning and strength.	*Although he spent three months searching for a job,* he didn't go hungry once. She went *because she didn't want to miss anything.*
climactic/climatic	*Climactic* refers to climaxes. *Climatic* refers to climate and weather.	The experience was *climactic.* *Climatic* conditions should improve.
collective noun	A collective noun names a group of persons, places, things, concepts, actions, or qualities.	army, committee, team, family, class, public, jury, crowd, group
	When a collective noun refers to a group as a whole, use a singular verb and pronoun.	The *committee* was confused; *it* had to seek outside help.
	When a collective noun refers to individuals within the group, use a plural verb and pronoun.	The *family* are eating *their* meals at different places tonight. (members of the family)
	Some collective nouns regularly take singular verbs. Others do not.	The *crowd* was cheering wildly. *People* are the earth's best asset.

THE ITEM . . .	EXPLAINED . . .	AND IN ACTION ! ! !
colon	A *colon* is a punctuation mark of anticipation that halts the reader, then connects the first statement to the following one.	

It can connect a series or list to the sentence.

I have four classes: math, biology English, and history.

It can link one statement to another to develop, illustrate, explain, or amplify it. When used in this way, the colon can even link two sentences.

Any large cafeteria can have two related problems: it must fix enough food but not too much, and it must keep the food from spoiling.

A colon can introduce a stacked list.

The following courses will be offered in the fall:
Math 103   Math 209   Math 308
Math 104   Math 210   Math 309

A colon adds emphasis to a phrase which describes a noun.

Only one thing can make me happy: a new camera.

Colons can separate chapters and verses as well as hours and minutes.

Genesis 1:1
9:30 A.M.

In proportions, colons mean ratios.

$8:4 = 12:x$

A colon follows salutations in letters.

Dear Sir: Dear Thornell:
Dear Ms. Geoffry:

When using colons with quotations, capitalize the first letter of the first word of the quotation if the quote originally began with a capital letter.

The sign stated: "No shoes, no shirt, no service."

A colon always goes outside quotation marks.

These are qualities he calls "good": wine, women, and song.

If you quote a statement that ends with a colon, drop the colon and add ellipses.

"Any large cafeteria can have two related problems . . .," an author contends.

comma

A comma can link, enclose, separate, and show omissions.

To link:

Place a comma before a coordinating conjunction (and, but, or, for, nor, so, yet) when it combines two sentences (independent clauses).

You can go to the dance if you want, but I'm going to the show.

To enclose:

A direct address is enclosed in commas.

Edgar, get out of that mud!
You should know, stupid, that $2 \times 2 = 4$.

Commas enclose phrases and clauses that are inserted in a sentence but are not essential to the meaning of the sentence (nonrestrictive clauses and parenthetical elements).

My favorite movie, which was nominated for an Academy Award, is a comedy. You will, of course, give me money.

Appositives (phrases that identify something) are enclosed in commas.

My favorite movie, *Star Wars*, is science fiction.

To separate:

Commas separate introductory elements from the rest of the sentence.

During the first game of the series, we had four runs, six hits, and no errors.
Finally, I'm finished.
Yes, I know I'm crazy.

Commas separate items in a series.

Cigarettes harm your lungs, my lungs, and everybody's lungs.
I learned how to be a leader, how to take orders, how to control my temper, and how to work with others.
I ate the big, juicy, wormless, delicious red apple.

Commas separate elements of an address written on the same line.

Sharon Simms, 1716 Arbor Lane, Dayton, OH 45401

Commas separate elements of numbers.

5,764,199

Commas separate elements of geographical names.

Lagos, Nigeria, West Africa

Commas separate names when the last name is first.

Williams, Barbara

To show omissions:

Sometimes a comma will replace a verb. This construction, however, is rarely used and is only used for a special effect.

Some were crisp; others, soggy. (The comma replaces *were*.)

A comma *always* goes inside quotation marks.

Although she thought the meal was "adequate," I thought it was mediocre.

comma fault/
comma splice

Both of these expressions mean the same thing: you have joined two independent clauses (sentences) with a comma. For example, *As a child, the alcoholic did not learn the things a child needs to learn, thus his life was destined to go bad* is a comma fault.

You can correct a comma splice in one of the following ways:

THE ITEM . . .	EXPLAINED . . .	AND IN ACTION ! ! !
	Rewrite the sentence as two independent sentences.	As a child, the alcoholic did not learn the things a child needs to learn. Thus, his life was destined to go bad.
	If the ideas of the sentences are closely related, replace the comma with a semicolon.	As a child, the alcoholic did not learn the things a child needs to learn; thus, his life was destined to go bad.
	Make one sentence dependent on the other by subordination.	Since the alcoholic did not learn as a child the things children need to learn, his life was destined to go bad.
commence	If you mean *start* or *begin*, say it. Commence is one of those $10 words that distracts the reader.	
common noun	See *noun*.	
compare/contrast	When you *compare* something, you look at two or more items to see how they are alike or different. When you *contrast* things, you look only at their differences.	
compare to/ compare with	*Compare to* usually emphasizes similarities. *Compare with* emphasizes relative values which can be alike or different.	He *compared* the classroom *to* a jail. He *compared* smoking cigarettes *with* smoking marijuana.
comparison	Adjectives and adverbs have endings to show comparison.	
	You can take an adjective or adverb and make it stronger (comparative) or strongest (superlative) through one of these methods:	
	1 Add -er for stronger and -est for strongest. strong healthy easy wise	stronger, strongest healthier, healthiest easier, easiest wiser, wisest
	2 Use *more* for the stronger and *most* for the strongest. useful beautiful gracious helpful	more useful, most useful more beautiful, most beautiful more gracious, most gracious more helpful, most helpful

THE ITEM . . .	EXPLAINED . . .	AND IN ACTION ! ! !
	3 Change the word to a new degree.	
	little	less, least
	far	farther, further; farthest, furthest
	much	more, most
	good/well	better, best
	bad	worse, worst
complected	Use *complexioned* or just say *Her complexion was dark.*	
complement/compliment	*Complement* refers to anything that completes the whole.	That scarf *complements* your dress perfectly.
	Compliment refers to praise.	I don't know how to take a *compliment.*
complex sentence	In a complex sentence, you join thoughts together by making one depend on another. It has one independent clause and one dependent clause.	When we won, we thought we were tops in the country. The car, which has the highest estimated miles per gallon, isn't very expensive.
	Complex sentences offer readers a break from simple sentences and help deepen relationships between thoughts in two sentences.	We bought a coke and two candy bars while we waited.
compose/comprise	*Compose* means to make up the whole or to create.	Mozart *composed* music. The library is *composed* of one million volumes.
	Comprise means to include.	The library *comprises* one million volumes.
compound sentence	A *compound sentence* has two or more independent clauses (sentences) that are related and equally important.	I want to go, but he wants to stay.
	Combine the independent clauses with a comma and a coordinating conjunction (and, but, or, nor, for, so, yet), a semicolon, or a semicolon, a conjunctive adverb, and a comma.	I want to stay, *but* he wants to go. I want to stay; he wants to go. I want to stay; however, he wants to go.
	Combining sentences to make them compound can add interest and variety to a paper.	
compound-complex sentence	When you combine two or more independent clauses (sentences) with at least one dependent clause, you've got a compound-complex sentence.	I want to go, but he wants to stay until his paycheck arrives. I like to dance; however, I can't find the time, and I can't afford those cover charges at the clubs.
	Mastery of this type of sentence can really add life and variety to writing.	

THE ITEM . . .	EXPLAINED . . .	AND IN ACTION ! ! !
	See *complex sentence* and *compound sentence.*	
comprehend/apprehend	See *apprehend.*	
concept/conception	A *concept* is a thought or idea. A *conception* is the sum of ideas, or concepts, on a subject.	My *conception* of a good life was formed from all of the *concepts* I was taught.
concern	Instead of saying *The subject of the book concerns good against bad,* say *The subject of the book is good against bad.* If you mean *is,* say it.	
concur in/concur with	*Concur in* decisions. *Concur with* people.	I *concur in* that decision to leave. He *concurred with* the class in their decision to take a walk.
confess/admit	See *admit.*	
conjunction	*Conjunctions* connect words, phrases, or clauses and show relationships between the elements they connect (*and* joins together, *but* shows contrast, *or* selects and separates).	

Types of conjunctions:

A *coordinating conjunction* is a word that joins two words, phrases, or clauses that have identical functions. There are seven.
and
but
or
for
nor
yet
so

Burgers *and* fries are my favorite.
Not one *but* two birds have escaped.
You can walk *or* fly, I don't care.
I'll go, *for* I'm scared to stay.
I don't know, *nor* do I care.
I love you, *yet* I hurt you.
I'll sleep, so you will stay awake.

Correlative conjunctions are coordinating conjunctions that are used in pairs. There are five.
either . . . or
neither . . . nor
not only . . . but also
both . . . and
whether . . . or

Either you *or* I will get the prize.
Neither you *nor* I will fail.
You make me *not only* mad *but also* happy.
I feel like *both* laughing *and* crying.
Whether I pass *or* fail is up to me.

Subordinating conjunctions connect sentence of different weights and strengths, usually an independent clause with a

THE ITEM . . .	EXPLAINED . . .	AND IN ACTION ! ! !

dependent clause. There are many, but some are used often.

although	than
after	since
because	as
if	unless
where	before
when	that
whereas	though

I'm going *although* I'm sick.
Since you're so smart, do it alone!
As you can see, I'm only teasing.
I'm leaving *unless* you need me.
Before you leave, listen to this.
The season *that* I love is spring.
I'm fat *whereas* you're skinny.

A *conjunctive adverb* is an adverb that has the strength of a conjunction because it joins two independent clauses (sentences). Some are very common.

however	consequently
moreover	besides
therefore	accordingly
further	also
then	too

The car is fast; *however,* it's expensive.

I am on scholastic probation; *therefore,* I have to post a 2.0.

I have to take out the garbage; *then,* I have to clean the garage.

To punctuate conjunctions:

1 Two independent clauses (sentences) separated by a coordinating conjunction must have a comma before the conjunction.

The project was finished, so I took a vacation.

2 If the two independent clauses joined by the conjunction have commas within the clauses, you can separate the independent clauses with a semicolon.

I wanted to run, skip, and shout; but he wanted to stomp, crawl, and pout.

3 When you join two main clauses with a conjunctive adverb, place a semicolon before the conjunctive adverb and a comma after the conjunctive adverb.

I'd like to order a banana split; however, I'm on a diet.

conscience/conscious

Conscience is a noun.
Conscious is an adjective.

His *conscience* bothers him.
She is *self-conscious.*

conscious/aware

See *aware.*

consensus

Consensus means *general agreement,* so statements like *a general consensus of opinion* are repetitious. Just say *the consensus* or *the general opinion.* A consensus is very close to being unanimous.

considerable

Avoid *considerable* to mean *many.*

consist of/consist in

Consist of means *to be made up of.*

An omelet *consists of* eggs, milk, and garnishes.

THE ITEM . . .	EXPLAINED . . .	AND IN ACTION ! ! !
	Consist in means *to lie in* or *exist in*.	Unity *consists in* standing together.
contemptible/contemptuous	If something is *contemptible*, it deserves contempt. If you're *contemptuous*, your contempt is showing!	Cheating is *contemptible*. Her *contemptuous* feelings are inexcusable.
continual/continuous	*Continual* means *recurring at intervals*. *Continuous* means *nonstop* or *uninterrupted*.	I don't even have a tan yet because of the *continual* rain this summer. Snow fell *continuously* for two hours this afternoon.
contraction	A contraction is a shortened version of a word or phrase. An apostrophe substitutes for the missing letters. Contractions are fine in informal writing, but they might create a tone that is too everyday in formal or business writing. Use your judgment. cannot I will will not have not it is	 can't I'll won't haven't it's
contrast	See *compare*.	
contributing factor/factor	A *factor* is something that actively *contributes* to the production of a result, so *contributing factor* is repetitive. Just say *factor*.	
convince/persuade	*Convince* means *to win agreement*. *Persuade* means *to move to action*.	I *convinced* Jared that the movie was worth watching. I *persuaded* Jared to watch the movie.
coordinating conjunction	See *conjunction*.	
coordination	*Coordination* means *to link sentence elements that are equal*. You can coordinate words, phrases, clauses, sentences.	 *Math and English* are supposed to be the hardest subjects for freshmen. They spent the evening *drinking beer and eating popcorn*. *Since he had nothing else to do and since he had promised her he would go*, John went to the gymnastics meet. I had planned to study while I was in the library, *but* I took a nap instead.

See also *compound sentence* and *conjunction* (coordinating conjunction).

correlative conjunctions   See *conjunction*.

could of   Actually, you mean *could've* (*could have*). Instead of saying *I could of won hours ago, but I wanted to give you a chance*, say *I could have* (or *could've*) *won hours ago . . .*

cope   You usually *cope with* some problem, so try not to use *cope* without *with*. Avoid saying *She just couldn't cope.*

correspond to/ correspond with   If you *correspond to* something, you match it. If you *correspond with* it, you write it a letter.

council/counsel   A *council* is an assembly or meeting. *Counsel* is advice or a lawyer to give advice.   She was elected to city *council*. The accused murderer's *counsel* said to plead not guilty.

couple/pair   *Couple* means *two things connected for consideration.* In a *pair*, the two items are always used together.   The *couple* got married last year.

I need a new *pair* of skis and a new *pair* of ski boots.

criteria/criterion   *Criteria* is plural. *Criterion* is singular.   Those *criteria* will be hard to meet. That *criterion* is unreasonable.

critique   As a verb, *critique* sounds very formal. Try using *criticized* instead.

crowd   See *bunch*.

crucial   *Crucial* means *essential to resolving a crisis.* It shouldn't be used as a substitute for *important; crucial* means much more critical than just *important.*

dangling modifier   Phrases that don't clearly and logically refer to a noun or pronoun are called dangling modifiers. You can correct dangling modifiers by adding a noun or pronoun to the sentence for the phrase to modify or by making the phrase a clause.

After finishing the test, the course was over.
After we finished the test, the course was over.

After finishing the test, *we knew* the course was over.
The course was over after we finished the test.

THE ITEM . . .	EXPLAINED . . .	AND IN ACTION ! ! !
	Sleeping soundly, the night was quickly over.	Sleeping soundly, *I felt that* the night was quickly over.
		Because I slept soundly, the night was quickly over.
	To improve tennis skills, practice is needed.	*To improve tennis* skills, *you need* to practice.
dash	When typing, use two hyphens (--) to indicate a dash. The dash has several functions:	
	It can indicate a sharp turn in thought.	That marks the end of that class—unless I failed the last test.
	It can add emphasis to a pause.	I'll get the job done—after I take another break.
	It can set off an explanatory series or an appositive series.	Two of the applicants—Steve and Lisa—will be offered jobs.
	Dashes can add emphasis to a parenthetical element (an item inserted in the sentence that isn't essential to meaning).	Only one person—you—can control what you say.
data	*Data* is generally considered as plural. *Datum*, singular, is rarely used. You could say *fact* for *datum* and sound just as smart.	
dates	Dates are traditionally listed with the month, day, and year. Separate the day and year with a comma.	April 8, 1981
	When you list just the month and the year, you don't need a comma.	April 1981
	The names of centuries can be confusing. The century always names the numbers of the years to come.	
	twentieth century = 1900s (1900–1999) nineteenth century = 1800s (1800–1899) the sixth century = 500s (500–599)	
deduce/deduct	*Deduce* means *infer*. *Deduct* means *subtract*.	How did you *deduce* that fact? I'd like to *deduct* the car on my income tax form.
defective/deficient	*Defective* means *faulty*. *Deficient* means *lacking in some ingredient*.	That rear axle is *defective*. My background in writing was *deficient*.
definite/definitive	*Definite* means *without question* or *positive*.	I'm going to Florida this summer, and that's *definite*.
	Definitive means *final*.	We've got to find a *definitive* answer to the parking problem.

THE ITEM . . .	EXPLAINED . . .	AND IN ACTION ! ! !
demonstrative pronoun	See *pronoun*.	
depend	Don't just say It *depends*. It must *depend on* something or *upon* something.	
desert/dessert	*Desert* is the dry land. *Desert* means *to leave*. *Dessert* is what some of us eat too much of.	If Las Vegas is the *desert*, send me! Don't *desert* me. I'll have three helpings of *dessert*.
device/devise	*Device* is a noun. *Devise* is a verb.	This *device* should save time and trouble. I must *devise* a way of convincing the prof that I know what I'm talking about.
dialogue	Avoid using *dialogue* in a sense of trading ideas. It means *conversation* in a strict, literary sense.	
differ from/differ with	*Differ from* means *to have some things that are different*. *Differ with* means *to disagree*.	
different	You sometimes use this word when it's obvious. Why say *I have three different excuses for being late*? If the excuses weren't different, then you wouldn't have three, would you?	
different from/different than	*Different from* is considered correct. *Different than* is appropriate in special cases.	These jeans are *different from* the ones I wanted. That sandwich tasted *different than* I had expected.
discreet/discrete	*Discreet* means *modest* or *with good judgment*. *Discrete* means *distinct*.	She was *discreet* about her success. We're talking about two *discrete* topics.
disinterested/uninterested	Both mean *not interested*, but *disinterested* has an element of not choosing sides.	
distinctive/distinguished	*Distinctive* means *unique*. *Distinguished* means *dignified*.	Her British accent is *distinctive*. He's trying to sound *distinguished* with his fake accent.
don't	Don't say *She don't know*. It's *She doesn't know*.	
doubtless(ly)	Since *doubtless* is an adverb, you don't need to write *doubtlessly*.	

THE ITEM . . .	EXPLAINED . . .	AND IN ACTION ! ! !
due to the fact that	If all you mean is *since* or *because*, that's all you have to say. *Due to the fact that* is much too wordy for such a simple meaning.	
duo/trio/quartet	A *duo* is made up of two people. A *trio* is made up of three. A *quartet* is made up of four. All of these expressions are considered formal. You wouldn't want to say *A quartet of birds just camped out in the birdhouse; Four birds . . .* sounds much more smooth.	
during the course of	*During the course of* is the longest way we can think of to just say *during*. Why waste all of that energy?	
economic/economical	*Economic* means *based on economics*. Use *economical* when you mean *thrifty*.	This store is an *economical* place to shop.
effect	See *affect*.	
e.g.	In footnotes or in information within parentheses, *e.g.* can be used to mean *for example*.	Don't substitute a noun for a verb (e.g., *job* for *run*).
egoism/egotism	*Egoism* is an ethical doctrine of self-interest. *Egotism* is an exaggerated view of yourself, or conceit.	We studied *egoism* in sociology. She's so *egotistic* that she won't ever admit that she could be wrong.
elicit/illicit	*Elicit* means *to bring forth or evoke*. *Illicit* means *not permitted*.	I can't *elicit* a response. This affair isn't *illicit;* we're married!
ellipsis (. . .)	*Ellipsis* is a punctuation mark that shows you've left out some words. When you quote only part of a statement, insert ellipsis to show where you've left the information out. It's not fair to leave any important information out of a quotation or to pull words from a quotation and change the meaning.	"Work . . . is the privilege of all citizens," the politician explained.
emigrant/immigrant	An *emigrant* has left a country. An *immigrant* has arrived in a country.	

THE ITEM...	EXPLAINED...	AND IN ACTION !!!
eminent/imminent/ immanent	*Eminent* means *outstanding* or *distinguished.* *Imminent* means *about to happen.* *Immanent* means *inherent* and is used mostly in religion and philosophy.	She is an *eminent* scientist. Success is *imminent.* Is God *immanent* in all things?
emphasis	Since all English sentences are formed from a simple pattern, you can change that pattern to emphasize an idea in the sentences.	
	Position: One of the simplest ways to create emphasis is to move a modifier in a sentence out of its usual position.	
	Put a phrase at the beginning of the sentence.	*In our society,* nothing seems to be unlawful.
	Try moving adverbs around in the sentence.	*Unfortunately,* that was the last of the water. That, *unfortunately,* was the last of the water. That was, *unfortunately,* the last of the water. That was the last of the water, *unfortunately.*
	Or change the position of conjunctive adverbs.	Marion went to the movie recommended by her prof. *However,* John refused to go. John, *however,* refused to go. John refused to go, *however.*
	You can even try *inversion* — placing a prepositional phrase at the beginning of the sentence so that it seems to function as the subject.	*At the end of the block* is the house where the murder occurred. *By the engine* stood a dark motionless being in a sort of trance. *Against the twilight* rises the trapezoidal top of the stack. *At the center of the enterprise* lies the hope of explaining a great past event.
	Balance: Balance is an important trick to know to vary your sentence structure. To make a sentence balance, repeat a pattern within the sentence. This can emphasize similarity or create contrast. Balanced sentences are easy to remember.	Ask not what your country can do for you; ask what you can do for your country. (John F. Kennedy's inaugural address) The world will little note, nor long remember, what we say here, but it can never forget what they did here. (Lincoln's Gettysburg Address)
	Make sure your idea is worth emphasizing.	To say that there are no real heroes left is to say that there is no hope left.

THE ITEM...	EXPLAINED...	AND IN ACTION !!!

Make sure the balanced parts are grammatically equal. What that means is to pair nouns with nouns, verbs with verbs, phrases with phrases, clauses with clauses, sentences with sentences.

Not only will it improve your strength, but it will also improve your looks.

Periodic Sentence:
In a periodic sentence, you emphasize a point by leaving the main sentence pattern for the end of the sentence. Such sentences create suspense and anticipation by sending the reader through a series of parallel introductory elements before she gets to the main thought. Periodic sentences make the subject seem very important.

Whether I shall turn out to be the hero of my own life, or whether that station will be held by anybody else, these pages must show. (Opening sentence of *David Copperfield*)

endeavor

Try sounds better, if that's what you mean.

enhance

Enhance means *to increase desirability* or *to make more attractive.*
You can't use *enhance* to increase everything. For example, you can't enhance your reading skills.

enormity

Enormity refers to something that is wickedly monstrous. If something is just huge, don't use this word.

ensure

See *assure.*

enthuse

Although *enthuse* is widely used, many experts think it's too informal for classroom writing. It's all right to use *enthuse* in your conversations, but go ahead and use *enthusiastic* in your writing.

We're *enthused* about this baseball season.

Response to the call for aid was *enthusiastic.*

epic

Reserve *epic* for special events. Everyday events are not monumental enough for epic.

equally as

Equally as means *as,* so there's no need to say both.

escalate

Escalation is intentional, not just a haphazard increase. Problems don't escalate unless someone planned them that way.

THE ITEM . . .	EXPLAINED . . .	AND IN ACTION ! ! !
especially/specially	*Especially* means *distinctively* or *outstandingly.* *Specially* means *with a certain purpose in mind.*	She is *especially* talented in dance. That steel was *specially* formed for support.
et al.	This abbreviation stands for *and others* It is mostly used in footnotes and bibliographies. *Et al.* refers to people.	
etc.	*Etc.* means *and other things.* Don't use unless it can't be avoided. Also, don't use etc. for people. See also *et al.*	
ever so often/every so often	*Ever so often* means *very often.* *Every so often* means *once in a while.*	I think of you *ever so often.* I remember to take that medicine *every so often.*
every day/everyday	*Every day* refers to something that you do every single day. *Everyday* means *commonplace.*	I have to work *every day.* Your temper is becoming an *everyday* problem.
exceedingly/excessively	*Exceedingly* means that you've surpassed a limit. *Excessively* means that you've gone overboard.	They're *exceedingly* thankful. We've been *excessively* wasteful.
except	See *accept.*	
excess	See *access.*	
exclamation point	Exclamation points are used at the end of sentences to show surprise, anger, or emphasis.	She's married! Hell, no, I'm not giving in! I'll never do that again!
exist	Avoid using *exist* when it doesn't add real meaning to the thought; for example, in *all the money that exists in the world* nothing would be lost if you just said *all the money in the world.*	
expect	*Expect* means *to anticipate.* If you mean *suppose,* say *suppose.*	
facet	*Facet* can't be substituted for *part* because facets mean that the perspective has shifted.	I see a new *facet* of the problem every time I approach it from a different angle.

THE ITEM . . .	EXPLAINED . . .	AND IN ACTION ! ! !
fact/fact that	Both of these items can only be used with statements that are true. For example, you can't say *the fact that the earth was square*.	
factor	See *contributing factor*.	
fail	*Fail* suggests that somebody was making an attempt to succeed. Don't say *She failed to do her homework* unless you know that she tried to get it done.	
fantastic	*Fantastic* is definitely overworked today. Only use it in the sense of fantasy.	
farther/further	*Farther* is an adverb which actually talks about distance. *Further* means *additionally* or *more*.	How much *farther* to the next town, Dad? We'll have to discuss this *further*.
fatal/fateful	*Fatal* refers to death. *Fateful* refers to destiny or fate.	That accident could have been *fatal*. The *fateful* act caused me to wonder about fortune telling.
faulty parallelism	If a portion of your writing is marked *faulty parallelism*, you have matched parts of a sentence that are not equal. If you wrote *Writing is very entertaining, educational, and it relieves tension,* you'd want to change it to *Writing is very entertaining, educational, and relaxing.* See also *parallelism*.	
few/little	**Use few when you're talking about things or people that you can count.** **And use** *little* **when you are talking about things that are measured.**	few hours, few failures, few kids, few radishes, few aardvarks little trouble, little time, little success, little interest
fewer/less	*Fewer* and *less* are like *few* and *little*. *Fewer* compares amounts that can be counted separately. *Less* compares amounts that can't be counted separately.	I have *fewer* marks on my paper than he does. I've got *less* sense than anybody.
field	See *area*.	
figure/calculate	Avoid using these words when you mean *guess* or *suppose*. If you figure or calculate something, it should be certain.	

THE ITEM . . .	EXPLAINED . . .	AND IN ACTION ! ! !
final	A conclusion, finding, result, ending, outcome is final. So you don't have to say *final ending*.	
flunk	The correct form is *fail*.	Thirty students failed algebra.
for free/for the purpose of/for the simple reason that	All of these expressions are wordy and can be eliminated.	
	I got the bike *for* free.	The bike was free.
	We are gathered *for the purpose of* raising money.	We are gathered to raise money.
	I'm tired *for the simple reason that* I haven't slept in three days.	I'm tired because I haven't slept in three days.
foreword/forward	A *foreword* is an introduction to a book. *Forward* means *up front*.	Nobody reads *forewords*. Put your best foot *forward*.
formally/formerly	*Formally* means *according to form*. *Formerly* means *previously*.	I haven't asked *formally*. She was *formerly* the president.
fragment	If your sentence is marked *fragment*, you've punctuated a part of a sentence as a complete sentence. Here's an example: *That and the fact that there is safety in numbers.*	
	To correct your fragment:	
	1 Link it to the sentence that comes before it.	Perhaps not having to think is why they conform, or perhaps they feel there is safety in numbers.
	2 Make the fragment a complete sentence.	Perhaps not having to think is why they conform. The feeling that there is safety in numbers may also explain why people conform.
	Although you should try to get rid of fragments in your writing, you should know that some good writers use fragments for emphasis, for a planned afterthought, or for transitions.	The King's English Band delights me. A joy to hear.
framework	Try not to overuse *framework* when it's not referring to a definite structure. The structure can be abstract, but it must be a structure.	
frightened	See *afraid*.	

THE ITEM . . .	EXPLAINED . . .	AND IN ACTION ! ! !
fulsome	*Fulsome* means disgusting or insincere, not full of something.	
funny	*Funny* refers to laughter. If you mean strange or odd, say so.	
further	See *farther*.	
fused sentence	See *run-on sentence*.	
gap	Just about everybody is tired of hearing *generation gap, credibility gap, communications gap.* Try to use *gap* only when you mean a *physical hole*.	
gay	If you mean anything other than *homosexual*, don't use *gay*. At best, your meaning may be misunderstood and the reader may snicker.	
gender	Although *gender* identifies and classifies words according to sex, don't use the word when you're referring to anything but grammar.	
general public	The public is a general group of people, so you can just say *public*.	
gerund	See *participle*.	
good/well	*Good* is an adjective. *Well* is an adverb. When you're talking about health, you can use either one.	This pie tastes *good*. You all did *well* on that assignment. Aren't you feeling *good*? Aren't you feeling *well*?
had better	*Had better* can't be shortened to better. Don't say *I better win the race*, say *I had better win the race*.	
had ought	Instead of saying *had ought*, say *ought to have*.	
hanged/hung	Back in the Wild West, men were hanged almost every day. Everything else (including the dirty laundry and the jury) was hung.	
hang-up	We all have *hang-ups*, but try to call them *problems* or *biases* or *inhibitions* in writing.	

THE ITEM...	EXPLAINED...	AND IN ACTION ! ! !
hardly . . . than	You probably mean *hardly . . . when.*	
	I had *hardly* finished my meat *than* she brought out some ice cream.	I had *hardly* finished my meat *when* she brought out some ice cream.
-has reference to	*Refers to* is simpler.	
head up	If you've hit a wild shot in golf and you want your partner to get her head up, that's fine. But if you want your partner to *head up* the foursome, use *direct* or *lead* instead.	
helping verb	See *verb.*	
historic/historical	*Historic* refers to events that helped shape history. *Historical* refers to events that pertain to history but didn't necessarily shape it.	The *historic* influence of the French Revolution can't be measured. What does that *historical* marker say about St. Simon's Island?
hopefully	In formal writing, avoid using *hopefully* to mean *I hope.* In personal writing and everyday speaking, *hopefully* is fine.	*I hope* that these concepts are clear. *Hopefully,* the referee will call a technical before this game gets too rough.
host	Avoid *host* as a verb. Some people say *entertain* sounds better.	
house/home	A *house* is something you can build; a *home* is something you can make.	
how ever/however	How will you *ever* build that fence? *However* means *no matter which way.*	*How ever* you look at it, it's correct. *However,* you look at it and it's correct.
human history	*When in the course of human history . . .* is wordy for *When in the course of history . . . .* History is considered to be human unless you state that it's otherwise.	
human/humane	*Human* means *having to do with mankind.* *Humane* means *having the good qualities of a human, especially kindness, compassion, or mercy.*	Act like a *human!* Saving that dog from the traffic was *humane.*
hyphen	Although hyphens are mostly used in spelling, they can also link or separate words. Hyphens have some main functions in the language:	able-bodied carry-all know-it-all mother-in-law

THE ITEM . . .	EXPLAINED . . .	AND IN ACTION ! ! !
	They join letter or number modifiers to a word.	T-square A-bomb 6-inch
	They are used with prefixes when the original word begins with the same letter.	re-elect re-enter
	They are used to join *ex-* to a word when you mean *former*.	ex-wife ex-student
-ics	Words like dynamics, mathematics, statics, economics, genetics that end in *-ics* and refer to bodies of knowledge are singular.	*Economics* is difficult to read.
idea/ideal	An *idea* is a conception or thought. An *ideal* is a principle.	What a brilliant *idea* you had! Your *ideals* are not the highest.
i.e.	This abbreviation means *that is*.	
if and when	You probably mean *if*/or you mean *when*. Use one or the other.	
ignorant/stupid	An *ignorant* person hasn't been taught much; a *stupid* person couldn't learn something if it were taught.	I may be *ignorant* in math, but I'm not *stupid;* if you'll teach me, I'll learn.
illicit	See *elicit*.	
illusion	See *allusion*.	
immanent	See *eminent*.	
immigrant	See *emigrant*.	
imminent	See *eminent*.	
immortal	Don't immortalize something that's not mortal (living). Songs, records, games, wins, and losses can't be immortal.	
imply/infer	*Imply* refers to what a statement means; an implication is not always stated in the original, but the idea is included in the meaning. *Infer* refers to an interpretation—a listener's or reader's judgment based on the statement.	Your criticism *implies* that she's not worth seeing. From what you said, I *inferred* that it would be a waste of money to eat at the Greasy Spoon.

THE ITEM . . .	EXPLAINED . . .	AND IN ACTION ! ! !
in to/into	These are different in that *in to* is usually part of an infinitive (to form of a verb). *Into* means *inside of*.	I'm going *in to do* my laundry. I'm going *into* that cave soon.
in a very real sense/ in all probability/ in all likelihood/ in order to/ in back of/ in regards to/ in terms of/ in connection with/ in excess of/ in spite of the fact that/ in this day and age/ in number/ in length/ in size/ in area/ in volume/	Avoid all such phrases. They are wordy and can cause confusion.	
incident/incidence	An *incident* is an event or occurrence. *Incidence* refers to how often something happens or rate of occurrence.	That was an unforgettable *incident*. The *incidence* of unwanted pregnancies is dropping in the Boston area.
incredibly	Don't overuse this word to try to make another word stronger. *He's incredibly strong* could just be *He's strong.*	
indefinite pronoun	See *pronoun*.	
individual	Don't use *individual* when you just mean *person*. Todd is an incredible *individual*.	Todd is an incredible person.
infer	See *imply*.	
infinitive	See *verbal*.	
input/output	These words are almost dead from overwork. Try using them only when you're talking about mechanically putting something in and out.	
inside of/outside of	*Inside* and *outside* mean the same as *inside of* and *outside of*. So why use the extra words?	
instance	See *case*.	

THE ITEM . . .	EXPLAINED . . .	AND IN ACTION ! ! !
insure	See *assure*.	
intensifier	See *adverb*.	
interjection	When you interject something, you interrupt the usual flow of a thought or sentence or conversation. Interjections are a part of speech that do just that— they interrupt the flow of the sentence by adding surprise, emotion or anger. Commas or an exclamation mark usually set interjections off from the rest of the sentence. Use interjections with care in your writing. They can seem overdramatic and out of place.	*Oh,* I didn't know you were waiting for me. *Alas,* I was doomed to fail my first swimming test. *Hey!* I think that might be the answer. *Heck no!* I'm not going to miss the party. advantage of me!
interrogative pronoun	See *pronoun*.	
inversion for emphasis	See *emphasis*.	
irregardless	*Irregardless* is actually *regardless*.	*Regardless* of the time, I'm going to wait for my friend.
italics	On a typed or handwritten page, under-line whatever is in *italics* on a printed page. Use italics: to refer to foreign words for emphasis to refer to words as words to indicate that a title names a book, a work of art, a movie, or a ship (airplanes are considered ships).	writ of *habeas corpus, in absentia* What do you mean *I* did it? Is *fulsome* a word or the name of that prison in Johnny Cash's song? *The Queen Mary, If Life Is a Bowl of Cherries What Am I Doing in the Pits, Grease, Starry Night*
join together	You can just say join or together. They both mean the same thing, so it's a waste to say both.	
kind of/sort of/type of	If you feel the urge to write these phrases, don't. They're not necessary, and you shouldn't lose any meaning if you leave them out of your sentence. So pick up your pencil, mark through them, and go on writing.	
lack for	*Lack for* can be simplified to *lack*. Yellowstone doesn't *lack for* bison.	Yellowstone doesn't *lack* bison.

THE ITEM . . .	EXPLAINED . . .	AND IN ACTION ! ! !
large	*Large* can be an adverb all by itself. There's no need to add the usual *-ly*.	Tomatoes grow *large*.
large number of/ large part/ large portion/ large share	If you mean *many*, just say *many*.	
later/latter	*Later* means *after a while.* *Latter* relates to the second of two things being referred to.	See you *later*, alligator. If I had to choose between spaghetti or lasagna, I'd choose the *latter*.
lay/lie	*Lay* means *to place or set down* (lay, laid, laid). *Lie* means *to recline* (lie, lay, lain).	Please *lay* the book on the table carefully. Yesterday, you *laid* it on the edge and it fell off. I should have *laid* it down myself. I want to *lie* down when I get home. Yesterday, I *lay* in bed until 9:00. I haven't *lain* in bed that late for a long time.
leave/let	As a verb, *leave* shouldn't mean *to allow:* *Leave* me have it my way.	*Let* me have your packages.
lend/loan	In formal writing, avoid *loan* as a verb. In informal writing and conversation, *loan* as a verb is accepted.	The bank will *lend* money at 9%. *Loan* me a quarter.
less	See *fewer*.	
let	See *leave*.	
let's us	*Let's* means *let us,* so you don't need to say *let's us*.	
liable	See *apt*.	
lie	See *lay*.	
like	See *as*.	
likely	See *apt*.	
linking verb	See *verb*.	
little	See *few*.	
loan	See *lend*.	
loose/lose	*Loose* is an adjective that means not fastened or unrestrained.	That screw is *loose*.

THE ITEM . . .	EXPLAINED . . .	AND IN ACTION ! ! !
	Lose is a verb that means the opposite of win or to be deprived of.	I hope you didn't *lose* your checkbook.
lot(s) of	These expressions, although common in informal writing, should be avoided in formal writing. Try to be more specific.	
mad/angry	Although *mad* is used to mean angry, mad goes one degree further to imply insane.	
may	See *can*.	
mean	See *average*.	
mechanics	*Mechanics* are rules that make your writing easier to read. In some cases they function as signals to the reader, but, in most cases, mechanics are simply conventions that standardize things like capitalization, the use of numbers, and abbreviations.	
	See *capitalization, abbreviations and symbols, dates, numbers, italics, apostrophe, hyphen, quotation marks*.	
media/medium	*Media* is plural.	The *media* are concerned with being objective.
	Medium is singular.	India ink is the *medium* for that sketch.
median	See *average*.	
mighty	*Mighty* means *imposing in size or extent*. Don't use it to mean *very*.	Mighty Mouse
misplaced modifier	When a modifier modifies, or appears to modify, the wrong word or phrase in a sentence, it is misplaced. As a rule of thumb, place modifiers as close to the words they will modify as you can get them. Misplaced modifiers can be words, phrases, or clauses.	
	We sent the car to a shop that had the flat tire. We took Dad to the hospital with a broken leg.	We sent the car that had the flat tire to a shop. We took Dad, with a broken leg, to the hospital.
modification	When words, phrases, or clauses that you add to the basic sentence pattern restrict	

or qualify the subject, verb, or complement, you are using the process of modification. Modification is an important means of expanding the basic sentence pattern because it increases the amount of information that one sentence can carry. Modifiers can be words, phrases, or clauses.

Notice what happens to this simple sentence when we add modifiers:

The driver yelled.

The driver, *white with rage,* yelled *angrily at the pedestrian who darted in front of the car.*

You can expand your sentence easily by adding relative clauses; they are easy to recognize because they contain a relative pronoun (who, which, that, whom), and that pronoun renames the noun that the clause modifies.

The boy *who broke the window* ran away before I could catch him.

Sometimes relative clauses are difficult to recognize because they have been reduced or simplified.

The girl (who is) wearing the red dress just moved here from Casper.

See also *dangling modifier, misplaced modifier,* and *relative clauses.*

more preferable	Just say *preferable.*	
most	See *almost.*	
muchly	One may think this is a word, but it's not. Use *much.*	
myself	Use *myself* only as a reflexive pronoun. Not as a substitute for *I* or *me.*	I told *myself* that I had to be a complete idiot.
	Don't say, *If you want a ride, call either Jane or myself.*	If you want a ride, call either Jane or me.
nature	When used to mean sort or kind, *nature* is often unnecessary and vague. Instead of saying *The nature of the disease caused discomfort,* say *The fever connected with the disease caused discomfort.*	
near future/not too distant future	*Soon* would probably work just as well, and it would certainly be simpler.	
need	See *lack.*	
nobody	See *anybody.*	

THE ITEM ...	EXPLAINED ...	AND IN ACTION ! ! !
nonrestrictive clause	See *restrictive clause*.	
nor/or	*Nor* will follow *neither* in a sentence of comparison. *Or* will follow *either*.	*Neither* rain *nor* snow will dampen my spirits. *Either* rain *or* snow could interfere with the barbeque.
not too/not that	If you mean *not very,* say it. *Not too* and *not that* sound sluggish. She's *not that* interested in going. She's *not too* interested in going.	She's *not very* interested in going.
noun	A noun names a person, place, thing, or idea. Nouns can be divided into two broad categories: proper nouns and common nouns.	
	Proper nouns name specific persons, places, things, or ideas.	Robert Redford, Chicago, King Tut, Holland, The Washington Monument
	Proper nouns are always capitalized.	The Incredible Hulk
	A common noun names a person, place, or thing that is ordinary, that is one of many others in a class.	assumption, toy, honesty, sky, mind, universe, railroad, job, jaguar.
	Nouns have certain features:	

	They can be abstract or concrete.
	    Abstract nouns name ideas, events, and other things that are intangible.
	    Concrete nouns name things that are tangible, that can be touched, felt, seen, or experienced in some way.
		joy, Civil War, growth, marriage, manner, category, motherhood
		pen, woman, sofa, house, head, dog, bull, piano

	They can be human or nonhuman.	man, nurse, Art Buchwald, Trigger, woman, waiter, elephant
	They can be masculine or feminine.	lion, tigress, actress, widow, gander, widower

	They may be animate or inanimate.
	    Animate nouns name living things.
	    Inanimate nouns name nonliving things.
		amoeba, animal, goldfish, engineer, teacher
		rock, ocean, chair, mountain, water, cloud

	Nouns have two basic functions in sentences: they may be subjects or objects.	
	As a subject, the noun announces the topic of a sentence.	When the sudden *rain storm* ended, the *swimmers* returned to the lake. The *president* will make an important foreign policy statement tonight.

THE ITEM . . .	EXPLAINED . . .	AND IN ACTION ! ! !

<table>
<tr><td></td><td></td><td>The desk is so cluttered that I can't even see your paper.</td></tr>
<tr><td></td><td>As an object, the noun completes the meaning of a verb or verbal, or it joins with a preposition to form a prepositional phrase.</td><td>I finally finished my term paper at 3 A.M.
Typing that paper was hard work.
I still plan to write a book someday.
During its last session, Congress gave itself a raise.
I asked the movers to put the couch against the wall in the living room.</td></tr>
<tr><td>noun clause</td><td>A noun clause is a subordinate clause (one that can't stand alone as a sentence) that functions in the sentence as a noun.</td><td></td></tr>
<tr><td></td><td>A noun clause can be used in a sentence anywhere you'd use a noun:
subject
direct object</td><td>That we had lost made us angry.
The other team admitted that the referees had made serious mistakes.</td></tr>
<tr><td></td><td>object of preposition
indirect object
appositive</td><td>After school, I'm going to wherever I want.
Take whoever signs up out to eat.
The people that we care about, those who can't care for themselves, must not be hurt.</td></tr>
<tr><td></td><td>objective complement</td><td>I made myself whatever I am today.</td></tr>
<tr><td>nowhere near</td><td>See not nearly.</td><td></td></tr>
<tr><td>numbers</td><td>Here are some general rules to follow when using numbers:</td><td></td></tr>
<tr><td></td><td>Spell out numbers from one to ten.</td><td>We have to read five books this semester; we may choose from a list of 25 novels.</td></tr>
<tr><td></td><td>Use figures to indicate exact sums, time, large figures, dates.</td><td>2:30 A.M., $8.65, 203,431, 1999, 500 B.C.</td></tr>
<tr><td></td><td>Avoid beginning a sentence with a number. If you can't rewrite the sentence so that the number is not at the beginning, then spell it out.</td><td></td></tr>
<tr><td></td><td>Avoid 1963 marked the beginning of an important era in American life.</td><td>In 1963, Americans began an important era in politics.</td></tr>
<tr><td></td><td>Numbers from 21 to 99 are hyphenated when spelled out. Make sure you spell forty and ninety correctly.</td><td>thirty-five, ninety-seven, forty-two</td></tr>
<tr><td></td><td>Twelve odd teachers of mine . . . .</td><td>Twelve-odd teachers of mine . . . .</td></tr>
<tr><td>of between/of from</td><td>Don't use two prepositions when one will do the job.</td><td>I'll give you a list of ten to 12 people.</td></tr>
</table>

THE ITEM . . .	EXPLAINED . . .	AND IN ACTION ! ! !
oftentimes	*Oftentimes* sounds great when you're sitting on the front porch swing telling tales. Otherwise, you should use often.	
on account of	*Because of* sounds better.	
on the part of	How did we ever get in the habit of saying *by* with so many words?	
orient/orientate	Both of these words mean the same thing, so use the shorter, simpler one — *orient*.	
ourself	Since *our* is plural, *selves* should also be plural. Always say *ourselves*.	
output	See *input*.	
outside of	See *inside of*.	
owing to the fact that	Such a long string of words might put the reader to sleep. Try *since*.	
pair	See *couple*.	
parallelism	When you join equal parts of a sentence to emphasize the relationship between structure and meaning, you use parallelism. Using parallelism, repeating a grammatical pattern in a series, makes the sentence stand out and reinforces its ideas. Parallelism can be used at any level: a series of nouns, modifiers, subordinate clauses. Parallelism adds emphasis. See also *emphasis*.	Personal growth brings great happiness, great expansion, and great rewards. If one person tries to be different, he will be labeled a freak; if five people do it, they are just a radical group; but if 30,000 people, perhaps the entire population of your home town, started being different, that would be called a "movement."
parens (parentheses)	Recently we discovered that the punctuation marks were called parens and the information inside the parens, along with the parens, was called parenthesis. This news is not earth-shattering, but it is interesting. Parens suggest a closeness between the writer and the reader and imply that you two know something that the rest of the world might not know. Parenthetical information is played down and de-empha-	Many American presidents (for example, Dwight Eisenhower) were military leaders. CUNY (City University of New York) offers a variety of programs.

sized; it may not be essential to a sentence, but it may be interesting or helpful to the reader.

Punctuation:

Parenthetical material does not affect the punctuation of a sentence. If a parenthetical clause comes at the end of a sentence, for example, the period to end the sentence would go outside of the parens.

I like some history courses (American), but hate others (ancient Greek).

When numbering a series of items in a sentence, use two parens, not one.

I'll eat (1) potatoes, (2) meat, (3) carrots, and (4) gravy.

When a complete sentence is parenthetical, the end punctuation goes inside the parens.

I want to know (You can tell me if you want to.) what I've got to do to improve.

If you have an item that you need to set off with parens inside of a parenthetical idea, use brackets.

I want to know (You can tell me [if you want to].) . . . .

participle   See *verbal.*

parts of speech   Words in English are classified into eight parts of speech. Each part of speech has a specific function in the language. The parts of speech are noun, pronoun, verb, adverb, adjective, preposition, conjunction and interjection.

See also *noun, pronoun, verb, adverb, adjective, preposition, conjunction,* and *interjection.*

passive voice   See *active voice.*

past/passed   *Past* is something that has already happened.
Passed is the past action of *passing.*

My *past* record isn't too great.

He *passed* the ball.

per   *Per* sounds a bit stiff for everyday classroom writing. Try to use it only when you're referring to math formulas.

percent/per cent   Either spelling is accepted. Spelling the word out rather than using the symbol is preferable in writing.

period   A period indicates a full stop at the end of a sentence.

Send me help.

THE ITEM . . .	EXPLAINED . . .	AND IN ACTION ! ! !
	A period always goes inside quotation marks.	"Send me help." This was the cry of my math teacher.
	Use periods after intitials in names.	Patricia R. Martin, Dr. Ernestine Hambrick
	Use periods as decimals in numbers.	17.65, 33.5, 3.25
	Use periods with abbreviations.	Inc., Ms., M.D.

	Use periods following the numbers or letters in lists or outlines.	1.
		2.
		   a.
		   b.

periodic sentence	See *emphasis*.	
persecute/prosecute	*Persecute* means *to harass because of a belief*. *Prosecute* means *to follow to the end*, or *to seek legal action for a crime*.	Hitler *persecuted* the Jews. Allied Nations *prosecuted* those in Hitler's regime for persecuting Jews.
personal/personnel	Your own belongings are your *personal* things. If you want a job, write to the company's *personnel* director.	
personal pronoun	See *pronoun*.	
persuade	See *convince*.	
phenomena/phenomenon	*Phenomenon* is singular.	
phrase	A phrase is a group of related words that acts together as one part of speech.	
	Prepositional phrases can be adverbs and adjectives. Participial phrases can be adjectives. Gerund and infinitive phrases can be nouns.	Put the money *on the counter*. *Riding bikes* is my hobby.
plan on	You *plan to* do something, not *plan on* doing it.	
poorly	Avoid *poorly* when referring to health.	
position for emphasis	See *emphasis*.	
possessive pronoun	See *pronoun*.	
possessive	See *apostrophe*.	
precede/proceed	*Precede* means *to go ahead of* or *to surpass*.	The secret servicemen *preceded* the president into the room.

THE ITEM . . .	EXPLAINED . . .	AND IN ACTION ! ! !
	Proceed means *to continue on.*	We *proceeded* on course.
predicate adjective	See *adjective.*	
predication	See *subject-verb-object agreement.*	
predominate/predominant	*Predominate* is a verb. *Predominant* is an adjective.	
prejudice/prejudiced	*Prejudice* doesn't always mean that you are against something; you could be prejudiced for something. Notice that the adjective is *prejudiced,* not *prejudice.*	I was *prejudiced* in favor of lowering bus rates.
preposition	Prepositions are words or groups of words that indicate relationships between the object of the preposition and some other word in the sentence. The preposition indicates time, cause, place, manner, agency, association, or other relationships. Usually, prepositions occur in phrases which function as adverbs or adjectives.	Tom lives *by* a noisy freeway. She sat *beside* me *at* the movies. *In* the summer, I'll be working full time *at* our local drugstore. *To* me, a summer job is a good way to prepare *for* a full time job *after* graduation. *In spite of* her mother's refusal, Jane went anyway.
	Sentences may end in a preposition when the preposition is separated from its object.	Who are you going to the party *with?* That's something I won't put *up with.*
	Verb Particles: Some prepositions have become so closely associated with certain verbs that the verb and preposition form a verb unit. In these sentences, *up* and *out* don't function as prepositions because they don't link an object to another part of the sentence. The prepositions are merely bound to the verb in such a way that they change its meaning. *Look* is different from *look up,* and *make* is certainly different from *make out.* Prepositions that are a part of the verb are called *verb particles.*	Would you *look up* this word? *Call* me *up* when you want to talk. I can't *make out* what number that is.
pretty	*Pretty* is overused. Don't use it to mean *very.*	
principal/principle	A *principal* is a leader, chief, or head.	My brother thinks he's the *principal* character in that story. That *principal* is a push-over.
	Principle is a noun that means *theory, concept, rule.*	Should moral *principles* be taught in school?

THE ITEM . . .	EXPLAINED . . .	AND IN ACTION ! ! !
proceed	See *precede*.	

pronoun

Pronouns are usually defined as noun substitutes because they frequently replace a noun mentioned earlier in a sentence or in a previous sentence.

As noun substitutes, pronouns are important in reducing redundancy in sentences.

John broke *his* leg as *he* was climbing down the mountain.

Pronouns are considered noun substitutes for another reason: they perform the same functions as nouns do. They serve as subjects of sentences and clauses or as objects of verbs and prepositions.

This is my favorite book.
I refuse to go to that class one more time.
I explained to *him* why *I* wasn't going.
You don't mean *that,* do you?
My jeans are different from *those.*

Personal Pronouns:
Personal pronouns occur in the same positions as nouns, but the form of the pronoun changes with its function in the sentence. If it is used as a subject, the nominative form is used: I, you, he, she, it, we, they.
But when the personal pronoun serves as an object, the objective form is used: me, him, her, us, them.

I, you, he, she, it, we, they, me, him, her, us, them

I answered the telephone when *you* called.
They plan to move into the room across the hall.
I will accompany *him* on the trip to New Mexico.
Tell *us* all about the trip.
Jennifer will take the trip with Joe and *me.*

Possessive Pronouns:

As indicators of ownership or possession, these pronouns function just as possessive nouns do. Essentially, they modify the nouns that they appear with.

my, mine, his, her, hers, its, our, ours, your, yours, their, theirs
his books, our time, my story

Reflexive Pronouns:

Reflexive pronouns occur only when a noun and pronoun or two pronouns in the same sentence or clause clearly refer to the same word before it. This is why the pronoun is called reflexive: it is grammatically bound to the noun or pronoun it refers to.

myself, himself, herself, itself, yourself, ourselves, themselves
Mary considers herself a good person.
Fred asks that Dave himself play the guitar.

Relative Pronouns:

This set of pronouns replaces the noun in a relative clause. Like all other pronouns, relative pronouns are referents, that is, there is always a noun to which the pronoun refers.

who, whose, whom, which, that, when, where, wherever
The dress *that* I worked on yesterday is still not finished.
The street *where* John lives is hard to find.

THE ITEM...	EXPLAINED...	AND IN ACTION ! ! !
	Notice that the relative pronoun is always the first word in the relative clause.	I remember the man *who* told me how to get there.

Demonstrative Pronouns:
Demonstrative pronouns function as nouns or as modifiers.

this, that, those, these
This is not what I had in mind when I suggested we have a party.
What did she mean by *that?*
Which of *those* did you want?
These are the best shoes I've ever owned.
Those flowers are the freshest in the shop.

Interrogative Pronouns:
Interrogative pronouns are used in questions to represent the information that is unknown. Like relative pronouns, interrogative pronouns always appear at the beginning of the clause or sentence since it is the unknown information that is the focus of the sentence. Unlike relative pronouns, however, the referent for these pronouns is unknown.

who, which, what, where, why, when
Who is the man you were talking to?
When do you plan to go home?
What are you writing your paper on?
Which guys were in the office?

Indefinite Pronouns:

Indefinite pronouns may function as nouns or as modifiers. They have no specific antecedent, but they are pronouns because they clearly function as noun substitutes.

each, everyone, anybody, either, some, somebody, one, no one, several, everybody, any, all
Give me three copies of *each.*
No one came to the party.
Anybody can answer that.
They ordered *several* kegs for the party.

pronoun reference

You might have an error marked on your paper that says *noun-pronoun agreement* or *pronoun reference.*
Remember that a pronoun is a noun substitute.
Usually, the sentence contains a noun to which the pronoun refers, and the pronoun must reflect the grammatical features of that noun. If the noun is plural, the pronoun must be plural; if it is feminine, the pronoun must be feminine; if the noun is an object, the pronoun must be an object. Most of the time, pronoun agreement presents no problems, but some sentence constructions make pronoun reference difficult to recognize.

Everybody, anyone, anybody, someone, no one, one, each and such indefinite pronouns are always singular. So they must be matched by singular pronouns:

THE ITEM . . .	EXPLAINED . . .	AND IN ACTION ! ! !
	Everybody finished *their* themes in 50 minutes. *Someone* left *their* umbrella here. Does *everyone* want *their* coffee black?	*Everybody* finished *his or her* theme in 50 minutes. *Someone* left *his or her* umbrella here. Does *everyone* want *his or her* coffee black?
	Pronouns can cause problems in sentences for one other reason. Sometimes, it's not clear what noun the pronoun refers to. Sometimes you may be misled by a word or phrase that appears to be an antecedent but actually isn't. The *Swiss* have not been at war for many years. *It* is a neutral country. He was opposed to *gun control* because he felt every citizen should have *one* for self-defense.	*Switzerland* has not been at war for many years. *It* is a neutral . . . . He was opposed to *gun control* because he felt every citizen should *be allowed to own firearms* for self-defense.
proper noun	See *noun*.	
prophecy/prophesy	*Prophecy* is the noun. *Prophesy* is the verb.	That *prophecy* will never come true. You *prophesy*, but your prophecies don't come true.
prosecute	See *persecute*.	
punctuation	Punctuation helps the reader follow your train of thought. See *period, question mark, exclamation point, comma, semicolon, colon, parens (parenthesis), dash.*	
quarrel	See *argue*.	
quartet	See *duo*.	
question mark	Use a question mark at the end of a sentence that asks a question.	What do you think of that surf?
	With quotations, when the writer who is doing the quoting is asking the question, the question mark goes outside of the quotation marks.	Did she say, "I wouldn't marry you if my life depended on it"?
	When the quotation is a question, the question mark goes inside the quotation marks.	She asked, "What do you think of that surf?"
quotation marks	Quotation marks enclose direct repetition of words. Avoid using quotation marks for emphasis.	

THE ITEM . . .	EXPLAINED . . .	AND IN ACTION ! ! !
	When you quote anything word for word from another source, enclose those words in quotation marks.	The report said, "Many high school graduates are going to college."
	If a quotation is longer than five lines, indent all of the lines of the quotation five spaces from the left margin, single-spaced. Don't use quotation marks with indented quotations.	

	If a quotation is more than one paragraph (and it is not indented because it's not more than five lines), put quotation marks at the beginning of every paragraph but at the end of only the last paragraph.	"I can't pay the rent, I can't pay the rent.
		    "My kids are hungry.
		    "My house is cold.
		    "My husband left me.
		    "I can't pay the rent."

	If you have a quotation within a quotation, use single quotation marks (the apostrophe key on a typewriter) on the inside quote.	Regan asked, "Did I hear him say 'Get lost'?"
	Use quotation marks to indicate titles of short stories, magazine and newspaper articles, songs, and television programs.	"The Death of a Salesman" "Captain Kangaroo" "Grease"
	Always put periods and commas inside closing quotation marks.	"The Death of a Salesman," "Grease." He said, "I'll go."
	Always put colons and semicolons outside closing quotation marks.	The agent said, "I'll pay the rent"; that surprised me. These are my favorite "classes": lunchtime, study hall, and rest period.
	For all other punctuation: If the punctuation is a part of the quotation, place it inside the quotation marks; if the punctuation is not a part of the quotation, place it outside the marks.	
	See *question marks*.	
quote	For most writing, *quote* is just fine. But if you want to be formal, use *quotation*.	
raise/rear	People used to say that you *raised* cattle but *reared* children. But now it's all right to say you *raised* children. However, use *raise* only with animals and crops.	
raise/rise	*Raise* means *to lift up.* *Rise* means *to get or go up.*	He *raised* that chair with his finger. I saw it *rise* above his head.

THE ITEM . . .	EXPLAINED . . .	AND IN ACTION ! ! !
rarely ever	Just say *rarely.*	
rather than	When you use *rather than,* be careful that your comparisons are parallel.	
	Rather than eating lunch, we decided to eat breakfast.	Rather than eat lunch, we decided to eat breakfast.
real/very	These words are overworked. Try to give them a rest as often as you can.	
rear	See *raise.*	
reason	See *cause.*	
reason is because	*Because* means the same thing and saves energy.	
reckon	*Reckon* is another one of those front porch words. It's fine for a down-home, yarn-spinning effect, but that's about all.	
reflexive pronoun	See *pronoun.*	
in regard to/with regard to	If you can just say *about,* or *concerning,* prefer one of those.	
relative clause	See *modification.*	
relative pronoun	See *pronoun.*	
relevant	Don't use *relevant* by itself. Your topic must be *relevant to* something.	
restrictive clause	Relative clauses may be restrictive or nonrestrictive, a distinction that is important to the meaning of a sentence. A restrictive clause is vital to the meaning of the sentence and can't be left out. Relative clauses make the nouns more specific.	The girl *who lives next door* is going to Europe this summer. *English class* will be the biggest part of our grade.
	Nonrestrictive clauses, on the other hand, don't restrict the meaning of the nouns they modify, they merely add information to it.	My professor, *who recently returned from France,* says the United States has a poor image abroad.
	Nonrestrictive clauses can be omitted without affecting the meaning of the sentences because they merely add information.	The theme, *which must be typed,* can be on any subject we choose.

THE ITEM . . .	EXPLAINED . . .	AND IN ACTION ! ! !
	Usually relative clauses used with proper nouns (Marcy) are nonrestrictive because a name is already specific.	Marcy, *who loves to travel,* will go to Grand Canyon next summer.
	Nonrestrictive clauses are always set off by commas. If a relative clause can be restrictive or nonrestrictive, these commas are the only way the reader can tell if the information is essential or just interesting.	The theme which is due next week can be on any subject we choose. The theme, which is due next week, can be on any subject we choose.
reticent	*Reticent* doesn't mean reluctant. It means inclined to be secretive or silent.	
rise	See *raise*.	
robber	See *burglar*.	
run-on sentence	A run-on sentence misleads readers. are much like comma splices except that in a run-on, all punctuation is omitted between the independent clauses (sentences):	
	Universities are an important part of our world for it is their teaching of our children that should someday bring about a better world.	
	A run-on sentence misleads the reader. With no period or semicolon to mark the end of one sentence, they read the attached sentence as if it were a part of the first one. A run-on is usually very confusing and hard to understand.	
	1 To correct run-ons: Rewrite the run-on as two separate sentences.	Universities are an important part of our world. It is their teaching of our children that should someday bring about a better world.
	2 Insert a semicolon between the fused sentences if the two sentences are closely related in content.	Universities are an important part of our world; it is their teaching of our children that should someday bring about a better world.
	3 If the sentences can be joined by a coordinating conjunction, separate them with a comma.	Universities are an important part of our world, for it is their teaching of our children that should someday bring about a better world.
	Use subordination to make one sentence dependent on the other.	Universities are an important part of our world since their teaching of our children may someday bring about a better world.

THE ITEM . . .	EXPLAINED . . .	AND IN ACTION ! ! !
same/the same	The words aren't pronouns. Don't say *I did the same.*	
scared	See *afraid.*	
scene	Try to avoid using scene in the sense of *drug scene.* A *scene* is a place where something has happened or will happen.	
semi-	See *bi-.*	
semicolon	A semicolon can join two sentences that are close in meaning. It indicates a greater pause than a comma but not as great a pause as a period. Semicolons can also add clarity to involved sentences. Place a semicolon to join closely related sentences.	I want to go; he doesn't.
	Use a semicolon to join closely related sentences combined with a conjunctive adverb.	I want to go; however, he doesn't.
	Use the semicolon to divide series in sentences that have several series.	This year I'm taking math, English, weightlifting, and biology; next year history, chemistry, drafting, and swimming.
	Use a semicolon to separate sentences joined by a coordinating conjunction if the sentences already have commas.	In most cases, I'll order steak, baked potato, and salad; but today I think I'll order fish.
sensual/sensuous	*Sensual* means *carnal* or *having to do with sex.* *Sensuous* refers to the senses.	Cavitene gum will make your mouth *sensual.* The symbols in that book were *sensuous.*
sentence	English sentences exist in an infinite variety of forms, lengths, and situations. Because of this variety it is difficult to define a sentence absolutely. In the appropriate context, even a word or phrase may be considered a sentence.	
	Despite differences in form and length, sentences share one thing: they all have a subject, which announces the topic, and a verb, which makes a comment upon that topic.	
	We can think of a sentence, then, as a topic and comment whose form is controlled by the writer's intention (how much information the writer wants to get across in one sentence).	English sentence = subject + verb + optional complement

The basic sentence pattern (subject + verb + optional complement) is flexible. In regular conversation or writing, we rarely use the basic pattern (s-v-c). Our real sentences are longer; they carry more information than the basic pattern can carry. We vary the basic pattern and add information to the sentence through expansion: modification, coordination, and subordination.

See also *modification, coordination,* and *subordination.*

sentence fragment   See *fragment.*

set/sit   *Set* means *to put something down.*   *Set* the book on the table.
Sit means *to occupy a place.*   *Sit* down.

shall/will   Once, people insisted on using *shall.*   I *shall* return. (formal)
should/would   Now, it's considered very formal, and   I *will* return. (normal)
will is considered perfectly all right.

sight   See *cite.*

similar to   If you mean *like,* say it; it's shorter and clearer.

sit   See *set.*

some time/sometime/   *Some time* means *an amount of time.*   I'll need *some time* to think.
sometimes   *Sometime* means *at any time.*   Bring it to me *sometime.*
Sometimes means *once in a while.*   I *sometimes* forget to go to class.

somebody   See *anybody.*

something   *Something* is usually overused and not clear. Avoid it.

somewheres   Drop the *s. Somewhere* is correct.

sort of   See *kind of.*

specially   See *especially.*

spelling rules   Despite the inconsistencies in English spelling, there are some rules that show spelling isn't as haphazard as it sometimes seems to be. Try to learn these.

THE ITEM . . .	EXPLAINED . . .	AND IN ACTION ! ! !
	-ie/-ei:	
	I before *e*	believe, retrieve, achieve
	Except after *c*	receive, conceive
	Or when sounded as *a*	sleigh, eight
	As in *neighbor* or *weigh*	
	A few exceptions . . .	weird, leisure, foreign, height
	final *e* + suffix:	
	When the suffix begins with a vowel, drop the final *e*.	
	stare + ing	staring
	note + able	notable
	Except when the word ends in -ce/-ge . . .	courageous, noticeable, knowledgeable
	When the suffix begins with a consonant, keep the final *e*.	wasteful, shameful, likeness, engagement, pavement, careful
	Exceptions . . .	abridgment, judgment, argument, acknowledgment
	final consonants:	
	When a suffix beginning with a vowel is added to short words or short accented syllables ending in a consonant, double the final consonant.	deferral, bugged, fitted, handicapped, stirring, beginning
	If the final syllable ends in a consonant but is not accented, don't double the final consonant.	bigoted, riveter, murderer
	When a suffix beginning with a consonant is added to a word ending in a consonant but is not accented, don't double.	deferment, fitness, capful
	final *y* + suffix:	
	Change *y* to *i*, except when the suffix is *-ing*.	beautiful, died, satisfied, lied, flying, dying, satisfying
	final *c* + suffix that begins with a vowel:	frolicking, trafficked, panicky, picnicking
	Change *c* to *ck*.	
stationary/stationery	*Stationary* means fixed.	That fixture is *stationary*.
	Stationery is the paper.	What cute *stationery!*
stupid	See *ignorant*.	
subject	See *area*.	
subject of sentence	The *subject* of the sentence announces the topic for the sentence.	This *paper* is getting long.

THE ITEM . . .	EXPLAINED . . .	AND IN ACTION ! ! !
	See also *sentence*.	
subject-verb agreement	Subject-verb agreement means that a singular subject must have a singular verb and a plural subject must have a plural verb. If your paper has subject-verb agreement marked on it, then somehow you got confused and gave your plural noun a singular verb or your singular noun a plural verb. When your subject and verb are separated in the sentence, this is easy to do.	
	The chef's salad and the baked chicken looks good.	The chef's salad and the baked chicken look good.
	Compound sentences joined by *or* and *nor* often cause agreement problems:	
	Neither John nor my brother are going to camp.	Neither John nor my brother is . . . .
	Indefinite pronouns can also cause problems when there is a prepositional phrase between the subject and the verb:	
	Each of the boys want to try out for the team.	Each of the boys wants to try out.
	Only one of the chairs need to be moved.	Only one of the chairs needs . . . .
	To avoid errors in subject-verb agreement, keep the subject as close to the verb as you can get it, and keep your subject clearly in mind—no matter what separates it from the verb.	
subject-verb-object agreement	Some people call these mismatches between the subject and the verb and the object predication. In sentence error, something is wrong with the agreement of your subject and verb and object: they disagree either grammatically or logi-	
	Any person absent on the final day of classes would have meant that the end-of-school picnic could not be held. (person is concrete, but verb and complement are abstract)	Any person's absence would have meant that the end-of-school picnic could not be held.
	The subject of his talk was about employment after graduation.	The subject of his talk was employment after graduation.
	When air fares are reduced, there will no longer be so many cars driving people to vacation spots.	When air fares are reduced, there will no longer be so many people driving cars to vacation spots.

THE ITEM . . .	EXPLAINED . . .	AND IN ACTION ! ! !
subordinating conjunction	See *conjunction*.	
subordination	Subordination, the process of reducing the grammatical rank of one sentence and joining it with another, is a major way to expand the basic sentence pattern. When we reduce the grammatical rank of a sentence, we make it dependent on another for its meaning:	
	We couldn't go to the show last night. The car wouldn't start.	We couldn't go to the show last night *because* the car wouldn't start.
	The function of subordination is to make relationships between sentences and ideas clear.	
	Subordinating conjunctions signal different relationships: time place cause contrast condition	 when, after, whenever, while, before where, wherever because, since, in order that, so that although, though, while if, unless, since, as long as
such as	See *as*.	
suppose	If you mean *supposed*, be sure you add the *d*.	We were supposed to go fishing, but the wind was blowing too hard.
surely	*Surely* is the adverb, but *certainly* sounds better.	
symbol	See *abbreviation*.	
take	See *bring*.	
that/which/who	*That* and *which* generally refer to non-human objects. *Who* refers to people.	
theirselves	Use *themselves* instead.	
thief	See *burglar*.	
thusly	*Thus* is correct.	
till/until	These words are correct. Don't use til or 'til.	
to/too/two	*Too* means also. *Two* is the number.	I want to go, *too*. I'll take *two* helpings.

THE ITEM . . .	EXPLAINED . . .	AND IN ACTION ! ! !
	To is everything else.	I plan *to* drive *to* town.
totally	Don't use *totally* just to mean very; it means entirely or completely.	
toward/towards	Both are fine!	
trio	See *duo*.	
type of	See *kind of*.	
under water/underwater	*Under water* is the prepositional phrase. *Underwater* is the adjective or adverb.	Ralph performs *under water*. Aquarena Springs has Ralph, the *underwater* pig.
underlining	See *italics*.	
uninterested	See *disinterested*.	
until	See *till*.	
use to/used to	Make sure you say *used to*.	She *used to* weigh 237 pounds. Her car *used to* have heavy-duty shocks, didn't it?
verb	The verb may be considered the heart of the sentence because it contributes to and affects meaning more than any other element in the sentence. It determines the number of nouns needed to make a sentence meaningful. It determines the time and the quality of the action. It sometimes focuses the reader's attention on a particular part of the sentence. So, when we talk about the verb, it is not enough to define it as an action word.	
	Verbs in English have four principal parts which form the basis of the tense system: present, past, perfect, present participle. Tense refers to the way we indicate when an action occurs.	
	Verbs may be regular or irregular depending on how the principal parts are formed. In regular verbs, the past and perfect are formed by adding *-ed* to the present.	

Present	Past	Perfect	Present Participle
alert	alerted	alerted	alerting
dress	dressed	dressed	dressing
cross	crossed	crossed	crossing
pass	passed	passed	passing

In irregular verbs, the past and perfect sometimes show changes in the main vowel, and sometimes, the past and perfect forms are entirely different from the present.

Present	Past	Perfect	Present Participle
go	went	gone	going
lie	lay	lain	lying
write	wrote	written	writing
do	did	done	doing
is	was/were	been	being

Principal parts are important in understanding how time (tense) is expressed by the verb:

Present expresses action going on right now.

I *pass* by his house every day.
Tom *is* sick today.

Past expresses completed action.

He *crossed* the street without looking.
Sue *wrote* me a long letter.

Perfect also expresses past action, but the addition of *have* as a helping verb changes the aspect (quality) of the past action.

He *has done* all he can do.
I *have crossed* that street many times.

The present participle is used with a form of *be* to convey the sense of continuing action or future action.

John *is going* home with me.
She *is* upstairs *dressing* for her important job interview.

The Auxiliary or Helping Verb:
As the sample sentences show, the principal parts alone allow only limited distinctions of time and quality of action. To increase the range of action expressed by the verb, we add auxiliaries to the main verb of the sentence. The English language has two kinds of auxiliaries: helping verbs and modals.

Helping verbs are forms of *have* and *be* used with the perfect and with the present participle to change the quality rather than the time of the action.

Past: I saw all I wanted to see at the museum.

I had seen all I wanted to see, so I went home. (past perfect)
Since I have seen all of these exhibits before, I will skip the museum tour. (present perfect)

Modals are special kinds of verbs used with any of the principal parts to express the mode of the action. The modal indicates whether action is possible, permitted, required, or desired.

can, could, may, might, must, ought, will, would, shall, should

Modals always appear before the main verb.

I *can* finish this tonight if I hurry.

When modals are used with helping verbs, the perfect or progressive markers (*-ed* or *-ing*) follow the modal.

He could have *been* a good writer.
You should have *been* sleeping instead of studying.

Modals must be used with other verbs; a modal does not express action. Try writing a sentence using only shall or might as the verb. Only when the context is understood do modals appear alone.

Mary asked me if I was going to her party. I said I *might.*

Subject-Verb-Complement Combinations: One of the most important functions of the verb is to indicate the number of nouns needed to complete the meaning of the sentence. We know that there must always be a noun to function as the subject for the verb, but some verbs require one noun, two nouns, or an adjective as a complement (completer of the action).

These verb-noun combinations are classified as intransitive, transitive, or linking.

When a verb is complete without a complement, it is an intransitive verb.

I *was talking* to my mother on the telephone.
Our congressman *voted* against the bill.
To get exercise, I *walk* to school.

When a verb requires a noun or nouns to complete its meaning, it is a transitive verb.

He *hit the ball* farther than he ever had before.

THE ITEM . . .	EXPLAINED . . .	AND IN ACTION ! ! !
	Direct objects are sometimes needed to complete the verb.	The president will almost certainly veto *the bill.*
	Indirect objects along with direct objects are often needed. To test if a word is an indirect object, simply re-word it as a prepositional phrase that indicates at whom the action of the sentence is directed: Mother taught the alphabet *to me.*	My mother taught *me* the alphabet.
	A small group of verbs require two objects, a direct object and an ob-jective complement which may either be a noun or an adjective.	She considered Tom *a bore.* We painted the town *red.*

When the complement renames or modi-fies the subject, the verb is a linking verb. We have two kinds of linking verbs in English: *be* verbs and verbs that deal with the senses or with states of being. What makes the complement of a linking verb different from the complement of a transitive verb is that it may be a noun (predicate nominative), an adjective (predicate adjective), or an adverb. Furthermore, this complement carries most of the meaning in a sentence whose verb is a linking verb. The function of the linking verb is to show identity be-tween the subject of the complement, so the verb itself carries little meaning and conveys little or no action.

Mary was sick today.
The truth is that I just didn't have time to do it.
Truth is evasive.
The heroine remained unmarried.
She became despondent when her lover died.
That person's clothes always look wrinkled. In his baggy pants and narrow ties he seems unconcerned about style.
I feel awkward every time I talk to her.

With most transitive and intransitive verbs, the verb is the heart of the sen-tence. With linking verbs, the absence of action makes the complement the heart of the sentence.

verb particles See *prepositions.*

verbal Although the verb usually functions as the predicate of a sentence, certain verb forms can serve as nouns and adjectives and adverbs. When a verb functions as a different part of speech, it is called a *verbal.* There are three kinds of verbals in English: participles, gerunds, and infinitives.

THE ITEM . . .	EXPLAINED . . .	AND IN ACTION ! ! !
	Participle: A participle is a verb used as an adjective. You can recognize participles when you notice the perfect form or the present participle of a verb used to modify some part of the sentence.	The *evaporating* mist made the morning seem muggy. The *tired* man trudged down the trail.
	Gerund: A gerund is a verb used as a noun. You can recognize a gerund when you notice an *-ing* form of a verb in a position generally filled by a noun.	*Studying* makes me sleepy. *Going to the lake and spending the day fishing* is my idea of a good time.
	Infinitive: An infinitive is formed by adding *to* to the present verb form. Infinitives function as nouns, adjectives, or adverbs.	*To quit* now would be unwise. The best way *to write* is to use a pen and paper. He is eating heavier meals *to gain* weight.
	Verbals can be either single words or phrases.	
very	See *real.*	
wake	See *awake.*	
want	See *lack.*	
ways	If you mean distance, *way* is the right word.	I've got a long *way* to go.
weather/whether	*Weather* is what's going on outside the window. *Whether* is the conjunction.	What's the *weather* like? *Whether* you go or not, I'm going.
well	See *good.*	
which	See *that.*	
who	See *that.*	
will/would	See *shall.*	
would like for	Save space; say *want*	

INDEX

INDEX

point of view, form, tone/mood, 487
theme, 489
Figurative language, 637
Figure, calculate, A27
Final, A28
Flow, revising for, 235-290
Flunk, A28
Footnotes, 741; 465
form, 461-465
for work previously cited, 466
Foreward, forward, A28
For free, for the purpose of, A28
Form, 139-154
in fiction and drama, 487, 488
mixed, 150
patterns of organization, 141
Formal language, 626
Formally, formerly, A28
Fragment, 622, A28
Framework, A28
French language, 626
Frost, Robert (poem by), 506
Fulsome, A29
Function paragraphs, 238, 269-282
uses, accommodate writer's style, 273
add drama, 270
break up long passages, 272
emphasize point, develop example, 274
make transitions, 271
set off dialogue, 271
Fused sentence, *see* Run-on sentences

Gap, A29
Gay, A29
Gender, A29
General public, A29
General-specific order, pattern of organization, 145
Gerund, 603
Good, well, 658, A29
Grammar, 651-654

Had better, A29
Had ought, A29

Haiku, 493
Hanged, hung, A29
Hang-up, A29
Hardly...than, A30
Has reference to, A30
Head up, A30
Hemisphericity, 11-12
Heuristics, *see* Creating techniques
Hierarchy of needs, 85
Historic, historical, A30
History of the English language, 626, 652
Homophones, 672
Hopefully, 658, A30
Host, A30
House, home, A30
How ever, however, A30
How-to essay, characteristics, 101
essays:
"A Beach Cure That Works in Mysterious Ways and Lasts Forever," 105
"Buying a Pickup Truck," 112
"How to Borrow Money and Build Credit in Your Own Name," 108
"How to Catch a Speckled Trout," 119
"How to Stop Procrastinating. Today.", 102
"Virgie Richardson's 68-Year-Old Soap Recipe," 107
how to write, 120-123
rules, 123
writing contexts, 120
How to write essay exam questions, 517
Human, humane, A30
Human history, A30
Hyphen, 679, A30

-ics, A31
Idea, ideal, A31
Idioms, 649
I.e., A31
If and when, A31
Ignorant, stupid, A31
Illusion, allusion, 656

Illustration, in essay/thesis development, 202
in paragraph development, 258
Imagery, in poetry, 492
Immortal, A31
Imply, infer, 658, A30
In a very real sense, A32
Incident, incidence, A32
Incredibly, A32
Indefinite pronoun, 596
errors in, 612
Indexes, general, 475
specialized, 475
Individual, A32
Induction, pattern of essay organization, 147
Infer, A32
Infinitive, 603
Informal word choice, 626
Information essay, 333-343
characteristics 333
essays:
"Don't Step on the Bugs," 340
"The Meanings of the Kiss," 334
"On the Track of the Devil Wind," 335
"Showing Off Prize Chickens," 339
how to write, 341-343
writing contexts, 341-342
Input, output, A32
Inside of, outside of, A32
Insider, for thesis, 129
In to, into, A32
Intransitive verb, 601
Introductions, essay, 173
Invent, definition, 2
Invention, 1-47
questions, 33
techniques, *see* Creating techniques
see also Creating stage
Irregardless, 658, A33
Italics, 678, A33
Its, it's, 658

Jargon, 357-358, 535-537, 647

INDEX

INDEX

INDEX

INDEX

ACKNOWLEDGMENTS

STAGE ONE: CREATING

"Four Kinds of Luck" by James Austin is based on information from CHASE, CHANCE, AND CREATIVITY by James Austin. Used by permission of Columbia University Press.

Material on Looping is drawn from WRITING WITHOUT TEACHERS by Peter Elbow, Oxford University Press, 1975. Used by permission of the author.

"The Journal as a Source for Ideas" is excerpted from Isobel Silden's article, "For Irving Wallace and Family—Readers and Royalties Are in the Millions" from the February 18, 1979 issue of *Family Weekly*. Reprinted by permission of *Family Weekly* magazine, 641 Lexington Avenue, New York, NY 10022.

"Aristotle's Common Topics" from THE LITTLE RHETORIC by Edward P. J. Corbett. Copyright © 1977 by John Wiley & Sons, Inc. Reprinted by permission of John Wiley & Sons, Inc.

"Creative Jogging" by Hugh Burns from April 1979 issue of *Runner's World*. Reprinted with permission from *Runner's World* Magazine, 1400 Stierlin Road, Mountain View, CA 94043.

"Questions to Ask About ..." from THE LITTLE RHETORIC by Edward P. J. Corbett. Copyright © 1977 by John Wiley & Sons, Inc. Adapted from "Discovery Through Questioning: A Plan for Teaching Rhetorical Invention" by Richard L. Larson from *College English*, November 1968.

THE PERSONAL EXPERIENCE ESSAY

"A Sketch of the Past" by Virginia Woolf from MOMENTS OF BEING by Virginia Woolf, edited by Jeanne Schulkind, copyright© 1976 by Quentin Bell and Angelica Garnett. Reprinted by permission of Harcourt Brace Jovanovich, Inc., the Author's Literary Estate, and The Hogarth Press Ltd.

"A Stranger Goes to the Soviet Union" by Hans Rütimann is reprinted by permission of the author.

"Uncle's Farm" by Mark Twain is abridged from pp. 96-104, 109-110 (under the title "Uncle's Farm") from MARK TWAIN'S AUTOBIOGRAPHY, Vol. I, Copyright 1924 by Clara Gabrilowitsch; renewed 1952 by Clara Clemens Samossoud. Reprinted by permission of Harper & Row, Publishers, Inc.

"Christmas at Home" by Liv Ullmann is reprinted from CHANGING, by Liv Ullmann. Copyright © 1976, 1977 by Liv Ullmann. Reprinted by permission of Alfred A. Knopf, Inc.

STAGE TWO: SHAPING

"The Bear" from THE JOURNALS OF LEWIS AND CLARK, A New Selection With an Introduction by John Bakeless. Copyright © 1964 by John Bakeless. Reprinted by arrangement with The New American Library, Inc., New York, N.Y.

"Growing Old" by May Sarton is reprinted from THE HOUSE BY THE SEA, A JOURNAL, by May Sarton by permission of W. W. Norton & Co., Inc. Copyright © 1977 by May Sarton.

"The Word, The Map, The Symbol" excerpted from LANGUAGE IN THOUGHT AND ACTION, Fourth Edition by S. I. Hayakawa, copyright © 1978 by Harcourt Brace Jovanovich, Inc. Reprinted by permission of the publisher.

"All through THE ELEMENTS OF STYLE ..." excerpted from THE ELEMENTS OF STYLE, Third Edition, by William Strunk, Jr. & E. B. White. Copyright © 1979, The Macmillan Publishing Co., Inc. and reprinted with their permission.

"John Cheever Says ..." is excerpted from the interview "Fiction Is Our Most Intimate Means of Communication" from the May 21, 1979 issue of *U. S. News & World Report*. Copyright © 1979 by U. S. News & World Report and used by their permission.

"Recent studies have provided reasons ..." is excerpted from "Periodisms in Mouse Spontaneous Activities ..." by Emma D. Terracini and Frank A. Brown, Jr. from PHYSIOLOGICAL ZOOLOGY, January 1962. Used by permission of The University of Chicago Press.

"One of the greatest riddles of the universe ..." is excerpted from "Life's Mysterious Clocks" by Frank A. Brown, Jr. from the December 24, 1960 issue of *The Saturday Evening Post*. © 1960 The Curtis Publishing Company.

"Everyone knows that there are individuals ..." is excerpted from "Biological Clocks and the Fiddler Crab" by Frank A. Brown, Jr. from the April 1959 issue of *Scientific American*. Copyright © 1959 by Scientific American, Inc. All rights reserved.

THE HOW-TO-ESSAY

"How to Stop Procrastinating" by Richard Grossman is from the June 1979 issue of *Family Health* Magazine. © All Rights Reserved. Reprinted with permission.

"A Beach Cure That Works in Mysterious Ways and Lasts Forever" by Joan K. Davidson is from the July 22, 1978 issue of *The New York Times*. © 1978 by The New York Times Company. Reprinted by permission.

"How to Borrow Money and Build Credit in Your Own Name" by Chris Barnett is from the February 1979 issue of *Playgirl Magazine*. Reprinted by permission of Playgirl Inc., 3420 Ocean Park Boulevard, Suite 3000, Santa Monica, CA 90405.

"Buying a Pickup Truck" by Noel Perrin is from FIRST PERSON RURAL by Noel Perrin. Copyright © 1978 by Noel Perrin. Reprinted by permission of David R. Godine, Publisher, Inc.

"The Process of Abstracting" and the "Abstraction Ladder" are excerpted from LANGUAGE IN THOUGHT AND ACTION, Fourth Edition by S. I. Hayakawa, copyright © 1978 by Harcourt Brace Jovanovich, Inc. Reprinted by permission of the publisher.

Quote from Randall E. Decker is from PATTERNS OF EXPOSITION by Randell E. Decker, 1978, Little, Brown & Company.

Quote from Henry Boettinger is from MOVING MOUNTAINS by Henry Boettinger. Copyright © 1969 by Henry M. Boettinger. Reprinted with permission of Macmillan Publishing Co., Inc.

THE PROBLEM/SOLUTION ESSAY

"How We Can Help Children Learn to Write" by Margaret Mead and Rhoda Metraux is from the November 1976 issue of *Redbook* Magazine. Reprinted by permission of Mary Catherine Bateson and Rhoda Metraux.

analysts..." excerpted from THE DIARY OF ANAIS NIN, Volume Two, copyright © 1967 by Anais Nin. Reprinted by permission of Harcourt Brace Jovanovich, Inc.

"The essayist is a self-liberated man..." excerpted from the Foreword of ESSAYS OF E. B. WHITE by E. B. White, 1977, Harper & Row, Publishers, Inc. Copyright © 1977 by E. B. White.

"Some 'inborn' defects—some defects..." is excerpted from Science and the Sanctity of Life" by P. B. Medewar from a 1966 issue of *Encounter*. © 1966.

"From the luscious coolness of a freshly cut ..." is excerpted from the August 1978 issue of *Gourmet*.

"Ideas are not truly alive ..." is excerpted from p. 5 in MOVING MOUNTAINS by Henry M. Boettinger. Copyright © 1969 by Henry M. Boettinger. Reprinted with permission of Macmillan Publishing Co., Inc.

"Reading is an act of communication..." is excerpted from p. 12 in UNDERSTANDING READING by Frank Smith, 1978, Holt, Rinehart & Winston.

"In that mysterious dimension where..." is excerpted from THE FEMALE EUNUCH by Germaine Greer. Copyright © 1970, 1971 by Germaine Greer. Used by permission of McGraw-Hill Book Company and McGibbon & Kee Ltd.

"As her little bird body revealed ..." is excerpted from DANCE TO THE PIPER by Agnes de Mille. Copyright © 1951, 1952 by Agnes de Mille. Reprinted by permission of Harold Ober Associates.

"Writers are driven by a compulsion..." is excerpted from p. 5 in ON WRITING WELL by William Zinsser. Copyright © 1976 by William K. Zinsser. Reprinted by permission of William Zinsser.

"How is aim determined? ..." is excerpted from A THEORY OF DISCOURSE by James Kinneavy, 1975, Prentice-Hall, Inc.

From the Dedication Page: "But I want first of all—in fact, as an end ..." is excerpted from pp. 23-24 in GIFT FROM THE SEA, by Anne Morrow Lindbergh. Copyright © 1955 by Anne Morrow Lindbergh. Reprinted by permission of Pantheon Books, a Division of Random House, Inc.

Grateful acknowledgment is made to the following students for permission to reprint their work:

Arthur Akard, Eric Ashbaugh, Mike Barbour, Craig Blackburn, Brian Burrer, Cheryl Cortney, Karen Davis, Patricia DeFloria, Thomas Dittman, Clifford Dorn, Wade Dunn, Beatrice Egle, Debbie Engelbrecht, Pam Evans, Laurie Farwell, Ray Fields, Barbara Folk, Jeanette Goodwin, Stephen Hall, Teresa Harbich, Mark Hart, Alan Harvey, David Hill, Paul Hughes, Nancy Hutson, Philip Jackson, Holly Jacobs, Tom Joner, Don Jones, Rick Jones, Lee Kleb, Wilson Lambert, Darrell Lane, Charles McDaniel, Mark Marino, Howard Marshburn, Paul Merriman, Ivan Meunnich, Julie Meyer, Mona Middleton, Michael Miller, Raymond Moltz, Edward Moore, Brent Murphy, Alvie Nichols, Russell Norris, Kara O'Connor, Gary Parsons, Leslie Persier, Debbie Philp, Eric Pitcher, Teri Reed, Cindy Rockford, Mary Russell, Nancy Rutledge, Floyd Schexnayder, Martha Schutt, Mark Shelton, Lynda Sizer, Brad Smith, Barbara Stov, Vicki Tatum, Karen Tepera, David Terrell, David Thomson, Kay Wallace, Lillian Wesley, Vicki White, Bradley Willingham, Tim Wold, Mary Wolff, Eugene Woo, and Joe Don Zant.

633 Concrete
Abstract
Diction
↑
636 Word List

ALPHABETICAL LIST OF CORRECTION SYMBOLS

agr/pn	faulty pronoun-noun agreement
agr/sv	faulty subject-verb agreement
apos	use apostrophe for possessive case of noun
awk	awkward expression
coh	coherence of the paragraph is weak
CS	comma splice
Da	use appropriate diction
dangl	dangling modifier
dev	inadequate development of the paragraph
div	improper division of word at end of sentence
Dx	use exact, precise diction
fig	faulty figure of speech
frag	sentence fragment
FS	fused sentence
hyph	use hyphen for the compound word
id	unidiomatic expression
ital	use italics
MS	improper manuscript form
num	improper use of Arabic number
p/c	use comma here
p/col	use colon here
p/d	use dash here
p/sc	use semicolon here
paral	breakdown of parallel structure
pass	questionable use of passive verb
pred	faulty predication
quot	quotation mark placed improperly in relation to punctuation mark
ref	faulty reference of pronoun
rep	careless repetition
sp	spelling error
trite	trite expression
U	unity of the paragraph is weak
wordy	unnecessarily wordy sentence
ww	wrong word

PROOFREADERS' MARKS

e	delete
^	insert here what is indicated in the margin
¶	start new paragraph
no ¶	no paragraph; run in with previous paragraph
⊙/	insert period
⋀/	insert comma
;/	insert semicolon
:/	insert colon
=/	insert hyphen
∨/	insert apostrophe
cap	use capital letter here